LYLE

OFFICIAL ANTIQUES REVIEW 2001

LYLE
OFFICIAL
ANTIQUES
REVIEW 2001

A PERIGEE BOOK

A Perigee Book
Published by The Berkley Publishing Group
A division of Penguin Putnam Inc.
375 Hudson Street
New York, New York 10014

First edition: December 2000
ISBN: 0-399-52641-2
ISSN: 1089-1544

Published simultaneously in Canada.

The Penguin Putnam Inc. World Wide Web site address is
http://www.penguinputnam.com

Printed in the United States of America

10 9 8 7 6 5 4 3 2 1

INTRODUCTION

This year over 100,000 Antique Dealers and Collectors will make full and profitable use of their Lyle Antiques Price Guide. They know that only in this one volume will they find the widest possible variety of goods – illustrated, described and given a current market value to assist them to BUY RIGHT AND SELL RIGHT throughout the year of issue.

They know, too, that by building a collection of these immensely valuable volumes year by year, they will equip themselves with an unparalleled reference library of facts, figures and illustrations which, properly used, cannot fail to help them keep one step ahead of the market.

In its thirty-one years of publication, Lyle has gone from strength to strength and has become without doubt the pre-eminent book of reference for the antique trade throughout the world. Each of its fact filled pages is packed with precisely the kind of profitable information the professional Dealer needs – including descriptions, illustrations and values of thousands and thousands of individual items carefully selected to give a representative picture of the current market in antiques and collectibles – and remember all values are prices actually paid, based on accurate sales records in the twelve months prior to publication from the best established and most highly respected auction houses and retail outlets in Europe and America.

This is THE book for the Professional Antiques Dealer. 'The Lyle Book' - we've even heard it called 'The Dealer's Bible'.

Compiled and published afresh each year, the Lyle Antiques Price Guide is the most comprehensive up-to-date antiques price guide available. THIS COULD BE YOUR WISEST INVESTMENT OF THE YEAR!

Anthony Curtis

While every care has been taken in the compiling of information contained in this volume, the publisher cannot accept liability for loss, financial or otherwise, incurred by reliance placed on the information herein.

All prices quoted in this book are obtained from a variety of auctions in various countries and are converted to dollars at the rate of exchange prevalent at the time of sale. The images and the accompanying text remain the copyright of the contributing auction houses.

The publishers wish to express their sincere thanks to the following for their involvement and assistance in the production of this volume.

ANTHONY CURTIS (Editor)

EELIN McIVOR (Sub Editor)

ANNETTE CURTIS (Editorial)

CATRIONA DAY (Art Production)

ANGIE DEMARCO (Art Production)

NICKY FAIRBURN (Art Production)

PHILIP SPRINGTHORPE (Photography)

CONTENTS

ACKNOWLEDGEMENTS

AB Stockholms Auktionsverk, Box 16256, 103 25 Stockholm, Sweden
Abbotts Auction Rooms, The Auction Rooms, Campsea Ash, Woodbridge, Suffolk
Academy Auctioneers, Northcote House, Northcote Avenue, Ealing, London W5 3UR
James Adam, 26, St Stephens Green, Dublin 2
Henry Aldridge & Son, Devizes Auction Rooms, Wine Street, Devizes SN10 1AP
Amersham Auction Rooms, 125 Station Road, Amersham, Bucks. HP7 OAH
Jean Claude Anaf, Lyon Brotteaux, 13 bis place Jules Ferry, 69456, Lyon, France
Anderson & Garland, Marlborough House, Marlborough Crescent, Newcastle upon Tyne NE1 4EE
Antiques Networking, Tel/Fax: 01384 378964
Atlantic Antiques, Chenil House, 181–183 Kings Road, London SW3 5ED
The Auction Galleries, Mount Rd., Tweedmouth, Berwick on Tweed
Auction Team Köln, Postfach 50 11 19, D-50971 Köln, Germany
Auktionshaus Arnold, Bleichstr. 42, 6000 Frankfurt a/M, Germany
Bearne's, St Edmunds Court, Okehampton Street, Exeter EX4 1DU
Biddle & Webb, Ladywood Middleway, Birmingham B16 0PP
Bigwood, The Old School, Tiddington, Stratford upon Avon
Black Horse Agencies Ambrose, 149 High Street, Loughton, Essex 1G10 4LZ
Black Horse Agencies, Locke & England, 18 Guy Street, Leamington Spa
Boardman Fine Art Auctioneers, Station Road Corner, Haverhill, Suffolk CB9 0EY
JW Bollom, PO Box 78, Croydon Rd, Beckenham CR3 4BL
Bonhams, Montpelier Street, Knightsbridge, London SW7 1HH
Bonhams Chelsea, 65–69 Lots Road, London SW10 0RN
Bonhams West Country, Dowell Street, Honiton, Devon
Bosleys, The White House, Marlow, Bucks SL7 1AH
Andrew Bottomley, The Coach House, Huddersfield Rd, Holmfirth, West Yorks.
Michael J. Bowman, 6 Haccombe House, Near Netherton, Newton Abbot, Devon
Bristol Auction Rooms, St John Place, Apsley Road, Clifton, Bristol BS8 2ST
British Antique Replicas, School Close, Queen Elizabeth Avenue, Burgess Hill, Sussex
Butchoff Antiques, 229–233 Westbourne Grove, London W11 2SE
Butterfield & Butterfield, 220 San Bruno Avenue , San Francisco CA 94103, USA
Butterfield & Butterfield, 7601 Sunset Boulevard, Los Angeles CA 90046, USA
Canterbury Auction Galleries, 40 Station Road West, Canterbury CT2 8AN
Cedar Antiques Centre, High Street, Hartley Wintney, Hook, Hants. RG27 8NY
Central Motor Auctions, Barfield House, Britannia Road, Morley, Leeds, LS27 0HN
H.C. Chapman & Son, The Auction Mart, North Street, Scarborough.
Chapman Moore & Mugford, 8 High Street, Shaftesbury SP7 8JB
Cheffins Grain & Comins, 2 Clifton Road, Cambridge
Christie's (International) SA, 8 place de la Taconnerie, 1204 Genève, Switzerland
Christie's France, 9 avenue Matignon, 75008 Paris
Christie's Monaco, S.A.M, Park Palace 98000 Monte Carlo, Monaco
Christie's Scotland, 164–166 Bath Street, Glasgow G2 4TG
Christie's South Kensington Ltd., 85 Old Brompton Road, London SW7 3LD
Christie's, 8 King Street, London SW1Y 6QT
Christie's East, 219 East 67th Street, New York, NY 10021, USA
Christie's, 502 Park Avenue, New York, NY10022, USA
Christie's, Cornelis Schuytstraat 57, 1071 JG Amsterdam, Netherlands
Christie's SA Roma, 114 Piazza Navona, 00186 Rome, Italy
Christie's Swire, 2804–6 Alexandra House, 16–20 Chater Road, Hong Kong
Christie's Australia Pty Ltd., 1 Darling Street, South Yarra, Victoria 3141, Australia
Clarke & Gammon, The Guildford Auction Rooms, Bedford Road, Guildford, GU1 4SE
Bryan Clisby, Andwells Antiques, Hartley Wintney, North Hants.
The Clock House, 75 Pound Street, Carshalton, Surrey SM5 3PG
A J Cobern, The Grosvenor Sales Rooms, 93b Eastbank Street, Southport PR8 1DG
Collins Antiques, Wheathampstead, St Albans AL4 8AP
Cooper Hirst Auctions, The Granary Saleroom, Victoria Road, Chelmsford, Essex CM2 6LH
Coppelia Antiques, Holford Lodge, Plumley, Cheshire.
The Cotswold Auction Co., Chapel Walk Saleroom, Chapel Walk, Cheltenham GL50 3DS
The Crested China Co., Station House, Driffield, E. Yorks YO25 7PY
Cundalls, The Cattle Market, 17 Market Square, Malton, N. Yorks.
Dargate Auction Galleries, 5607 Baum Blvd., Pittsburgh PA 15206
Julian Dawson, Lewes Auction Rooms, 56 High Street, Lewes BN7 1XE
Dee & Atkinson & Harrison, The Exchange Saleroom, Driffield, Nth Humberside YO25 7LJ
Garth Denham & Assocs. Horsham Auction Galleries, Warnsham, Nr. Horsham, Sussex
Diamond Mills & Co., 117 Hamilton Road, Felixstowe, Suffolk
David Dockree Fine Art, The Redwood Suite, Clemence House, Mellor Road, Cheadle Hulme, Cheshire
Dorking Desk Shop, 41 West Street, Dorking, Surrey

William Doyle Galleries, 175 East 87th Street, New York, NY 10128, USA
Douglas Ross, Charter House, 42 Avebury Boulevard, Central Milton Keynes MK9 2HS
Dreweatt Neate, Donnington Priory, Newbury, Berks.
Dreweatt Neate, Holloways, 49 Parsons Street, Banbury
Hy. Duke & Son, 40 South Street, Dorchester, Dorset
Du Mouchelles Art Galleries Co., 409 E. Jefferson Avenue, Detroit, Michigan 48226, USA
Sala de Artes y Subastas Durán, Serrano 12, 28001 Madrid, Spain
Eldred's, Box 796, E. Dennis, MA 02641, USA
R H Ellis & Sons, 44/46 High Street, Worthing, BN11 1LL
Ewbanks, Burnt Common Auction Rooms, London Road, Send, Woking GU23 7LN
Fellows & Son, Augusta House, 19 Augusta Street, Hockley, Birmingham
Fidler Taylor & Co., Crown Square, Matlock, Derbyshire DE4 3AT
Finarte, 20121 Milano, Piazzetta Bossi 4, Italy
John D Fleming & Co., The North Devon Auction Rooms, The Savory, South Molton, Devon
Peter Francis,19 King Street, Carmarthen, Dyfed
Fraser Pinney's, 8290 Devonshire, Montreal, Quebec, Canada H4P 2PZ
Freeman Fine Arts, 1808 Chestnut Street, Philadelphia PA19103, USA
Galerie Koller, Rämistr. 8, CH 8024 Zürich, Switzerland
Galerie Moderne, 3 rue du Parnasse, 1040 Bruxelles, Belgium
GB Antiques Centre, Lancaster Leisure Park, Wynesdale Rd, Lancaster LA1 3LA
Geering & Colyer (Black Horse Agencies) Highgate, Hawkhurst, Kent
The Goss and Crested China Co., 62 Murray Road, Horndean, Hants PO8 9JL
The Grandfather Clock Shop, Little House, Sheep Street, Stow on the Wold 9L54 1AA
Graves Son & Pilcher, Hove Auction Rooms, Hove Street, Hove, East Sussex
Great Grooms Antiques Centre, Parbrook, Billingshurst, Kent Rh14 9EU
Great Grooms Antiques Centre, Riverside House, Charnham Street, Hungerford, Berks.
Green Dragon Antiques Centre, 24 High Street, Wincanton, Somerset BA9 9FJ
Greenslade Hunt, Magdalene House, Church Square, Taunton, Somerset, TA1 1SB
Hampton's Fine Art, 93 High Street, Godalming, Surrey
Hanseatisches Auktionshaus für Historica, Neuer Wall 57, 2000 Hamburg 36, Germany
William Hardie Ltd., 141 West Regent Street, Glasgow G2 2SG
Andrew Hartley Fine Arts, Victoria Hall, Little Lane, Ilkley
Hastings Antiques Centre, 59–61 Norman Road, St Leonards on Sea, East Sussex
Hauswedell & Nolte, D-2000 Hamburg 13, Pöseldorfer Weg 1, Germany
Muir Hewitt, Halifax Antiques Centre, Queens Road/Gibbet Street, Halifax HX1 4LR
Hobbs Parker, New Ashford Market, Monument Way, Orbital Park, Ashford TN24 0HB
Holloways, 49 Parsons Street, Banbury OX16 8PF
Hotel de Ventes Horta, 390 Chaussée de Waterloo (Ma Campagne), 1060 Bruxelles, Belgium
Jackson's, 2229 Lincoln Street, Cedar Falls, Iowa 50613, USA.
Jacobs & Hunt, Lavant Street, Petersfield, Hants. GU33 3EF
P Herholdt Jensens Auktioner, Rundforbivej 188, 2850 Nerum, Denmark
G A Key, Aylsham Saleroom, Palmers Lane, Aylsham, Norfolk, NR11 6EH
George Kidner, The Old School, The Square, Pennington, Lymington, Hants SO41 8GN
Kunsthaus am Museum, Drususgasse 1–5, 5000 Köln 1, Germany
Kunsthaus Lempertz, Neumarkt 3, 5000 Köln 1, Germany
Lambert & Foster (County Group), The Auction Sales Room, 102 High Street, Tenterden, Kent
W.H. Lane & Son, 64 Morrab Road, Penzance, Cornwall, TR18 8AB
Langlois Ltd., Westaway Rooms, Don Street, St Helier, Channel Islands
Lawrence Butler Fine Art Salerooms, Marine Walk, Hythe, Kent, CT21 5AJ
Lawrence Fine Art, South Street, Crewkerne, Somerset TA18 8AB
Lawrence's Fine Art Auctioneers, Norfolk House, 80 High Street, Bletchingley, Surrey
David Lay, The Penzance Auction House, Alverton, Penzance, Cornwall TA18 4KE
Gordon Litherland, 26 Stapenhill Road, Burton on Trent
Lloyd International Auctions, 118 Putney Bridge Road, London SW15 2NQ
Lots Road Chelsea Auction Galleries, 71 Lots Road, Chelsea, London SW10 0RN
Duncan McAlpine, Stateside Comics plc, 125 East Barnet Road, London EN4 8RF
McCartneys, Portcullis Salerooms, Ludlow, Shropshire
John Mann, Bruntshielbog, Canonbie, Dumfries DG14 0RY
Christopher Matthews, 23 Mount Street, Harrogate HG2 8DG
John Maxwell, 133a Woodford Road, Wilmslow, Cheshire
May & Son, 18 Bridge Street, Andover, Hants
Morphets, 4–6 Albert Street, Harrogate, North Yorks HG1 1JL
Neales, The Nottingham Saleroom, 192 Mansfield Road, Nottingham NG1 3HU
D M Nesbit & Co, 7 Clarendon Road, Southsea, Hants PO5 2ED
Newark Antiques Centre, Regent House, Lombard House, Newark, Notts.
John Nicholson, Longfield, Midhurst Road, Fernhurst GU27 3HA

The Old Brigade, 10a Harborough Rd, Kingsthorpe, Northampton NN1 7AZ
The Old Cinema, 157 Tower Bridge Rd, London SE1 3LW
Old Mill Antiques Centre, Mill Street, Low Town, Bridgnorth, Shropshire
Olivers, The Saleroom, Burkitts lane, Sudbury, CO10 1HB
Onslow's, The Depot, 2 Michael Road, London, SW6 2AD
Pendulum of Mayfair, 51 Maddox Street, London W1
Phillips Manchester, Trinity House, 114 Northenden Road, Sale, Manchester M33 3HD
Phillips Son & Neale SA, 10 rue des Chaudronniers, 1204 Genève, Switzerland
Phillips West Two, 10 Salem Road, London W2 4BL
Phillips, 11 Bayle Parade, Folkestone, Kent CT20 1SQ
Phillips, 49 London Road, Sevenoaks, Kent TN13 1UU
Phillips, 65 George Street, Edinburgh EH2 2JL
Phillips, Blenstock House, 7 Blenheim Street, New Bond Street, London W1Y 0AS
Phillips Marleybone, Hayes Place, Lisson Grove, London NW1 6UA
Phillips, New House, 150 Christleton Road, Chester CH3 5TD
Pieces of Time, 26 South Molton Lane, London W1Y 2LP
Potteries Specialist Auctions, 271 Waterloo Road, Cobridge, Stoke-on-Trent
Harry Ray & Co, Lloyds Bank Chambers, Welshpool, Montgomery SY21 7RR
Peter M Raw, Thornfield, Hurdle Way, Compton Down, Winchester, Hants SC21 2AN
Remmey Galleries, 30 Maple Street, Summit, NJ 07901
Rennie's, 1 Agincourt Street, Monmouth
Riddetts, 26 Richmond Hill, Bournemouth
Ritchie's, 429 Richmond Street East, Toronto, Canada M5A 1R1
Derek Roberts Antiques, 24–25 Shipbourne Road, Tonbridge, Kent TN10 3DN
Romsey Auction Rooms, 56 The Hundred, Romsey, Hants 5051 8BX
Russell, Baldwin & Bright, The Fine Art Saleroom, Ryelands Road, Leominster HR6 8NZ
St. James Antiques Market, 197 Piccadilly, London W1V OLL
Schrager Auction Galleries, 2915 N Sherman Boulevard, PO Box 10390, Milwaukee WI 53210, USA
Selkirk's, 4166 Olive Street, St Louis, Missouri 63108, USA
Skinner Inc., Bolton Gallery, Route 117, Bolton MA, USA
Allan Smith, Amity Cottage 162 Beechcroft Rd. Upper Stratton, Swindon, Wilts.
Soccer Nostalgia, Albion Chambers, Birchington, Kent CT7 9DN
Sotheby's, 34–35 New Bond Street, London W1A 2AA
Sotheby's, 1334 York Avenue, New York NY 10021
Sotheby's, 112 George Street, Edinburgh EH2 2LH
Sotheby's, Summers Place, Billingshurst, West Sussex RH14 9AD
Sotheby's, Monaco, BP 45, 98001 Monte Carlo
Southgate Auction Rooms, 55 High Street, Southgate, London N14 6LD
Spink & Son Ltd., 5–7 King Street, St James's, London SW1Y 6QS
Michael Stainer Ltd., St Andrews Auction Rooms, Wolverton Rd, Boscombe, Bournemouth BH7 6HT
Michael Stanton, 7 Rowood Drive, Solihull, West Midlands B92 9LT
Street Jewellery, 5 Runnymede Road, Ponteland, Northumbria NE20 9HE
Stride & Son, Southdown House, St John's Street, Chichester, Sussex
G E Sworder & Son, 14 Cambridge Road, Stansted Mountfitchet, Essex CM24 8BZ
Taviner's of Bristol, Prewett Street, Redcliffe, Bristol BS1 6PB
Tennants, Harmby Road, Leyburn, Yorkshire
Thomson Roddick & Laurie, 24 Lowther Street, Carlisle
Thomson Roddick & Laurie, 60 Whitesands, Dumfries
Thomson Roddick & Medcalf, 44/3 Hardengreen Business Park, Esbank, Edinburgh EH22 3NX
Thimbleby & Shorland, 31 Gt Knollys Street, Reading RG1 7HU
Charles Tomlinson, Tel/Fax 01244 318395. Email charles.tomlinson@lineone.net
Tool Shop Auctions, 78 High Street, Needham Market, Suffolk IP6 8AW
Truro Auction Centre, City Wharf, Malpas Rd., Truro TR1 1QH
Venator & Hanstein, Căcilienstr. 48, 5000 Köln 1, Germany
T Vennett Smith, 11 Nottingham Road, Gotham, Nottingham NG11 0HE
Garth Vincent, The Old Manor House, Allington, nr. Grantham, Lincs. NG32 2DH
Wallis & Wallis, West Street Auction Galleries, West Street, Lewes, E. Sussex BN7 2NJ
Wells Cundall Nationwide Anglia, Staffordshire House, 27 Flowergate, Whitby YO21 3AX
West Street Antiques, 63 West Street, Dorking, Surrey
Whitworths, 32–34 Wood Street, Huddersfield HD1 1DX
Wilkinsons Auctioneers, The Old Salerooms, 28 Netherhall Road, Doncaster DN1 2PW
A J Williams, 607 Sixth Avenue, Central Business Park, Hengrove, Bristol BS14 9BZ
Peter Wilson, Victoria Gallery, Market Street, Nantwich, Cheshire CW5 5DG
Wintertons Ltd., Lichfield Auction Centre, Fradley Park, Lichfield, Staffs WS13 8NF
Woolley & Wallis, The Castle Auction Mart, Salisbury, Wilts SP1 3SU
Worthing Auction Galleries, 31 Chatsworth Road, Worthing, W. Sussex BN11 1LY

ANTIQUES
REVIEW
2001

The Lyle Antiques Price Guide is compiled and published with completely fresh information annually, enabling you to begin each new year with an up-to-date knowledge of the current trends, together with the verified values of antiques of all descriptions.

We have endeavored to obtain a balance between the more expensive collector's items and those which, although not in their true sense antiques, are handled daily by the antiques trade.

The illustrations and prices in the following sections have been arranged to make it easy for the reader to assess the period and value of all items with speed.

You will find illustrations for almost every category of antique and curio, together with a corresponding price collated during the last twelve months, from the auction rooms and retail outlets of the major trading countries.

When dealing with the more popular trade pieces, in some instances, a calculation of an average price has been estimated from the varying accounts researched.

As regards prices, when 'one of a pair' is given in the description the price quoted is for a pair and so that we can make maximum use of the available space it is generally considered that one illustration is sufficient.

It will be noted that in some descriptions taken directly from sales catalogs originating from many different countries, terms such as bureau, secretary and davenport are used in a broader sense than is customary, but in all cases the term used is self explanatory.

A Japanese Tiger four-function manual calculator, with 9-place insertion and 18 place result, circa 1938.
(Auction Team Köln) $335

An Omega Model 3 large manual calculating machine with nine pushrod entry system, by Justin Bamberger, München, 1904.
(Auction Team Köln) $1,340

A very rare Double Odhner Model 35 4-function calculating machine, produced in very small numbers, with 2 x 8 insertion levers and 2 x13 results, circa 1937.
(Auction Team Köln) $2,179

A Walther EMKD barrel calculating machine, electrically powered, by Carl Walther, Zella-Mehlis, Thüringen, 1926.
(Auction Team Köln) $435

A Russian Original Odhner Model 1 'Arithmometer', made in St. Petersburg by the Swedish pioneer Willgodt Odhner, 1886.
(Auction Team Köln) $5,249

A Triumphator Model H 3 Z manual Leipzig calculator with 6, 6 or 11 place working, 1935.
(Auction Team Köln) $289

An Adix 3-place adding machine with latch drive and nine keys, by Pallweber & Bordt, Mannheim, with cancellation mechanism and case, 1903. (Auction Team Köln)
$593

A black Curta Type II miniature four-function cylinder calculating machine, produced in Liechtenstein by Curt Herzstark, with original metal case, 1948. (Auction Team Köln) $628

An early Adix pocket calculator, with 9 keys and zeroing facility, in original blue velvet Danish case, 1903.
(Auction Team Köln) $557

An Olivetti-Divisumma 28 designer four-function calculating machine, electronic, with print-out, circa 1968.
(Auction Team Köln) $590

A very rare original Addo Model I adding machine, on original base, serial no. 3875, 1920.
(Auction Team Köln) $2,179

An unusual undocumented Mercedes Euclid Model 19 calculating machine, circa 1928.
(Auction Team Köln)
$198

A rare Multifix Norwegian barrel calculator, circa 1950.
(Auction Team Köln) $603

A Unitas four function step-roller calculator with double scale and 10 place full keyboard, on cast iron base plate, by Ludwig Spitz, Berlin, 1912.
(Auction Team Köln) $788

A bakelite Adix nine place adding machine by Pallweber & Bordt, Mannheim, circa 1935.
(Auction Team Köln) $248

A Brunsviga Model 10, the smallest Brunsviga four-function calculator with split step rollers, with 6 insertion levers, 10-place results and 5-place conversion, 1932.
(Auction Team Köln) $459

Mercedes Euklid Model 1 four function machine with proportional levers, by Christel Hamann, Berlin, with 9,8 or 16 place working, 1905.
(Auction Team Köln) $1,574

A rare French Chateau barrel calculating machine with 9-place insertion and 13 place result, circa 1909. (Auction Team Köln)
$660

A Comptometer 8-place ready reckoner with direct display, in copper case, circa 1920.
(Auction Team Köln) $72

An Adix 3 place adding machine with latch drive and 9 keys, by Pallweber & Bordt, Mannheim, on/off switch and in original velvet case, 1903.
(Auction Team Köln) $524

A Saldorita Swedish manual adding machine with print-out and 7-place insertion, in bakelite case, circa 1955.
(Auction Team Köln) $917

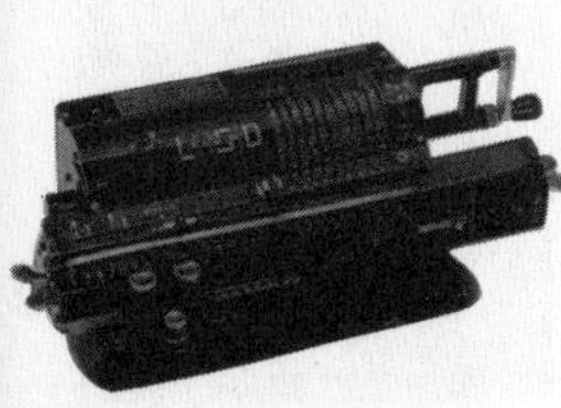

A LuSiD Original Odhner Model H adding machine, a version produced in small numbers for the British market, 1928.
(Auction Team Köln) $1,123

A TIM-Unitas sliding cylinder calculating machine with 8-place lever insertion, 2 x 12-place result and 7-place conversion, by Ludwig Spitz, Berlin, 1912.
(Auction Team Köln) $858

A Double Brunsviga Model D 13 R/1 compound calculator for special calculations such as registry work, in original box, 1961.
(Auction Team Köln) $569

Unusual painted wooden sign, early 20th century, *Bean Supper Sat. Night at__*, with a small hanging sign below for time or location. Black and white lettering, with a red hand pointing to the right, 46in. long. (Eldred's) $352

An advertising display for Wrigley's Juicy Fruit Chewing Gum, Art Deco style colored card with cardboard support to rear, 50 x 73cm., 1920. (Auction Team Köln) $251

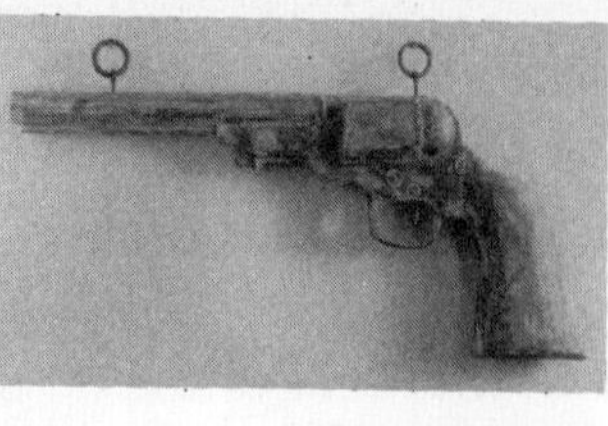

A carved and painted Colt pistol gun trade sign, American, 20th century, carved in the round, a realistic depiction of a Colt pistol, 41in. long. (Sotheby's) $4,312

Macfarlane, Lang & Co. counter display Baker Boy, a Pytram Ltd. composition boy standing astride holding wooden tray and *ML & Co* on hat, painted features, 30in. (Christie's) $727

A polychrome iron and tin shop sign, early 20th century, modelled with a semi-naked female bust holding a lantern with eagle to the rear and plate inscribed *BROCANTE*, 32in. high. (Christie's) $1,097

An original display figure for Leonhardi's Inks, the hand-painted figure of a schoolboy carved in the round in papier mâché, holding up a bottle of ink, 83.5cm. high, circa 1900. (Auction Team Köln) $1,717

Painted zinc trade sign, American, late 19th century, in the form of a pocket watch labelled *C.W. Hallett*, white dial and gold case, 20½in. diameter. (Skinner) $488

A rare small cartridge display board, by Eley, displaying sporting shot gun and rifle rounds centred around the painted registered trademark, 43.5 x 51cm. (Bonhams) $6,280

A cartridge display mirror, by Kynoch, displaying cartridges, centered around the registered trademark, the bevelled mirror with wooden frame, 68 x 78cm. (Bonhams) $1,099

A rare wooden Kodak stool in the form of a film box, painted in yellow, red and black, with imitation leather seat, 61cm. high, circa 1930.
(Auction Team Köln) $302

An American leather shoe shop sign or model, early 20th century, the brown leather brogue with gilt signature to inside *Field and Flint Co. Brockton. Mass.*, 25¾in. long.
(Christie's) $3,160

A painted wooden shop sign with applied carving, Thomas Penn, High Class Photographer, circa 1870, 58 x 92cm.
(Auction Team Köln) $133

Gilt copper pawn shop trade sign, possibly America, late 19th century, the three gilt balls with beaded detail mounted on an iron bracket, replaced bracket, diameter of each ball 13½in.(Skinner) $2,415

La Feria, signed *A[dolphe] Thomasse*, shaped chromo-lithographic advertising fan for the restaurant in the Pavillon Royal d'Espagne, published by Duvelleroy, circa 1900.
(Christie's) $265

**Sheet metal painted trade sign, probably America, late 19th century, the shield-form convex panel with a beaded gilt border, inset panel of gilded metal-worker's tools, 41in. wide.
(Skinner) $1,725**

A folding Kodak advertising display card for the Brownie Flash, USA, 1950s, with two Verichrome cards, French, 31 x 46.5cm.
(Auction Team Köln) $88

A painted tin camera trade sign, American, third quarter 19th century, in the form of an old fashioned 'Brownie' camera painted yellow, 9in. high.
(Sotheby's) $2,875

A fine Eley travelling salesman's cartridge, shot and powder display-case, with a range of Eley proprietary shot cartridges, the lower section displaying a range of rifle and pistol cartridges.
(Christie's) $11,810

Hopi Pottery jar, inscribed on base *Nampeyo,* dated *1986,* 9¾in. diameter. (Eldred's) $660

A Tlingit ceremonial dancing blanket, Chilkat, woven in black, ivory, yellow and blue green commercial wool and cedarbark fibre in a crest pattern, 69in. long. (Christie's) $18,975

Acoma Pottery Jar, by I. Chino, in ovoid form with black and white star design, 8½in. high. (Eldred's) $264

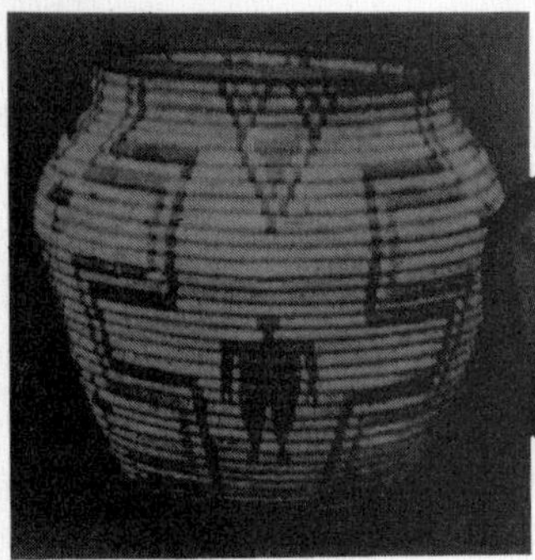

A Western Apache pictorial polychrome coiled storage jar, olla, Arizona, with rounded shoulder, woven in martynia (devil's claw), red yucca and willow, 20cm. high. (Bonhams) $1,492

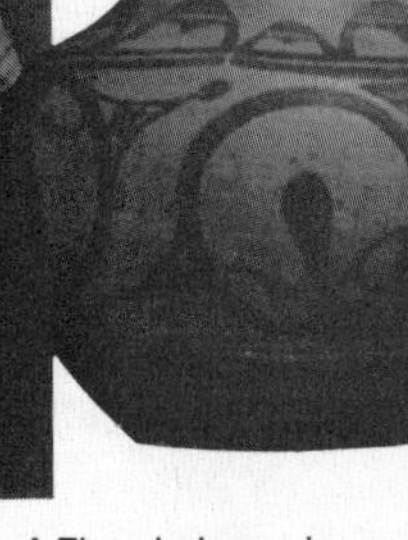

A Zia polychrome jar, possibly Trios, thick walls painted in red and black over a creamy white slip, a broad central band composed of elaborate scrolled motifs, 11¼in. diameter. (Christie's) $9,200

A Western Apache pictorial coiled storage jar, olla, Arizona, with rounded shoulder, woven in devil's claw and willow with four registers of triangular panels, 26.5cm. high. (Bonhams) $5,024

A Sioux beaded buckskin fringed waistcoat, North American Plains, the front panels decorated with stylized flowers and stems, 48cm. long. (Bonhams) $1,178

A pair of quilled hide moccasins, Eastern Woodlands, the supple hide adorned with a single band bisecting vamp and three bands along ankle cuffs, varying shades of faded red, black and cream plaited quillwork, 27cm. long. (Bonhams) $28,260

A pair of beaded and fringed hide leggings, possibly Arapaho, Eastern Colorado, North American Plains, the yellow dyed hide embroidered with red banded white strips to the edges and knee, 75cm. long. (Bonhams) $2,512

A German Totomat machine by Günter Wulff, Berlin, finger operated machine, wooden case, 61 x 82 x 16cm., 1950.
(Auction Team Köln) $1,246

An Atlantic coin-operated electric shock machine by the Sächsische Automaten Industrie Wötzel u. Fickert, *A Way to Power and Beauty,* 31 x 17 x 30cm., circa 1910.
(Auction Team Köln) $1,050

A Treff mechanical 3-cylinder games machine with starting button, wooden case with cast front, 54 x 72.5 x 26cm., 1955.
(Auction Team Köln) $426

An Astoria-Rubin mechanical three-cylinder machine by Günter Hiltgens, Moers, with one start and two brake buttons, wooden case with painted metal mounts, 50 x 71.5 x 23cm, 1962.
(Auction Team Köln) $459

A Mills Twelve gaming machine by the Mills Novelty Co., Chicago, red painted cast aluminium front, wooden back and base for old pennies, 1955.
(Auction Team Köln) $2,179

An Addomat games machine by Günther Wulff, Berlin, electric single disc machine with stop button, wooden case with glass front, 50 x 74 x 22cm., 1966.
(Auction Team Köln) $328

A Bajazzo pinball machine by Jenzsch & Meerz, Leipzig, dark brown wood case with green playing surface and brass mountings, 45 x 63 x 17cm., post 1904. (Auction Team Köln)
$2,972

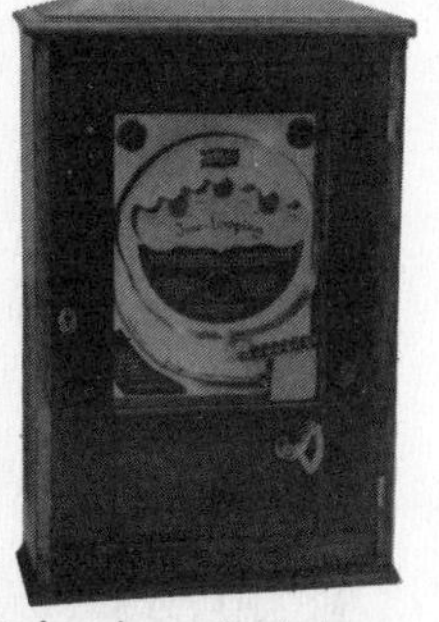

An Imo-Looping early electro-mechanical catapult action machine with points/win display with three lamps and an electric bell, wooden case, 51.5 x 78 x 20cm., circa 1930.
(Auction Team Köln) $2,296

A Rouletta gaming machine by Th. Bergmann & Co., Hamburg, face of molded mirrored glass and gold painted aluminium, wooden casing, circa 1960, 49 x 72 x 23cm.
(Auction Team Köln) $297

A Ludus mechanical three-cylinder games machine by Hans Lindl, Kelheim, wooden case with metal parts and brass mounts, 51 x 74 x 24cm. 1964.
(Auction Team Köln) $557

A Bravo coin-operated catapult machine, putting the ball in the basket wins a cigar, no spring mechanism, 22 x 22 x 35cm., circa 1900.
(Auction Team Köln) $1,969

A Duo-Lett gaming machine by Wulff, Berlin, mechanical two-dial machine, wooden casing, with start button and crank drive, 1958, 48 x 74 x 21cm.
(Auction Team Köln) $595

A Derby Luxus games machine by T.H. Bergmann, Hamburg, three cylinder machine with selection button, wooden case with molded glass front, 49 x 72.5 x 25cm., 1962.
(Auction Team Köln) $492

A Diplomat games machine by O.J. Hoffmann, Düsseldorf, electric 3-cylinder machine with stop-button, for 10pfg. pieces, wooden case with cast front, 49.5 x 63 x 21cm., 1955.
(Auction Team Köln) $184

A Roulomint machine by Löwen automaten, Braunschweig, Roulette machine with number and color selection buttons, wooden case, 50.5 x 71 x 24cm., 1955.
(Auction Team Köln) $170

A Neomat Select by O.J. Hoffmann, Hellenthal, an electric 3-cylinder machine with stop and start buttons, for 10pfg. pieces, wooden case, 50.5 x 67.5 x 23cm., 1963.
(Auction Team Köln) $328

An electro-mechanical Bingolett catapult machine, for 10pfg. pieces, wooden case with pressed glass front, 50 x 73.5 x 25cm., 1959.
(Auction Team Köln) $426

An Rotomat Juwel gaming machine by Günter Wulff, Berlin, 3-cylinder machine with start button and two stop buttons, wooden case, 55 x 71.5 x 25cm., 1953.
(Auction Team Köln) $590

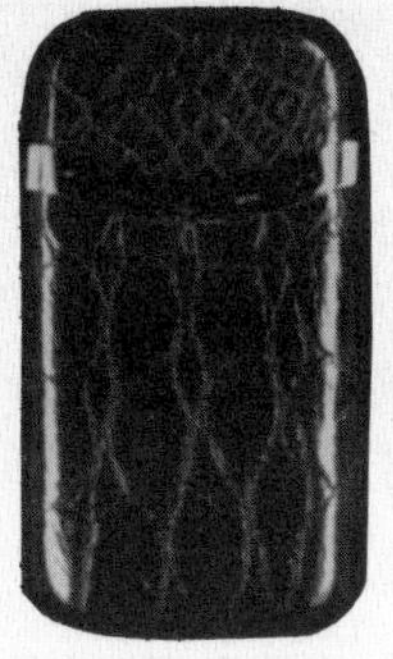

A silver mounted crocodile skin cigar case, London 1912, maker's mark worn, rectangular form, plain mount, 13.8cm. high. (Bonhams) $272

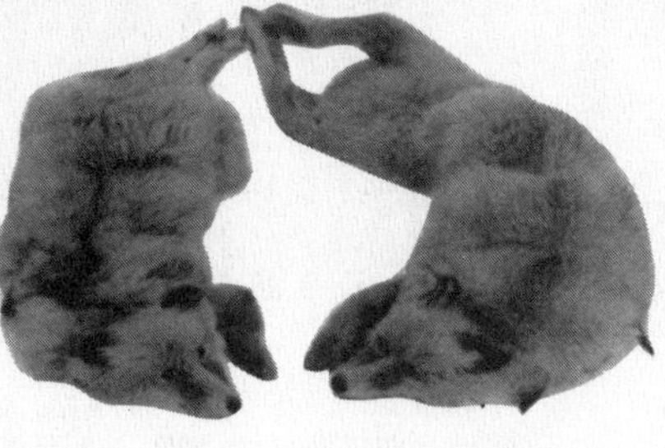

1920s fox collars with heads and fore and hind legs and glass eyes. 70cm. long excluding legs. (Auction Team Köln) $220

A mallard in a glass dome, set on reed foliage, 19½ x 23in. (Bonhams) $480

A fine cased mallard drake, by Rowland Ward, 167 Piccadilly, London, on a realistic setting of reeds and grasses within a slab-sided case, retailer's oval to base 20in. wide. . (Bonhams) $785

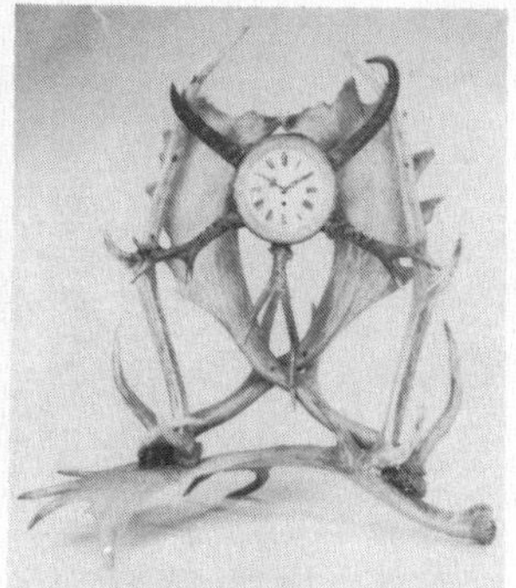

An unusual French antler mounted mantel timepiece, early 20th century, with single barrel movement, later vertically positioned platform escapement, 24in. high. (Christie's) $1,120

A case containing a male snowy owl perched on a tree stump with moss and heather foliage, labelled *Kenneth Pemberton, Onibury*, 25 x 29in. (Russell Baldwin & Bright) $521

A fine cased hybrid cock pheasant, by Rowland Ward, 167 Piccadilly, London, on a realistic setting of leaves and grasses, within a slab-sided case, retailer's oval to base 35½in. wide. (Bonhams) $644

A spherical dinosaur egg, Saltasaurus Cretaceous, from Patagonia, Argentina, 7¼in. diameter. (Christie's) $11,265

A cased fox plucking the body of a white goose, against a dusky sky and naturalistic surroundings. (Wintertons) $412

A Sumerian white stone recumbent bull with incised naturalistic details, the eyes recessed, 3rd Millennium B.C., 1½in. (Bonhams) $1,127

A pale blue Roman glass jug, with cylindrical body and broad combed strap handle folded at right angles to the body, 2nd-3rd century A.D., 13.7cm. (Bonhams) $805

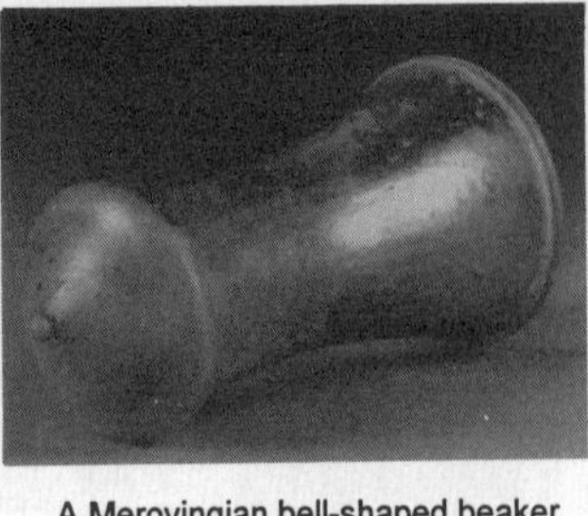

A Merovingian bell-shaped beaker, of bubbly pale green glass, the flaring mouth with a thickened fire-rounded rim, circa 6th century A.D., 5¼in. (Bonhams) $4,508

A large late Roman pale green glass lamp with curved sides tapering to a narrow base, with a row of applied blue glass blobs around the shoulder, 4th-5th century A.D., 4in. high. (Bonhams) $2,898

A Roman terracotta fragmentary relief showing a standing draped female molded in high relief wearing a long himation pulled over her head, circa 1st century A.D., 16½in. (Bonhams) $11,270

An Egyptian gesso-painted wood mask with black-painted headdress, ochre face and details in black with black and white eyes, Late Period – Ptolemaic, 10½in. (Bonhams) $644

A large Attic black glazed hydria with finely ribbed body, the plain neck and shoulder decorated with a chain of interlinked lotus buds, 5th-4th century B.C., 20½in. (Bonhams) $8,050

A Roman cobalt blue glass drinking cup with out-turned lip and ground-down rim, scratched lines below the rim, first half of the 1st century A.D., 3in. diameter. (Bonhams) $2,093

An important Anglo-Saxon gold and garnet pectoral Cross, the cellwork is filled with shaped garnets held in place by calcium carbonate paste and pointillé gold, early 7th century A.D., 5.3cm. (Bonhams) $88,550

A Byzantine glazed pottery dish, with straight, slightly flaring sides, of orange clay with cream slip on the interior decorated with an incised pattern, first part of the 12th century A.D., 23.8cm. diameter. (Bonhams) $1,127

A Roman purple mould-blown glass grape flask, realistically molded in the form of an asymmetrical bunch of grapes, Eastern Mediterranean, A.D. 150-200, 11.5cm. (Bonhams) $4,508

A New Kingdom fragmentary limestone relief showing two registers of offering bearers, the upper carved with the legs of two figures walking with a dog and a horned goat, circa 1567-1200 B.C., 13 x 15½in.(Bonhams) $1,256

An Attic Red-Figure bell krater, attributed to the Komaris Painter decorated on Side A with a semi-erotic komos scene, circa 410 B.C., 30cm. high. (Bonhams) $23,345

An Alexandrian hollow-backed terracotta head with thick tightly curled hair and beard, with furrowed brows, circa 1st century B.C./A.D., 8cm. high. (Bonhams) $403

An Egyptian bead mummy mask, composed of disc-shaped glazed composition spacer beads strung together, the face of pale yellow, Late Period – Ptolemaic, circa 500-30 B.C., 19.3 x 18.2cm. (Bonhams) $2,898

A large black basalt weight, of spherical form with flattened top and bottom, bronze bands wrapped around the body and fixed together enabling suspension, weight 3.4kg, height 4½in. (Bonhams) $885

A Roman marble fragmentary relief carved in sunk relief showing Herakles standing naked, leaning on a large hydria or urn, 1st-2nd century A.D., 13½ x 9 x 2¾in. (Bonhams) $2,254

A Villanovan Bucchero ware amphoriskos, on a pad base with strap handles, the incised decoration of a figure-of-eight spiral on either side of the body, 8th-7th century B.C., 3in. (Bonhams) $885

Maximilian-style horse armour, Schmidt Workshop, late 19th /early 20th century copy of a 16th century type, chanfron, hammered plate steel with fluting roped edging, galleried orbits, floral boss containing a corkscrew spike.
(Skinner) $2,415

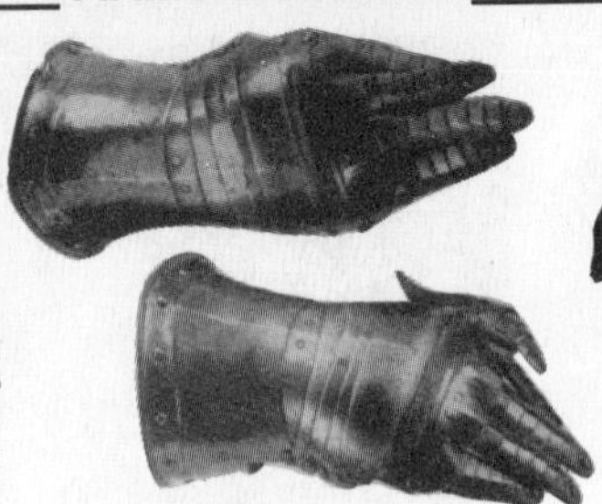

A pair of German fingered guantlets mid-late 16th century, of bright steel, each comprising a flared boxed cuff made in two pieces, 29cm. (Bonhams) $1,208

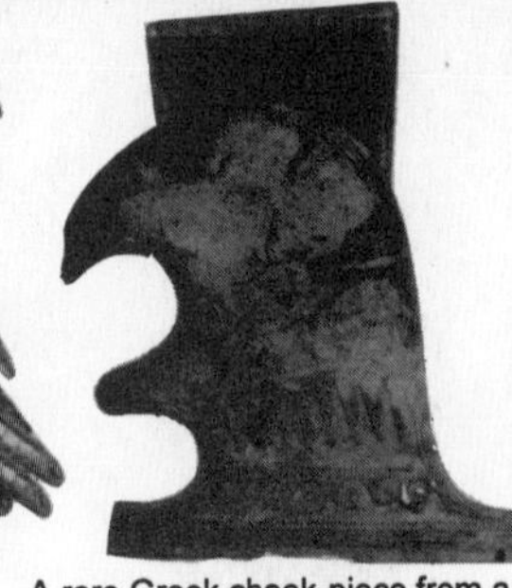

A rare Greek cheek-piece from a helmet, 4th – 3rd century B.C., of bronze and in excavated condition, shaped to the cheek and decorated with line borders, 16.1cm.
(Bonhams) $1,208

A Menpo (Half Mask), Edo Period (Late 17th/early 18th century), the russet iron mask of good form and modelled with ears in one piece.
(Christie's) $3,562

An interesting Indian mail shirt, probably 18th century, made from tiny riveted rings, vent to rear, open front, red velvet collar with embroidered edges.
(Wallis & Wallis) $825

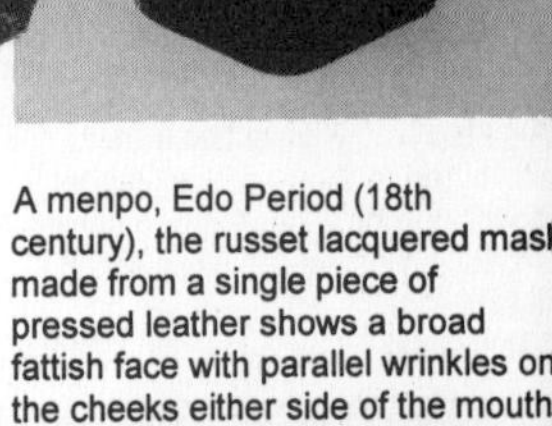

A menpo, Edo Period (18th century), the russet lacquered mas[k] made from a single piece of pressed leather shows a broad fattish face with parallel wrinkles on the cheeks either side of the mouth
(Christie's) $2,16[6]

A composed half armor, predominantly 16th century, including a closed helmet, Italian, circa 1600; a breastplate, backplate, collar and tassets, all Italian, gauntlets, 19th century.
(Tennants) $6,840

A fine heavy 17th century Indian chain mail and lamellar shirt, the mail of alternate rows of thickly forged solid rings and riveted rings, taken at the Siege of Adoni in 1689.
(Wallis & Wallis) $1,492

A complete armor for an officer of Pikemen, morion, breastplate, backplate and tassets all decorated en suite, English, first half 17th century. (Tennants) $10,64

A magnificient somen, Muromachi Period (Late 15th/early 16th century), the large iron mask is modelled on the shishiguchi-men used in the noh drama hyakkyo. (Christie's) $45,712

An Indian gold-damascened top and dastana (arm-guards) 18th century, of watered steel, the first with domed skull decorated around the rim with gold-damascened bands of running arabesques and foliage. (Bonhams) $1,449

A 17th century English cavalry trooper's breastplate, of traditional form with medial ridge, slightly flared narrow skirt, raised edge to neck and arm cusps. (Wallis & Wallis) $769

A fine menpo, Edo Perod (18th century), the russet iron mask boldly forged with deep repoussé wrinkles, the nose detachable with hooks and fitted with rings on the cheeks. (Christie's) $6,320

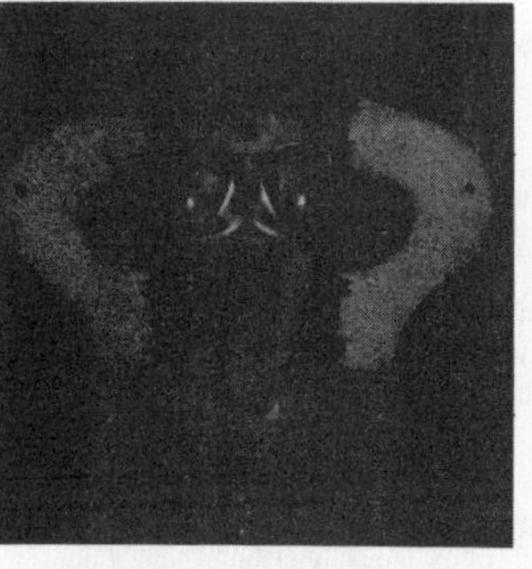

A fine horse armor (bagai) with mask (bamen) Edo Period (17th century), the horse armor made in two sections, one to protect the neck and shoulders, the other for the croup, flank and thighs, the mask 14¾in. long. (Christie's) $27,082

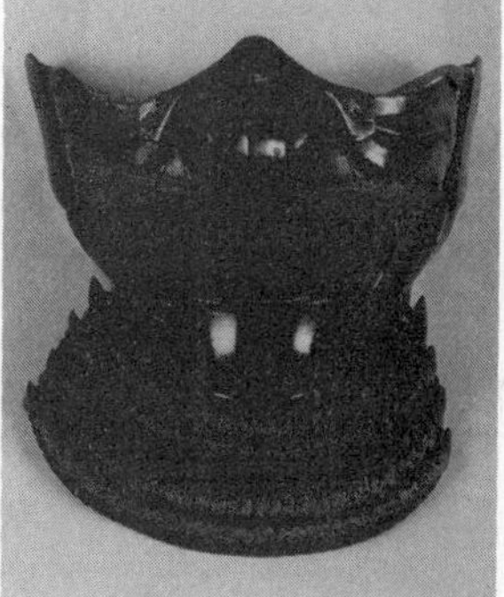

A menpo [half mask], Edo Period (Late 18th/early 19th century), the black lacquered iron mask with a hair moustache. (Christie's) $2, 236

A French Carabinier's breast and backplate, circa 1830, heavy steel plate faced with brass bearing oval brass badge of eagle clutching thunderbolt. (Wallis & Wallis) $1,413

An Eastern mail shirt, perhaps Turkish, 16th/17th century, of riveted iron rings, knee-length, the skirt split front and rear, elbow-length sleeves. (Bonhams) $837

Household Cavalry Trooper's front cuirass plate, this front plate has been adapted as a wall ornament, made of nickel silver, edged with a brass band and ornamented with brass studs. (Bosleys) $437

A composite Silesian flintlock ax pistol Fokos, 32in., part octagonal barrel 18¾in, head engraved with bird, snail, wolf's head and rabbit, pierced shaped peen. Stock inlaid with engraved staghorn plaques, lock signed *S Havschca.* (Wallis & Wallis) $3,062

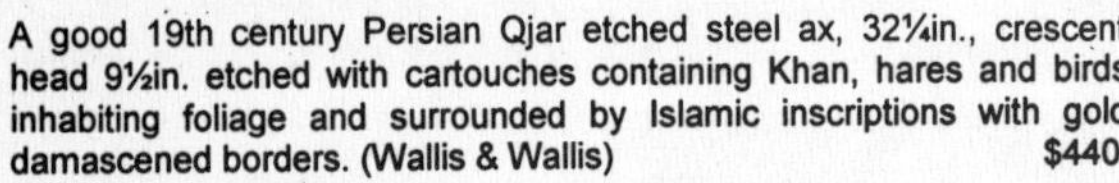

A good 19th century Persian Qjar etched steel ax, 32¼in., crescent head 9½in. etched with cartouches containing Khan, hares and birds inhabiting foliage and surrounded by Islamic inscriptions with gold damascened borders. (Wallis & Wallis) $440

A European fighting ax, possibly 16th century, head 7½in. with slightly backward facing 5½in. cutting edge, large eye with cover stepped over back of haft. Later wooden haft. (Wallis & Wallis) $242

A naval boarding ax, steel head stamped with WD and arrow, inspector's stamp and *W Gilpin*, rounded wooden haft, mounted with brass rack number stamped *5*, overall length 23in., head 4½in. (Wallis & Wallis) $597

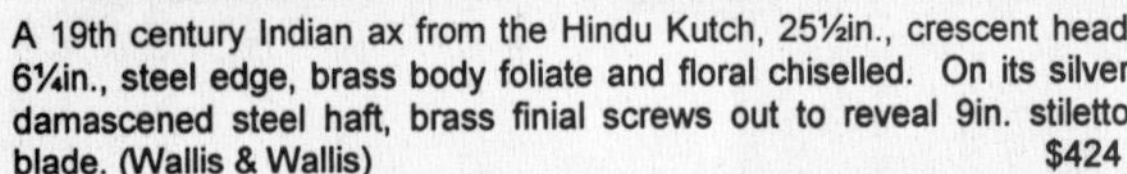

A 19th century Indian ax from the Hindu Kutch, 25½in., crescent head 6¼in., steel edge, brass body foliate and floral chiselled. On its silver damascened steel haft, brass finial screws out to reveal 9in. stiletto blade. (Wallis & Wallis) $424

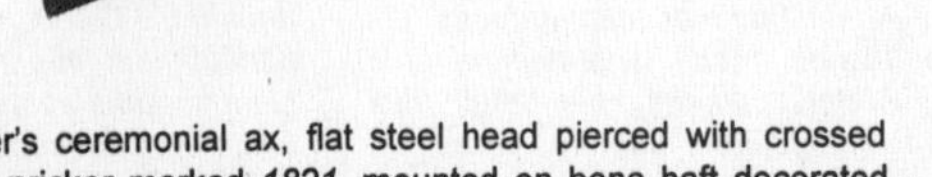

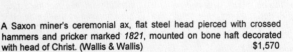

A Saxon miner's ceremonial ax, flat steel head pierced with crossed hammers and pricker marked *1821*, mounted on bone haft decorated with head of Christ. (Wallis & Wallis) $1,570

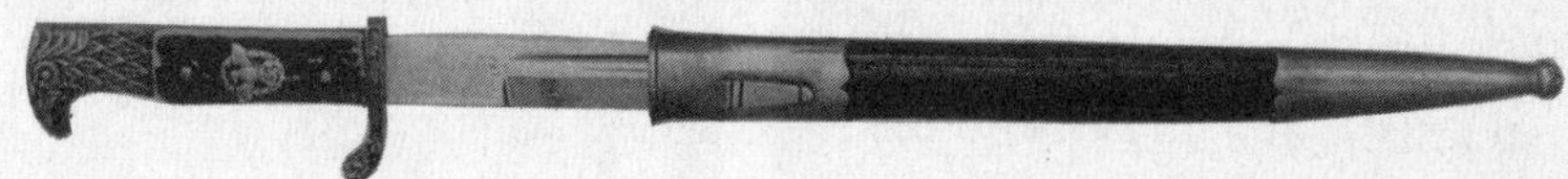

A Nazi Police carbine length dress bayonet, by Carl Eickhorn, plated blade 10in., gray metal stylized eagle's head pommel and mounts, staghorn grips with police emblem, in its black leather sheath with plated mounts. (Wallis & Wallis) $393

Imperial German Ersatz conversion bayonet, Great War period example. The triangular blade is fitted into an all steel Ersatz pattern hilt with simulated ribbed grip and threequarter muzzle ring. Blade length 18in. (Bosleys) $196

A Nazi Wehrmacht dress bayonet, by E Pack & Sohne, plated blade 9½in., etched *Zur Erinnerung An Meine Dienstzeit*, bordered with oak leaves and German soldier. (Wallis & Wallis) $226

Imperial German Ersatz conversion bayonet, Great War period example, Enfield style triangular blade fitted into an all steel Ersatz pattern hilt, with flat smooth sides and threequarter muzzle ring. Blade length 18in. (Bosleys) $196

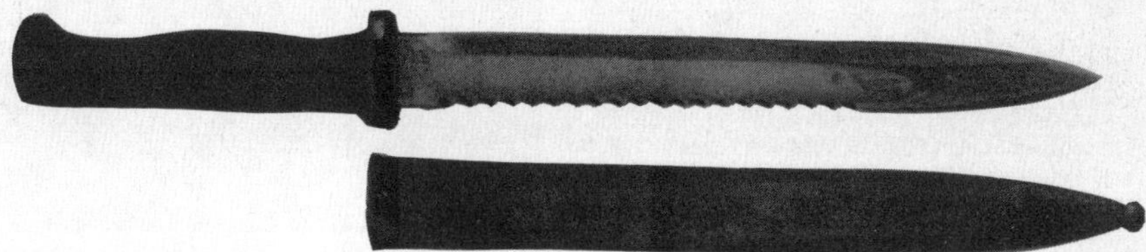

An Imperial German Seitengewehr M1884/98 bayonet with saw back blade, maker's stamp *Gebr Heller Marienthal*. Two piece wooden grip with two rivets, complete with metal scabbard. (Bosleys) $118

A Nazi Wehrmacht dress bayonet, plated blade 10in., marked Solingen, etched with *Zur Erinnerung An Meine Dienstzeit* within scroll, machine gun team etc, and *Inf Regt 115 Worms A RH*, plated hilt, diced black grips. (Wallis & Wallis) $283

A Nazi police dress bayonet, by Weyersberg Kirschbaum, German silver hilt with staghorn grips and police emblem, eagle's head pommel, the crosspiece and scabbard locket stamped *L A1 129*. (Wallis & Wallis) $240

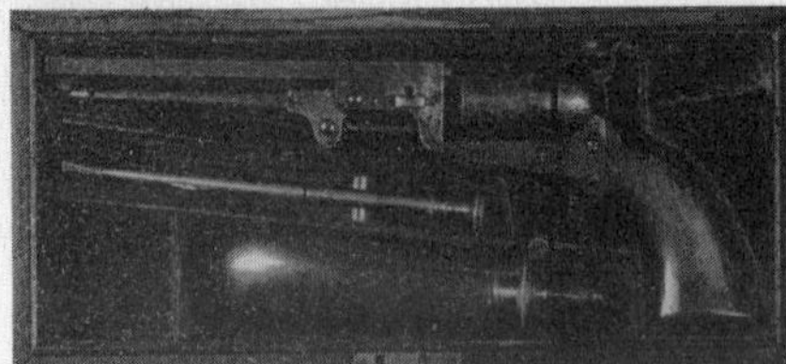

A cased Colt 1851 Model Navy percussion revolver, No. 25523 for 1855, with octagonal sighted barrel with London address, cylinder with naval engagement scene, rammer, steel trigger-guard and back-strap, varnished walnut grips, 33cm.
(Bonhams) $2,737

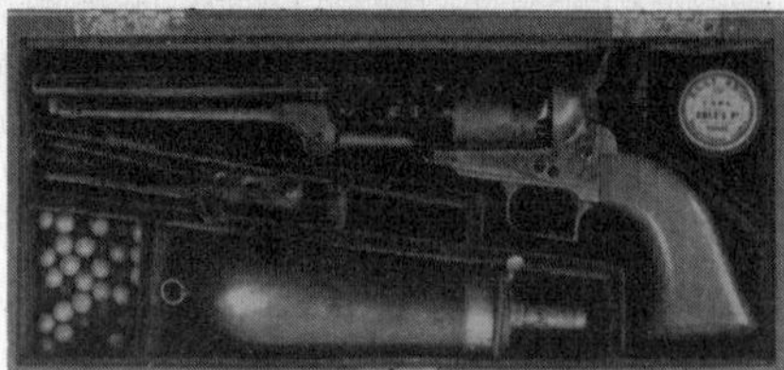

A cased reproduction .36 Navy percussion revolver by Colt, serial no. 1306, for 1971, a commemorative model to Ulysses S. Grant with 7½in. blued barrel with rolled name and address and commemorative details, blued chamber engraved by W.M. Ormsby depicting a Naval scene. (Bonhams) $448

A cased pair of Irish 80-bore percussion box-lock turn-over pistols by Wm. & Jn. Rigby, 24 Suffolk Street, Dublin, Nos. 9568/9 for 1846, with turn-off barrels engraved at the muzzles and numbered from 1 to 4, foliate engraved case-hardened breeches, hammers and actions, in original fitted mahogany case. (Bonhams) $5,152

A rare cased pair of silver mounted American saw-handled flintlock duelling pistols, by B. & J. Cooper, New York, circa 1820, octagonal twist steel barrels set with silver fore-sights, gold lined touch holes and double gold bands at breeches, locks with inlaid gold ovals engraved *B&J COOPER*, finely engraved borders. (Bonhams) $20,700

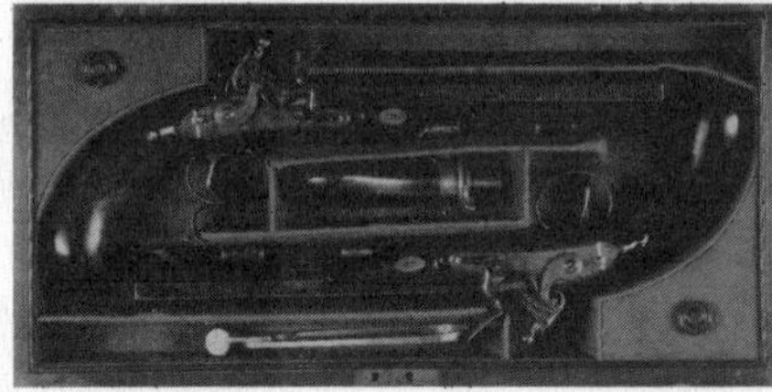

A cased pair of 25-bore flintlock duelling pistols, by Sykes, Oxford, early 19th century, with rebrowned twist octagonal sighted barrels, tangs finely engraved with foliage and a starburst, roller, rainproof pan and engraved safety-catch, Birmingham private proof marks, 37cm. (Bonhams) $6,923

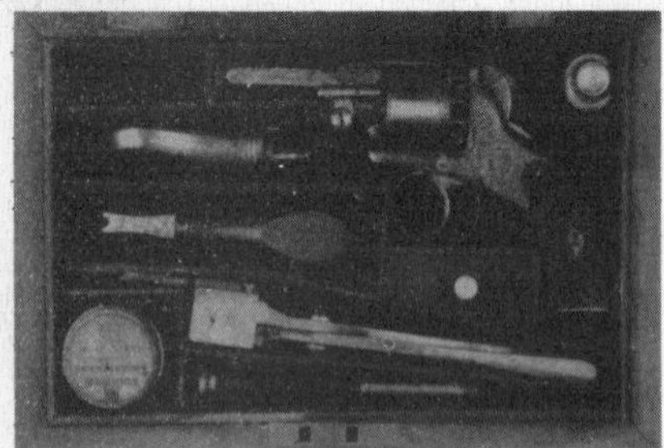

An unusual cased 105-bore Bentley Patent five-shot self-cocking percussion pocket revolver, unsigned, No. 5, circa 1855, with blued octagonal sighted barrel retained by a wedge, engraved at the muzzle and with scrollwork on the top-strap, 16.5cm.
(Bonhams) $1,530

A cased 25-bore percussion saw-handled duelling pistol, by J. Probin, Maker to His R.H. The Prince of Wales, early 19th century, converted from flintlock, with rebrowned octagonal sighted barrel signed in full on the top flat, in lined and fitted mahogany case, Birmingham private proof marks.
(Bonhams) $2,737

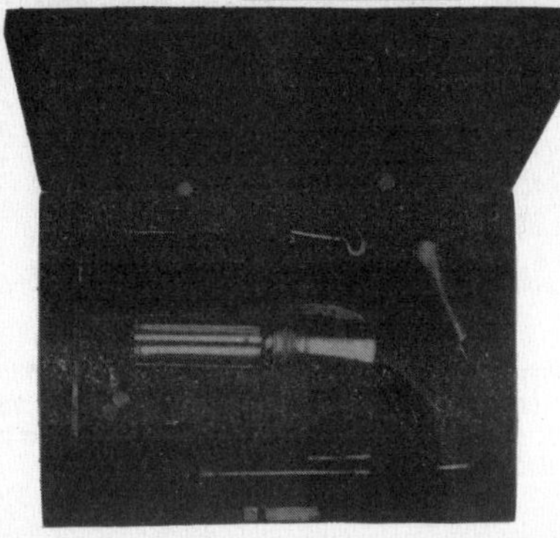

A scarce 6 shot 100 bore nickel framed and barrelled self cocking percussion pepperbox revolver, 7¾in., fluted barrels 3in. Birmingham proved, fern tip engraved muzzles. Foliate engraved rounded frame with *Collins Maker*. (Wallis & Wallis) $942

A cased pair of 25-bore percussion travelling pistols by Thomas Cartmell of Doncaster, early 19th century, rebuilt from flintlock, with short rebrowned sighted barrels each engraved with foliage in front of the sighting flat, 23cm. (Bonhams) $2,576

An unusual cased Irish six-shot saw-handled percussion pepperbox revolver by Wm. & Jn. Rigby, Dublin, No. 9149 for 1843, the barrels engraved with scrolls at the breech, blued signed action engraved with characteristic scrollwork, 20.4cm.
(Bonhams) $5,152

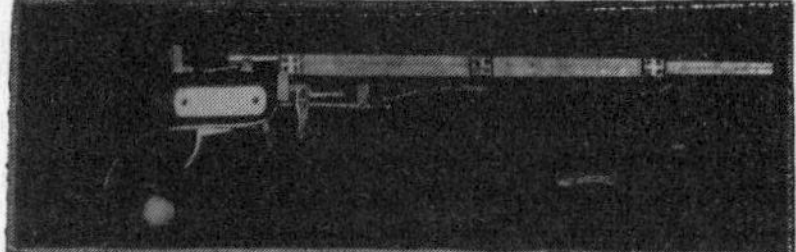

A most unusual Swiss precision made magician's pistol, 14½in. two piece brass octagonal barrel 9¾in., the two halves secured by screwed steel plates. Coil sprung plunger 'cocked' by bone tipped ebony 'ramrod'. Ebonized checkered stock.
(Wallis & Wallis) $1,610

A cased pair of 18-bore flintlock officer's pistols, by James Stevens, 43 High Holborn, London, No. 1008, circa 1820, with browned twist sighted barrels each signed in full on the top flat, platinum touch-holes, engraved case-hardened tangs each incorporating a back-sight, in original fitted oak case, 28.6cm.
(Bonhams) $3,220

A cased pair of 18-bore percussion pistols by Thomas Gill, London, early 19th century, rebuilt from flintlock, with browned twist octagonal sighted barrels, case-hardened breeches, in lined and fitted oak case, Tower private proof marks, 36.5cm.
(Bonhams) $2,737

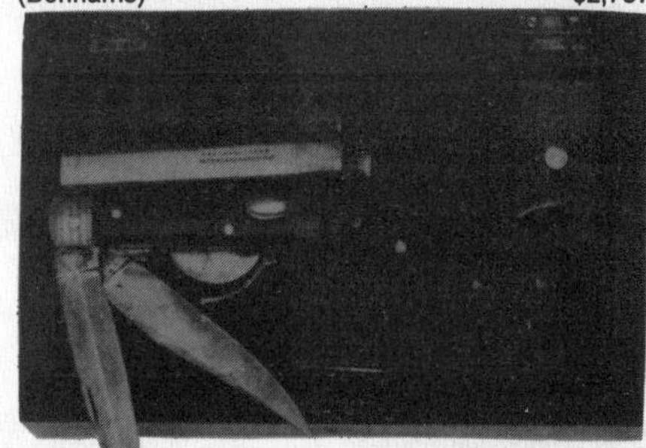

A good cased Unwin & Rodgers 7mm rimfire combination knife pistol, with two blades, checkered hobnail grips, hinged butt trap and folding trigger, hexagonal barrel Birmingham proved, in its hinged case with brass escutcheon.
(Wallis & Wallis) $1,530

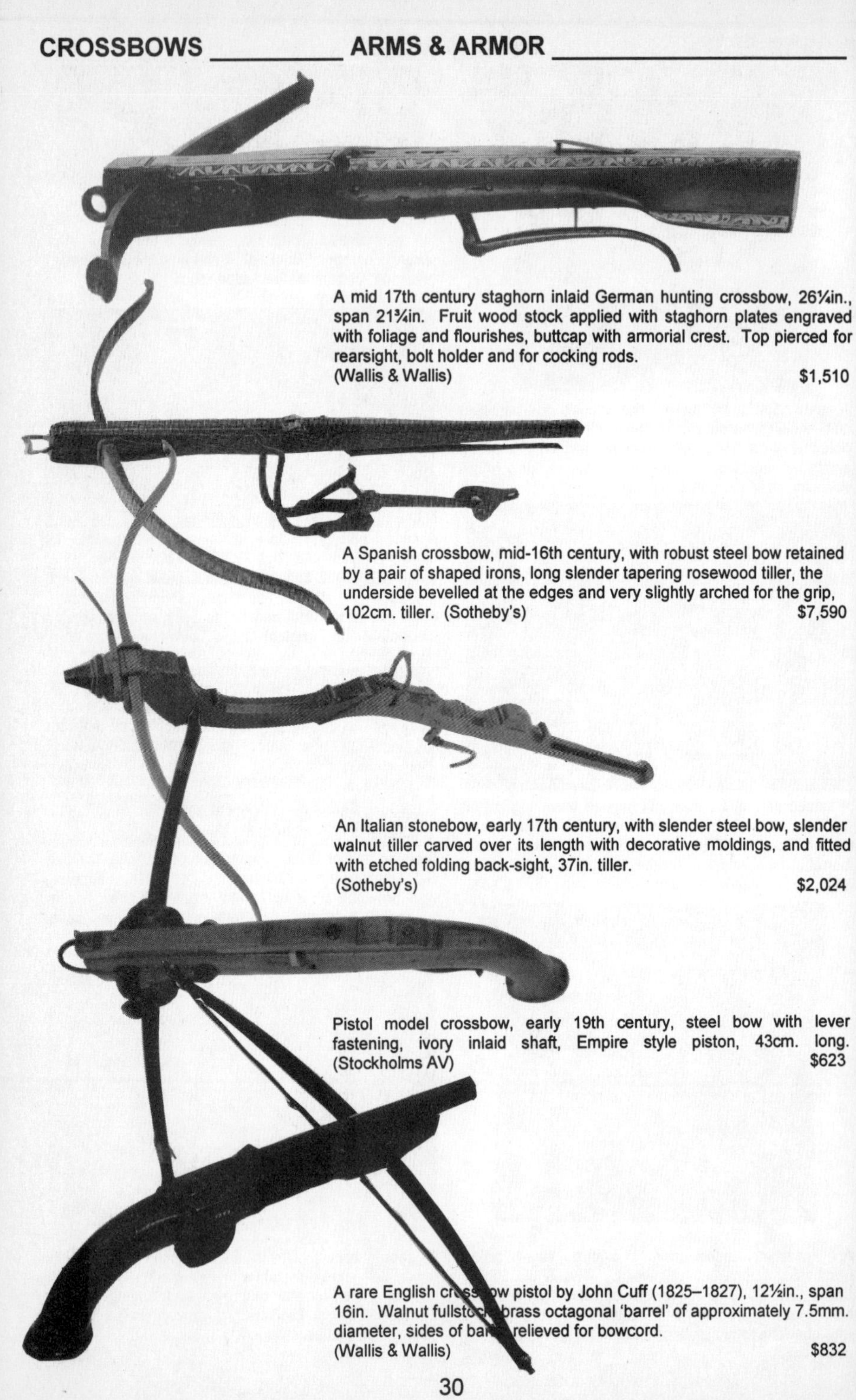

A mid 17th century staghorn inlaid German hunting crossbow, 26¼in., span 21¾in. Fruit wood stock applied with staghorn plates engraved with foliage and flourishes, buttcap with armorial crest. Top pierced for rearsight, bolt holder and for cocking rods.
(Wallis & Wallis) $1,510

A Spanish crossbow, mid-16th century, with robust steel bow retained by a pair of shaped irons, long slender tapering rosewood tiller, the underside bevelled at the edges and very slightly arched for the grip, 102cm. tiller. (Sotheby's) $7,590

An Italian stonebow, early 17th century, with slender steel bow, slender walnut tiller carved over its length with decorative moldings, and fitted with etched folding back-sight, 37in. tiller.
(Sotheby's) $2,024

Pistol model crossbow, early 19th century, steel bow with lever fastening, ivory inlaid shaft, Empire style piston, 43cm. long.
(Stockholms AV) $623

A rare English crossbow pistol by John Cuff (1825–1827), 12½in., span 16in. Walnut fullstock, brass octagonal 'barrel' of approximately 7.5mm. diameter, sides of barrel relieved for bowcord.
(Wallis & Wallis) $832

A good gold damascened 19th century jade hilted Indian dagger pesh kabz, 18¼in., T section polished blade 12in. with thickened tip and raised rib, etched with watered pattern. Four piece shaped green jade grips with ivory spacers. (Wallis & Wallis) $543

A good gold and silver mounted 19th century Indian kukri, swollen single edged fullered blade 12in., carved bone hilt, in its black leather sheath, bone handled companion knives and leather wallet. (Wallis & Wallis) $471

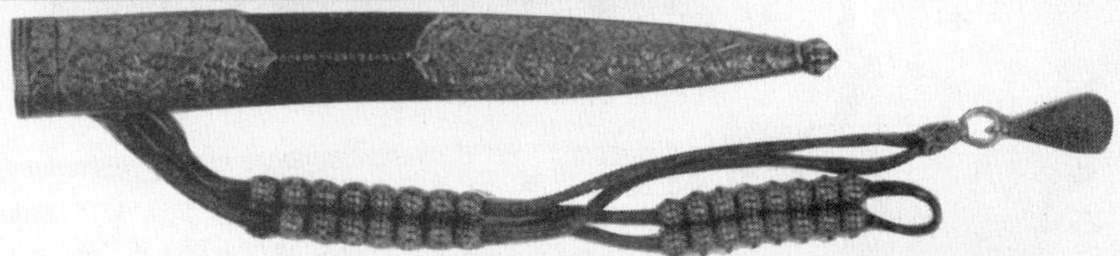

A Turkish silver-mounted dagger, struck with Tughra mark of Mahmud I (1730-54 A.D.), with finely watered single-edged blade struck with a mark at the forte and decorated with three small groups of encrusted gold foliage, 39cm. (Bonhams) $4,991

A 19th century silver mounted kukri, swollen polished blade 16in., steel mounted polished one piece horn hilt. In its black leather covered sheath with large silver mounts. (Wallis & Wallis) $247

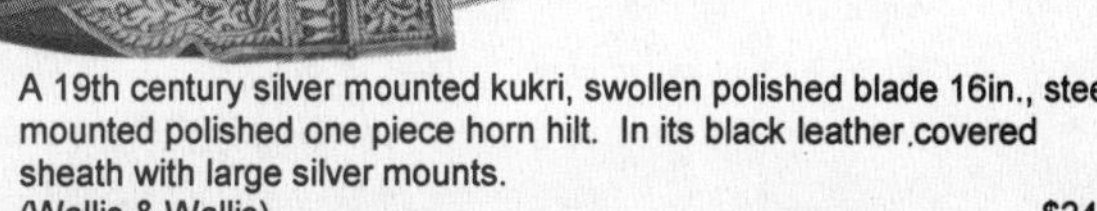

An Italian Gil 1938 model Youth leader's dagger, plated blade 7½in., aluminium hilt, black central panel inset with brass fasces, eagle head pommel, in its blue painted metal sheath. (Wallis & Wallis) $496

A late 19th century Siamese dagger, straight single edged blade 12¼in., brass hilt, elephant's head pommel with inlaid eye, 2 piece checkered ivory grips, crosspiece with dragon's head finials. (Wallis & Wallis) $173

A large 18th century Indo Persian dagger kard, blade 11in. back edge fluted. Steel gripstrap and ferrules, two piece ivory grips stained for effect. (Wallis & Wallis) $194

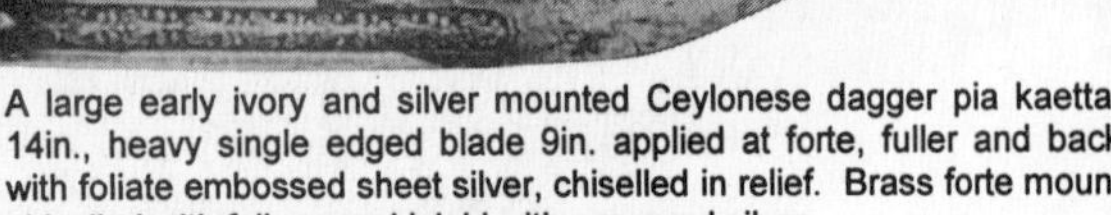

A large early ivory and silver mounted Ceylonese dagger pia kaetta, 14in., heavy single edged blade 9in. applied at forte, fuller and back with foliate embossed sheet silver, chiselled in relief. Brass forte mount chiselled with foliage and inlaid with engraved silver. (Wallis & Wallis) $667

A 17th century Indian dagger khanjarli from Vizianagram, 12¾in., recurved blade 8¼in. with swollen armor piercing tip, deep shaped fullers and raised ribs, foliate chiselled device at forte. (Wallis & Wallis) $981

A Spanish left-hand dagger, second half of 17th century, the blade with 9in. edge along back edge having also a finely formed spine, robust forte with two pierced circular holes and punched decorations forming a cross, 17in. blade. (Christie's) $12,650

A good 19th century all steel Sudanese dagger etched with thuluth script overall, 19¼in., curved blades 7½in., steel grip. In its twin crocodile skin covered sheaths with steel mounts etched en-suite. (Wallis & Wallis) $565

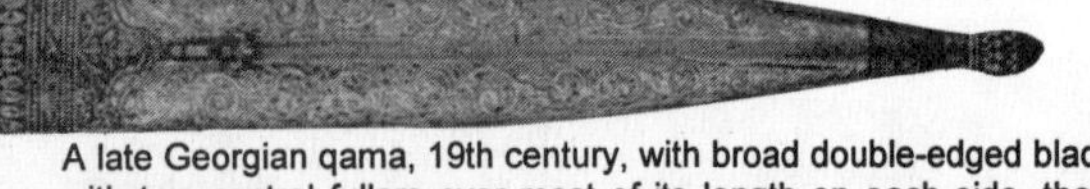

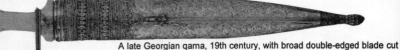

A late Georgian qama, 19th century, with broad double-edged blade cut with two central fullers over most of its length on each side, the forte struck with a mark and damascened in silver, 59.5cm. (Bonhams) $1,368

A good 18th century Spanish main gauche dagger, 20¾in., blade 16in. of diamond section, ricasso with serrated edges, hollow depression for thumb, stamped with crowned *S* and *Caino.* Guard finely pierced and chiselled. (Wallis & Wallis) $2,898

A Japanese WWII pilot's hara kiri dagger, blade 15cm., mumei, inscribed in the hi with 4 characters, wavy hamon. Wooden shirasaya with bone fuchi and koi guchi, in leather cover. (Wallis & Wallis) $1,359

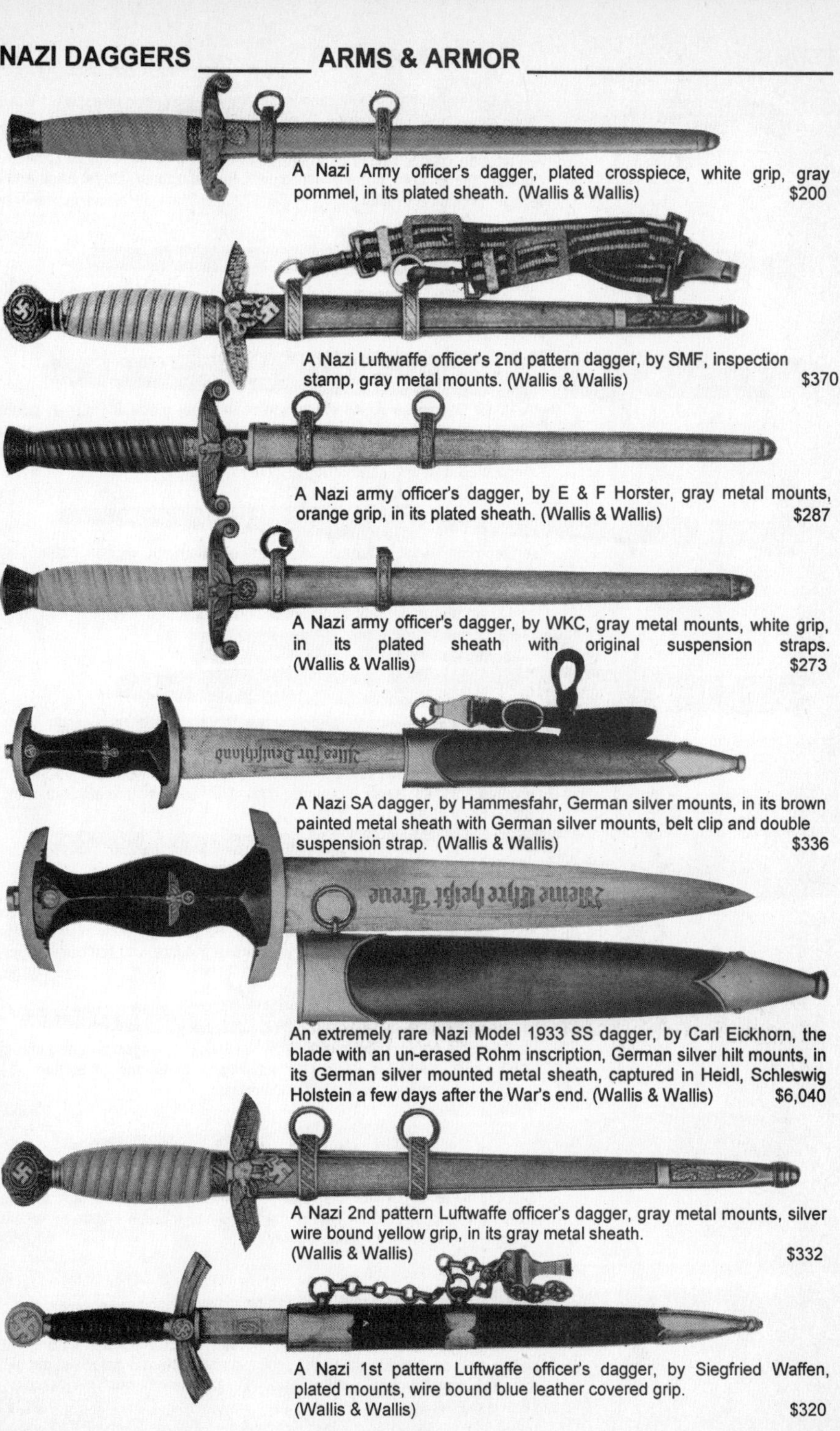

A Nazi Army officer's dagger, plated crosspiece, white grip, gray pommel, in its plated sheath. (Wallis & Wallis) $200

A Nazi Luftwaffe officer's 2nd pattern dagger, by SMF, inspection stamp, gray metal mounts. (Wallis & Wallis) $370

A Nazi army officer's dagger, by E & F Horster, gray metal mounts, orange grip, in its plated sheath. (Wallis & Wallis) $287

A Nazi army officer's dagger, by WKC, gray metal mounts, white grip, in its plated sheath with original suspension straps. (Wallis & Wallis) $273

A Nazi SA dagger, by Hammesfahr, German silver mounts, in its brown painted metal sheath with German silver mounts, belt clip and double suspension strap. (Wallis & Wallis) $336

An extremely rare Nazi Model 1933 SS dagger, by Carl Eickhorn, the blade with an un-erased Rohm inscription, German silver hilt mounts, in its German silver mounted metal sheath, captured in Heidl, Schleswig Holstein a few days after the War's end. (Wallis & Wallis) $6,040

A Nazi 2nd pattern Luftwaffe officer's dagger, gray metal mounts, silver wire bound yellow grip, in its gray metal sheath. (Wallis & Wallis) $332

A Nazi 1st pattern Luftwaffe officer's dagger, by Siegfried Waffen, plated mounts, wire bound blue leather covered grip. (Wallis & Wallis) $320

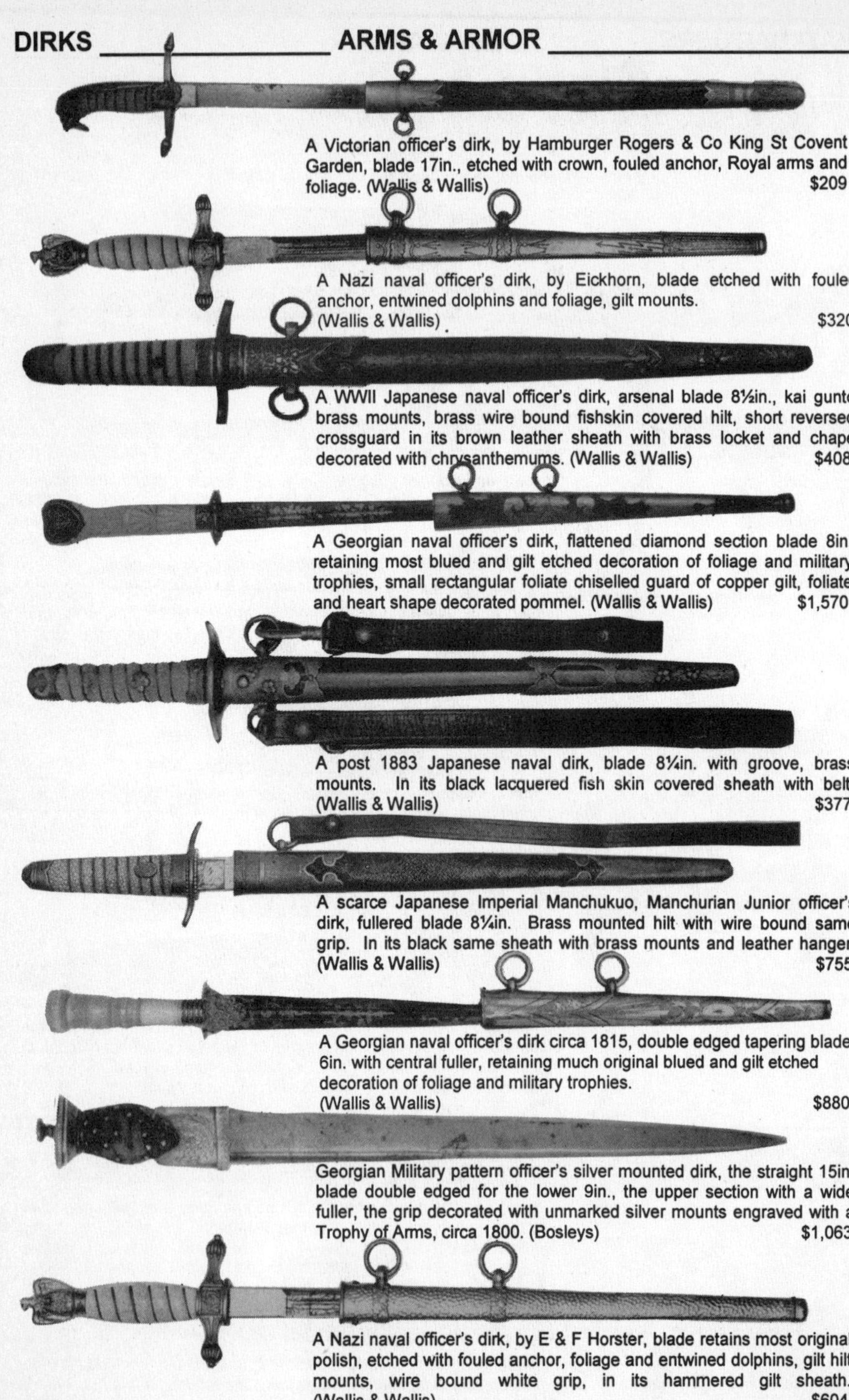

A Victorian officer's dirk, by Hamburger Rogers & Co King St Covent Garden, blade 17in., etched with crown, fouled anchor, Royal arms and foliage. (Wallis & Wallis) $209

A Nazi naval officer's dirk, by Eickhorn, blade etched with fouled anchor, entwined dolphins and foliage, gilt mounts. (Wallis & Wallis) $320

A WWII Japanese naval officer's dirk, arsenal blade 8½in., kai gunto brass mounts, brass wire bound fishskin covered hilt, short reversed crossguard in its brown leather sheath with brass locket and chape decorated with chrysanthemums. (Wallis & Wallis) $408

A Georgian naval officer's dirk, flattened diamond section blade 8in. retaining most blued and gilt etched decoration of foliage and military trophies, small rectangular foliate chiselled guard of copper gilt, foliate and heart shape decorated pommel. (Wallis & Wallis) $1,570

A post 1883 Japanese naval dirk, blade 8¼in. with groove, brass mounts. In its black lacquered fish skin covered sheath with belt. (Wallis & Wallis) $377

A scarce Japanese Imperial Manchukuo, Manchurian Junior officer's dirk, fullered blade 8¼in. Brass mounted hilt with wire bound same grip. In its black same sheath with brass mounts and leather hanger. (Wallis & Wallis) $755

A Georgian naval officer's dirk circa 1815, double edged tapering blade 6in. with central fuller, retaining much original blued and gilt etched decoration of foliage and military trophies. (Wallis & Wallis) $880

Georgian Military pattern officer's silver mounted dirk, the straight 15in. blade double edged for the lower 9in., the upper section with a wide fuller, the grip decorated with unmarked silver mounts engraved with a Trophy of Arms, circa 1800. (Bosleys) $1,063

A Nazi naval officer's dirk, by E & F Horster, blade retains most original polish, etched with fouled anchor, foliage and entwined dolphins, gilt hilt mounts, wire bound white grip, in its hammered gilt sheath. (Wallis & Wallis) $604

A Regimental Scottish dirk and plaid brooch of the 4th Volunteer Battalion of the Black Watch, by Anderson & Sons, George Street, Edinburgh, the first with single-edged blade fullered and notched along the back-edge, baluster-shaped dark wood hilt carved with basketwork, the last cast, pierced and chased with regimental badge and motto, the first 44.5cm. (Bonhams) $1,530

A silver-mounted Scottish dirk, a dress skean dhu, and a sporran, the first with Edinburgh silver hallmarks for 1888, maker's mark *TJ*, single-edged blade fullered and notched along the back-edge, baluster-shaped dark wood hilt carved with basketwork, the first 36cm. (Bonhams) $1,224

A good early 18th century Scottish dirk, straight double edged blade 14¼in. deeply struck *Andrea Farara* with four deep king's head maker's stamps on both sides, with two pairs of short fullers. Bog oak hilt nicely carved with woven Celtic strapwork design. (Wallis & Wallis) $3,864

A silver mounted Scottish dress dirk, fullered blade 11in. with scalloped back edge. Basket weave carved bog oak grip, in its leather sheath with companion knife and fork en-suite. (Wallis & Wallis) $1,610

A Scottish dirk set, plain, scallop backed blade 11¼in. retaining all original polish, corded black wood hilt, decorated with brass studs, carved at base with Scottish thistle and Highland bonnet, gilt mounts with thistle decoration, imitation Cairngorm faceted pommel. (Wallis & Wallis) $830

An unusual mid 19th century Scottish silver mounted dirk, multi fullered polished blade 11½in. stamped with maker *Mason*, pierced fuller, scalloped back edge. Horn grip (possibly waterbuck), silver mounted embossed and chased with thistles and laurel. (Wallis & Wallis) $2,174

A boy's Highland dirk, and a dress skean dhu the first dated *Novr. 1868*, maker's mark *TJ*, the first with single-edged blade notched along the back-edge at the forte, baluster-shaped wooden grip carved with basketwork and set with silver studs, the last with silver-mounted grip carved with basketwork and set with silver studs on the outside. (Bonhams) $805

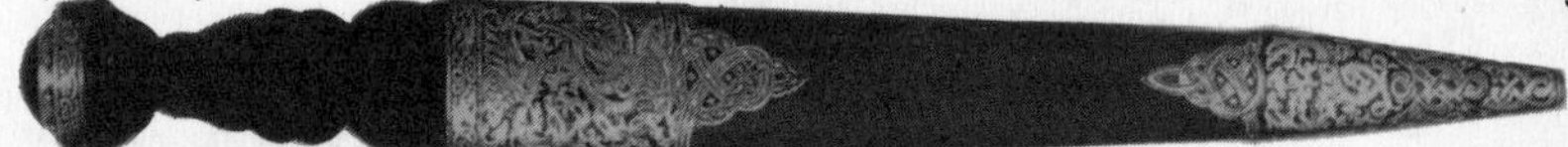

An unusual late 19th century silver mounted Scottish dirk, fullered blade 12in., scalloped back edge. Nicely carved boxwood grip, cabochon cut dark glass pommel. (Wallis & Wallis) $2,093

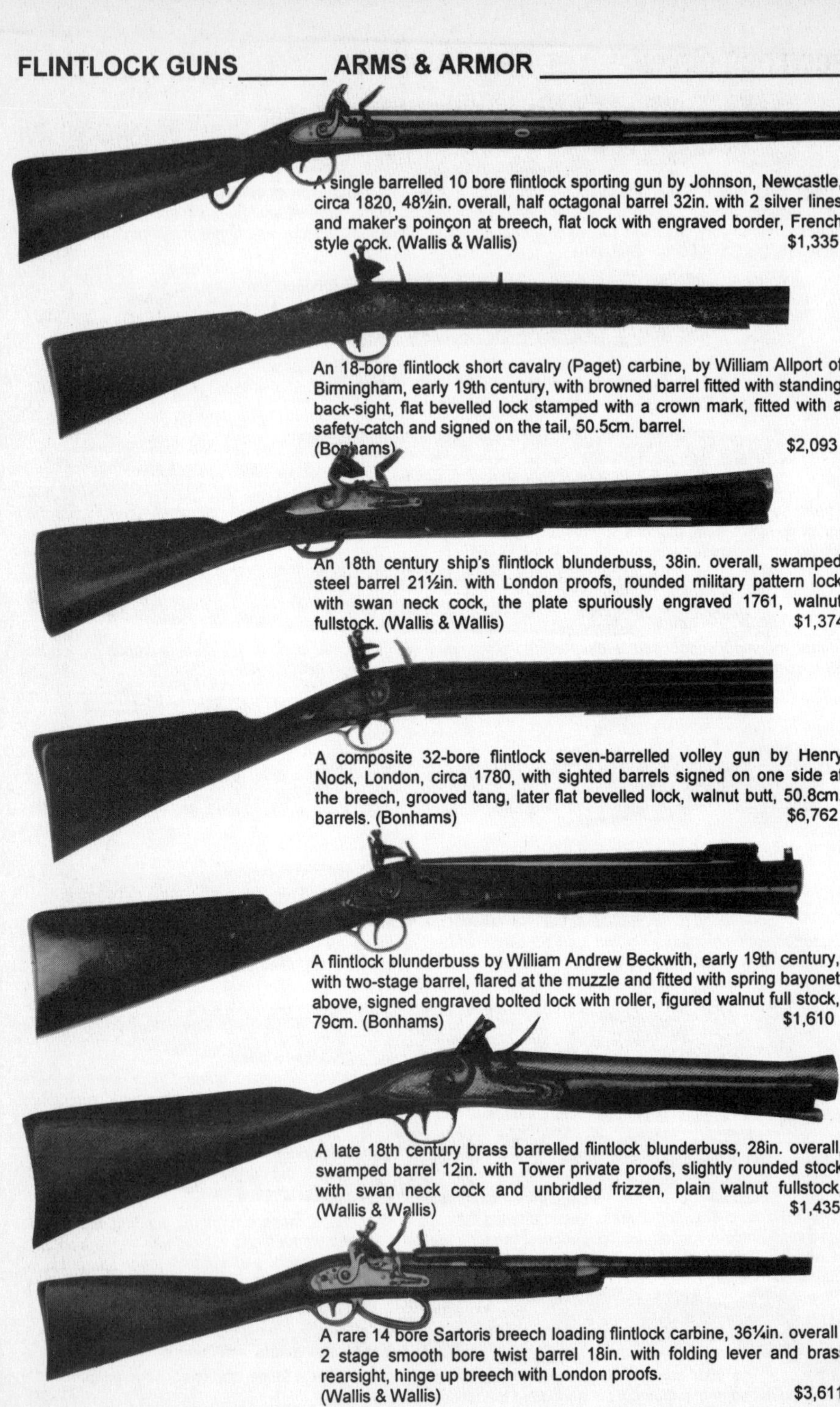

A single barrelled 10 bore flintlock sporting gun by Johnson, Newcastle, circa 1820, 48½in. overall, half octagonal barrel 32in. with 2 silver lines and maker's poinçon at breech, flat lock with engraved border, French style cock. (Wallis & Wallis) $1,335

An 18-bore flintlock short cavalry (Paget) carbine, by William Allport of Birmingham, early 19th century, with browned barrel fitted with standing back-sight, flat bevelled lock stamped with a crown mark, fitted with a safety-catch and signed on the tail, 50.5cm. barrel. (Bonhams) $2,093

An 18th century ship's flintlock blunderbuss, 38in. overall, swamped steel barrel 21½in. with London proofs, rounded military pattern lock with swan neck cock, the plate spuriously engraved 1761, walnut fullstock. (Wallis & Wallis) $1,374

A composite 32-bore flintlock seven-barrelled volley gun by Henry Nock, London, circa 1780, with sighted barrels signed on one side at the breech, grooved tang, later flat bevelled lock, walnut butt, 50.8cm. barrels. (Bonhams) $6,762

A flintlock blunderbuss by William Andrew Beckwith, early 19th century, with two-stage barrel, flared at the muzzle and fitted with spring bayonet above, signed engraved bolted lock with roller, figured walnut full stock, 79cm. (Bonhams) $1,610

A late 18th century brass barrelled flintlock blunderbuss, 28in. overall, swamped barrel 12in. with Tower private proofs, slightly rounded stock with swan neck cock and unbridled frizzen, plain walnut fullstock. (Wallis & Wallis) $1,435

A rare 14 bore Sartoris breech loading flintlock carbine, 36¼in. overall , 2 stage smooth bore twist barrel 18in. with folding lever and brass rearsight, hinge up breech with London proofs. (Wallis & Wallis) $3,611

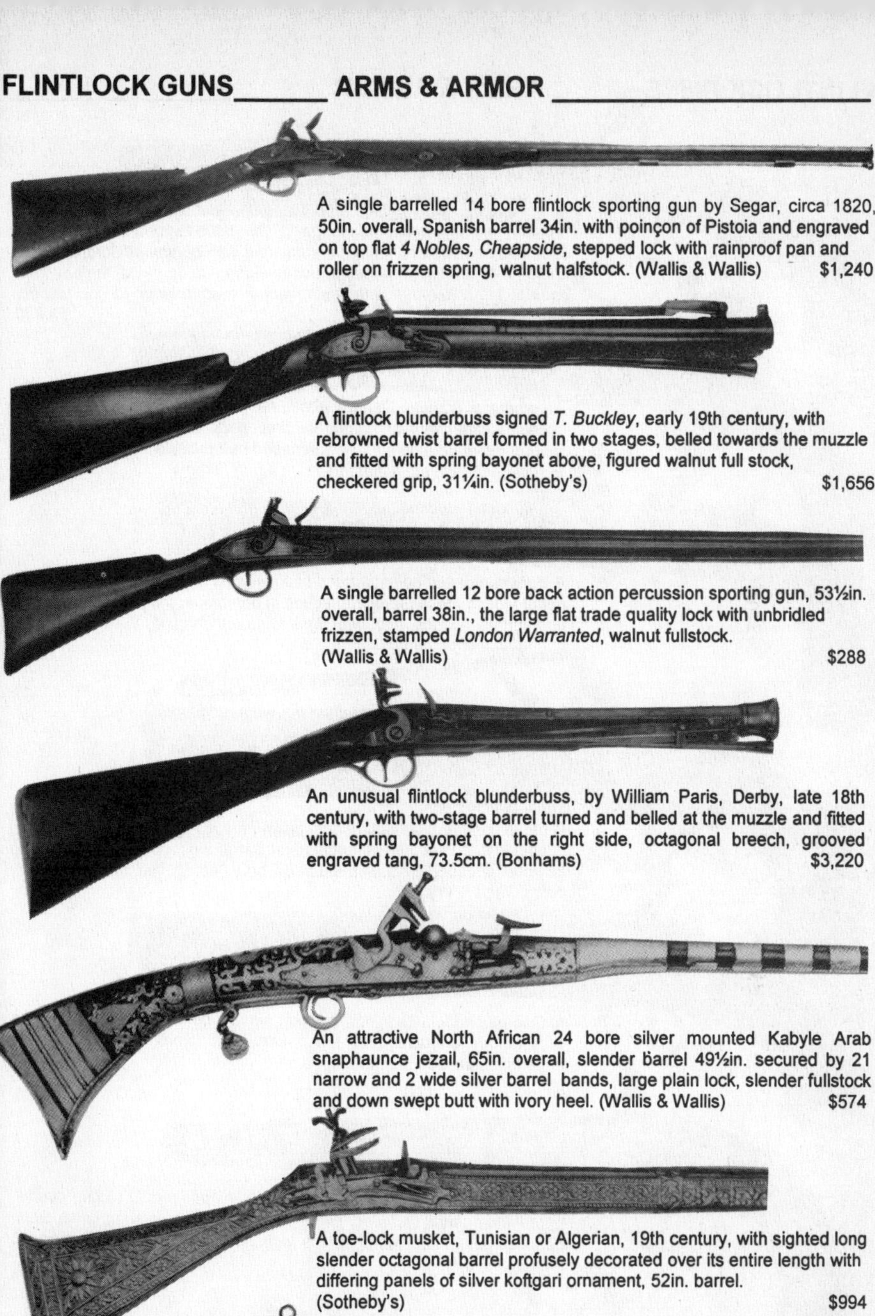

A single barrelled 14 bore flintlock sporting gun by Segar, circa 1820, 50in. overall, Spanish barrel 34in. with poinçon of Pistoia and engraved on top flat *4 Nobles, Cheapside*, stepped lock with rainproof pan and roller on frizzen spring, walnut halfstock. (Wallis & Wallis) $1,240

A flintlock blunderbuss signed *T. Buckley*, early 19th century, with rebrowned twist barrel formed in two stages, belled towards the muzzle and fitted with spring bayonet above, figured walnut full stock, checkered grip, 31¼in. (Sotheby's) $1,656

A single barrelled 12 bore back action percussion sporting gun, 53½in. overall, barrel 38in., the large flat trade quality lock with unbridled frizzen, stamped *London Warranted*, walnut fullstock. (Wallis & Wallis) $288

An unusual flintlock blunderbuss, by William Paris, Derby, late 18th century, with two-stage barrel turned and belled at the muzzle and fitted with spring bayonet on the right side, octagonal breech, grooved engraved tang, 73.5cm. (Bonhams) $3,220

An attractive North African 24 bore silver mounted Kabyle Arab snaphaunce jezail, 65in. overall, slender barrel 49½in. secured by 21 narrow and 2 wide silver barrel bands, large plain lock, slender fullstock and down swept butt with ivory heel. (Wallis & Wallis) $574

A toe-lock musket, Tunisian or Algerian, 19th century, with sighted long slender octagonal barrel profusely decorated over its entire length with differing panels of silver koftgari ornament, 52in. barrel. (Sotheby's) $994

A good 20 bore Turkish gold inlaid miquelet flintlock rifled carbine, dated *1811 AD*, 39½in., damascus twist octagonal barrel 27in., gold inlaid at breech and muzzle with scrolls and cypress trees, with inlaid cabochon turquoise. Fullstocked in striped walnut. (Wallis & Wallis) $1,099

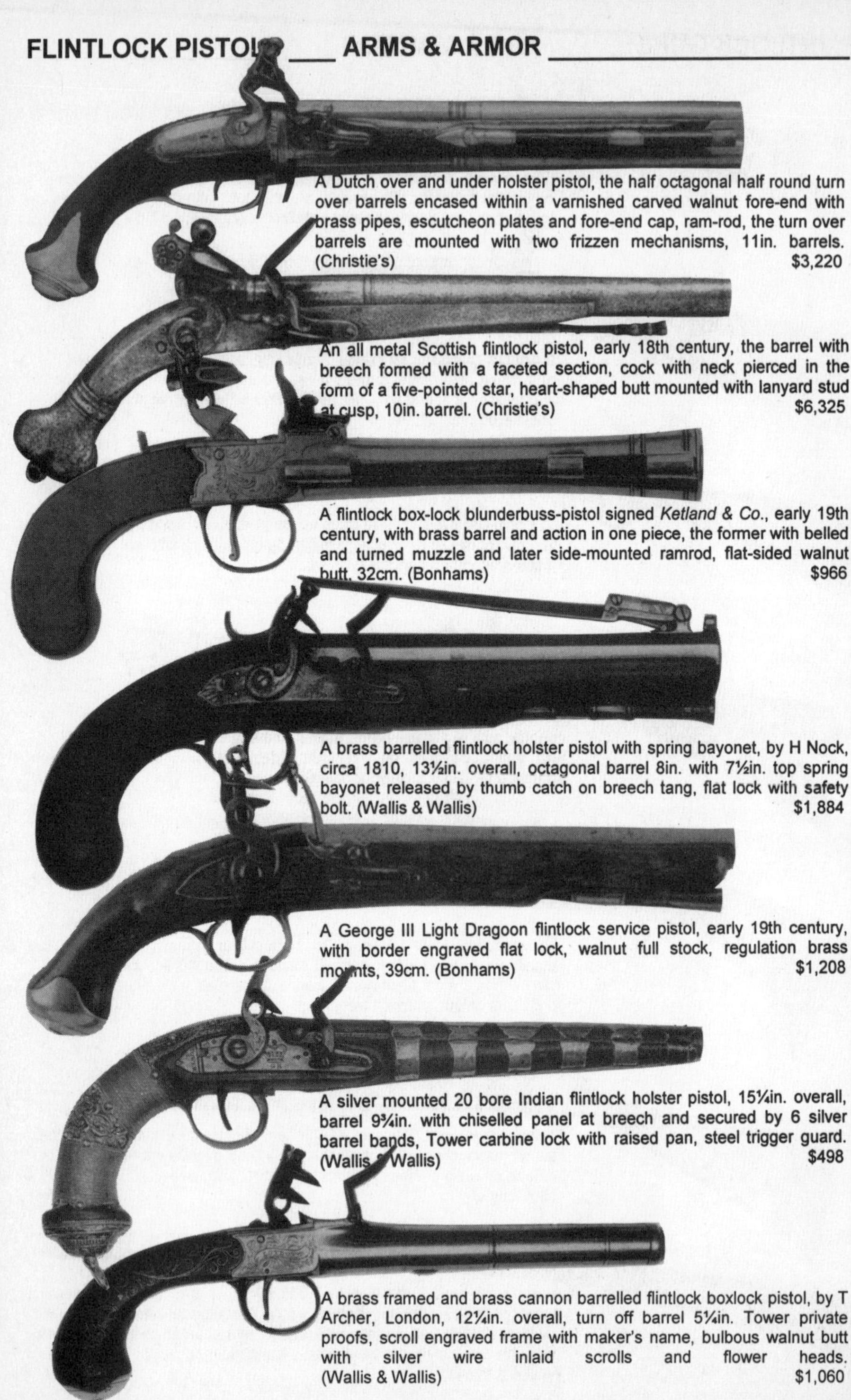

A Dutch over and under holster pistol, the half octagonal half round turn over barrels encased within a varnished carved walnut fore-end with brass pipes, escutcheon plates and fore-end cap, ram-rod, the turn over barrels are mounted with two frizzen mechanisms, 11in. barrels. (Christie's) $3,220

An all metal Scottish flintlock pistol, early 18th century, the barrel with breech formed with a faceted section, cock with neck pierced in the form of a five-pointed star, heart-shaped butt mounted with lanyard stud at cusp, 10in. barrel. (Christie's) $6,325

A flintlock box-lock blunderbuss-pistol signed *Ketland & Co.*, early 19th century, with brass barrel and action in one piece, the former with belled and turned muzzle and later side-mounted ramrod, flat-sided walnut butt, 32cm. (Bonhams) $966

A brass barrelled flintlock holster pistol with spring bayonet, by H Nock, circa 1810, 13½in. overall, octagonal barrel 8in. with 7½in. top spring bayonet released by thumb catch on breech tang, flat lock with safety bolt. (Wallis & Wallis) $1,884

A George III Light Dragoon flintlock service pistol, early 19th century, with border engraved flat lock, walnut full stock, regulation brass mounts, 39cm. (Bonhams) $1,208

A silver mounted 20 bore Indian flintlock holster pistol, 15¼in. overall, barrel 9¾in. with chiselled panel at breech and secured by 6 silver barrel bands, Tower carbine lock with raised pan, steel trigger guard. (Wallis & Wallis) $498

A brass framed and brass cannon barrelled flintlock boxlock pistol, by T Archer, London, 12¼in. overall, turn off barrel 5¼in. Tower private proofs, scroll engraved frame with maker's name, bulbous walnut butt with silver wire inlaid scrolls and flower heads. (Wallis & Wallis) $1,060

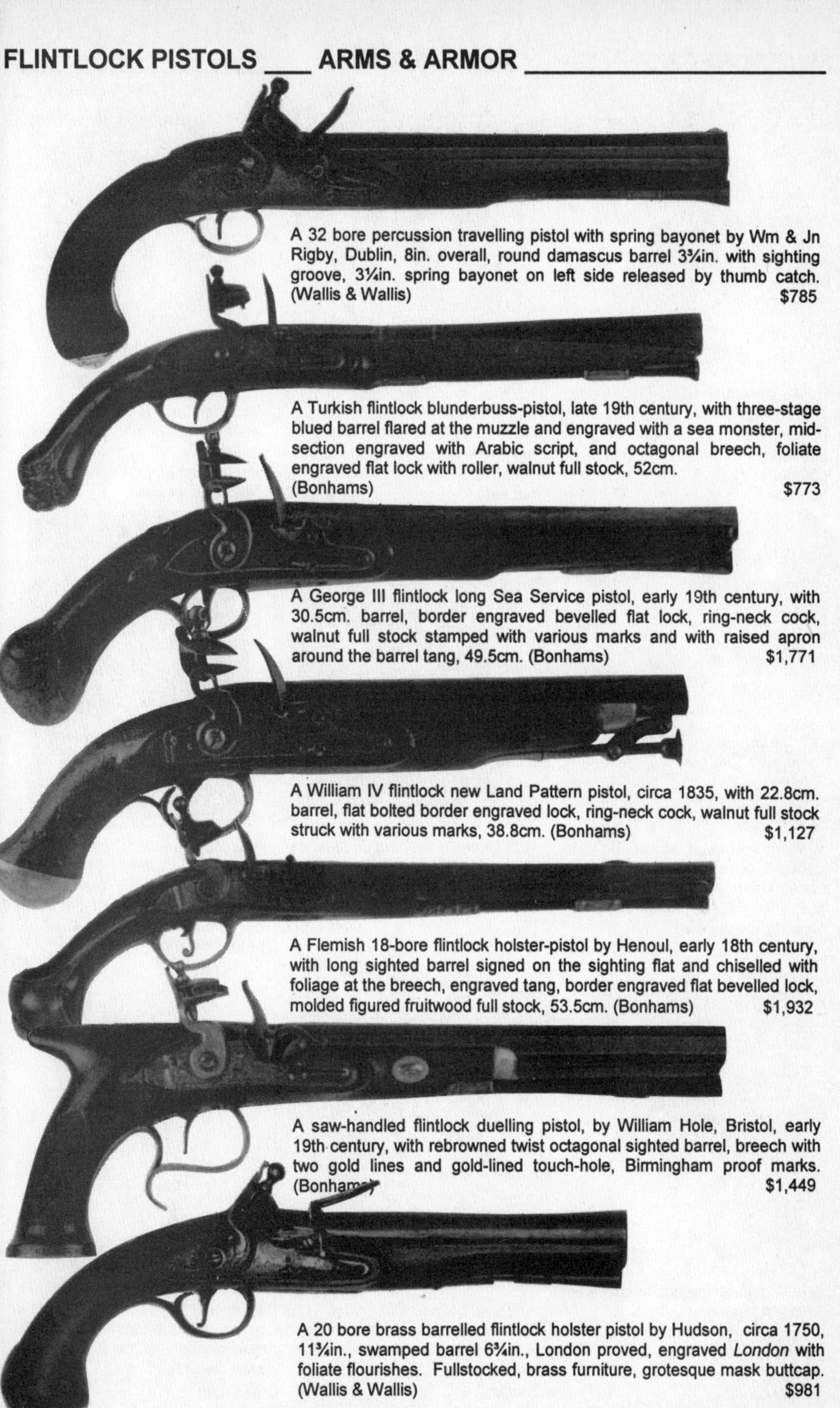

A 32 bore percussion travelling pistol with spring bayonet by Wm & Jn Rigby, Dublin, 8in. overall, round damascus barrel 3¾in. with sighting groove, 3¼in. spring bayonet on left side released by thumb catch. (Wallis & Wallis) $785

A Turkish flintlock blunderbuss-pistol, late 19th century, with three-stage blued barrel flared at the muzzle and engraved with a sea monster, mid-section engraved with Arabic script, and octagonal breech, foliate engraved flat lock with roller, walnut full stock, 52cm. (Bonhams) $773

A George III flintlock long Sea Service pistol, early 19th century, with 30.5cm. barrel, border engraved bevelled flat lock, ring-neck cock, walnut full stock stamped with various marks and with raised apron around the barrel tang, 49.5cm. (Bonhams) $1,771

A William IV flintlock new Land Pattern pistol, circa 1835, with 22.8cm. barrel, flat bolted border engraved lock, ring-neck cock, walnut full stock struck with various marks, 38.8cm. (Bonhams) $1,127

A Flemish 18-bore flintlock holster-pistol by Henoul, early 18th century, with long sighted barrel signed on the sighting flat and chiselled with foliage at the breech, engraved tang, border engraved flat bevelled lock, molded figured fruitwood full stock, 53.5cm. (Bonhams) $1,932

A saw-handled flintlock duelling pistol, by William Hole, Bristol, early 19th century, with rebrowned twist octagonal sighted barrel, breech with two gold lines and gold-lined touch-hole, Birmingham proof marks. (Bonhams) $1,449

A 20 bore brass barrelled flintlock holster pistol by Hudson, circa 1750, 11¾in., swamped barrel 6¾in., London proved, engraved *London* with foliate flourishes. Fullstocked, brass furniture, grotesque mask buttcap. (Wallis & Wallis) $981

An Eboshi-Nari kabuto, Edo Period (18th century), the helmet gold lacquered over leather and lacquer above an iron bowl in the form of a courtier's cap.
(Christie's) $10,246

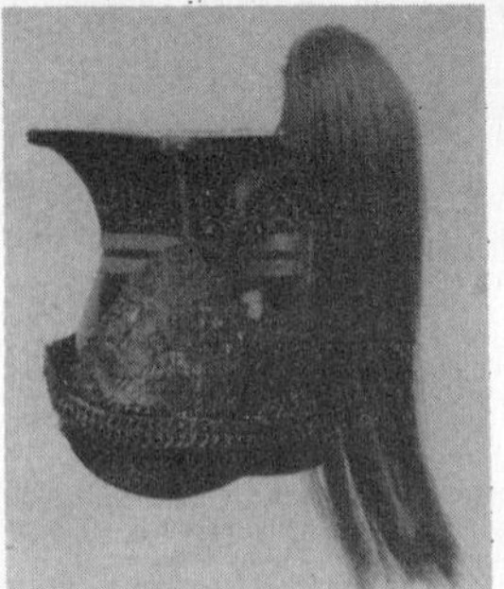

12th Prince of Wales Royal Lancers Victorian lance cap, with black patent leather body, peak and crown with ornate gilt metal fleur bosses to each corner.
(Bosleys) $1,170

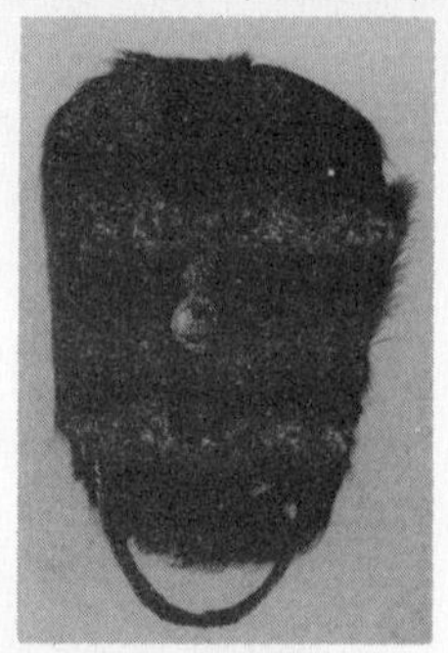

Victorian 3rd VB Lancashire Fusiliers officer's fur cap, bearing silvered flaming grenade to front, the ball mounted with gilt metal Sphinx. (Bosleys) $1,288

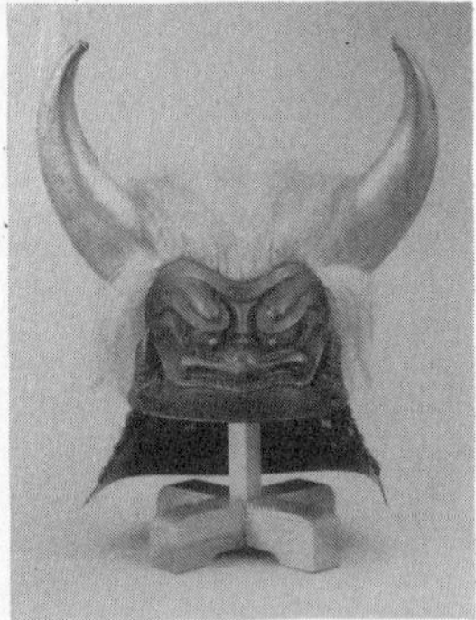

A Kawari kabuto, Edo Period (18th century), covering the entire helmet is a mane of white hair, possibly yak, through which a pair of gilded wood horns appear.
(Christie's) $30,693

16th Queen's Lancers OR's lance cap, post 1901 example, patent leather body, peak and crown with ornate gilt metal fleur bosses.
(Bosleys) $1,127

A Korean helmet, Choson Period (19th century), the leather bowl black lacquered, the lower edge bordered by a deep iron rim cusped over the eyes and with a shallow peak riveted on.
(Christie's) $5,624

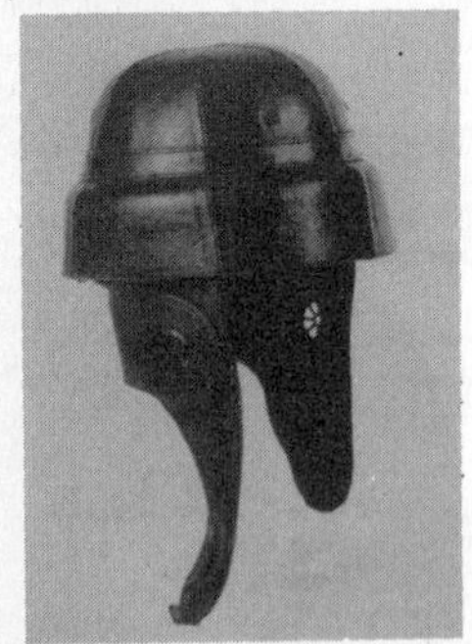

A rare 'Warren' pattern aviator's RNAS flying helmet, made by Christy's hatters of London, black hardened leather shell with padding, leather ear flaps.
(Bosleys) $437

An unusual helmet, Edo Period (18th century), the russet lacquered iron bowl of low rounded form with decreasing horizontal ridges.
(Christie's) $4,514

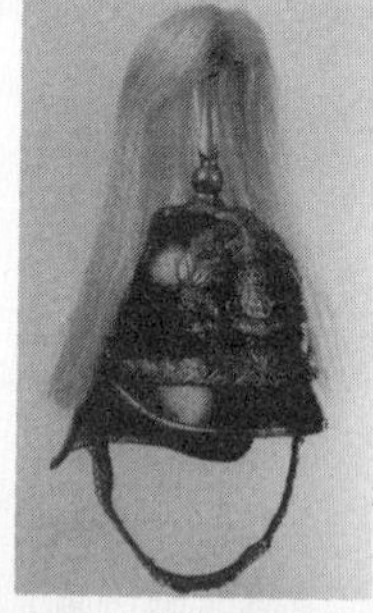

King's Own Norfolk Imperial Yeomanry OR's helmet, Edward VII period example, black leather skull, mounted with gilt metal laurel leaf band decoration.
(Bosleys) $1,288

A Prussian N.C.O.'s Garde du Corps helmet, with white-metal mounted copper skull, surmounted by a silvered crowned eagle. (Bonhams) $4,025

A Nobuiye suji kabuto, signed and dated *1539*, the thirty-two plate russet iron Suji Bachi bowl with russet iron peak and haraidate. (Christie's) $67,981

Merryweather pattern brass Fireman's helmet, with a variation on the Universal pattern brass badge to front, with crossed axes, hoses etc. (Bosleys) $686

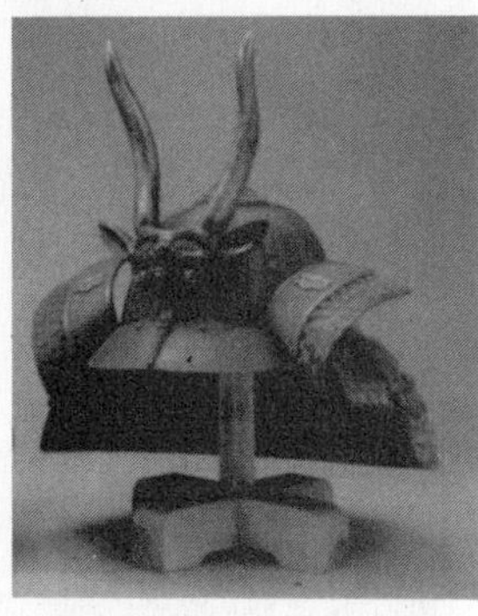

A Suji Bachi kabuto, Edo Period (18th century), the thirty-eight plate bowl of russet iron mounted with a six stage tehen kanamono. (Christie's) $4,694

Victorian Gothic Revival close helmet, a fine quality example of a French late 16th early 17th century style close helmet, embossed with rich detailed decoration. (Bosleys) $562

Coldstream Guards officer's Foreign Service helmet, an important example worn by Colonel Baron Edward Kenelm Digby, whilst Military Secretary to the Governor General and Commander in Chief Australia 1921 to 1923. (Bosleys) $1,368

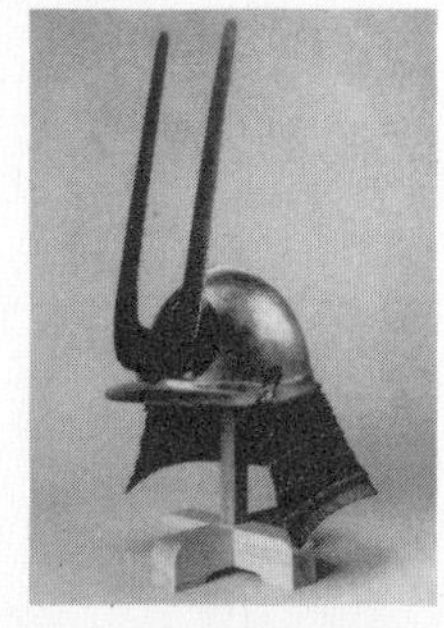

A four plate helmet, Edo Period (18th century), the heavy bowl gold lacquered with a black lacquer disc to the front and fitted with a simple black lacquered elongated 'horseshoe' crest. (Christie's) $6,319

A rare Nambokucho hoshi bachi (bowl with standing rivets), Nambokucho Period (circa 1350), the simple thirty-eight plate russet iron bowl of typical shape with hoshi (standing rivets) on each plate. (Christie's) $14,444

Merryweather style fireman's helmet, brass skull surmounted by floral ornamented brass comb. To the front a shield bearing the Universal pattern fire device. (Bosleys) $644

Royal Air Force officer's full dress busby, rare pre war example, skull of black chromed leather, trimmed with seal dyed nutria, plume of dyed ostrich feathers.
(Bosleys) $848

17th (Duke of Cambridge's Own) Lancers Victorian lance cap, pre 1901 Troop Sergeant-Major's example, black patent leather body and peak, white patent leather crown. (Bosleys) $1,460

Tower Hamlets Rifle Volunteers officer's helmet, a scarce attributed example of an officer's pre 1901 Home Service Pattern blue cloth helmet, with silvered metal spike.
(Bosleys) $1,248

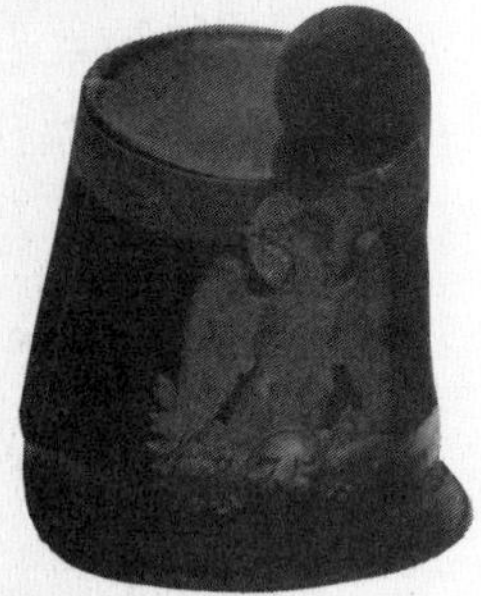

A French OR's 1852 pattern shako of the 35th Infantry, stiffened black cloth body, leather peak, headband and top, scarlet top band, brass eagle plate.
(Wallis & Wallis) $193

An imperial Bavarian Lancers officer's tschapka, silvered helmet plate, single cockade, leather backed brass chinscales, scarlet cloth mortarboard base mount.
(Wallis & Wallis) $1,046

A French OR's all leather shako circa 1855, of the 4th Infantry Regt, brass crowned eagle plate with *4* in the ball, red, white and blue painted metal cockade.
(Wallis & Wallis) $338

Victorian South African ZAR Police Officer's helmet, rare white foreign service pattern made by Christy's of London, The white cotton covered helmet is mounted with a gilt metal helmet plate and gilt spike.
(Bosleys) $502

A Japanese Kon-Ito Odoshi Haruta-No-Kabuto, Haruta style Hachi, probably from Kaga province, end of 17th or beginning of 18th century, with fine chrysanthemum moulding.
(Wallis & Wallis) $7,567

A French Gendarmerie trooper's brass helmet, white metal ear to ear plate bearing grenade within wreath, ornamental white metal with Medusa head finial and black brush crest.
(Wallis & Wallis) $1,099

A French Cuirassier's model 1874 helmet, plated skull, brass mounts, including ear to ear plate with grenade in wreath.
(Wallis & Wallis) $1,510

Boer War Orange Free State Artillery Other Rank's Pickelhaube, worn by members of the Orange Free State Artillery, polished black leather, circular spike base with gilt ball. (Bosleys) $1,138

A scarce Omani Royal Bodyguard officer's tropical full dress helmet, covered in maroon cloth, green linen puggaree, green horsehair plume. (Wallis & Wallis) $580

A fine embossed German morion circa 1900, two piece skull with tall comb, embossed with cabled ribs, geometrically punched borders, plume socket.
(Wallis & Wallis) $2,898

An English Civil War period 'Dutch pot', one piece skull embossed with 6 radial lines, 4 plate articulated neck guard, adjustable nasal bar, pierced ear flaps, suspension loop to crown, ear flap leathers.
(Wallis & Wallis) $982

An officer's 1855 (French) pattern shako of the 22nd (Cheshire) Regiment, black beaver body, patent leather peaks, headband and top, gilt shako plate with 22 in center.
(Wallis & Wallis) $1,167

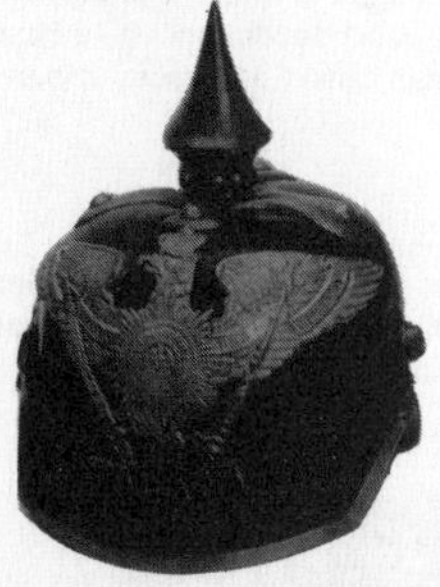

A Prussian Dragoon Reservist ORs Pickelhaube, gilt helmet plate with white metal Garde star, leather chinstrap, brass spike and mounts.
(Wallis & Wallis) $483

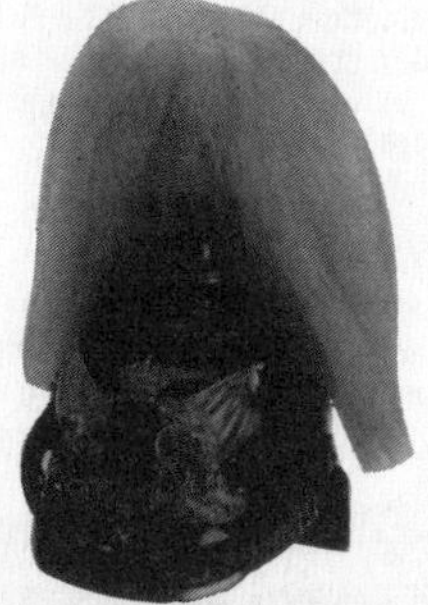

Swedish Senior Officer's helmet of the Foot Guards circa 1880, polished black leather skull with front and rear peaks, yak hair white plume.
(Wallis & Wallis) $1,208

A Prussian state official's Pickelhaube, brass helmet plate in the form of the Imperial German eagle, fluted brass spike.
(Wallis & Wallis) $580

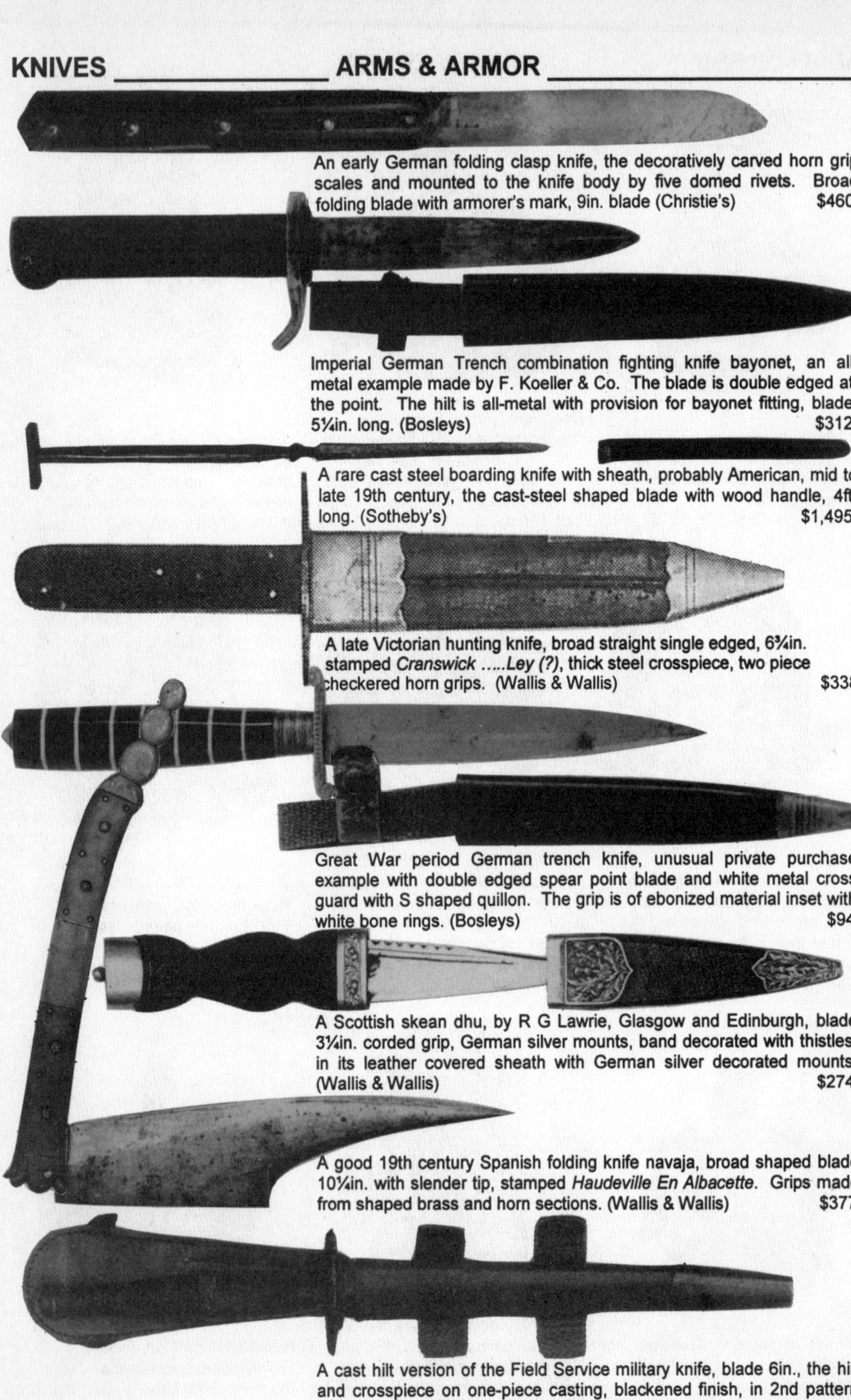

An early German folding clasp knife, the decoratively carved horn grip scales and mounted to the knife body by five domed rivets. Broad folding blade with armorer's mark, 9in. blade (Christie's) $460

Imperial German Trench combination fighting knife bayonet, an all metal example made by F. Koeller & Co. The blade is double edged at the point. The hilt is all-metal with provision for bayonet fitting, blade 5¼in. long. (Bosleys) $312

A rare cast steel boarding knife with sheath, probably American, mid to late 19th century, the cast-steel shaped blade with wood handle, 4ft. long. (Sotheby's) $1,495

A late Victorian hunting knife, broad straight single edged, 6¾in. stamped *Cranswick .....Ley (?)*, thick steel crosspiece, two piece checkered horn grips. (Wallis & Wallis) $338

Great War period German trench knife, unusual private purchase example with double edged spear point blade and white metal cross guard with S shaped quillon. The grip is of ebonized material inset with white bone rings. (Bosleys) $94

A Scottish skean dhu, by R G Lawrie, Glasgow and Edinburgh, blade 3¼in. corded grip, German silver mounts, band decorated with thistles, in its leather covered sheath with German silver decorated mounts. (Wallis & Wallis) $274

A good 19th century Spanish folding knife navaja, broad shaped blade 10¼in. with slender tip, stamped *Haudeville En Albacette*. Grips made from shaped brass and horn sections. (Wallis & Wallis) $377

A cast hilt version of the Field Service military knife, blade 6in., the hilt and crosspiece on one-piece casting, blackened finish, in 2nd pattern Field Service military knife sheath with blackened chape and belt tongue. (Wallis & Wallis) $198

A Bowie knife, spear point blade 7in., with part blued surface containing *VR* cypher by H G Long, German silver oval crosspiece, staghorn hilt with plated foliate mounts, in its leather sheath.
(Wallis & Wallis) $746

A very large Bowie knife, by Butcher Sheffield with kangaroo stamp, pronounced clipped backed blade 13¼in, reversed German silver crosspiece, ivory foliate carved swelling hilt.
(Wallis & Wallis) $1,570

A folding Bowie knife, clipped back blade 7½in., marked *J Rodgers & Son* (feint) *Cutlers to Their Majesties No 6 Norfolk Street, Sheffield England*, German silver short crossguard, the blade folding into staghorn grip hilt with thumb release button, in its leather sheath.
(Wallis & Wallis) $471

A rare Michael Price San Francisco Bowie knife, circa 1870, clip point blade with abbreviated back edge, *M. Price/San Francisco* marked ricasso, walrus ivory grip scales, with three German silver pins, 6in. blade. (Christie's) $4,370

A Victorian folding Bowie knife in its hallmarked silver mounted sheath, swollen single edged clipped back blade 7¼in., folding two-piece white metal crosspiece, two-piece checkered horn grips with oval white metal locking catch. (Wallis & Wallis) $336

A good Bowie knife by J Rodgers & Sons, polished clipped back blade 8in. stamped *GR* with small crown, and *J Rodgers & Sons 6 Norfolk St (S)heffield England.* White metal crosspiece with ball finials.
(Wallis & Wallis) $765

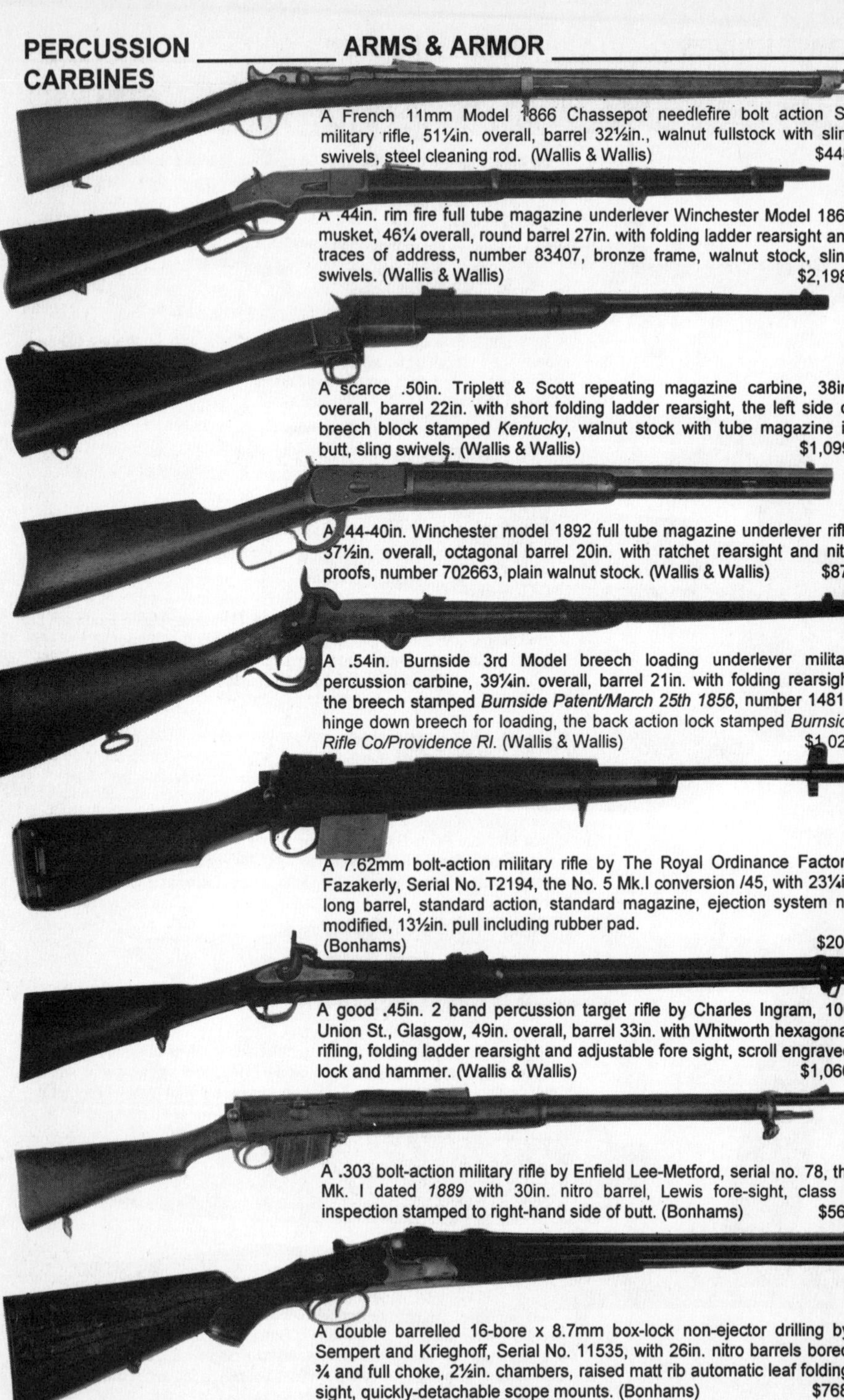

A French 11mm Model 1866 Chassepot needlefire bolt action SS military rifle, 51¼in. overall, barrel 32½in., walnut fullstock with sling swivels, steel cleaning rod. (Wallis & Wallis) $448

A .44in. rim fire full tube magazine underlever Winchester Model 1866 musket, 46¼ overall, round barrel 27in. with folding ladder rearsight and traces of address, number 83407, bronze frame, walnut stock, sling swivels. (Wallis & Wallis) $2,198

A scarce .50in. Triplett & Scott repeating magazine carbine, 38in. overall, barrel 22in. with short folding ladder rearsight, the left side of breech block stamped *Kentucky*, walnut stock with tube magazine in butt, sling swivels. (Wallis & Wallis) $1,099

A .44-40in. Winchester model 1892 full tube magazine underlever rifle 37½in. overall, octagonal barrel 20in. with ratchet rearsight and nitro proofs, number 702663, plain walnut stock. (Wallis & Wallis) $876

A .54in. Burnside 3rd Model breech loading underlever military percussion carbine, 39¼in. overall, barrel 21in. with folding rearsight the breech stamped *Burnside Patent/March 25th 1856*, number 14811 hinge down breech for loading, the back action lock stamped *Burnside Rifle Co/Providence RI*. (Wallis & Wallis) $1,020

A 7.62mm bolt-action military rifle by The Royal Ordinance Factory, Fazakerly, Serial No. T2194, the No. 5 Mk.I conversion /45, with 23¼in. long barrel, standard action, standard magazine, ejection system not modified, 13½in. pull including rubber pad. (Bonhams) $208

A good .45in. 2 band percussion target rifle by Charles Ingram, 100 Union St., Glasgow, 49in. overall, barrel 33in. with Whitworth hexagonal rifling, folding ladder rearsight and adjustable fore sight, scroll engraved lock and hammer. (Wallis & Wallis) $1,060

A .303 bolt-action military rifle by Enfield Lee-Metford, serial no. 78, the Mk. I dated *1889* with 30in. nitro barrel, Lewis fore-sight, class 1 inspection stamped to right-hand side of butt. (Bonhams) $560

A double barrelled 16-bore x 8.7mm box-lock non-ejector drilling by Sempert and Krieghoff, Serial No. 11535, with 26in. nitro barrels bored ¾ and full choke, 2½in. chambers, raised matt rib automatic leaf folding sight, quickly-detachable scope mounts. (Bonhams) $768

A 6.5mm Italian Mannlicher Carcano Terni Model 1891 bolt action military rifle, 50½ overall, barrel 30½in., number KH 1034, adjustable ratchet rearsight, walnut fullstock with inlaid brass plate in butt. (Wallis & Wallis) $560

A 12 bore Russian Crimean War period military percussion musket, 58in. overall, barrel 42½in. with small eagle stamp, date *1848*, the butt plate tang bearing Russian eagle. (Wallis & Wallis) $863

A .45-90in. Winchester Model 1886 half tube magazine underlever sporting rifle, 44in. overall, round barrel 26in., 2 folding leaf rearsights and blade foresight, plain walnut stock with bronze butt plate. (Wallis & Wallis) $1,060

A good French 14 bore Charleville military pattern percussion musket, which was exhibited at the Great Exhibition in 1851, 55½in. overall, barrel 40½in. with proof marks and date *1850* at breech, back action lock with oval stamp of *Jacquemart & Freres a Charleville*, Ardennes. (Wallis & Wallis) $1,295

A rare .303 bolt-action military rifle, by Winchester, Serial No. W199502, the No. 3 Mk. 1 with 26in. nitro barrel, extremely rare marking *'IW* / PATT.. '14'* to right hand side of butt, plain peep-sight and Aldis Bros. scope on Alex.Martin mounts. (Bonhams) $2,560

A good light weight .45in. percussion sporting rifle, by Joseph Harkom, 32 Princes Street, Edinburgh, 44¼in. overall, octagonal barrel 28½in. with 3 folding leaf rearsights, scroll engraved lock with safety bolt, nicely figured walnut halfstock. (Wallis & Wallis) $1,295

A .22 LR bolt-action target rifle by Anschutz, Serial No. 103408, the Match 54 model with 26in. nitro barrel, Anschutz sights, 13¼in. pull. (Bonhams) $240

A 12 bore Russian Crimean War period military percussion musket, 58in. overall, barrel 42½in. with small eagle stamp, date *1849* and *No 11533* at breech. (Wallis & Wallis) $785

A good .303in. SMLE bolt action military pattern prize rifle, by BSA Co, 44½in. overall, barrel 25in., nitro proved, magazine cut off, walnut fullstock with pull through. (Wallis & Wallis) $544

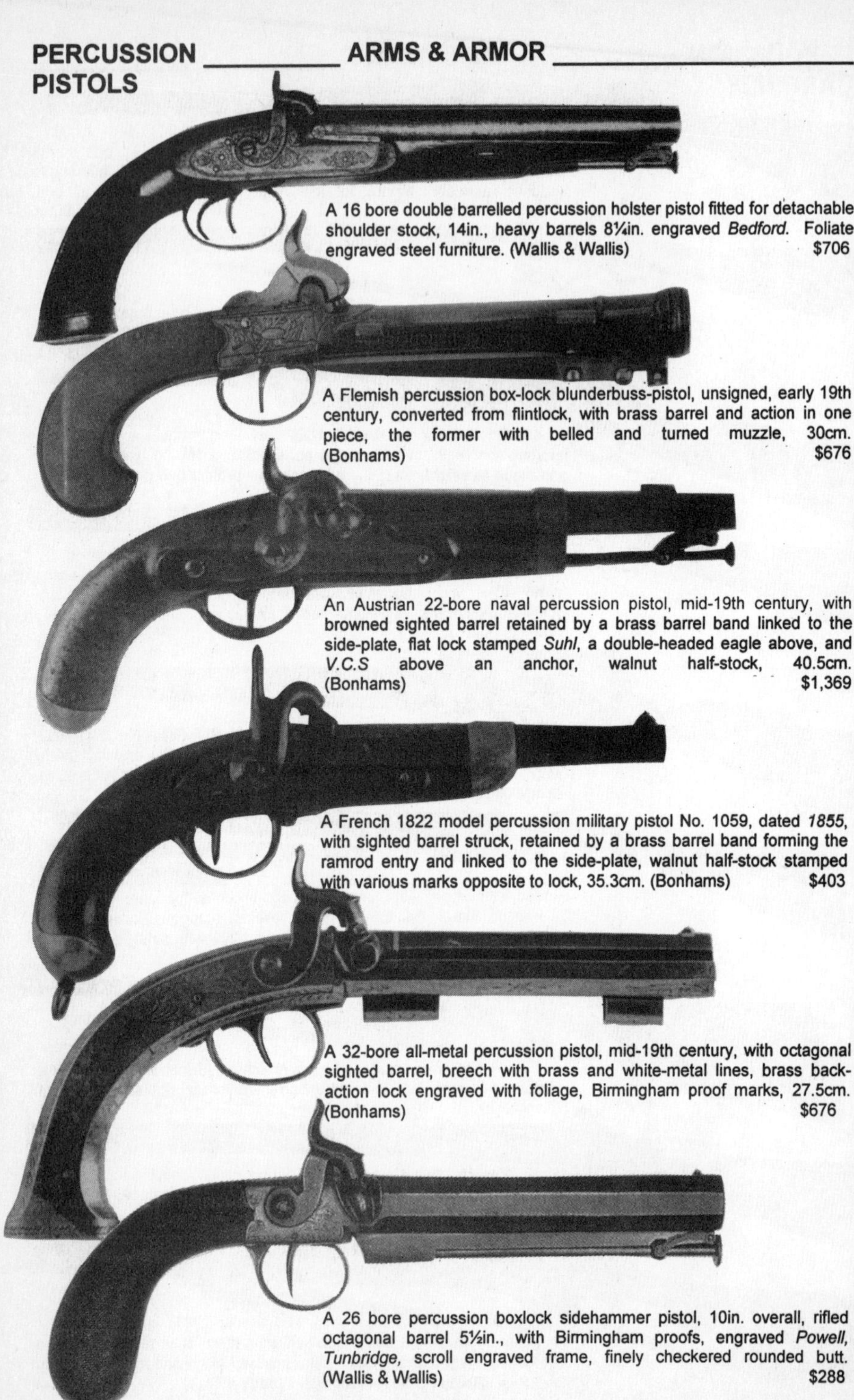

A 16 bore double barrelled percussion holster pistol fitted for detachable shoulder stock, 14in., heavy barrels 8¼in. engraved *Bedford*. Foliate engraved steel furniture. (Wallis & Wallis) $706

A Flemish percussion box-lock blunderbuss-pistol, unsigned, early 19th century, converted from flintlock, with brass barrel and action in one piece, the former with belled and turned muzzle, 30cm. (Bonhams) $676

An Austrian 22-bore naval percussion pistol, mid-19th century, with browned sighted barrel retained by a brass barrel band linked to the side-plate, flat lock stamped *Suhl*, a double-headed eagle above, and *V.C.S* above an anchor, walnut half-stock, 40.5cm. (Bonhams) $1,369

A French 1822 model percussion military pistol No. 1059, dated *1855*, with sighted barrel struck, retained by a brass barrel band forming the ramrod entry and linked to the side-plate, walnut half-stock stamped with various marks opposite to lock, 35.3cm. (Bonhams) $403

A 32-bore all-metal percussion pistol, mid-19th century, with octagonal sighted barrel, breech with brass and white-metal lines, brass back-action lock engraved with foliage, Birmingham proof marks, 27.5cm. (Bonhams) $676

A 26 bore percussion boxlock sidehammer pistol, 10in. overall, rifled octagonal barrel 5½in., with Birmingham proofs, engraved *Powell, Tunbridge,* scroll engraved frame, finely checkered rounded butt. (Wallis & Wallis) $288

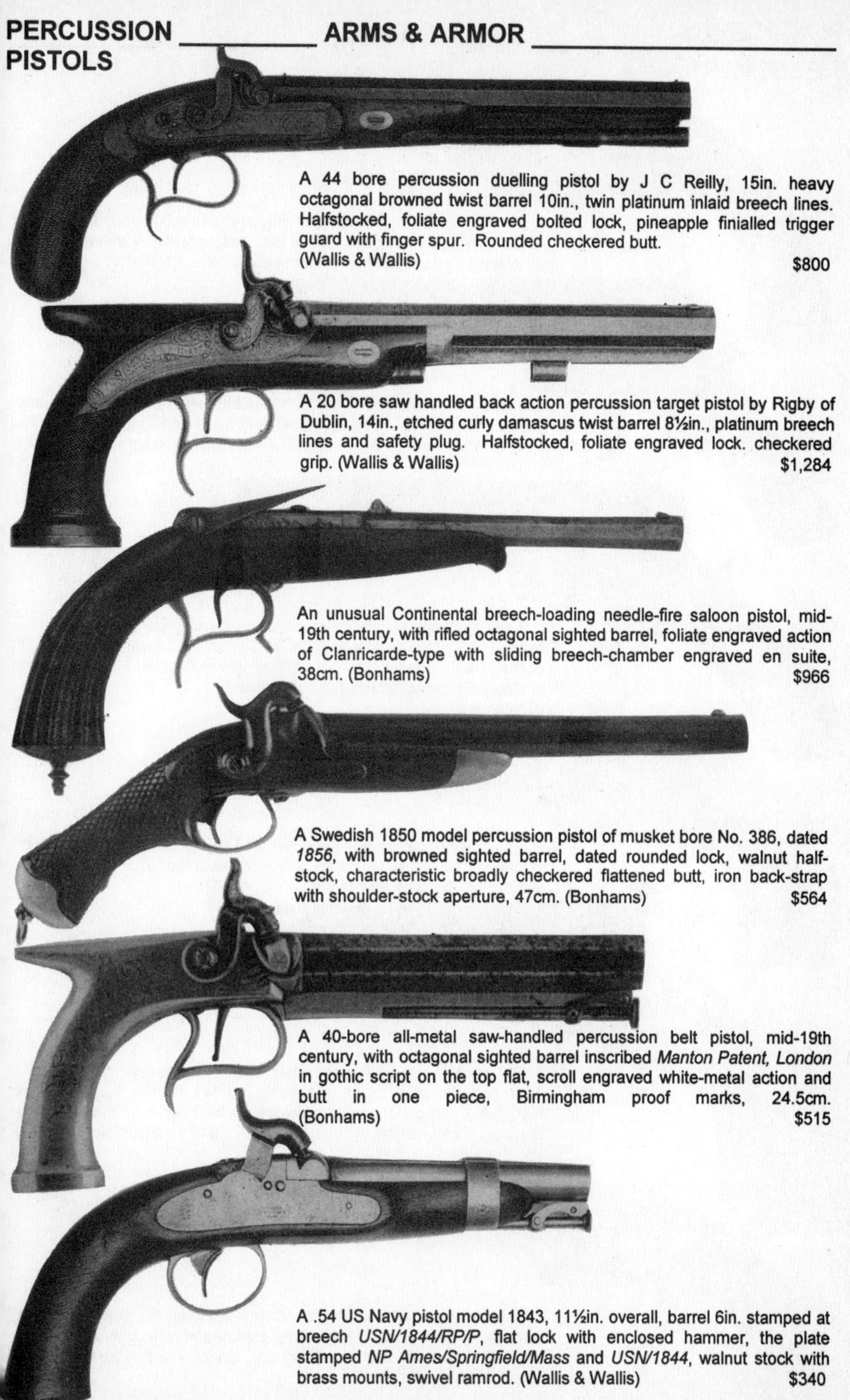

A 44 bore percussion duelling pistol by J C Reilly, 15in. heavy octagonal browned twist barrel 10in., twin platinum inlaid breech lines. Halfstocked, foliate engraved bolted lock, pineapple finialled trigger guard with finger spur. Rounded checkered butt. (Wallis & Wallis) $800

A 20 bore saw handled back action percussion target pistol by Rigby of Dublin, 14in., etched curly damascus twist barrel 8½in., platinum breech lines and safety plug. Halfstocked, foliate engraved lock. checkered grip. (Wallis & Wallis) $1,284

An unusual Continental breech-loading needle-fire saloon pistol, mid-19th century, with rifled octagonal sighted barrel, foliate engraved action of Clanricarde-type with sliding breech-chamber engraved en suite, 38cm. (Bonhams) $966

A Swedish 1850 model percussion pistol of musket bore No. 386, dated *1856*, with browned sighted barrel, dated rounded lock, walnut half-stock, characteristic broadly checkered flattened butt, iron back-strap with shoulder-stock aperture, 47cm. (Bonhams) $564

A 40-bore all-metal saw-handled percussion belt pistol, mid-19th century, with octagonal sighted barrel inscribed *Manton Patent, London* in gothic script on the top flat, scroll engraved white-metal action and butt in one piece, Birmingham proof marks, 24.5cm. (Bonhams) $515

A .54 US Navy pistol model 1843, 11½in. overall, barrel 6in. stamped at breech *USN/1844/RP/P*, flat lock with enclosed hammer, the plate stamped *NP Ames/Springfield/Mass* and *USN/1844*, walnut stock with brass mounts, swivel ramrod. (Wallis & Wallis) $340

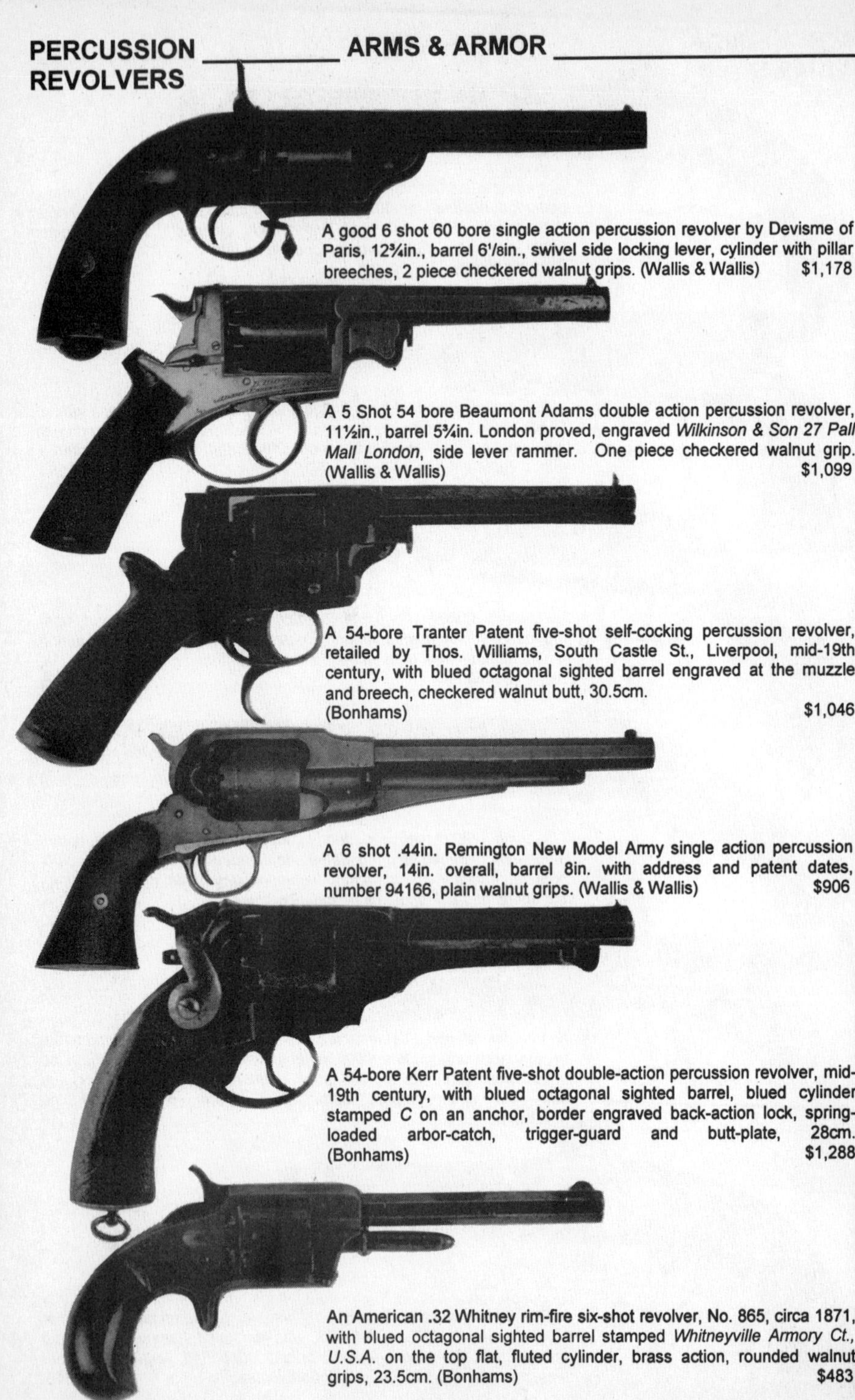

A good 6 shot 60 bore single action percussion revolver by Devisme of Paris, 12¾in., barrel 6⅛in., swivel side locking lever, cylinder with pillar breeches, 2 piece checkered walnut grips. (Wallis & Wallis) $1,178

A 5 Shot 54 bore Beaumont Adams double action percussion revolver, 11½in., barrel 5¾in. London proved, engraved *Wilkinson & Son 27 Pall Mall London*, side lever rammer. One piece checkered walnut grip. (Wallis & Wallis) $1,099

A 54-bore Tranter Patent five-shot self-cocking percussion revolver, retailed by Thos. Williams, South Castle St., Liverpool, mid-19th century, with blued octagonal sighted barrel engraved at the muzzle and breech, checkered walnut butt, 30.5cm. (Bonhams) $1,046

A 6 shot .44in. Remington New Model Army single action percussion revolver, 14in. overall, barrel 8in. with address and patent dates, number 94166, plain walnut grips. (Wallis & Wallis) $906

A 54-bore Kerr Patent five-shot double-action percussion revolver, mid-19th century, with blued octagonal sighted barrel, blued cylinder stamped *C* on an anchor, border engraved back-action lock, spring-loaded arbor-catch, trigger-guard and butt-plate, 28cm. (Bonhams) $1,288

An American .32 Whitney rim-fire six-shot revolver, No. 865, circa 1871, with blued octagonal sighted barrel stamped *Whitneyville Armory Ct., U.S.A.* on the top flat, fluted cylinder, brass action, rounded walnut grips, 23.5cm. (Bonhams) $483

A good 6 shot .44in. Remington single action percussion army revolver No 93912, 14in. barrel 8in., underlever rammer, brass trigger guard, 2 piece walnut grips struck with government inspector's initials. (Wallis & Wallis) $1,727

A 50-bore five-shot double-action percussion revolver, mid-19th century, with blued octagonal sighted barrel, blued cylinder, border engraved frame and mounts, rammer, checkered walnut grips, 29cm. (Bonhams) $885

A 12 shot 9mm. double action pin fire revolver, 11in., barrel 6in., Birmingham proved. Open frame, sidegate loading, frame with a little foliate engraving. Two piece bag-shaped checkered walnut grips. (Wallis & Wallis) $667

A very rare and historic Confederate revolver, by Augusta Machine Works, Augusta Georgia, Serial Letter *K*, circa 1862, sighted octagonal barrel, rifled in 6 grooves, color case hardened frame, blued cylinder, varnished walnut grips. (Christie's) $92,700

A factory engraved .45 Colt single action army revolver, the blued and color case hardened revolver engraved overall with bold scrolls, stippled fields, fan patterns and intertwining lines, by Cuno Helfricht, mounted with the Colt sunken medallion ivory grip panel, apparently carved by the owner, 5½in. barrel. (Christie's) $10,350

A good scarce 6 shot 7mm pinfire Belgian double action revolving knife pistol, 10in. folding blade 2½in., barrel 3¼in. Liège proved. Frame and cylinder engraved with flowers, foliage and strapwork cartouches. Folding trigger, sidegate loading, two piece ebony grips. (Wallis & Wallis) $2,198

A copper three way powder flask, 3¾in. overall, common top with fixed nozzle, swivel lid reveals compartment for lead balls.
(Wallis & Wallis) $193

A Scottish cowhorn dress powder-flask, 19th century, with body of curved flattened form, silver mounts comprising base-mount cast and chased with thistles, 34cm.
(Bonhams) $885

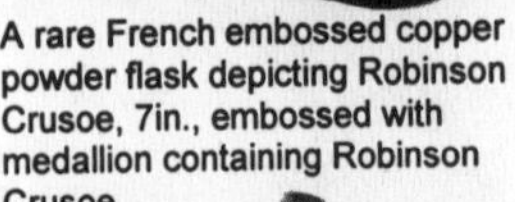

A rare French embossed copper powder flask depicting Robinson Crusoe, 7in., embossed with medallion containing Robinson Crusoe.
(Wallis & Wallis) $554

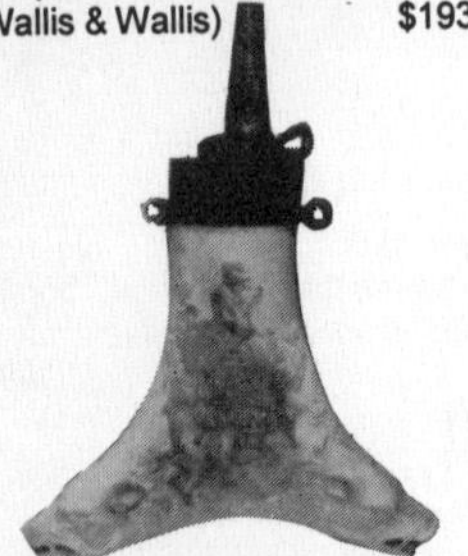

A carved bone wheel-lock powder flask, the body of bone carved with the image of a lady and her assistant, between two snarling boar's-head finials, 7 x 9in.
(Christie's) $1,265

A Caucasian silver-mounted priming-flask, 19th century, with curved dark horn body with shims of dark horn and walrus-ivory forming the base-plate, 17.5cm.
(Bonhams) $1,208

An Eastern European powder-flask, Carpathian Basin, 18th century, with forked body of natural staghorn, the outerside polished and engraved with concentric designs. (Bonhams) $563

A fine decorated large steel wheel-lock powder horn, of triangular form, the powder flask wrapped in red felt encased with two steel panels chased with scenes of Minerva, surrounded by florals and putti with scrolling ribands, 9½ x 10½in. (Christie's) $2,875

A large wooden wheel-lock powder flask of circular form, the flask is mounted with a pierced steel plate bearing the crest surmounted with a stylized crown, 6½in.
(Christie's) $863

An East European powder-flask, Carpathian Basin, 18th century, with forked body of polished natural staghorn, the outerside carved and engraved with a concentric design, 19.4cm. (Bonhams) $805

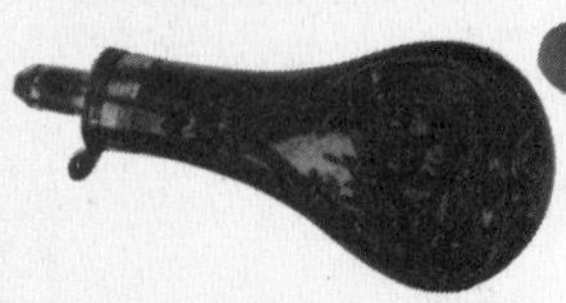

An American brass-mounted powder-flask, by Frary, Benham & Co., 19th century, with lacquered bag-shaped body embossed on one side with a covey of partridges, 21cm. (Bonhams) $676

A good Crimean War period Russian gunner's powder horn,15½in. overall including the boxwood stopper. Thick brass mounts, sprung lever charger, base cap with scalloped edge.
(Wallis & Wallis) $2,825

An 18th century Continental flattened cow horn powder flask, 8¼in. engraved with scrolling foliage, wooden base plug, spring side lever charger, iron suspension loop. (Wallis & Wallis) $196

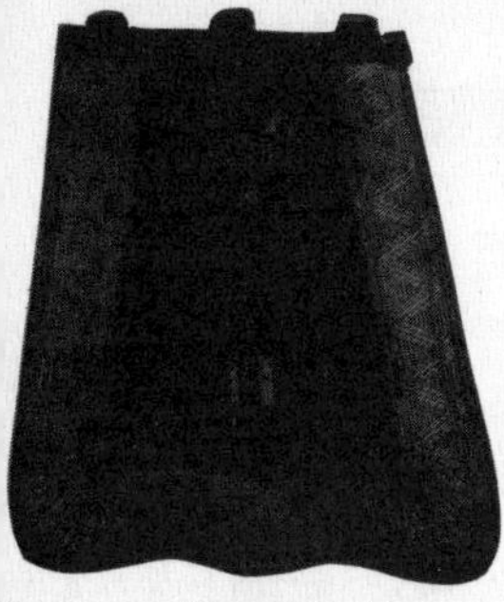

'ictorian Northumberland Hussars fficer's sabretache, the scarlet loth face edged with two inch ilver lace of zig-zag pattern.
Bosleys) $1,208

Victorian East Lothian Yeomanry cavalry sabretache, full dress sabretache worn by an officer from 1846 until the title of the regiment changed in 1888.
(Bosleys) $1,449

Victorian Royal Artillery officer's sabretache of dark blue melton ground embroidered with bullion Royal Arms and oak leaf and acorn.
(Bosleys) $370

n officer's full dress embroidered lue sabretache of the 1st Troop, st Brigade, Bengal Horse Artillery, irca 1845, broad lace border, riginally gilt), embroidered *Sphinx Egypt,* scroll *Ava.*
Wallis & Wallis) $1,771

A large size early Victorian officer's full dress embroidered scarlet cloth sabretache of the 8th The Kings Royal Irish Hussars, 15 x 12½in., gilt lace border, embroidered Guelphic crowned VR cypher with superimposed Royal Crest.
(Wallis & Wallis) $1,690

A sabretache of an officer of the Northumberland Hussars, circa 1895, of red Morocco leather faced in red cloth embroidered in silver and gilt bullion with the crowned monogram and badge of the regiment.(Bonhams) $1,610

n officer's black patent leather abretache of the 12th Bengal avalry, bearing brass crowned BC onogram and 5 battle honour crolls to Afghanistan 1878-80.
Wallis & Wallis) $1,510

Queen's Own Glasgow Yeomanry Cavalry Victorian sabretache, officer's example, face of dark blue melton cloth embroidered in gold bullion with entwined initials *QOGYC.* (Bosleys) $1,170

Royal 1st Devon Yeomanry post 1855 sabretache, officer's full dress example, the dark blue cloth face bears heavily embroidered VR cypher surmounted by a bullion crown. (Bosleys) $1,288

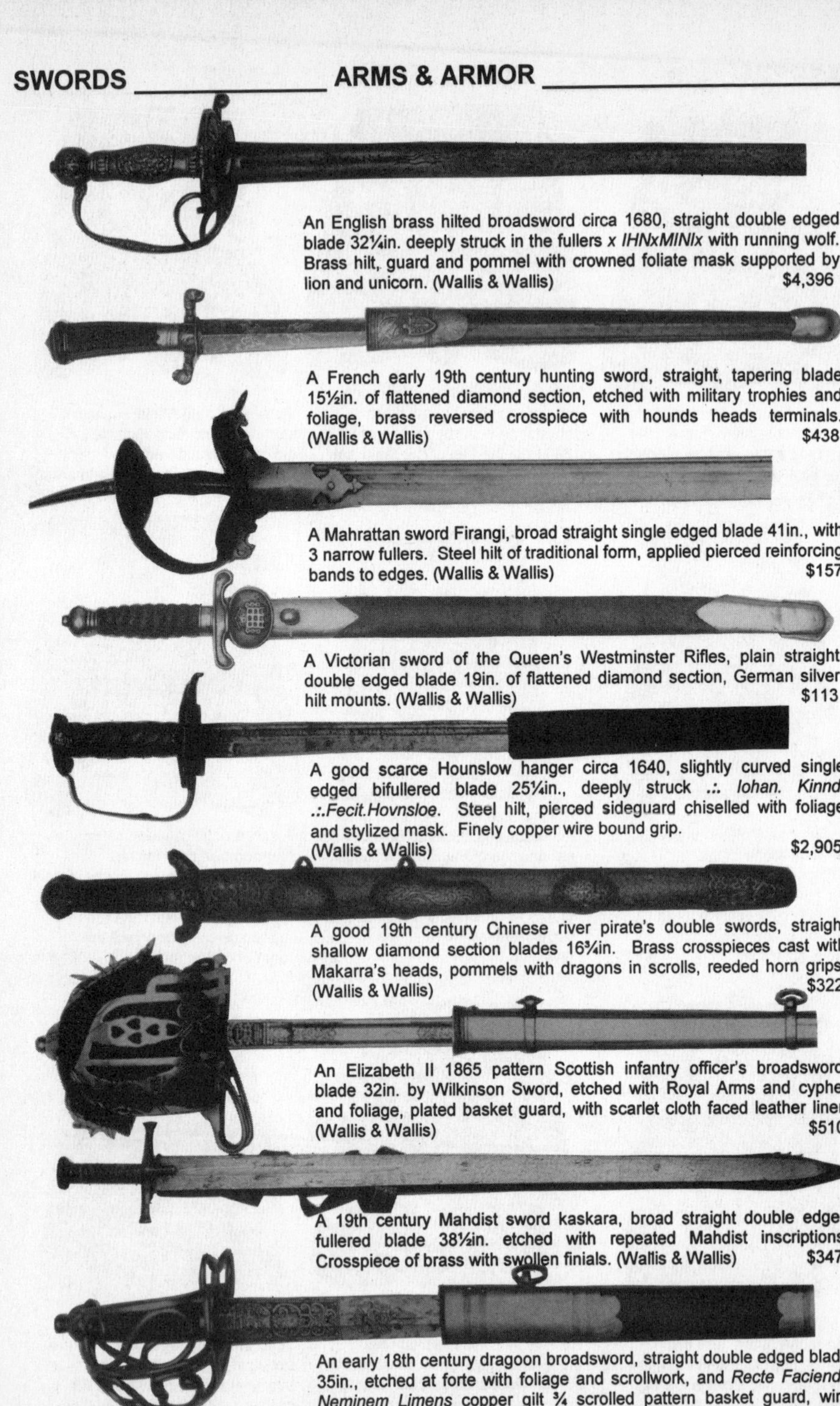

An English brass hilted broadsword circa 1680, straight double edged blade 32¼in. deeply struck in the fullers *x IHNxMINIx* with running wolf. Brass hilt, guard and pommel with crowned foliate mask supported by lion and unicorn. (Wallis & Wallis) $4,396

A French early 19th century hunting sword, straight, tapering blade 15½in. of flattened diamond section, etched with military trophies and foliage, brass reversed crosspiece with hounds heads terminals. (Wallis & Wallis) $438

A Mahrattan sword Firangi, broad straight single edged blade 41in., with 3 narrow fullers. Steel hilt of traditional form, applied pierced reinforcing bands to edges. (Wallis & Wallis) $157

A Victorian sword of the Queen's Westminster Rifles, plain straight double edged blade 19in. of flattened diamond section, German silver hilt mounts. (Wallis & Wallis) $113

A good scarce Hounslow hanger circa 1640, slightly curved single edged bifullered blade 25¼in., deeply struck *.:. Iohan. Kinndt .:.Fecit.Hovnsloe.* Steel hilt, pierced sideguard chiselled with foliage and stylized mask. Finely copper wire bound grip. (Wallis & Wallis) $2,905

A good 19th century Chinese river pirate's double swords, straight shallow diamond section blades 16¾in. Brass crosspieces cast with Makarra's heads, pommels with dragons in scrolls, reeded horn grips. (Wallis & Wallis) $322

An Elizabeth II 1865 pattern Scottish infantry officer's broadsword, blade 32in. by Wilkinson Sword, etched with Royal Arms and cypher and foliage, plated basket guard, with scarlet cloth faced leather liner. (Wallis & Wallis) $510

A 19th century Mahdist sword kaskara, broad straight double edged fullered blade 38½in. etched with repeated Mahdist inscriptions. Crosspiece of brass with swollen finials. (Wallis & Wallis) $347

An early 18th century dragoon broadsword, straight double edged blade 35in., etched at forte with foliage and scrollwork, and *Recte Faciendo Neminem Limens* copper gilt ¾ scrolled pattern basket guard, wire bound black leather covered grip. (Wallis & Wallis) $2,355

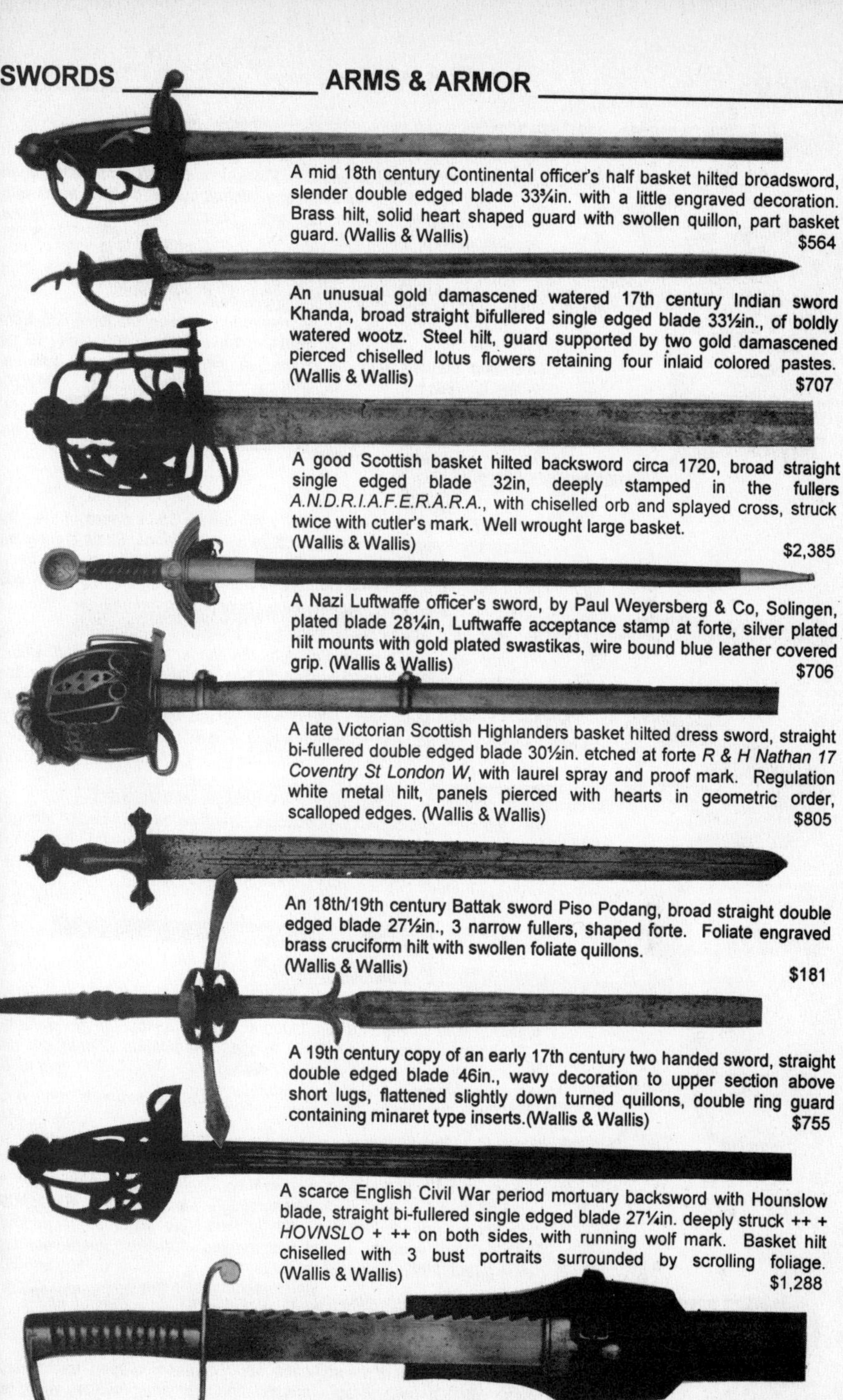

A mid 18th century Continental officer's half basket hilted broadsword, slender double edged blade 33¾in. with a little engraved decoration. Brass hilt, solid heart shaped guard with swollen quillon, part basket guard. (Wallis & Wallis) $564

An unusual gold damascened watered 17th century Indian sword Khanda, broad straight bifullered single edged blade 33½in., of boldly watered wootz. Steel hilt, guard supported by two gold damascened pierced chiselled lotus flowers retaining four inlaid colored pastes. (Wallis & Wallis) $707

A good Scottish basket hilted backsword circa 1720, broad straight single edged blade 32in, deeply stamped in the fullers *A.N.D.R.I.A.F.E.R.A.R.A.*, with chiselled orb and splayed cross, struck twice with cutler's mark. Well wrought large basket. (Wallis & Wallis) $2,385

A Nazi Luftwaffe officer's sword, by Paul Weyersberg & Co, Solingen, plated blade 28¼in, Luftwaffe acceptance stamp at forte, silver plated hilt mounts with gold plated swastikas, wire bound blue leather covered grip. (Wallis & Wallis) $706

A late Victorian Scottish Highlanders basket hilted dress sword, straight bi-fullered double edged blade 30½in. etched at forte *R & H Nathan 17 Coventry St London W*, with laurel spray and proof mark. Regulation white metal hilt, panels pierced with hearts in geometric order, scalloped edges. (Wallis & Wallis) $805

An 18th/19th century Battak sword Piso Podang, broad straight double edged blade 27½in., 3 narrow fullers, shaped forte. Foliate engraved brass cruciform hilt with swollen foliate quillons. (Wallis & Wallis) $181

A 19th century copy of an early 17th century two handed sword, straight double edged blade 46in., wavy decoration to upper section above short lugs, flattened slightly down turned quillons, double ring guard containing minaret type inserts.(Wallis & Wallis) $755

A scarce English Civil War period mortuary backsword with Hounslow blade, straight bi-fullered single edged blade 27¼in. deeply struck ++ + *HOVNSLO* + ++ on both sides, with running wolf mark. Basket hilt chiselled with 3 bust portraits surrounded by scrolling foliage. (Wallis & Wallis) $1,288

An 1856 pattern brass hilted pioneer sidearm, saw backed blade 22½in., ribbed grip, stirrup knucklebow, in its brass mounted leather scabbard with frog. (Wallis & Wallis) $282

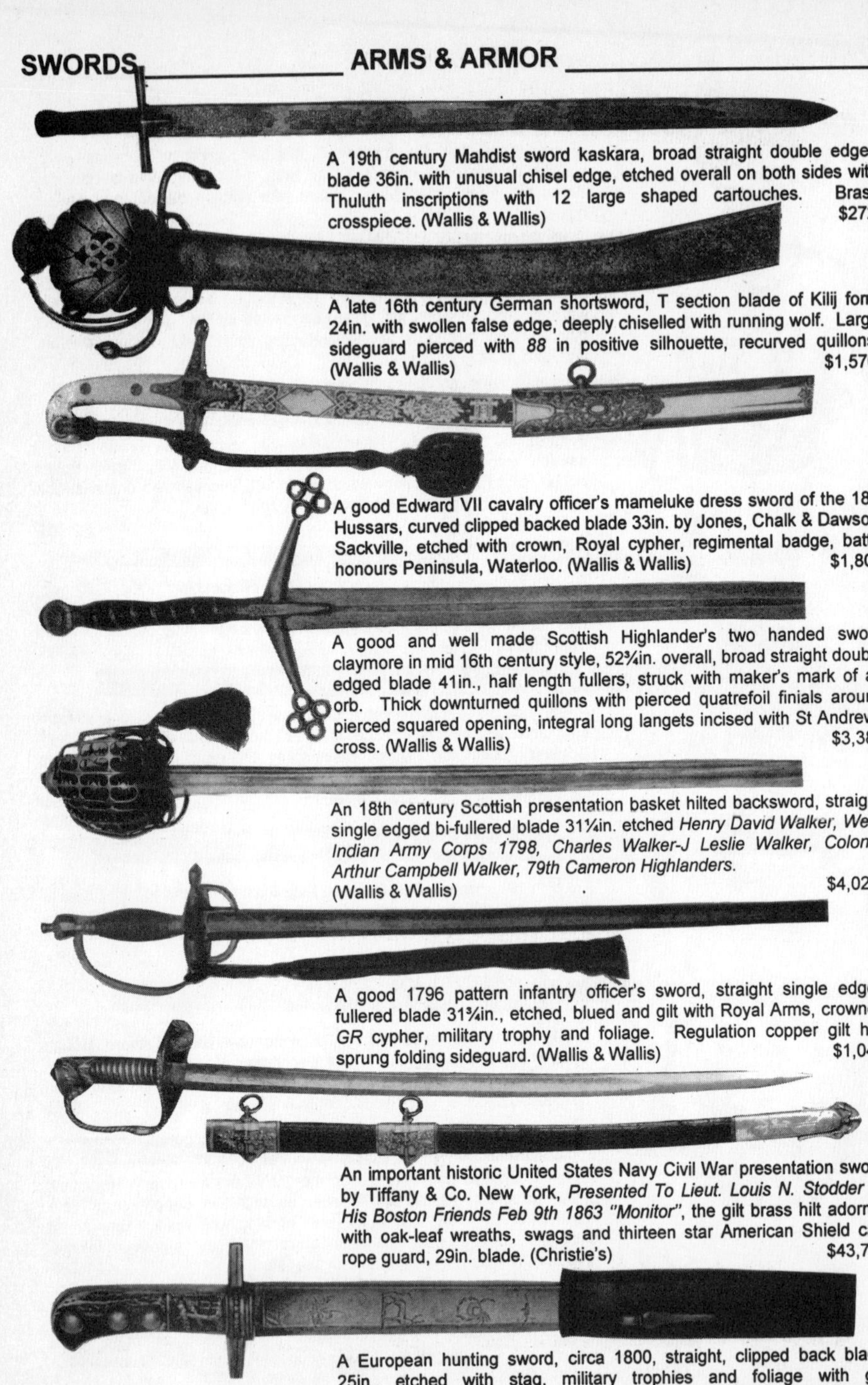

A 19th century Mahdist sword kaskara, broad straight double edged blade 36in. with unusual chisel edge, etched overall on both sides with Thuluth inscriptions with 12 large shaped cartouches. Brass crosspiece. (Wallis & Wallis) $272

A late 16th century German shortsword, T section blade of Kilij form 24in. with swollen false edge, deeply chiselled with running wolf. Large sideguard pierced with *88* in positive silhouette, recurved quillons. (Wallis & Wallis) $1,570

A good Edward VII cavalry officer's mameluke dress sword of the 18th Hussars, curved clipped backed blade 33in. by Jones, Chalk & Dawson, Sackville, etched with crown, Royal cypher, regimental badge, battle honours Peninsula, Waterloo. (Wallis & Wallis) $1,805

A good and well made Scottish Highlander's two handed sword claymore in mid 16th century style, 52¾in. overall, broad straight double edged blade 41in., half length fullers, struck with maker's mark of an orb. Thick downturned quillons with pierced quatrefoil finials around pierced squared opening, integral long langets incised with St Andrews cross. (Wallis & Wallis) $3,381

An 18th century Scottish presentation basket hilted backsword, straight single edged bi-fullered blade 31¼in. etched *Henry David Walker, West Indian Army Corps 1798, Charles Walker-J Leslie Walker, Colonel Arthur Campbell Walker, 79th Cameron Highlanders.* (Wallis & Wallis) $4,025

A good 1796 pattern infantry officer's sword, straight single edged fullered blade 31¾in., etched, blued and gilt with Royal Arms, crowned *GR* cypher, military trophy and foliage. Regulation copper gilt hilt sprung folding sideguard. (Wallis & Wallis) $1,046

An important historic United States Navy Civil War presentation sword by Tiffany & Co. New York, *Presented To Lieut. Louis N. Stodder By His Boston Friends Feb 9th 1863 "Monitor"*, the gilt brass hilt adorned with oak-leaf wreaths, swags and thirteen star American Shield cap rope guard, 29in. blade. (Christie's) $43,700

A European hunting sword, circa 1800, straight, clipped back blade 25in., etched with stag, military trophies and foliage with gilt heightening, silvered brass hilt mounts, short crosspiece, forest scene panel to grip, staghorn grips secured with three domed brass rivets, in its leather scabbard with brass belt lug. (Wallis & Wallis) $330

A late 18th century European dress hunting sword, straight tapering double edged blade 15½in. marked *1414,* rococo copper gilt hilt with short reversed eagle's head crosspiece, boar to center. (Wallis & Wallis) $274

A 9th Lancers Georgian officer's 1822 pattern mameluke full dress sword by Prosser, clipped back single edged blade 31¼in. etched with crowned cross lances above *IX Lancers*, copper gilt mounts chiselled with scrolls in relief, two piece ivory grips. (Wallis & Wallis) $1,256

A good heavy Nepalese sacrificial sword kora, circa 1800, 'elephant's ear' blade 21in., with raised central rib, chiselled intermittent fullers, red filled chiselled 'seeing eye'. Cylindrical steel grip and twin disk guards. (Wallis & Wallis) $338

A late 19th European dress hunting sword, straight plain blade 22½in retaining most polish, solid brass cruciform hilt, rectangular straight crosspiece decorated with oak leaf sprays. (Wallis & Wallis) $204

A rare Georgian 1796 Light Cavalry officer's sabre of the 8th Light Dragoons, curved blade 32½in., etched with crown, *GR* 1801-16 Royal Arms, military trophies and foliage, Pegasus, mounted cavalry trooper, regimental device of crowned Irish Harp, plain steel stirrup hilt. (Wallis & Wallis) $2,576

A scarce 18th century silver hilted Arab sword Saif, broad curved single edged blade 26in. with narrow fuller. Silver hilt of traditional form, canted bi-furcated pommel with reinforced borders. (Wallis & Wallis) $628

A 19th century African Ngala tribal execution sword, 22½in., broad sickle shaped blade 15in. with back projections, deeply incised with geometric decoration. Wooden hilt of traditional form, with brass studs, brass and steel wire bound grip. (Wallis & Wallis) $242

A Victorian 1887 Heavy Cavalry officer's undress sword, by Henry Wilkinson, Pall Mall, blade 35in., etched with crown, Royal Arms, interlaced cypher, foliage, Prince of Wales feathers. (Wallis & Wallis) $353

A Japanese sword katana, blade 65.7cm., signed *No Shu Seki Zenjo Ke* (Zenjo family) *Echizen No Kami Yoshi Kado*, also signed first month lucky day; 2 smiths sign in thin manner, both circa 1645-1700. Tape bound gold lacquered same tsuka, partly gilt shakudo menuki, iron fuchi kashira inlaid with silver foliage, fuchi applied with 2 silver mons; inscribed iron tsuba. (Wallis & Wallis) $1,117

A richly mounted katana, Mei: Inscribed in red lacquer *Kunikane*, the blade, honzukuri and torii-zori with full-length wide grooves, in a fine kin ikakeji scabbard decorated in hiramakie with dragons, and aoi mon. (Christie's) $18,958

A Japanese WWII army officer's sword katana, blade 66.5cm. signed *Koa (or Okitsgu) Issin Mantetsu Wo Motte Kore Wo Saku 18th Year 1941 Kanoto Mi* (Spring). Straight hamon in shin gunto mounts with silver mon of Fukawa and other families on menuki. (Wallis & Wallis) $1,510

A Wakizashi in aikuchi silver mounts, Mei: Yasutsugu oite Echizen saku kore, Edo Period (17th century) 15½in., with an old silver covered habaki carved with waves. (Christie's) $14,059

A fine daisho, the Katana Mei: Inscribed *Bishu ju Osafune, But Ise-Kuwana Uchi, the wakisashi Mei: Izumi No Kami* (and the remainder: Fujiwara Kunisada cut off), Edo Period (17th century). (Christie's) $16,249

A Japanese WWII army officer's sword katana, blade 65cm., signed *Sukemitsu (Showa to)*, gunome hamon, good polish. (Wallis & Wallis) $604

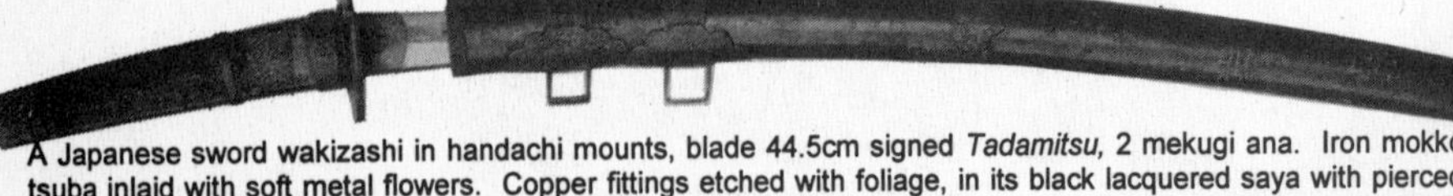

A Japanese sword wakizashi in handachi mounts, blade 44.5cm signed *Tadamitsu,* 2 mekugi ana. Iron mokko tsuba inlaid with soft metal flowers. Copper fittings etched with foliage, in its black lacquered saya with pierced oshi. (Wallis & Wallis) $438

A katana Mumei, probably Bizen School, Momoyama Period (16th century), the blade, honzukuri and koshizori with itame hada, komidare hamon of nie with midare utsuri and slightly pointed komaru boshi, suriage nakago with three mekugi-ana, 26¼in. (Christie's) $5,055

A Japanese WWII naval officer's sword katana, blade 59.8cm. signed *Ishi Hara Masanao,* inscribed *Kinsaku Taka Yama Katana Tosho Kenshi Ishihara Masanao Konuma Jotaro* (polished by Konuma Jotaro), In Kyo-gunto mounts with leather covered saya. (Wallis & Wallis) $906

A William IV painted wooden truncheon, black painted body, painted in gold with *WRIV* and *Ely*, turned wood grip, leather wrist strap, 18in. (Wallis & Wallis) $224

A William IV polychrome painted turned wooden truncheon, 18¼in., decorated with *IV WR* and crowned *St Pancras Middx 362.* (Wallis & Wallis) $267

A George VI painted wood truncheon, painted in gold and colors with GRIIII crown, and 1826, club shaped barrel body, 16in. (Wallis & Wallis) $209

A Victorian painted wooden tipstave, rounded head painted in gold and colors with crown, VR and Cheetham, swelling wood grip, 8¼in. (Wallis & Wallis) $496

A fine George IV painted boxwood truncheon, painted with elaborate crown, Royal Arms, Arms of Birmingham, *GIVR* within cartouche, turned grip, 16½in. (Wallis & Wallis) $370

A Victorian wood and polychrome decorated truncheon, 19¾in., painted with shield shape containing red cross and device. (Wallis & Wallis) $173

A George IV turned and polychrome decorated wooden truncheon, 20½in., decorated in gilt with post 1816 Royal Arms, Garter motto, crowned *IV GR* and *Crown.* (Wallis & Wallis) $314

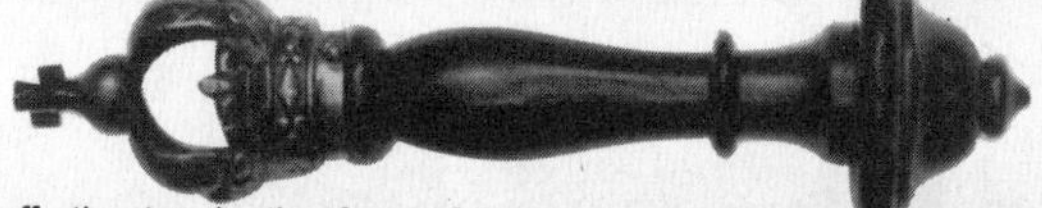

A Georgian tipstaff, the top in the form of brass openwork crown, polished turned wood grip, 8½in. (Wallis & Wallis) $520

A Victorian black painted wooden truncheon, painted *VR No 14K*. (Wallis & Wallis) $224

A George V World War 1 rosewood commemorative painted truncheon, painted in gold and colors with crown, Royal Cypher, armorial shield, motto *In Principio Erat Verbum,* and date *1914-1918,* shaped handle grip, 15in. (Wallis & Wallis) $258

A Victorian painted wood truncheon, painted in gold and colors with crown, VR and within cartouche Hundred of *Hundreds Barrow*, plain wooden handle, 17in. (Wallis & Wallis) $435

1891 6th Inniskilling Dragoons officer's tunic, scarlet melton cloth, with white facing to the collar and cuffs. The collar retains original bullion devices of the Castle of Inniskilling. (Bosleys) $550

Royal Navy Vice Admiral's tailcoat, post 1902 full dress tail coat, each sleeve ornamented with two narrow and one broad band of gold lace backed by purple cloth. (Bosleys) $780

Women's Royal Naval Service Officer's tunic. World War Two period double breasted example of dark blue cloth, to each cuff Lieutenant's rank lace of light blue. (Bosleys) $94

NSDAP Ober-Einsatzleiter's tunic, belt and holster, with original insignia applied for display purposes, light brown four pocket tunic with golden yellow cord piping around the collar which bears a pair of collar badges for a State level Upper action-Leader. (Bosleys) $659

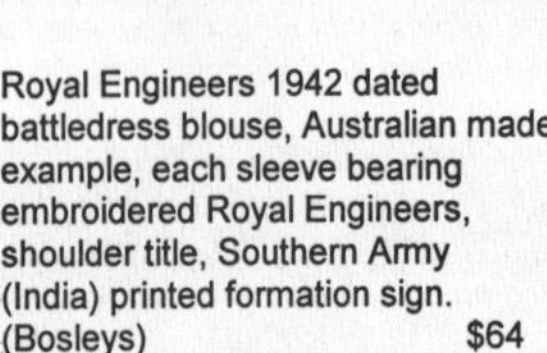

Royal Engineers 1942 dated battledress blouse, Australian made example, each sleeve bearing embroidered Royal Engineers, shoulder title, Southern Army (India) printed formation sign. (Bosleys) $64

A dress tunic and accessories of an officer of the Northumberland Hussars, circa 1895, including a tunic of dark blue cloth with silver bullion lacings, and sky blue mess waistcoat, two pairs of dark blue overalls. (Bonhams) $1,770

Derbyshire Regt (Sherwood Foresters) VB 1881 tunic. Field Officer's transitional example of the 1881 pattern tunic with rounded collars. Scarlet melton cloth with white facings.(Bosleys) $283

A Danish Ambassador's full dress uniform worn by His Excellency M.F.L. De Bille, former Danish Minister to the court of St. James's 1890-1909, including a silk-lined and padded coatee of red cloth, and a black silk velvet cocked hat. (Bonhams) $1,771

Mechanised Transport Corps WW2 khaki tunic, with pockets to breast and waist. The cuffs are with blue piping and an embroidered five pointed star. (Bosleys) $157

RFC aviator's flying coat and helmet, soft brown leather, with plastron front, slanted map pocket to the chest and single pocket to the waist. (Bosleys) $644

Bedfordshire Imperial Yeomanry officer's full dress tunic, post 1902 plastron fronted tunic, dark blue cloth with white facings to the collar and cuffs. (Bosleys) $580

A rare late Georgian OR's scarlet coatee of The Royal Marines, blue facings, gray false turnbacks to chest with 5 white lace loops. (Wallis & Wallis) $1,178

A Nazi NCO's full dress 4 pocket tunic, scarlet piping, dark green collar with scarlet collar patches with silver cloth bars, epaulettes of the 4th company of the 290th Regiment.
(Wallis & Wallis) $393

A good double breasted brown leather flying jacket with map pocket to chest as worn by The Royal Flying Corps, fastening right across the chest, with 2 pleated flap pockets to front.
(Wallis & Wallis) $226

A scarce WW1 sergeant's khaki SD uniform of The Gordon Highlanders, comprising: 1907 pattern doublet, tartan kilt stamped *Sgt C E R Moseley*, and another similar, glengarry cap, sporran, with pair hose; leather covered baton.
(Wallis & Wallis) $1,225

TOP TIPS

Uniforms remain one of the most undervalued areas of militaria collecting and can sometimes prove the most unpredictable. A fine scarlet officer's uniform of the Victorian army can be bought for as little as £100. Often uniforms bear the original owner's name and his full military history can often be traced, bringing to life famous battles read about in history books or taught to us in school.

Always try to buy uniforms in good condition, retaining original badges. Moth balls or insect repellants are recommended to help preservation, and also try to keep them away from direct sunlight. (Bosleys)

Westmoreland and Cumberland Yeomanry scarlet patrol tunic, Officer pattern scarlet serge patrol tunic introduced to the regiment in 1897 and worn until the start of the Great War in 1914.
(Bosleys) $484

A Nazi Army officer's 4 pocket dress tunic, scarlet piping, dark green collar with scarlet collar patches with silver braid bars, bullion wove breast eagle.
(Wallis & Wallis) $468

A Nazi General's 4-pocket tunic, field gray color, General's bullion wove scarlet collar patches, Iron Cross 1st class, tunic stated to be that of General Von Thoma, who was taken prisoner when the Germans surrendered in North Africa.(Wallis & Wallis) $1,095

1858 12th (East Suffolk) officer's shell jacket, a scarce mid 19th century example, attributed to Lt Reuben Frederick Magor. Scarlet cloth with white facings. (Bosleys) $500

A good WWI OR's khaki serge 1907 pattern SD jacket of the Border Regt, white embroidered slip on shoulder titles, brass German silver buttons, double pleats below collar. (Wallis & Wallis) $314

An early 19th century Cavalry officer's tunic, dark blue cloth with scarlet facings to the collar and cuffs, cuffs decorated with scrolling gilt embroidered cord. (Bosleys) $640

A California Highway patrol officer's complete uniform, comprising: fawn peaked cap, crash helmet, khaki green jacket, fawn breeches, belt with holster, pouches etc, shirts, Deputy Sheriff badge. (Wallis & Wallis) $338

Home Guard Wiltshire battledress blouse, 1937 pattern, to each sleeve a printed Home Guard title and two piece designation *WTS 2.*, epaulettes bear cloth Major's rank crown. (Bosleys) $80

City of London Yeomanry Rough Riders uniform, trooper's example of the Lancer pattern tunic, blue gray material with purple facings. (Bosleys) $354

A good and very rare bandsman's gray cloth uniform of the 14th Bn(Young Citizens Volunteers) The Royal Irish Rifles. (Wallis & Wallis) $1,000

SAS Irish Guards officer's scarlet tunic, post 1953 Major's example with dark blue facings to the cuff and collar. (Bosleys) $628

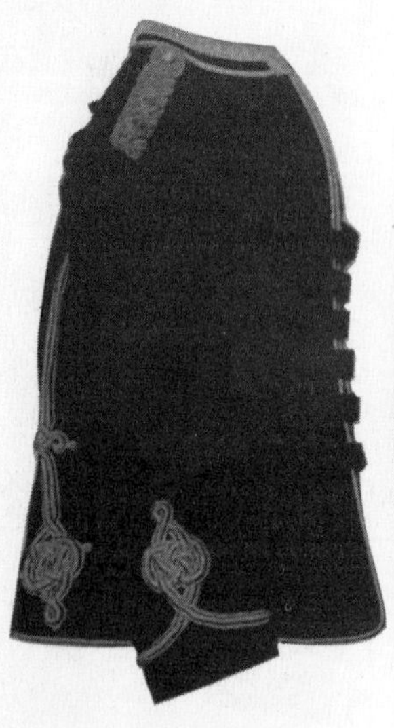

A good Captain's full dress blue tunic of the 12th Bengal Cavalry, blue facings, gilt lace, cord and braid trim including heavy ornamentation to back, 6 black cord loops to chest. (Wallis & Wallis) $1,812

Westmoreland & Cumberland Yeomanry tunic, 1845 pattern Other Rank's issue full dress tunic worn by Quarter Master Hesket. Scarlet melton cloth. (Bosleys) $445

A rare and possibly unique Georgian Irish Yeomanry officer's full dress scarlet coat of the Drogheda Association, apple gree facings and turnbacks to double breasted front. (Wallis & Wallis) $1,12

A scarce General Officer's 1856 pattern scarlet tunic, worn from 1856 to 1868, scarlet melton cloth with dark blue facings to the cuff and collar. (Bosleys) $546

An officer's full dress scarlet coatee circa 1854, of the 2nd West Yorkshire Light Infantry Militia, white facings, silver lace trim. (Wallis & Wallis) $1,040

Westmoreland & Cumberland Yeomanry officer's tunic, scarlet melton cloth with white facings to the cuff and collar. (Bosleys) $780

An officer's scarlet coatee, circa 1828, of the 20th (East Devon) Regt, yellow facings and turnbacks to chest, 10 narrow braid loops with buttons, in pairs, to chest. (Wallis & Wallis) $1,072

York & Lancaster Regiment officer's scarlet tunic, post 1902 example worn by Lt Col G.E. Branson, Volunteer Decoration, scarlet melton cloth, with white facings. (Bosleys) $258

An officer quality OR's grey cloth uniform of the 5th Middlesex (London Welsh) Rifle Volunteers, circa 1863, comprising: pill box hat, tunic, shoulder belt, waistbelt. (Wallis & Wallis) $885

A head of a Japanese polearm Su Yari, 14.2cm., signed (2 characters) single mekugi ana to nakago. Head of traditional form, slightly swollen, tempered edge. (Wallis & Wallis) $361

Two whistling arrows, Edo Period (late 18th/early 19th century), the first turnip headed of two pronged shape, the other [flat] shaped fletched with hawk's feathers, 40³/₈in. and 41in. long. (Christie's) $2,049

A 19th century, Japanese polearm yari, head 9.7cm., details of nakago not available, black lacquered with red lacquered hi. Wooden haft, top covered with mother of pearl segments and 3 brass bands. (Wallis & Wallis) $256

A French double barrelled Dumouthier's Patent percussion knife pistol, 12¹/₈in., blade 8in. with central fuller, barrels 3¼in. Steel crosspiece, one pair of quillons forming the hammers, concealed trigger, steel gripstrap, two piece ribbed horn grips screwed to gripstrap. (Wallis & Wallis) $1,449

A halberd circa 1600, 96in. overall, blade pierced with quatrefoil, scalloped rear spike with pierced device, thickened point, riveted straps.(Wallis & Wallis) $468

A fine Northwest Coast yew bow, tapering at each notched end, narrowing at center, rounded front, 5½ft. high. (Christie's) $9,775

A very rare and unusual folding boar spear head, possibly Neapolitan, sprung hollow ground blades 6in. released by upturned crosspiece with baluster finials. Springs with brass covers, 4 small oval plates with studded edges. (Wallis & Wallis) $4,396

A fine Yumidai (Archery set), Edo Period (late 18th/early 19th century), the matching pair of bows in black lacquer, one wrapped at intervals with red lacquered bamboo, the other with natural bamboo, within the strung bows a double quiver in metal and gilt leather with three crests of the Maru ni Amagasaki Fuji family, overall 90in. (Christie's) $14,059

A halberd circa 1600, 96in. overall, blade pierced with 5 holes, scalloped rear spike with pierced device. Thickened point, riveted straps. (Wallis & Wallis) $559

Yasser Arafat, signed 7 x 5, half-length looking downwards, 21st Jan. 1981.
(Vennett-Smith) $93

Rodgers & Hammerstein, signed 10 x 8, by both Richard Rodgers and Oscar Hammerstein individually, half-length standing alongside each other. (Vennett-Smith) $496

Pete Sampras, signed color 7.5 x 11.5, three quarter length about to serve. (Vennett-Smith) $71

Neil Armstrong, signed color 8 x 10, half-length standing in white spacesuit, with large image of moon in background.
(Vennett-Smith) $434

Andrew Lloyd Webber, signed 8 x 10, head and shoulders, in silver ink, together with a signed and inscribed 8 x 10 of Julian Lloyd Webber, half-length with cello.
(Vennett-Smith) $108

Judy Resnik, signed and inscribed color 8 x 10, head and shoulders wearing blue NASA overalls, with model of space shuttle in background.
(Vennett-Smith) $85

Winston S. Churchill, a fine, wartime signed 5 x 7.5, in full, to lower photographer's mount, 1945, the celebrated image of Churchill seated half-length at his desk by Walter Stoneman.
(Vennett-Smith) $2,015

The Three Tenors, signed color 11 x 8, Pavarotti, Carreras and Domingo, also signed by conductor James Levine, three quarter length standing in row.
(Vennett-Smith) $114

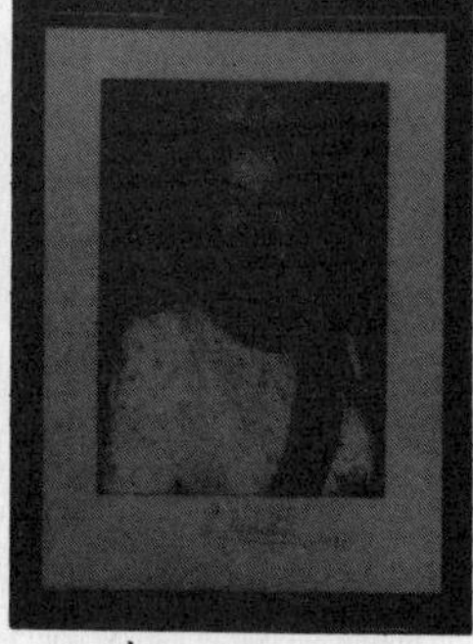

Queen Elizabeth II, a color 11 x 15 photo of the Queen, half-length smiling in ceremonial robes, boldly signed to ivory mount, Elizabeth R 1993, framed and glazed.
(Vennett-Smith) $775

Pope John Paul II, signed color 4 x 6, half-length in white robes, with hands clasped, 12th July 1992.
(Vennett-Smith) $288

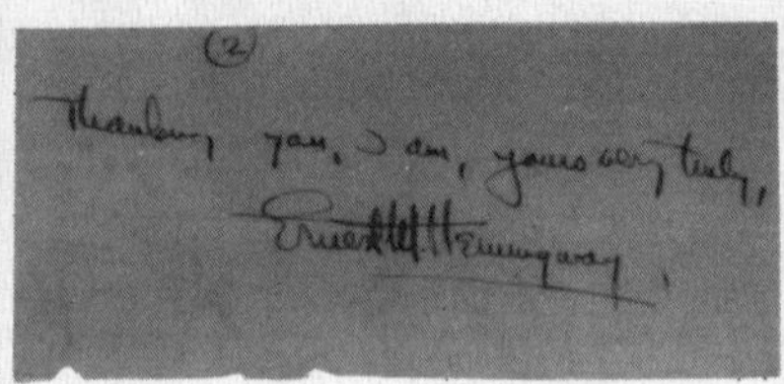

Ernest Hemingway, 5 x 2 piece, cut from end of letter, with additional words *Thanking you I am yours very truly*.
(Vennett-Smith) $656

Robert Kennedy, signed and inscribed 4 x 6, half-length with arms folded, signed against very dark portion.
(Vennett-Smith) $272

Prince Charles, signed edition of Highgrove, Portrait Of An Estate, First Edition 1993, signed and dated 1996, with a covering letter from the Prince's Secretary, sending the book to help raise funds at a Parachute Regiment Association Open Day.
(Vennett-Smith) $318

Pierre Auguste Renoir, autographed signed letter, one page, July 1892, to an unidentified friend, in French, stating that he has just had some teeth removed, 16.5 x 14.5 overall.
(Vennett-Smith) $1,520

William Booth, a fine signed 6 x 8, head and shoulders in Salvation Army uniform, signed with additional words in his hand *with thanks for kindly arrangements for my comfort on the Campania, dated 14th March 1903.*
(Vennett-Smith) $155

Mikhail Gorbachev, signed color 8 x 11, standing speaking from a podium at the Ronald Reagan Presidential Library.
(Vennett-Smith) $124

Queen Victoria, a fine signed sepia cabinet photo, half-length seated in semi-profile, framed and glazed in the original gilt frame (6 x 8.5).
(Vennett-Smith) $1,027

Muhammad Ali, signed color 8 x 10, head and shoulders in bare-chested pose, wearing black boxing gloves and Everlast head protection, signed in gold ink.
(Vennett-Smith) $201

Bruce Bairnsfather, signed postcard, half-length in army uniform wearing cap and smoking cigarette, scarce in this form. (Vennett-Smith) $124

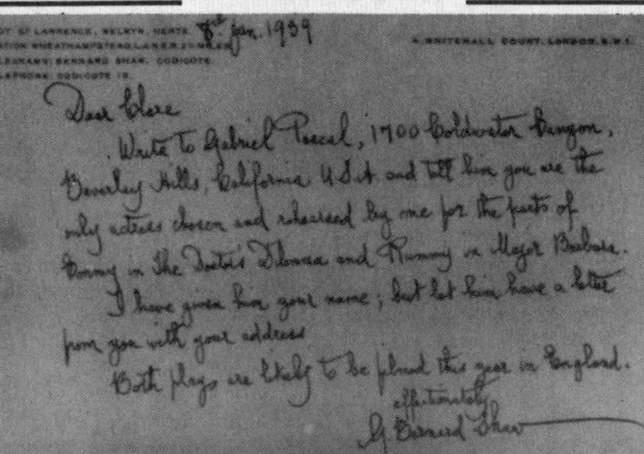

Ayot St Lawrence, Welwyn, Herts.
Station Wheathampstead L.N.E.R.
Telegrams: Bernard Shaw, Codicote.
Telephone: Codicote 18.

8th Jan. 1939

4, Whitehall Court, London, S.W.1.

Dear Clare

Write to Gabriel Pascal, 1700 Coldwater Canyon, Beverley Hills, California U.S.A. and tell him you are the only actress chosen and rehearsed by me for the parts of Jenny in The Doctor's Dilemma and Rummy in Major Barbara.

I have given him your name; but let him have a letter from you with your address.

Both plays are likely to be filmed this year in England.

affectionately
G. Bernard Shaw

George Bernard Shaw, autograph signed letter, one page, 8th Jan. 1939, to Dear Clare, suggesting that she write to Gabriel Pascal and providing his address in Beverley Hills. (Vennett-Smith) $632

Lillie Langtry, signed postcard, half length wearing hat and with one gloved hand raised to her shoulder. (Vennett-Smith) $341

Enrico Caruso, a good original pen and ink self-caricature, 5.5 x 8.5 head and shoulders in profile, on reverse of a sheet of notepaper, London 1905. (Vennett-Smith) $1,072

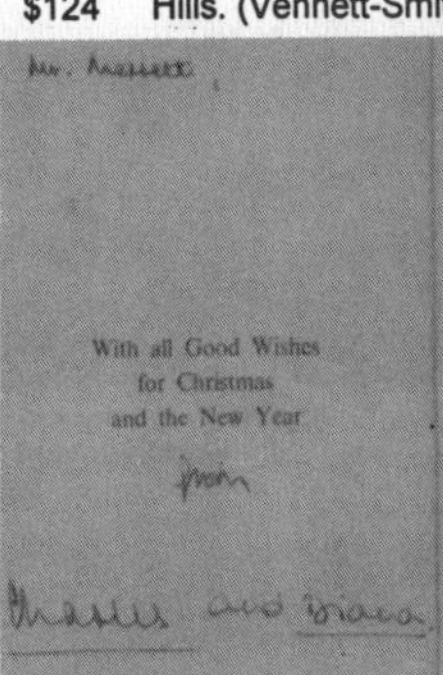

Prince Charles and Princess Diana, signed and inscribed Christmas greetings card by both Charles and Diana individually, featuring a color photo of the royal couple on their wedding day. (Vennett-Smith) $1,550

Neil Armstrong, signed color 6 x 3 three quarter length seated in white spacesuit, neatly trimmed down from 8 x 10 of the Apollo XI crew. (Vennett-Smith) $160

Jacques Villeneuve, signed color 8 x 11.5 in Williams Renault overalls at Melbourne 1977 (first race of the season in which Villeneuve became World Champion). (Vennett-Smith) $54

Vladimir Komarov, signed 6 x 4, full-length standing in uniform with group of cosmonauts, inc. Gagarin, rare due to his death whilst piloting Soyuz I. (Vennett-Smith) $336

The White House

AN HISTORIC GUIDE

PUBLISHED BY
WHITE HOUSE HISTORICAL ASSOCIATION
WASHINGTON, D.C.

Jacqueline Kennedy, hardback edition of The White House An Historic Guide, signed and inscribed by Jacqueline Kennedy to title page, whilst First Lady. (Vennett-Smith) $1,343

Charles Dickens, small signed irregularly cut piece from envelope, laid down to page with photo.
(Vennett-Smith) $237

Lawrence Oates, autograph signed note, with initials L.O., on a picture postcard of a ruined castle, 28th Aug. 1902, addressed in his hand to Miss V.E. Oates, in full.
(Vennett-Smith) $434

M. Fangio, signed 4 x 6, head and shoulders in racing helmet, modern reproduction signed in later years.
(Vennett-Smith) $141

Al Jolson, signed sepia postcard (slight stain and creasing), together with a signed postcard of George Formby Snr. and another of Edward G. Robinson with secretarial signature.
(Vennett-Smith) $108

Ayrton Senna, signed 7 x 4.5, head and shoulders in profile, wearing helmet and seated in racing car, 1994, together with a typed signed letter, one page, 8th March 1994, to Hamlin.
(Vennett-Smith) $496

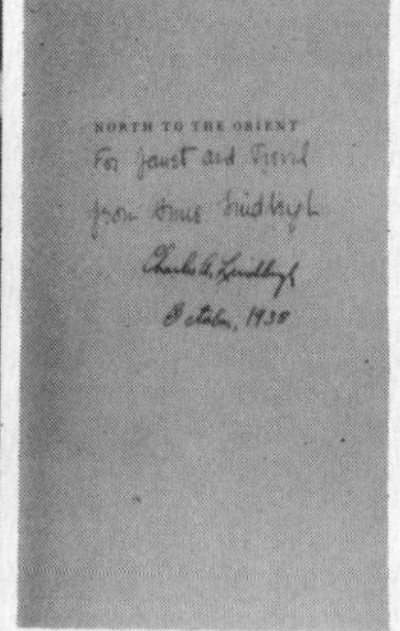

Charles & Anne Lindbergh, hardback edition of North To The Orient, signed and inscribed to half title page by Anne and Charles Lindbergh, Oct. 1935.
(Vennett-Smith) $1,264

Maria Callas, signed 4 x 6, half-length in profile from Il Trovatore, at La Scala, photo by Piccagliani, signed with full married name to lower white border.
(Vennett-Smith) $911

Boxing, a signed 20 x 16 by both Muhammad Ali and Joe Frazier, showing them three quarter length in ring during fight, 24x 20 overall.
(Vennett-Smith) $208

Winston S. Churchill, signed 6.5 x 4.5 to lower mount, in full, half-length seated at desk, photo by Stoneman.
(Vennett-Smith) $840

Pope John Paul II, signed color 6 x 4, half-length wearing white robes and with one hand raised.
(Vennett-Smith) $434

Neil Armstrong, signed color 8 x 10 of Apollo 4 launch.
(Vennett-Smith) $272

Al Jolson, signed sepia 5 x 7, head and shoulders wearing suit, New Year 1952.
(Vennett-Smith) $178

Adolf Hitler, a very fine signed 7 x 9.5, head and shoulders, wearing a tiepin featuring the swastika and Nazi eagle, dated in Hitler's hand, Berchtesgaden, 5th September 1936.
(Vennett-Smith) $3,100

Babe Ruth, an excellent signed 9.5 x 7.5 by Babe Ruth, Dizzy Dean, Frank Frisch, Mickey Cochrane and L.T. 'Schoolboy' Rowe individually, showing Ruth standing full-length, in suit in a dugout during the 1934 World Series, 15 x 23 overall.
(Vennett-Smith) $3,040

Yuri Gagarin, signed color 4 x 6 postcard, head and shoulders in military cap and coat, smiling, with facsimile signature and printed caption in Russian to lower border.
(Vennett-Smith) $490

Al Jolson, signed postcard, full-length seated in suit and bow-tie, with Davey Lee seated on his knee (Sonny Boy).
(Vennett-Smith) $160

Charles Schultz, hardback edition of I Need All The Friends I Can Get, by Schultz, 1964, signed and inscribed by Schultz to flyleaf, with an original pencil sketch of Snoopy.
(Vennett-Smith) $416

Woodrow Wilson, signed sepia 6 x 4, to lower white border, half-length wearing spectacles, minor silvering to top edge.
(Vennett-Smith) $263

Nellie Melba, signed postcard, half-length holding a fan to her chin.
(Vennett-Smith) $46

Pele, signed color 11.5 x 8.5, full-length sitting on astra turf in tracksuit.
(Vennett-Smith) $141

Muhammad Ali, signed color 8 x 10, full-length standing over Sonny Liston in a boxing ring, signed in gold ink.(Vennett-Smith) $217

Nelson Mandela, signed color 8 x 11.5, to lower white border, head and shoulders, in suit and tie, 9th Nov. 1996.
(Vennett-Smith) $474

Prince Charles autograph signed letter, two pages, Buckingham Palace, 30th March 1981, Princess Diana typed signed letter, one page, Buckingham Palace, 12th March 1981, each mentioning their engagement.
(Vennett-Smith) $2,370

Prince Charles & Princess Diana, a good signed 6 x 7.5 color photo, by both to lower photographer's mount, 1989, showing the couple three quarter length arm in arm.
(Vennett-Smith) $1,896

and believe me yours
faithfully
Jefferson Davis

Jefferson Davis, autograph signed letter, two pages, 26th February 1874, to Mrs Von Amien.
(Vennett-Smith) $668

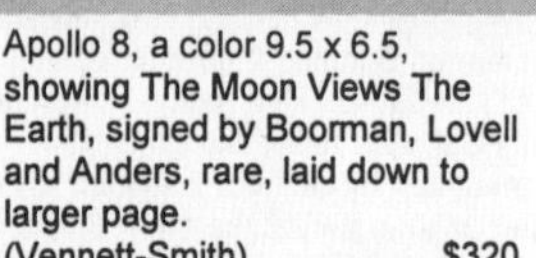

Apollo 8, a color 9.5 x 6.5, showing The Moon Views The Earth, signed by Boorman, Lovell and Anders, rare, laid down to larger page.
(Vennett-Smith) $320

Bobby Darin, signed color postcard, half-length in suit.
(Vennett-Smith) $372

Mike Tyson, signed color 8 x 10, half-length in bare-chested pose. (Vennett-Smith) $72

Adolf Hitler, signed real photographic postcard of German Destroyer at sea, also signed by Von Blomberg and Erich Raeder. (Vennett-Smith) $928

Nat King Cole, signed concert program, to front cover portrait, Concert Tour Spring 1954. (Vennett-Smith) $155

Willy Messerschmitt, signed 5 x 7, half-length seated. (Vennett-Smith) $221

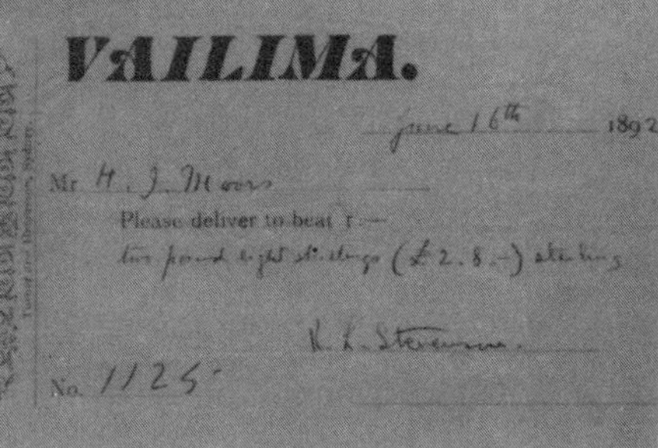

VAILIMA.

June 16th 1892

Mr H. J. Moors

Please deliver to bearer:—

two pound eight shillings (£2.8.–) sterling

R. L. Stevenson

No. 1125

Robert Louis Stevenson, receipt with printed heading Vailima made out to Harry Moors (Stevenson's business agent), for two pounds eight shillings, 16th June 1892, in Stevenson's hand. (Vennett-Smith) $558

Yitzhak Rabin, signed color 7 x 9, to lower white border, head and shoulders standing in front of bookcase. (Vennett-Smith) $90

Sarah Vaughan, signed and inscribed 8 x 10, half-length wearing shoulderless dress, early. (Vennett-Smith) $70

Queen Elizabeth and Prince Philip, signed 7 x 8, by both individually, to lower border, 1955, three quarter length seated with the young Prince Charles and Princess Anne standing alongside. (Vennett-Smith) $502

William McKinley (1843-1901), autographed lithograph of McKinley, circa 1900, by L. Parker, 8 x 6in. framed; bleeding to signature. (Skinner) $431

A French coin slot singing bird in cage, with yellow plumage, domed square brass cage with bevelled corners and giltwood base, 22½in. high.
(Christie's) $2,576

A piano player, with blue eyes, bisque head, brown mohair wig and composition limbs wearing original silk and lace dress, with hand and head movement, 14in. high.
(Christie's) $1,090

A rare Vichy musical figure playing the balalaika to a harlequin doll, with composition head, blue eyes and beard, dressed as a Russian, before a rock, 19½in. high.
(Christie's) $6,360

A Lambert musical smoker, as the music plays he brings his cigarette to his lips, blows smoke and turns his head from side to side, 23in. high. (Christie's) $4,724

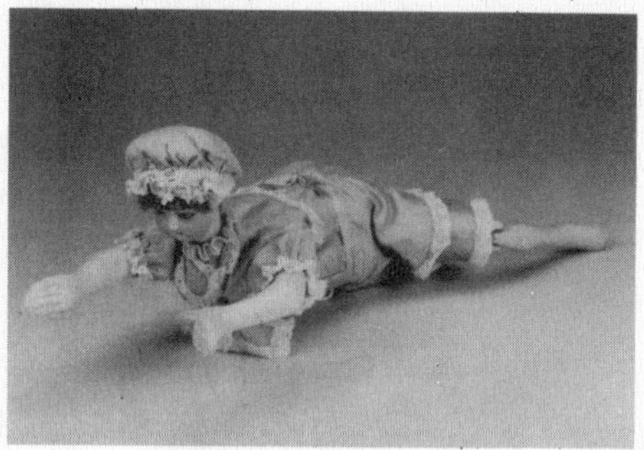

A fine Simon & Halbig mechanical swimming Ondine, German, circa 1910, pin-jointed wooden limbs and cork torso containing swimming mechanism, 16½in. high.
(Sotheby's) $1,171

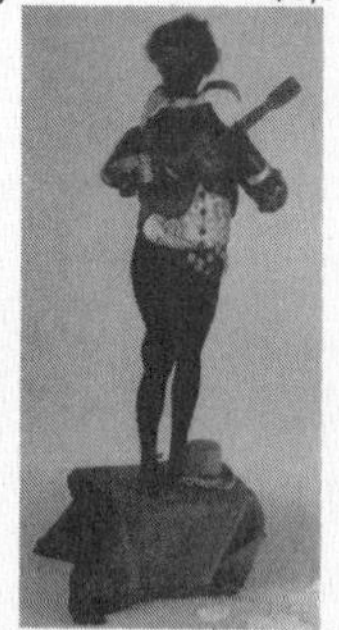

A Lambert black guitar player with composition head and lower limbs, black hair and beard and smiling mouth, with eye, jaw, head, shoulder and hand movements, 28in. high.
(Christie's) $5,088

A Roullet & Decamps dancing girl automaton, French, circa 1910, Simon & Halbig bisque swivel head, clockwork mechanism causing her to pirouette and raise her left leg, 19in. high.
(Sotheby's) $1,712

A rocking ship automaton, the ship in a river-mouth between a windmill and a watermill, with musical movement playing two airs, 19½in. high. (Christie's) $920

A Leopold Lambert musical automaton of a girl with her doll, French, 1900, the German bisque head child with blue glass eyes, head turns from side to side, eyes open and shut, and arms moving towards the doll as if to give her doll a kiss, 18in. tall.
(Bonhams) $1,343

Late 19th century mother of pearl clock picture inset with motif of Big Ben with mother of pearl chip detail, 19 x 14½in. (G.A.Key) $192

A cyclist musical automaton by Leopold Lambert, the doll with porcelain head and original clothing, 36 tone comb, circa 1890, unrestored. (Auction Team Köln) $25,236

A Bontems musical bocage with clock, singing birds in a tree and waterfall, 28½in. high, 18in. wide. (Christie's) $1,999

A clockwork musical automaton, the bisque bébé's head with closed mouth and fixed brown eyes, polichinelle papier mâché body and bisque hands playing the cymbals, 17½in. high. probably by Lambert, redressed. (Christie's) $2,544

A coin-operated musical carousel automaton, in hexagonal glazed case with turned ebonized frame on inlaid burr walnut base, 26in. high, circa 1890. (Christie's) $14,720

A fine automaton of a clown playing the violin, French, circa 1890, the painted clown papier mâché face with blue glass eyes, hollow wooden torso containing key wind, stop- start musical mechanism, 23in. tall. (Bonhams) $3,160

A Vichy Triboulet black banjo player, with brown composition head and hand with a dragonfly painted on his forehead, brown glass eyes, white silk top hat, red and white striped trousers, 30in. high. (Christie's) $9,085

A Phalibois clockwork musical monkey acrobat, of composition, lying on his back twirling a barrel on his foot in a natural setting with silk flower arch above him and head, arm, leg and barrel movement, 33in. (Christie's) $1,362

A clockwork smoking monkey, with composition head and body, dressed in Arabian costume, smoking from a hookah and holding a fan, with head and arm movements, 13½in. high. (Christie's) $1,544

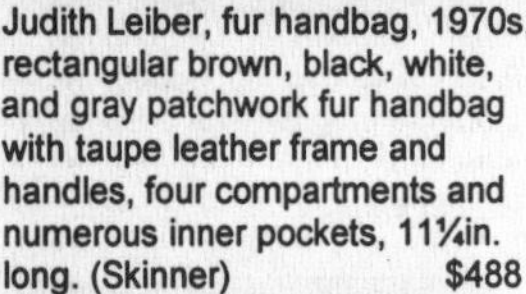

Judith Leiber, fur handbag, 1970s, rectangular brown, black, white, and gray patchwork fur handbag with taupe leather frame and handles, four compartments and numerous inner pockets, 11¼in. long. (Skinner) $488

Louis Vuitton, black Epi leather satchel, 1990s, with short handles, one exterior pocket, goldtone padlocked zipper top closure, and suede interior, 13in. long. (Skinner) $230

Hermès black leather Kelly bag, 1980s, black pebble grain leather Kelly bag, black leather interior with three inner pockets, 13in. long. (Skinner) $1,840

Nantucket bag, 1970s, woven basket bag with top lid, wooden handle, and leather and bone toggle closure, scrimshaw embellishment on top of lid depicts jockey on horse vaulting fence, 8in. long. (Skinner) $460

Hermès, crocodile Kelly bag, 1980s, with lock and key and detachable shoulder strap, black leather lining, 12½in. long. (Skinner) $6,900

Barry Kieselstein-Cord, dog-embellished leather bag, 1990s, black leather handbag with rounded bottom, flap closure with matte goldtone dog closure and short leather handle, 10½in. long. (Skinner) $862

Gucci burgundy Mallette bag, 1960s, leather jewelry case with gold-plated hardware and decorative saddle stitching, four inner pockets, 13⅛in. long. (Skinner) $546

Cartier, a lady's gold and diamond mounted evening bag, the ribbed black silk bag with reeded yellow metal mounts, carrying chain and diamond mounted clasp, stamped *CARTIER 14KT*. (Bearne's) $1,573

Judith Leiber, brown crocodile suitcase bag, circa 1990, with top closure and short goldtone chain handle interwoven with brown crocodile, 7½in. long. (Skinner) $373

A Kelly handbag of black leather, with padlock and keys, *HERMÈS PARIS*, 12.5in.
(Christie's) $1,805

A teddy bear purse with golden mohair, black shoe button eyes, pronounced snout, felt pads and purse opening to back of teddy, 9in. tall, circa 1910.
(Christie's) $1,635

Nettie Rosenstein, taupe leather bag, 1950s, with short handle, flap closure, and three-compartment interior, four inner pockets, 9½in. long. (Skinner) $86

Straw bag, 1940s, woven basket bag from Nantucket with bamboo handle and silver metal hardware, large center front closure with heart motif and fish-shaped clasp, 10in. long. (Skinner) $57

Lilly Pulitzer, 'The Lilly', brightly colored box bag, 1960s, hard-sided box bag covered with patchwork of multicolored Pulitzer fabrics, goldtone frame.
(Skinner) $488

Myles Originals multicolored lucite handbag, 1950s, olive green, red, and metallic gold with top flap, goldtone hardware and top handle, 7½in. long. (Skinner) $431

Gucci bamboo day bag, mid-1970s, burgundy leather handbag with rounded top flap and bamboo toggle closure and handle, mustard leather interior, 10in. long.
(Skinner) $460

Hermès, alligator Kelly bag, 1970s, with lock and key and detachable shoulder strap, brown leather lining, 12½in. long.
(Skinner) $9,200

A shaped knapsack of black ostrich skin, with leather straps and a carrying handle, the interior fitted with pockets and with a metal chain with key ring, stamped *ASPREY*, 11in. base. (Christie's) $198

A mahogany and inlay wheel barometer, English, circa 1860, 94cm.
(Bonhams) $626

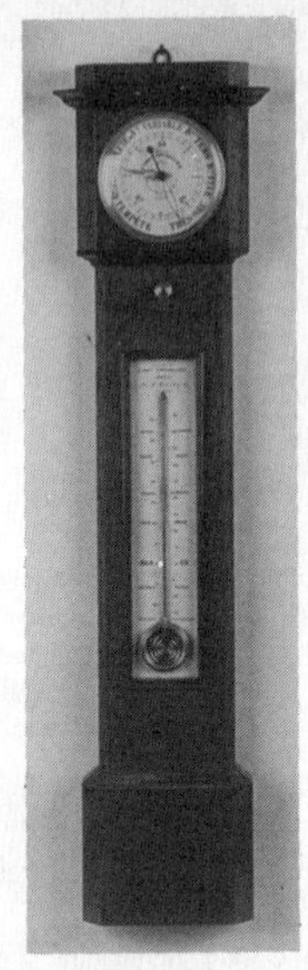

A rosewood wall barometer, Chevallier, Paris, circa 1840, 37½in.
(Bonhams) $1,254

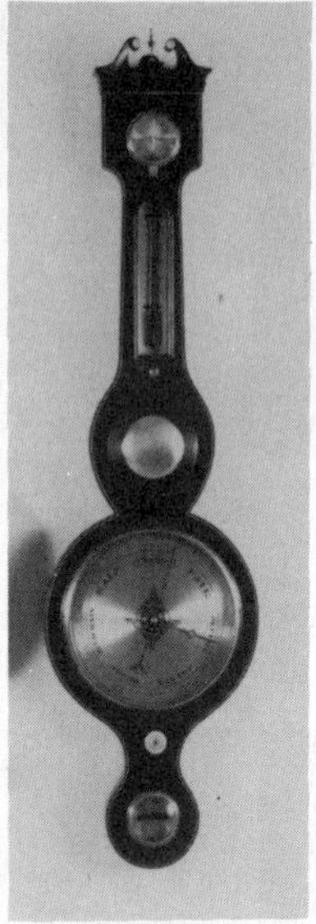

A George III mahogany mercury wheel barometer, with ebony and boxwood edge lining, 96cm. high.
(Wintertons) $718

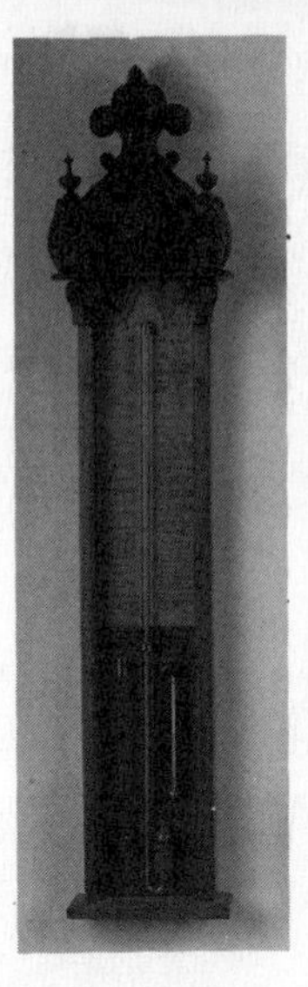

A carved oak wall barometer, English, Admiral Fitzroys 19th century, 49½in.
(Bonhams) $1,492

A mahogany five- dial wheel barometer, English, mid 19th century, signed *Dubini London*, 99cm.
(Bonhams) $412

A mahogany and inlay wheel barometer, English, circa 1860, signed *Jones London*, 98cm.
(Bonhams) $610

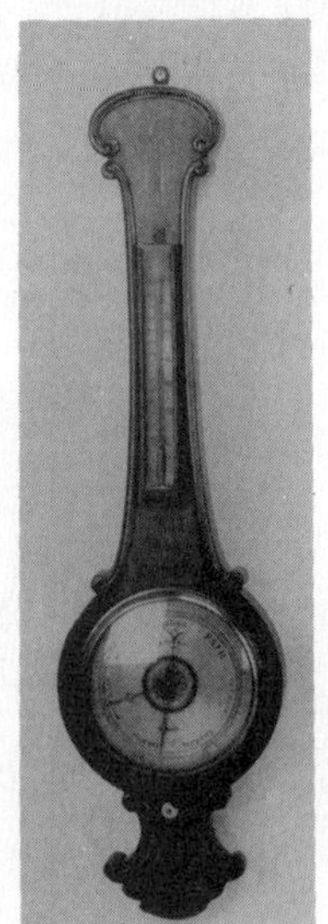

An oak cased wheel barometer, English, circa 1860, signed *J. & L. Pini & Co.*, 94cm.
(Bonhams) $280

A mahogany wheel barometer, Dutch, circa 1900, signed *Willemsen & ZN Gravenhage*, 97cm.
(Bonhams) $395

Thos. Corti, Exeter, a late George III mahogany banjo barometer, 38in. high. (Dreweatt Neate) $661

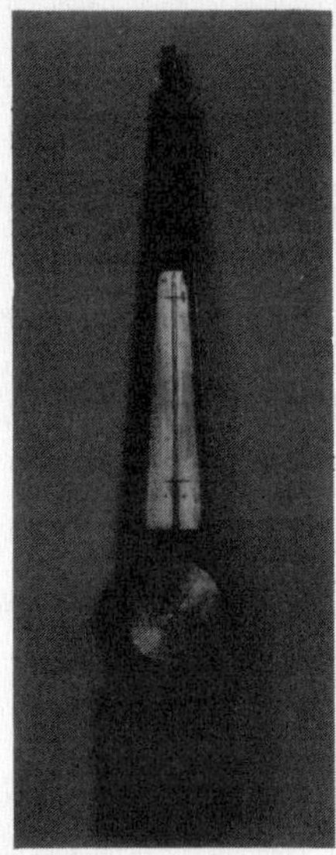

A Regency mahogany and chequer strung wheel barometer, first quarter 19th century, 42in. high. (Christie's) $20,044

A George III mahogany wall barometer by J. Currotty, 99cm. (Bearne's) $566

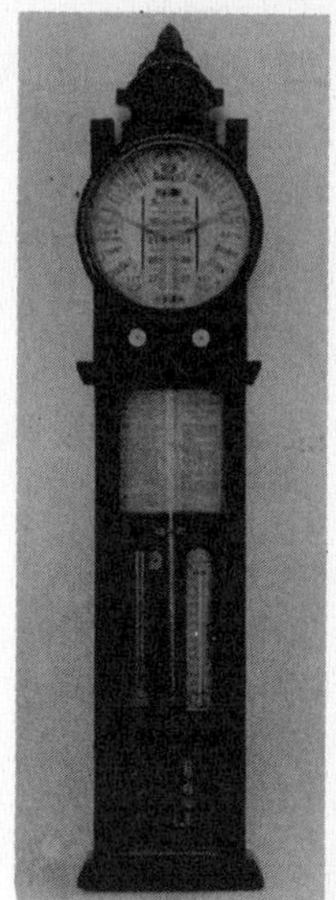

A carved mahogany Admiral Fitzroy's barometer, English, 19th century, 112cm. (Bonhams) $1,071

A mahogany five dial wheel barometer, English, circa 1860, signed *Spiegelhalter 9 Mount Place Whitechapel,* 96cm. (Bonhams) $626

An oak cased aneroid wheel barometer, Welsh, circa 1880, enamel dial signed *Heitzmann & Sons Cardiff,* 103cm. (Bonhams) $527

A George III mahogany wall barometer by P & P Gally, No. 9 Turnmill St. Clerkenwell, London, 103cm. (Bearne's) $1,510

A mid Victorian mahogany mercury wheel barometer with scroll top, signed *A. Burt, Tunbridge Wells,* 91cm. (Wintertons) $638

Nantucket basket, interior bottom stamped *R. Folger Maker Nantucket Mass.*, 6¾in. high, 10in. long. (Skinner) $1,380

Late Edwardian wicker picnic set. (Christie's) $1,380

Large double melon basket, 21in. across. (Eldred's) $330

Nantucket lightship purse basket, America, 20th century, oval form with lid, swing handle, ivory whale decoration on walnut oval lid medallion, 6¾in. high. (Skinner) $3,565

Two 19th century Chinese rice baskets, bronze mounted basketwork, each with four compartments, 65cm. high. (Arnold) $2,642

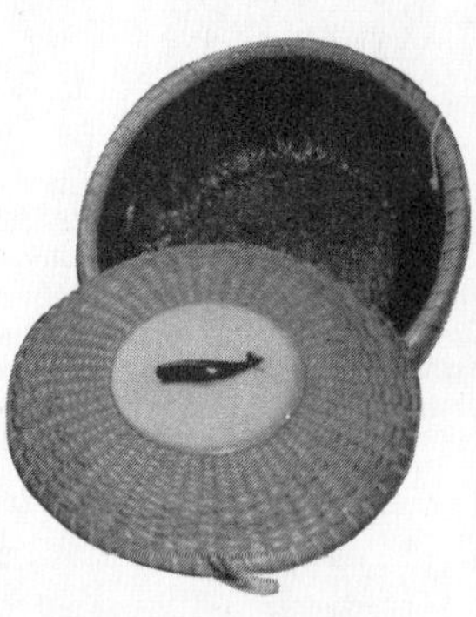

Round Nantucket covered sewing basket, made by Jose Formoso Reyes, America, mid-20th century, the basket with round wooden button on cover with ebony whale decoration, hasp and ebony latch pin closure, 10¼in. diameter. (Skinner) $3,450

A Regency inlaid rosewood oval 'birdcage' work basket with bentwood handle and ivory finial knob, 24.5cm. (Bearne's) $2,202

Splint bamboo ikebana basket, early 20th century, in crescent form, 13in. long. (Eldreds) $550

Nantucket basket, America, 20th century, round basket with wooden swing handle and brass ear assembly, 9⅝in. diameter. (Skinner) $747

Nantucket basket, 19th century, 3in. high, 7¼in. diameter. (Skinner) $1,150

Splintwork gathering basket, 19th century, with swing handle, marked *J. Folger Nantucket*, 9½in. diameter. (Eldred's) $143

Nantucket basket, oval form, 3½in. high, 9¾in. diameter. (Skinner) $632

Two Nantucket baskets, America, early 20th century, includes a large round and small oval basket with a paper label *Made by William D. Appleton…*, both with swing handles, round basket, diameter 11in., oval basket 9in. long. (Skinner) $3,450

New England Indian woven splint basket, 19th century, cylindrical-shaped basket, with alternating blue and natural staves, and blue, natural and yellow weft, 14¼in. diameter. (Skinner) $575

Two round Nantucket baskets, 20th century, *R. Folger Maker Nantucket Mass.*, both stencilled on the base interior, single swing handle with faceted carved ears, 4 x 6 and 4½ x 6¾in. (Skinner) $4,600

Imbricated splint basket with loop handle and relief banded design, 9½in. high. (Eldred's) $253

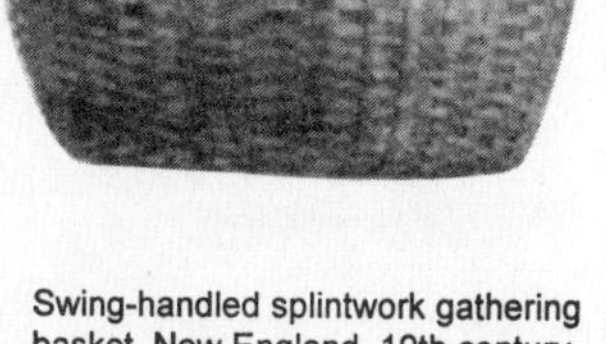

Swing-handled splintwork gathering basket, New England, 19th century, 7½in. diameter. (Eldred's) $176

Two-handled splint egg basket of ovoid form, 5¾in. diameter. (Eldred's) $143

Ferrari C35 – A rare limited edition lightweight racing bicycle, constructed in collaboration with Ferrari Engineering and Colnago, 16-speed gears and special 5-spoke wheels.
(Christie's) $20,342

A Flyer Cresta delivery bicycle by Brown & Brown, Wainik, NZ, 18in. front wheels, 26in. rear wheel, with rear wheel brake and large basket.
(Auction Team Köln) $602

Tornedo, bicycle, wooden frame with Brooks plastic saddle, marked *Tornedo, Schweinfurt, Made in Germany.*
(Sotheby's) $1,379

A 19th century English Safety bicycle with triangular frame, curved handlebars, wooden grips, solid rubber tyres, single brake and 29in. wheels. Although extensively corroded this bicycle retains some original features, such as a leather mudflap and rubber footrests.
(David Lay) $2,700

'Hercules' boneshaker bicycle, circa 1870, an early 'Vélocipède' after Michaux, who invented the 1st bicycle in the world, wooden spoke wheels with iron bands, cast iron pedals, frame and wooden saddle. Brake on rear wheel.
(Auction Team Köln) $7,270

Jan Olsen & Lars Samuelsen; Sweden, a plastic Itera bicycle designed 1978, for Itera A.B., in association with Volvo, two-tone blue plastic bicycle with metal components.
(Christie's) $275

BIRDCAGES

Victorian Gothic Revival carved and painted wood and wire birdcage, 19th century, with removable carved acanthus leaf base, 20¼in. wide. (Skinner) $1,380

An Indian hardwood birdcage on stand, 100cm. wide x 100cm. deep x 197cm. high.
(Bonhams) $816

A bamboo, rattan and metal bird cage, late 19th/early 20th century, of pagoda shape, on outswept feet, 32in. wide, 48in. high.
(Christie's) $736

A pair of Venetian parcel-gilt blackamoor torchères, each with arms raised supporting a circular platform with mask and drape tapering column, 20th century, 128cm. (Bearne's) $4,710

A North Italian blackamoor side table, late 19th century, the shaped top supported by an acrobatic figure on cushion base, 18½in. high. (Christie's) $4,542

A pair of blackamoors, Venice, circa 1860, each gondoliere holding a painted paddle, his hat inscribed *Venezia*, upholding a five-branch gilt-metal candelabrum, 248cm. high. (Sotheby's) $26,243

A pair of Italian giltwood and gilt-composition polychrome-painted blackamoor torchères, mid-20th century, each with a small boy holding aloft an acanthus-wrapped six light torchère, 68in. high. (Christie's) $4,903

A pair of painted ebonized stools in the form of blackamoors, Italian, late 19th century, each with upholstered rectangular top above seated blackamoor on shaped base, 66cm. wide. (Sotheby's) $9,085

A pair of late 18th century ebonized and giltwood blackamoor figures, their arms extended to hold a container (missing), on later faux marble stands, Venice, 146cm. high overall. (Finarte) $15,136

A costumed blackamoor figure in costume, probably Italian, late 19th or early 20th century, with velvet jacket and jeweled head-dress and shoes, 51in. high. (Christie's) $1,998

A pair of Venetian polychrome-decorated, parcel-gilt and ebonized blackamoors, 19th century, each dressed in Venetian gold damask tunics, standing on a spreading stepped square plinth, 49in. high. (Christie's) $76,320

A pair of Venetian painted and giltwood blackamoor figures, dressed in red and gold, their upraised arms holding a lobed dish, 19th century, 222cm. high overall. (Finarte) $24,596

Sir William Edward Parry, (1790-1855) Journal of a Voyage for the Discovery of The North-West Passage..., London, 1821, 4to, cloth, with fourteen plates and six charts and maps.
(Skinner) $805

James Riley (1777-1840), Loss Of The American Brig Commerce..., London, 1817, 8vo, half calf with gilt spine, fold out map.
(Skinner) $345

Alfred, Lord Tennyson (1809-1892), Poems by Two Brothers, London, 1827, First edition, 8vo, original gray boards with paper label, with autographed note tipt in to front of volume. (Skinner) $4,600

Houel (Jean-Pierre-Louis-Laurent), Voyages Pittoresque des Isles de Sicile, de Malte et de Lipari, illustrated with 263 mostly aquatint plates, 1782-87, 5 volumes, folio, tree calf. (Bearne's) $11,797

Belcher, Edward, Sir (1799-1877), The Last of the Arctic Voyages: being a narrative of the expedition in the H.M.S. Assistance...., London, 1855, 8vo, two volumes, half calf with marbleized boards.
(Skinner) $1,840

Pub. E.A.W. Zimmermann, Description and Formation of an unborn elephant, and other unpublished papers on elephants, Erlangen, 1783.
(Stockholms AV) $308

Rambles among our Industries: Wool and the Weaver, the cover designed by Charles Rennie Mackintosh, published by Blackie and Son Ltd, 1912.
(Bonhams) $126

François André Michaux, (1770-1855) The North American Sylva..., Paris, 1817-19, three volumes, 8vo, contemporary gilt half morocco, with 156 hand colored plates; minor foxing, edge wear.
(Skinner) $2,185

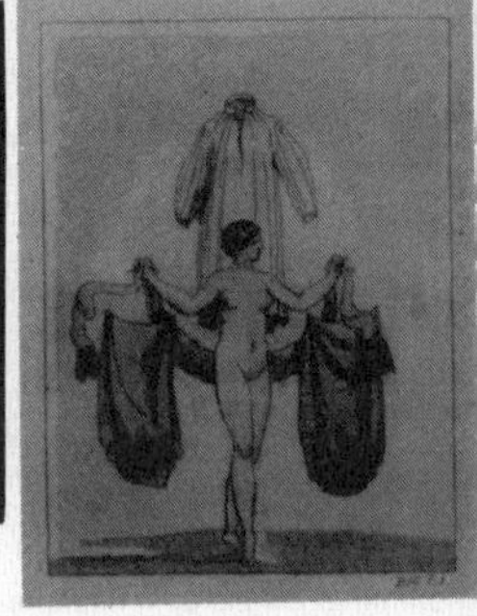

C.A. Ehrensvärd, Italian Journey, 1780, 1781,1782, pub. Stralsund 1819, 38 hand colored plates.
(Stockholms AV) $853

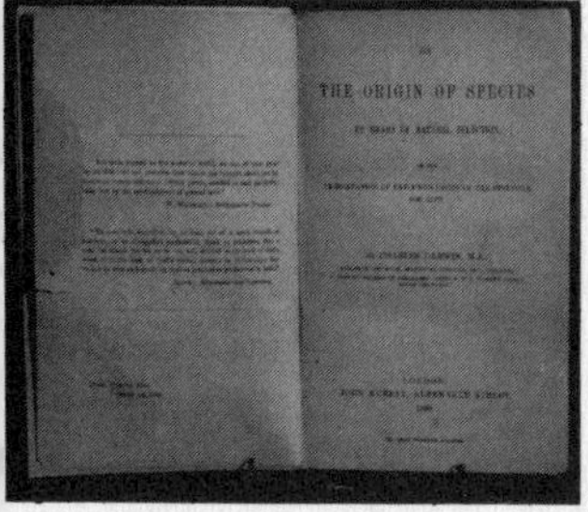

Charles Darwin, (1809-1882) On the Origin of Species..., London, 1859, First edition, John Murray, half morocco with marbled boards, all with gilt highlights.
(Skinner) $5,175

William Taplin, The Sportsman's Cabinet, London, 1803-04, two volumes, 4to, gilt tooled morocco with frontispieces and twenty-four plates. (Skinner) $632

Johann Baptist Homann (1663-1724) Atlas Novus Terrarum Orbis Imperia..., Nuremberg, circa 1720, folio, two volumes, contemporary vellum, with engraved title, portrait and 282 hand colored maps.
(Skinner) $64,100

Countee Cullen, (1903-1946), Copper Sun, New York & London, 1927, 8vo, cloth, signed and numbered 91 of 1000 copies with dust jacket and slipcase.
(Skinner) $575

Ferrari, Giovanni Battista (1584-1655) Flora, Overo Cultura Di Fiori, Romer, 1638, First edition, 4to, engraved frontispiece and forty-five plates, old vellum.
(Skinner) $2,415

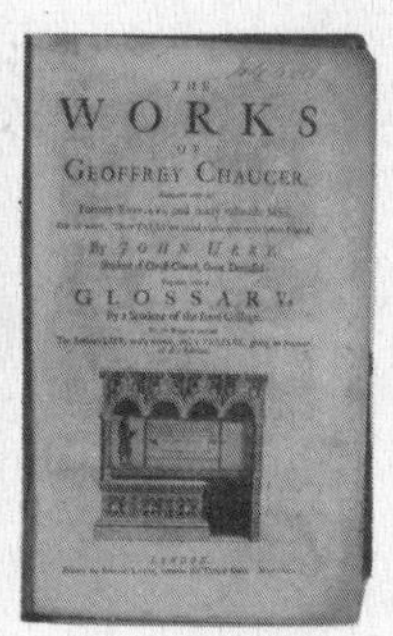

Geoffrey Chaucer, (1340?-1400), Works, London, 1721, compiled by John Urry, folio, calf, with engraved frontispiece and portrait of Chaucer, illustrated throughout with small engravings.
(Skinner) $402

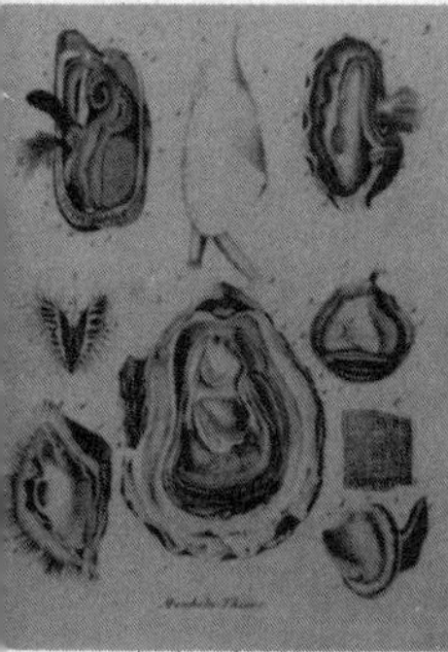

F. Berge, Conchylienbuch, a general study of mussels and snails, Stuttgart, 1847, 44 color plates.
(Stockholms AV) $568

Io. B. Portae, De Humana Physiognomonia libri III, Hanoviae (apud G. Antonium, impensis P. Fischeri Fr.) 1593, 534pp.
(Stockholms AV) $498

A.H. de Sallengre, Novus Thesaurus Antiquitatum Romanorum, I-III, Hagae Comitum, 1716-19, 3 vols. leather bound with gilt tooled arms of Count de Bessans.
(Stockholms AV) $1,090

Robert Tait McKenzie, American (1867-1938), Modern Discus Thrower, signed and dated *1926*, 28½ x 19in.
(Sotheby's) $15,495

Louis-Ernest Barrias, French (1841-1905), La Terre Dévoilant ses Trésors (Earth revealing her Treasures), signed, figure 17¾in. high. (Sotheby's) $18,230

Claire Jeanne Roberte Colinet, 'Theban Dancer', 1920s, cold painted bronze and ivory modelled as a seated scantily clad dancer, 10½in. (Sotheby's) $10,764

A bronze group Le Crepuscule by Émile André Boisseau (1842-1923), French, late 19th century, of a nude winged female figure upholding an oil lamp and sheltering two infants, dated *1880*, 72cm. high.
(Sotheby's) $26,243

A parcel gilt bronze encrier modelled as a helmet, late 19th century, the hinged crown surmounted with a dragon, cast in relief overall with trailing foliage and mythical beasts, 7in. high.
(Christie's) $1,304

Alexander Kelety, dancer, 1930s, silvered bronze modelled as a naked female dancer in mid leap, her arms intertwined in the leaves of a stylized hedge, 48.5cm.
(Sotheby's) $16,146

A bronze figure of a songbird, perched on a branch with outstretched wing, raised on rustic oval base, signed *Moigniez,* 4¾in. high. (Andrew Hartley) $606

'Dancer with Thyrsus', a bronze figure cast from the model by Pierre Le Faguays, 1920s, the Grecian maiden poised on one foot, 55.5cm. high. (Christie's) $7,728

A late bronze Victorian parcel gilt and silvered bronze inkwell, late 19th century, modelled as a cat's head, with a bow tied to its neck, 4in. high.
(Christie's) $2,544

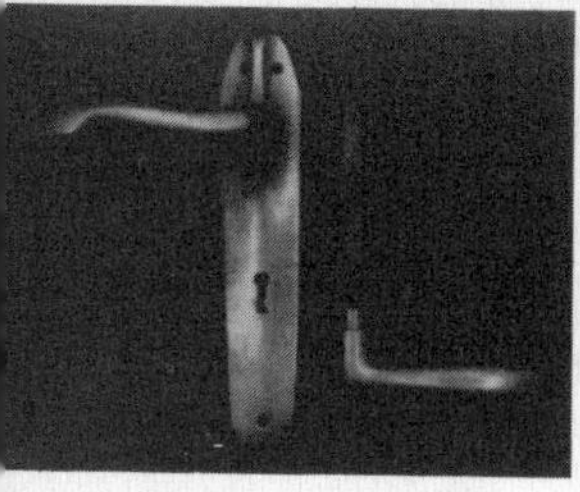

A bronze door handle and lock plate designed by Henry van de Velde, 1904, the handles of sculptural organic form, 8¾in. high.
(Christie's) $2,318

Pierre-Jules Mêne, French (1810-1879), L'Accolade (an Arab mare and stallion), signed, dark brown patina on a red velvet base, 17¼ x 26½in.
(Sotheby's) $21,876

A Boutarel figure of a hoop dancer, 1920s, cold painted, silvered bronze modelled as a naked woman poised on one foot holding a large hoop, 28¾in.
(Sotheby's) $2,708

A gilt-bronze and rouge marble ewer by Sormani, Paris, circa 1880, of baluster form, with a lobed body, the spout and the handle cast with foliage and a shell motif, 42cm. high.
(Sotheby's) $14,996

Maurice Bouval, pair of candelabra 'Obsession' and 'Dream', circa 1900, silvered bronze modelled as two naked women supporting candle holders in form of an iris, 44.8cm., 45.5cm. respectively.
(Sotheby's) $14,352

A pair of Japanese Meiji bronze models of circus elephants, late 19th or early 20th century, each with ivory tusks, shown standing on a sphere above a colored tapering plinth, 11⅛in. high.
(Christie's) $3,540

'Ophelia', a gilt bronze and porcelain bust cast from the model by Maurice Bouval, manufactured by Sèvres, circa 1900, 43cm. high.
(Christie's) $19,320

Alfred Boucher, French (1850-1934), 'Au But', signed, on green-black marble base, group 10¾in. high. (Sotheby's) $2,917

'Charm of the Orient', a bronze and ivory figure cast from the model by A. Godard, 1920s, 19¼in. high.
(Christie's) $8,694

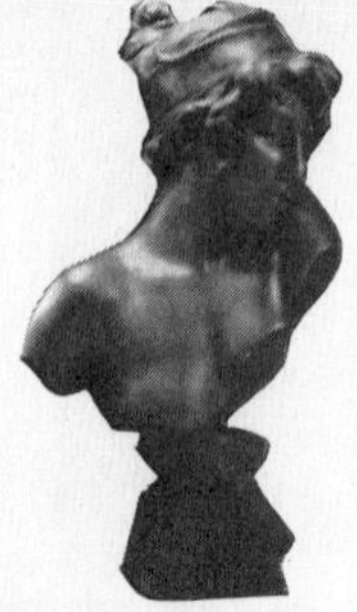

'Sapho', a patinated bronze bust, cast from the model by E. Villanis, circa 1900, the young girl resting her head against her raised shoulder, 22¾in. high.
(Christie's) $3,726

'The Treasure', a bronze sculpture, cast from the model by Charles van der Stappen, 1900, the young girl gazing, with hands resting on a ledge, 14in. high.
(Christie's) $5,216

A Gual figure of an archer, circa 1930, silvered and gilt bronze, cast as a kneeling female archer taking aim, on black slate base with two green onyx 'feet', 10¾in.
(Sotheby's) $812

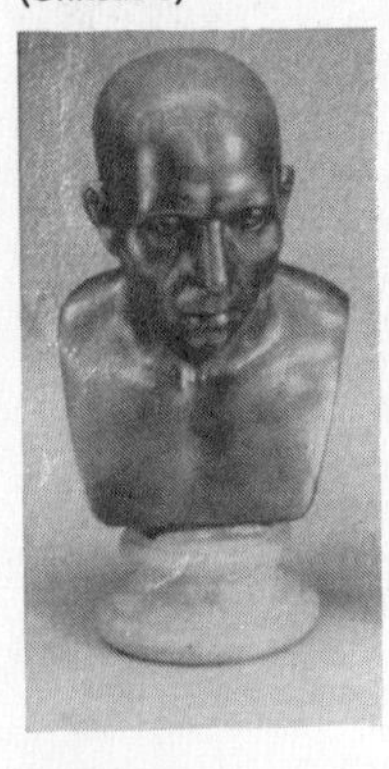

Bronze bust of a man, early 20th century, unpatinated, incised to back *Masulli*, on marble socle, bust 8¼in. high.
(Skinner) $172

A pair of bronze handles from a stamnos or hydria, the pętal-shaped attachments decorated with stylized palmettes, Hellenistic – Roman, circa 2nd century B.C.-2nd century A.D., 5½in.
(Bonhams) $805

François Alphonse Piquemal (early 20th century), bust of a Renaissance woman, French gilt bronze and ivory, signed, on onyx socle, 10¾in. high.
(Skinner) $1,61

A pair of 19th century French gilt bronze candlesticks, the sconces supported by figures of cherubic musicians. (Academy) $704

An Art Deco bronze figure of a dancer balanced on tiptoe, with a stylised wavy cast and gilt painted drape, on a deep oval marble base, green patina, 46.5cm.
(Bearne's) $5,024

A Swedish bronze 8 pound weight, mid 18th century, Gabriel Esping, 1764.
(Stockholms AV) $1,670

Continental bronze bust of a gentleman, late 19th century, signed A. Svoy, 23½in. high.
(Skinner) $747

An English bronze figure of a saddled stallion, cast from a model by John Willis-Good, on shaped grassy base, 30.2cm. long.
(Bristol) $1,887

Bronze and marble bust figure, 19th century, signed *Calendi*, French, doré cap and blouse, 18in. high.
(Du Mouchelles) $2,250

'Ophelia', a gilt bronze bust, cast from the model by Maurice Bouval, manufactured by E. Colin & Cie., circa 1900, modelled with serene expression, her flowing tresses bedecked with poppies, 17in. high.
(Christie's) $12,109

'Les Amis de Toujours', a gilded bronze and ivory figure cast and carved from a model by D.H.Chiparus, of a young woman wearing medieval style dress and skull cap, standing with two attendant borzoi, 41cm. high.
(Christie's) $12,512

'Juggler', a gilt bronze figure, cast from a model by C.J.R.Colinet, of a naked young woman poised on tiptoe and balancing three balls, 34.6cm. high.
(Christie's) $1,011

A pair of Louis Philippe gilt and patinated bronze candlesticks, circa 1840, with engine turned nozzles and drip pans on tapering reeded shafts, 12in. high.
(Christie's) $1,723

A gilt bronze cherub wall applique, early 20th century, the sconce as a rose-bud held by the winged figure, 17in. wide.
(Christie's) $3,992

TRICKS OF THE TRADE

A bronze in good condition can be cleaned with soapy water and a soft brush which will penetrate the detail. After rinsing, it should be dried in dry air (a central heating or electric radiator) then hot waxed with melted beeswax.
When the work has cooled completely remove excess wax with a brush and rub it with a woollen duster.
(Hobbs Parker)

Marcel Bouraine, figure of a bather, circa1925, green patinated bronze with textured surface modelled as a naked kneeling woman, 62cm.
(Sotheby's) $6,458

An Austrian cold painted bronze group of a lady with attendant, late 19th or early 20th century, shown standing on a carpet, 7½in. high.
(Christie's) $4,099

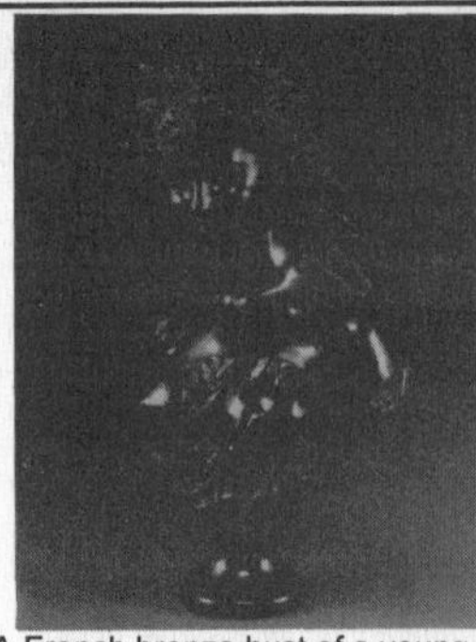

A French bronze bust of a young woman, last quarter 19th century, after a model by Mathurin Moreau, portrayed with flowers in her hair, signed, 24½in. high.
(Christie's) $3,816

Ferdinand Preiss, 'Cabaret Girl', 1920s, cold painted bronze and ivory modelled as a female dancer in a short tight-fitted bodysuit, 40.4cm.
(Sotheby's) $12,558

'Lantern Dancer', a bronze figure cast from the model by Claire-Jeanne-Roberte Colinet, 1920s, the scantily clad silvered female dancer poised on one foot with arms outstretched holding lanterns, 23in. high. (Christie's) $15,456

Demêtre H. Chiparus, 'Delhi Dancer', 1920s, gilt bronze and ivory modelled as a female figure turned to one side with her arms stretched to either side, 35.4cm.
(Sotheby's) $5,382

Professor Otto Poertzel, 'Butterfly Dancers', 1930s, cold painted bronze and ivory, modelled as two confronting female dancers, each poised on one leg, base 41.7cm.
(Sotheby's) $19,734

'Starlight', a bronze and ivory figure cast from the model by Demêtre Chiparus, 1920s, the young woman standing in patinated costume, her green pleated skirt with handkerchief points, 23¼in. high.
(Christie's) $17,388

Marcel Bouraine, 'Harlequin' table lamp, 1920s, cold painted bronze and ivory figure of a dancer in a checkered harlequin costume, 21¾in.(Sotheby's) $28,70

A Continental cold-painted bronze model of a cockerel, late 19th century, mounted on a wooden branch, 22½in. high.
(Christie's) $5,996

'Toboggan', a bronze group cast from the model by Bruno Zach, 1920s, five men in a toboggan racing downhill, 10¼in. high.
(Christie's) $18,354

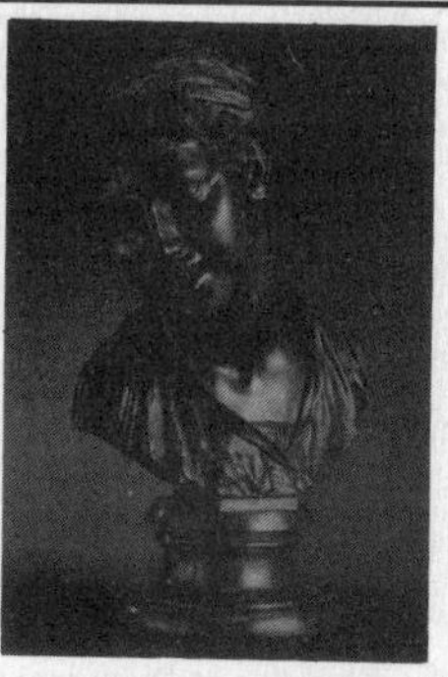

Vincenzo Gemito, Italian (1852-1929), Carmella, a bust, signed, bronze, clear mid-brown patina, 19¼in. (Sotheby's) $5,469

Gerdago, exotic dancer, 1920s, cold painted bronze and ivory figure modelled as a dancer, wearing an ornate jacket, trousers with long tassels and a pointed hat, 14in.
(Sotheby's) $8,611

A fine pair of gilt-bronze and onyx urns by Eugene Cornu, Paris, circa 1870, each with a bulbous turned body, upheld by a base cast with foliage and three cherubs, 108cm. high. (Sotheby's) $29,992

'Beach Ball Girl', a bronze and ivory figure, cast from the model by Ferdinand Preiss, 1930s, the dancer in fringed bathing costume, cold-painted with metallic aqua, 14¼in. high.
(Christie's) $17,388

Ferdinand Preiss, 'The Stile', 1930s, cold painted bronze and ivory, modelled as a female figure in sportswear, 25cm.
(Sotheby's) $16,146

'Nubian Dancer', a bronze and ivory figure cast from the model by Demêtre Chiparus, 1920s, the female figure in Egyptian-inspired costume, 41.5cm. high.
(Christie's) $23,184

A German bronze figure of Mercury, late 19th century, shown standing with an anchor and barrel at his feet, the base inscribed *Moos*, 26¼in. high.
(Christie's) $2,236

A silvered bronze figure cast from a model by Bouraine, of naked young girl dancing with birds, on stepped onyx base, signed in the bronze, numbered *4*, 53.5cm. high.
(Christie's) $3,611

A patinated bronze bust cast from a model by Raoul Larche, of a young girl, green onyx oval base, signed in the bronze, foundry seal, 41cm. high. (Christie's) $1,534

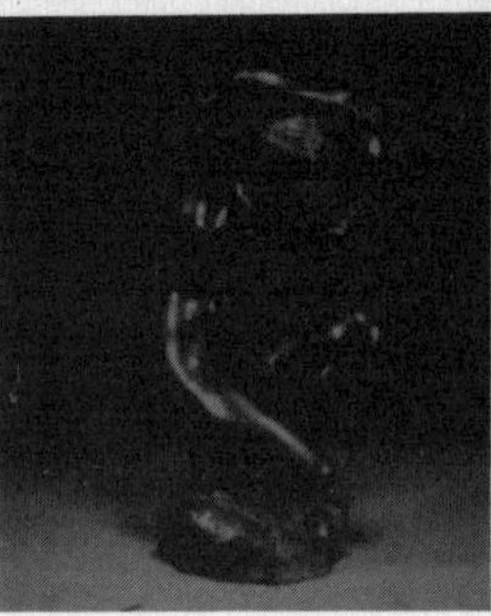

A patinated bronze figure cast from a model by Prochaska, signed in the bronze, 39cm. high.
(Christie's) $631

'Ayouta' a gilded and patinated bronze and ivory figure, cast from a model by D.H.Chiparus, of a poised dancer, on stepped onyx base, 46.3cm. high.
(Christie's) $19,860

A patinated bronze figure group cast after a model by A.Puyt, signed in the bronze, dated *1907*, incised *H.Nonhoff*, stamped foundry seal, 70.8cm. high.
(Christie's) $4,333

A patinated bronze figure cast from a model by H. Muller, signed in the bronze, 14cm. high.
(Christie's) $903

A gilt bronze figural jug, cast from a model by A. Vibert, signed in the bronze, stamped foundry seal, 42cm. high.
(Christie's) $3,069

A silver bronze figure cast from a model by G. Daverny, base with incised signature *Editions Revevaolis Paris*, 69cm. high.
(Christie's) $3,611

A Hagenauer gilt metal face mask, stamped marks, 23cm. high.
(Christie's) $1,083

A silvered bronze bust cast from a model by Dakon, of stylized female, signed in the bronze, 35.2cm. high.
(Christie's) $2,528

A patinated bronze figure cast from a model by Godard, base with incised signature, stamped *Bronze*, 53cm. diameter.
(Christie's) $1,806

A gilt bronze bust cast from a model by Horejc, signed in the bronze, 22.5cm. high.
(Christie's) $306

A Hagenauer silvered bronze and ebonized wooden figure of a stylized girl and panther, stamped marks, 52.3cm. high.
(Christie's) $3,430

A patinated spelter figure group cast from a model by Limousin, of an elegant woman and lion, on rectangular black onyx base, impressed signature, 45cm. high.
(Christie's) $361

A silvered bronze figure group cast from a model by L.Heuvelmans, signed in the bronze, stamped foundry seal, 43.2cm. high.
(Christie's) $2,166

A gilt patinated bronze figure cast from a model by Charron, signed in the bronze *Calf* (?) *Charron*, 40.5cm. high.
(Christie's) $1,625

'Young Grape Harvesters' a silvered and gilded bronze figure group, cast from a model by D.H. Chiparus, on onyx base with bronze plaque, incised and impressed signature, 49cm. high.
(Christie's) $6,861

A silvered and cold-painted bronze and ivory figure cast and carved from a model by Gerdago, of a dancer in elaborate costume, signed in the bronze, foundry mark *AR*, 27cm. high.
(Christie's) $7,583

A brass bound mahogany plate bucket, 19th century, with swing handle and liner, 12in. high. (Christie's) $1,472

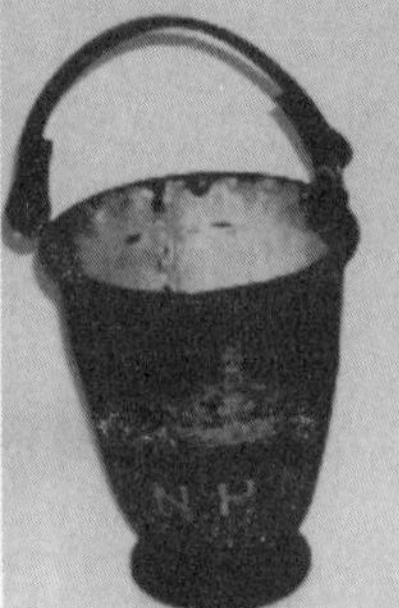

A pair of early 19th century painted leather fire buckets, with gilded crown and initials *N.H.M.* 29cm. high. (Cheffins) $1,506

An Irish George III mahogany and brass-bound bucket with hinged handle and the brass liner also with handle, 16in. high. (Christie's) $4,600

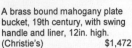

A George III Irish brass bound mahogany plate bucket with swing handle, 16.5in. high. (Russell Baldwin & Bright) $1,683

A pair of George III style brass bound mahogany wine coolers, of tapering cylindrical form with twin ring handles, 10in. high. (Christie's) $2,944

A leather fire bucket, emblazoned to front and reverse with the royal coat-of-arms, 13½in. high. (Christie's) $695

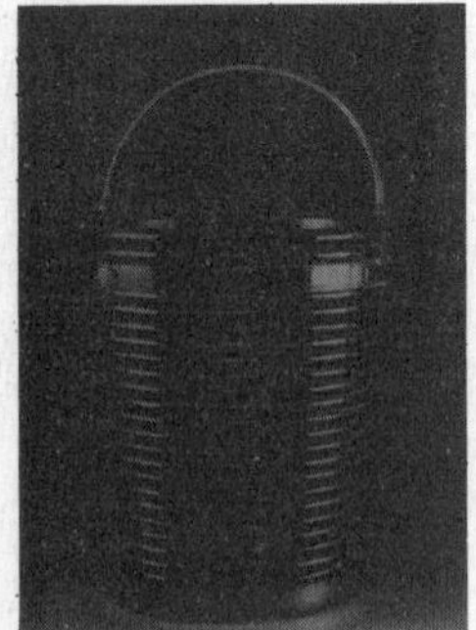

A George III brass bound mahogany peat bucket, late 18th century, the ribbed tapering cylindrical body of coopered construction, with loop handle, 16¼in. high. (Christie's) $5,087

Two George III brass-bound mahogany buckets, of circular tapering form with a carrying-handle and later metal liner, one: 15½in. high; the other: 15in. high. (Christie's) $7,406

A George III brass bound mahogany peat bucket, late 18th century, the cylindrical ribbed body of coopered construction, with twin brass handles, 15¾in. high. (Christie's) $5,087

Art Nouveau period oak stationery slope, the front with hallmarked silver Art Nouveau panels to each corner and a central panel depicting an owl with cartouche surround, 11in. tall, Birmingham 1904.
(G A Key) $463

Red painted pine six-drawer spice chest, 19th century, three tiered construction with overhanging molded edges, 15½in. wide.
(Skinner) $1,840

A George III mahogany knife box, with slope top and chequer strung edges, the serpentine front with two line inlaid panels, 23cm.
(Tennants) $1,440

An early 19th century tortoiseshell octagonal tea caddy with two interior lidded divisions on ball feet, 5.5in. (Russell Baldwin & Bright) $1,505

A pair of late Victorian mahogany urns, each with pine cone and acanthus finial above a swirled gadrooned cover with floral rim, 32½in. high.
(Christie's) $12,512

Capo di Monte porcelain and metal mounted casket, Italy, 19th century, of rectangular form, panelled sides of gilt and enamel decorated in relief, 13¾in. long.
(Skinner) $4,025

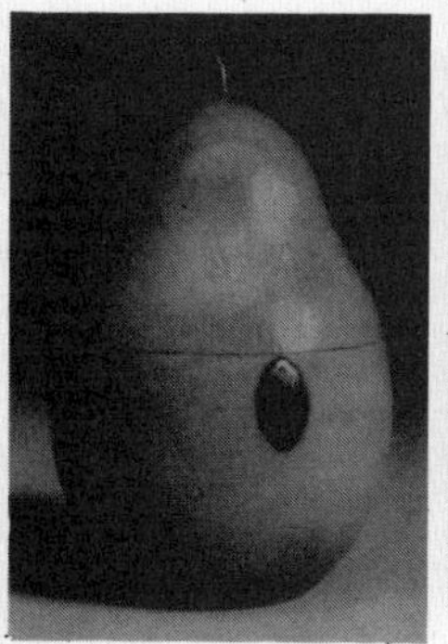

Turned fruitwood tea caddy, England, late 18th century, in the form of a pear, 6¼in. high.
(Skinner) $5,750

Anglo-Indian/British Colonial antler, ivory and sandalwood tea caddy, mid-19th century, with fitted interior of etched ivory and a glass mixing bowl, 14in. long.
(Skinner) $3,335

A wallpaper-covered box, American, 19th century, covered with brown, green and white paper depicting a mounted male figure shooting an arrow at a tiger in a jungle landscape, 11in. diameter.
(Christie's) $920

A walnut casket mounted with silver and lapis lazuli, marked for Leo Horovitz and dated *1905*, the sides with panels of German cities, the canted corners with fluted columns, 30 x 35 x 28cm.
(Arnold) $2,113

Victorian coromandel travelling writing case, 19th century, with brass edging, opening to fitted interior with ivory utensils and writing slates.
(Skinner) $862

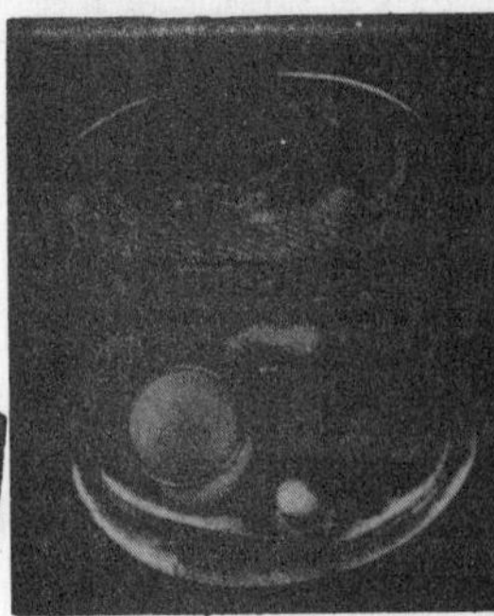

A gilt-metal mounted walnut shell, fitted with a variety of sewing tools and accessories, French, mid 19th century, 5cm.
(Christie's) $973

Federal inlaid maple knife box, England or America, early 19th century, serpentine front, slant lid top with shell inlay, 15½in. high.
(Skinner) $690

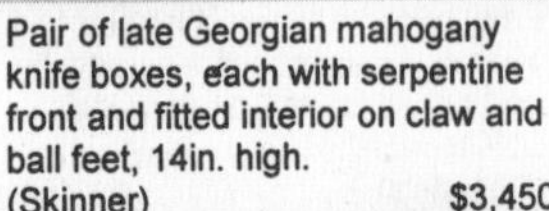

Pair of late Georgian mahogany knife boxes, each with serpentine front and fitted interior on claw and ball feet, 14in. high.
(Skinner) $3,450

Paint decorated tin snuff box, 19th century, the domed lid decorated with a portrait reserve of General Scott, 3⅛in. long.
(Skinner) $1,035

An American brass posting box, comprising thirty hinged and glazed compartments, and nine more of double size, 35in. wide.
(Christie's) $827

A late Regency tortoiseshell veneered necessaire, second quarter 19th century, with ivory banding and domed engine milled cover, on foliate capped ball feet, with later associated musical movement, 5¼in. wide.
(Christie's) $1,090

A maroon velvet lace box, the lid worked in colored beads and silver thread with a design of birds, butterflies and flowers, 18th century, 35cm. long.
(Dreweatt Neate) $74

A Victorian crocodile skin cased dressing table box, circa 1854, brass bound walnut veneered case, the interior with silver mounted glass jars and trays, 11¾in. wide. (Christie's) $1,635

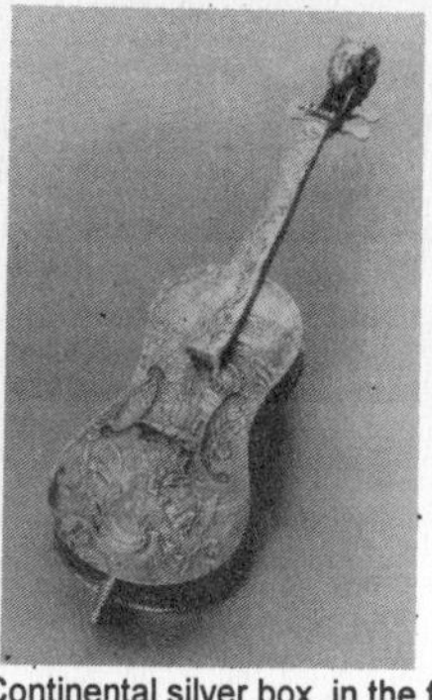

A Continental silver box, in the form of a cello, repoussé decorated with a noblewoman bathing with attendants in rococo landscape, 9in., late 19th century. (Bristol) $684

A small Spanish iron strongbox, the strap hinges to the cover with floret bosses and applied scroll and pierced shaped escutcheon plates, the sides with swing handles, 10in. (Woolley & Wallis) $481

Carved and painted mirrored walnut wall box, Pennsylvania or Connecticut, circa 1830/40, the arched cornice molding flanks a carved device above tasselled pendants and curving sides, 12in. wide. (Skinner) $1,955

A fine pair of George III satinwood-inlaid and silver-mounted figured mahogany knife boxes, circa 1790, each with an oblong top inlaid with a conch shell, 15in. high. (Sotheby's) $9,200

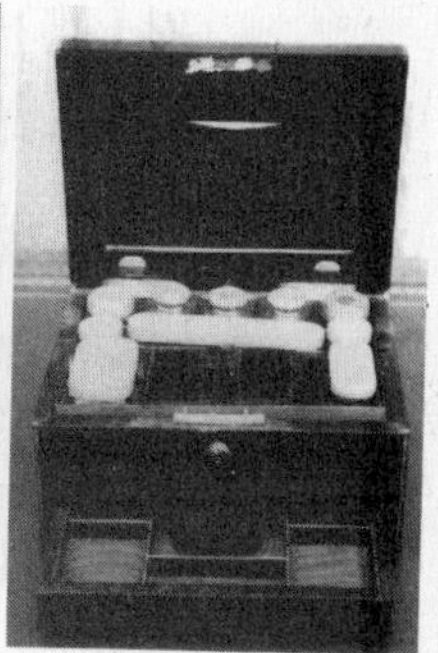

A Victorian coromandel and brass mounted vanity box with ten glass and silver plate mounted jars and bottles, lift out tray and secret drawer. (Academy) $368

Pair of late George III chequer, crossbanded and inlaid knife urns, early 19th century, with fitted interior and carved finial, 25½in. high. (Skinner) $4,600

A Regency tortoiseshell tea caddy with cavetto lid above breakfront and concave chamfered corners, 8in. wide. (Russell Baldwin & Bright) $2,202

A pair of Regency ebony-inlaid mahogany cutlery-boxes, each of square tapering form with concave corners and telescopic top, 24in. high. (Christie's) $8,332

Tropical Una hand camera, James A. Sinclair, London; quarter-plate, polished wood body, lacquered brass binding strips, with a Ross, London Xpres 5½in. f/4.5 lens. (Christie's) $1,666

Makina 67 camera, Plaubel, Germany; 120-rollfilm, with a Nikon Nikkor f/2.8 80mm. lens no. 50936 and instruction booklet, in case. (Christie's) $889

Carte-de-visite camera, J H Dallmeyer, London; 1⅝ x 3½in., mahogany body, lacquered brass binding, with a Dallmeyer brass-bound lens no.8972 and two single darkslides. (Christie's) $6,480

Travelling camera set, English; 6½ x 3¼in., mahogany body, brass fittings, the upper section with removable focusing screen rack and pinion focusing. (Christie's) $9,258

Sigriste camera, J G Sigriste, Paris, 9 x 12cm., wood body, tan leather body panels, with a Berthiot, Paris, Eurygraphe Anastigmat No 1. Serie IVb f/4 lens. (Christie's) $3,703

The Marquis field camera, England, half-plate, brass and mahogany, red leather bellows, with a Swift & Son, London Rapid Paragon 8 x 5 lens. (Christie's) $222

Stereo Xit camera, J F Shew & Co., London, 6½ x 3in., polished mahogany body, aluminum fittings with a pair of Carl Zeiss Anastigmat 110mm. f/8 lenses. (Christie's) $2,962

Tropica no. H.82121, Zeiss Ikon. Germany; 10 x 15cm., polished teak body, nickel-metal fittings, with an interrupted-thread fitting Meyer Plasmat f/5.5 10 x 15cm. lens. (Christie's) $823

Leicaflex SL2 no. 1421567, black, with a Leitz Summicron-R f/2 50mm. lens no. 2367909, lens hood and cap. (Christie's) $889

Canon new F1 no. 264210, black, with a Canon FD L 50mm f/1.2 lens no. 24118.
(Christie's) $1,018

Studio camera no. 702, English, 5 x 5in., mahogany body, with contained focusing screen and single darkslide, and a brass bound lens no. 4101 signed *Jabez Hughes, London.*
(Christie's) $2,592

Horizon 202 camera, Horizon KMZ, USSR; with an MC f/2.8 28mm. lens no. 920359, and grip, in case, in maker's box.
(Christie's) $518

The 1904 BB Instantograph field camera, J Lancaster & Son, Birmingham; quarter-plate, brass and mahogany, with lens in shutter.
(Christie's) $314

Tropical reflex camera no. R297, Ross Ltd., London; half-plate, teak and lacquered brass fittings, red leather viewing hood and bellows, with Ross/Zeiss patent Convertible Anastigmat 11.5/16.5in. lens.
(Christie's) $2,222

Tropical Klapp no. 1131611, Ernemann, Germany; quarter-plate, polished teak body, brass fittings, tan leather bellows, and an Ernemann Ernotar f/4.5 13.5cm. lens. (Christie's) $832

Tropical Deck-Rullo no. S10747, Contessa-Nettel, Germany; 6 x 9cm., polished teak body, nickelled fittings, tan leather bellows, with Carl Zeiss Jena Tessar lens.
(Christie's) $555

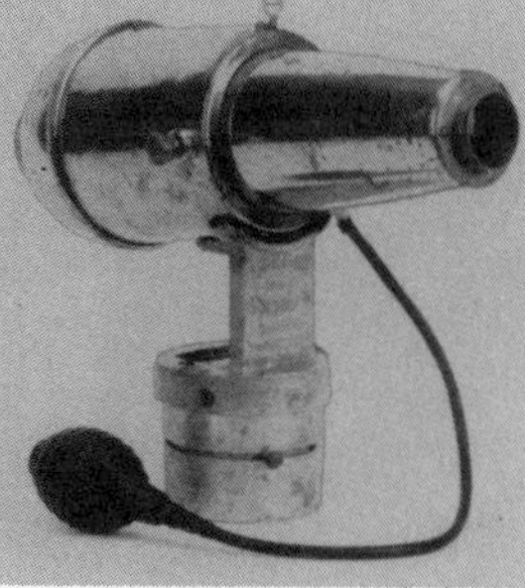

Wonder Photo Cannon camera, Chicago Ferrotype Co., USA; 1in. diameter, bright nickelled body lens, sprung plate holder, and base mounted development tank.
(Christie's) $1,018

MB No. 2 field camera, Marlow Brothers, Birmingham; quarter plate, mahogany body, brass fittings, black square cut bellows.
(Christie's) $314

A Contaflex TLR camera by Zeiss Ikon, Dresden, with Zeiss 2.8/8 focusing lens and Zeiss Sonnar 2/5cm. taking lens, post 1935. (Auction Team Köln) $1,995

Stereo tailboard camera, J T Chapman, Manchester; 7½ x 4½in. mahogany body, brass fittings, red leather square cut bellows, with a pair of Ross, London lenses. (Christie's) $1,388

A rare Eastman Kodak No. 5 folding Kodak Improved Stereo camera for 5 x 7in. roll film, the interior with changeable film cassette and counter to 23 prints, 1893. (Auction Team Köln) $8,522

Fujica G690 no. 9060252, Fuji Photo Film Co., Japan, 120-rollfilm, with a Fuji Fujinon f/3.5 100mm. lens no. 105443. (Christie's) $444

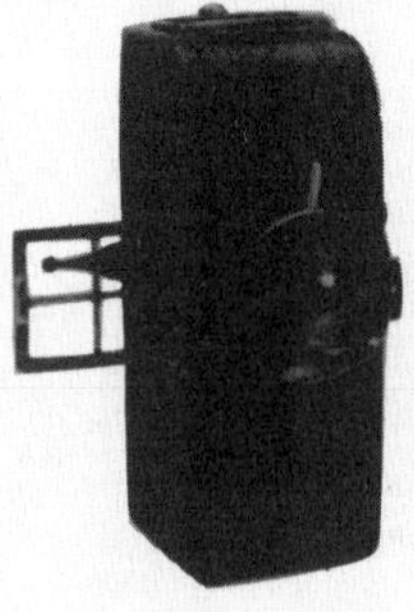

A Levy-Roth, Berlin, Minigraph small print camera, 18 x 24mm. on 135 film in special cassettes, in leather covered wooden and tin body, incomplete, circa 1915. (Auction Team Köln) $171

Street camera, W J Thompson Co. Inc., New York; leather covered wood body, with base-mounted processing tank, lens and shutter. (Christie's) $370

Window pattern sliding box camera no. 489, J H Dallmeyer, London; 7¼ x 4½in., mahogany body, brass fittings, removable focusing screen. (Christie's) $11,109

A Zeiss Ikon Contaflex camera, with Sonnar 1:1,5/5cm. lens, with original cover and case, 1934. (Auction Team Köln) $2,343

Vitessa camera, 35mm., with a Voigtländer Ultron f/2 50mm. lens no. 3777433, in maker's ever ready case. (Christie's) $368

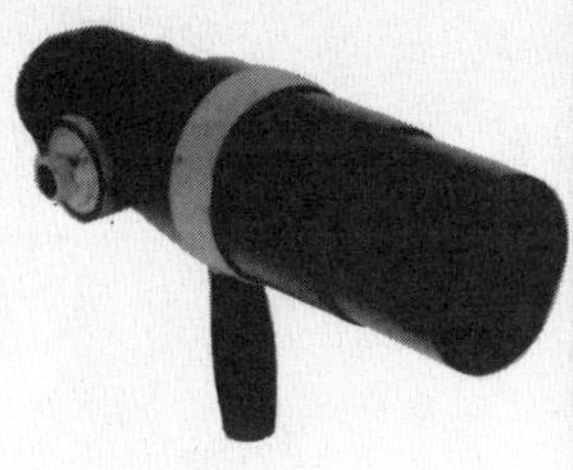

A rare Zeiss Tele-Tessar 1:5.6/400mm. lens for Contarex, with hand grip, covers and leather case, one of only 366 ever made, 1970. (Auction Team Köln) $2,645

Nydia no. 342, Newman and Guardia, London; quarter-plate, mahogany integral magazine plate holder and lens, in maker's leather case. (Christie's) $555

A Kodak Brownie box camera, Century of Progress World's Fair Souvenir, 1933 special edition. (Auction Team Köln) $210

Exakta-Stereo equipment, comprising Zeiss close-up stereo lens, Ihagee Stereflex binocular interchangeable viewfinder and Exacta Varex IIa, 1957. (Auction Team Köln) $1,998

An Eastman Dry Plate & Film Co. original Kodak Rollfilm box camera for 100 pictures, 1888, the model which made amateur photography a reality. (Auction Team Köln) $2,410

Kodak Boy Scout Brownie camera, an Eastman Kodak box camera in olive green with Scout symbol on the front, a rare model for 120 film, 1932. (Auction Team Köln) $301

A Cycle Montauk I hardwood leather covered movable base plate camera, by Gennert, New York, with unattributed lens, red bellows, circa 1900. (Auction Team Köln) $182

Deceptive Angle Graphic no. 9, Folmer & Schwing Mfg. Co., New York, NY; 3¼ x 4¼in., pebble-grained-leather body covering, red-leather internal bellows. (Christie's) $11,040

An American mahogany and brass-mounted Ray Special travel camera with red leather bellows and leather covered case, with 4 x 5in. double wood casette. (Auction Team Köln) $177

19th century horse drawn phaeton with sprung wheels and raised driver's seat, front and rear facing seats behind. (Ewbank) $3,960

Painted and decorated wood, leather and cast iron perambulator, America, 1860, the convertible leatherette top above a faille tufted and upholstered seat. (Skinner) $460

19th century bath-chair with upholstered seat, small front directional wheel and two large rear wheels with spokes. (Ewbank) $1,023

A Sicilian polychrome wood cart, the planked body with figural finials overall, the side panels with battle scenes, 90in. long. (Christie's) $8,176

A painted wood ice cream hand cart, with metal sides, decorated in red, blue and yellow, advertising *Antonio Rossi*, with canopy held by spiral twist brass poles, 72½in. long, 72in. high. (Christie's) $2,656

A green painted governess car, the scroll and pierced back foot plate to a panelled door, leatherette squab cushions and sides, and a pair of brass carriage lanterns. (Woolley & Wallis) $863

'Gröningen', a carpet by Barbro Nilsson, 1954, shades of green squares on a gray ground, 375 x 278cm.
(Stockholms AV) $23,875

Serapi carpet, Northwest Persia, last quarter 19th century, large rosette medallion surrounded by palmettes and serrated leaves, on the terracotta red field, 12ft.2 x 9ft.2in. (Skinner) $9,200

An Oushak carpet, pale green field with all over large beige and ivory medallions within a beige foliage main border and pale blue foliage guards, 9ft.4in. square.
(Woolley & Wallis) $2,514

An Omega Workshops woollen carpet, designed by Roger Fry, 1914, abstract design in pastel shades with mustard and coral on a complementary chocolate brown ground, 94½ x 74¼in.
(Christie's) $22,356

A Chinese Art Deco design carpet, terracotta field bordered on two sides with a series of black lines with a rosette of flowerheads and circles in one corner, 10ft.4in. x 11ft. (Woolley & Wallis) $747

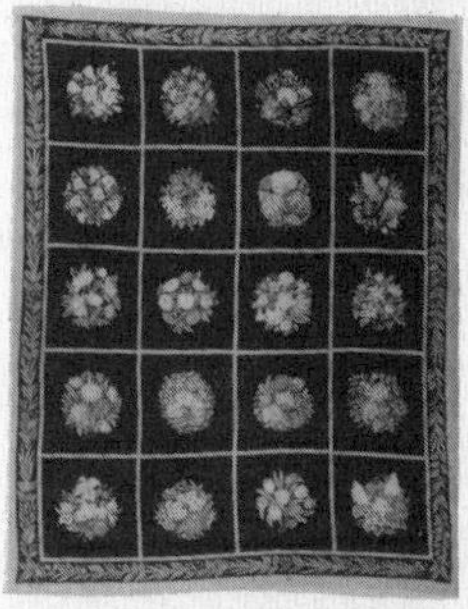

A needlework carpet, colored wools worked in half cross stitch, gobelin and tent stitch; black field composed of twenty squares each with a differing floral spray, possibly French, late 19th century, 9ft.4 x 7ft.9in.
(Woolley & Wallis) $1,328

An Arts and Crafts carpet, probably manufactured in Ireland, circa 1900, indigo blue central field, with bold floral border decorated with fruits and birds, 12ft.10in. by 10ft.
(Christie's) $10,246

A Donegal carpet, the central brick red field with repeating stylized onion design within a sea-green border, 344cm. x 258cm.
(Bearne's) $6,921

Ivan da Silva Bruhns, Modernist carpet, 1930-33, wool, tufted, with a decoration of lines and waves in shades of gray, brown and champagne, 558 x 340cm.
(Sotheby's) $45,051

1931 Lincoln Model K Dual Cowl Phaeton, gray with blue fenders and trim and blue leather upholstery. Engine: V–8, side valve, 384ci., gearbox: three speed manual with free wheeling device; Brakes: four wheel drums. Left hand drive.
(Christie's) $64,100

1929 Packard 645 Dual Cowl Phaeton, coachwork by Dietrich, black with red striping and red leather interior, Engine: straight eight, 384.8ci., 120bhp at 3,200rpm; Gearbox: three speed manual; Brakes: four wheel drum. Left hand drive.
(Christie's) $112,500

1934 Ford V-8 Deluxe Roadster, tan with dark brown upholstery, Engine: L–head V–8, 221ci., Gearbox: three speed manual; Brakes: four wheel drums. Left hand drive. (Christie's) $29,900

1973 Jaguar E–Type V–12 Series III Roadster, silver with black leather interior. Engine: V–12, 5,343cc; Gearbox: four speed manual; Brakes: hydraulic disc. Left hand drive. (Christie's) $26,450

1913 Mercer Type 35 J Raceabout, canary yellow with black striping and black leather upholstery, Engine: four cylinder T–head, dry sump lubrication, 300ci, (5 litre); Gearbox: four speeds forward plus reverse; Brakes: two wheel drum and a contracting shoe on the drive shaft. Right hand drive.
(Christie's) $926,500

1924 Rolls-Royce Silver Ghost Pall Mall Tourer, coachwork by Rolls-Royce Custom coachworks, maroon and black with black leather interior. Engine: six-cylinder, side valves, 7,428cc, Gearbox: three speed manual with overdrive; Brakes: two wheel drum. Right hand drive.
(Christie's) $96,000

1932 Plymouth Convertible, white with black fenders and maroon and red interior. Engine: in-line four cylinder, 196.1ci., Gearbox: sliding gear three speed manual; Brakes: four wheel Lockheed hydraulic. Left hand drive. (Christie's) $18,400

1941 Cadillac Series 62 Coupé, blue metallic with striped gray cloth upholstery, Engine: eight cylinder L-head, 346ci., Gearbox: three speed manual; Brakes: hydraulic drums all around. Left hand drive.
(Christie's) $17,250

1932 Lincoln KB Convertible Coupé, coachwork by LeBaron, dark blue with black fenders and brown leather interior. Engine: V–12, 448ci., 150bhp at 3,400rpm; Gearbox: three speed manual; Brakes: four wheel drum. Left hand drive.
(Christie's) $129,000

1951 Jaguar XK 120 fixed head coupé, Twilight blue metallic with tan leather interior, Engine: six cylinder in-line, double overhead camshaft, 3,422cc, Gearbox: four speed manual; Brakes: hydraulic four wheel drum. Left hand drive.
(Christie's) $56,350

Circa 1929 Stutz Vertical eight series BB Black Hawk Speedster, green with black fenders and tan leather interior. Engine: eight cylinder, in-line, overhead camshaft, 4,900cc, 298ci; Gearbox: four speed manual; Suspension: semi-elliptic all round; Brakes: four wheel hydraulic. Left hand drive.
(Christie's) $40,250

1939 Lasalle Coupé, metallic blue with striped gray and blue cloth interior. Engine: eight cylinder L-head, 322ci., Gearbox: three speed manual; Brakes: hydraulic drums all around. Left hand drive.
(Christie's) $8,625

1960 Bentley S2 Standard saloon, black with green leather interior, Engine: V-8, overhead valve, single central camshaft, 6,230cc, c.200bhp at 4,500rpm; Gearbox: four speed automatic; Suspension: front independent, rear elliptic; Left hand drive.
(Christie's) $16,100

1956 Mercedes-Benz 300SL Gullwing, red with tan leather interior and tan leather fitted luggage, Engine: six cylinder, in-line, 2,996cc., 240bhp at 6,100rpm; Gearbox: four speed manual; Suspension; independent front and rear; Brakes: hydraulic drum. Left hand drive. (Christie's) $167,500

1940 Lasalle Series 52 Special 'Torpedo' Convertible Coupé, gray with red leather interior. Engine: eight cylinder L–head, 322ci., 130bhp at 3,400rpm; Gearbox: three speed manual; Suspension: leaf springs all around; Brakes: hydraulic drums all around. Left hand drive.
(Christie's) $20,700

1954 Buick Skylark Model–X100 Luxury Sports Car Convertible, gull gray poly with red interior, Engine: Fireball V–8, 322ci., Gearbox: Dynaflow three speed automatic; Brakes: hydraulic drums all around. Left hand drive. (Christie's) $90,500

1963 Avanti, turquoise with light blue vinyl interior, Engine: V-8 overhead valve, Paxton supercharger, Gearbox: four speed manual; Brakes: front disk, rear drum. Left hand drive.
(Christie's) $5,520

1966 Ford Mustang 289 Convertible, red with red and white interior. Engine: V–8, overhead valves, 289ci., 225bhp at 4,800rpm; Gearbox: automatic transmission; Brakes; four wheel drum. Left hand drive. (Christie's) $14,950

1950 Allard J2, acquamarine with black interior, Engine: 90 degree V–8, side valve; Gearbox three speed, synchromesh on second and third; Brakes: four wheel hydraulic drum. Right hand drive. (Christie's) $32,200

1930 Lincoln Model L Sport Phaeton, coachwork by Lincoln, Engine L–head 60 degree V–8, 385ci., Gearbox: three speed manual; Brakes: four wheel drum. Left hand drive.
(Christie's) $29,900

1928 Lincoln Model L Sport Phaeton, coachwork by Locke, Engine: L–head V–8, 385ci., 95bhp at 2,900rpm; Gearbox: three speed manual; Brakes: four wheel drum. Left hand drive.
(Christie's) $57,500

1941 Cadillac Series 62 Deluxe Convertible coupé, coachwork by Fisher, bronze with red interior. Engine V–8, 346.3ci, 150bhp at 3,400rpm; Gearbox: three speed manual; Brakes: four wheel drum. Left hand drive. (Christie's) $32,200

1957 Jaguar XK140 MC Roadster, dark blue with red leather interior, Engine: six-cylinder, twin overhead camshafts, 3,442cc, Gearbox: four speed manual synchromesh with overdrive; Brakes: Lockheed four wheel drum. Left hand drive.
(Christie's) $79,500

1934 Rolls-Royce Phantom II Henley coupé, coachwork by Brewster, black with leather tan canvas covered fixed head. Engine: six cylinder, 7,668cc, Gearbox: four speed manual; Brakes: four wheel drum. Left hand drive.
(Christie's) $321,500

1963 Cadillac Fleetwood Sixty Special 4-door hardtop sedan, black with light blue interior. Engine 90 degree V–8, 390ci., 325 bhp at 4,800 rpm; Gearbox: three speed automatic. Left hand drive.
(Christie's) $1,610

1920 Mercer Series 5 22-73HP Raceabout, yellow with black leather upholstery. Engine: four cylinder L-head, dry sump lubrication; Gearbox: four speeds plus reverse; Brakes: two wheel drums. Left hand drive.
(Christie's) $79,500

1956 Bentley S1, silver with red coachline and beige leather interior, Engine: six cylinder in-line, 4,887cc, 178bhp at 4,500rpm; Gearbox: four speed automatic; Brakes: four wheel drum. Left hand drive.
(Christie's) $11,500

1954 Citroen Traction Avant 15 Six Saloon, black with gray cloth upholstery, Engine: six cylinder in line, 2,867cc; Gearbox: three speed manual; Brakes: four wheel drum. Left hand drive.
(Christie's) $6,325

1953 Ford F100 pickup truck, sea haze green with tan Connolly leather interior, Engine: overhead valve six cylinder, 223ci., Gearbox: four speed; Brakes: four wheel drums. Left hand drive.
(Christie's) $44,850

1959 Morris Minor 1000 Convertible, white with tan interior and black top. Engine: in–line four cylinder, 948cc., 37hp at 4800rpm; Gearbox: four speed manual; Brakes: four wheel drum. Left hand drive.
(Christie's) $8,050

1958 Chevrolet Corvette Roadster, silver blue with light blue interior, Engine: V-8, 283ci., 245hp at 4,800rpm; Gearbox: four speed manual; Suspension: independent front with rear semi-elliptic leaf springs; Brakes: four wheel drum. Left hand drive.
(Christie's) $46,000

1971 Lamborghini P400 S Miura GT Berlinetta, red with gold SV trim and blue cloth and vinyl interior. Engine: V–12, transverse rear-mounted four overhead-camshaft with four valves per cylinder, six twin-choke Weber carburettors, 3929cc; Brakes: four wheel disk. Left-hand drive.
(Christie's) $85,000

1937 Bugatti Type 57 Ventoux, coachwork by Gangloff, silver and black with maroon leather interior. Engine: eight cylinders in-line, twin overhead camshaft, 3,257cc giving circa 140bhp at 4,500rpm; Gearbox: 4-speed; Brakes: mechanical to all wheels. Right hand drive. (Christie's) $200,500

1959 Cadillac Fleetwood Sixty Special Sedan, metallic blue with two-tone blue upholstery, Engine: overhead valve V-8, 390ci., 345bhp at 4,800rpm; Gearbox: automatic; Suspension: independent front with coil springs all around; Brakes four wheel drums all around. Left hand drive.
(Christie's) $19,550

1937 Cord 812 supercharged Sportsman cabriolet coupé, maroon with tan leather interior. Engine: V8, L-head 288.6ci (4.7 litres); Gearbox: four-speed preselector by Bendix; Brakes: four wheel drum. Left hand drive.
(Christie's) $142,200

1964 AC Cobra with Paxton Supercharger, white with blue racing stripes and black leather interior. Engine: V8, 4,727cc; Gearbox: four speed manual; Brakes: four wheel discs. Left hand drive.
(Christie's) $127,900

1957 Ford Thunderbird factory supercharged 'F' Series, baby blue with white leather interior. Engine: V8 supercharged, 312ci, giving 300bhp at 4,800rpm; Gearbox: Ford-O-Matic; Brakes: four wheel power-assist. Left hand drive.
(Christie's) $88,300

1967 AC Cobra 427 SC 'Semi-Competition', blue with white racing stripes. Engine: V8, iron block and heads, pushrod operated overhead valves, 427ci; Gearbox: four speed manual; Brakes: four wheel disc, 11.6in. front, 10.75in. rear. Left hand drive.
(Christie's) $283,000

1948 Ford Super Deluxe Woody Station Wagon, body by Ford Iron Mountain, green, Honduras mahogany panels, Michigan hard maple stiles, ash roof slats with tan interior. Engine: V–8 flat–head, 239ci, Gearbox: three speed column shift; Brakes drums all round. Left hand drive. (Christie's) $35,650

1954 Corvette Removable Plexiglass Bubbletop Roadster, sportsman red with red interior. Engine: Blue Flame six-cylinder, 235ci.; Gearbox: automatic; Brakes: front and rear drums. Left hand drive.
(Christie's) $51,750

1967 Corvette Stingray L71 Convertible, ermine white with red stinger and red interior. Engine: L71 V8 427ci, giving 435bhp, single four barrel carburettor; Gearbox: four speed manual; Brakes: four wheel disc. Left hand drive.
(Christie's) $72,900

1968 Mercedes Benz 600 six-door pullman limousine, black with red interior. Engine: V8 single overhead camshaft per bank, fuel-injected, 6,332cc; Gearbox: four speed automatic; Suspension: self levelling air independent; Brakes: servo-assisted twin circuit disc. Left hand drive. (Christie's) $59,700

1990 Ferrari F40, coachwork by Pininfarina, Ferrari red with red and black interior. Engine: 90 degree V8, two belt driven overhead camshafts per bank operating four valves per cylinder; Gearbox: five-speed; Brakes: four wheel discs. Left hand drive.
(Christie's) $266,500

1969 Corvette Stingray L88, Riverside gold with black interior. Engine: Chevrolet overhead valve V8, 427ci; Gearbox: automatic turbo hydromatic transmission; Brakes: four wheel disc. Left hand drive.
(Christie's) $64,100

1955 Mercedes Benz 300 SL gullwing, Daimler Benz strawberry red metallic with tan leather interior. Engine: six-cylinder, in line, 2,996cc, 240bhp; Gearbox: four speed manual; Suspension: independent front and rear; Brakes: hydraulic drums. Left hand drive. (Christie's) $272,000

1957 Mercedes Benz 300SL Roadster, white with red leather interior. Engine: six cylinder, in line, 2,996cc; Gearbox: four speed manual; Suspension: independent front and rear; Brakes: hydraulic drums. Left hand drive.
(Christie's) $140,000

1972 Lancia Stratos Rally, orange with black interior. Engine: V6, 2,418cc, four overhead camshafts, mid-engine transversely mounted; Gearbox: ZF limited slip differential, 5-speed close ratio Ferrari competition gearbox; Brakes: four wheel discs. Left hand drive.
(Christie's) $43,700

1953 Corvette Roadster, polo white with sportsman red interior. Engine: Blue Flame six-cylinder, 235ci; Gearbox: two speed automatic; Brakes: front and rear drums. Left hand drive.
(Christie's) $81,700

1939 Packard Six (1700) Station Wagon (Woody) coachwork by J.T. Cantrell, black with wooden sectioned bodywork, Engine: six cylinder, in line, side valve, L head, 245ci., 100bhp at 3200rpm. Gearbox: three speed Packard selective with synchromesh; Brakes: four wheel drum. Left hand drive. (Christie's) $63,000

1948 Plymouth Special Deluxe Woody station wagon, Balfour green with leatherette interior, white ash rails and frames with mahogany panels, Engine: six cylinder L–head, 218ci., 95hp at 3,600rpm; Gearbox: column mounted three speed manual. Left hand drive.
(Christie's) $40,250

Circa 1911 Daimler 38hp Tourer, red with beige upholstery, Engine: four-cylinder sleeve valve, 124mm x 130mm bore and stroke, 6280cc., 383 ci.; Gearbox: four speed and reverse, cone clutch, shaft transmission with worm final drive; Brakes: internal expanding on rear wheels and foot operated on transmission. Right hand drive.
(Christie's) $40,000

1966 Ford F–100 'Good Humor' Ice Cream truck, white with blue and white cloth interior, Engine: six cylinder, 240ci., 150bhp at 4000rpm; Gearbox: column shift three speed automatic; Brakes: drums all around. Left hand drive. (Christie's) $10,925

1936 Morris 8 h.p. Series 1 Saloon Reg. No. AUP 520, the Morris Eight was the product of the mighty Nuffield Empire to compete with the products of competitors Ford and Austin.
(Tennants) $3,344

1955 Mercedes-Benz 300SL Gullwing, Mercedes Red with black leather interior, Engine: inline six cylinder, single overhead camshaft, 2,996cc., 240bhp at 5,800rpm; Gearbox: four speed synchromesh manual; Brakes: vacuum assisted four wheel finned drums.Left hand drive. (Christie's) $184,000

A National Model 452 bronzed cast metal cash register with mahogany base, for US currency, circa 1913. (Auction Team Köln) $569

A brass 'National' cash register, no.95 and serial no.516301, width 60cm. (Bristol) $576

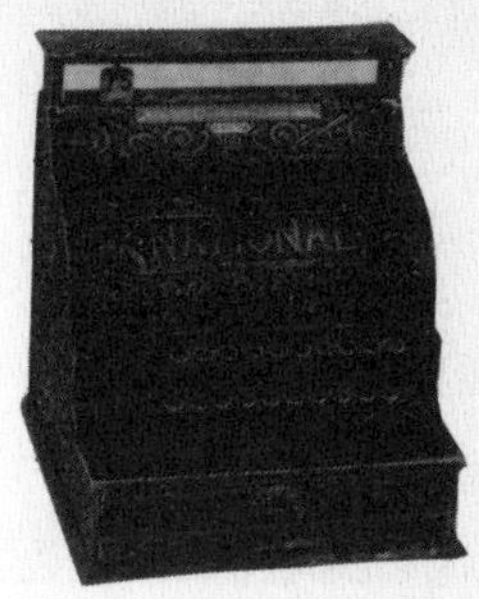

An early National Model 13 cash register of unusual mechanical construction, with original manufacturer's label dated *1901*. (Auction Team Köln) $837

A National Model 92 press button cash register with 5-place keyboard, bronzed brass, with print out and till receipt, 1898. (Auction Team Köln) $1,004

A National Model 652 nickel plated cash register, Art Nouveau style on wooden base, four insertion levers for currency up to DM99.99, till receipt, 1914. (Auction Team Köln) $660

National Model 562-X-6C Art Nouveau plated cash register, with drawers for six cashiers, for German currency, with receipt dispenser and handle, circa 1910. (Auction Team Köln) $1,003

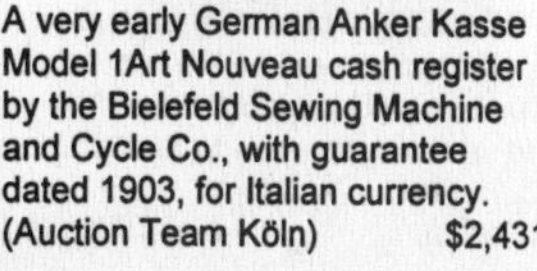

A very early German Anker Kasse Model 1Art Nouveau cash register by the Bielefeld Sewing Machine and Cycle Co., with guarantee dated 1903, for Italian currency. (Auction Team Köln) $2,431

A National Model 453 cash register, bronzed and silvered with mahogany base, for British currency, 1912. (Auction Team Köln) $1,004

National Model 642 plated cash register on mahogany base, in the Art Nouveau style, print-out with receipt dispenser, German-made, circa 1910. (Auction Team Köln) $1,473

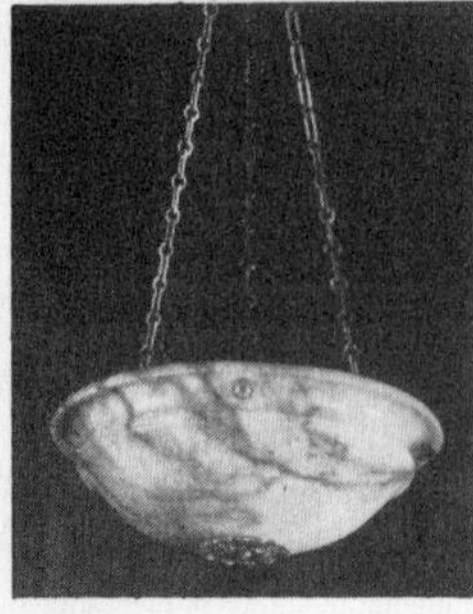

An alabaster ceiling light, 20th century, the circular dish with a gilt-bronze anthemion cast terminal, with suspension chains, 19½in. diameter.(Christie's) $1,687

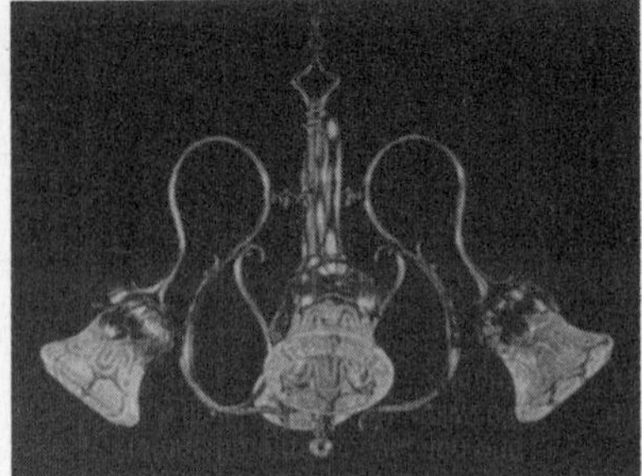

W.A.S. Benson and James Powell & Sons, four-light chandelier, 1880s, brass with copper detail, the four arms modelled as scrolling flower stems, 25¼in. (Sotheby's) $8,998

A Régence style gilt-bronze eight-light chandelier, early 20th century, with campana nozzles and gadrooned drip pans on scroll branches, 29in. high. (Christie's) $3,187

A Continental neo-classic style ormolu and cut-glass sixteen-light chandelier, the pierced corona issuing scrolls suspending tassels above faceted chains and drops , 52¾in. high. (Christie's) $18,400

Art Nouveau gilded and patinated hammered copper chandelier, first quarter of the 20th century, with six Quezal iridescent ribbed bell form shades, decorated around the ring form fixture with Egyptian style figures and animals, 24½in. diameter.(Freemans) $5,750

A brass chandelier, designed by Leopold Bauer, circa 1909, hemispherical open design, the curving ribs interspersed with scrolling spirals, white glass shades, 24in. maximum width. (Christie's) $5,796

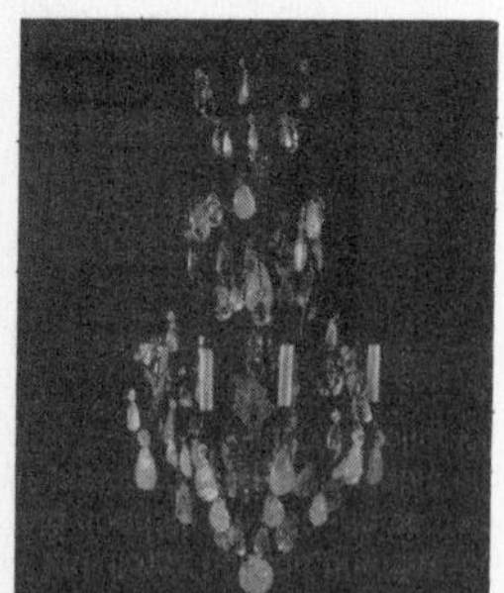

A Louis XV style patinated bronze six-light chandelier, early 20th century, with a scrolling frame hung with faceted drops centering a cut-glass finial, 44in. high. (Christie's) $4,025

A German carved giltwood seven light chandelier, 18th century, with naturalistic branches radiating about a pierced spherical well, 41in. high. (Christie's) $6,560

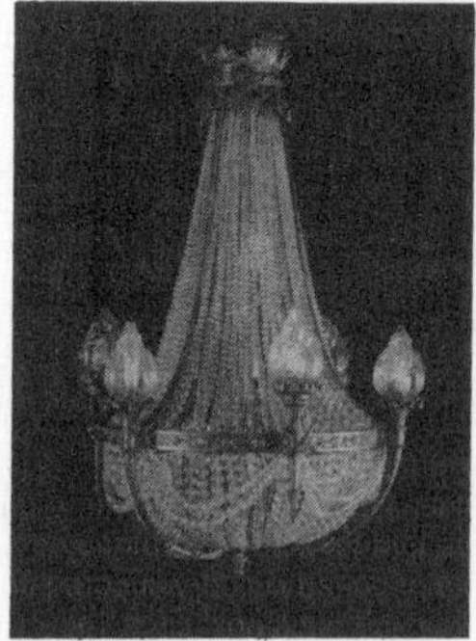

A French gilt-bronze and glass six branch chandelier, 20th century, the trumpet-shaped frame with strings of graduated faceted beads, 33in. high. (Christie's) $2,437

A French bronze eighteen-light chandelier, late 19th century, of naturalistic form, the branches grouped in three registers, 30in. high. (Christie's) $2,249

Bronze figural bat chandelier, 20th century, three full-bodied flying bats in a triangular formation suspended from bronze chains, drop 21½in. (Skinner) $7,187

An Empire style bronze and brass eight light chandelier, 20th century, with scroll branches about the circular well, 45in. high. (Christie's) $3,997

A fine cut glass and gilt-bronze chandelier, circa 1825, possibly Spanish, the outer ring supporting eighteen candle nozzles and cast with masks and cornucopiae, 140cm. high. (Sotheby's) $14,584

An antler chandelier, early 20th century, the frame of entwined antlers fitted with nine sconces, 37in. high. (Christie's) $2,907

Ettore Sottsass, a painted metal chandelier, designed 1956-7 for Arredoluce, composed of a graduated series of conical shades, 40in. wide. (Christie's) $23,515

One of a pair of cut-glass and gilt-bronze chandeliers, Italian, circa 1890, each with eighteen scroll branches arranged in two tiers, approximately 118cm. high. (Sotheby's) (Two) $22,494

A gilt-patinated tôle six-light chandelier, 20th century, the curvaceous openwork frame with leaf mounts and glass drops suspended overall, 28in. high. (Christie's) $1,184

One of a pair of Empire style gilt and patinated bronze six-light, of recent manufacture, the branches modelled as swans about the spherical bodies, 35½in. high. (Christie's) (Two) $5,216

A late 19th century brass rise and fall gasolier, 47in. drop, incomplete. (Dockrees) $2,160

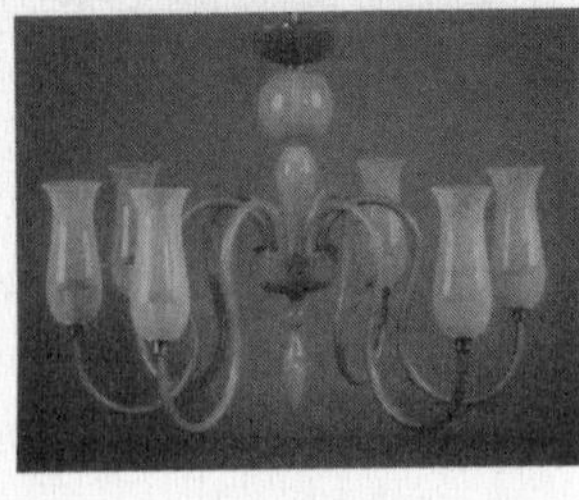

Italian Art Glass chandelier, circa 1960, baluster shaped shaft with six curved armatures supporting flared oviform shades in pearlescent pink, 18in. long. (Skinner) $747

Baccarat clear and turquoise cut and molded glass eight-light chandelier, with central turned standard and S-scrolled arms, 34in high. (Skinner) $4,600

Art Glass chandelier, Italy, mid 20th century, trumpet and baluster shaped shaft with thirty two branching floral and leaf glass armatures in white, yellow, transparent green and colorless glass, 29in. high. (Skinner) $862

A large Louis XV style gilt bronze eighteen light chandelier, early 20th century, with scroll branches issuing from the openwork triform frame with entwined berried foliage, 51in. high. (Christie's) $13,041

A late Regency gilt bronze and glass colza chandelier, second quarter 19th century, the arms with tulip shaped part-frosted shades below a hexagonal reservoir of architectural form with gothic tracery and crocketed finial, 36in. high. (Christie's) $7,62

A French gilt bronze thirty light chandelier, second half 19th century, with lanceolate leaf clasped nozzles and beaded drip pans, 52in. high. (Christie's) $7,452

A bronze mounted alabaster dish light, early 20th century, the domed shade with a ribbon tied reeded border, 18in. diameter. (Christie's) $5,814

A gilt-bronze and glass bead chandelier, French, circa 1900, of bell form, the leaf-cast corona suspending beaded glass strands 118cm. high. (Sotheby's) $10,938

Exceptional Rookwood Pottery vellum glaze vase, 1907, decorated by Edward Timothy Hurley, cylindrical form depicting palm trees reflected in water, 9½in. high.
(Skinner) $5,750

Spongeware jardinière, late 19th/early 20th century, 12in. high, 15½in. diameter.
(Eldred's) $176

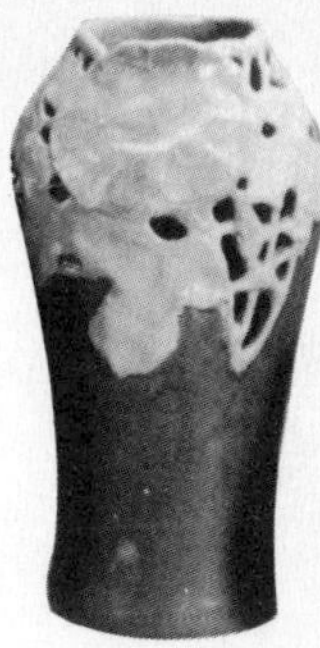

Art Pottery vase, applied red floral design, green glazed openwork on a dark matte green ground, unmarked, 12in. high, 6in. diameter. (Skinner) $230

Figure of Benjamin Franklin, mid 19th century, figure standing in a cobalt blue coat holding his hat and a document, 14¼in. high.
(Freeman) $1,456

A fine and large glazed sewer tile lion, probably Ohio, late 19th/early 20th century, the recumbent figure posed on rectangular base with canted corners, 34in. long.
(Sotheby's) $3,450

Figure of Benjamin Franklin, mid 19th century, figure holding a hat and a document, titled on base *General Washington*, 15¼in.
(Freeman) $1,120

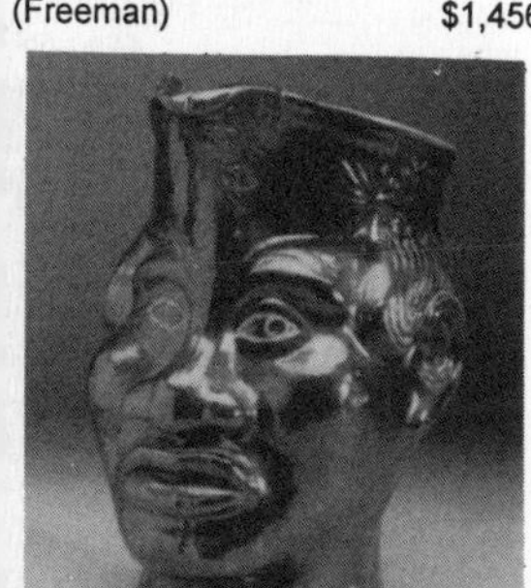

Brown glazed stoneware face jug, Medford, Massachusetts, first half 19th century, molded and incised features purportedly a likeness to Henri Christophe 1767-1820, Haitian President, 10in. high.
(Skinner) $7,000

George Ohr puzzle mug, mottled brown glaze, reticulated circular pattern near rim, stylized rabbit-form handle, 3½in. high.
(Skinner) $1,150

Tucker China water pitcher, circa 1830, modified Grecian form with gilt rim, mid band and handle, wide summer flower mid band and reserve to lip, 8¼in.
(Freeman) $392

An Amphora porcelain flower holder in the form of a basket, a goat at one side, a woman standing at the back, late 19th century, 46cm. high.
(Bearne's) $288

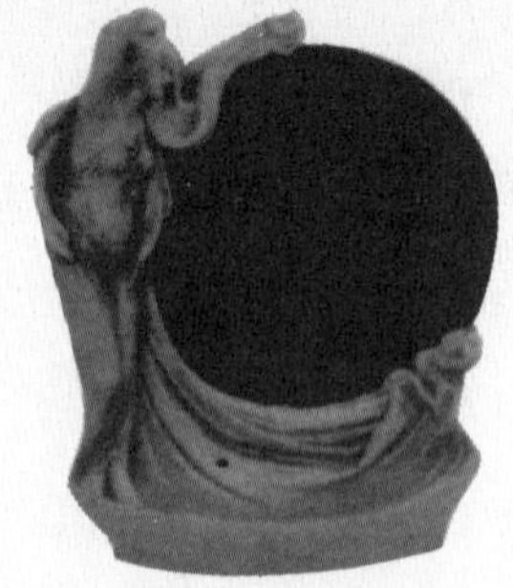

An Austrian Art Nouveau stylized mirror by Amphora Porzellanfabrik, circa 1910, 13in. high.
(Lyle) $600

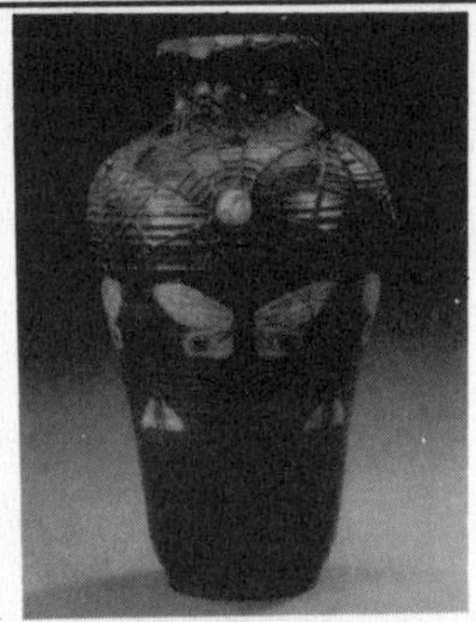

Reissner, Stellmacher & Kessel, 'Amphora' iridescent vase, circa 1905, glazed earthenware washed in pink/green/blue iridescence, decorated with spiders' webs, 12½in. (Sotheby's) $1,703

ARITA

A large porcelain dish, Arita Ware, Edo Period, (1660-80), decorated in underglaze cobalt blue and in polychrome enamels over clear glaze with flowers and with a large peony spray in the circular well, 12in. diameter.
(Christie's) $11,500

Two Arita models of rabbits, Meiji Period (19th century), seated and realistically rendered, decorated in light iron-red and black enamels, 5¾in. and 3¾in.
(Christie's) $3,353

A large porcelain bowl, Arita Ware, Edo Period (1670-90), decorated in vivid polychrome enamels over clear glaze with three Chinese lions and lotuses surrounding pomegranates, 26.3cm. diameter.
(Christie's) $29,900

An Arita sake bottle, late 17th/early 18th century, decorated in iron-red, brown enamels and gilt, and modelled as Hotei smiling and holding a fan, seated on a large gourd, 8in. high.
(Christie's) $3,972

A globular porcelain jar, Arita Ware, Edo Period (1660-70), decorated in polychrome enamels over clear glaze with a frieze of birds and flowers above latticework and fretwork, 5¾in. high.
(Christie's) $8,625

A porcelain gorgelet (Kendi), Arita Ware, Edo Period, (1670-1700), painted in polychrome enamels over clear glaze with two lotus panels separated by blue and green phoenixes, 8in. high.
(Christie's) $3,450

A pair of KPM Berlin two handled vases and covers, painted with roundels of maidens and putti, each emblematic of The Seasons, 35cm. (Christie's) $5,488

A Berlin black-ground cabinet cup and saucer, circa 1830, boldly painted with colorful stylised flowers, butterflies and a parrot between gilt borders. (Sotheby's) $1,005

A pair of Berlin porcelain figures of children, representing Spring and Winter, the young girl sitting by a basket of flowers, her companion warming himself by a brazier, 14.5cm. high. (Bearne's) $450

A German rectangular plaque of 'Clementine', Berlin (K.P.M.), late 19th/20th century, signed *Von L. Schünzel* after C. Kiesel, painted with the mythic beauty.29.4 x 22.6cm. (Christie's) $6,900

A German rectangular plaque of the penitent Magdalene, Berlin (K.P.M.), 19th century, signed *Wagner*, after Pompeo Batoni, painted with the partially clad recumbent saint deep within a grotto, 10¾ x 16½in. (Christie's) $2,760

A German rectangular plaque of 'Good Night' Berlin (K.P.M.), late 19th/20th century, signed *Wagner*, painted with a young girl in her night gown aglow with the light of her candle, 33.3 x 20.2cm. (Christie's) $6,900

A rare Berlin pâte-sur-pâte circular dish, circa 1900, finely decorated by H.M., signed, in low relief on a shaped green-ground panel with a lady clad in diaphanous robes, 30.3cm. (Sotheby's) $6,319

A German oval plaque of the Madonna and Child, Berlin (K.P.M.), 19th century, signed *Wagner*, after Raphael, finely painted with a detail of 'The Sistine Madonna', 42.9 x 34cm. (Christie's) $4,370

A German two-handled ice-pail, Berlin (K.P.M.), circa 1860, each handle as a Maenad holding ripe grapes, a fruiting vine at her waist, 32.4cm. high. (Christie's) $3,450

A Beswick 'Mickey Mouse' Walt Disney figure, painted in colors, printed gilt marks (restoration), 10cm. high.
(Christie's) $640

'Snow White and the Seven Dwarfs' eight Beswick Walt Disney figures, painted in colors.
(Christie's) $5,152

A Beswick Beatrix Potter figure of Duchess with flowers, painted in colored enamels, printed gilt marks, 9.5cm.
(Woolley & Wallis) $1,694

BOW

An English porcelain sparrow beak jug, probably Bow, the baluster body painted with a Chinese river landscape with a fisherman and figures in a garden, 8cm. high, mid 18th century.
(Bearne's) $598

A pair of Bow blue-ground two-handled vases and covers, circa 1770, of slender ovoid form with scroll handles and leaf-molded borders, the domed covers with berry finials, 11in.
(Sotheby's) $1,444

A Bow powder-blue-ground plate painted with a roundel of a stylized Oriental landscape with fan-shaped and circular panels painted with vignettes of huts and sprigs of flowers, circa 1765, 18cm. diameter. (Christie's) $469

An octagonal soft-paste porcelain dish, English, Bow Ware (circa 1754-58), decorated in polychrome enamels and gilt over clear glaze in the 'Hob in the well' pattern, 20.7cm. diameter.
(Christie's) $7,475

A pair of Bow models of horned cows, modelled recumbent before bocage, on oval flower-encrusted bases, circa 1765, 8.5cm. wide.
(Christie's) $2,024

A Bow leaf shaped pickle dish, painted in blue with two leaves and a bunch of grapes on a blue ground, the serrated rim with a blue edge, no mark, circa 1765 – 70, 8.5cm.
(Woolley & Wallis) $440

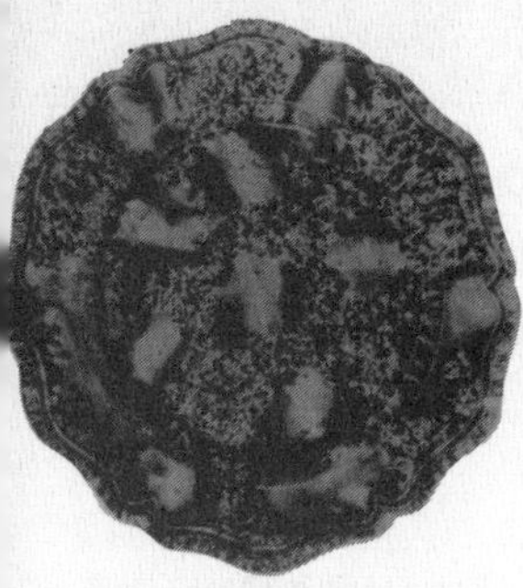

Whieldon 18th century plate abstractly decorated in yellow and green on brown speckled ground, 9in. (G.A. Key) $222

English ironstone two handled covered rectangular soup tureen and stand, the whole printed in blue with panels of flowering foliage, Ashworths or Ridgways coat of Arms mark, 14in.
(G.A. Key) $299

A Della Robbia charger circa 1900, incised with herons amongst bullrushes picked out in shades of green and brown on a green ground, 15in.
(Sotheby's) $1,104

Mocha ware pitcher, England, 19th century, marbled pattern in blue, black, brown, white, with blue band at rim, white handle with pressed ends, 7¾in. high.
(Skinner) $2,415

A Fieldings, Devon Sylvan Lustrine ovoid jar and cover, each piece boldly painted in enamel colors and gold with butterflies amongst dark trees against a deep red ground, 23cm. high.
(Bearne's) $492

MONEY MAKER

Buying antique or old dinner services can be a shrewd investment, and the price per unit appreciably less than their modern counterparts. However, you can always replace breakages from your new service, but not your antique alternative. When buying old dinner services therefore always ensure you have at least six, eight or even ten or more of all the major parts to ensure you have a worthwhile and resaleable investment. (David Dockree)

A Caughley blue and white cylindrical mug printed with the 'Fisherman' pattern beneath a cell pattern border, circa 1790, 14cm. high. (Christie's) $478

One of two dipped blue Jasper cheese bells and stands, relief molded in white, one with cherubs the other classical figures, 27cm. high and smaller.
(Bonhams) (Two) $518

Mocha ware pitcher, England, 19th century, with brown, cream and ocher cat's eye pattern on blue ground, 6¾in. high.
(Skinner) $1,495

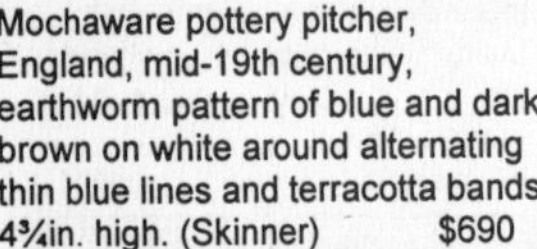

Mochaware pottery pitcher, England, mid-19th century, earthworm pattern of blue and dark brown on white around alternating thin blue lines and terracotta bands, 4¾in. high. (Skinner) $690

Christopher Dresser Art Pottery vase, late 19th century, long round neck on bulbous base with double angular handles in turquoise brown, glossy drip glaze, 20in. high.
(Skinner) $2,070

A blue and white shaped meat platter, 19th century, printed in the 'Mesopotamia' pattern, with a group of armed Persian men resting under coconut trees, inside a square panel, 52cm.
(Bonhams) $314

A George III tea caddy, Prattware, circa 1790, relief molded with profile portraits of the King, facing to dexter, above satyr masks and flowers, 16.5cm.
(Bonhams) $2,156

Large Mocha ware mug, England, 19th century, earthworm pattern on orange and yellow striped ground, green glazed impressed band around top, 5¾in. high.
(Skinner) $2,760

A pair of Burmantofts faience vases, circa 1900, each of bottle form, finely incised with a frieze o blue flowers on a bright yellow ground, 13¾in.
(Sotheby's) $442

A highly important large Indus jar by William Staite Murray, dark green with reddish brown markings, 14½in. high.
(Bonhams) $7,078

Eight G. Leonardi hand painted plaster figures of Snow White and the Seven Dwarfs, late 1930s, each dwarf 7½in. high, Snow White 12½in. high.
(Christie's) $579

Blue and white transfer decorated pearlware round serving dish, England, early 19th century, scene depicts a child and a dog feeding ducks in a stream, diameter 13½in
(Skinner) $747

An English slipware boar, early 19th century, modelled seated on its haunches, with snout ring, harness and chain, restored, 24in. high. (Bonhams) $1,727

An English blue and white pottery oval meat dish, the centre decorated with a panel depicting a night sea battle between 'Blanche' and 'La Pique', 54.5cm. wide. (Bearne's) $1,925

A Scottish creamware figure of a Billy-goat with long brown horns, standing on a multi-colored rocky mound, 21.5cm. high. (Bearne's) $647

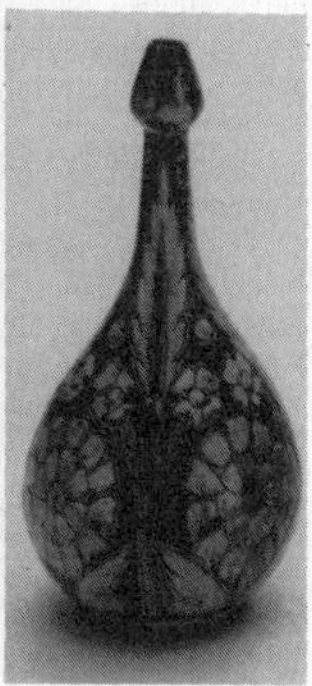

A mid 19th century Della Robbia bottle shaped vase, stylized flower heads, tulip top, initialled *ELL 184*, 34cm.(Locke & England) $730

A Hicks and Meigh Ironstone soup tureen, cover and stand, compressed circular body molded with acanthus leaves, painted in polychrome with stylized flowers and leaves, circa 1810-20, 13½in. (Woolley & Wallis) $800

A Sampson Hancock & Sons Morris Ware pottery vase, the shaped cylindrical body decorated with rhododendrons on a blue wash ground, 31.5cm. high. (Bearne's) $1,386

A majolica figural comport, the shell shaped bowl held aloft by a putto riding a dolphin, on fluted oval base, 13in. high. (Andrew Hartley) $396

A Fieldings Crown Devon musical tankard, circa 1930, entitled *Daisy Bell*, decorated in colors and relief with a courting couple and a tandem, 12.5cm. high, working. (Bonhams) $298

A 19th century commemorative jug transfer printed in purple with King William IV and Queen Adelaide flanking a crown titled *Crowned Sep 8 1831*, 20cm. high. (Cheffins) $254

Rose Canton diamond shaped fruit tazza, China, 19th century, 14¼in. diameter. (Skinner) $747

Canton enamel tea kettle and stand, China, early 19th century, globular form with continuous figural scenes, 12¼in. high to top of handle. (Skinner) $977

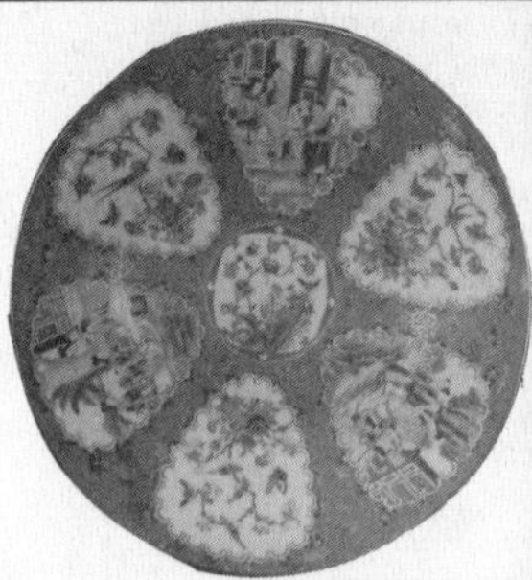

A large Cantonese dish painted and gilt with shaped panels of ladies and dignitaries in gardens of pavilions and birds and butterflies, 15in. diameter, 19th century. (Christie's) $770

A pair of Canton famille rose vases, each with a domed cover, Qing Dynasty. (Bonhams) $1,309

A Cantonese cider jug and cover, painted and gilt with butterflies and insects amongst scattered lotus, peonies, ears of corn and fruit sprays, 11½in. high, 19th century. (Christie's) $2,656

A pair of Chinese Canton famille rose baluster vases, each decorated with shaped panels of figures on verandas and smaller panels of birds and insects, mid 19th century, 17in. (Woolley & Wallis) $1,600

CAPODIMONTE

Capodimonte porcelain plaque, Italy, 19th century, cut-corner rectangular form with classical subject, 6¼ x 8½in., set in a brass mounted ebonized wood frame inset with colored porcelain medallions. (Skinner) $900

A softpaste Capodimonte (Carlo III period) cup and saucer, the cup painted with a market scene, the saucer with a mythological scene, possibly by Caselli, 1750/55. (Finarte) $6,068

A Capodimonte (Carlo III) ormolu-mounted oviform vase, circa 1750, the mounts probably 19th century, richly painted by Giovanni Caselli, each side with butterflies and other insects fluttering around flowers, 17½in. high overall. (Christie's) $21,804

'Floral Comets' a footed Carlton Ware bowl and stand pattern no. 3387, printed and painted in colors on a mottled brown and yellow ground, 24.8cm. diameter.
(Christie's) $2,024

A Carlton Ware Guinness advertising toucan figure, standing beside a pint, painted in colors, printed factory mark, 22.5cm. high.
(Bonhams) $628

'Egyptian Fan' a Carlton Ware globular jug with strap handle, pattern no. 3695, shape no. 696, printed and painted in colors 17cm. high.
(Christie's) $2,080

'Rainbow Fan' a shouldered ovoid Carlton Ware vase, pattern no. 3699, printed and painted in colors and gilt on an orange ground, printed script marks, 18.6cm. high.
(Christie's) $11,960

'Mandarins chatting' a Carlton Ware globular vase with strap handle, pattern 3653, printed and painted in colors and gilt on a black ground, 17.3cm. high.
(Christie's) $957

'Floral Comets', a vase by Carlton Ware, circa 1934, pattern 3422, shouldered form with everted rim, printed and painted in colored and gilt on a blue ground, 5.5in. high.
(Christie's) $1,625

'Red Devil' a conical Carlton Ware bowl mounted on three triangular feet, printed and painted in colors and gilt on a pale turquoise-green ground, 23cm. diameter.
(Christie's) $6,256

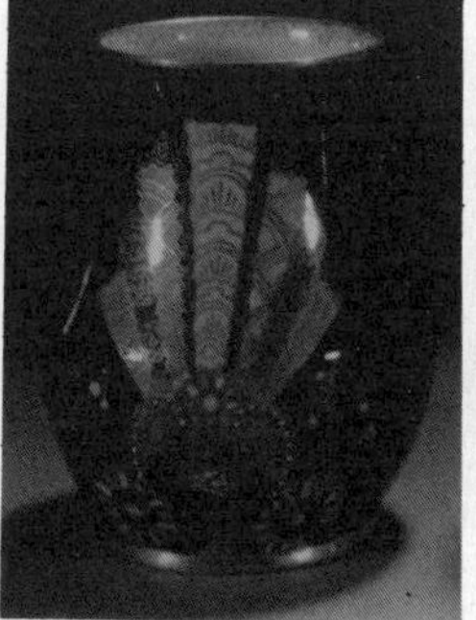

'Fan', a vase by Carlton Ware, circa 1935, pattern no.3559, shape no.468, printed and painted in colors and gilt on a red luster ground, 6in. high.
(Christie's) $1,353

'New Chinese Bird', a wall charger by Carlton Ware, 1933, pattern no. 3320, printed and painted in colors and gilt on a matt blue ground, 15in. diameter.
(Christie's) $1,806

An Italian maiolica dish in the Castelli style, painted with Hannibal addressing his troops, the border painted with a coat of arms among trophies, 41cm. diameter.
(Christie's) $331

An 18th century maiolica albarello, with polychrome allegorical decoration of Chastity, Castelli, 19cm. high.
(Finarte) $617

A Castelli saucer painted with a gallant and companion with attendant in an Italianate landscape, circa 1740, 13.2cm. diameter.
(Christie's) $578

CHARLOTTE RHEAD

Charlotte Rhead large handled mug, England, Persian rose design in colors of blue, pink, green, and orange on mottled gray ground, Crown Ducal mark, 7⅛in.
(Skinner) $172

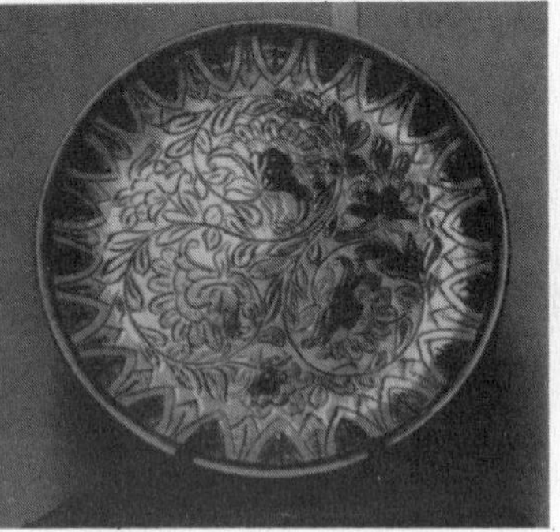

Charlotte Rhead, charger plate, 15½in. diameter.
(Whitworths) $432

Charlotte Rhead large handled jug, England, dragon design in colors of dark green and red with gilt highlights, Crown Ducal mark, 10¼in. high. (Skinner) $172

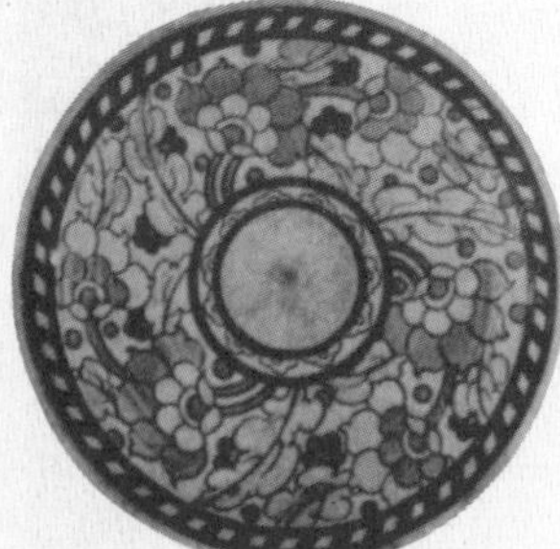

Charlotte Rhead (Crown Ducal) circular charger with slightly dished border, the rim decorated with a blue chevron band, over a panel of stylized foliage, 12½in.
(G A Key) $277

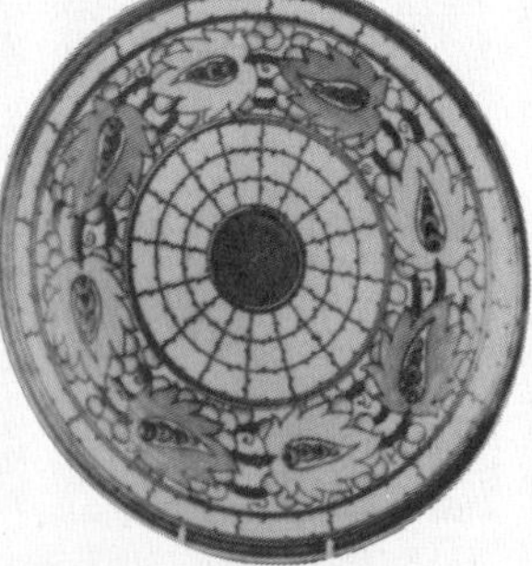

A Crown Ducal Charlotte Rhead plate having stylized leaves in orange and yellow with a web center design, 32cm.
(Locke & England) $247

A Bursley Ware charger tube lined and painted with a stylized fruit/flowers design in pale greens, lemons, pink and blues, after a design by Charlotte Rhead, 36cm. diameter. (Wintertons) $352

Chelsea fluted teabowl, circa 755, Red Anchor mark, painted by effreyes Hamett O'Neale with two gures beside a ruined obelisk in a vooded river landscape, 2½in. igh. (Christie's) $4,710

A Chelsea fluted oval dish, circa 1755, Red Anchor mark, painted in puce camaïeu by Jefferyes Hamett O'Neale with a seated and standing figure beside a tree and rockwork with a tree and mountain in the distance, 6½in. wide.
(Christie's) $6,280

A Chelsea leaf-shaped dish, circa 1755, Red Anchor mark, with green stalk handle, the five lobed green-edged leaf with puce and molded veins, painted with a bouquet of flowers, 8¼in. long.
(Christie's) $1,884

An hexagonal soft-paste porcelain ar and cover, English, Chelsea Ware, circa 1752-55, red anchor mark, painted with three panels of pine, plum and bamboo alternating with three other panels of scrolling chrysanthemums, 10½in. high.
(Christie's) $11,500

A pair of Chelsea rectangular section vases, with scroll handles, each painted in polychrome with flowers, gilt line rims, gold anchor marks, circa 1760, 7in.
(Woolley & Wallis) $1,440

A Charles Vyse figure of 'The Tulip Woman', 1921, standing on a circular base, holding a basket of tulips under one arm, 10½in.
(Sotheby's) $1,288

An octagonal molded soft-paste porcelain dish, English, Chelsea Ware, circa 1745-58, raised anchor mark, decorated in Kakiemon-style n polychrome enamels, with two spiky-tailed birds, 9¼in. diameter.
Christie's) $8,050

A small Chelsea flared cylindrical cream jug, with a loop handle, painted in polychrome with a flower spray and smaller sprigs, circa 1755, 6cm. high.
(Woolley & Wallis) $251

Two Chelsea 'Red Anchor' plates, circa 1752-58, painted with fruit, flowers and insects; and four others plates, various marks.
(Bonhams) $942

A pair of gilt-bronze mounted Chinese famille verte porcelain vases, last quarter 19th century, decorated with birds amidst flowers, 12½in. high.
(Christie's) $3,997

A Chinese Export porcelain chamfered rectangular soup tureen, cover and stand, circa 1780, each piece painted in iron-red and gilding with an allover floral pattern, 14in. long and 14½in.
(Sotheby's) $2,300

Rose mandarin covered cider jug, China, 19th century, with woven double strap applied handle, lid with foo dog finial, 9½in. high.
(Skinner) $2,990

A Yuan blue and white flattened circular ewer, early 14th century, painted on both sides with a central roundel enclosing two phoenix in flight, 8½in. high.
(Christie's) $14,621

An ormolu-mounted Chinese blue-ground and Continental porcelain table font, 19th century, the baluster vase with shell-form cover and mask spout entwined with a tôle branch set with porcelain flowerheads, 11¼in. high.
(Christie's) $2,530

A late 18th/early 19th century Islamic pottery kendi, painted in the Chinese style in blue and black, with mandarin ducks and water foliage, 7¼in. high.
(Dreweatt Neate) $3,975

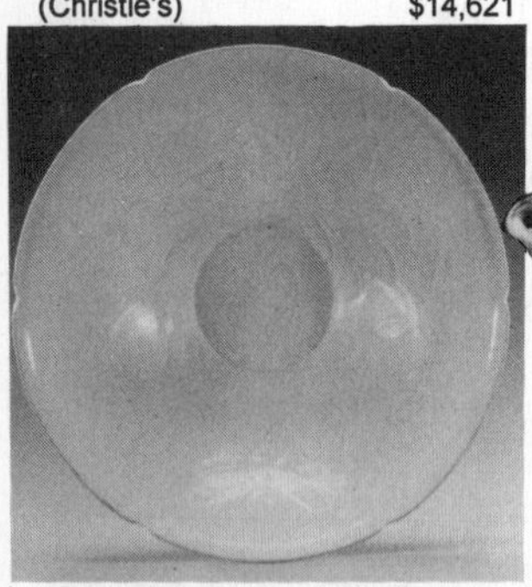

A Dingyao lobed bowl, Northern Song Dynasty (960 – 1127), with rounded sides rising from a low foot to a foliate rim, the interior carved with a lotus and leaves, 22cm. diameter.
(Christie's) $31,475

A pair of Chinese export 'Rockefeller Pattern' oval octagonal warming dishes with molded entwined handles, painted and gilt with scenes of figures on riverbanks and at leisure in gardens, 13in. wide, 18th century.
(Christie's) $3,611

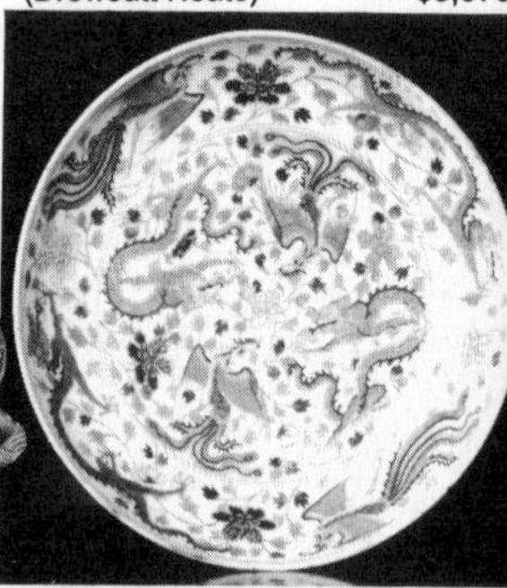

A large Wucai 'Dragon and Phoenix' saucer-dish, Kangxi six-character mark and of the period, painted and enamelled with pairs of confronted dragons and phoenix, 12⅝in. diameter.
(Christie's) $2,812

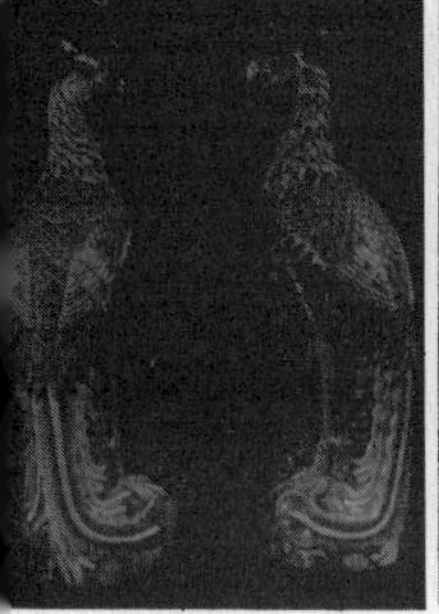

A pair of Qianlong polychrome porcelain fong-huangs perched on a rocky base, 62cm. high. (Galerie Moderne) $7,563

Chinese Export porcelain platter and pierced inset, 19th century, blue and gilt vintage border decoration, monogramed, 17½in. long. (Skinner) $1,265

A large pair of Chinese Export polychrome painted plaster nodding-head figures, 19th century, in the form of a man with detachable weighted head, 31½in. high. (Christie's) $6,992

TOP TIP

When examining 18th century porcelain teapots, Chinese examples can be distinguished from English by the hole found in the crook of the handle, which is hollow.

Also the Chinese teapot has an unglazed rim, as does the underside of the lid - very necessary as they were fired with the lids on!

(Cotswold Auction Co.)

An impressive pair of Chinese cockerels, each with a celadon glaze, and naturalistic head, set on a pierced light brown base, 38.5cm. high, 19th century. (Bearne's) $2,517

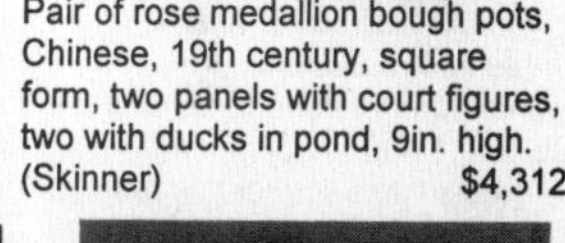

Pair of rose medallion bough pots, Chinese, 19th century, square form, two panels with court figures, two with ducks in pond, 9in. high. (Skinner) $4,312

Chinese underglaze red, blue and white vase, well painted with deer in a rocky landscape, six character seal mark of Q and of the period (1735-96). (Academy) $1,680

A Chinese Export blue and white porcelain Armorial tureen and cover, painted with panoramic lakeland views, circa 1755, 36cm. (Tennants) $942

A Chinese famille verte hexagonal section ewer, handle modelled as a dog of Fo standing on a reticulated ball holding the ewer at its neck, 19th century, 9in. (Woolley & Wallis) $454

A Clarice Cliff 'Fantasque' pottery vase of ogee form with inverted rim, painted with the 'Floreat' pattern, 20cm. high. (Bearne's) $739

'Age of Jazz', a rare 'Bizarre' double dancing figures centerpiece, model no.434, painted in shades of green, orange, black and yellow, two drilled holes to base, 18cm. high. (Christie's) $17,043

A Clarice Cliff Oranges and Lemons conical sugar sifter, 14cm. printed marks. (Bonhams) $3,100

A Clarice Cliff 'Lucerne' pattern jug, early 1930s, of 'Lotus' shape, painted with a castle in a mountainous landscape against a blue sky, 11½in. (Sotheby's) $8,125

A Clarice Cliff circular wall plaque, molded as flower heads and leaves and pierced with five holes, decorated with orange, yellow, brown and green, 33.5cm. (Woolley & Wallis) $539

A Clarice Cliff 'Autumn Balloon Trees' Lotus jug, early 1930s, painted in orange, yellow and brown, and outlined in blue with a continuous landscape scene, 29.5cm. (Sotheby's) $1,472

A Clarice Cliff Farmhouse single handled Lotus jug, 28.8cm. printed mark. (Bonhams) $2,945

A Clarice Cliff Crocus Beehive honey pot and cover, 10cm. printed marks. (Bonhams) $264

A Clarice Cliff House & Bridge pattern vase, shape 358, Newport Pottery, 8in. high. (Michael J. Bowman) $1,968

ʌn English porcelain ice pail, ɔossibly Coalport, with cornucopia ınd scroll handle, the cover with a ɔinecone knop, 26.5cm. high, early 19th century.
Bearne's) $944

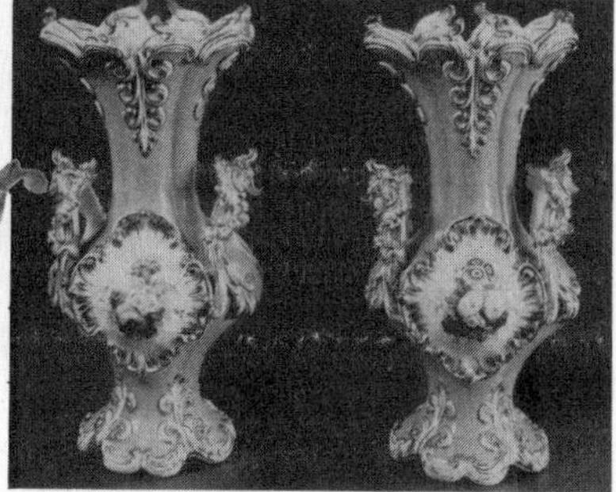

Pair of Coalport rococo style baluster vases, with apple green ground, applied quatrefoil panels to the front and back painted with floral bouquets, 14in. high.
(Russell Baldwin & Bright) $1,436

A 19th century porcelain jug of ovoid form painted with exotic birds in landscape, possibly Coalport, 10in. high.
(Andrew Hartley) $302

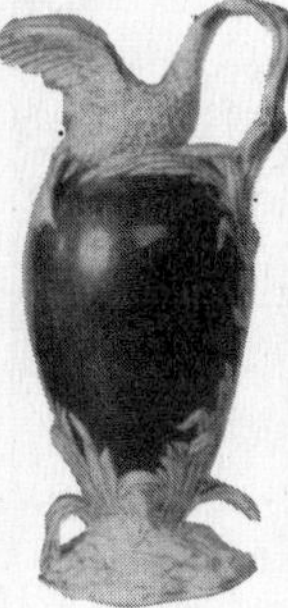

A Coalport Sèvres style ewer, the neck, spout and handle formed as a swan which sits on a large egg, which forms the body, the egg cerise, 2nd half 19th century, 27cm.
(Woolley & Wallis) $471

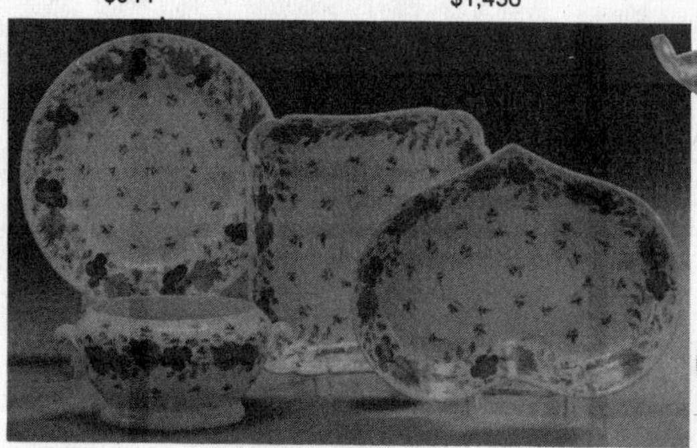

A Coalport part dessert service, circa 1800, each piece painted with a border of poppies and trailing foliage, comprising 19 pieces, dessert plate 22cm.
(Sotheby's) $1,884

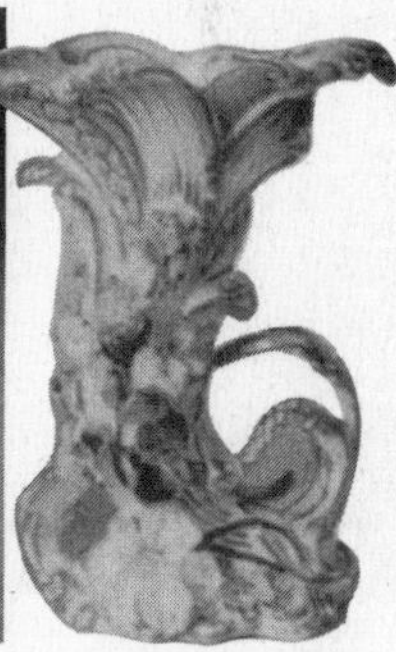

A good Coalport cornucopia vase, modelled as scrolling leaves, detailed in orange and gilt and applied with colorful flowers, circa 1825 – 35, 15cm.
(Woolley & Wallis) $659

COPELAND

A Copeland and Garrett pearlware ɔot pourri vase and cover, with an nternal lid, the circular body with oop side handles and a berry finial, 1833-47, 12iin.
(Woolley & Wallis) $608

'Mending the Nets', a Copeland Art Union of London Parian figure, modelled by Edward W Wyon, dated *1873,* girl seated with net across her lap and basket of fish to one side, 43.5cm. high.
(Bonhams) $2,198

A Copeland reticulated teapot and cover of lobed section, pierced with panels of leafy bamboo canes, enriched in turquoise and gilt, printed marks, circa 1875, 18cm. high. (Christie's) $744

A Davenport pearlware dated flask of circular form, inscribed *P.F.* and dated *1827*, the reverse with sprays of flowers, 19cm. high.
(Christie's) $397

A Davenport bough-pot and cover of D section, painted in puce monochrome with vignettes of figures and buildings in rural landscapes, circa 1810, 22cm. wide. (Christie's) $542

A Victoria Royal Service cake basket, Davenport, 1837, painted with a gilt and iron red scrolling VR monogram inside a floral wreath, the border with tooled gilt scrolling acanthus leaves, 25cm. diameter.
(Bonhams) $2,310

DE MORGAN

A ruby lustre charger, circa 1880, attributed to William De Morgan, painted with five chrysanthemums issuing from a central vase, 14in.
(Sotheby's) $1,431

A William De Morgan 'Isnik' jug, circa 1888-97, painted by Fred Passenger in blue, turquoise, manganese and black with a band of eagles each clutching a lizard by the tail, 11¼in.
(Sotheby's) $5,055

A William De Morgan ruby and pink luster dish, Fulham Period, 1888-1898, painted by Charles Passenger, with an eagle attacking a snake, 12in.
(Sotheby's) $2,527

DEDHAM

Dedham Pottery day lily plate, blue stamp, 8½in. diameter.
(Skinner) $1,092

Dedham Pottery mushroom pattern plate, decorated by Maud Davenport, Blue Rabbit stamp, 8½in. diameter.
(Skinner) $805

Dedham Pottery round grape pattern platter, blue stamp and one impressed rabbit, 12in. diameter.
(Skinner) $201

Delft style circular charger, abstractly decorated in manganese, underglazed blue, lemon, stylized floral design, 18th/19th century, 12in. (G A Key) $160

A delft blue and white pedestal cup, the globular body painted with insects and sprays of flowers above a foliate scroll band, mid 18th century, 9cm. high. (Bearne's) $398

An English delftware blue and white Royal portrait charger, circa 1705, possibly Brislington, the center painted with a three-quarter length portrait of Queen Anne, flanked by *Q A*, 13in. (Sotheby's) $9,508

An English blue and white Delft mug, probably Lambeth, the globular body inscribed *God Bless King William* on a ribbon reserve, the slightly tapering cylindrical neck encircled with vertical brush strokes, 9.7cm. high, late 17th century. (Bearne's) $10,780

A pair of Dutch (De Porceleyne Klaeuw) Delft butter tubs and covers, circa 1763, possibly for Lambertus Sanderus, each cover surmounted by a recumbent manganese spotted horse, 4½in. wide. (Christie's) $32,200

A London delftware wine bottle, dated *1649*, the compressed globular body with a loop handle, inscribed in blue *SACK 1649* above a flourish, 6in. (Sotheby's) $11,885

A Lambeth delftware plate, mid 18th century, decorated with a swimming duck, before a bridge with trees either side, 22.5cm. (Bonhams) $691

A Lambeth polychrome delftware ballooning plate, circa 1785, painted in blue, green, manganese and ocher with Vincenzo Lunardi's balloon rising above a fenced terrace of a house and gardens, 25.9cm. (Bonhams) $2,310

An English delftware punch bowl, probably Bristol, circa 1760-70, the interior painted in underglaze-blue with an extensive farmyard scene, within a scroll and diaper border, 12in. (Sotheby's) $13,714

An English delft tulip charger, painted with tulips, other flowers and leaves, probably London, late 17th century, 34.5cm.
(Tennants) $1,804

A Dutch delft puzzle-jug, early 18th century, the neck pierced with four stylized flowers with lozenge and heart-shaped petals, 6¼in. high.
(Christie's) $1,150

An English delft plate, painted in blue with a Chinaman presenting a Chinese lady with a gift, 1st half 18th century, 8¾in.
(Woolley & Wallis) $35

An English delftware 'Adam and Eve' charger, circa 1720-30, probably Liverpool, painted in blue, green, yellow and red with the figures of Adam and Eve below the Tree of Life, 34cm.
(Sotheby's) $1,736

A pair of Dutch delft polychrome plates, late 18th century, each painted in the center with a stylized flowering plant on a green plateau, $9\frac{3}{8}$in. diameter.
(Sotheby's) $1,725

A Bristol delftware plate, circa 1740, painted in blue, green and iron-red with a cockerel standing in a landscape flanked by manganese sponged foliage.
(Sotheby's) $7,31

A delft blue and white colander bowl, the side with a rectangular pouring hole, decorated with panels of flowers, diaper and with a flower and fence design, mid 18th century, 8¾in. (Woolley & Wallis) $640

A delftware bottle vase, of ovoid form, blue painted with a band of scrolling foliage between similar, smaller bands and concentric circles, 23cm.
(Bonhams) $220

An English delftware bowl circa 1720, probably Bristol, the center painted in polychrome enamels with a sun motif within stylized foliate borders and a 'pie-crust' rim, 7in.
(Sotheby's) $5,77

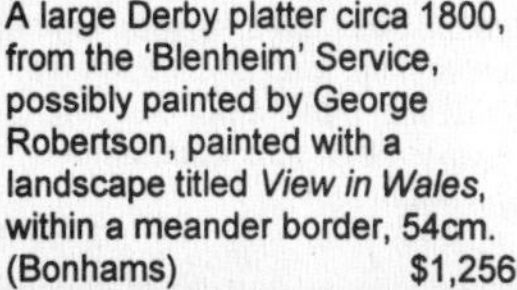

A large Derby platter circa 1800, from the 'Blenheim' Service, possibly painted by George Robertson, painted with a landscape titled *View in Wales*, within a meander border, 54cm.
(Bonhams) $1,256

Early 19th century Derby sauce tureen and cover of oval shape, the handles all molded with lion mask terminals, painted throughout in colors with sprays of garden flowers, circa 1820, 6½in.
(G.A. Key) $477

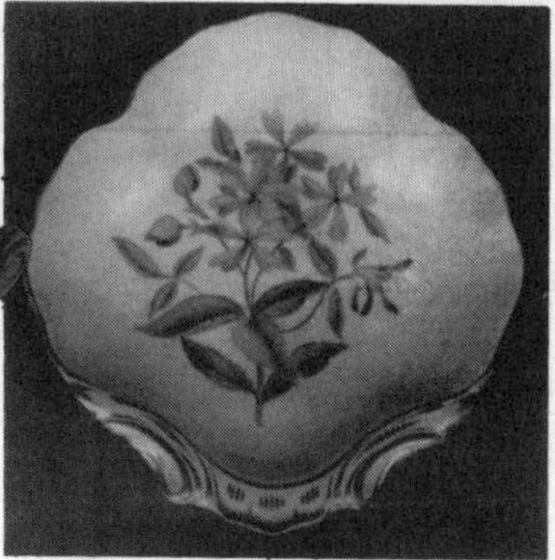

A Derby botanical trefoil shaped dish, painted with a floral specimen with small mauve flowers and green leaves, early 19th century, 10in.
(Woolley & Wallis) $302

A pair of Derby figures of a piper and a guitar player, both on turquoise and gilt openwork scroll bases, William Duesbury and Co., circa 1775, 14.5cm.
(Tennants) $1,394

A Derby figure of Britannia, circa 1765, standing with a lion at her feet, among patriotic attributes, 10½in. (Sotheby's) $1,920

A pair of Royal Crown Derby porcelain table candlesticks, painted in the Imari palette, 25cm. high, printed mark and date code for 1910. (Bearne's) $862

A Derby centerpiece, modelled with a boy wearing a turquoise jacket sitting high on shell encrusted coral, holding a scallop shell upon his head, circa 1765, 9.5in.
(Woolley & Wallis) $1,280

A Derby topographical plate, circa 1797-1800, probably painted by George Robertson with a gilt-edged circular panel enclosing a titled view of Scaleby Castle near Carlisle, 9¼in.
(Sotheby's) $1,188

A fine Royal Crown Derby two-handled vase and cover, circa 1899, well painted by D. Leroy, signed, with panels of flowers in rectangular gilt cartouches, 9½in.
(Sotheby's) $8,228

Royal Doulton stoneware liquor vessel, molded with Viking ship motif and inscribed *Special Highland Whisky*, impressed marks, 7½in. (G.A. Key) $120

A Royal Doulton pottery wall plaque, depicting the smiling face of Friar Tuck in a brown cowl, 25.5cm high. (Bearne's) $661

Royal Doulton Lambeth grog jug of baluster form, inscribed with verse, molded with Pan mask and sovereign head motifs, circa late 19th century, 8in. (G.A. Key) $159

A Hannah Barlow Doulton Lambeth stoneware tankard of baluster form, the buff glaze incised with a scene of a chase with two geese and a terrier within a geometric border, 14cm. high. (Wintertons) $627

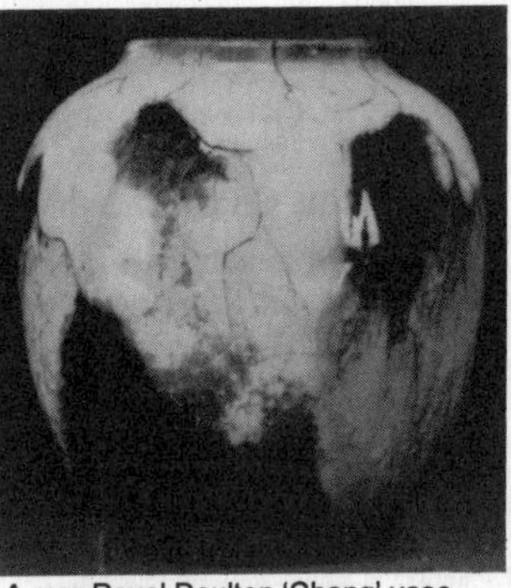

A rare Royal Doulton 'Chang' vase, circa 1925-30, by Charles Noke and Harry Nixon, covered in dripping layers of thick crazed ash-white glaze with blue veining over a red and ocher mottled ground, 22.5cm. (Sotheby's) $1,840

Art Nouveau period Doulton Lambeth ewer, molded and decorated in green geometric foliate design, on a deep blue ground, by Mark V Marshall, circa 1879/1912, 7in. (G A Key) $651

A rare Royal Doulton Lambeth dish mounted with a koala bear for the Australian market, Number 8902, signed *MB* (Maud Bowden ?), circa 1925. (Academy) $464

A large Royal Doulton character jug, the 'Toothless Granny', issued 1935. (Bearne's) $385

A Royal Doulton two handled loving cup, depicting The Three Musketeers, 25.5cm. high, No.305 of an edition limited to 600. (Bearne's) $975

'Fate', a Royal Doulton porcelain mask, designed by Richard Garbe, 1921, produced in a limited edition of 100, modelled in relief, covered in a matt green glaze, 10¼in. high. (Christie's) $992

A Royal Doulton Limited Edition figure 'The West Wind', by Richard Garbe A.R.A, in a matt ivory finish, no. 5 of 25, 39cm. high. (Wintertons) $4,704

A Royal Doulton pottery Toby jug, in the form of Charlie Chaplin wearing a detachable bowler hat, 29cm. high, issued circa 1918. (Bearne's) $2,618

A Royal Doulton Art Nouveau barrel-shaped jug molded with flowers in low relief having green, pink and brown glazes, 7½in. (G.A. Key) $159

A pair of Doulton stoneware vases by Eliza Simmance and Rosina Brown, each bottle shape vase incised and painted with exotic fruiting and leafy plants, 30.5cm. high. (Bearne's) $801

A Royal Doulton stoneware ginger wine barrel and stopper, *Ginger Wine* applied on a deep blue ground, a band of leaves above and below, 24.5cm. high. (Bearne's) $330

Royal Doulton jug of baluster form, elaborately molded with panels of groups of figures in cycling poses, impressed mark, circa early 20th century, 6in. (G A Key) $200

'Sunshine Girl' HN 1344, a Royal Doulton porcelain figure designed by Leslie Harradine, 1929, modelled seated wearing spotted bathing suit, holding a sun parasol, 5in. high. (Christie's) $4,514

A Doulton three handled mug, with silver plated rim, olive green Art Deco design, signed *EES* and dated *1884*. (George Kidner) $353

A pair of Dresden models of parrots facing left and right, naturalistically modelled perched on tree stumps, 20th century, 39.5cm. high. (Christie's) $2,479

Dresden 20th century early morning tea set, comprising: sucrier; teapot; cream jug; 2 cups and saucers, with matching two handled tray, all decorated in colors in the manner of Kauffman.(G A Key) $814

Dresden group of two embracing putti, one clutching a floral garland, both painted in colors on a Rococo gilded scrolled base. (G A Key) $622

A Dresden 'Yardley's Old English Lavender' group typically modelled with a woman and two girls with lavender baskets standing on a scroll-molded titled base, impressed marks, post WWII, 30.5cm. high. (Christie's) $471

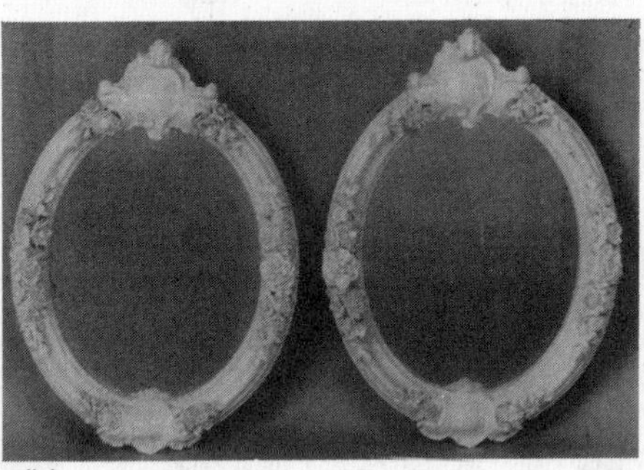

A Dresden pair of oval wall mirrors, 19th century, white glazed with cartouche to top and base and encrusted with flowers, blue crossed swords mark, 40.2 x 30cm. (Bristol) $410

A pair of Dresden porcelain floral encrusted vases, late 19th century, each of footed baluster form applied with cherubs and flowers on a blue repeating rococo panel ground, with loop handles, 33.4cm. (Bristol) $225

Pair of Dresden porcelain vases and covers, Germany, circa 1900, alternating panels of lovers and turquoise ground floral bouquets, 14in. high. (Skinner) $600

Dresden porcelain group of two artistic putti, one painting canvas on an easel, the other clutching a scroll, cross swords mark in underglazed blue, 6in. (G A Key) $622

Dresden porcelain vase and cover, Germany, 19th century, Thieme factory, enamel decorated classical panels surrounded by applied flowers, insects, and fruits, a bird perched to branch knop on cover, 12¾in. high.(Skinner) $1,200

Continental porcelain boat shaped pedestal centerpiece, crested with motif of a winged putto blowing a horn and molded throughout with foliate scrolls etc. and painted in colors, 10in.
(G A Key) $112

Ceramic mermaid, in dark celadon green and brown glaze, signed on base *O. Wilhelmson, Strommen, 1966*, 20½in. long.
(Eldred's) $522

An Austrian porcelain plate, the center painted with Paris, Venus and Helen in a palace within a blue and magenta border, 24.3cm. diameter. (Bearne's) $739

A large pottery bust, of a stylized youth, with wavy hair, angular features and medieval style costume, indistinct impressed factory marks, 38.5cm. high.
(Christie's) $294

A European pottery clock, late 19th century, unmarked, slight damage, 35cm. high.
(Bonhams) $816

A glazed earthenware centerpiece, by Süe et Mare, 1925, the bowl formed with stylized leaves, on four semi-spherical feet, 14¼in. high.
(Christie's) $2,236

A Royal Danish Porcelain Factory group 'Bølge og Strand', by Patrik Nordström, a girl emerging from the sea embracing a man tied to a rock, blue, white and beige glazes, early 20th century, 47cm. high.
(Stockholms AV) $1,312

A pair of Holitsch apothecary jars and matched pierced covers circa 1770-80, each of shouldered form, painted with polychrome landscapes within scrolling floral cartouches, 8¾in.
(Sotheby's) $1,828

A 19th century Continental porcelain plaque, painted with a portrait of a young lady wearing a white headscarf and fur trimmed jacket, 6¾ x 5in.
(Andrew Hartley) $2,268

A Belleek commemorative chamber pot, printed in black in the base of the interior with a portrait of Gladstone, wearing a high collared shirt and spotted bow tie, and a miserable expression, 13.5cm. diameter. (Bonhams) $847

An Austrian pottery centerpiece, modelled as a scantily clad woman seated on a shell with a cherub behind, 36.5cm. (Bonhams) $292

A European-subject, famille-rose teabowl and saucer, decorated with Cupid presenting his heart to a seated lady, together with a blue and white saucer dish, with Chenghua six-character mark. (Christie's) $235

FASCINATING FACT

The five senses are often represented allegorically as women in art and are found, for example, in paintings, tapestries and china groups. Learning to identify these can add a totally new dimension to our appreciation and understanding of a piece.

Hearing is associated with music and may be found with a bowed or stringed instrument. Sight often holds a mirror or on occasion a flaming torch. Taste can be portrayed with a basket of fruit, while Smell may hold a bunch of flowers or sometimes a bottle of perfume. Touch is depicted in many ways, sometimes with a bird on her hand.

Other birds and animals are also often used to depict the senses. An eagle, for example, can represent sight, while a dog can be emblematic of smell and a stag of hearing.

(Cotswold Auction Co.)

A pair of 19th century Continental porcelain strut mirrors, of oval form, each surmounted by a pair of applied cherubs holding a floral festoon, 13in. high. (Andrew Hartley) $692

A rare Venetian figure of a Turk, Hewelcke Factory, circa 1758-63, modelled standing wearing a striped head-dress surmounted by a crescent and long flowing robes, 13cm. (Sotheby's) $13,714

A Dutch red stoneware teapot and cover, workshop of Arij de Milde, 1680-1708, of compressed shouldered form with short spout and loop handle, applied with prunus sprigs and insects, impressed mark, 8cm. (Sotheby's) $1,645

A 19th century Continental porcelain plaque, of oval form, painted with Ruth in the Cornfield, unsigned, 5 x 3¼in. (Andrew Hartley) $1,141

Famille rose porcelain teapot, circa 1780, with rectangular reserves and bamboo-form handle and spout, bud finial, 7½in. high.
(Eldred's) $2,640

A Chinese famille rose chamfered rectangular tureen, cover and stand, decorated with two peacocks, ornamental rockwork and peony, Qianlong, 1736-95, 15½in.
(Woolley & Wallis) $11,520

A pair of famille rose baluster vases and covers, painted with baskets of peonies and foliage within borders of lappets reserved with lotus, phoenix and scattered blossom, 20½in. high, 19th century.
(Christie's) $3,542

FAMILLE VERTE

A pair of famille verte stepped square vases painted and gilt with shaped panels of insects in flight above sprays of peonies, prunus, chrysanthemums and lotus, 8½in. high, Kangxi.
(Christie's) $1,204

A pair of famille verte dogs of Fo, one with a brocade ball, the other with a cub, both decorated on the biscuit in green, aubergine, yellow, Kangxi, 1662-1722, 13in.
(Woolley & Wallis) $24,800

A famille verte kendi, painted with sprays of chrysanthemums, lotus, peonies and prunus, 8¼in. high, Kangxi. (Christie's) $924

FRANKENTHAL

A Frankenthal teacup and saucer, painted in the manner of Andreas Dettner with a lady and a gallant in a parkland setting, circa 1765.
(Tennant) $1,394

A pair of Frankenthal figure groups, circa 1770, modelled by W.J.Lanz, as groups of two putti playing musical instruments, supported on scrolling bases, 7½in.
(Sotheby's) $1,272

A Frankenthal figure of a boy throwing a ball, circa 1760, modelled by J.W. Lanz, in a black hat, pink suit and pale iron-red waistcoat, 5⁵/16in. high.
(Christie's) $2,185

A pair of Chantilly plates painted in colors with sprays of flowers within osier-molded borders and shaped rims, third quarter 18th century, 24cm. diameter.
(Christie's) $478

A Continental porcelain group, probably French, modelled with a Renaissance man and companion standing with two seated male companions, circa 1900, 32cm. wide. (Christie's) $1,771

A St. Cloud coffee cup and trembleuse saucer, painted in underglaze blue with Berainesque scroll borders and half-fluted molding, circa 1730.
(Tennants) $492

A pair of French turquoise-ground two-handled baluster vases and stands, late 19th century, painted with an eighteenth century vignette of an amorous couple and a maiden, 31½in. high.
(Christie's) $8,050

A French bronze mounted Imari style porcelain coupe, last quarter 19th century, the gadrooned tapering bowl with gilt heightened foliate decoration on a blue and red ground with white reserves, 14¼in. high. (Christie's) $1,490

A pair of French turquoise-ground baluster vases and stands, Paris, mid-19th century, signed indistinctly __*Vernoy,* elaborately decorated in the Jacob Petit style, the handles as satyrs holding garlands of fruit, 23½in. high.
(Christie's) $5,750

C. Fauré Art Deco enamelled vase, Limoges, France, decorated with geometric shapes in foil under shades of blue, black and opalescent white enamel,11½in. high. (Skinner) $3,565

A pair of French porcelain figural scent bottles, mid 19th century, modelled as the seated figures of a pasha and his lady, the stoppers inset in their turbans, 9in. high.
(Christie's) $9,993

A gilt-bronze and biscuit porcelain centerpiece, Paris, circa 1880, of circular form with scroll, foliate and mask handles, 40cm. high.
(Sotheby's) $8,998

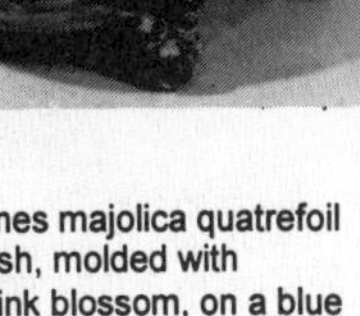

A George Jones majolica quatrefoil strawberry dish, molded with leaves and pink blossom, on a blue and brown ground, 12in. wide.
(Andrew Hartley) $1,268

George Jones majolica covered cheese dish, the cover modelled as a haystack, applied with brown rope molded ties, the base molded with fence borders, 19th century, 8in. (G A Key) $8,319

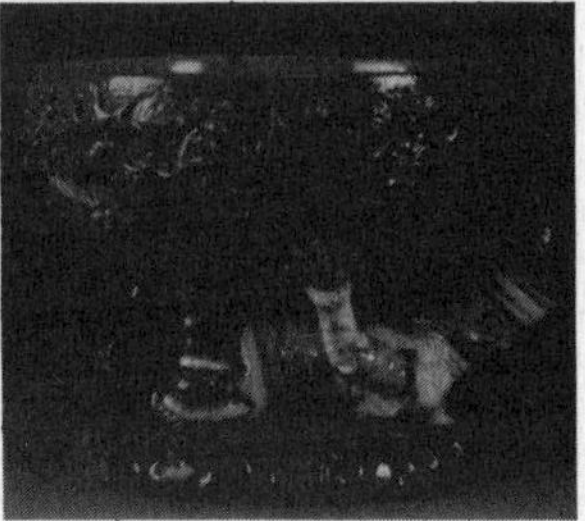

A George Jones majolica 'Punch' bowl, the bowl formed as an orange half molded with a continuous branch of fruiting holly, supported by a recumbent Mr Punch lying on his back, circa 1873, 28.5cm. diameter.
(Christie's) $13,282

A George Jones majolica cheese bell and cover of domed form, naturalistically molded with ferns and grasses within scallop-shell borders, circa 1873, 30cm. high.
(Christie's) $15,939

A graduated set of three George Jones majolica jugs molded in relief with bullrushes and other aquatic plants, circa 1870, 16cm., 18.5cm. & 21cm. high.
(Christie's) $4,959

A majolica jardinière and low stand, possibly by George Jones, each facet of the square section body molded and painted with lily-of-the-valley against a pink ground, total height 22.5cm.
(Bearne's) $3,080

A George Jones majolica cheese dish and cover, modelled as a castellated turret with turquoise pennant forming the handle, 1873, 33cm. (Tennants) $2,355

A George Jones majolica card-tray, the finial formed as two dolphins with entwined tails, between two shells supported on branch feet, impressed mark, circa 1870, 25cm. wide. (Christie's) $2,479

A George Jones majolica 'Daisy' cheese dome and stand, the rustic twig handle entwined with fruiting brambles, circa 1870, 31cm.
(Tennants) $8,164

A white tulip vase with polychrome floral decoration, with five spouts, the central one with pewter ring, unmarked, Thuringia, mid 18th century, 15.8cm. high.
(Lempertz) $733

A large Sitzendorf piano recital group, the figures wearing 18th century dress, mostly modelled seated before a child at a piano, his music master beside him, 20th century, 22cm. wide.
(Christie's) $1,355

A 17th century German salt glazed stoneware bellarmine jar with bulbous body and molded in relief with mask above circular leaf paterae, 8¼in. high.
(Canterbury) $410

A German faience tankard with pewter mount and cover, the cylindrical body brightly painted with a Chinese scene within a foliate cartouche, 20cm. high, early 18th century.
(Bearne's) $503

A garniture of three German bisque porcelain figures of 'The Farm Boy' and 'The Farm Girl' both with sheaves of wheat, figures 12in. high, domes 21in. high.
(Canterbury) $640

A blue, yellow, manganese and iron red decorated faience ewer, the pewter lid by J.P. Weiss, surmounted by the figure of a peasant, Hanau, early 18th century.
(Lempertz) $2,358

A Nymphenburg matt pale-blue ground cabinet-cup and saucer, circa 1815, an oval gilt cartouche, enclosing a finely stippled portrait by Christian Adler of Crown Prince Ludwig of Bavaria.
(Christie's) $3,270

Otto Lindig for the Keramikwerkstätte Bauhaus, Weimar, Dornburg, four piece cocoa service, 1923, comprising cocoa pot and cover, cup, saucer and plate, glazed terracotta, cocoa pot 8½in. high.
(Sotheby's) $10,812

A Höchst ormolu-mounted oval biscuit portrait plaque of Baron von Groschlag, circa 1772, modelled by J.P. Melchior, with a half-length portrait of a gentleman in profile to the right, the plaque 6in. high.
(Christie's) $21,804

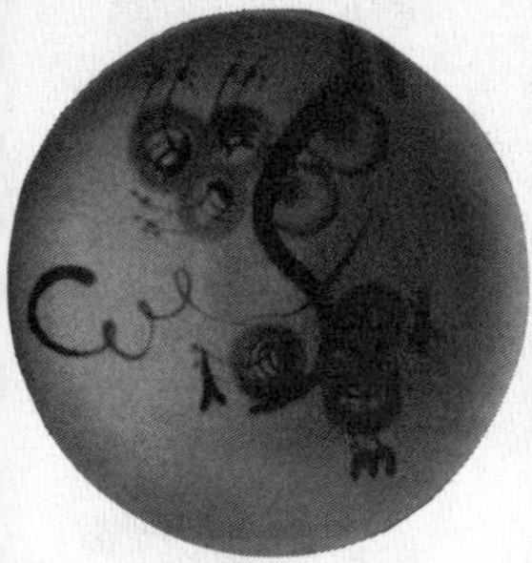

Margarete Marks, an earthenware dish, designed circa 1930, for Hael Werkstätte, with abstract underglaze painted in colors, 14¾in. diameter.
(Christie's) $939

A rare pair of Limbach figures of the Virgin Mary and St. John, circa 1780, each modelled standing wearing long flowing robes, colored in tones of pink and puce, 9in. (Sotheby's) $951

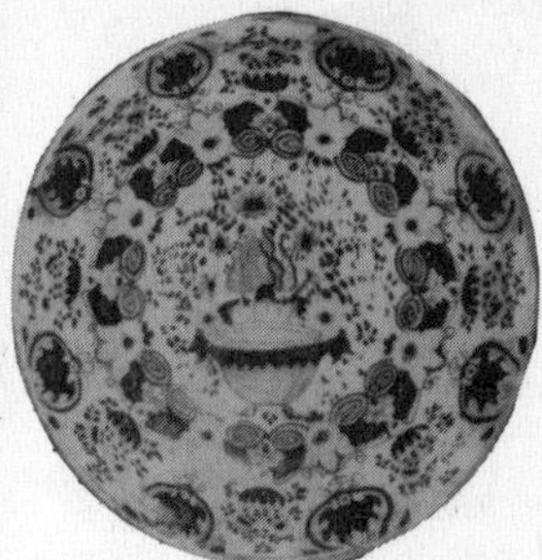

One of a pair of Ansbach blue and white circular dishes, circa 1720, the centers with a bowl of flowers, within a shaped panel of radiating flowers and scroll ornament, 10¼in. diameter.
(Christie's) (Two) $1,635

A Hanau spirally-molded Hausmalerei Enghalskrug, circa 1720, iron-red M mark to base, painted with the flaying of Marsyas and Diana appearing to Pan, 11½in. high.
(Christie's) $3,997

A pair of Ludwigsburg figures of musicians, circa 1765, from the series of the 'Kleine Musiksoli' modelled by C.F. Beyer, the young man playing a cello, with female musician, playing a mandolin, 4¾in.
(Sotheby's) $2,862

A saltglazed Westerwald stoneware tankard, relief decorated with foliate motifs on separate fields, hinged pewter lid with monogram *AFB* and date *1784*, late 18th century, 22cm. high. (Lempertz) $628

A Salzburg faience pewter-mounted jug, circa 1700, of stout baluster form with pinched spout and applied handle, painted in turquoise, ocher, manganese and blue with a sportsman and deer, 7in. (Sotheby's) $8,045

A Böttger red stoneware bust of Vitellius, circa 1712, perhaps modelled by Paul Heermann, half turned to the right and with incised hair, 4¼in. high.
(Christie's) $6,359

A German brown salt glazed stoneware jug dated *1609*, the bulbous body decorated with a band of chevrons and a band of florets above three oval armorials, 8¾in.
(Woolley & Wallis) $1,458

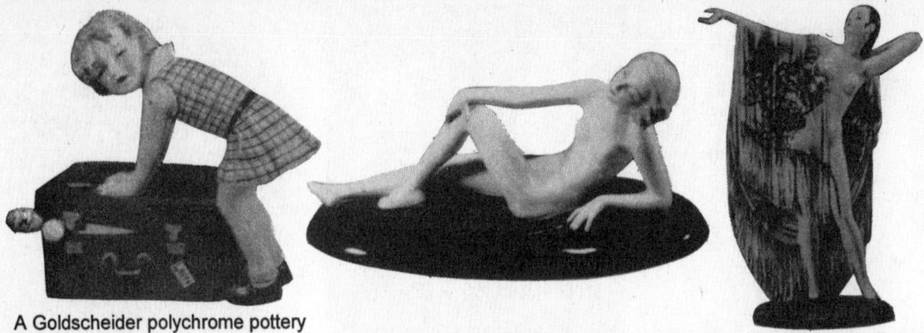

A Goldscheider polychrome pottery figure, modelled as a young girl with blond ringlet hair and green plaid dress, standing packing a large suitcase with puppet emerging, 18cm. high. (Christie's) $1,472

A Goldscheider polychrome pottery figure, from a model by Lorenzl, of a naked young woman reclining on black oval base, printed factory marks, 42cm. diameter. (Christie's) $1,195

A Goldscheider figure of a woman, 1930s, polychrome glazed earthenware, modelled as a semi-naked young woman striking a pose in front of a short plinth, 16½in. (Sotheby's) $1,533

A Goldscheider polychrome pottery figure from a model by Lorenzl, incised signature, printed factory marks, impressed numerals *6227 25 10* and *20*, 35cm. high. (Christie's) $1,805

A Goldscheider polychrome pottery figure modelled as a lady with blue flower costume, printed factory marks, impressed numerals *8459 42 7*, 40cm. high. (Christie's) $4,333

A Goldscheider polychrome pottery figure from a model by Lorenzl, printed marks, impressed numerals *7058 153 19*, 31cm. high. (Christie's) $397

A Goldscheider polychrome pottery figure from a model by Dakon, of girl in blue dress, printed and impressed factory marks, numbered *6330 364 19*, 31cm. high. (Christie's) $342

A Goldscheider polychrome pottery figure from a model by Rosé, incised signature, printed factory marks, impressed numerals *5171 375 9*, 25.5cm. high. (Christie's) $1,083

A Goldscheider patinated terracotta bust of Art Nouveau maiden, with lilies across chest, impressed factory marks, numbered *2385 84 19*, 59cm. high. (Christie's) $1,534

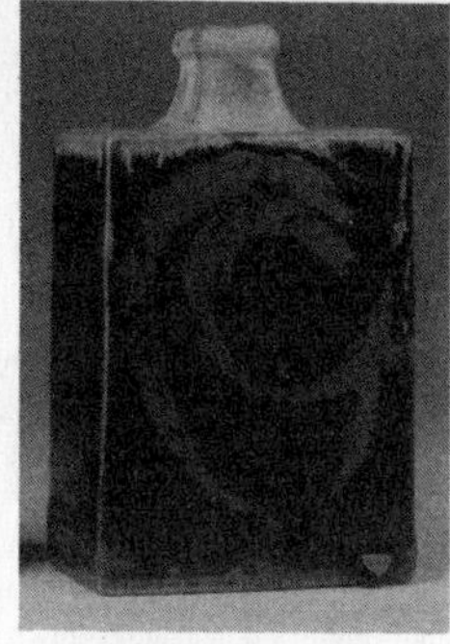

A stoneware bottle vase by Shoji Hamada, iron glaze on brown with 'finger-wipe' design, the top, neck and rim white, circa 1958, 8in. high. (Bonhams) $3,932

A stoneware pouring bowl by Shoji Hamada, thick crawling glaze, beige with free painted brown foliate decoration, circa 1960, 9½in. wide. (Bonhams) $2,202

A stoneware bottle vase by Shoji Hamada, brown and black with an abstract green design on two surfaces, circa 1959, 8in. high. (Bonhams) $7,550

A highly important stoneware squared vase, by Shoji Hamada, thrown round and paddled square, wax resist of bamboo and sugar cane patterns, circa 1960, 230mm. high. (Bonhams) $9,437

A stoneware footed bowl by Shoji Hamada, olive green crawling glaze with all round painted flower motifs in hakeme, rust and green, 193mm. diameter. (Bonhams) $4,719

An early St. Ives stoneware vase by Shoji Hamada, shiny brown with a band of black around the unglazed foot, circa 1923, 130mm. high. (Bonhams) $5,033

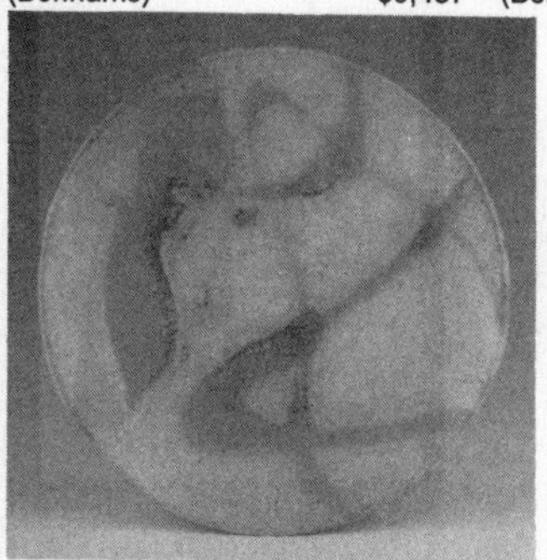

An exceedingly rare stoneware plate, by Shoji Hamada, wheel thrown, nuka rice glaze with ladle poured design in green copper glaze, circa 1930, 250mm. diameter. (Bonhams) $7,078

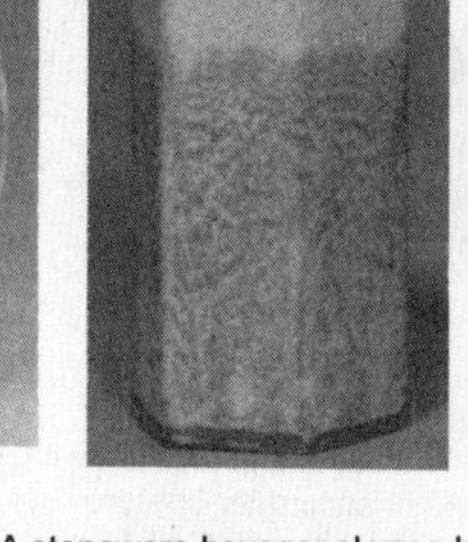

A stoneware hexagonal vase by Shoji Hamada, double dipped rice husk ash glaze, two toned gray, circa 1955, 7½in. high. (Bonhams) $5,977

A stoneware dish by Shoji Hamada, wheel thrown, shiny black glaze with khaki ladle poured design, circa 1960, 27mm. diameter. (Bonhams) $5,977

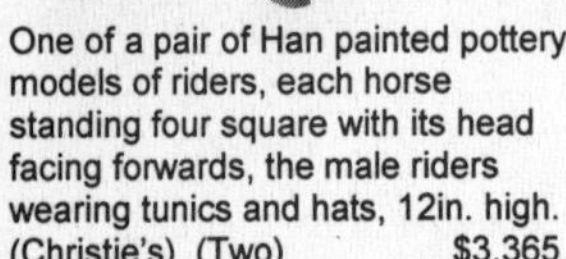

One of a pair of Han painted pottery models of riders, each horse standing four square with its head facing forwards, the male riders wearing tunics and hats, 12in. high. (Christie's) (Two) $3,365

A Han group of an ox with cart, 206BC -220AD, pottery with traces of paint, 34cm. long, 21cm. high. (Stockholms AV) $775

A Han figure of a dog, 206BC-220AD, traces of coloring, 20cm. high, 30cm. long, (Stockholms AV) $835

A set of four Han gray pottery models of a ram and three ewes, the recumbent beasts with their heads inclined to one side, the ram 7½in. long. (Christie's) $850

A pair of large lead glazed baluster vases, Hu, Han Dynasty (206 BC – 220 AD), decorated at the shoulder with raised triple-bands above another geometric band, divided by two applied taotie handles, 17½in. high. (Christie's) $8,332

A pair of Han painted pottery models of attendants each standing wearing a tunic and with the hair pulled back, with one hand by his side, 18in. high max, perspex stands. (Christie's) $2,479

A Han pottery group of a pair of horses standing with their driver, traces of black paint with details in red and white, on plexiglass stand, driver 27.5cm. high. (Stockholms AV) $4,655

A large Chinese sectional buff pottery model of a compound with double entrance door opening onto a walled courtyard flanked by two terraced outbuildings and two connecting two-tiered pavilions, 33 x 24 x 17¾in., Han Dynasty. (Christie's) $3,250

Two Chinese buff pottery models of dancing ladies, each wearing long flowing robes tied at the waist and with their hair pulled back, 19¾in. and 22in. high, Han Dynasty. (Christie's) $1,805

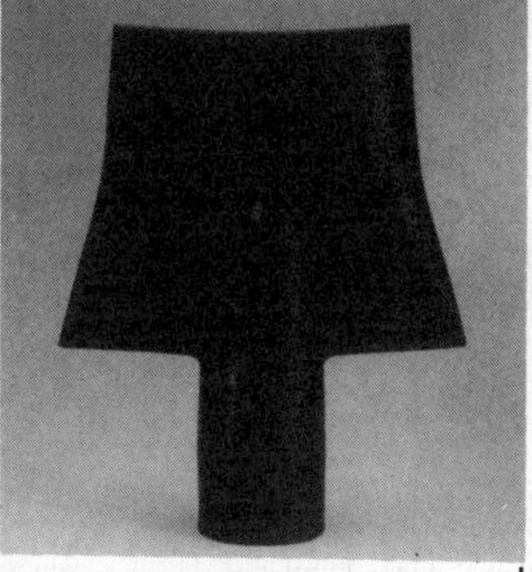

A black stoneware 'spade' form by Hans Coper, the flattened body widening towards the cylindrical base, circa 1971, 9in. high.
(Bonhams) $18,875

Hans Coper, a rare stoneware vase of spherical body with horizontal disc, covered in a matt black manganese glaze, circa 1970, 8.1cm. high.
(Christie's) $3,726

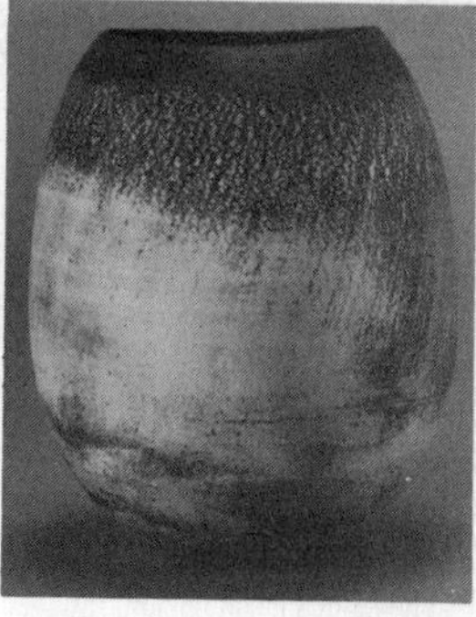

A stoneware black goblet form by Hans Coper, mounted on a square white base, circa 1961, 6¼in. high.
(Bonhams) $7,865

A 'tripot' by Hans Coper, the three cylindrical volumes each with a differently incised design to the foot, circa 1956, 8¼in. high.
(Bonhams) $5,977

A tapered stoneware barrel vase, by Hans Coper, white with vertical lines against a brown slip, above an incised brown spiral, circa 1955, 10½in. high.
(Bonhams) $22,021

An important black stoneware pot by Hans Coper, of composite form, impressed *HC* seal, 1974, 8¼in. high. (Bonhams) $15,729

Hans Coper (1920-1981), a stoneware shallow bowl, covered in a mushroom colored glaze with stylized sgraffito decoration to the well, 18.1cm. diameter.
(Christie's) $2,049

Hans Coper, a stoneware squeezed sack form vase, the matt buff glaze covered with white slip and deeply burnished to reveal manganese, circa 1970, 19.8cm. high. (Christie's) $9,200

A unique off-white dish by Hans Coper with the powerful design of a swan, open-winged with bent neck and face, circa 1953, 375mm. diameter.
(Bonhams) $15,729

An Imari dish, painted with fan shaped panels, containing garden scenes with birds and mythical creatures around central peony medallion, 45.5cm. diameter. (Bearne's) $541

An Imari tapering cylindrical cistern and slightly domed cover, painted and gilt with a quatrefoil panel of scrolling foliage flanked by two ho-o in flight, 10¾in. high, circa 1700. (Christie's) $1,386

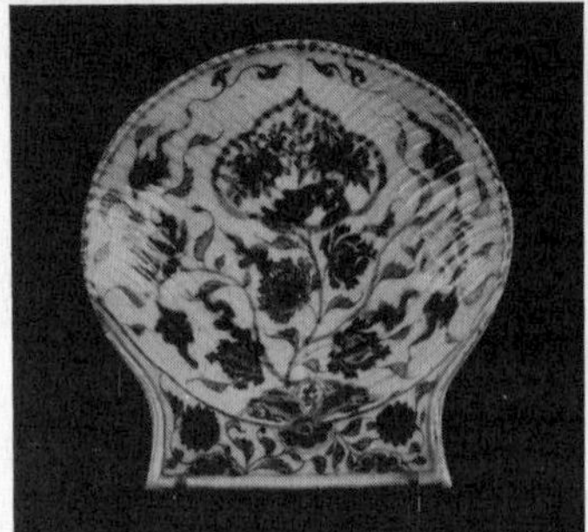

A Chinese Imari shell shaped ribbed dish, painted and gilt with sprays of lotus, chrysanthemums and trailing foliage, 7¾in. wide, 18th century. (Christie's) $800

A Chinese Imari jar and cover, the globular body boldly painted in underglaze blue, iron red and gold with peonies and a willow in a fenced garden, 24cm. high, Qianlong.(Bearne's) $1,652

A pair of reticulated ormolu mounted Imari vases, late 17th century, mounts later, the openwork body with ho-o birds and paulownia flowerheads, 40.4cm. high. (Christie's) $13,541

An Imari bottle, late 17th century, decorated in underglaze blue with a large band of arabesque with peony flowerheads, 16in. high. (Christie's) $12,800

An Imari porcelain and gilt-bronze mounted vase, the domed cover with bud finial, the vase with running guilloche pierced gallery below an overhanging rim, 18th century, mounts 20th century, 17in. high. (Christie's) $7,268

A pair of Imari jars and covers, late 17th/early 18th century, each decorated with a large shishi on a branch within two shaped panels, each approximately 25in. high. (Christie's) $5,778

An Imari Dutch-style pancake dish, late 17th/early 18th century, decorated in iron-red, black enamels and gilt on underglaze blue with a central panel containing a peony emerging from a vase, 14½in. diameter. (Christie's) $6,319

An Italian maiolica portrait dish painted with a portrait of a warrior, in profile to the left, within a scale and scroll pattern border, 42.5cm. diameter. (Christie's) $368

A pair of Caltagirone waisted albarelli painted in yellow and green and outlined in manganese with flowers and scrolling leaves on a blue ground, 17th century, 15cm. high. (Christie's) $939

An Urbino maiolica dish, circa 1560, painted with Diana and Cupid before a wooded landscape, within an ocher rim, 9½in. (Sotheby's) $2,743

n Italian maiolica dish, painted verall in landscape in brown, cher, yellow, blue and green, epicting a-man in contemplation efore a shrine, Angarano circa 700, 12in. diameter. Michael J. Bowman) $5,248

A South Italian maiolica holy water stoop, perhaps Cerrito Sanita, typically formed, painted with a full-length portrait of a saint, between leaf-molded sections, late 18th century, 24.5cm. high. (Christie's) $542

A pair of Nove vases and stands early 19th century, signed *GBV*, painted with scenes of a romantic couple inside a molded and brown painted scrolling cartouche, 60cm. (Bonhams) $2,618

n Italian maiolica plate painted in e Urbino style in shades of ellow, ocher and iron-red with a ortrait bust of a lady, with two bons titled *Giovanna Bella*, late 9th century, 23cm. diameter. hristie's) $785

A Venice waisted albarello painted with a three quarter-length portrait of a saint, in profile to the left, within an oval panel on a ground painted with flowers, circa 1570, 13cm. high. (Christie's) $1,445

An Urbino istoriato tondino of cardinal's hat form, painted with Venus, Cupid and Mars in landscape, circa 1550, 17cm. diameter. (Christie's) $4,335

A Nabeshima footed dish painted in underglaze blue, black, red, yellow and green enamels with two birds among foliage and waves, 6in. diameter, 19th century.
(Christie's) $722

A Japanese model of a recumbent rabbit, decorated in brown and white glazes to simulate the mottled fur, 6in. long, 19th century.
(Christie's) $942

A Makuzu Kozan dish, Meiji Period (late 19th century), decorated in various colored enamels and gilt, finely molded in high relief with two pigeons perched on a blossoming tree, 30.8cm. diameter.
(Christie's) $1,829

A Fukugawa waisted jug with flaring shaped rim and coiled dragon handle, painted in underglaze blue and gilt, 8½in. high, 19th century.
(Christie's) $924

A Makuzu Kozan bottle vase, Meiji Period (late 19th century), modelled in the form of an old hat in Bizen style biscuit ware and glaze splashes, a small snail at the side, with wood box, 10¾in.
(Christie's) $3,611

An earthenware model of Benkei, Taisho Period (early 20th century), lifting the bell of Mii Temple, painted in polychrome enamels and gilt over a clear crackled glaze, 6½in. high.
(Christie's) $1,840

A Japanese earthenware koro and cover, painted with panels to the front and reverse enclosing scenes of a courtesan family in a garden, circa 1900, 14cm.
(Tennants) $628

A pair of earthenware vases, Taisho Period (early 20th century), each painted with mice in samurai costume, some mounted on rats subduing an enraged cat, 25½in. high. (Christie's) $10,925

An Oribe koro, Momoyama Period (late 16th century), cover later, of elegantly waisted form on three feet decorated in underglaze ocher, white and green, 7.5cm. high.
(Christie's) $33,534

Shakuzara Nabeshima dish, Edo eriod (late 17th/early 18th entury), decorated in underglaze ue with a repeated motif of a each branch with blossom and liage,12¼in. diameter.
hristie's) $118,260

An Ao-Kutani figure of a young boy, seated on the back of a water buffalo, and playing a flute in the guise of Roshi [Lao Tsze], Meiji Period, 10½ in. long.
(Bonhams) $200

A rare Nabeshima koro, Edo Period (18th century), elegantly decorated in a pale celadon glaze, the rounded rim in a rich underglaze blue, 3¼in. diameter.
(Christie's) $10,805

Japanese brown glazed baluster ase, with short slightly everted eck, decorated in gilt with a bird erched on the branch of a owering magnolia tree, 11¾in. gh, signed.
hristie's) $628

A Makuzu Kozan ewer, impressed seal, Meiji Period (late 19th century), modelled in the form of a longevity turtle decorated in underglaze blue, the top of the body with takaramono within a honey-comb pattern, 6¾in. long.
(Christie's) $3,657

An interesting clobbered Imari double gourd ewer, with loop handle, decorated with two Yamato Nadeshko, the porcelain Genroku period. (Bonhams) $431

Hirado blue and white ewer and med cover with dragon head out and tail handle, painted with o scholars in a bamboo grove, 1. high, 19th century.
hristie's) $770

A Japanese trefoil globular tripod censer with everted rim and short knub feet, decorated in underglaze blue and copper red with the Three Friends, 7½in. high, 19th century.
(Christie's) $2,302

A large and rare Japanese porcelain model of a recumbent deer, the blueish glaze over a textured body, the head with sockets to receive real antlers, 19th century or earlier, 70.5cm. overall height.
(Woolley & Wallis) $18,055

An octagonal porcelain bowl, Arita Ware, Kakiemon style, Edo Period (late 17th century), decorated with two panels of Chinese boys, one panel of two Chinese men, and one panel of a bird and plum, 7in. diameter.
(Christie's) $5,750

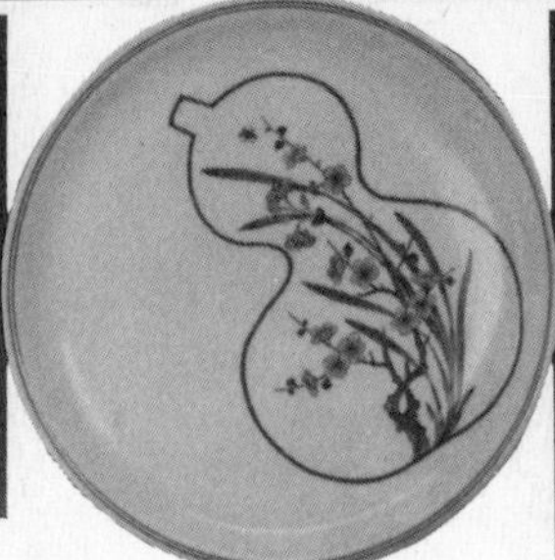

A Kakiemon blue and white dish, Edo Period (late 17th century), decorated in underglaze blue with sprays of plum blossom among grasses within a large panel shaped as a double gourd, 8½in. diameter. (Christie's) $8,125

A porcelain cuspidor, Arita Ware, Kakiemon style, Edo Period (1680-1700), the bowl with a blue bird, prunus, rock and bamboo, and the lower body with two butterflies and flowering grasses, 10.4cm. high.
(Christie's) $3,450

A rare Kakiemon sixteen-sided vase, Edo Period (late 17th century), decorated in iron-red, blue, turquoise and black enamel with a continuous band of long-tailed birds flying over sprays of hibiscus, 7½in. high.
(Christie's) $51,198

A pair of rare Kakiemon models of Shishi, Edo Period, each similarly decorated in iron-red, blue, green, yellow and black enamels, approximately 8¼in. and 8in. high respectively.
(Christie's) $46,943

A pair of Kakiemon flower vases in the form of ladies, Edo Period (late 17th century), each decorated in iron-red, green, blue and black enamels, standing, wearing kimono decorated with stylized clouds, each 11¾in. high.
(Christie's) $25,600

A Kakiemon incense burner, Edo Period (late 17th century), modelled as a circular insect basket raised on three shaped feet with a ribbon tied around the top, 3in. high.
(Christie's) $13,541

Two porcelain dishes, Arita Ware, Kakiemon style, Edo Period (circa 1700), 15.1 and 15.2cm. diameters.
(Christie's) $12,650

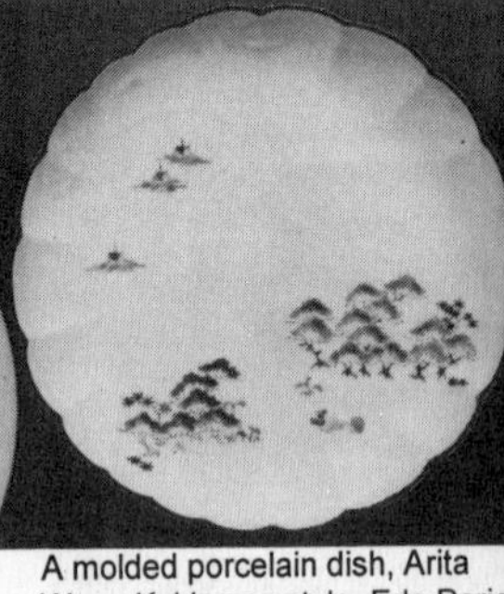

A molded porcelain dish, Arita Ware, Kakiemon style, Edo Period (circa 1670), molded with twenty-one rim facets, a large trefoil leaf, two gingko leaves and six small leaves in the shape of inverted hearts, 17.4cm. diameter.
(Christie's) $63,000

A stoneware pitcher in the medieval style by Bernard Leach, light green and brown speckled ash glaze, 10¼in. high.
(Bonhams) $865

A porcelain hexagonal lidded box by Bernard Leach, the lid with a domed cover, celadon with a dark blue lid, an incised flying bird motif, 650mm. diameter.
(Bonhams) $1,258

Bernard Leach, a tall stoneware press molded bottle vase with short cylindrical neck and everted rim, 35.5cm. high.
(Christie's) $3,726

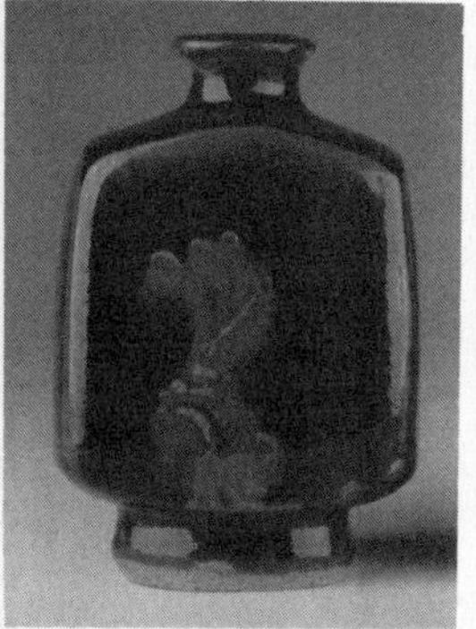

A stoneware bottle vase by Bernard Leach, tenmoku with a different zig-zag finger-wipe design to both sides, 7½in. high.
(Bonhams) $2,989

A highly impressive lidded stoneware jar by Bernard Leach, tenmoku with vertical flute decoration, circa 1962, 230mm. high. (Bonhams) $4,719

A stoneware tea-caddy by Bernard Leach, darkest blue with two sides decorated with three wavy red lines, 6¾in. high.
(Bonhams) $1,180

An impressive stoneware dish 'The Pilgrim', by Bernard Leach, olive blue and orange-brown, with stencil figure and mountains, circa 1965, 328mm diameter.
(Bonhams) $13,842

A stoneware flattened bottle vase by Bernard Leach, running green and brown ash glaze with an incised design of mountains, 7¾in. high. (Bonhams) $1,022

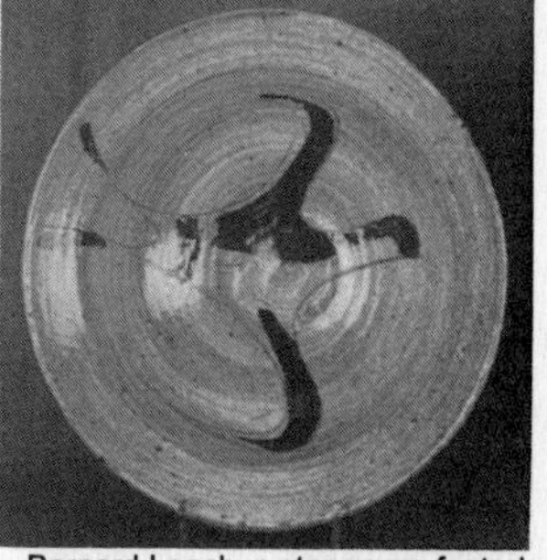

Bernard Leach, a stoneware footed bowl, the interior covered in a translucent mushroom peppered glaze, the well decorated with incised 'bird in flight', 27.1cm. diameter.
(Christie's) $1,771

An English creamware oviform teapot and cover, probably Leeds, painted with a loose spray of flowers among scattered sprigs, with a leaf-molded spout, circa 1775, 13.5cm.
(Christie's) $699

A Leeds creamware teapot and cover, circa 1770, of shouldered cylindrical form with tapering spout and entwined reeded handle, the cover with a convolvulus knop, 5in.
(Sotheby's) $1,188

A Leeds creamware baluster jug painted with a vignette of two gentlemen at a cock fight, among scattered sprigs of flowers, circa 1785, 21cm. high.
(Christie's) $3,612

LENCI

A Lenci pottery jug in the form of a fierce rotund man with tall black hat being attacked by children, 30cm. high, 1930. (Bearne's) $1,076

A Lenci polychrome pottery figure, painted factory mark, impressed numerals *899*, 33.5cm. high.
(Christie's) $866

A hand painted porcelain figure modelled as Pinocchio, inscribed underneath *Lenci, Made in Italy*, early 1940s, 7½in. high.
(Christie's) $1,085

LINTHORPE

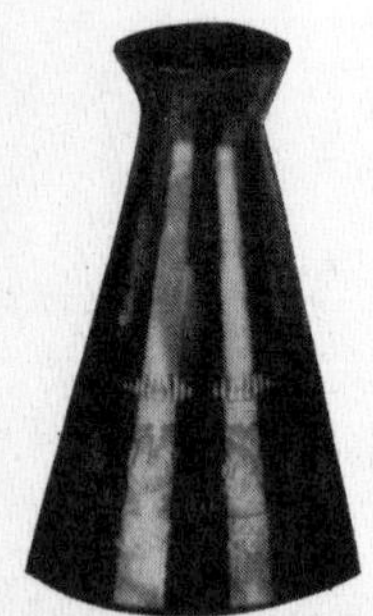

A Linthorpe Pottery vase designed by Christopher Dresser, covered in a running turquoise, brown and dark green glaze, the base decorated with incised stylized leaf banding, 21.6cm. high.
(Christie's) $773

A Linthorpe tall pottery vase, after a design by Dr Christopher Dresser, decorated to the exterior with a streaky green glaze and in relief with irises, circa 1880, 48.5cm.
(Tennants) $1,476

A Linthorpe pottery jug, designed by Christopher Dresser, cylindrical neck and pulled rim, covered in a running brown glaze to green, 14.4cm. high.
(Christie's) $184

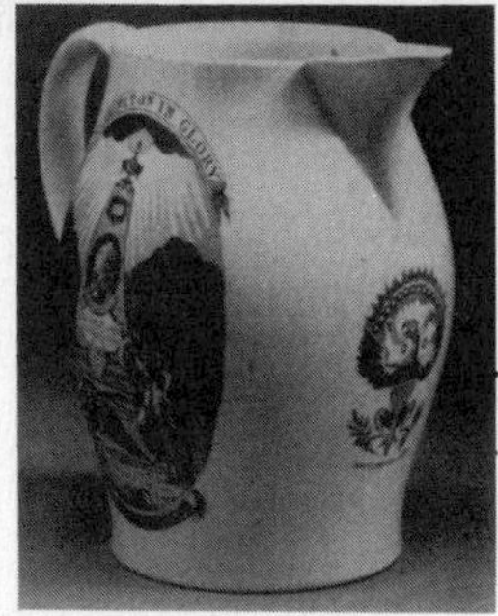

Transfer decorated Liverpool pitcher, England, early 19th century, depicting a ship on one side, Masonic emblems on the other, 11in. high.
(Skinner) $4,025

A Liverpool delftware pickle dish set, circa 1760, comprising: a central petal-shaped dish and four fan-shaped dishes, each piece painted in underglaze-blue with oriental flowers and foliage, 8in.
(Sotheby's) $3,140

Liverpool jug, early 19th century, black transfer decorated with 'Seasons' spring and autumn, 7½in. high. (Skinner) $632

LONGWY

A pottery charger by Longwy, for Pomone, 1920s, incised and glazed in shades of brown, yellow, amethyst and cream, with design of two stylized elephants in jungle landscape, 15in. diameter.
(Christie's) $6,861

A pottery vase by Longwy, for Primavera, 1920s, the front incised and glazed in shades of blue, white and black with stylised female nude before two peacocks, printed marks, 11½in. high.
(Christie's) $3,972

A pottery charger by Longwy, for Primavera, 1920s, the shallow circular dish incised and glazed in shades of blue, black, amethyst and cream with three naked females in stylized jungle landscape, 14½in. diameter.
(Christie's) $1,444

LOWESTOFT

An 18th century mug of slight bell shape painted in underglaze blue with foliage, circa 1760-70, possibly Lowestoft, 8.5cm. high.
(Cheffins) $1,256

A Lowestoft teapot and cover, circa 1775, each side finely painted by the 'Tulip Painter' with a spray of flowers, including a tulip, 16.8cm.
(Sotheby's) $6,765

A Lowestoft teapot and cover, circa 1780, painted on each side in underglaze-blue with a pagoda and fenced garden in a chinoiserie landscape, 15cm.
(Sotheby's) $1,188

A spectacular golden vase by Dame Lucie Rie, a ring of terracotta and two white sgraffito lines to both interior and exterior, 7¼in. high. (Bonhams) $8,651

A fine stoneware 'knitted' bowl by Dame Lucie Rie, white and pale green with inlaid brown criss-cross lines, circa 1982, 7in. diameter. (Bonhams) $6,292

An early earthenware teapot by Dame Lucie Rie, with flat lid and two loops to hold the cane handle, brown with a white interior, circa 1947, 7¾in. wide overall. (Bonhams) $2,045

A rose-petal pink porcelain bowl by Dame Lucie Rie, with fine radiating inlaid lines rising from a ring of turquoise blue around the well, circa 1981, 7½in. diameter. (Bonhams) $15,729

A golden vase with inlaid blue lines by Dame Lucie Rie, the shoulder with a band of light brown crossed with white sgraffito lines, 257mm. (Bonhams) $11,797

A small round stoneware bowl by Dame Lucie Rie, white pitted glaze, impressed *LR* seal, 5¾in. diameter. (Bonhams) $2,831

A porcelain vase by Dame Lucie Rie, bronze with wide blue rim and blue shoulder decorated with sgraffito lines, circa 1980, 7¼in. high. (Bonhams) $4,404

An important white stoneware pitted vase by Dame Lucie Rie, rounded base rising to an oval lip, diagonal fluting, 7in. high. (Bonhams) $4,404

A superb porcelain vase by Dame Lucie Rie, bronze glaze, with upper part with diagonal sgraffito bordered with horizontal lines, circa 1958, 8¼in. high. (Bonhams) $5,033

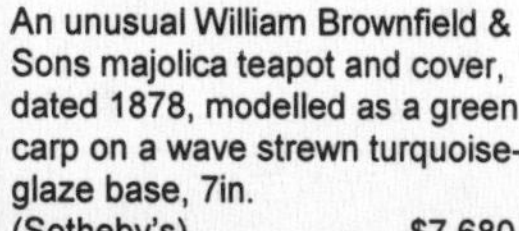

An unusual William Brownfield & Sons majolica teapot and cover, dated 1878, modelled as a green carp on a wave strewn turquoise-glaze base, 7in.
(Sotheby's) $7,680

A majolica basket vase with simulated bamboo handle and framing, molded bird and inset design on a blue ground, pale blue interior, 10in. long.
(G.A. Key) $167

An unusual majolica character jug, modelled as a balding figure with a long brown overcoat, his lilac collar forming the spout, circa 1880, 27cm. (Tennants) $706

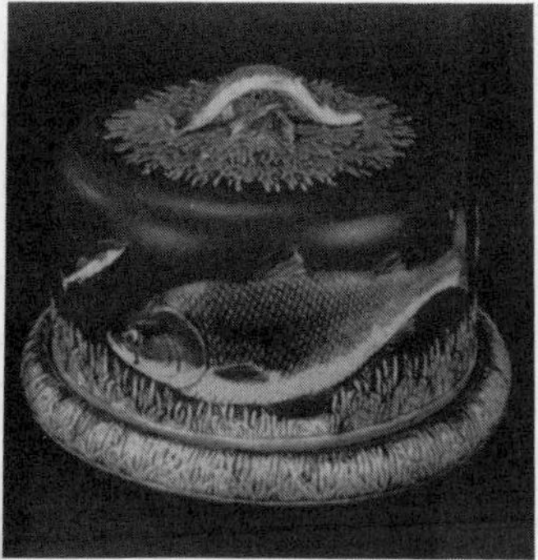

A Joseph Holdcroft majolica cheese dish and cover, molded and painted with varied fish, above reeds on a blue ground, 1870, 19cm. (Tennants) $2,041

An English majolica garden seat of baluster form, with a band of pierced oval cartouches among acanthus leaves, beneath a band of vine leaves, circa 1875, 53cm. high.
(Christie's) $1,078

A majolica cheese bell and stand naturalistically molded as a knarled tree stump and molded in relief with a band of leaves, late 19th century, 29cm. high.
(Christie's) $885

A pair of English polychrome-decorated majolica jardinières on stands, by Minton's dated *1883*, each with an ovoid body centered to the front and back by ribbon-tied medallion, flanked to each side by a ram's mask, overall 65½in. high.
(Christie's) $129,525

A Joseph Holdcroft majolica jardinière molded with continuous frieze of water lilies issuing from four feet, the rim molded with a band of leaves, above a deep lilac interior, circa 1875, 30cm. high.
(Christie's) $796

A pair of Joseph Holdcroft majolica bird umbrella stands, circa 1875, each modelled as a heron standing on one leg by a clump of bulrushes, 84.2cm.
(Sotheby's) $23,699

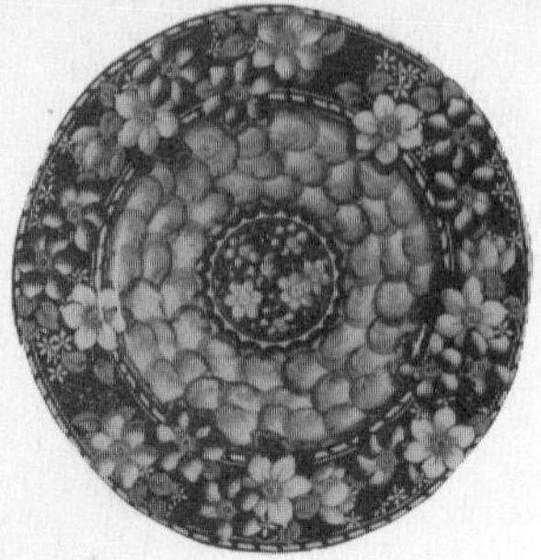
A Maling luster Clematis design plate, 10in. diameter, circa 1948.
(Lyle) $320

A fine pair of Maling two handled luster comports with floral decoration, 10in. wide.
(Lyle) $400

Maling circular bowl, luster decorated in colors with the 'Oriental' pattern, printed mark, pattern No. 5920, 8in.
(G.A. Key) $262

Maling for Ringtons Tea commemorative octagonal jardinière, the whole printed in blue with scenes of Bamburgh and Durham castles etc., 6½in.
(Aylsham) $136

Maling for Ringtons Tea, tea canister of hexagonal baluster form, printed in blue with panels of scenes of Selby Abbey, Yorkminster, Carlisle Cathedral etc, 4½in. (G A Key) $198

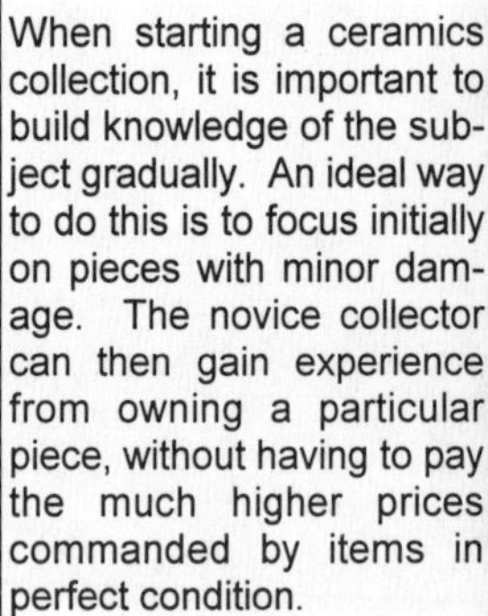
TOP TIPS

When starting a ceramics collection, it is important to build knowledge of the subject gradually. An ideal way to do this is to focus initially on pieces with minor damage. The novice collector can then gain experience from owning a particular piece, without having to pay the much higher prices commanded by items in perfect condition.
(Amersham Auction Rooms)

MARCEL GUILLARD

A polychrome terracotta figure group, by Editions Etling, potted by Marcel Guillard, designed by Kelety, of small girl seated with teddy bear, leaning against Alsatian dog, 11in. high.
(Christie's) $1,444

A pottery vase by Editions Etling, potted by Marcel Guillard, designed by Jose Martin, circa 1925, of flattened octagonal form, molded with central roundel of Bacchanalian mask, 8in. high.
(Christie's) $942

A large terracotta figure from a model by Marcel Guiraud-Riviere, 1920s, modelled as a harlequin clown, striding forth wearing long mottled blue cape, mask and checkered costume, 26½in. high.
(Christie's) $3,611

A rare Martin Brothers saltglaze stoneware 'Toby' jug, the figural form of a seated man with grotesque face, a pipe and drinking horn. (Bonhams) $9,437

A Martin brothers saltglaze stoneware jug, by Roberrt Wallace Martin and Brothers, light brown with an incised and painted design of three birds on a branch, 9¾in. high. (Bonhams) $1,887

A Martin Brothers bird jar and cover, dated 1903, modelled standing, his feathers picked out in ocher, blue and brown enamels, 9¼in. (Sotheby's) $6,400

MASONS

Mason's Ironstone large jug of octagonal baluster form, applied with a snake moulded handle, decorated in Imari colors, with oriental style botanical design with gilded detail, 19th century, 8½in. (G A Key) $236

A Mason's Patent Ironstone wash jug and bowl, with matching soap dish and drainer, printed with Oriental motifs on a rich blue gilded ground. (Wintertons) $447

A rare Mason's Ironstone 'Mogul Pattern' punch jug and cover, circa 1820-1830 decorated with three figures, the smallest holding a parasol, seated beside a table with a large vase of flowers, 24.5cm. (Bonhams) $1,884

A Masons ironstone dinner plate, 19th century, profusely decorated in underglaze blue, green and salmon, with central star point flower surrounded by vegetation and butterflies, 26cm. diameter. (Bonhams) $157

A large pair of Mason's Ironstone blue ground baluster vases and covers, the bodies decorated in gilt with butterflies and other insects above peony, chrysanthemum and a fruiting tree, circa 1830, 62cm. (Woolley & Wallis) $3,542

One of a pair of large Masons ironstone plates, 19th century, the orange ground decorated in underglazed blue and gilt with dragons, 32cm. diameter. (Bonhams) (Two) $502

A Meissen figure group. late 19th century, modelled as a rustic maiden seated against a tree stump defending her love letters from a prying dandy, 15.5cm. (Christie's) $1,176

A Meissen porcelain group in the form of a young man with a basket of flowers handing a posy to his seated companion, 19cm. high. (Bearne's) $1,416

A Meissen figural group, late 19th century, modelled as a courtly couple seated on a large settee, playing instruments, a pug dog seated between them, 14.4cm. high. (Christie's) $1,725

A Meissen figure of a cook, circa 1750, modelled by J.J.Kändler and P. Reinicke, wearing a double-breasted white jacket, puce breeches and a white apron, 7in. high. (Christie's) $4,542

A Meissen ormolu-mounted dove, circa 1735, the mounts Louis XV, modelled by J.J. Kändler to the right, 32cm. high overall. (Christie's) $25,438

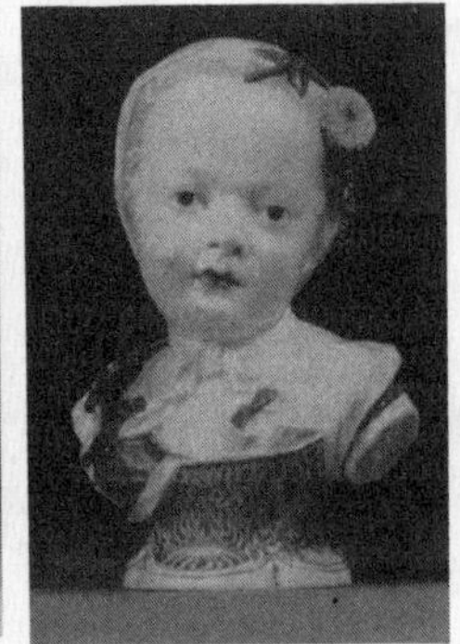

A Meissen bust of Princess Marie Zepherine de Bourbon, circa 1753, modelled by J.J. Kändler, looking slightly to her left, wearing a white headscarf with a chrysanthemum, 9¼in. high. (Christie's) $3,270

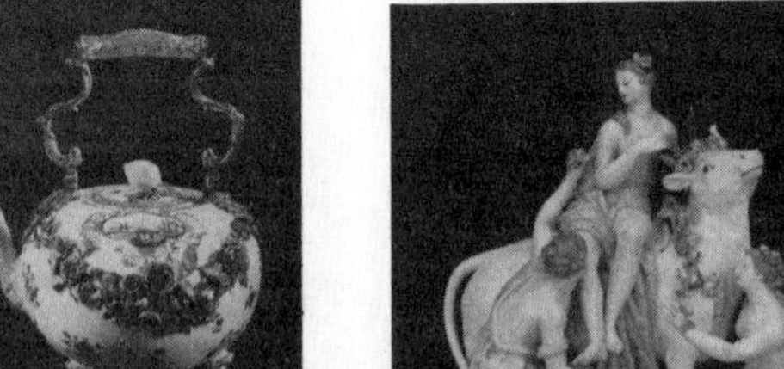

A Meissen ormolu mounted tea kettle, cover and stand, the porcelain 18th century, decorated circa 1880, the globular form painted with harbor scenes, 16½in. high, (Sotheby's) $4,922

A Meissen figural group of Europa and the Bull, late 19th century, she modelled seated on the bull's back, two attendants kneeling beneath, 22cm. high. (Christie's) $1,725

A Meissen chinoiserie arbor group, circa 1750, modelled by P. Reinicke, he wearing a conical hat and a long puce gilt and purple flowered tunic, 7½in. high. (Christie's) $11,810

A Meissen figure group, after a model by Schoenheit, as a musician playing an instrument to his companion, 14.5cm.
(Christie's) $1,254

A pair of late 19th century Meissen porcelain figures of dancers, the gentleman and his companion both in 18th century dress, 24½in. high.
(Canterbury) $3,629

A Meissen figure of a boy and goat, after a model by Schoenheit, attired in green breeches and red jacket, resting against the animal's back, 14.5cm. (Christie's) $706

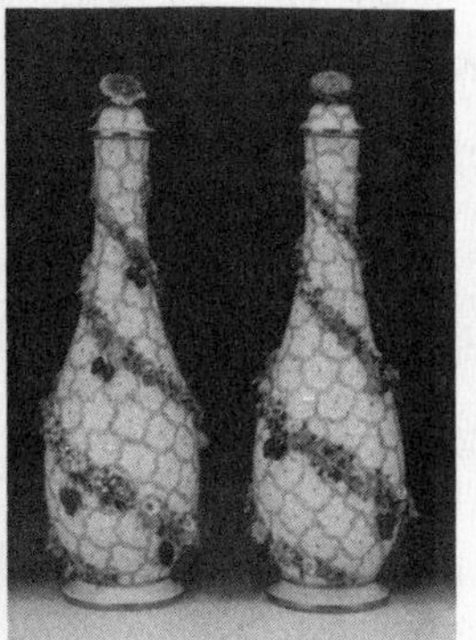

A pair of 'Meissen' bottle vases and covers, late 19th century, encrusted with spiralling floral meanders laden with fruit and berries, 38cm.
(Christie's) $1,882

A 'Meissen' pagoda figure, circa 1880, after an original by J. J. Kändler, outside decorated, seated cross legged, her left breast exposed, 31cm. high.
(Christie's) $6,586

A German figure group allegorical of 'Lessons in Love', Meissen, 19th century, after a model by M.V. Acier, modelled in the round with Cupid standing on a pedestal before an altar, 11½in. high.
(Christie's) $6,325

A Meissen figure of Count Brühl's tailor, circa 1740-5, modelled by J.J. Kändler, wearing a black tricorn hat and a long pale-yellow coat with indianische blumen, seated astride a billygoat, 8¼in. high.
(Christie's) $3,997

A German white figure group of a young man on a donkey, Meissen, circa 1930, L. Nick, modelled in the Art Deco style with a barefoot figure seated on the back of the animal, 16in. high.
(Christie's) $2,760

A German figure group emblematic of Love, Meissen, 19th century, modelled in the round with young couples playing music and celebrating, 14½in. high.
(Christie's) $4,830

A pair of Meissen figures, 19th century, modelled as a man and a woman standing beside beer barrels, raised on tree trunks, 17cm. high.
(Bonhams) $1,805

A 19th century Meissen figure modelled as a young lady seated on rockwork beside a large ewer encrusted and painted with flowerheads, 18cm. high.
(Cheffins) $317

Pair of Meissen porcelain cupids, late 19th century, each holding a flaming heart, one with love bird, painted in multicolors, 11½in. high. (Skinner) $3,737

A pair of large Meissen style figures of a gallant and his lady, each in floral costume with basket of flowers and a posy, late 19th century, 46cm. high.
(Bearne's) $1,248

A Meissen figure of Count Bruhl's tailor, circa 1880, after an 18th century model by J.J.Kändler, the bewigged and bespectacled gentleman wearing a yellow floral coat, boots and a tricorn hat, 17in. (Sotheby's) $11,764

AUCTIONEER'S ADVICE

Good quality porcelain is always in demand, especially if it is fresh to the market or if there is anything unusual about it.

Condition, as ever, is vital to value.

Collections of blue and white have been selling well, as have Royal Worcester, Meissen, Chinese Export and Derby.

(Woolley & Wallis)

A rare Meissen model of a scruffy dog, sitting on the top of his kennel, his head turned to the side and with a chain from his collar to the roof, circa 1740, 4¼in.
(Woolley & Wallis) $1,272

A Meissen model of a peacock, late 19th century, the male bird modelled standing displaying his tail feathers, naturalistically colored, on a tree stump base, 9in. (Sotheby's) $2,560

A large Meissen ewer emblematic of Earth, after a model by Kăndler, modelled with figures of Diana and Pan and modelled with animals of the Chase, circa 1860-70, 26in.
(Woolley & Wallis) $4,000

A Longquan celadon dish, Ming Dynasty (1368-1644), molded with a floral roundel at the center, the fluted well rising toward a wide everted rim, 15in. diameter.
(Christie's) $2,592

A late Ming blue and white lobed jar and cover, Wanli, painted in subtly changing washes of underglaze blue with squirrels among pomegranates and leafy branches, 8in. high.
(Christie's) $8,000

A Ming blue and white 'Dragon' saucer-dish, Wanli six-character mark and of the period, painted in pale cobalt blue washes with dark outlines to the center with three cloud swirls, 7½in. diameter.
(Christie's) $4,800

An early Ming blue and white ewer, Yongle (1403 – 1425), the pear-shaped body painted with two quatrefoil cartouches enclosing fruiting and blossoming peaches on one side and loquats on the other, 10½in. high.
(Christie's) $59,087

An early Ming blue and white dish, Yongle (1403 – 1425), with shallow rounded sides rising from a slightly tapering foot to an everted rim, the center of the interior painted in dark blue tones with a budding and flowering peony stem, 14¾in. diam.
(Christie's) $24,070

A Chinese blue and white vase, Hu, of hexagonal section, the neck with slightly swollen tubular lugs, painted in the Ming style with stylized peony and leafy stems, Qianlong six-character mark and of the period.
(Bonhams) $2,041

One of a pair of Ming porcelain water droppers in the form of birds, with lids on their backs and pierced beaks, 1368-1644, 10cm. high.
(Stockholms AV) (Two) $620

A Frankfurt blue and white baluster jar, finely painted in the Ming manner with three panels depicting Chinese figures in river landscapes, 33cm. high, circa 1690.
(Bearne's) $1,966

A blue and white saucer dish, decorated in the early Ming style with a tied bunch of lotus, Qing Dynasty, 11in. diameter.
(Christie's) $173

A Minton majolica dark-blue-ground inverted baluster vase molded with seaweed and supported by three tritons above a stepped circular base, year cypher for 1868, 37cm. high.
(Christie's) $619

One of a pair of Minton majolica urn-shaped blue-ground jardinières designed by Gottfried Semper, with serpent handles, molded with rope-twist borders, date codes for 1858, one damaged, 25cm. high.
(Christie's) (Two) $973

A Minton majolica jug, molded and colored with vine leaves and grapes in green, purple and brown on a straw yellow ground, circa 1870, 23cm. (Tennants) $1,413

A garniture of three Minton pink-ground vases, circa 1830, the central two-handled vase reserved with a gilt scroll-edged canted rectangular panel finely painted with a basket of summer flowers, 8¼in. (Sotheby's) $4,694

A pair of Minton majolica shell vases, circa 1869, each shell supported on a seaweed stem entwined with two dolphins, 9in.
(Sotheby's) $5,120

A Minton majolica circular bread plate molded with a spray of corn within a blue-glazed border molded with the motto *Seed Time And Harvest Shall Not Cease,* year cypher for 1859, 37cm. diameter.
(Christie's) $1,771

A Minton style majolica jardinière, decorated in colors and relief with flowers, 40cm. high.
(Bonhams) $471

A Minton majolica jug, molded with flowering lilies and painted in green, white and yellow on a claret ground, circa 1870, 20cm.
(Tennants) $2,355

A fine Minton majolica ice stand, circa 1865, the scalloped circular dish supported by three stag's heads, 14in.
(Sotheby's) $27,345

A Moorcroft MacIntyre 'Dura Ware' jug and cover, circa 1902, of 'Sicilian' shape, tube-lined with blue flowers and scrolling foliage on celadon ground, 7in.
(Sotheby's) $505

A Moorcroft 'Claremont' footed bowl, circa 1913-16, the interior and exterior tube-lined with clusters of toadstools in shades of red, pink, yellow and blue, 8¼in. diameter.
(Sotheby's) $2,167

A Moorcroft MacIntyre 'Dura Ware' hot water jug and cover, circa 1902, of 'Edwardian shape, tube-lined with blue poppies on a celadon ground, 8½in.
(Sotheby's) $542

A Moorcroft MacIntyre 'Hazeldene' tankard, circa 1902-1903, tube-lined with tapering trees, in a gently rolling landscape, 5¼in.
(Sotheby's) $3,611

Moorcroft Pottery 'Peter The Pig' a figure, 31cm. wide.
(Christie's) $1,078

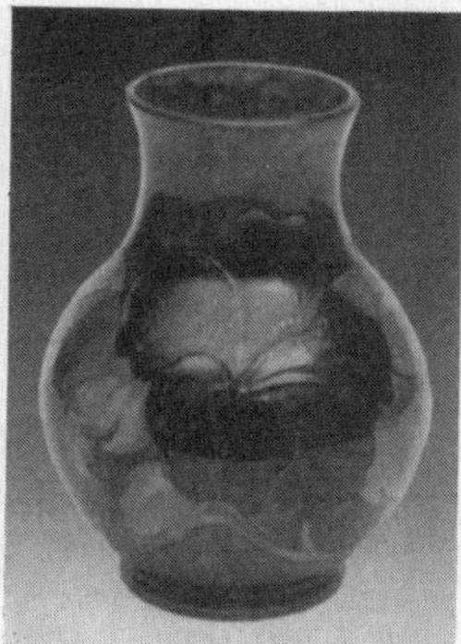

A Moorcroft Pottery vase, hibiscus design with different colored blooms on a blue wash ground, 24cm. high.
(Bearne's) $1,081

A Moorcroft MacIntyre 'Florian Ware' vase, circa 1902, the ample body tube-lined with sprays of blue and mauve lilacs, 10in.
(Sotheby's) $5,778

A Macintyre Moorcroft pewter-mounted jug, circa 1910, of ovoid form with pewter-mounted cover, decorated in deep pink and ocher with the 'Cornflower' pattern, 13.7cm.(Sotheby's) $3,312

A Moorcroft silver overlay 'Pomegranate' teapot and cover, circa 1912, tube-lined with fruit and foliage against a mottled green ground, 6½in.
(Sotheby's) $4,333

One of a pair of Naples creamware (Giustiniani) hexafoil serving dishes each with a scallop-shell handle, painted in shades of brown with Etruscan figures within palmette band border, 19th century, 25cm. wide. (Christie's) (Two) $939

Pair of Naples porcelain groups of loving couples, both dressed in 18th century costume, painted in colors, 20th century, 9in. (G A Key) $431

Naples or Capodimonte porcelain covered small Stein, the lid applied with a Napoleon plumed hat finial, elaborately decorated in colors with a biblical hunting or battle scene, 6in. (G A Key) $113

A Naples creamware group of Europa and the bull, Europa modelled seated with attendants on a recumbent bull, late 19th century, 36cm. high.(Christie's) $1,150

A Naples portrait cup circa 1800-1810, finely painted with an oval bust portrait of Ferdinand IV, against a band of trailing flowers between tooled gilt borders. (Sotheby's) $4,333

A late 18th century Naples (Real Fabbrica Ferdinandea) porcelain group of two peasant children with a basket of fruit, on a rockwork base. (Finarte) $4,471

PALISSY

A French Palissy style tobacco jar and cover, modelled as a knarled stump, applied with a serpent, toad, butterflies, insects and flowers, circa 1880, 19cm. high. (Christie's) $1,505

A Palissy style bough pot, probably French, naturalistically modelled as a wooden rectangular trough with foliage growing over it, late 19th century, 17.5cm. wide. (Christie's) $1,240

A Palissy style 'Grotesque' dish decorated with a central fish on a mottled blue ground, also with a snake, toad, stag beetle, 11in. (Academy) $1,472

A Walton pearlware 'Rustic' group in the form of a young boy and girl by a tree stump on a grassy mound with a dog and sheep, 17cm. high. (Bearne's) $770

An English pearlware oval tureen, cover and stand, printed in blue with the 'Goldfinch' pattern, early 19th century, 18in. (Woolley & Wallis) $1,536

A Staffordshire pearlware female figure, circa 1820-30, the fashionable young lady modelled seated reading a book, wearing an ostrich-plumed head-dress and empire-style dress, 9in. (Sotheby's) $1,280

An unusual Belfast pearlware plate probably Downshire Pottery, Belfast, circa 1787-1805, painted with a brown and beige stag standing before a small fence and sponged foliage, 26.7cm. (Bonhams) $2,464

A Staffordshire pearlware bust of Maria Foot, Countess of Harrington, circa 1820, of Obadiah Sherratt type, modelled with downcast gaze to sinister, wearing a pink dress edged in green, 11½in. (Sotheby's) $4,754

A polychrome pearlware jug with simulated bamboo handle, inscribed under the spout *James Wood 1819*, painted in Pratt enamels, 19cm. high. (Bearne's) $354

PLAUE

A Plaue porcelain flower-encrusted clock case molded en rocaille with C-scrolls and applied with three putti, printed Schierholz & Sohn mark, 46cm. high. (Christie's) $903

Pair of Plaue porcelain trunk formed vases, each applied with figures of courting couples in various poses, heavily encrusted with flowers, circa late 19th century, 16in. (G A Key) $1,120

Plaue porcelain centerpiece of campana form, pierced surround, encrusted throughout with flowers and painted in colors, the base applied with three winged putti, 12in. (G A Key) $1,218

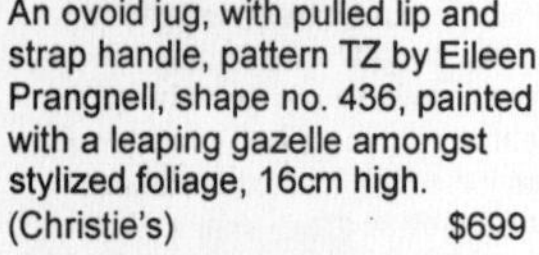

An ovoid jug, with pulled lip and strap handle, pattern TZ by Eileen Prangnell, shape no. 436, painted with a leaping gazelle amongst stylized foliage, 16cm high. (Christie's) $699

A Carter, Stabler, Adams pedestal bowl, pattern ED by Ruth Pavely, the exterior painted with stylized flowers in shades of green, yellow, pink, purple, black and blue, 12cm. high. (Christie's) $400

A Carter Stabler Adams shouldered vase, by Anne Hatchard, pattern ZB, painted with stylized flowers and foliage in shades of yellow, green, brown and black, 28cm. high. (Christie's) $920

A tapering Poole Pottery cylindrical jug with pulled lip and strap handle, pattern GPA by Hilda Hampton, shape no. 321, painted with stylized foliate design in shades of green, gray and black, 12.2cm. high. (Christie's) $699

A Carter, Stabler, Adams large charger, pattern Z by Anne Hatchard, shape no. 538, painted with a deer amongst stylized foliate design in shades of beige, purple, blue, yellow, and green, 37.5cm. diameter.(Christie's) $1,656

A Carter, Stabler, Adams large vase, pattern AX, shape no. 456, decorated with stylized foliate design in shades of blue, beige and gray on an off-white ground, 27.7cm. high. (Christie's) $1,846

A Carter, Stabler, Adams cylindrical vase, pattern YO by Winifred Collett, decorated with stylized foliage between bands in shades of blue, purple, pink, yellow, black and green, 16.4cm. high. (Christie's) $368

Carter, Stabler, Adams hexagonal vase, pattern by FZ by Eileen Prangnell, painted with stylized foliate design in shades of blue, yellow, green, purple, pink and black on an off-white ground, 13.5cm. (Christie's) $480

A Carter, Stabler, Adams vase, pattern AX by Mary Brown, shape no. 970, the body decorated between bands with stylized foliate design in shades of blue, beige and black, 24.6cm. high. (Christie's) $2,392

A famille rose coral-ground bowl, Qianlong seal mark and of the period (1736 – 1795), the exterior brightly enamelled with a profusion of flowers, including narcissus, hibiscus, peony and lotus, 13cm. diameter. (Christie's) $8,331

A rare quatrefoil tea-dust glazed jardinière, Qianlong seal mark and of the period (1736-1795), overall glazed with finely mottled olive green and russet brown glaze, 9in. wide. (Christie's) $18,515

A fine yellow-ground iron-red 'Dragon' bowl, Qianlong seal mark and of the period (1736 –1795), finely enamelled around the exterior with five five-clawed dragons entwined among flame and cloud-scrolls, 4¾in. diameter. (Christie's) $15,738

A fine and rare blue and white vase, Qianlong seal mark and of the period (1736 – 1795), the waisted neck applied with two dragon handles, each side of the body finely painted with a central and supplementary lotus heads, 11¾in. high. (Christie's) $55,545

A blue and white 'Dragon' dish, Qianlong seal mark and of the period (1736 – 1795), with shallow rounded sides and slightly flaring rim, the interior painted with a five-clawed dragon chasing a flaming pearl, 10in. diameter. (Christie's) $2,777

A fine Ming-style blue and white moonflask, Qianlong seal mark and of the period (1736 – 1795), each side painted around a central boss in strong blue tones with a stylized flower-head surrounded by key-pattern and lappet bands, 19½in. high. (Christie's) $69,713

A fine blue-glazed bottle vase, Qianlong seal mark and of the period (1736 – 1795), with tall cylindrical neck, all under a rich dark blue glaze stopping neatly above the spreading foot, 26.3cm. high. (Christie's) $9,660

A pair of Doucai octagonal jardinières and stands, Qianlong seal marks and of the period (1736 – 1795), each bowl and stand raised on four ruyi legs, enamelled around the exterior with stylized lotus sprays, 6¾in. diameter. (Christie's) $7,406

A large famille rose powder-blue and gilt-decorated baluster vase, iron-red Qianlong seal mark and of the period, enamelled around the body with fruiting branches of peach, pomegranate, finger citrus and persimmon, 27in. high. (Christie's) $73,255

A fine slip-trailed and combed redware charger, Pennsylvania, 1790-1810, the circular dished form with incised edge covered in a light orange-brown glaze, 13½in. diameter.
(Sotheby's) $8,625

A glazed redware vase impressed *S. Bell & Son, Strasburg, Virginia,* mid 19th century, covered in a yellow glaze with dabbings of brown and green, 8½in. high.
(Sotheby's) $3,162

A rare glazed redware deep dish, John Stockburger, Bethania, North Carolina, circa 1810, decorated with a stylized bird within a compass drawn interlacing stellate device, 15in. diameter.
(Sotheby's) $6,325

A fine glazed and molded redware pitcher impressed *John Bell, Waynesboro, Pennsylvania*, circa 1850, decorated with a hunting scene with stags and hounds, 8in. high. (Sotheby's) $4,025

A rare group of three glazed redware covered pots, probably Berks County, Pennsylvania, 19th century, in an orange-brown glaze with black and yellow splotches.
(Sotheby's) $8,050

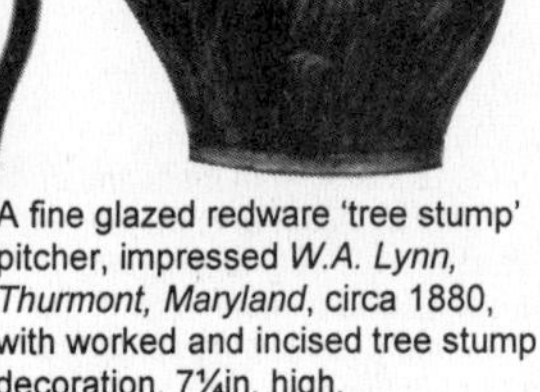

A fine glazed redware 'tree stump' pitcher, impressed *W.A. Lynn, Thurmont, Maryland*, circa 1880, with worked and incised tree stump decoration, 7¼in. high.
(Sotheby's) $9,200

ROSENTHAL

The Fright, a Rosenthal porcelain group of a faun surprised by a stag beetle on his hand, by Ferdinand Liebermann, circa 1910, 42cm. high. (Lempertz) $2,720

A Rosenthal figure of a recumbent elk, signed *Theodor Kärner* (1885-1966), 43cm. long.
(Arnold) $372

A Rosenthal white bisque porcelain sculpture of a crouching girl, signed *Fritz Klimsch* (1870-1960), 42cm. high. (Arnold) $399

Royal Dux Bohemia Art Deco period group of dancers, decorated in the manner of Chiparus, 12½in. (G A Key) $317

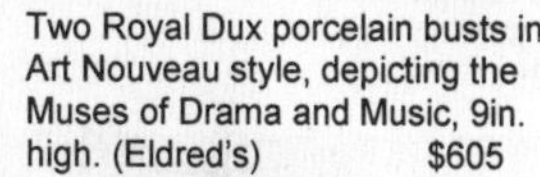

Two Royal Dux porcelain busts in Art Nouveau style, depicting the Muses of Drama and Music, 9in. high. (Eldred's) $605

A Royal Dux porcelain figure of a female dancer, standing wearing a green/gold and pink costume and holding up her skirt tail, raised on circular base, 13in. high. (Andrew Hartley) $1,022

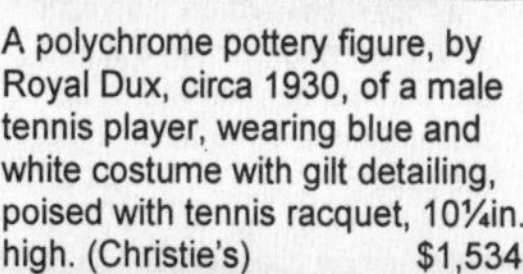

A polychrome pottery figure, by Royal Dux, circa 1930, of a male tennis player, wearing blue and white costume with gilt detailing, poised with tennis racquet, 10¼in. high. (Christie's) $1,534

A pair of Royal Dux porcelain figures of a boy and girl kissing, in green/gold and pink dress, the boy raised on a circular base, 5½in. high. (Andrew Hartley) $582

Pair of Royal Dux figural groups, late 19th/early 20th century, one a shepherd with pipes and sheep, the other a shepherdess with staff and goats, 16½in. high. (Skinner) $747

A Royal Dux figural group, of man seated on a camel with his servant below, 48.6cm. (Bonhams) $567

A Royal Dux figural group, of a woman seated on an upturned shell, playing a flute, 26.5cm. (Bonhams) $356

A Royal Dux figural group, of a young boy on horseback, 34cm. (Bonhams) $389

A Ruskin high-fired vase, dated *1909*, covered in a mottled crimson and lilac glaze freckled overall with green spots, 18.2cm.
(Sotheby's) $3,250

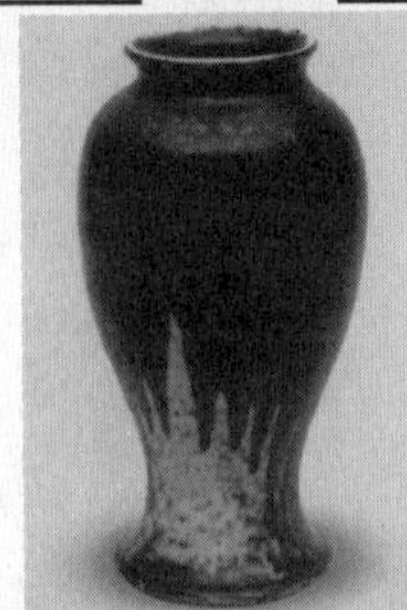

A fine Ruskin stoneware vase, the baluster body covered in a rich red flambé glaze with blue/green spots, 36cm. high, dated *1926*.
(Bearne's) $5,505

A Ruskin Pottery high-fired ginger jar and cover, 1910, the shoulder pierced with repeating flowerhead motifs, all covered in a mottled green and red glaze, 6¼in.
(Sotheby's) $2,578

RUSSIAN

A porcelain scent bottle from the Orlov service by the Imperial Porcelain Factory, St. Petersburg, period of Catherine II, circa 1763, shaped quatrefoil, 10cm. high.
(Christie's) $14,404

A Soviet porcelain cup and saucer by the Imperial Porcelain Factory, St. Petersburg, period of Nicholas II, later decorated, circa 1921, with gilt ciselé flowerheads on dark blue ground, saucer 15.5cm. diameter.
(Christie's) $3,841

A St. Petersberg (Imperial Porcelain Factory) teapot, cover and stand, modelled as a stylized elephant, seated holding a scroll-shaped shield painted with a spray of flowers, circa 1840, 26cm. high.
(Christie's) $1,682

SAMSON

A pair of Samson figures in porcelain with gilt-bronze bases, modelled as two musicians in rustic dress, 19th century, 40cm. high.
(Finarte) $1,661

A 19th century Samson porcelain and ormolu mounted covered urn, painted with a scene of rustics dancing, the cover with putto and dolphin finial, 51cm. high.
(Finarte) $3,578

A pair of Samson figures, 19th century, modelled as comic musicians playing animals; and a similar parrot, 19cm.
(Bonhams) $277

An earthenware vase, Meiji Period (late 19th century), gilt mark Kozan Zo, decorated with folding fans painted with animals and flowers, 19.8cm. high.
(Christie's) $3,680

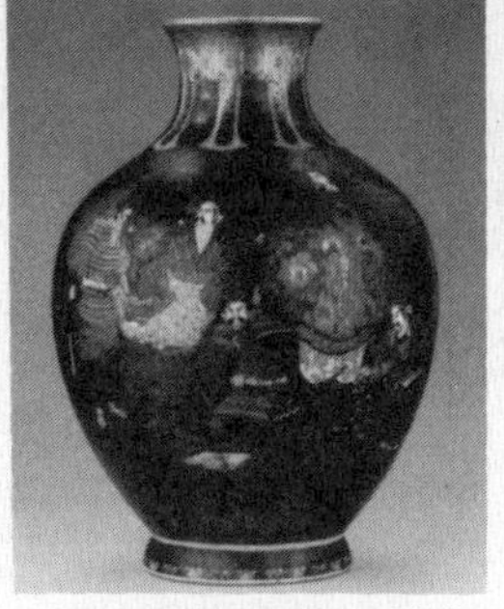

A large earthenware vase, Meiji Period (late 19th century) impressed mark *Kinkozan Zo,* painted with warriors, 15½in. high.
(Christie's) $5,000

A large Satsuma earthenware incense burner, (Koro) Meiji Period (late 19th century), painted with the Seven Sages of the Bamboo Grove, 13½in. high.
(Christie's) $10,000

A Satsuma vase, signed Satsuma Yaki, Katsuyama Ga, Meiji Period (late 19th century), decorated in various colored enamels and gilt with a carriage with tomoe crest design and a brocade cloth with a large drum, 14¼in. high.
(Christie's) $7,222

An earthenware model of an elephant, Meiji Period (late 19th century), gilt mark Dai Nippon Satsuma Kizan, its back, shoulders and haunches draped with a tasselled caparison, 6½in. high.
(Christie's) $4,370

A Satsuma vase, Meiji Period (late 19th century), the ovoid body decorated in various colored enamels and gilt with butterflies hovering among large sprays of peonies growing behind a brushwork fence, 13½in. high.
(Christie's) $4,333

An earthenware ewer, Meiji Period (late 19th century), molded with two dragons forming the spout and handle and decorated on the body with sprays of chrysanthemums, 18.5cm. high.
(Christie's) $1,610

A Satsuma earthenware jar and cover, Meiji Period (late 19th century), painted with Chinese immortals in a bamboo grove, 35.9cm. (Christie's) $4,025

An Satsuma earthenware vase, Taisho Period (early 20th century), painted with peonies and chrysanthemums on bamboo trellises, 11¼in. high.
(Christie's) $3,220

A Sèvres style gilt-metal-mounted blue-ground pedestal bowl on tripartite gilt-metal foliate stand, late 19th century, 46cm. high.
(Christie's) $1,327

A Sèvres matt-red-ground plate from a service commissioned by Napoleon-Joseph-Charles-Paul Bonaparte, painted with a vignette of a dove perched on the side of a dish, 1853, 24cm. diameter.
(Christie's) $3,896

A Sèvres style pottery dark-blue-ground gilt-metal-mounted oviform vase and cover, painted with a Watteauesque scene, and a couple in a landscape to the reverse, circa 1900, 93cm. high.
(Christie's) $5,313

'Narcisses', a porcelain vase, designed by Henri Rapin, decorated by Augustin Carrier, manufactured by Sèvres, 1900, 9½in. high.
(Christie's) $1,545

A large pair of ormolu mounted 'Sèvres' vases and covers, late 19th century, by Leber, signed, in two sections, the domed cover with bud finial, 45¼in.
(Sotheby's) $58,177

A 'Sèvres' blue-ground coffee cup and saucer, late 19th century, the cup reserved with an oval panel painted with a shepherdess and her sheep seated in a landscape.
(Sotheby's) $867

A Sèvres white biscuit porcelain group, in the form of Leda sitting on a rocky outcrop with Jupiter in the form of a swan at her side, 40cm. high, mid 18th century.
(Bearne's) $899

A pair of Sèvres porcelain Nile vases and covers, urn shaped with gilt metal mounts, the semi-lobed body painted with puce floral pendants, reserved on a gilded bleu celest ground, 13in. high.
(Andrew Hartley) $1,196

A Sèvres biscuit figure of Maréchal de Turenne from the Serie des Grands Hommes, on a bleu nouveau rectangular plinth, 1783, modelled by A. Pajou, 55cm. high. overall. (Christie's) $11,810

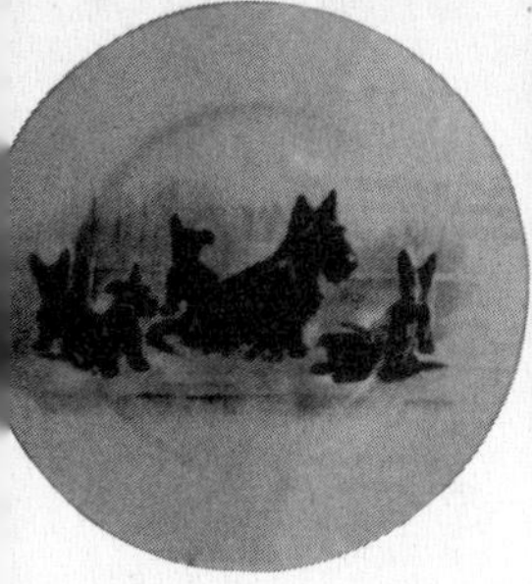

Spode 'Royal Jasmine' circular plate, decorated with a scene of terriers, printed mark, 10in.
(G A Key) $48

A Spode pearlware broth bowl, cover and stand, blue printed from the Caramanian Series, the bowl with the very rare scene of 'Sepulchre with Annexe', early 19th century.
(Woolley & Wallis) $1,540

Spode plate, printed in blue with the 'Death of the Bear' pattern, (Indian Sporting Series), titled verso, early 19th century, printed and impressed marks, 9½in.
(G A Key) $326

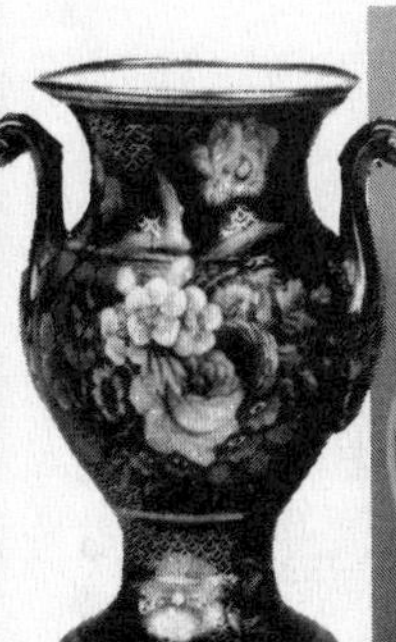

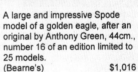

A Spode blue-ground two-handled oviform vase painted with loose bouquets of luxuriant flowers and scattered flower-sprays, circa 1820, 15.5cm. high.
(Christie's) $2,080

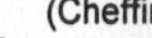

An early 19th century Spode part dinner service, transfer printed in underglaze blue and overpainted in yellow enamel with the Etruscan Trophies pattern, circa 1825.
(Cheffins Grain & Comins) $832

A large and impressive Spode model of a golden eagle, after an original by Anthony Green, 44cm., number 16 of an edition limited to 25 models.
(Bearne's) $1,016

A Spode oval meat platter, with a well to one end, blue printed with the 'Triumphal Arch of Tripoli' from the Caramanian Series, impressed Spode mark, early 19th century, 52cm.(Woolley & Wallis) $400

A Spode porcelain conical pastille burner, with a gilt flame finial, painted in enamels with flower sprigs and sprays, circa 1820, 4¾in.
(Woolley & Wallis) $302

A Spode earthenware octagonal meat plate, blue printed with the 'Buffalo' pattern, impressed Spode mark, early 19th century, 46cm.
(Woolley & Wallis) $123

A Staffordshire pottery group, 'Tee Total', modelled with a couple and a baby sat beside a tea table with a twin turreted castle behind with bocage, circa 1820, 18cm.
(Tennants) $2,826

One of a pair of Staffordshire figures of standing grayhounds holding rabbits, with painted details, 6in. high.(Russell, Baldwin & Bright) $370

A group of Heenan and Sayers, the boxers wearing breeches and long stockings, modelled standing in combat, sparsley-colored and gilt, on gilt-titled base, circa 1860, 23.5cm. high.
(Christie's) $885

A Staffordshire figure group of 'Saint Peter', modelled kneeling in prayer wearing a purple sponged gown with a cockerel and a bible at his side, bocage beyond, circa 1830, 21cm.
(Tennants) $471

A Staffordshire solid agateware teapot and cover, circa 1750-60, of lozenge section, with molded spout and loop handle, the cover with a recumbent lion knop, 5¾in.
(Sotheby's) $7,314

An early 19th century Staffordshire pearlware (Wood & Caldwell) figure of child with mother seated wearing a green dress and white head-dress, 14½in. high.
(G.A. Key) $1,431

An early Staffordshire pottery group, possibly Walton, potted in the form of a man and woman by a tree, he with bagpipes, she with a mandolin, 20cm. high.
(Bearne's) $493

The figure of a British sailor with an ensign and an anchor at his side, his girl companion with a tricolor and an anchor, 25.4cm. high.
(Bearne's) $472

A Staffordshire figure of a standing man beside a basket and pierced trellis, lightly painted, 4in. high.
(Russell Baldwin & Bright) $72

An equestrian figure of Napoleon III wearing cocked hat and uniform, modelled seated with his left hand on the horse's head, on gilt-titled base, circa 1854, 34cm. high. (Christie's) $265

Historic blue and white transfer decorated Staffordshire platter, Enoch Wood & Sons, Burslem, 1819-46, 'Niagara from the American Side', early 19th century, 'Detroit', unknown maker, 14½in. long. (Skinner) $2,070

A group of Napoleon III and Prince Albert wearing military uniform, modelled clasping hands and standing either side of a brick wall with a pile of shells at its base, circa 1854, 35.5cm. high. (Christie's) $336

TOP TIPS

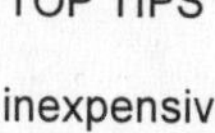

When inexpensive white ceramics become discolored through staining, immerse the piece in a solution of diluted bleach. Leave for twenty-four hours and then rinse.

This will invariably bring back the white ground.

(Amersham Auction Rooms)

A pair of royal figures, each standing by a table, the Princess Royal with a bird, the Prince of Wales with a model yacht, 15.5cm. high. (Bearne's) $409

Pair of 19th century figures of a washer boy and woman, both with baskets on their backs and standing by a stream, painted in colours, 9in. (G.A. Key) $167

A 19th century Staffordshire blue and white porter mug, printed with figures beside a monument in an Italianate lakeland landscape, circa 1830, 12cm.(Tennants) $408

A boat in the form of a winged horse on a blue wavy sea, carrying two figures, the young man with a hunting horn, his companion with a bird, 23.2cm. high. (Bearne's) $315

Friendly Society(?). A Staffordshire pottery twin-handled mug, printed and painted with vignettes 'The real Cabinet of Friendship', 'Brother be of good Cheer' and 'Justice and Equality', 21.3cm. (Bristol) $264

DAVID LEACH

A stoneware spherical vase by David Leach, tenmoku with orange and brown foliate motifs, 13½in. high. (Bonhams) $1,730

A stoneware teapot by David Leach, globular form, red rust and tenmoku, with a looped cane handle, 8¼in. high including handle. (Bonhams) $346

A spherical stoneware vase by David Leach, with a collar neck, cream and blue with a painted design of branches in brown and orange, 10¾in. high. (Bonhams) $1,101

ELIZABETH FRITSCH

A 'Lachrymatory' vase by Elizabeth Fritsch, geometric design to front in blues, yellow, brown and white, brown sides, 14¼in. high. (Bonhams) $4,719

A stoneware 'Moonpocket' by Elizabeth Fritsch, the exterior orange with a light blue and pink band around the rim, 180mm. high. (Bonhams) $4,719

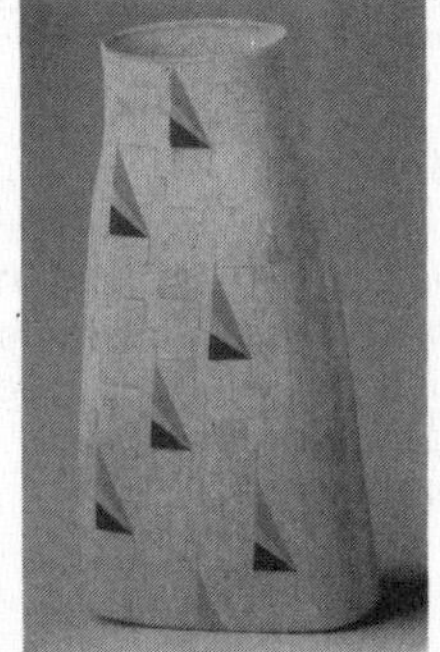

A stoneware flattened vase by Elizabeth Fritsch from the 'Jazz Piano, series, white with a light green, blue, yellow, violet and black stepped design, 256mm. high. (Bonhams) $7,393

JANET LEACH

A squared stoneware pot by Janet Leach, all-over gray-green glaze with several vertical blue stripes, circa 1965, 5½in. (Bonhams) $551

A rounded stoneware vase by Janet Leach, the heavily textured body with large vertical cuts, the neck cylindrical, green and brown, 9in. high. (Bonhams) $629

A porcelaneous flattened bottle form by Janet Leach, two discs with a square aperture at the top, light celadon with a brown vertical splash to either side. (Bonhams) $708

KATHERINE PLEYDELL-BOUVERIE

A stoneware round pot by Katherine Pleydell-Bouverie, blue-green and cream, impressed seal, 6¾in. high.
(Bonhams) $598

A stoneware vase by Katherine Pleydell-Bouverie, the bulbous central section with vertical fluting, a wide flaring rim, 136mm. high.
(Bonhams) $346

A fine stoneware round pot by Katherine Pleydell-Bouverie, shiny brown with a frieze of fine carved silhouettes of panther-like creatures, key design above and below, circa 1930, 3½in. diameter.
(Bonhams) $1,101

MICHAEL CARDEW

A large stoneware Abuja vase by Michael Cardew, light green and metallic brown seed pod design, circa 1959, 320mm. high.
(Bonhams) $786

Two early earthenware cups and saucers by Michael Cardew, light cream glaze with a brown slip design to both cups and saucers, circa 1930, 5¾in. diameter.
(Bonhams) $661

An important earthenware dish by Michael Cardew, with a slip trailed design in yellow of a stag, circa 1930, 440mm. diameter.
(Bonhams) $8,651

WILLIAM STAITE MURRAY

A stoneware bulbous vase by William Staite Murray, glossy olive green glaze, cream interior, 4¼in. high. (Bonhams) $1,022

An impressive stoneware bowl by William Staite Murray, conical form with a large underglazed foot, blue and indigo Chun glaze, 12½in. diameter.
(Bonhams) $3,460

A stoneware tall vase, 'Autumn Leaves', by Wiillam Staite Murray, of baluster form with an elongated neck, orange-brown, 1935, 14in. high. (Bonhams) $629

A Sunderland pink luster pottery Masonic jug printed in black with a panel of Masonic devices and two panels of verse, within borders of stylized leaves, circa 1840, 18.5cm. high. (Christie's) $708

A Sunderland pink luster pottery plaque printed in black and painted in colors with Britannia and a sailor supporting a compass rose, inscribed above *The Mariner's Compass,* mid 19th century, 17cm. x 19.5cm. (Christie's) $390

A Sunderland pink luster pottery Masonic jug printed in black with a view of the Iron Bridge, Masonic devices, and a panel of verse, circa 1840, 23cm. high. (Christie's) $744

A Sunderland luster jug, mic 19th century, the helmet shaped lip printed in black with a lady feeding poultry, a verse 'England, England, glorious name' beneath the spout, 25.2cm. (Bonhams) $523

A purple luster jug, printed under the spout with a nautical verse, on one side a sailor returning to his family, 18.5cm. high. (Bearne's) $330

A Sunderland pink luster pottery jug printed in black and painted in black and painted in colors with a view of the Iron Bridge, The Sailor's Farewell and panel of verse, circa 1840, 18cm. high. (Christie's) $390

TANG

A Sancai-glazed figure of a horse and rider, Tang dynasty, the sturdy animal carrying in its saddle a slender female figure with an unglazed head, 16½in. high. (Christie's) $11,247

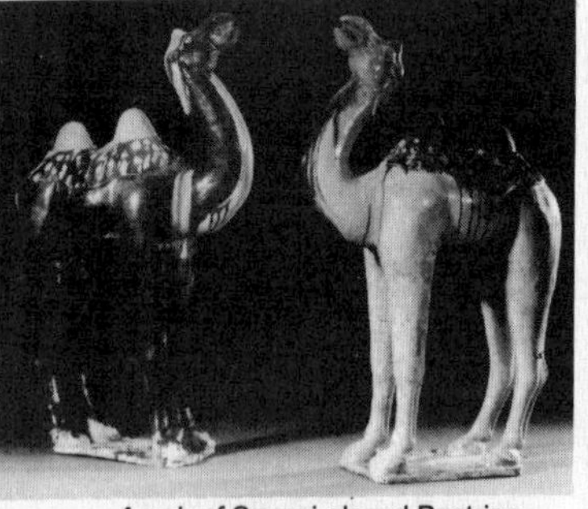

A pair of Sancai-glazed Bactrian camels, Tang Dynasty (618 – 907), the body of one glazed amber, the other straw-glazed, the humps surrounded by a blanket splashed green and amber over straw, 25½in. high. (Christie's) $4,629

A Sancai-glazed pottery equestrian figure, Tang dynasty, the horse covered with an amber glaze, the rider seated upright with arms and hands raised, 13³/8in. wide. (Christie's) $10,310

Vienna plate with claret and gilt flower decorated border, the center painted with 'Solitude', a female figure with long blonde hair, signed A. *Becker*, 9½in. diameter.
(Ewbank) $801

A pair of Vienna porcelain pot pourri vases and covers, the body painted with scenes from classical mythology reserved on a lemon ground with gilt embellishment, 11¾in. high.
(Andrew Hartley) $2,140

A fine Victoria Diamond Jubilee porcelain charger, Vienna, circa 1897, signed *R Diettrich*, well painted with a head and shoulders portrait of Victoria, wearing a lace head-dress under a gold tiara, 40.3cm. (Bonhams) $5,544

A Vienna figure of a huntswoman, circa 1760, modelled by J.J.Niedermayer, the young woman holding a rifle in one hand, her cap in the other, 8¼in.
(Sotheby's) $658

A Vienna cabaret set, circa 1801, each piece painted with a silhouette profile beneath swags of cornflowers and pansies, gilt rims, the tray 32cm.
(Sotheby's) $3,474

A 19th century Viennese porcelain figural group depicting Europa and the Bull, Europa with floral lemon shawl with two semi nude maiden attendants.
(Andrew Hartley) $542

A Vienna topographical cabinet cup and saucer, circa 1821, the cup finely painted with a rectangular panel of a monument in parkland and figures walking before a lake.
(Sotheby's) $1,714

A rare Vienna group of 'Les Mangeurs de Raisins', circa 1770, after Boucher, the shepherdess seated on a grassy mound, her apron filled with bunches of grapes, leaning back on a shepherd.
(Sotheby's) $3,474

A large 'Vienna' cabinet plate, 19th/20th century, painted after Asti, with a bust portrait of a scantily clad maiden in diaphanous shawl, 31.5cm.
(Christie's) $2,509

Wade china novelty teapot 'Scottie', the cover formed as a pale green tartan hat, silver Wade transfer mark, circa 1953/4, 4in.
(G.A Key) $78

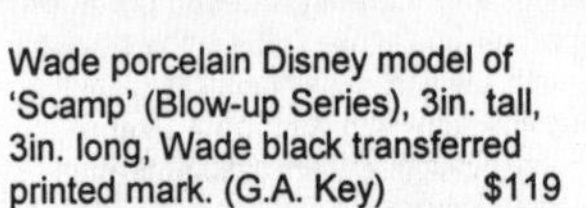

Wade porcelain Disney model of 'Scamp' (Blow-up Series), 3in. tall, 3in. long, Wade black transferred printed mark. (G.A. Key) $119

Large Wadeheath decorative china jug, molded with '3 Pigs' handle formed as the wolf, black Wadeheath ink stamp marks, circa 1928/37, 10in.
(G.A. Key) $365

Wade earthenware figurine 'Pavlova', number 9 (cellulose finish), Wade black ink stamp mark, circa 1920/30,10in.
(G.A. Key) $143

Seven pieces of Wade, Heath & Co. Mickey Mouse nursery ware, each transfer printed with various Disney characters, 10.5cm. high, in original box.
(Christie's) $1,085

A Wade, Heath & Co. hand painted porcelain figure of Mickey Mouse, 1935, the base hand painted with a black *K*, 3¾in. high.
(Christie's) $1,085

WANLI

A rare large late blue and white 'Kraak Porselein' armorial dish, Wanli, painted centrally with a double-headed eagle below a coronet amidst flower sprays, 20in. diameter.
(Christie's) $70,579

A rare polychrome fish bowl, Wanli six-character mark, the deep, thickly potted sides well painted in inky underglaze blue with two spirited five-clawed dragons striding towards clumps of lotus plants amidst yellow-glazed sprigs of lingzhi fungus, 55cm. diameter.
(Christie's) $40,250

A rare Ming wucai hexafoil box and cover, Wanli six-character mark and of the period (1573 – 1619), painted and enamelled around the exterior with cats sitting on incense burners with other cats prowling around, 15cm. high.
(Christie's) $73,255

Wedgwood Fairyland luster ooted bowl, enamelled and gilt with airies, goblins and birds in a antastic landscape, 22.1cm. iameter. (Bristol) $715

Pair of Wedgwood black basalt urns, circa 20th century, of neoclassical form with the 'Dancing Hours' pattern, domical lids, square plinths, 13in. high.
(Freeman) $868

A rare Wedgwood three colored jasperware teapot and cover, with a cylindrical body decorated with a dice pattern in blue and white with applied green flower heads, 1st half 19th century, 6¼in.
(Woolley & Wallis) $2,470

mps on a Bridge', a Wedgwood airyland luster Lincoln plate, esigned by Daisy Makeig Jones, rinted and painted in colors and ilt, 27cm. diameter.
Christie's) $7,222

'Candlemas', a pair of Wedgwood Fairyland luster vases, shape no.3148, in colors and gilt on a black luster ground, 26.5cm. high.
(Christie's) $15,347

A Wedgwood charger by Alfred H Powell, painted with a clipper at sea in silver luster on a black ground painted marks, March 1926, 31cm. diameter.
(Christie's) $451

A stylistic Art Deco bulbous Wedgwood vase, hand painted bright flowerheads and leaves on a pale cream ground, 9in. high.
(Dee Atkinson & Harrison) $388

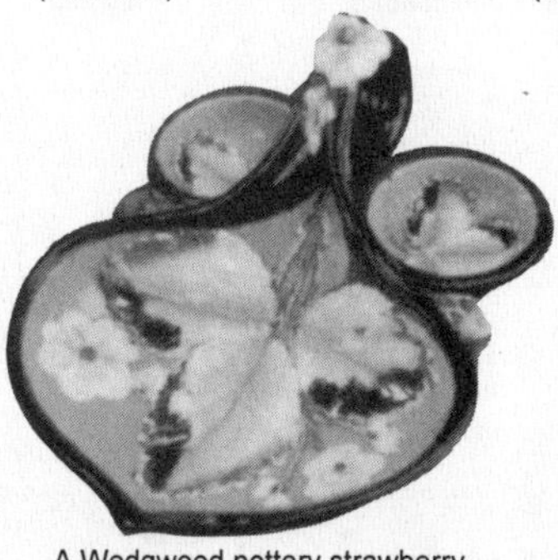

A Wedgwood pottery strawberry dish with branch handle, leaf-shaped bowl and two circular wells, molded with leaves and blossom on a green ground, date codes for 1869, 25cm. long.
(Christie's) $265

A Staffordshire creamware rouletted and green-glazed baluster jug and cover, possibly Wedgwood, gilt with a flowerspray, circa 1765, 14cm. high.
(Christie's) $483

Wedgwood blue jasper dip lidded urn, circa 20th century, of campagna form with domical lid and bas relief figural frieze, impressed *WEDGWOOD, ENGLAND*, 8¼in. high. (Freeman) $280

A Wedgwood John Skeaping figure of a bison standing on a rectangular base with foliage by legs, rust glaze on a gray body, 22.5cm. (Wintertons) $376

Wedgwood blue jasper dip pitcher circa early 19th century, with well molded bas relief frieze of a version of the 'Sacrifice to Ceres', 8 1/16in. (Freeman) $14

Wedgwood black jasper dip vase, circa mid 19th century, acanthus leaf pattern, grape vines around the flaring mouth, impressed *WEDGWOOD*, 10in. high. (Freeman) $448

A pair of Wedgwood Fairyland Luster trumpet vases, 1920s, designed by Daisy Makeig-Jones, decorated with the 'Butterfly Women' pattern, 9½in. (Sotheby's) $4,333

A Wedgwood majolica dark-blue-ground jardinière molded with quarter-length busts of Galileo, Montaigne, Henry IV and a Renaissance gentleman, within circular cartouches, date code for 1875, 33cm. high. (Christie's) $2,310

WEMYSS

Wemyss cylindrical covered preserve jar and stand, decorated in colors with foliage and grapes, within deep puce borders, 7in. (G A Key) $600

A pair of Wemyss relief decorated and rose painted candlesticks. (Locke & England) $684

A large Wemyss pottery three-handled mug, boldly painted with boughs of cherries in typical enamel colors, 23cm. high, impressed *Wemyss Ware, R.H & S* (Bearne's) $585

A Royal Worcester Royal commemorative plaque, molded in relief with two oval profile portraits of Edward VII and Queen Alexandra and inscribed *June 1902,* 8in. across.
(Woolley & Wallis) $334

Locke's Worcester biscuit barrel, silver plated cover, rim and handle, molded below and decorated in puce with gilded detail, 7½in.
(G.A. Key) $230

A George III cup and saucer, Flight, Barr and Barr, Worcester, the cup of two-handled ovoid form, well painted with an oval profile bust portrait of George III in a border of jeweled flowers.
(Bonhams) $3,080

A George III porcelain mug, Worcester, circa 1760, black printed with a profile portrait of George III to dexter, the reverse with a similar portrait of Queen Charlotte, 8.5cm.
(Bonhams) $4,312

A Chamberlain's Worcester beaker, circa 1800-10, finely painted with rectangular panel of a bird standing in landscape within a gilt dotted green border above the brown painted title *BUSTARD*, 10.4cm.
(Sotheby's) $1,625

A Royal Worcester plate, early 20th century, hand painted in colors by Rushton with Anne Hathaway's cottage at Shottery, 27cm. diameter. (Bonhams) $141

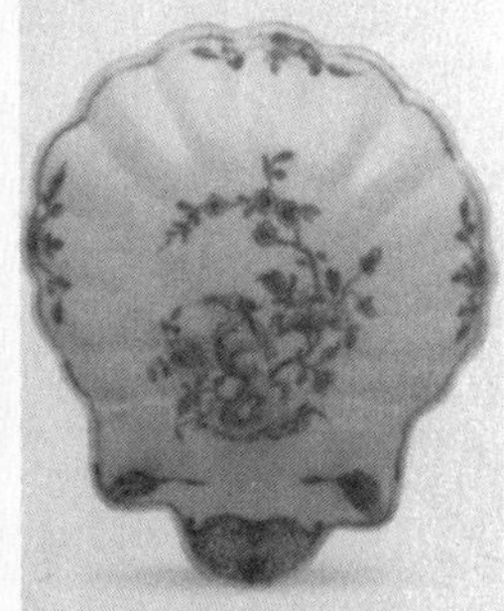

A Worcester blue and white pickle dish, the interior painted with the two peony rock bird pattern within a flower spray and blue line rim, 13.5cm. wide, mid 18th century.
(Bearne's) $277

TOP TIP

When you come face to face with a piece of blue and white porcelain showing an oriental man standing in a boat and holding a fish, with another seated fisherman in the background, it could well be a piece of Worcester or Caughley porcelain depicting the 'Fisherman and Cormorant' pattern. The same pattern was used by both factories, but has minor differences as follows:

If the fish held by the standing fisherman is long and thin and the seated fisherman's line is wiggly, then the pattern is most likely to have been made by Worcester.

If the fish is short and fat and the second fisherman's line is straight, then the pattern is likely to come from the Caughley factory.

The pattern is fairly common and was made in large quantities by both factories.
(Cotswold Auction Co.)

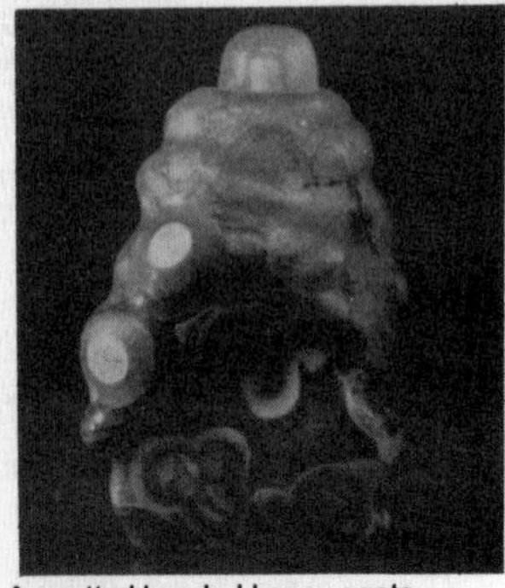

A spotted banded honey agate bottle, the light honey-green stone with a pattern of disks and wavy bands in a cell-like pattern. stopper, 5.3cm. high. (Christie's) $817

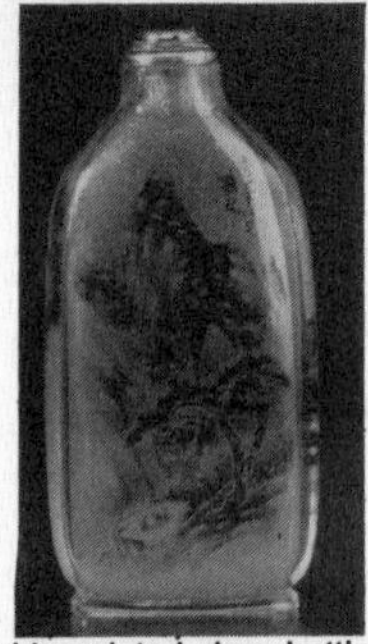

An inside-painted glass bottle, signed *Zhou Leyuan*, circa 1884, painted to one side with a rocky landscape, three figures sitting on a hillside clearing, 2¾in. high. (Christie's) $8,176

A fine celadon and russet jade bottle, 1740-1790, Master of The Rocks School, cleverly carved using the brown skin and dark inclusions with a high relief chilong to each of the narrow sides, 2¼in. high. (Christie's) $17,262

A rare turquoise enamelled blue and white and underglaze-copper-red bottle, Qianlong four-character seal mark in a line and of the period, the body enamelled in turquoise and gilt, 2½in. high. (Christie's) $11,810

An inside-painted rock crystal bottle, signed *Ma Haoxuan* and dated corresponding to1895 and of the period, delicately painted to one side with the so-called ba-po (eight broken things) and butterflies and flowers, 6.6cm. high. (Christie's) $19,987

A Japanese gilt red lacquer bottle, 1820-1900, with a recessed panel on each side, one depicting Zhonggui subduing a demon and the other shows a male immortal on the back of a fish, 6.2cm. high. (Christie's) $9,085

An inside-painted rock crystal bottle, signed *Ye Zhongsan* and dated *JIA YIN* year corresponding to 1914, painted in bright colors with four ladies seated at a table in a garden with a male attendant, 6.2cm. high. (Christie's) $980

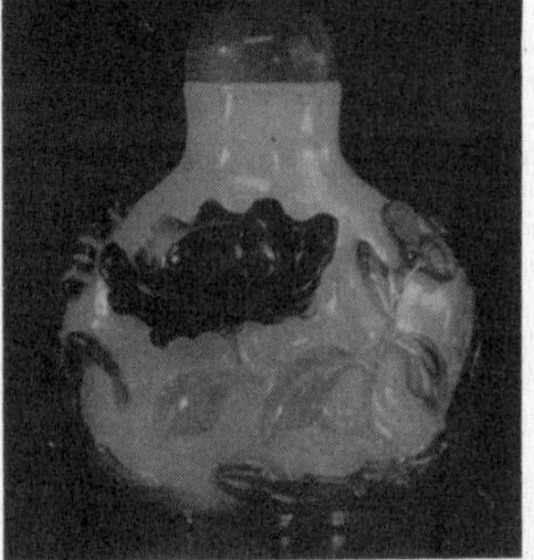

Four-color overlay semi-transparent glass bottle, 1750-1800, carved through overlays of blue, green, yellow and red in a continuous scene with peony to one side, 4cm. high. (Christie's) $2,362

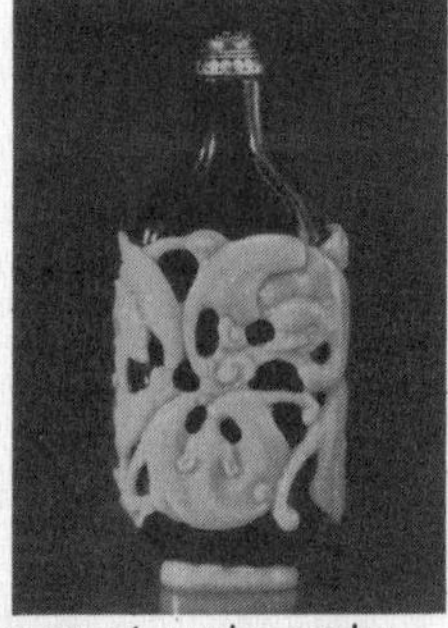

An opaque turquoise overlay transparent red glass bottle, 1770-1830, carved through the opaque turquoise overlay in a continuous scene with five bats, wufu, flying amidst clouds, 6.6cm. high. (Christie's) $8,722

A rare Japanese horn figural bottle, 1800-1880, as a fisherman-farmer, with exquisite details to all parts, holding a small tortoise in his clasped hands and also his sandal, 8.3cm. high.
(Christie's) $12,719

A small carved ivory bottle, 1850-1920, with a recessed panel to each side carved with a standing official on a wave ground near a censer on stand, 4.7cm. high.
(Christie's) $1,543

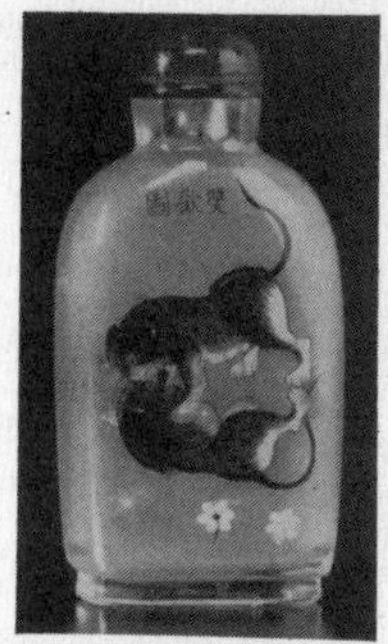

An inside-painted glass bottle, signed *Ma Shaoxian* and dated *XIN YOU* year corresponding to 1921, painted to one side with two scuffling felines below a three-character inscription, 2½in. high.
(Christie's) $2,166

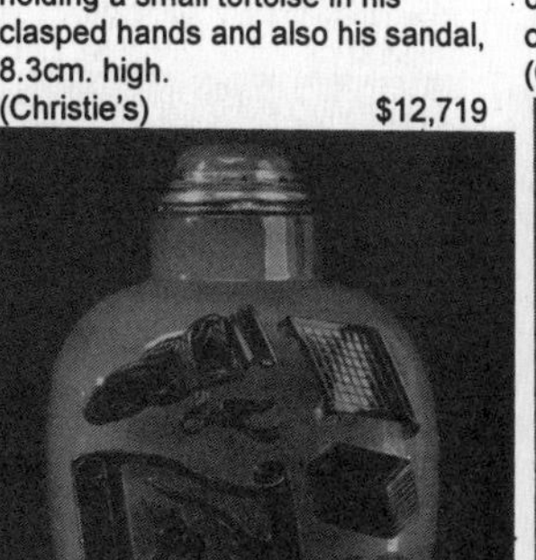

A carved shadow agate bottle, 1800-1880, orange russet inclusions to one side carved in high relief to depict the four gentlemanly accomplishments, 2¼in. high.
(Christie's) $5,088

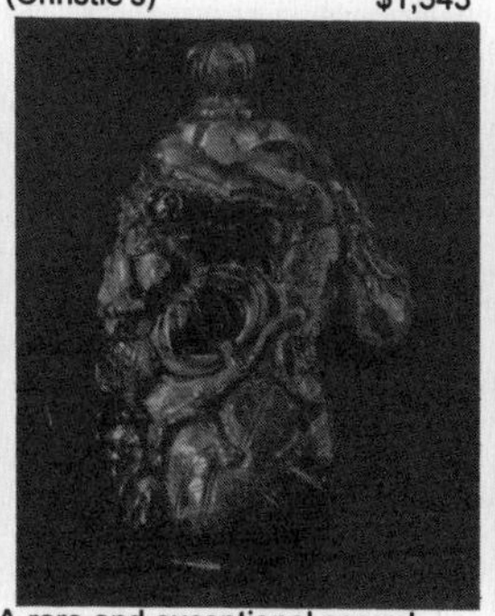

A rare and exceptional carved figural amber bottle, 1750-1850, representing the Daoist immortal Litiegui, with his traditional attributes of a staff and gourd, 5.7cm. high.
(Christie's) $8,176

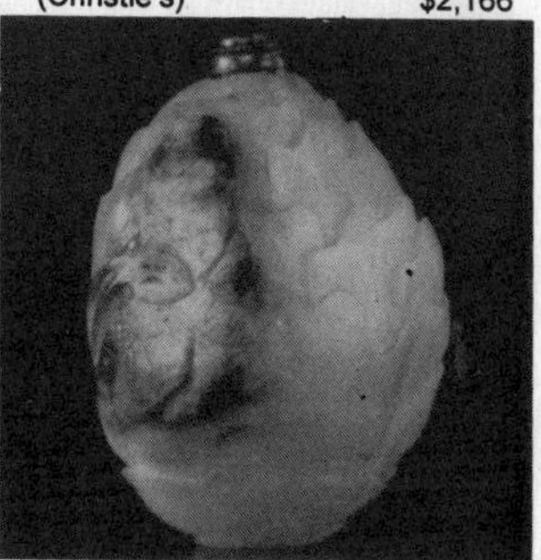

A rare white and russet jade bottle, 1750-1850, carved in low relief in the form of a large peony flower head, a russet inclusion to one side carved as a butterfly, stopper, 5.9cm. high.
(Christie's) $5,451

An Imperial white jade inscribed bottle, incised Qianlong Yi Chi Yu Ti mark and Qianlong seal and of the period, with a continuous Imperial poem in clerical script to each side, 6.3cm. high.
(Christie's) $10,902

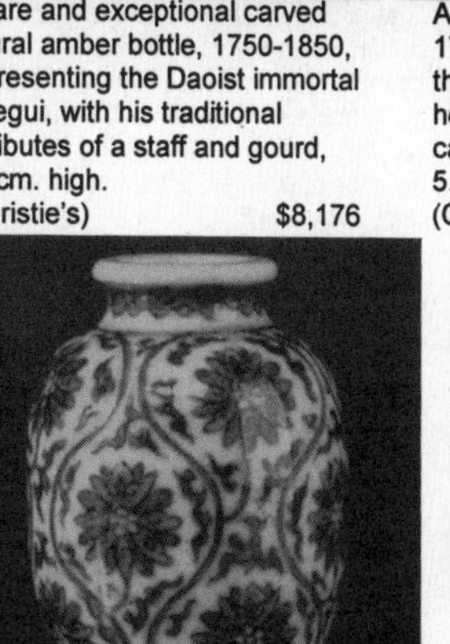

A blue and white and gilt porcelain bottle, Yongzheng four-character mark in underglaze blue, 1780-1880, painted all around with lotus flowers separated by winding stems, 5cm. high.
(Christie's) $545

A fine semi-translucent apple-green jadeite bottle, 1800-1900, translucent cool green stone is attractively shot through with darker apple and emerald-green veining, superb smooth finish, stopper 2in. high. (Christie's) $16,353

A carved shadow agate bottle, 1780-1880, carved in relief from a russet inclusion with a horse tethered to a post, 2¼in. high. (Christie's) $1,090

A rare crystal coin bottle, 1781-1810, the translucent rock crystal finely carved on both sides, following the design of a Spanish Eight Reales coin, 5.6cm. high. (Christie's) $10,902

A 'thumb-print' agate bottle, 1800-1900, the semi-transparent stone with fine concentric bands ranging from white to gray, 2¼in. high. (Christie's) $1,725

A molded enamelled porcelain bottle, 1870-1920, shaped as a folded lotus leaf with long stems and buds carved in varying relief emerging from the mouth and curving around the base, 6.9cm. high. (Christie's) $727

A rare and unusual inscribed agate bottle, Zhenwan incised mark to base, infilled in red, 1800-1880, the dark stone with an attractive natural pattern of geometric veining in shades of orange, pink, green and gray, 5cm. high. (Christie's) $17,262

A rare inside-painted fluorite bottle, signed *Ye Zhongsan* and dated corresponding to 1911, the clear pale-blue semi-precious stone painted on both sides with carp, fan-tailed fish, and other fish, 6.2cm. high. (Christie's) $9,085

A white-glazed molded porcelain bottle, 1800-1850 finely molded in medium relief with eighteen luohan, each with his respective animal stopper, 6.3cm. high. (Christie's) $5,451

A honey and green agate half bottle, 1780-1850 cleverly carved in high relief through a dark green skin with a cricket on a beet near lotus, 7.2cm. high. (Christie's) $763

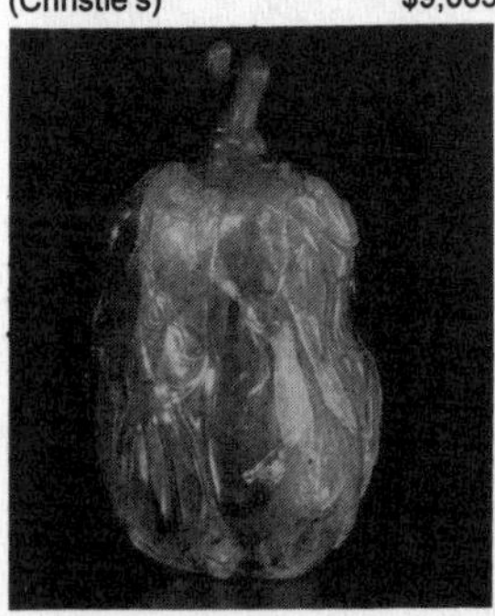

A rare and unusual rose and clear quartz bottle, 1750-1830, the unusual bi-colored tone cleverly cut with a large melon cut from the clear stone, 6.5cm. high. (Christie's) $8,176

An 'East Frisian sailor' electric cigarette lighter, on marble base, 10cm. high.
(Auction Team Köln) $59

Victorian silver cigar lighter in the form of a Roman oil lamp with eagle headed flying handle, scrolled engraved decoration, 5in. long, London, 1854.
(G.A. Key) $432

A good 18ct. gold Dunhill cigarette lighter decorated with sunburst design of alternating panels of gold and red enamel decorated with foliated scrolls.
(Anderson & Garland) $1,138

A Victorian spirit lighter, in the form of an Inniskilling dragoon guardsman's helmet on an oval base, lacking taper holder, by J. Vickery, 1888, 12.5cm. high.
(Christie's) $1,256

An electro-plated cast spirit lighter in the form of a camel resting on its haunches, on a hardstone base, with a central lighter and two slave lighters with 'minaret' covers, circa 1870, 18cm. long.
(Christie's) $992

A Dunhill large chrome table lighter, marked *Patent Number 143752*, upright rectangular form, engine turned decoration, 10.5cm. high.
(Bonhams) $96

A chromed brass band lighter by Köhlers, Germany, with original band, circa 1885, 5.5cm. high.
(Auction Team Köln) $247

A Dunhill petrol pocket lighter, chrome with guilloché ornament, folding cover with flint wheel, Swiss.
(Auction Team Köln) $100

A lighter in the form of a gent's pocket watch by Emil Deutsch, Vienna, marked for 1911.
(Auction Team Köln) $330

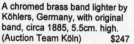

A Bull Dog American cinematograph 35mm. film projector, in red metal case, by AB-Cum-O-graph with Maltese cross transport.
(Auction Team Köln) $220

An unattributed American wooden film camera, 35mm. but converted to 16mm., hand wound, with two intergal wooden cassettes, 1929.
(Auction Team Köln) $468

A Rectaflex Rotor camera, with triple change rotor and Angenieux Retrofocus Type R 11 lens, grip and shoulder support.
(Auction Team Köln) $3,239

A Bolex H16M 16mm film camera with Pan-Cinor, by Paillard Bolex, Switzerland, for 30m. daylight reels, in original case with instructions and tables, 1958.
(Auction Team Köln) $334

An Ernemann portable 35mm. film camera for 30m film in wooden cassettes, in brass-mounted oak case, post 1914.
(Auction Team Köln) $1,473

An Arriflex 16ST film camera by Arnold & Richter, with Zeiss accessories and four lenses.
(Auction Team Köln) $2,963

A Bolex H16 Reflex camera by Paillard Bolex, Switzerland, 16mm. on 30m. daylight spools, wind-up mechanism.
(Auction Team Köln) $401

An Ertel Filmette 35mm. film camera by Ertel Werke, Munich, in brass-mounted walnut case, 1923.
(Auction Team Köln) $1,473

A Kinamo N 25 35mm. film camera by Zeiss Ikon, Dresden, for 25m. Zeiss Ikon cassettes, removable clockwork motor, 1926.
(Auction Team Köln) $535

A Louis XV style boulle bracket clock, the gilt-bronze mounted boulle case surmounted with a putto, 19th century, 58cm.
(Bearne's) $1,159

S D Neill (Belfast) early 20th century mahogany cased bracket clock, arched silvered face with circular Roman chapter ring, 11in.
(G.A. Key) $556

A late Regency mahogany bracket clock with strike silent, 8in. painted dial with twin fusee movement, 17½in. overall.
(Dockree's) $1,680

A George II ebonized striking bracket, Daniel Delander, London, mid 18th century, Indian mask-and-foliate spandrels, strike/silent ring in the arch, 18¾in. high.
(Christie's) $4,963

A Regency mahogany striking bracket clock, Thomas Earnshaw London, first quarter 19th century, the case with handle to breakarch top, trellis-pierced gilt-brass sound frets to the sides, 30cm. high.
(Christie's) $2,290

A late Victorian bracket clock with eight-day three train fusee movement chiming on gongs and bells, in walnut architectural case by W.T. Strong, Barrow-in-Furness, 29in. high.
(G.A. Key) $3,816

Mahogany bracket clock, the pagoda top over an arched face, circular Roman chapter ring and painted with rural scene, eight day movement by Robert Beels of King's Lynn, circa late 18th/early 19th century, 12in.
(G A Key) $2,002

A mahogany cased small size pad top verge repeating bracket clock, John Ireland, London, circa 1770, 6in. replaced dial with a silvered chapter ring, matted center with a silvered sector, 15in.
(Bonhams) $4,620

Late 18th/early 19th century mahogany bracket clock, the pagoda pediment crested with gilt metal pineapple finial, eight day movement by Thomas Purnell of Camberwell, 23in.
(G.A. Key) $5,247

A mahogany cased bracket clock, unsigned, early 19th century, in a single pad top case with a brass carrying handle, side and front fish scale frets, 16½in.
(Bonhams) $2,983

A Regency mahogany quarter striking bracket clock, Ellicott, London, first quarter 19th century, the brass-lined case with handle to break-arch triple-pad top, 18¼in. high. (Christie's) $12,999

A Regency mahogany striking bracket clock, Matthew Harris Junr., Bath, the case with handle to the break arch top, fishscale frets to the sides and on bracket feet, 17¼in. high. (Christie's) $3,430

A George II ormolu mounted ebonised grande sonnerie bracket clock, Joseph Martineau Senior, London, third quarter 18th century, the case with foliate ormolu mounts to the bell top surmounted by an ormolu figure of Chronos, 19in. high. (Christie's) $48,748

An unusual Provincial mahogany cased quarter repeating and alarm bracket timepiece, B Allin, Newcastle, late 18th/19th century, 9in. painted dial with a concentric calendar, and alarm setting hand with floral painted spandrel, 23in.
(Bonhams) $2,826

A George III green japanned bracket clock, the re-decorated case with handle and pineapple finials to the bell top, associated dial with silvered Roman and Arabic chapter ring, 18in. high.
(Christie's) $2,528

A Charles II ebony bracket timepiece with pull quarter repeat, Thomas Tompion, London. No. 77, the case with foliate ormolu mounts to the cushion-molded top with foliate-tied handle, 12¾in. high.
(Christie's) $88,705

A George III mahogany quarter chiming bracket clock, W. Bull, Stratford, fourth quarter 18th century, the breakarch top with four brass ball finials on pedestals to the angles, 23in. high.
(Christie's) $7,222

A Queen Anne ebony striking bracket clock with pull quarter repeat, Joseph Windmills, London, the case with a brass double-S baluster handle to the cushion molded top, 16in. high.
(Christie's) $30,693

A mahogany mantel timepiece, mid 19th century, 7½in. painted dial with Roman numerals signed *Hy Ballard Cranbrook*, single fusee movement, 17in. (Bonhams) $706

A rosewood striking bracket clock, Wiltshire, 182 Oxford Street, 19th century, in an arched top case with applied carved foliage decoration, brass edge lower panelled front, 13½in. (Bonhams) $1,884

A mahogany striking bracket clock, James Stone, Windsor, circa 1800, in a break arch case with molded cornice, brass carrying handle, 17in. (Bonhams) $3,454

A walnut and marquetry striking bracket clock, the case inlaid overall with arabesque scrolling foliage within stylized acanthus borders, backplate signed *John Stanton London*, circa 1690, case and dial of later date, 13¾in. high. (Christie's) $10,833

A George III mahogany balloon bracket clock with automata, Joseph Dudds, London, the center dial painted with a romantic landscape with lovers in the foreground, 22in. high. (Christie's) $11,194

A William and Mary walnut striking bracket clock of phase III type Joseph Knibb London, circa 1695, the case with foliate-tied brass handle on later walnut molding to the domed top, 12in. high. (Christie's) $109,429

A George III walnut Dutch striking bracket clock, Thomas Hunter, London, the case with handle to the inverted bell top, finely pierced walnut sound frets to the sides and to the front and rear door, 18in. high. (Christie's) $30,694

A Queen Anne ebony bracket timepiece with pull quarter repeat, Thomas Tompion, London, knife-edge verge escapement, restored? pull quarter repeat on two bells on Tompion's system from either side, 14¾in. high. (Christie's) $45,137

A William and Mary ebonized quarter striking bracket clock, Adamson, London, circa 1695, the case with foliate cast handle and repoussé mounts to the cushion-molded top, 13½in. high. (Christie's) $8,666

A Regency mahogany striking bracket clock, circa 1825, the case with pineapple finial to the stepped and chamfered top, 19¼in. high. (Christie's) $3,312

Kienzle, a late 19th century German mahogany bracket clock, the eight-day movement with Westminster strike on five rods, 16½in. high. (Dreweatt Neate) $456

Victorian oak bracket clock with matching bracket, signed *W. & M. Dodge Manchester*, 31in. high including bracket. (Lawrences) $1,690

An 18th century ebonized bracket clock by William Hill of St. Margaret's Hill, Southwark, the 7in. gilt brass dial with silvered chapter ring, date aperture and strike/silent dial to arch, 19½in. high, circa 1740. (Canterbury) $4,561

A George II mahogany striking table clock with full calendar, Thomas Ogden, Halifax, second quarter 18th century, the case with ogee-molded top with gilt-metal rosette finial mounts, 22¾in. high. (Christie's) $21,953

Late 19th/early 20th century brass mounted mahogany bracket clock, the cover crested with heavy brass anvil mount, the handle modelled as garland swag, French chiming movement, 17in. (G A Key) $638

A late Victorian gilt metal mounted ebonized bracket clock with silvered ring dial 'numbered' *FOREVERNEVER*, with floral basket top on scroll feet, 18in. (Graves Son & Pilcher) $2,558

A late Victorian carved oak bracket clock with masks, beasts and flowers, inscribed *West & Son, Dublin,* on bracket feet, 20½in. (Graves Son & Pilcher) $957

Large English ormolu mounted ebonized quarter striking and chiming clock, mid 19th century, with pull repeat, Westminster chimes on eight/ten bells, 30in. high. (Skinner) $4,312

A French gilt-metal and cloisonné enamel striking carriage clock, Drocourt, circa 1920, the case with twist moldings and handle, the sides decorated with high relief multicolored cloisonné enamel panels, 6½in. high.
(Christie's) $5,778

A presentation brass repeating carriage clock numbered *7966*, the foliate and white enamelled dial inscribed *R.R. Rowell & Son. Oxford*, 17cm.
(Bearne's) $1,476

A Swiss gilt-metal digital sub-miniature striking carriage clock, Swiss, last quarter 19th century, the foliate engraved gilt dial mask with a central lobed recess with apertures displaying the digital hours and minutes, 3in. high.
(Christie's) $16,249

An early Victorian gilt-metal striking giant carriage clock, Black & Murray, third quarter 19th century, the gilt dial mask and center profusely engraved with flower heads amongst scrolling foliage, 7¾in. high.
(Christie's) $7,222

A Victorian ormolu-mounted ebonized quarter chiming travelling clock with calendar alarm, French, Royal Exchange, London, the arched top surmounted by cast handle of two confronting dolphins' heads, 13in. high.
(Christie's) $27,083

A French gilt-metal and champlevé enamel striking carriage clock, retailed by Carl Suchy & Söhn, Wien, fourth quarter 19th century, the anglaise riche case entirely decorated with multi-colored enamels in a foliate design, 7in. high. (Christie's) $5,416

A French gilt engraved brass grande sonnerie carriage clock, Charles Oudin, Paris; third quarter 19th century, the gorge case engraved overall with swags of flowers on a pounced ground, 5¾in. high. (Christie's) $7,222

An engraved and jeweled porcelain mounted oval cased repeating grand sonnerie carriage clock with alarm, French, Drocourt, circa 1870, porcelain dial with alarm setting subsidiary below, 7½in.
(Bonhams) $7,065

A French gilt-brass striking small carriage clock, Grohé, Paris, third quarter 19th century, the white enamel Roman chapter disc with blued steel moon hands, alarm disc beneath, 5in. high.
(Christie's) $1,986

Fine late 19th century brass and glass cased grande sonnerie carriage clock, oval shaped with hand painted porcelain panels to the sides, possibly by Jacot, 6in. tall. (G A Key) $2,356

Fine late 19th century ormolu cased carriage clock barometer combination, also featuring a thermometer and compass, the face inscribed *J & W Mitchell, Glasgow*, overall size 6¾in. tall, with leather travelling case. (G.A. Key) $1,034

French brass carriage clock, painted enamel dial marked *Bigelow Kennard & Co.*, gilt bronze face and body, hour repeat and alarm movement, 6in. high. (Eldred's) $2,530

Geo Shreye & Co, San Francisco, a 19th century French brass repeating carriage clock with alarm, the molded case with rectangular enamel dial painted in the Japanese taste, 15cm. high. (Cheffins) $1,590

A miniature silver cased carriage clock, 'C' scroll carrying handle, engine turned decoration, on four bun feet, bears import marks for London 1913, 8.5cm. high. (Wintertons) $494

Liberty & Co., carriage clock, circa 1905, pewter, rectangular, the clock face enamelled in shades of turquoise/green and copper, 4½in. (Sotheby's) $5,382

Louis Philippe ormolu grande sonnerie striking chronometer carriage clock with alarm, Breguet Neveu & Cie., circa 1844, the one-piece case entirely engraved with scrolling foliage, 5¾in. high. (Christie's) $37,720

A late Victorian boudoir timepiece, the case embossed and chased profusely with birds, floral scrolls and a vacant cartouche, by W. Wright & F. Davis, 1890, 10cm. high overall. (Christie's) $850

A Victorian gilt-metal striking chronometer giant carriage clock, Dent, London, circa 1862, the case with tiny bracket feet, molded base, bevelled glazed sides, 21cm. high. (Christie's) $29,233

A French gilt-brass grande sonnerie striking carriage clock with alarm, Bourdin, Paris, case engraver Gemengeot, second quarter 19th century, 6½in. high.
(Christie's) $11,316

A cylinder carriage timepiece, with alarum, the dials with gilt mask, in an oval case, 13cm.
(Tennants) $288

A repeating lever carriage clock, by Jacot , with bimetallic balance, in corniche case, 12cm.
(Tennants) $576

An Edwardian tortoiseshell cased carriage clock by William Comyn, the fascia inlaid with ribbon tied festoons, husk edging and bun feet, 4in. high, London 1908.
(Andrew Hartley) $1,512

A late Victorian carriage timepiece, with trompe l'oeil textured surface, resembling woven raffia-work, L. Emmanuel, Birmingham 1892, 9.25cm. high overall.
(Christie's) $1,195

A late 19th century French repeating carriage clock by Drocourt, dial inscribed *Edwards & Sons. Glasgow*, 15cm.
(Bearne's) $5,977

A French striking and repeating carriage clock, with white enamel Roman dial inscribed *Mappin & Webb Ltd. Paris,* early 20th century. (Bearne's) $880

A Victorian gilt-metal Egyptian carriage timepiece with calendar, second quarter 19th century, the case on sphinx feet supporting detached fluted columns, 13.5cm. high. (Christie's) $5,281

Large French brass and glass panelled carriage clock with good quality movement, 5in. tall, late 19th century. (G.A. Key) $320

A 19th century French clock garniture, the ormolu case set with Sèvres style porcelain panels painted with romantic figures with pink surround, 14in., pair of vases and covers having ram's head mask. (Russell Baldwin & Bright) $1,195

Louis XVI style gilt metal and porcelain three piece clock and garniture, circa 1900, the case mounted with putti and foliate scrolls, the two urn-form garnitures similarly decorated, clock 20in. high (Skinner) $805

A 19th century French porcelain, gilt metal and ormolu mounted clock garniture, the dark blue ground enamel dial with Roman numerals and Japy Frères bell-striking movement, the case surmounted by an urn above a pair of putti and cornucopiae, 55cm. high. (Cheffins) $2,385

A 19th century gilded spelter clock garniture, the clock with French eight day movement striking to bell, the decorative clock case surmounted by a pink and floral porcelain urn with gilt metal handles, clock height 14in. (Dee Atkinson & Harrison) $842

Ornate ormolu and Paris porcelain 19th century garniture, comprising: clock and pair of matching urn formed covered vases, the central clock crested with two winged putti, clock 19in.
(G.A. Key) $1,610

A 19th century French gilt brass and champlevé enamel three-piece clock garniture by Japy Frères, the clock contained in case with domed scrolled cupola to top, slender turned columns to sides supported by Cupids, the pair of three-light candelabra with leaf capped scroll branches, 15¾in. (Canterbury) $1,736

A bronze and gilt-bronze clock garniture, Napoleon III, circa 1855, the white enamelled dial signed *Gleizes à Paris Place Vêndome 3,* the case allegorical of the sea surmounted by Neptune in a shell upheld by winged mermaids, flanked by a pair of candelabra in the form of cherubs upholding eight scroll branches, clock: 91cm. high.
(Sotheby's) $19,682

Three piece garniture comprising Bonn porcelain cased clock with circular Roman chapter ring and decorated with floral designs, with a pair of similar two-handled balustered vases, both decorated with panels in the manner of Kauffmann, clock 13½in. high. (G.A. Key) $235

French gilt bronze and rouge royale marble three piece mantel clock and garniture, circa 1860, Raingo Frères, Paris, with urn form finial, glass case and quiver form stiles, with enamelled face, the garnitures each with four nozzles, clock 18in. high.
(Skinner) $2,645

A gilt-bronze and white marble clock garniture, Louis Philippe, circa 1845, the molded cast dial surmounted by the figure of a young woman and cherub, flanked by a pair of tazze, clock 76cm. high.
(Sotheby's) $5,834

German Black Forest carved walnut clock and garniture, 19th century, carved with deer in a naturalistic setting, with pheasant and foliage candlesticks, clock, 24in. high.
(Skinner) $3,335

A 19th century Empire style clock garniture, the black and rouge marble case inlaid with Egyptian motifs similar decorative designs to the twin bronze mounted classical urns ensuite, the case surmounted by a cast bronze parcel gilt figure of an Egyptian noblewoman, height of clock 68cm. (Wintertons) $2,901

A brass lantern style mantel clock, Winterhaulter & Hoffmeier, 1900s, 41cm. (Bonhams) $960

A silver plated lantern timepiece, French, 1920s, 31cm. (Bonhams) $480

A brass lantern clock with later movement, T. Ansell, Abingdon, 22cm. (Bonhams) $283

A French brass miniature lantern timepiece with alarm, signed *Roland Hynar AParis*, fourth quarter 17th century, the movement with verge escapement and alarm striking on the replaced bell above, 8in. high. (Christie's) $7,222

A brass lantern clock with balance wheel control, English 17th/18th century, 6¼in. silvered chapter ring and a tulip engraved center with an alarm setting disk, in a case with corner tapered columns and turned finials, 15in. (Bonhams) $3,080

A George I brass lantern timepiece with alarm, Thomas Moore, Ipswich, the case of typical proportions with four columnar pillars supporting the bell secured with four straps to urn finials and pierced gallery frets, 15in. high. (Christie's) $7,272

A Queen Anne brass striking lantern clock, John Knibb, Oxon, the case of typical form with four brass columns supporting the bell on four straps secured to four urn finials, 15½in. high. (Christie's) $7,583

An early electric lantern timepiece, Eureka Clock Co Ltd, 1910s, the movement with a large balance wheel moving behind the dial in a case with corner tapered columns, 16½in. (Bonhams) $1,463

A Charles II brass miniature lantern clock, Joseph Knibb, London, third quarter 17th century, the movement with later verge and short bob pendulum escapement, 9¼in. high. (Christie's) $2,708

A carved case tubular chiming longcase clock, English, unsigned, circa 1890, 8ft.10in. (Bonhams) $10,990

A Dutch walnut musical longcase clock, H. Dykstra, Sneek, third quarter 18th century, 8ft.10in. high. (Christie's) $9,027

An inlaid mahogany tubular chiming clock, S Smith & Son, London, circa 1900, 8ft.10in. (Bonhams) $9,734

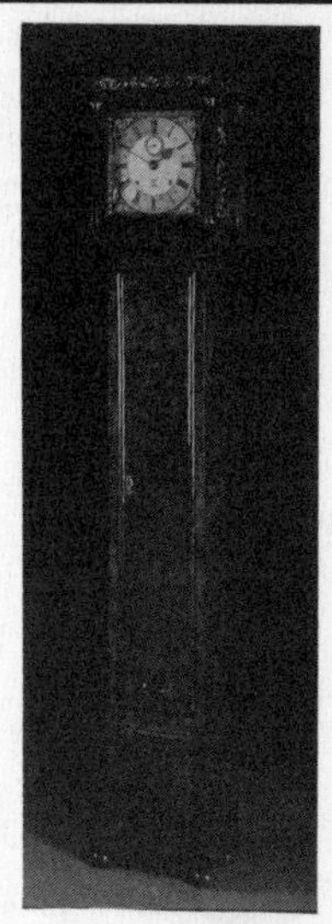

A William and Mary walnut month-going longcase clock, John Knibb, Oxford, circa 1690, 6ft.6in. high. (Christie's) $54,165

A Chippendale carved walnut tall-case clock, Frederick Town or Hagerstown, Maryland, 1780-1800, 95¼in. high. (Christie's) $10,925

An inlaid mahogany longcase clock, William Moore London, early 18th century movement in a later case, 7ft.4in. (Bonhams) $4,396

A Georgian mahogany longcase clock, 8-day mechanism by James Sandiford, Manchester. (Russell Baldwin & Bright) $7,475

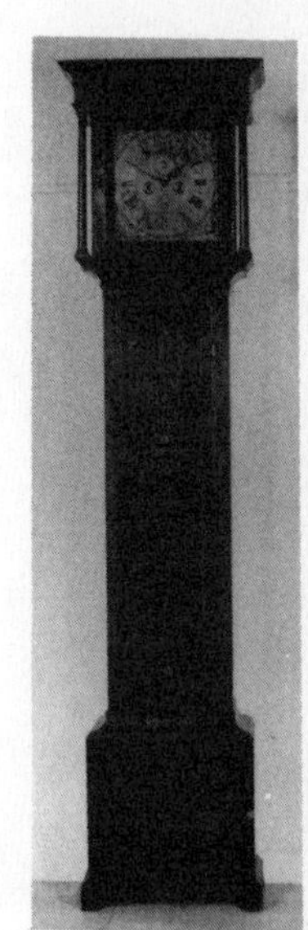

An early 18th century walnut and marquetry 8-day longcase clock by Peter Garon, London. (Russell Baldwin & Bright) $4,077

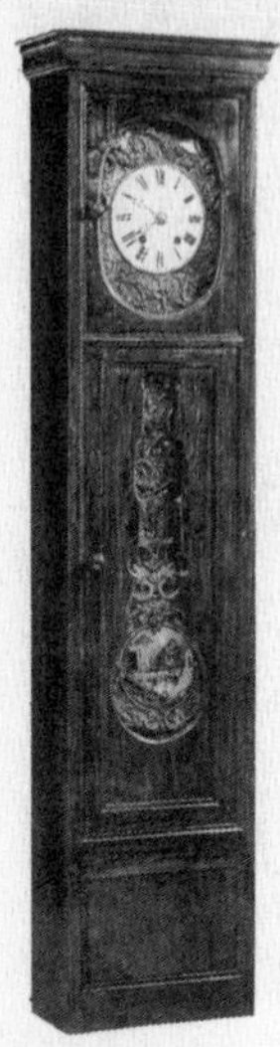

A French long case clock inscribed *Michel Roullier à Plancoet*, 86in. high. (Anderson & Garland) $1,023

A grandmother clock, 8 day movement, black and gold colored lacquer case, 5ft.8in. high.(Woolley & Wallis) $1,254

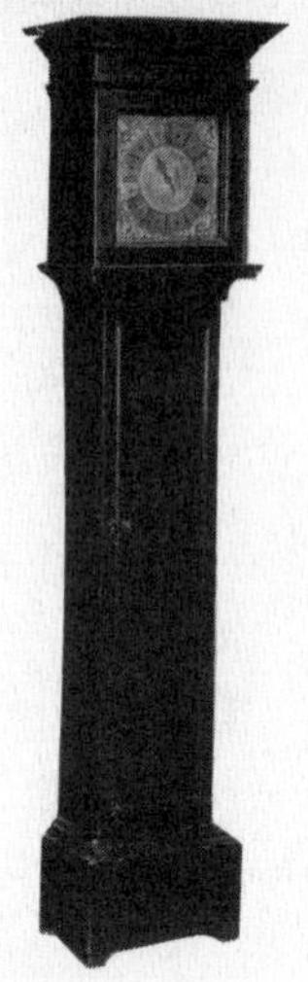

William Shortland, Stoney Stratford, an early 18th century ebonized pine thirty hour longcase clock, 76¾in. high.(Dreweatt Neate) $1,022

An eight day mahogany longcase clock by George Hardy, Fraserburgh, lacks plinth, 75½in. high. (David Lay) $4,508

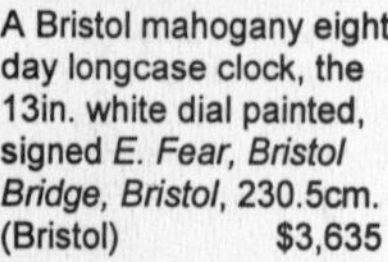

A Bristol mahogany eight-day longcase clock, the 13in. white dial painted, signed *E. Fear, Bristol Bridge, Bristol*, 230.5cm. (Bristol) $3,635

German Renaissance Revival walnut tall case clock, circa 1900, the hood with fruit and scroll carving, 79in. high. (Skinner) $1,955

A late 18th century mahogany longcase clock, 8 day movement, *Edm'd Whittingham, London*, 7ft.2in.high. (Woolley & Wallis) $4,455

An 18th century mahogany longcase clock by Emanuel Solomon of Canterbury, 84in. high. (Canterbury) $3,360

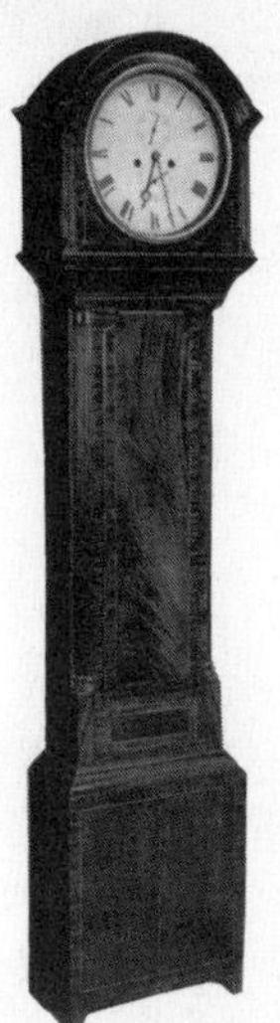

A 19th century Scottish 8-day mahogany longcase clock, 80in. high.(Dreweatt Neate) $1,573

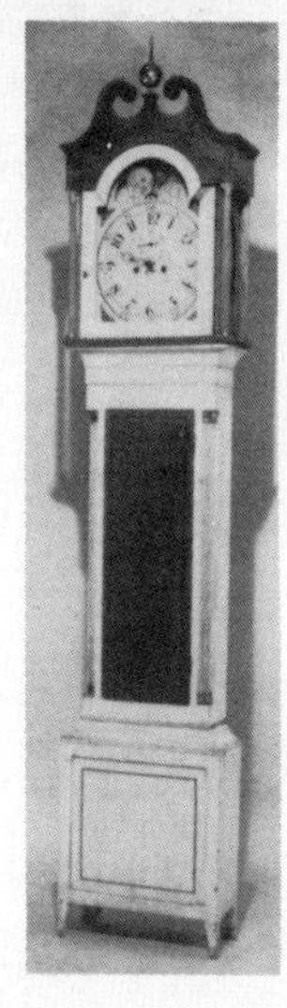

American mahogany long-case clock, brass works, 92¾in. (Eldred's) $2,860

A japanned longcase clock with eight day movement, dial signed *Hindley, York*, 92in. high. (Andrew Hartley) $2,640

Colonial Revival style walnut tall case clock, brass mounted face with phases of the moon, (Skinner) $2,070

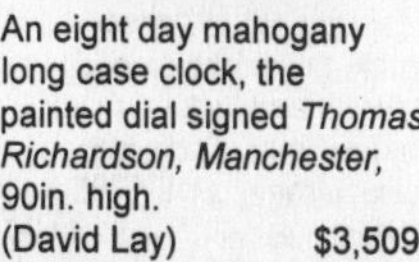

An eight day mahogany long case clock, the painted dial signed *Thomas Richardson, Manchester,* 90in. high. (David Lay) $3,509

Edwardian carved mahogany chiming tall case clock, signed *Walter Burfee*, 95in. high. (Skinner) $11,500

A George III oak longcase clock, early 19th century, signed *D. Hatfield H. BOSWORTH*, 81in. high. (Christie's) $2,208

Pine cased dwarf clock, attributed to Noah Ranlet, Gilmanton, New Hampshire, early 19th century, 48in. high. (Skinner) $6,325

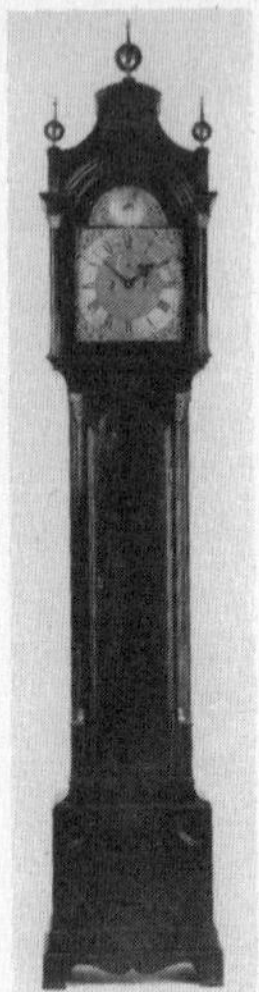

A fine 18th century style mahogany longcase clock, H W Webb, London, late 19th century, 8ft.1in.
(Bonhams) $11,775

A mahogany longcase clock, Samuel Abdell, Richmond, late 18th century, 6ft.6in.
(Bonhams) $3,140

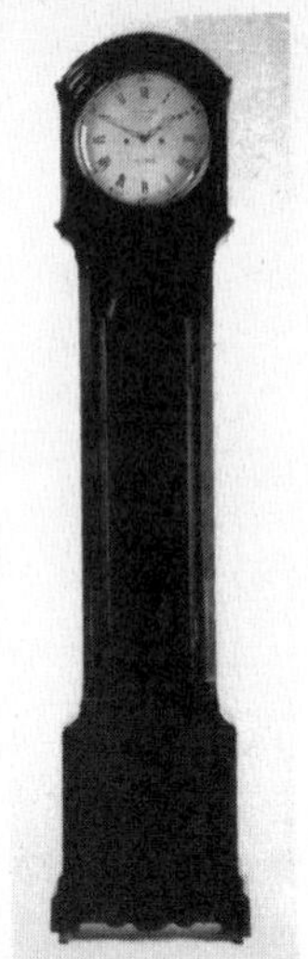

A mahogany longcase clock, Barraud, London, circa 1820, 6ft.9in.
(Bonhams) $8,164

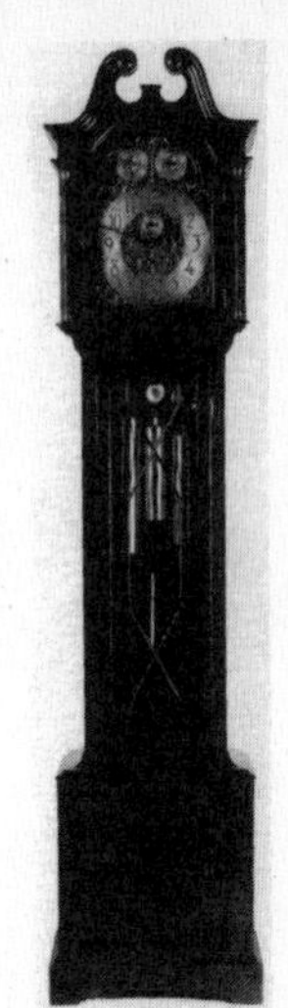

An oak cased tubular chiming longcase clock, R Stewart Glasgow, 7ft. 10in.
(Bonhams) $3,454

A late 18th century West Country eight-day mahogany striking longcase clock, the painted dial inscribed *Sam'l Hart. Devizes*, 219cm.
(Bearne's) $2,674

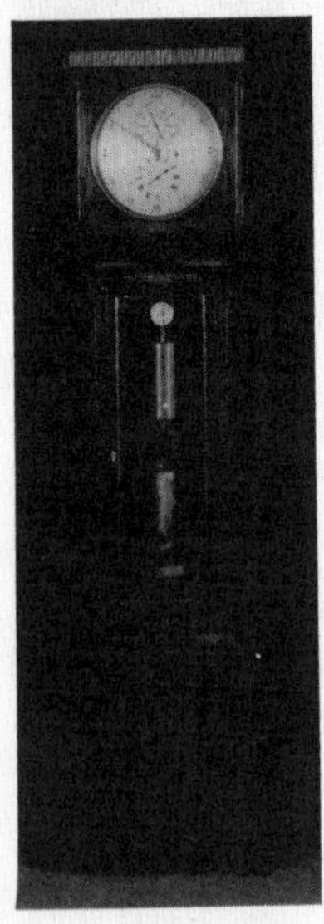

A Regency mahogany longcase regulator, E.J. Dent, London, circa 1830, 6ft.5in. high.
(Christie's) $12,638

An early 19th century mahogany and satinwood longcase clock, 8-day movement, by James Davis, Leominster.
(Russell Baldwin & Bright) $2,666

A Chippendale carved and inlaid walnut tall-case clock, the works signed *Joseph and John Hollinshead, Burlington, New Jersey*, circa 1785.
(Christie's) $18,400

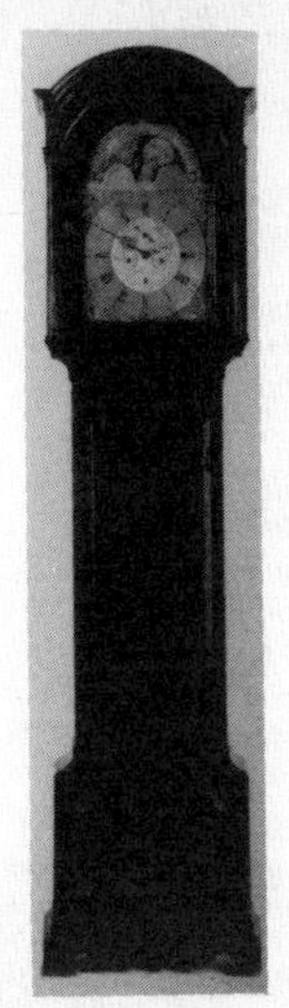

A mahogany longcase clock with a Rolling Moon, Edward Courter, Ruthin, circa 1780, 7ft.4in.
(Bonhams) $6,594

A late 18th century crossbanded oak long case clock, by Jno Shepley, Stockport, 85in. high.
(John Maxwell) $6,153

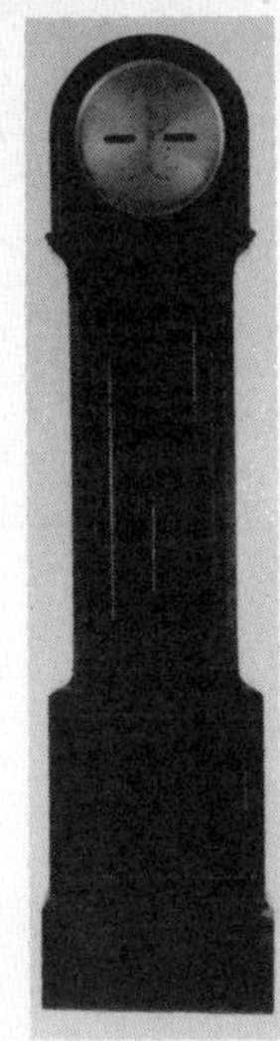

An ebonized longcase regulator, English, mid 19th century, 6ft.11in.
(Bonhams) $3,454

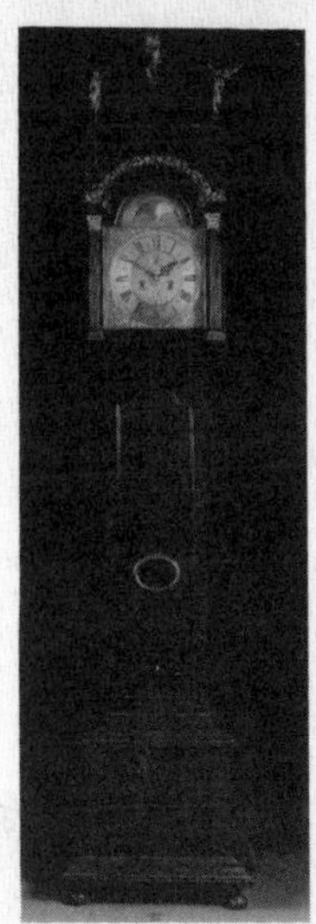

A Dutch walnut longcase clock, Symon Van Leeuwen, Amsterdam, circa 1750, 8ft. high.
(Christie's) $6,319

High style Philadelphia Chippendale mahogany long case clock, mid 18th century, by James Warne, London, 100½in. high.
(Freeman) $78,400

A Victorian mahogany longcase clock, eight day movement striking on a bell, 238cm. high.
(Bearne's) $1,304

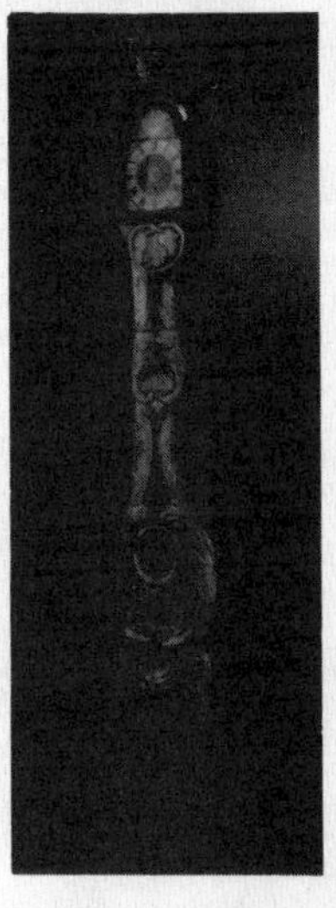

A Swedish ebonized and ormolu mounted longcase clock, signed *Johan Norberg*, 18th century, 219cm. high.
(Stockholms AV) $3,223

A George III mahogany longcase clock, having a good quality carved mahogany case and associated brass dial and movement. (G. E. Sworder) $4,000

French gilt bronze and porcelain mounted Gothic Revival mantel, with porcelain plaques depicting figures and foliage, works signed *Japy*, 12in. high.
(Skinner) $690

Ornate gilded spelter mantel clock, crested with a figure of a maiden, with circular Arabic chapter ring, 19th century, 12in.
(G A Key) $476

Gothic mahogany double steeple mantel clock, Birge & Fuller, 1844-48, the peaked case with two glazed doors enclosing a painted zinc dial and eight day movement, 13¹/8in. wide.
(Skinner) $3,105

French gilt bronze figural mantel clock, second quarter 19th century, the movement signed *J.B. Blanc, Paris*, featuring a classical maiden and portrait roundel, 15in. high.
(Skinner) $2,300

Lalique glass clock, attributed to René Lalique, model created in 1926, two etched figurines in frosted colorless glass surrounding the central clock, 13¼in. high.(Skinner) $6,900

A 19th century French musical mantel timepiece, the bronze and ormolu case depicting Napoleon standing by glass fountain in a rock, 13in.
(Woolley & Wallis) $1,485

Decorative ormolu mantel clock, crested with figure of a seated maiden, Roman chapter ring, flanked on either side by Sèvres style porcelain panels, early 19th century, 15½in.
(G.A. Key) $768

An adzed oak clock by Robert 'Mouseman' Thompson, with modern battery operated movement, square dial with gilded Roman numerals, 19½in. high.
(Andrew Hartley) $1,506

A French 19th century mantel clock, by Japy Frères, for Wartenberg, Paris, in an ormolu case of oval straight sided section heavily cast with figures and other Renaissance motifs, circa 1870, 46cm. (Tennants) $1,727

.ouis XVI style gilt and patinated ronze mantel clock, third quarter 9th century, depicting a young acchante seated on an orb, 14¾in. high.
Skinner) $2,300

A heavy spelter figural gilt and alabaster clock in the French style, with painted enamel dial, Roman numerals to face.
(Academy) $320

An easel backed square desk clock, domed top, engraved date, maker C.ET, Birmingham 1922, 10cm. high. (Wintertons) $104

A 19th century French mantel clock, eight day movement, having two piece enamel dial with open Brocot escapement, 17¼in. high.
(Andrew Hartley) $1,490

A Louis XVI style ormolu-mounted 'jeweled' turquoise-ground porcelain mantel clock, third quarter 19th century, the circular dial with Roman numerals signed *RAINGO FRES/PARIS*, 21¼in. high.
(Christie's) $6,325

A gilt metal and porcelain mounted 30 hour mantel timepiece, the floral painted white enamel dial inscribed *Frodsham, 20771*, within a ribbon tied wreath to waisted oval basket decorated case, 10¼in. high.
(Woolley & Wallis) $1,410

Federal mahogany pillar and scroll clock, Seth Thomas, circa 1825, the scrolled cresting joining three brass iron finials above the glazed door, 32in. high.
(Skinner) $2,185

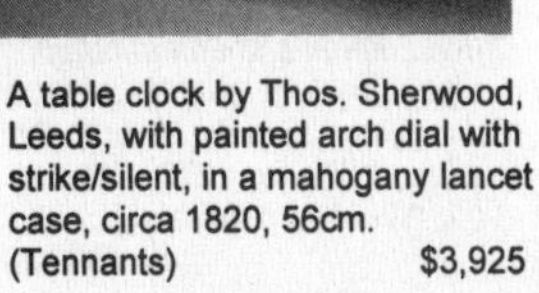

A table clock by Thos. Sherwood, Leeds, with painted arch dial with strike/silent, in a mahogany lancet case, circa 1820, 56cm.
(Tennants) $3,925

French carved giltwood mantel clock, first quarter 19th century, the base carved with paterae, with foliate urns to each side, 20in. high.
(Skinner) $2,645

A late 19th century French ormolu and porcelain striking mantel clock, the Japy Frères movement with Sèvres-style Roman dial painted with Cupid, 28cm.
(Bearne's) $1,195

A black lacquer and chinoiserie mantel clock, English, 1930s, 22cm. (Bonhams) $345

A cloisonné and gilt mantel clock with inlaid dial, French, 1890s, 27cm. (Bonhams) $1,020

A brass framed clock, thermometer, barometer and compass, in the form of a three-sided lamp on turned supports, 10½in.
(Russell Baldwin & Bright) $633

'Pomone', a rare silvered and patinated bronze mantel clock, cast from the model by Richard Guino, circa 1920, surmounted by a nymph bearing a cornucopia of fruit, 18¼in. high.
(Christie's) $9,660

A rouge marble and gilt-bronze mantel clock, Paris, circa 1880, the black marble dial with snake hands within a case of architectural form surmounted by an urn, 94cm. high.
(Sotheby's) $14,996

A French mother of pearl veneered timepiece modelled as a cathedral, mid 19th century, the clock face set within the gothic decorated façade, 13¼in. high.
(Christie's) $2,907

'The Magnus', a Liberty & Co. 'Cymric' silver and enamel clock, designed by Archibald Knox, the rectangular case with flared base and top, 6¼in. high, Birmingham 1902. (Woolley & Wallis) $30,020

A French carved walnut striking mantel clock, last quarter 19th century, case entwined with trailing oak leaves and surmounted by a cowled figure of Father Time, 18¾in. high.
(Christie's) $1,817

A large four glass clock, mercury pendulum, visible escapement, Roman numerals to base.
(Academy) $976

A gilt brass and glazed cased mantel timepiece, Jaeger-Le-Coultre, 'Atmos', 22cm.
(Bonhams) $471

A Victorian 'Aesthetic' ebonized chiming mantel clock, ceramic dial inscribed *John Mortlock & Co. Oxford St. London*, 56cm. high.
(Bearne's) $1,590

A fine Neoclassical ormolu 'Washington' mantel clock, Jean-Baptiste Dubuc, Paris, circa 1800, depicting a figural image of Washington clad in military regalia, 14½in. wide.
(Sotheby's) $156,500

An American crystal and ormolu mantel timepiece, late 19th century, possibly by J.E. Caldwell & Co., the drum case and glass dial supported by two dolphins on a breakfront plinth, 16in. high.
(Christie's) $7,825

Marcel Louis Baugniet and E. van Tonderen, clock, before 1930, silver and black painted wood, with three layered circular discs incorporated into an upright support, 18¼in.
(Sotheby's) $8,280

A Louis XVI bronze mounted marble portico clock, circa 1790, the drum case with eagle finial between a breakfront pediment surmounted with recumbent lions, 24¾in. high.
(Christie's) $8,570

Archibald Knox for Liberty & Co., clock, 1905, silver, the front decorated with a border of stylized honesty, clock face enamelled in shades of turquoise, blue and orange, 13cm.
(Sotheby's) $30,498

A Restauration ormolu striking mantel clock, first quarter 19th century, the drum-shaped case loosely engraved with designs emblematic of the continents, 21½in. high.
(Christie's) $1,998

A French ormolu pendule d'officer, Le Roy, Paris, the hollow cornered case with handle and urn finials to the top, foliate engraving to the six sides and on paw feet, 6in. high.
(Christie's) $5,055

A late Victorian or Edwardian bronze traveller's compendium in the form of a suitcase, late 19th or early 20th century, 6¾in. wide.
(Christie's) $2,362

A Swedish rococo green painted and gilt mantel clock, dial marked *Jacob Kock, Stockholm*, second half, 18th century, 68cm. high.
(Stockholms AV) $5,013

A French gilt-metal, enamel and white marble Bras en l'Air clock, A. Rousseau, early 20th century, the robed lady standing against a multi-colored enamel background, arms pointing to enamel sectors for the hours and minutes, 16½in. high.
(Christie's) $16,250

A mahogany mantel chronometer, Charles Frodsham, London, circa 1925, the single chain fusee movement with conical double-screwed gilt pillars securing the thick spotted plates, 10¼in. high.
(Christie's) $9,027

An ebonized and porcelain mantel striking clock, the design attributed to Henry and Lewis F. Day, circa 1870, ebonized with turned and incised decoration, 16½in. maximum height.
(Christie's) $2,608

A gilt ormolu elephant clock, French, early 19th century, in a cast drum case surmounted by the figure of Bacchus, mounted on the back of an elephant, 17in.
(Bonhams) $2,826

A late 18th/early 19th century ormolu and Meissen clock/ink stand in the rococo manner, the raised back in the form of a tree with porcelain flowers, 11in. high. (John Maxwell) $5,680

A brass cased 4 glass mantel clock, French, 1900s, 3¾in. enamel dial with Arabic numerals and floral decoration, gong striking movement, 12½in.
(Bonhams) $628

A gilt-bronze and porcelain mantel clock, French, circa 1860, the circular dial above a panel painted with lovers in a landscape, 47cm. high. (Sotheby's) $8,203

A 19th century red boulle marquetry clock standish, the square engraved brass dial engraved *Martin Baskett & Co, Cheltenham*, fitted with eight day striking drum movement, 14in. across. (Michael J. Bowman) $2,050

A gilt-bronze mantel clock with figure of George Washington, signed by *Stiennon, Paris*, second half 19th century, 13in. high. (Christie's) $12,650

An alabaster and ormolu mounted architectural mantel clock with six sculptured figures, the dial with automatons, signed *Peter Rau in Wien*, late 18th century, 66cm. high. (Finarte) $10,090

A Lalique clock 'Insepérables', after 1926, clear opalescent glass, molded with two pairs of birds perched on branches flanking the circular clock face, 4¼in. sq. (Sotheby's) $1,472

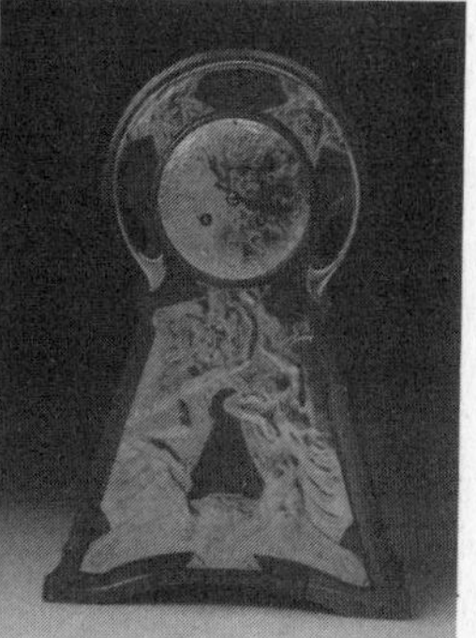

A tropical wood and ormolu mounted Art Nouveau style mantel clock, the spreading base with gilt bronze reliefs of Art Nouveau maidens, Paris, Japy Frères, circa 1900, 38cm. high. (Lempertz) $2,093

A French mahogany and gilt brass mystery timepiece, early 20th century, the four pillar going-barrel movement with square plates stamped *A*C Paris No. 198*, 14¼in. high. (Christie's) $12,999

An unusual French silver revolving cube desk compendium, circa 1900, twin thermometers, aneroid barometer, calendar and compass, cased, 7.5cm. (Bonhams) $4,160

A gilt ormolu and bronzed figural mantel clock, French, circa 1830, the drum bell striking movement with a silk suspension in a bronzed drum case with bow and quiver, 15in. (Bonhams) $2,433

An oak cuckoo desk clock, with enamel dial with Roman numerals, steel hands, pierced brass works with anchor escapement, circa 1930.
(Auction Team Köln) $196

An enamel and silver gilt minute repeating desk timepiece, Swiss, 1920s, the fine nickel 8 day movement repeating on two wire gongs, in a 6 sided case with blue and black enamel with chinoiserie decoration, 8in.
(Bonhams) $2,772

Jaeger Le Coultre 'Atmos' Swiss made brass revolving pendulum mantel clock, glazed case, 7in.
(G.A. Key) $556

A carved beech cuckoo mantel clock, Black Forest, mid 19th century, 4½in. chapter with raised figures, the brass movement with twin going barrels, pierced plates stamped *GHS*, 17½in.
(Bonhams) $659

A gilt metal quarter striking table clock, signed *Antoni Barisch, Fecit, Cracovie,* first half 18th century, in a case with a molded and scalloped edge, glazed lower panels with silvered borders, 3in. high. (Bonhams) $9,106

A carved beech cuckoo mantel clock, Black Forest, circa 1870, the twin fusee wooden posted movement sounding on a cuckoo and wire gong in a typical chalet style case, 20in.
(Bonhams) $455

A French brass and champlevé enamel eight-glass striking mantel clock, last quarter 19th century, the glasses divided by reeded pilasters, on stepped and molded bow-sided base, 17in. high.
(Christie's) $1,398

A black onyx, gold and diamond set desk timepiece, Cartier, 1920s, gilt dial with pierced diamond set hands, 8 day damascened nickel 19 jewel movement, 3in.
(Bonhams) $8,624

Federal mahogany pillar and scroll mantel clock, Seth Thomas, Plymouth, Connecticut, circa 1825, the scrolled cresting joining three plinths and brass urn finials, 31½in. high. (Skinner) $2,415

A Victorian 16in. double fusee brass skeleton clock striking on a gong. (Dockree's) $2,062

19th century single train skeleton clock, bell striking movement, circular Arabic chapter ring by Thwaites, within an oval glass dome on ebonized socle, 12½in. (G A Key) $1,600

Victorian brass skeleton timepiece, 19th century, with scrolled supports and rosewood base, with glass dome, 14½in. high. (Skinner) $1,955

A chiming skeleton clock with a triple calendar, English, unsigned, 19th century, triple fusee movement with a polished rafter type frame, on an ebonized base under a glass dome, 17½in. (Bonhams) $2,983

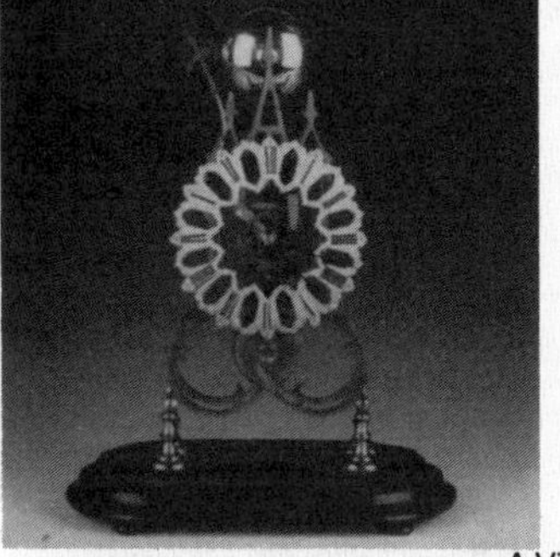

A brass skeleton timepiece with passing strike,English, mid 19th century, 42cm. (Bonhams) $628

A Victorian brass and mahogany skeleton timepiece, unsigned, third quarter 19th century, the pierced brass frame with six double-screwed pillars with single chain fusee and anchor escapement, 13in. over dome. (Christie's) $903

Victorian brass skeleton clock, mid-19th century, single fusee with Gothic spire arches, on a marble base with glass dome, 14in. high. (Skinner) $1,200

A Regency brass skeleton timepiece, first quarter 19th century, with skeletonized Arabic chapter ring, on oval base signed *John Pace Bury St. Edmunds No. 251*, 9¾in. high overall. (Christie's) $1,619

A 19th century cathedral skeleton clock with double fusee repeater movement, striking on a gong and bell. (Andrew Hartley) $3,864

A Viennese oak long duration wall regulator, Anton Kauba; third quarter 19th century, the movement with rectangular plates with four pillars, deadbeat escapement and maintaining power, 57in. high.
(Christie's) $3,069

A 19th century French vineyard wall clock, the 30cm. circular repaired alabaster dial in a case with brass and tortoiseshell inlays, 61cm. high.
(Bonhams) $680

An Edwardian mahogany wall regulator, Dent, London, circa 1915, the case with molded base and double locks to the glazed door, 4ft.7½in. high.
(Christie's) $5,778

A Black Forest carved and painted wood cuckoo and quail wall clock, early 20th century, the case of chalet form, with cresting of crossed rifles centered by a calf's head, 36in. high.
(Christie's) $2,236

A French glass dial mystery clock, Henri Robert, Paris, fourth quarter 19th century, the silvered metal counter-balanced hands containing watch movements, 16in. high.
(Christie's) $4,333

An eight day wall timepiece, the convex painted 12in. dial inscribed *Cattaneo & Co., Stockton*, in a mahogany case, 55cm.
(Tennants) $1,648

A mahogany and gilt-bronze clock and barometer, French, circa 1880, in the Empire style, the clock with a Japy Freres movement striking on a coiled gong, each 151cm. high.
(Sotheby's) $20,873

A George III ormolu mounted mahogany large wall clock, Brockbanks, London, the case with a central cream painted Roman dial with pierced and chased brass hands, 49in. square.
(Christie's) $9,027

A Biedermeier walnut month-going wall regulator, Anton Lorenz, Tornau, the case with concave-molded caddy top to the hood with glazed sides to the trunk, 59in. high. (Christie's) $46,943

\ mahogany wall timepiece signed
. *Mears & Co. Camden Town*,
9th century, 16in.
Bonhams) $474

A George II black japanned tavern clock, Sumart, the octagonal dial with Roman and Arabic chapters, the trunk decorated with raised gilt Chinoiserie figures above a glazed lenticle, 4ft. 4in. high.
(Christie's) $6,319

A mahogany dial fusee wall timepiece, English 1900s, 40cm.
(Bonhams) $480

Louis XV style gilt bronze cartel
ɔck, late 19th century, the case
ıst with scrolls and foliage to the
ırders, the white enamel dial
scribed *P. Lombard A Paris, 26*
'ace Vendôme, 31in. high.
:hristie's) $3,200

A bronzed case striking bulk wall clock with a mahogany travelling box, Dent, circa 1875, the twin fusee movement with owl shaped plates, fitted in a square mahogany box with a sliding back and flush top handle, 9¾ x 9¾in.
(Bonhams) $5,544

A French gilt bronze cartel clock, 19th century, the rectangular case with outset fluted pilasters surmounted by a garlanded cherub holding a dolphin, 27½in. high.
(Christie's) $2,760

ı oak cased single fusee wall
ɔck, the 33cm. painted dial with
ɔman numerals signed *Dent,61*
'rand. London 1682, set in a
olded oak case, 46cm. diameter.
ıonhams) $1,134

A Victorian dial clock, the twin fusee movement striking on a bell, the dial inscribed *John Monks Bolton*, in a mahogany case, with integral carved fretwork bracket, 44cm. (Bearne's) $1,113

A brass cased ship's style wall clock, fitted with a 18cm. circular dial with Roman numerals and a brass shaped bezel, 23cm. diameter. (Bonhams) $308

Important regulator calendar clock in walnut veneers, by Seth Thomas Clock Co., patent date of March 4th, 1862, 41½in. high.
(Eldred's) $2,200

A George I chinoiserie-decorated 'Act of Parliament' wall clock, Edward Pinchbeck, early 18th century, the waisted case below with figures and animals in an architectural niche, 5ft 8in.
(Sotheby's) $6,900

B.B. Lewis walnut calendar clock, 19th century, carved elements at top, sides and bottom, 29½in. long
(Eldred's) $3,080

A rosewood and mother of pearl inlaid striking wall clock, Marshall, Sunderland, circa 1860, the double fusee movement with shaped plates and striking on a bell, the chamfered bezel decorated with mother of pearl inlay, 29in.
(Bonhams) $1,309

Continental giltwood wall clock, mid 19th century, with gilt composition foliate decoration and a shadowbox frame.
(Skinner) $460

An oak cased drop dial railway wal timepiece, John Walker, 20th century, the single fusee movemen with shaped plates in a case with a turned surround with pegged back and drop trunk, 17in.
(Bonhams) $1,09

A rare No. 25R Symphonion and wall clock combination for 30cm. tinplate disks, 84-tone double comb, clock with 14 day movement, circa 1900, 165cm. high.
(Auction Team Köln) $5,024

A mahogany and brass inlaid octagonal wall timepiece, English, early 19th century, restored 10in. convex painted dial signed for Collier Commercial Rd London, single fusee movement.
(Bonhams) $1,884

An electromagnetic pendulum clock, silvered dial with arabic numerals, oak case with glazed door, with Swedish instructions, circa 1930.
(Auction Team Köln) $25

Waterbury Clock Co. drop regulator clock, 19th century, in walnut with geometric inlay, 27½in. high. (Eldred's) $440

A Victorian mahogany drop dial timepiece with eight day fusee movement, 12in. circular dial, 24in. overall. (Dockrees) $576

A French 19th century wall clock with striking mechanism, 29in. overall. (Dockrees) $272

A Federal mahogany and églomisé banjo clock, E. Howard & Company, Boston Massachusetts, circa 1840, the circular molded frame opening to a white enamelled dial with Roman numerals, approximate height 28in. (Sotheby's) $1,955

A mahogany case wall dial timepiece, English, 1920s, 11in. painted dial, the single fusee movement in a case with a turned surround and pegged back. (Bonhams) $539

A gilt ormolu cartel wall clock, French, 19th century, 5½in. convex enamel dial, the bell striking movement in a drum case surmounted with acanthus C scroll foliage, 23in. (Bonhams) $1,884

A weight driven quarter striking wall clock, Black Forest, early 19th century, 8in. shaped dial decorated with flowers in the corners, with wooden movement with twin bells striking on the quarters, 11in. (Bonhams) $706

An oak cased drop dial railway wall timepiece, English, 20th century, 8in. restored painted dial marked *LNER* and numbered *6061*, single fusee movement, 13in. (Bonhams) $1,020

A 19th century walnut Vienna regulator wall clock, the three train movement with a dead beat escapement, 4ft.4in. (Woolley & Wallis) $1,320

An early 20th century Swiss lever in a gold and enamel dress watch with equine decoration, signed *Union Horlogere*, circa 1920, diameter 46mm.
(Pieces of Time) $1,829

A late 18th century verge with polychrome enamel dial in silver repoussé pair cases and decorative underpainted horn protective outer, signed *Seamoure London*, 51mm. diameter, 14mm. deep.
(Pieces of Time) $2,783

A gold enamel verge pocketwatch signed *Terrot & Thuillier à Geneve*, 1780s, the frosted gilt chain fusee movement with bridgecock and square baluster pillars, 44mm. diameter. (Christie's) $2,167

A Rolex Prince Imperial steel and black enamel barrel-shaped pocket watch with 'Duo-Dial' and Observatory movement, circa 1935, 37 x 41mm.
(Finarte) $3,087

A white gold slim openface keyless pocketwatch with a length of white gold chain, signed *Vacheron & Constantin*, 1930s, 46mm. diameter. (Christie's) $1,714

A silver gilt, enamel and seed pearl minute repeating chronograph hunter pocketwatch, unsigned. 55mm. diameter, London 1815.
(Christie's) $2,708

A fine and rare gold quarter repeating cylinder hunter pocketwatch, signed *Breguet*, 1810s, the frost gilt movement with three armed monometallic balance, Breguet's temperature curb.
(Christie's) $32,499

A mid 18th century English verge with polychrome painted dial in silver pair cases, white enamel dial, a rural polychrome enamel scene at the center, signed *J Garnet London* circa 1754, 49in. diameter.
(Pieces of Time) $1,080

A fine slim 18ct. open faced keyless minute repeating chronograph pocketwatch, signed *Cartier*, 1910s, the frosted gilt movement jeweled to the hammers with bimetallic balance, 50mm. diameter.
(Christie's) $16,250

Napoleonic gold openface two minute tourbillon pocketwatch with modified ruby Duplex escapement, signed *E. Buffat, Fec: & Inven.*, 1860s, 52mm. diameter. (Christie's) $67,981

A late 17th century English verge with silver champlevé sun and moon dial in silver consular case, signed *Jon Williamson*, circa 1695, 56mm. diameter. (Pieces of Time) $5,247

A gold and enamel verge pocketwatch, inscribed *Breguet*, early 19th century, in openface gold case, the back with a painted scene of two ladies in a park, 48mm. diameter. (Christie's) $2,166

A gold repoussé quarter repeating pair case verge pocketwatch, signed *Hen Hester, London*, 1720s, chased and pierced inner case with floral design incorporating mythical birds, 46mm. diameter. (Christie's) $5,055

A silver pair case and tortoiseshell pocketwatch, signed *John Knibb at Oxon,* late 17th century, in plain silver case, in a tortoiseshell outer case with silver pinwork and silver wire inlay, movement signed, 52mm. diameter. (Christie's) $10,472

An early 19th century Swiss quarter repeating automaton verge with concealed erotic scene in a gold open face case, full plate fusee movement, signed *Girod Columby a Geneve*, 56mm. diameter. (Pieces of Time) $18,682

An important 22ct. gold calendar and moonphase à tact pocket watch with regulator dial, temperature indication and stopwatch facility, signed *Hunt & Roskell,* 1838, 53mm. diameter. (Christie's) $30,693

A fine late 17th century English verge with silver champlevé sun and moon dial in decorative silver and tortoiseshell pair cases, signed *Smith London*, circa 1685, 54mm. diameter, 18mm. deep. (Pieces of Time) $9,301

A fine 22 carat gold, enamel and diamond set quarter repeating triple cased verge pocket watch for the Turkish market, signed on the movement *Edward Prior, London*, 1810s, 50mm. diameter outer case. (Christie's) $9,027

A 19th century English verge in silver pair cases, full plate fusee movement with round pillars, signed John Stubbs Keyworth, 59mm. diameter.
(Pieces of Time) $676

Large plated cased travelling watch with button wind in fitted leather and silver fronted case, bearing the Sheffield hallmark for 1909.
(G.A. Key) $159

An early 20th century American railroad lever in a rolled gold open face case, signed *B W Raymond Elgin Illinois*, circa 1910, 54mm. diameter.
(Pieces of Time) $464

A rare early 17th century German verge clockwatch with the bell under the dial in a gilt metal and rock crystal case, signed *MK*, circa 1620, 37 x 77 x 35mm.
(Pieces of Time) $26,400

A fine Swiss cylinder watch with offset dial set in a silver Prussian coin, signed *S Friedeburg Sohne Berlin*, circa 1855, diameter 34mm.
(Pieces of Time) $3,176

A late 18th century French verge ir a gilt and enamel form watch, on reverse of the case the dial is replaced by a polychrome enamel scene of a native figure holding a longbow, signed *Breguet a Paris*, circa 1790, 71 x 115mm.
(Pieces of Time) $5,600

A Swiss lever watch set into a gilt petrol cigarette lighter, the watch housed in the lower section of the reeded case, wound and set by a flat button in the base, signed *Colibri*, circa 1960, 41 x 52mm. (Pieces of Time) $517

A late 19th century Swiss quarter repeating lever automaton in a gold full hunter case, either side of the dial are of cupid and a larger winged figure holding a scythe, signed *Volta*, circa 1890, 54mm. diameter.
(Pieces of Time) $5,406

An early 20th century Swiss lever gold octagonal dress watch, circula keyless nickelled bar movement with going barrel, hallmarked London 1922, 47mm. diameter.
(Pieces of Time) $1,03

Large nickel cased eight day travelling watch with button wind, in silver travelling case with hinged front, easel back, 3½ x 3½in., London 1920 by the Goldsmiths and Silversmiths Co.
(G A Key) $207

A mid 19th century Swiss crab tooth duplex with mock pendulum dial in a silver full hunter case, the white enamel dial with a representation of a French mantel clock, circa 1850, 51mm. diameter.
(Pieces of Time) $1,760

An unusual gold and pearl set pendant watch, unsigned 1820s, in diamond shaped case, the pearl set bezel secured by two screws to the band, 33 x 22mm.
(Christie's) $3,818

A late 19th century Swiss cylinder in a gunmetal open face case, on reverse a small glazed aperture revealing rotating disk bearing photographically reproduced nudes. circa 1890, 51mm. diameter.
(Pieces of Time) $2,320

An Ingersoll Mickey Mouse pocket watch depicting Mickey on the face, the animated hour and minute hands as his arms with yellow painted hands, 1930s, 2in. diameter. (Christie's) $687

A 19th century keyless fusee English lever with up/down dial in a watertight silver case, signed *Lund & Blockley To the Queen 42 Pall Mall London* , $\frac{2}{958}$ hallmarked *London 1878*, 59mm. diameter.
(Pieces of Time) $6,042

A late 19th century Swiss cylinder with Hebrew dial in an open face case, the cast back depicting a Rabbi reading from the Torah, signed *Wizard Levy – Swiss*, circa 1890, 51mm. diameter.
(Pieces of Time) $720

A gold montre à tact pocketwatch with eccentric dial, signed Breguet, 1830, in engine-turned case with gold à tact hand to the reverse and platinum touchpieces in the band for the hours, 38mm. diameter.
(Christie's) $28,888

An early 20th century Swiss goliath 8 day lever in a silver open face case, nickelled split three quarter plate keyless movement with going barrel, signed *Octava Watch Co. Switzerland*, 67mm. diameter.
(Pieces of Time) $596

A lady's diamond and ruby set wristwatch, signed *Piaget*, 1970s, oval bark effect gilt dial with Roman numerals, mechanical movement, oval case, Piaget bracelet, 29 x 25mm. (Christie's) $4,361

A gentleman's 9ct. gold octagonal wristwatch, signed *Rolex Oyster*, 1926, engine turned silvered dial with Arabic numerals, 33 x 32mm. (Christie's) $1,999

A gentleman's 14ct gold triple calendar center seconds wristwatch, signed *Movado,* circa 1950, two-tone silvered dial with gilt dot and Arabic numerals, 34mm. diameter. (Christie's) $1,272

A pink gold wristwatch, signed *Patek Philippe*, 1950s, the nickel plated movement jeweled to the center with gyromax balance and the Geneva seal of quality, micrometer regulation, 35 x 28mm. (Christie's) $5,055

An 18ct. gold self-winding minute repeating wristwatch, signed *Patek Philippe*, recent, the nickel plated self-winding movement, with 22ct. gold micro-rotor, 41 jewels, 33mm. diameter. (Christie's) $192,325

A gilt/steel self-winding and water resistant calendar chronograph wristwatch, signed *Breitling*, recent, with self-winding movement, the white dial with raised gilt Arabic numerals, 39mm. diameter. (Christie's) $1,805

A gentleman's 18ct. gold tonneau shaped automatic center seconds wristwatch, signed *Franck Muller, Geneve, Chronometro*, engine turned silvered dial with Roman numerals, blued steel hands, 43 x 30mm. (Christie's) $6,905

A gentleman's pink gold reversible wristwatch signed *Jaeger-LeCoultre*, Model Reverso, recent, with mechanical movement, the black dial with stylized Arabic numerals, 38 x 23mm. (Christie's) $3,972

A stainless steel and yellow metal top automatic center second wristwatch, Rolex, Bubbleback, 1930s, refinished black dial, the nickel chronometer movement in a case with an engraved bezel, 31mm. (Bonhams) $1,099

An 18ct. gold self winding and water resistant calendar wristwatch, signed *Audemars Piguet*, model Millenary, recent, with self winding mechanical movement, 39 x 34mm. diameter. (Christie's) $3,611

A gentleman's 18ct. gold wristwatch, signed *Audemars Piguet*, 1980s, white dial with Roman numerals, dauphine hands, with gold buckle, 30mm. (Christie's) $1,454

Mido, a gentleman's rare and early 9ct. gold wristwatch in the form of a car radiator, 1926, silver engine turned dial with applied gilt Arabic numerals, 34 x 25mm. (Christie's) $3,634

A gentleman's stainless steel automatic dual time zone and calendar wristwatch, signed *Rolex, model: Oyster Perpetual GMT-Master*, 1970s, diameter of bezel 39mm, with a Rolex box. (Christie's) $1,999

A rose precious metal chronograph wristwatch, Universal, Aero-Compax, 1940s, discolored silvered dial with subsidiaries for running seconds, 30 minutes, 12 hours and elapsed setting dial, 37mm. (Bonhams) $1,570

A bi-color automatic center seconds calendar bracelet watch, Rolex, Perpetual date, black dial, the nickel 28 jewel chronometer movement with 5 adjustments in a case with a bright cut bezel, 26mm. (Bonhams) $864

An 18ct. gold diamond and ruby set water resistant quartz wristwatch, signed *Chopard, Model St. Moritz*, 1980s, with quartz movement, the pavé diamond gold dial with ruby set five minute markers, 32 x 32mm. (Christie's) $9,027

Cartier, a rare gold reversible wristwatch, signed *Cartier*, 1940s, with nickel plated movement, jeweled to the center with gold alloy balance, adjusted to three positions, 25 x 24mm. (Christie's) $9,028

A gentleman's stainless steel quartz chronograph wristwatch, signed *Jaeger Le Coultre, Chronographe, model: Kryos*, circa 1990. white dial with baton markers, 35mm. (Christie's) $1,272

A chrome octagonal cased wristwatch, Rolex, Oyster, 1930s, the 17 jewel nickel movement in a case with screw down button and back, 33mm.
(Bonhams) $659

A gentleman's 18ct. gold automatic calendar wristwatch, signed *Patek Philippe*, circa 1980, cushion shaped gilt dial with applied gilt baton markers, 35mm.
(Christie's) $6,360

An 18ct. pink gold water resistant self-winding chronograph wristwatch, signed *Breguet Type XX, Model Aeronavale*, recent, with self-winding movement, 40mm. diameter. (Christie's) $8,125

A slim white gold wristwatch signed *Audemars Piguet*, 1970s, the nickel plated movement, jeweled to the center with gold alloy balance, adjusted to temperatures and to four positions, 35mm. diameter.
(Christie's) $1,625

An 18ct. yellow gold self-winding moonphase wristwatch with power reserve indication, signed *Patek Philippe*, recent, the nickel plated self-winding movement with gold micro-rotor, 29 jewels, 35mm. diameter.
(Christie's) $10,833

A gentleman's platinum tourbillon wristwatch with calendar and power reserve, signed *Blancpain Tourbillon, No. 100,* recent, subsidiary calendar dial and power reserve sector, 34mm. diameter.
(Christie's) $29,072

An 18 carat gold wristwatch, signed *Audemars Piguet, model Carnegie,* recent, with mechanical movement, white enamel dial with stylized Arabic quarter hour marks and raised gold five minute indexes, 24 x 25mm. (Christie's) $1,986

A gentleman's steel and gilt automatic calendar wristwatch, signed *Rolex Oyster Perpetual date*, 1970s, self-winding movement, steel case with gold casing, 32mm.
(Christie's) $1,272

A gold electronic calendar wristwatch, signed *Omega, Constellation Megaquartz,* 1960s, with electronic movement, the gray textured dial with baton minute ring, 48 x 31mm.
(Christie's) $2,708

A limited edition stainless steel self-winding water resistant calendar chronograph wristwatch, signed *Longines, Model Lusitania 75*, recent, 40mm. diameter.
(Christie's) $3,430

A stainless steel center seconds military wristwatch, International Watch Company, MK X1, 1952, black dial, the damascened nickel movement jeweled to the center, 38mm. (Bonhams) $1,884

A fine steel calendar chronograph water resistant wristwatch, signed *Rolex, Oyster Chronograph Anti-Magnetic*, 1930s, with mechanical movement, 36mm. diameter.
(Christie's) $14,444

A steel water resistant self winding calendar wristwatch in asymmetric case, signed *Breitling, Model Chronomatic*, 1960s, with self winding movement, the two tone and brown dial with raised luminous baton numerals.
(Christie's) $1,444

A gentleman's steel and gold automatic dual time zone and calendar wristwatch, signed Rolex, model: Oyster Perpetual Date GMT-Master II, 1990s, black dial with luminous dot and baton markers, diameter of bezel 40mm.
(Christie's) $3,997

A rare yellow gold perpetual calendar and chronograph wristwatch, signed *Patek Philippe*, 1960s, the nickel plated movement with bimetallic balance and micrometer regulation, 37mm. diameter.
(Christie's) $67,981

A limited edition platinum self-winding and water resistant perpetual calendar and moonphase wristwatch with carousel, signed *Audemars Piguet*, model Royal Oak, 1990s, 39 x 39mm.
(Christie's) $30,693

A 14ct gold automatic center seconds wristwatch on a gold bracelet, Rolex, Oyster perpetual chronometer, 1960s, gilt dial with dagger marks, the nickel movement in a polished case, 34mm.
(Bonhams) $1,649

An 18ct gold automatic center seconds calendar watch on a gold bracelet, Omega, Constellation, 1970, gilt dial, the pink gilt 24 jewel movement adjusted to 6 positions, 18ct gold mesh bracelet, 35mm x 185mm. (Bonhams) $785

A stainless steel limited edition self-generating quartz water resistant calendar chronograph wristwatch, signed *Seiko, Model Kinetic Chronograph,* 42mm. diameter. (Christie's) $1,986

A gentleman's 18ct. gold automatic wristwatch with hooded lugs, signed *Rolex Oyster Perpetual Certified Chronometer*, 1940s, 30mm. (Christie's) $6,360

A rare pink gold asymmetric wristwatch, signed *Cartier*, 1930s, the nickel plated movement jeweled to the center with gold alloy balance, signed *LeCoultre*, 36 x 20mm.(Christie's) $14,444

An 18 carat gold self-winding wristwatch with 24 hour and astronomic indications, signed *Ulysee Nardin, Model Astrolabium Galileo Galilei*, 1990s, chased and engraved gilt movement, 40mm. diameter.(Christie's) $13,541

A stainless steel chronograph bracelet watch, Omega, Speedmaster, 1970s, black dial, the pink gilt 17 jewel movement in a case with a tachymeter scale on the bezel, 40mm.(Bonhams) $754

An 18ct gold rectangular cased quartz wristwatch, Cartier Française, recent, silvered dial, the Swiss made movement in a curved polished case with box and paper work, 25mm x 30mm. (Bonhams) $1,884

A rare platinum rectangular wristwatch, signed *Rolex*, model Prince Brancard, 1930s, the nickel plated extra prima movement numbered *77657* with bimetallic balance jeweled to the third, 42 x 24mm. (Christie's) $18,055

A large pink gold water resistant chronograph wristwatch, signed *Longines*, 1950s, the nickel plated movement jeweled to the center with gold alloy balance, 38mm. diameter. (Christie's) $2,705

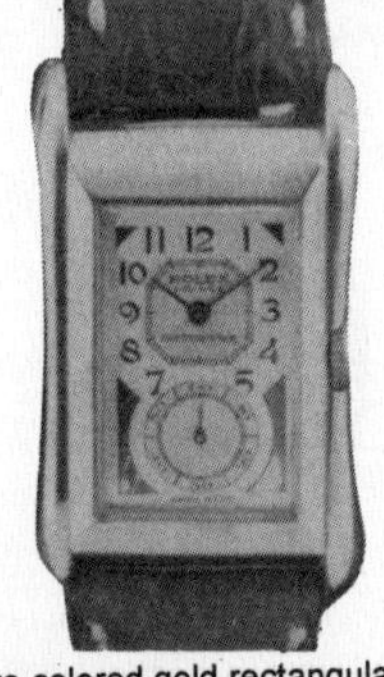

A two colored gold rectangular wristwatch with waisted case, signed *Rolex*, model Prince Brancard, 1930s, nickel plated chronometer movement with gold alloy balance, 42 x 26mm. (Christie's) $10,833

One of a pair of large cloisonné enamel censers, early 19th century, each of ovoid outline, decorated with various animals on a turquoise background, supported by three cranes, on black marble bases, 32in. high.
(Christie's) (Two) $14,720

A pair of Qianlong cloisonné polychrome aquaria, decorated with cypress trees, aquatic creatures, wading birds and flowers, on 19th century bronze stands.
(Galerie Moderne) $11,569

A Chinese cloisonné moon flask with globular neck and twin gilt metal dragon handles, decorated with a multitude of peonies and foliage, on a turquoise ground, 15½in. high, 18th century.
(Christie's) $2,725

A large Chinese cloisonné and gilt bronze tripod censer and domed cover, with seated Buddhistic lion finial, pierced angular handles and lion head and paw feet, turquoise ground, 40in. high, Qianlong six-character mark, 19th century.
(Christie's) $3,634

A cloisonné vase and cover, attributed to Namikawa Yasuyuki, 19th century, decorated in gold and silver wire and various colored enamels with bands of stylized geometric design and another with ho-o birds, 9.2cm. high.
(Christie's) $6,860

Cloisonné enamel covered jar, Meiji period, in inverted pear shape with butterfly and flower reserves on an aventurine ground, 4½in. high.
(Eldreds) $121

Cloisonné enamel plate, Meiji period, depicting a chrysanthemum garden surrounded by a floral border, diameter 9¾in.
(Eldreds) $192

A cloisonné and en plein enamel casket marked *K. Fabergé*, Moscow 1908-17, the domed hinged cover with an enamel plaque depicting The Return from Church, 15cm. wide.
(Christie's) $46,092

A cloisonné enamel napkin ring marked with the cyrillic initials of Fedor Rückert, Moscow, 1896-1908, enamelled with geometric motifs, 4.8cm. diameter.
(Christie's) $1,249

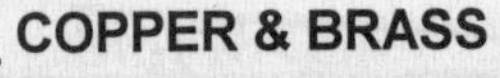

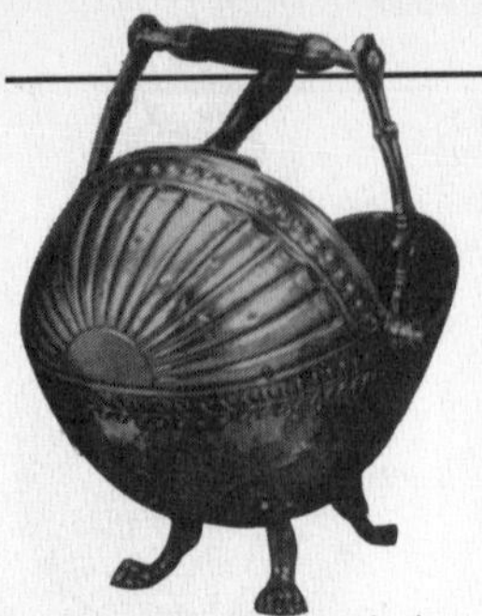

An Edwardian brass purdonium, early 20th century, the ovoid body with turned handle and on paw feet, the canopy impressed with stylised fan paterae, with integral handle, 20in. long. (Christie's) $817

A Northern European oval repoussé decorated copper jardinière, late 19th century, the sides with a flowering urn and dolphins, 27in. wide. (Christie's) $1,453

An American gilded copper figure of a cockerel, late 19th/early 20th century, naturalistically moulded, one leg lacking a spur, 25¼in. high. (Bonhams) $1,120

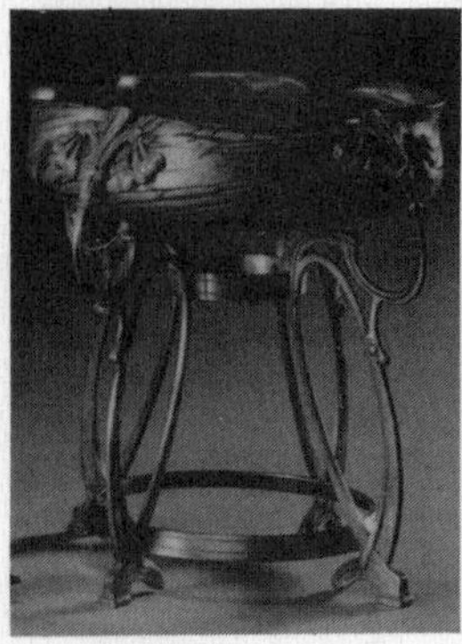

A Loetz iridescent coupe and mount, circa 1900, openwork brass mount modelled as stylized floral forms with berried terminals, 27.5cm. high. (Sotheby's) $2,167

A pair of rock crystal and silvered brass six light candelabra, late 19th or early 20th century, the scrolling branches supporting faceted nozzles and hexagonal drip pans, 21in. high. (Christie's) $12,701

Peter Behrens for AEG, electric tea kettle and cover, designed 1908, manufactured circa 1908, nickel plated brass, of octagonal section, decorated with beading, wicker covered handle, 20cm. (Sotheby's) $901

A Dutch brass carriage or foot warmer, possibly late 17th or early 18th century, of octagonal form, with pierced cover and embossed sides, the doors with rolled rivets, with loop handle, 8¼in. wide. (Christie's) $638

Walter Gropius and Adolf Mayer, one of four sets of nickel-plated brass door furniture, designed 1928, manufactured by Wehag and S.S. Loewy, each comprising a pair of door handles and a pair of escutcheons. (Christie's) (Four) $1,625

An English copper-alloy mortar, 17th century, the flared reeded body cast twice with the Royal Carolean Arms, within a circlet, 4½in. high. (Christie's) $1,090

19th century brass casket, domed rectangular form, elaborately molded with Art Nouveau style scrolls, foliage etc., enclosing a plush lined interior, 7½in.
(G.A. Key) $159

Peter Behrens, a nickel-plated electric kettle, designed 1909 for AEG, with turned wooden finial and cane-bound handle, 7¼in. high.
(Christie's) $992

Copper slave tax badge, Charleston, South Carolina, early 19th century, stamped *Charleston 2083 Servant 1835*, 2 x 2in.
(Skinner) $1,840

A copper tea and coffee service, with brass handles and feet, comprising coffee pot, tea pot sucrier, milk jug, and tray.
(Bonhams) $259

A Regency bronze and brass samovar, the oval molded lid with pierced finial surmounted by a sphinx, enclosing a pierced cover with a funnel and a well, the stepped sides with Greek-key molding, 15½in. high.
(Christie's) $1,272

A W.A.S. Benson kettle and cover, of compressed ovoid form with banded decoration and wicker covered handle, 18cm.
(Bonhams) $243

A Merry Phipson & Parker's Letter Clip, cast brass with steel spring, decorated with cast English arms, after 1843. (Auction Team Köln)
$178

A pair of French copper-bound brass ice-pails, of Regency style, late 19th/20th century, each with lappeted top and lion-mask handles on each side, 8in. high.
(Christie's) $2,011

A WMF brass tea kettle and burner, angular black wooden handle, Germany, circa 1910, 23.5cm. high.
(Stockholms AV) $298

19th century copper two handled circular samovar, applied with bone handles, brass tap, raised on quadruped base with balustered feet, 12½in.
(G A Key) $362

A late Victorian brass log bin, late 19th century, of cylindrical form, with bulbous base, with handle to slightly domed cover, 34in. high.
(Christie's) $4,360

A pair of 17th century Flemish brass candlesticks, each with a circular nozzle and wide drip pan on turned column, 24cm.
(Bearne's) $464

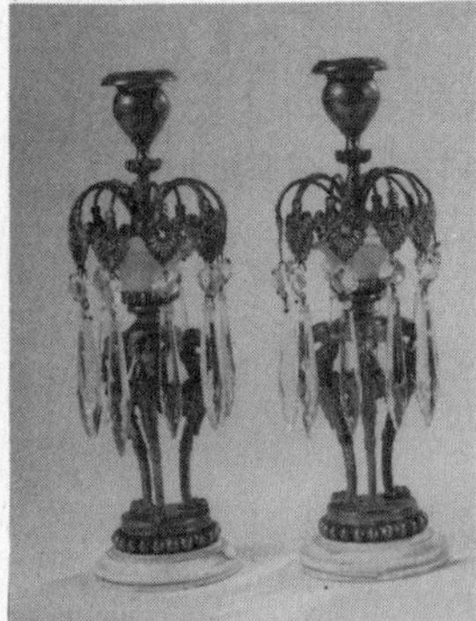

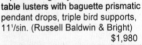

A pair of Regency brass framed table lusters with baguette prismatic pendant drops, triple bird supports, 11⅕in. (Russell Baldwin & Bright) $1,980

Continental brass basin on pedestal, 18th century, with wide flared lip and turned body and standard on a stepped circular foot, 10¼in. diameter.
(Skinner) $488

An early 19th century copper samovar, the campana shape body with stylized leaf borders, a detachable part ribbed cover to tinned liners, 14in. high.
(Woolley & Wallis) $304

Roycroft copper fruit tray, no. 805, East Aurora, New York, circa 1918, circular form of hammered copper with stylized rim decoration, 9¾in. diameter. (Skinner) $517

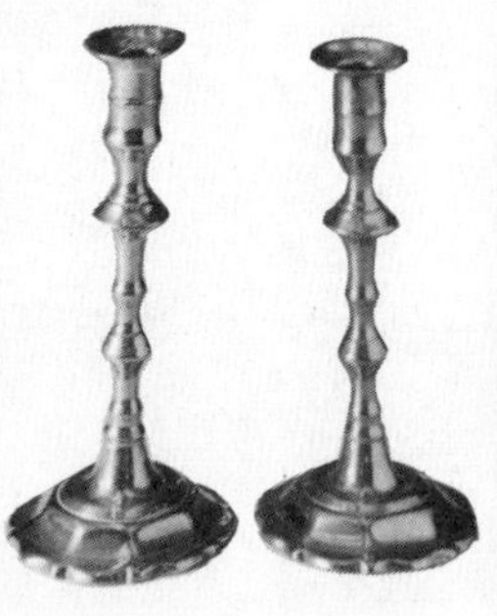

A pair of brass candlesticks, 18th century, each with flared candlecups and baluster stems above a scalloped domed base, 9½in. high.
(Sotheby's) $2,645

An English 'ball knop' candlestick, circa 1660, the ribbed stem with spherical knop above a spreading circular base, 5½in. high.
(Christie's) $6,400

Copper jelly mold, molded with central rosette design, 19th century, 5½in. (G A Key) $279

A brass curfew, Anglo-Flemish, late 17th/early 18th century, of typical outline, the handle and border repoussé and punch decorated with geometric ornament, 15¼in. wide. (Christie's) $515

A brass lion sejant, Low Countries, 17th century, either formerly a foot from a lectern or a Paschal candlestick, 8in. high. (Christie's) $1,280

Brass cigar lighter, in the form of Puck, 7½in. high. (Eldred's) $231

A pair of copper and green enamelled vases by Sir Hubert Von Herkomer, depicting figure scenes within raised banding, on circular foot, 10in. high. (Andrew Hartley) $1,944

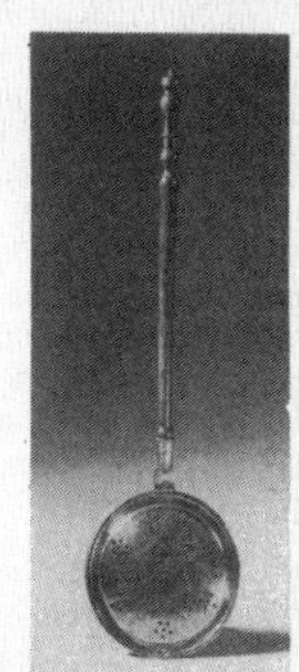

A good turned maple and bright-cut brass bedwarmer, probably New England, late 18th century, the ball finial above a shaped handle and tapering shaft, 44in. long. (Sotheby's) $1,725

A brass tinder box, 18th century, the cylindrical case with domed ends, with chain suspension loop, 4in. long. (Christie's) $549

Pair of brass candlesticks, England, mid-18th century, petal form base, 7½in. high. (Skinner) $805

A brass-bound mahogany oval churn, 19th century, with double handled two piece top enclosing a metal lined interior, 27in. wide. (Christie's) $4,600

A fine gentleman's Court suit of lime green ribbed velvet, comprising coat and breeches applied with silver thread trimmed with pink spangles, sequins and blue paste, the coat lined with pink satin, and waistcoats, circa 1770. (Christie's) $8,280

A Victorian dinner gown of pink shot silk, applied with black bands of fur pile, circa 1850s. (Woolley & Wallis) $797

Yves Saint Laurent, circa 1980, burgundy velvet Edwardian-inspired skirt and jacket ensemble, fitted jacket with high collar with taffeta neck ruffle, and full peplum three-quarter length skirt. (Skinner) $287

Oscar de la Renta, black and white evening dress, 1980s, one-shouldered floor-length dress, white bodice with diagonal rows of white beads and rhinestones, black silk organza skirt. (Skinner) $632

Christian Dior, periwinkle blue cocktail dress, mid-1950s, silk taffeta with round neckline, short sleeves, and full skirt, large bow at center front bodice with fringed ends hanging below waist. (Skinner) $690

Molyneux, orange and gold evening gown with wrap, late 1960s, orange silk with metallic gold trapunto quilting in abstract pattern, floor-length dress with camisole bodice. (Skinner) $373

Balenciaga, charcoal gray cocktail ensemble, 1950s, black brocaded silk three-piece ensemble, below-the-knee length straight skirt and boxy sleeveless top, boxy jacket.
(Skinner) $575

A Victorian three-piece ball gown in pink watered silk, last quarter of 19th century.
(Woolley & Wallis)
$1,162

Nettie Rosenstein, circa 1958, black silk cocktail-length sleeveless sheath dress, high-waisted cap-sleeved bodice of black guipure lace over flesh-colored net.
(Skinner) $287

Emilio Pucci, silk jersey cocktail dress, 1970s, with black skirt and printed bodice in black, white, and shades of gray and pink.
(Skinner) $517

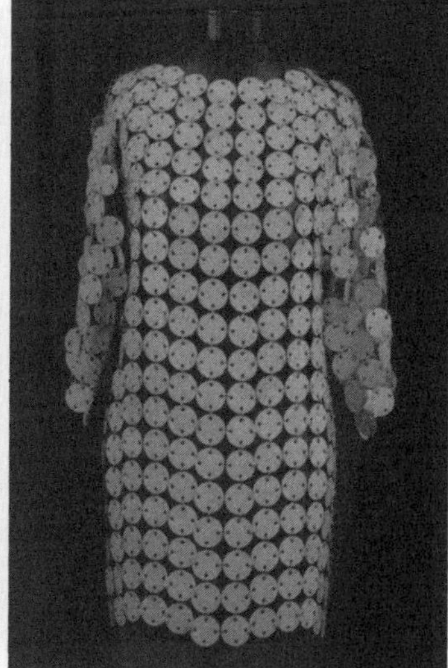

White plastic 'Disk' dress, 1960s, short-sleeved mini-dress composed of white plastic disks and small goldtone rings.
(Skinner) $431

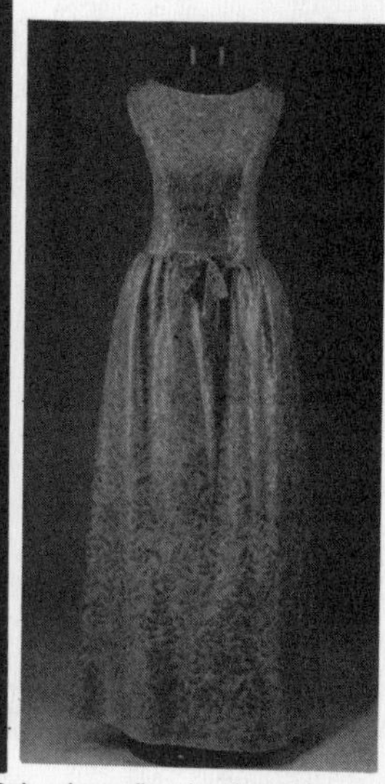

Balenciaga silver lamé evening gown, late 1950s, with matching jacket, sleeveless fitted bodice with jewel neckline and low round back, bow at center front waist.
(Skinner) $747

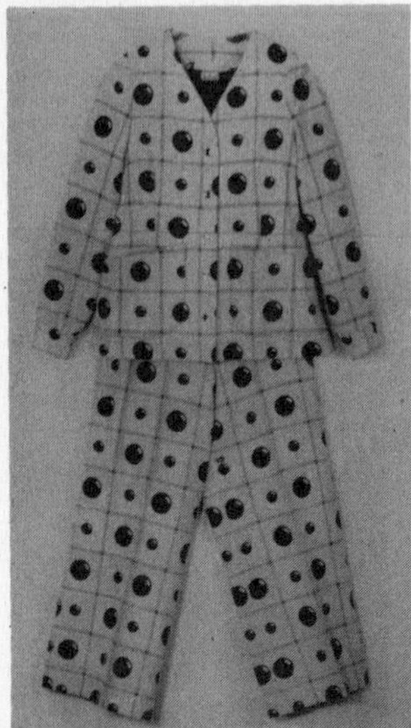

Stephen Burrows, yellow wool 'Bowling Ball' pantsuit, circa 1972, pale yellow and red wool jacket and pants set printed with a black bowling ball pattern.
(Skinner) $517

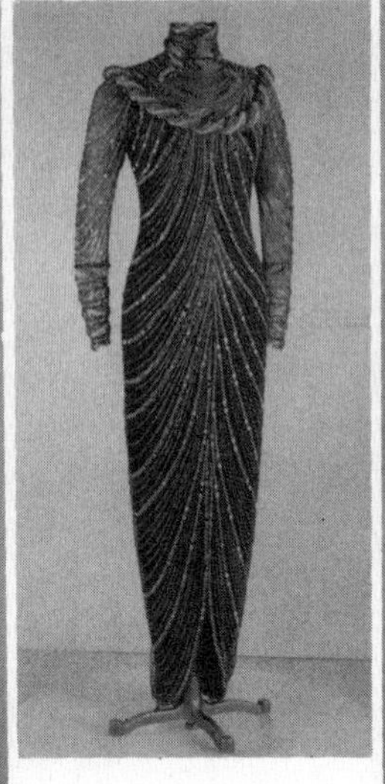

Bob Mackie, beaded evening dress, late 1970s, brown, gold, white, and silver beaded floor-length dress, brown net beaded with bugle beads and rhinestones, high-necked bodice adorned with trompe l'oeil necklace and twisted bead rope.
(Skinner) $747

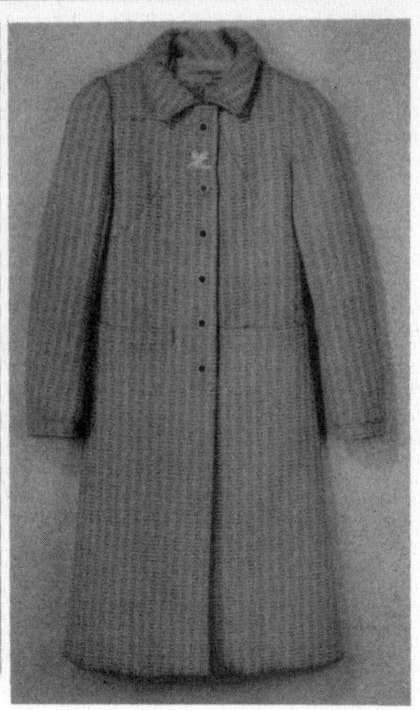

Courrèges, green and white wool coat, 1970s, three-quarter length, fitted silhouette with center front button closure, long sleeves, and pointed collar. (Skinner) $920

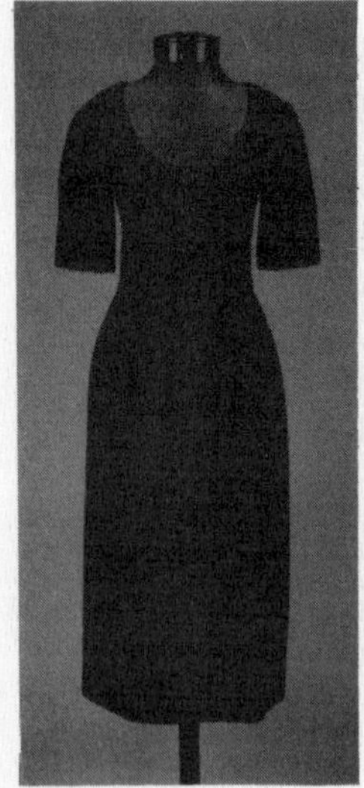

Norman Norell, salmon pink wool dress, 1970s, salmon pink wool bouclé three-quarter length dress, fitted bodice with round neckline and short sleeves.
(Skinner) $86

Valentino, sequinned cocktail suit, early 1980s, jacket and skirt with allover sequinned leopard and floral pattern in black, white, shades of gold, red, yellow, and purple.
(Skinner) $575

Ostrich feather evening dress, 1950s, black silk crepe and organza floor-length dress, fitted sheer black bodice with black ostrich feathers at shoulders, ostrich feather-trimmed net peplum.
(Skinner) $920

Jacques Heim, mint green evening gown with matching cape worn to John F. Kennedy inaugural celebration, 1961, with jewel neckline and plunging back. (Skinner) $575

Christian Dior, brown suede coat, 1970s, light brown double-breasted below-the-knee length fitted coat with brown fur lining, collar, and cuffs. (Skinner) $546

Christian Dior, black velvet evening gown, late 1950s, strapless fitted bodice with 2½in. grosgrain band extending horizontally around bust, grosgrain band at dropped waistline with bow to left side, US size 6. (Skinner) $1,150

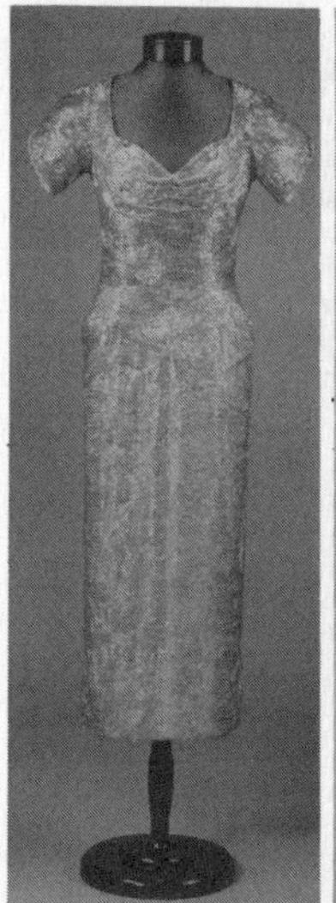

Howard Greer, silver cocktail dress, 1950s, ivory cotton dress with allover silver bugle beads and rhinestones in wave-like pattern, fitted silhouette with sweetheart neckline, short sleeves. (Skinner) $690

Chanel, red jacket and two-piece ensemble, circa 1985, wool blanket jacket with two large front pockets and red, white, and blue trim at collar, closure, pockets, cuffs and hem. (Skinner) $402

Sally Milgrim, 1937, black satin floor-length dress with net overdress, sleeveless satin dress with V-neck and plunging V-back and bias-cut skirt. (Skinner) $488

A Simon & Halbig character mold 1469, blue sleeping eyes, long blonde wig and adult jointed body wearing black and white striped dress, 14in. high. (Christie's) $924

An Ideal composition Shirley Temple doll, American, 1930s, with weighted green glass eyes, curly blonde wig, 21¼in. high.(Sotheby's) $541

A 'Reliable Toy' composition Shirley Temple doll, American, circa 1935, with weighted green eyes and real lashes, a five piece body with swivel head, 16in. (Bonhams) $174

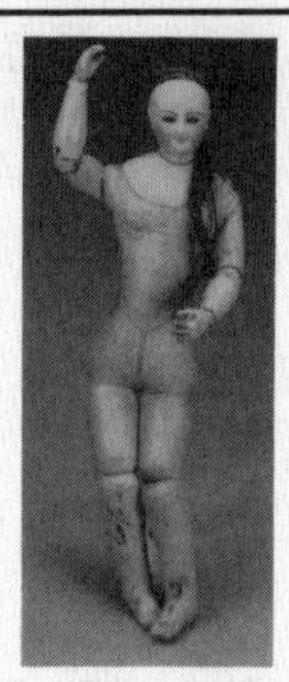

A smiling Bru swivel head doll, French, circa 1875, impressed *F*, with fixed blue glass eyes, cork pate, blonde wig, 17½in. high. (Sotheby's) $2,344

A 'Mon Tresor' bisque doll in original Jumeau box, French, circa 1900, the German head impressed *Mon Tresor 29,8*, blonde ringletted wig, 21in. high. (Sotheby's) $2,164

A S.F.B.J. mold 236, with brown sleeping eyes, open/close mouth, jointed composition body with the big toe detached from other toes, 24in. high. (Christie's) $619

A Jumeau bisque doll, French, circa 1895, with fixed blue paperweight eyes, open mouth, cork pate with dark brown wig, 27in. (Sotheby's) $1,803

A very rare Lucy Peck poured wax portrait doll modelled as the young Queen Victoria, dressed as Mary Queen of Scots, 32in. high. (Christie's) $13,628

A very rare George II wooden doll, English, circa 1740, the head and torso carved in one piece with enamelled glass eyes, 21¾in. high. (Sotheby's) $50,490

An Alt, Beck & Gottschalk bisque shoulderhead doll in Fresian costume, German, circa 1895, with domed head, cloth body with bisque lower arms, 18½in. high.(Sotheby's) $811

A fine poured wax doll of Queen Victoria as a child, English, circa 1830, blue glass eyes, cloth body with wax lower arms and legs, 22in. tall. (Bonhams) $869

A rare J.D. Kestner bisque character doll, German, circa 1910, with blue painted eyes, on a jointed wood and composition body, 14in. high. (Sotheby's) $3,246

ɬoreen, a Norah Wellings ‿ittle Bo Peep, with blue ɟide-glancing eyes, curly ɔrown wig and jointed felt ɔody, 30½in. high.
Christie's) $763

A pair of German celluloid dolls in traditional Norwegian dress, with blue sleeping eyes, open mouth, blonde and brown hair and stuffed body, 21in. high.
(Christie's) $796

A Schoenhut character child, with painted blue eyes, painted features, closed mouth, short blonde hair and jointed spring-jointed body, 15in. high.
(Christie's) $763

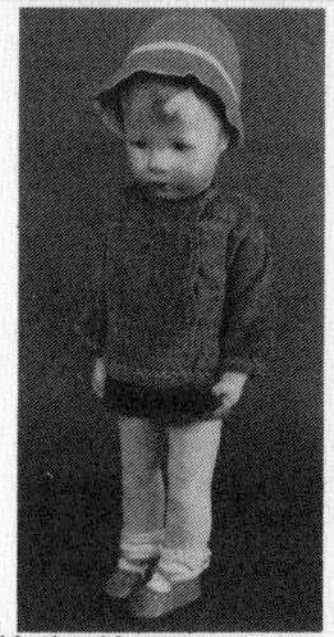

A Kathe Kruse Hampelchen doll XII, with painted #1 head sewn on, cloth body with button arrangement on back to let him stand, circa 1930s, 18in.
(Christie's) $1,817

)fficer, a Harwin felt 1st Vorld War soldier doll, fter Steiff, with center face eam, button eyes and riginal khaki felt uniform ith American cloth Sam rowne, 13½in. high.
Christie's) $763

A Jumeau walking doll, with fixed brown eyes, jointed composition body with walking mechanism in the stomach, with ticket dated *1879*, 22in. high.
(Christie's) $3,270

An Ideal Shirley Temple composition doll with green decal lashed sleeping eyes, blonde curly mohair wig and original red and white spotted dress, shoes and socks, 15in. high.
(Christie's) $265

A Simon & Halbig shoulder-head with brown lashed sleeping eyes, open mouth, pierced ears, short auburn hair, kid body and composition lower lims, 29in. high.
(Christie's) $635

A small Kämmer & Reinhardt bisque character doll, German, circa 1911, impressed *K*R 117/A 26*, with weighted blue eyes, 10½in. high.
(Sotheby's) $1,532

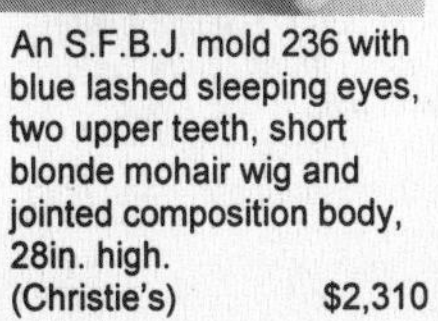

An S.F.B.J. mold 236 with blue lashed sleeping eyes, two upper teeth, short blonde mohair wig and jointed composition body, 28in. high.
(Christie's) $2,310

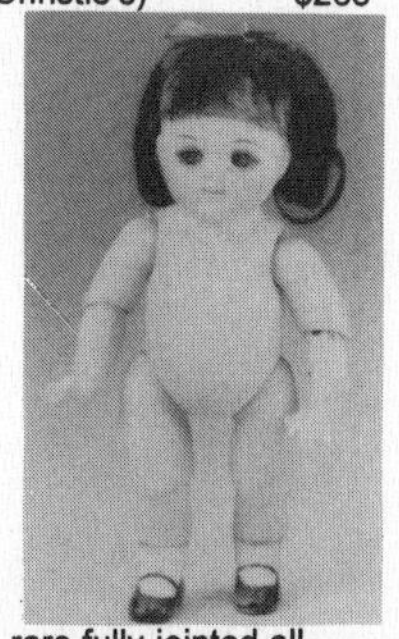

A rare fully-jointed all-bisque googly-eyed doll, German, circa 1915, probably Kestner, *111 0* on head and tops of legs, 4¾in. high.
(Sotheby's) $1,262

A fine Tête Jumeau bisque doll in original box, French, circa 1890, jointed wood and composition body, in original pale pink satin flounced dress, 28in. high.
(Sotheby's) $6,311

A large Jumeau type S.F.B.J. bisque head doll, French, circa 1900, with weighted blue glass eyes, on a fully jointed wood and composition body, 36in. tall. (Bonhams) $948

A Rabery & Delphieu pressed bisque doll, French, 1890s, impressed *R4/0 D*, good jointed wood and composition body, 14in. high. (Sotheby's) $3,606

An Armand Marseille black mold 341 with sleeping brown eyes, closed mouth, black spray paint hair and jointed composition body wearing cream suit, 9in. high. (Christie's) $474

A Jumeau mold bisque doll, French, 1900-10, impressed *8*, jointed wood and composition body, in dress of 1890s red and ivory satin, 19¾in. (Sotheby's) $1,171

A Wagner & Zwetsche character doll, 'Hansi', German, circa 1925, with painted molded composition head, intaglio eyes, jointed pink calico body, 15¾in. (Sotheby's) $180

A fine glazed china head doll, German, circa 1890, with painted features, molded black hair in ringlets, to cloth body with bisque lower arms and legs, 11in. tall. (Bonhams) $869

A Bahr and Proschild mold 309 bisque head child doll, German, circa 1909, with weighted blue glass eyes, open mouth, blonde kid leather body with bisque lower arms, 18in. tall. (Bonhams) $553

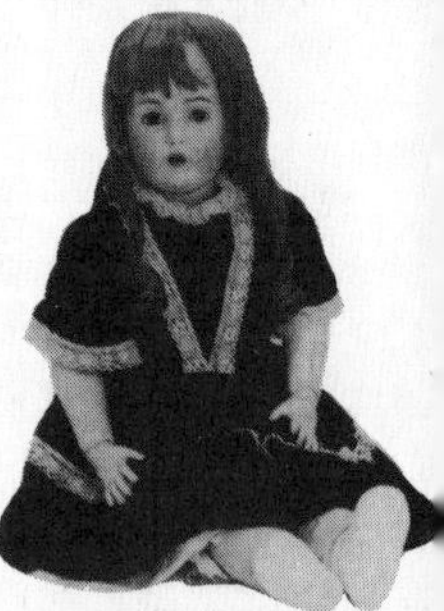

A large Kestner porcelain-headed doll, with brown sleeping eyes, painted open mouth with two glass teeth, blonde real hair wig, 84cm. high, after 1900. (Auction Team Köln) $1,574

A Simon & Halbig all-bisque dolls' house doll, with closed mouth, fixed blue eyes, blonde wig, neck, shoulder and hip joints, 5½in. high. (Christie's) $708

Hildchen, a Kathe Kruse Doll XII H, Hampelchen, with Doll 1 head, varnished green eyes, short blonde hair wig, 17in. high, circa 1931. (Christie's) $4,724

A Simon & Halbig walking doll, German, circa 1900, with blue flirting eyes, jointed wood and composition body with rigid legs, 24½in. (Sotheby's) $630

A Grodnerthal painted wooden doll, with carved and gilded comb, wearing contemporary red and white printed cotton tiered frock, circa 1830s, 13in. (Christie's) $711

A Schildkröt rattle doll, with fixed arms and legs, blue painted eyes and painted brown hair, in swimsuit, red shoes and white socks, 1954. (Auction Team Köln) $171

All-bisque twins, modelled as a boy and girl with molded hair, 5½in. high. (Christie's) $442

A Käthe Kruse doll, German, 1950s, painted magnesit face, blonde wig in pony-tail, jointed at neck and hips, 14½in. (Sotheby's) $685

A musical marotte with shoulder head, turned wood whistle handle, fixed blue eyes, blonde curly wig and blue and white streamers, 17in. high. (Christie's) $873

A Limbach googlie eye character doll, with sleeping brown eyes, closed mouth, short brown hair and jointed composition body, 7in. high. (Christie's) $1,453

Fiekchen, a Kathe Kruse doll XII, Hampelchen, with Doll 1 head, button on back holding the legs straight, 17in. high, circa 1931, in original box. (Christie's) $2,907

Maggie & Jiggs, by Bucherer, Switzerland, based on an American cartoon series, metal jointed bodies, 17 and 19cm. high, circa 1920. (Auction Team Köln) $3,608

A Kammer & Reinhardt child doll with blue lashed sleeping eyes, fair mohair wig, jointed composition and wood body and contemporary pink silk frock, 17in. high. (Christie's) $1,362

Swiss Lenci girl, with ainted brown eyes, stuffed elt body wearing Swiss egional costume, circa 939-41, 14in. high, riginal Lenci ticket. Christie's) $872

Two IX Kathe Kruse small German children, in original regional costume, short blonde hair, painted features, the boy with gray eyes, the girl with brown eyes, 15in. (Christie's) $3,088

A Grodnerthal painted wooden doll, with carved and painted yellow comb, wearing cotton seaweed print frock with red slippers, circa 1830s, 13in. high. (Christie's) $1,635

An Armand Marseille mold 390 with sleeping brown eyes, open mouth, brown mohair wig and jointed composition body wearing white cotton frock and bonnet, 21in. (Christie's) $308

'Portobello', English, 1700-1710, an impressive early dolls' house consisting of four high ceiling rooms fully furnished in late 18th and early 19th century furniture and fittings. (Bonhams) $34,712

'The Pediment House', English, 1827, a baby house having four rooms, the interior having some original wallpapers, overall: 57in. high. (Bonhams) $3,945

'St Faith's', English, circa 1870, unusual country Victorian Vicarage built in two halves and hinged at the center, no front door, overall: 32in. high, excluding stand. (Bonhams) $9,467

'Farnham House' English, late 18th century, a well proportioned professionally made house in good decorative order, the façade finished in a red brick effect with heavy quoining, overall: 49in. high. (Bonhams) $29,978

'The Cedars, Woodbridge', English, late 19th century, with a double-layer of rooms, as can be found in a 'real' house resulting in entrances to either side and the roof, overall:48in. high, including stand. (Bonhams) $7,100

BUYER BEWARE

Beware when buying dolls at auction as many are now being faked.
The quality of painting of the facial features is usually a giveaway, especially the eyes and lips.
Sometimes the quality of the composition hands and feet can also be an indication. Some companies were known for the lack of quality on their limbs, but only a few.

(Clarke Gammon)

'Carpenter's Cottage' English, circa 1880, a small scale cottage typical of the early artisan cottages that can still be found in the suburbs of London, overall: 15½in. high. (Bonhams) $5,522

'Durward's Hall', English, early 19th century, a charming baby house with a one-piece façade which detaches to reveal three spacious rooms on three levels. (Bonhams) $5,996

'Shell Villa', English, circa 1870, a brightly pink-painted seaside retreat used as a lodging house for cats, kept by Tabitha, Selina and Branwell Twitchett, overall: 30½in. high. (Bonhams) $6,627

'The Dower House', English, mid 18th century, an elegant and well proportioned country residence with four large rooms lit by generous windows, overall: 37in. high. (Bonhams) $11,834

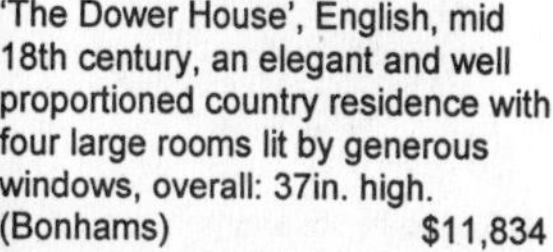

An English wooden dolls' house of circa 1830, opening at the front to reveal four rooms with doorways, the kitchen with concealed staircase, 36½in. wide. (Christie's) $1,011

'The Edwardian Villa', English, circa 1905, impressive wooden dolls' house, twelve rooms, with conservatory at rear, 29in. high overall.(Bonhams) $17,356

'Strawberry Hill Gothick', English, 1820-30, the pink paintwork is a reference to Horace Walpole's Gothick Villa on Strawberry Hill Twickenham, overall: 25in. high. (Bonhams) $5,996

'The Mahogany House', English, 1730-40, resting on its original stand, the polished mahogany façade with three steps leading up to the marquetry six-panelled front door, overall: 51in. high, including stand. (Bonhams) $37,867

'Van Haeften', English, 1740-1750, a detailed and finely proportioned Palladian Mansion standing on its original arcaded base. (Bonhams) $31,556

'Ivy Lodge', English, 1886, professionally built with Gothic staircase, original wallpapers to most of the rooms and attractive bay windows, overall: 78in. high. (Bonhams) $8,678

'Coburg', European, 19th century, a grand residence with large scale stucco markings and painted in a sandstone color, with kitchen and stables annexes, 78in. high, with stand, 97½in. wide. (Bonhams) $7,100

'The Original Swan', English, 1865-70, This once plain house has been converted into a fine country hotel, overall:64in. high including stand. (Bonhams) $10,256

A decorative cast iron coffee grinder by the Enterprise Mfg. Co., Philadelphia, unrestored, 29cm. high. (Auction Team Köln) $557

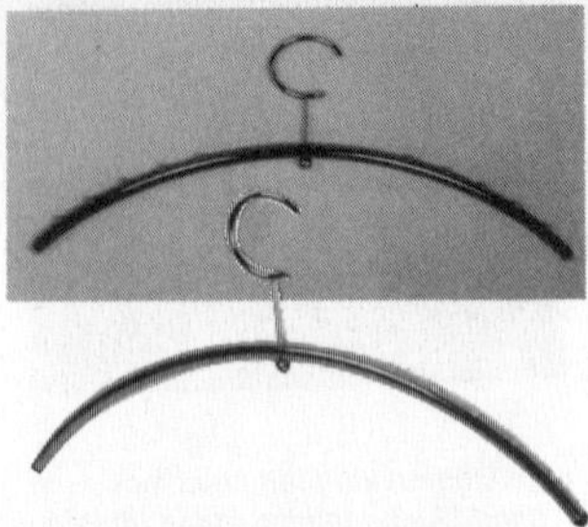

Shiro Kuramata, Japan, a pair of clothes hangers, designed 1989, for 'Spiral', electric blue anodized aluminum arched hanger with five turquoise rubber 'grippers' to each side, 450mm. long. (Bonhams) $236

A Roneo pencil sharpener, on a massive socle, with attractive decoration and rotating knife. (Auction Team Köln) $491

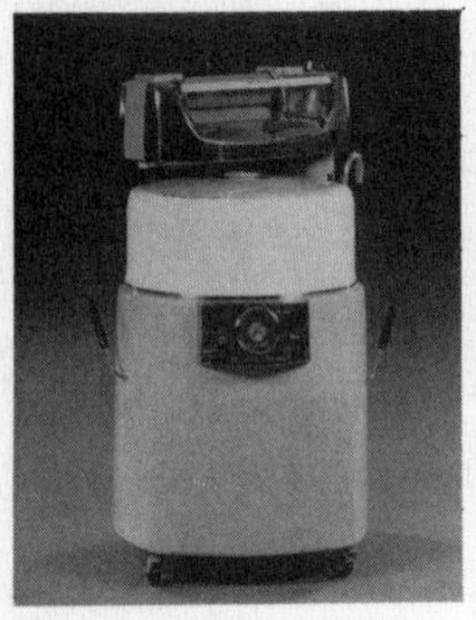

Anon, washing machine 'Lady Kenmore Visimatic', turquoise and white metal, two-speed, dial to front, swivelling top unit with mangle, top-loading. (Sotheby's) $736

Robert Mallet-Stevens, pair of waste paper baskets from the Villa C. at Croix, 1931-32, chromium plated metal, cream painted interior and underside, 34.5cm. approximately. (Sotheby's) $10,812

A stylistic Art Deco electric fire, in the form of a yacht with chrome sails and white painted hull 'The Bunting', 31in. high. (Dee Atkinson & Harrison) $97

An unusual Coca Cola Dispenser, by the Dole Valve Co., Chicago, for counter mounting, in the shape of an outboard motor 62cm. high, circa 1950. (Auction Team Köln) $602

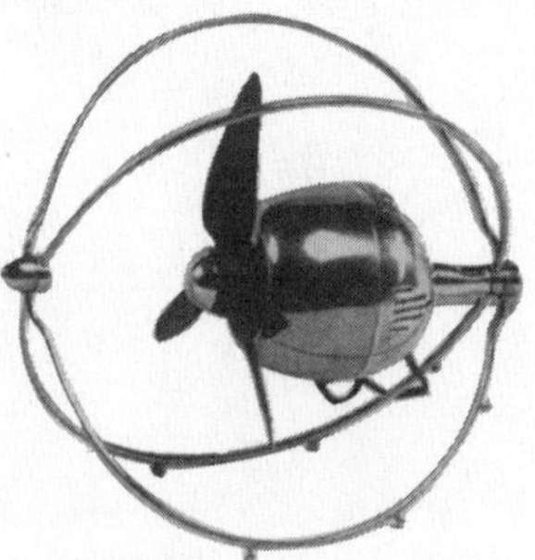

Ezio Pirali, a metal table fan, designed 1954 for Zerowatt, the aluminum case with rubber blades, within chromed wire cage. (Christie's) $2,351

A 'Cochon electriseur', by Philippe Leoni, France, with painted tin figure of a pig, for 10 centime pieces, 75cm. high, 1898. (Auction Team Köln) $10,034

An early 75 American cast iron apple peeler, to patents of 1868-76, lacks handle, with table clamp, circa 1876.
(Auction Team Köln) $79

Cranberry scoop, early 20th century. (Eldred's) $275

A Continental silver corkscrew, with double pistol handle type grips, knopped stem with sheath of chamfered square section, probably by Adrianus Steffens, Rotterdam, 1775, 87mm.
(Tennants) $1,067

Peter Behrens for AEG, fan 'GB 1', circa 1912, dark green painted iron, brass, 11¾in. high.
(Sotheby's) $901

A 19th century ivory handled and brass mounted corkscrew, applied brass crest *Ne plus ultra patent*, length fully open 19cm.
(Wintertons) $558

An aluminium Atomic coffee machine, circa 1947, for A. & M.G. Sassoon, the cast aluminum form with chromed metal and colored plastic fittings, 9½in. high.
(Christie's) $361

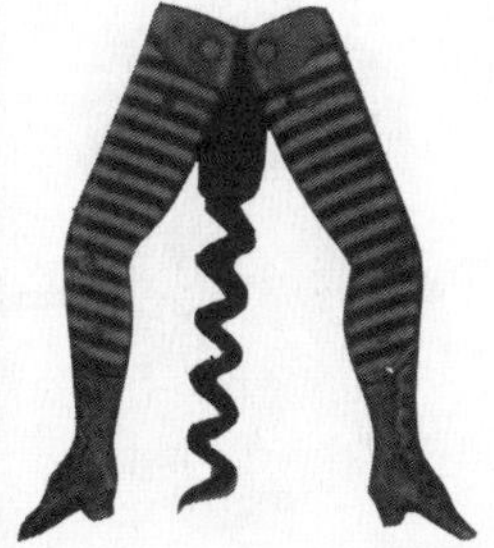

A late 19th century lady's legs corkscrew, folding form, full length blue and white stockings, length open 13.2cm.
(Bonhams) $237

Shaker blue and ivory painted wash tub, circular form with projecting pierced handles continuing to body with iron staves, 27in. diameter including handles.
(Skinner) $3,680

A cast iron Enterprise Mfg. No. 10 coffee grinder, painted blue and gold with brass container for beans, the base with wooden drawer, 84cm. high, 1898.
(Auction Team Köln) $1,981

A pair of South Staffordshire enamel candlesticks, circa 1770, finely painted with colorful sprays and sprigs of flowers between blue-ground panels, 12⅝in. high.
(Sotheby's) $2,300

A large Viennese Renaissance Revival silver and enamel-mounted ebonized jewelry casket, by Hermann Bohm, Vienna, circa 1875, profusely decorated overall with enamel on copper plaques, 18¼in. wide.
(Christie's) $43,700

A silver-mounted Viennese enamelled jug, painted with reserves depicting classical figural studies including Europa and the Bull, Austrian, late 19th century, 26cm. high.
(Christie's) $9,209

A Viennese enamel and gilt-metal centerpiece, late 19th century, in the form of a galleon, the sails, body and base painted with vignettes of allegorical figures, the rigging and deck modelled with crew, 13¾in. high.
(Christie's) $5,520

A Limoges champlevé enamel reliquary châsse, circa 1195-1200, retaining its original wood core, cresting and much original gilding, enamelled on a blue ground, 21.5cm. wide.
(Sotheby's) $275,000

A rare and fine George III South Staffordshire enamel tea caddy, circa 1760-61, well painted with a head and shoulders portrait of the King facing to sinister, the reverse painted with a similar portrait of Queen Charlotte, 11cm.
(Bonhams) $24,640

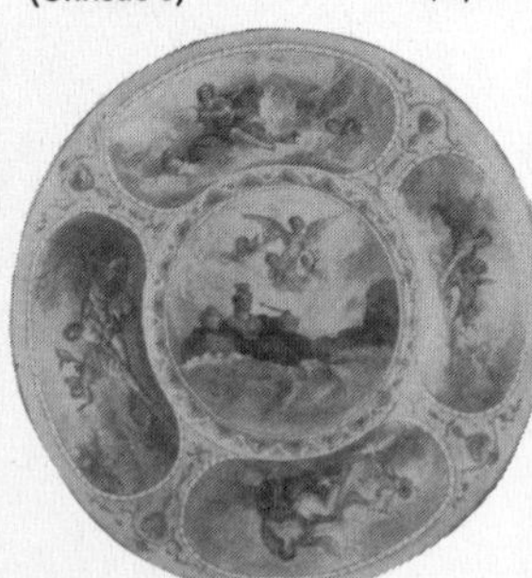

A silver-mounted Viennese enamelled plate painted with five reserves depicting amongst others the safe carriage of Arion by a dolphin, Austrian, late 19th century, 22.2cm. diameter.
(Christie's) $1,417

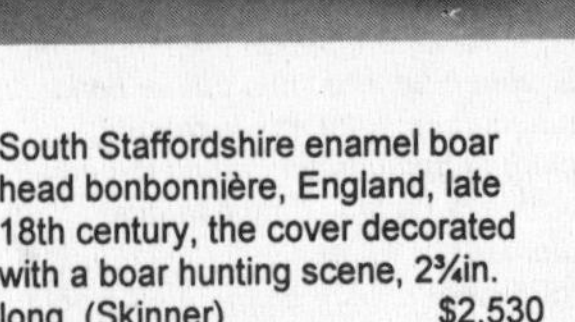

South Staffordshire enamel boar head bonbonnière, England, late 18th century, the cover decorated with a boar hunting scene, 2¾in. long. (Skinner) $2,530

A silver-gilt mounted Viennese enamelled sedan chair, the cover hinged to reveal two small silver gilt topped clear glass scent bottles in a lift out container, Simon Grunwall, Austria, late 19th century, 9cm. high. (Christie's) $2,303

A yellow gold, green enamelled box set with older enamel panels in the form of putti amid foliage, 20th century, 214gm., 9.4cm. long. (Finarte) $3,153

A silver-gilt mounted Viennese enamelled bowl of lobed oval form, on conforming pedestal foot and supported by two dolphins and a central pillar, Herman Boehm, Austrian, late 19th century, 21cm. across. (Christie's) $2,479

A silver-mounted Viennese enamelled lobed bowl, the center stamped in relief and painted with a scene of Galatea on her dolphin-drawn cockle shell carriage, Austrian, late 19th century, 16cm. diameter. (Christie's) $1,327

Pair of South Staffordshire enamel candlesticks, English, late 18th century, deep blue ground, polychrome pastoral scenes of figures in landscapes, 14½in. high. (Skinner) $2,300

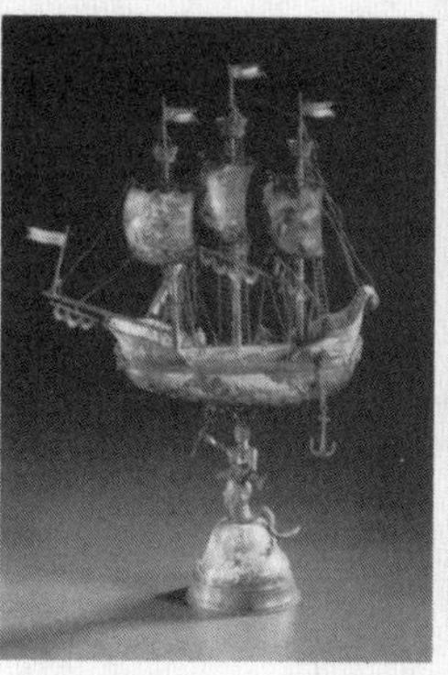

An enamelled nef, Vienna, circa 1880, with gilt-metal mounts, rigging and crew, supported by the figure of a fish and trident-bearing melusine, height overall 22in. (Sotheby's) $15,585

A pair of George III style enamelled candlesticks, 19th century, the knopped baluster stems on spreading circular bases, the royal blue ground with white reserves painted with landscapes and foliage, 8in. high. (Christie's) $1,920

A silver-gilt mounted Viennese enamelled ewer, the body and base painted with various classical figural studies, J.F., Austrian, late 19th century, 20.5cm. overall. (Christie's) $1,593

Pair of Continental enamelled green glass vases, late 19th century, probably Czechoslovakia, decorated with gilded scalework highlighted in blue, red, and white. (Skinner) $3,737

A pair of Viennese enamelled candlesticks on circular pedestal bases, painted with several reserves depicting scenes from classical mythology, Herman Boehm, Austrian, late 19th century, 20.5cm. high. (Christie's) $4,959

A Canton tortoiseshell brise fan with crest of a sun and *per via rectas*, carved and pierced with figures, animals and buildings both recto and verso, 7in., circa 1820. (Christie's) $827

A fan signed *A. Cavolo*, the silk leaf painted with a silhouette of a couple tap-dancing and a sweep, and caricatures of nine tradespeople, bone sticks painted with flowers, 13in., circa 1890. (Christie's) $731

Tarare, a printed fan, the leaf hand-colored etchings with two scenes recto and one verso from the Opera by Baumarchais and Salieri and with words and music, with wooden sticks with bone filets, 11in., 1787. (Christie's) $1,948

A magnificent brise fan, painted with two couples wit Cupid at the Altar of Love, the reserves pierced an silvered and painted with four simulated jasperwar plaques, 10.5in., circa 1795.
(Christie's) $5,31

Au Bon Marché, an advertising fan composed of leaf-shaped panels of crêpe paper each applied with an oval lithograph printed in orange with sporting ladies motoring, skating, riding, etc., by A. Boucicaut, M. Planvet, Av., 10in., circa 1910.
(Christie's) $353

Papillons de Jour, a fine Art Nouveau fan signed *H Poulin*, the canepin leaf partly applied with rea butterfly wings, partly painted, the ivory sticks finel carved with a sunburst and silvered, signed *J. Vaillan* at the front and *A. Rodien, Paris* on the verso, 14in circa 1895. (Christie's) $5,667

Late 17th century fan depicting Solomon and the Queen of Sheba, with pierced tortoiseshell sticks. The ivory guardsticks inlaid with mother of pearl and pique with silver, circa 1690, 26cm.
(Bonhams) $2,464

A fine fan, the leaf painted with three shaped vignette of travellers by ruins, alternating with two chinoiserie vignettes, the ivory sticks carved and pierced with chinoiserie, the closed fan resembles a dagger, 10in., French, circa 1750. (Christie's) $4,60

Le Gouter, a miniature fan, the leaf a hand-colored stipple engraving, the horn sticks gilt with stars, 6in., circa 1815, in early 20th century Vanier Chardin box. (Christie's) $425

King George III and his family at the Royal Academy, an unmounted printed fan leaf, a stipple engraving part printed in color after J.H. Ramberg, 19in. wide, 1790. (Christie's) $2,024

A fine fan, the leaf painted with an artist painting a lady in classical dress, the reserves with vignettes of fishermen by a harbor, the verso with a hero in a landscape, the guardsticks backed with mica, 11in., French, circa 1770. (Christie's) $4,250

Naples, a fan, the canepin leaf painted with the public gardens, with carriages in the foreground and the bay on the left, the verso with the city from the bay, the gilt metal sticks cast and pierced, 7in. Neapolitan, circa 1810. (Christie's) $2,833

A rare fan set with a thermometer and dated *1778*, the satin leaf painted with two groups of elegant musicians, their faces painted on paper and applied, their clothes outlined with gold braid, the verso painted with flowers, the upper guardstick set with a thermometer calibrated in centigrade and reaumur, the lower guardstick carved with a weather vane, 11in., 1778. (Christie's) $15,939

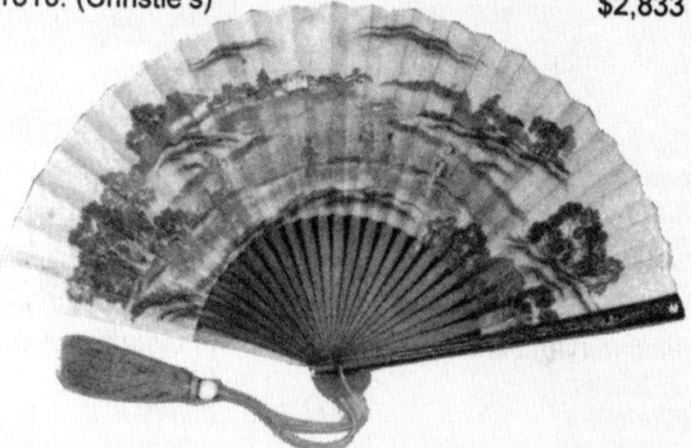

A fan signed *Kunihisa*, the leaf painted with a lady flying a kite, two others playing shuttlecock and battledore, with bamboo sticks and one ivory guardstick, the other set with a Shibayama work caterpillar and butterfly, 11in., Japanese, late 19th century. (Christie's) $3,128

The Toilet of Venus, a fine ivory brise fan painted and lacquered with three vignettes within gilt frames, the verso painted with the outlines of the recto and inscribed *Venus sa Toilette*, 8in., circa 1730. (Christie's) $3,188

A fan, the leaf a hand-colored stipple engraving of vignettes of a lady dressing and dancing, inscribed *Belleville*, the verso with a lady at her toilette helped by putti, with mother of pearl pagoda sticks with a spy hole, 8½in., circa 1830. (Christie's) $744

Saving Private Ryan, an American regulation-type khaki army helmet, signed in silver felt pen by Tom Hanks, Steven Spielberg, Giovanni Ribisi, Adam Goldberg, Jeremy Davies. (Christie's) $8,125

Marilyn Monroe, red silk purse with elaborate red feathers, silk-lined, with stitched leather interior pocket in soft cream with the monogram *MM* in silver on the pocket, with Gentlemen Prefer Blondes, 20th Century Fox, 1953, lobby card, 8 x 11in. (Christie's) $25,300

The Man In The Iron Mask/Leonardo DiCaprio, a pair of 18th century style gauntlets of tan leather trimmed at the cuff with gilt braid and fringing. (Christie's) $3,430

Gold plated metal statue on black base with front plaque, inscribed *Academy First Award / to / Herman J. Mankiewicz / for Writing / Original Screenplay of / Citizen Kane.* Statue is a substantial 7.5lbs, lightly patinated and bears the inscription *G. Stanley*. (Christie's) $244,500

Vivien Leigh, a cancelled British passport, issued on 20th December, 1932 for five years and extended until 20th December, 1940, with a black and white photograph of bearer, [Vivien Leigh] 6½ x 4cm. (Christie's) $6,319

Dr Who, a prop Cyberman helmet of silver painted fibreglass, made for the T.V. series Dr Who, possibly for the story The Tomb Of The Cybermen, 1967. (Christie's) $812

Audrey Hepburn, a Gucci handbag of fawn and white cotton check with brown leather clasp decorated with a gilt metal Gucci emblem, gilt-stamped inside *Gucci*. (Christie's) $1,083

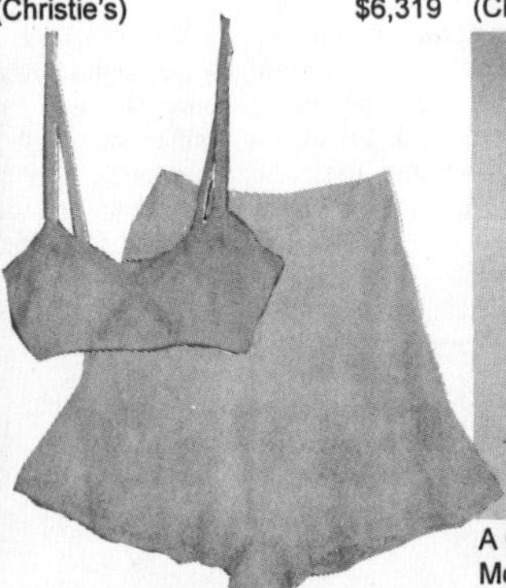

Jean Harlow, a set of matching bra and french knickers in peach silk, elaborately trimmed and inset with soft peach lace. (Vennett-Smith) $651

A Clockwork Orange, Malcolm McDowell's ever-present swordcane, ebonized with large walnut burl at apex, 36in. tall. The top reveals a highly finished 7in. stainless steel blade by Wilkinson Sword. (Christie's) $23,000

Marilyn Monroe, Family Circle Magazine, 26 April, 1946, complete and in very fine condition. Marilyn Monroe's very first appearance on the cover of a magazine.
(Christie's) $1,610

The Hunger/David Bowie, a pair of black leather with black patent leather detail, each boot inscribed inside in black ballpoint pen *D. Bowie,* purchased for Bowie in his role as vampire John Blaylock.
(Christie's) $680

Frank Sinatra, a shirt of pink cotton, with mother of pearl buttons and double cuff detail, labelled *Nat Wise of London.. Sunset Strip, Calif*, additionally labelled *Frank Sinatra, April 1971*.
(Christie's) $992

Absolutely Fabulous/Jennifer Saunders, an outfit comprising a tailored jacket of brightly colored Syrian satin ikat, a pair of black and white jersey palazzo pants, worn by Jennifer Saunders as Edina.
(Christie's) $631

The Man In The Iron Mask/Leonardo DiCaprio, an 18th century style gentleman's shirt of cream silk, the cuffs trimmed with antique Irish crochet.
(Christie's) $1,083

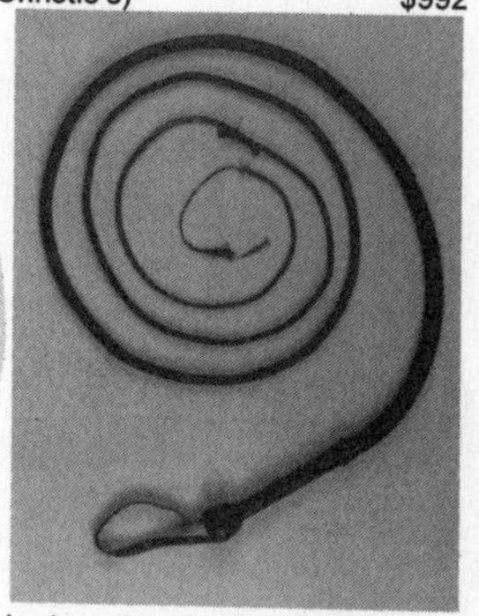

Harrison Ford/Indiana Jones, a hand-made sixteen-plait bull-whip of kangaroo hide with 106in. long lash, used by Harrison Ford as Indiana Jones in all three adventure films. (Christie's) $43,332

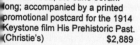

Charlie Chaplin, a bamboo cane marked *1932*, the cane 36½in. long; accompanied by a printed promotional postcard for the 1914 Keystone film His Prehistoric Past.
(Christie's) $2,889

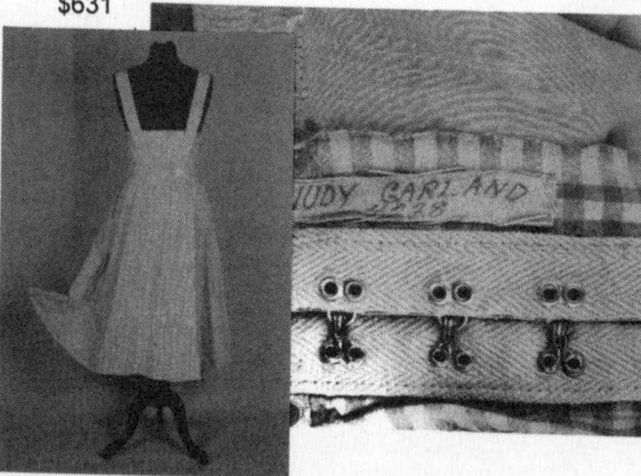

Judy Garland/The Wizard of Oz, a pinafore dress of blue and white gingham, with cotton wardrobe label inside inscribed in black ink *Judy Garland 4228*.
(Christie's) $313,215

Notting Hill, a 19th century blue painted pine door, ring-handled knocker and numbers 280, William Thackery's [Hugh Grant] front door in the 1999 production Notting Hill.
(Christie's) $9,028

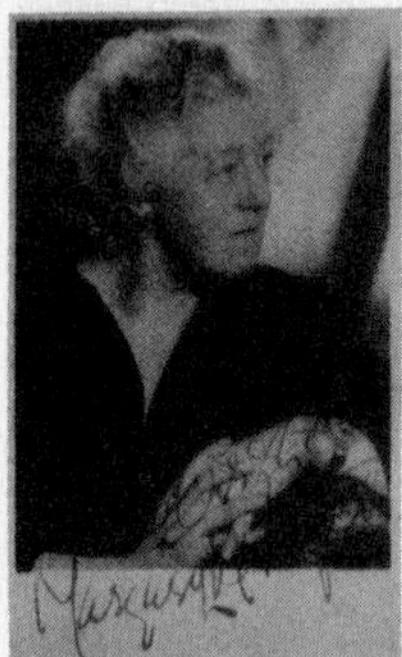

Margaret Rutherford, signed postcard, half-length in semi-profile, photo by Vivienne.
(Vennett-Smith) $147

Abbott & Costello, signed album page, 5 x 3.5, by both Bud Abbott and Lou Costello with small attached magazine photos.
(Vennett-Smith) $240

Sonja Henie, signed postcard, full-length standing on ice skates in a scene from Lovely To Look At.
(Vennett-Smith) $93

Shirley Temple, signed postcard head and shoulders smiling, signed as young girl, corner creasing and small tear to edge of image.
(Vennett-Smith) $204

Laurel & Hardy, signed and inscribed p/c by both Stan Laurel and Oliver Hardy individually, head and shoulders in characteristic pose wearing bowler hats.
(Vennett-Smith) $656

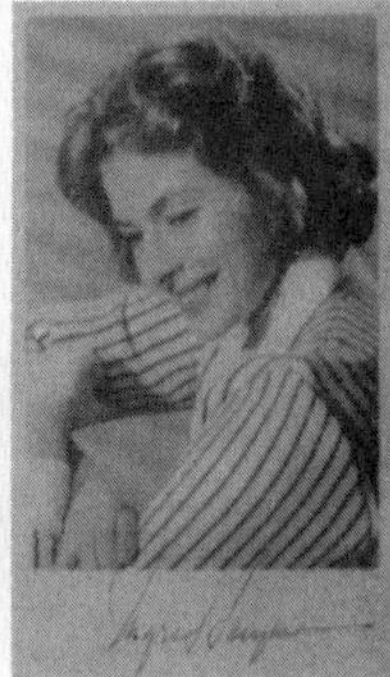

Ingrid Bergman, signed postcard, to lower white border, head and shoulders smiling, looking downwards.
(Vennett-Smith) $132

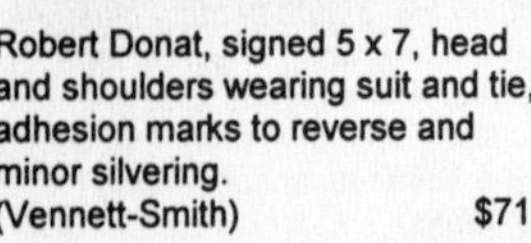

Robert Donat, signed 5 x 7, head and shoulders wearing suit and tie, adhesion marks to reverse and minor silvering.
(Vennett-Smith) $71

Easy Rider, signed 10 x 8, by Jack Nicholson, Peter Fonda and Dennis Hopper, showing them full-length seated on motor cycles.
(Vennett-Smith) $240

Vivien Leigh, signed 6 x 4.75, head and shoulders resting on one hand, irregularly trimmed, just affecting signature.(Vennett-Smith) $144

Frank Sinatra, signed and inscribed 8 x 10, half-length, 1982. (Vennett-Smith) $411

Stephen Spielberg, signed color 8 x 10, half-length looking through camera. (Vennett-Smith) $74

Phil Silvers, signed and inscribed 8 x 10, head and shoulders laughing. (Vennett-Smith) $174

Cruise & Kidman, signed color 8 x 10, by both Tom Cruise and Nicole Kidman, in gold and silver, half-length hugging. (Vennett-Smith) $98

Laurence Harvey, signed and inscribed 8 x 10, head and shoulders, smoking, slight creasing. (Vennett-Smith) $110

Judy Garland, signed 7 x 9, full-length performing on stage, holding microphone in later life, signed in green ink. (Vennett-Smith) $608

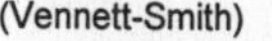

Dean Martin, signed 8 x 10, three-quarter length from a western, purportedly obtained in person. (Vennett-Smith) $101

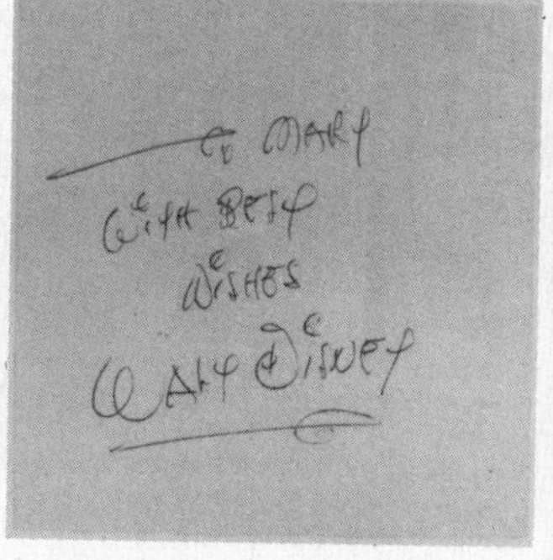

Walt Disney, large signed and inscribed piece, neatly laid down to card. (Vennett-Smith) $713

Alan Ladd, signed and inscribed 8 x 10, three quarter length reclining on sun lounger. (Vennett-Smith) $104

Betty Grable, signed and inscribed 8 x 10, head and shoulders wearing furs, in later years.
(Vennett-Smith) $139

Laurel and Hardy, a rare black and white head and shoulders portrait photograph of Laurel and Hardy by Stax, signed in blue ink by subjects, additionally inscribed in Laurel's hand *Hello Jimmy!,* 8 x 10in.
(Christie's) $1,714

Frank Sinatra, signed postcard, half-length in suit and tie, with lit cigarette in one hand.
(Vennett-Smith) $416

Vivien Leigh, a good signed 7.5 x 9.5 head and shoulders, unusual early portrait, photo by Dorothy Wilding.
(Vennett-Smith) $480

Rita Hayworth, signed 8 x 10, full-length riding on the horse of a carousel, together with an unsigned 10 x 8 of Hayworth meeting Anthony Eden, Douglas Bader etc at the premiere of Down To Earth in London.(Vennett-Smith) $411

Rudolph Valentino, a black and white half-length publicity portrait photograph of subject in The Eagle, 1925, signed and inscribed in black ink, 15½ x 10¾in.
(Christie's) $1,444

Alan Ladd, signed and inscribed sepia 5 x 7, head and shoulders wearing suit, New Year 1952.
(Vennett-Smith) $46

Star Wars, signed color 10 x 8 by Harrison Ford, Carrie Fisher and Mark Hamill individually, half-length standing together in a row in costume from 'Star Wars'.
(Vennett-Smith) $256

Lionel Barrymore, signed sepia 7.5 x 9.5, head and shoulders wearing bow tie. (Vennett-Smith) $94

Brigitte Bardot, signed postcard, head and shoulders looking backwards over bare shoulder. (Vennett-Smith) $43

François Truffaut, signed and inscribed 4.75 x 3.5, full-length standing with camera with two other men. (Vennett-Smith) $256

Pearl White, signed and inscribed postcard, three quarter length seated wearing hat, rare. (Vennett-Smith) $102

Marlene Dietrich, a black and white head and shoulders portrait photograph of Marlene Dietrich circa early 1930s, probably Paramount Studios, signed and inscribed in blue ink in German. (Christie's) $2,708

Titanic, signed color 10 x 8, by Leonardo Di Caprio (silver), Kate Winslet and James Cameron (gold) individually, standing on set of the Titanic. (Vennett-Smith) $240

Diana Dors, signed postcard, to lower white border head and shoulders looking back over one shoulder. (Vennett-Smith) $178

Friends, signed color 8 x 10, by all six, Jennifer Aniston, Courtney Cox, Lisa Kudrow, Matt le Blanc, David Schwimmer and Matthew Perry. (Vennett-Smith) $237

George Clooney, signed color 8 x 10, half-length in costume as Batman with one arm raised. (Vennett-Smith) $76

Sabu, signed p/c, head and shoulders as young boy, smiling, wearing turban. (Vennett-Smith) $46

FILM STAR AUTOGRAPHS

Leigh & Olivier, signed 6.5 x 4.75 by both Vivien Leigh and Laurence Olivier individually, half-length seated gazing into each other's eyes. (Vennett-Smith) $325

Titanic, signed color 10 x 8, by Kate Winslet, James Cameron and Leonardo Di Caprio, from The Golden Globe Awards. (Vennett-Smith) $163

Bela Lugosi, a signed postcard, to lower white border, in red ink, head and shoulders wearing hat and overcoat, smoking a cigar. (Vennett-Smith) $372

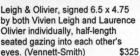

Sean Connery, signed and inscribed postcard, head and shoulders, early, rare in this for form. (Vennett-Smith) $93

Laurel & Hardy, signed and inscribed sepia 7 x 5 by both Stan Laurel and Oliver Hardy individually, half-length together in characteristic pose wearing bowler hats. (Vennett-Smith) $465

Margaret Rutherford, signed postcard to lower white border, half-length resting her chin on one hand, photo by Vivienne. (Vennett-Smith) $160

Richard Burton, signed postcard, head and shoulders, early, Picturegoer W912. (Vennett-Smith) $126

Cary Grant, signed and inscribed 10 x 8, half-length alongside, but not signed by, Ingrid Bergman, modern reproduction signed in later years. (Vennett-Smith) $279

Marlon Brando, signed postcard, head & shoulders wearing suit and tie, slight thinning to center, rare. (Vennett-Smith) $333

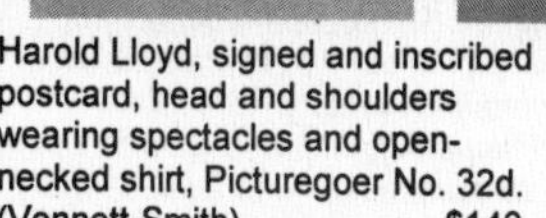

Harold Lloyd, signed and inscribed postcard, head and shoulders wearing spectacles and open-necked shirt, Picturegoer No. 32d.
(Vennett-Smith) $140

Harrison Ford, signed color 10 x 8 head and shoulders smiling.
(Vennett-Smith) $71

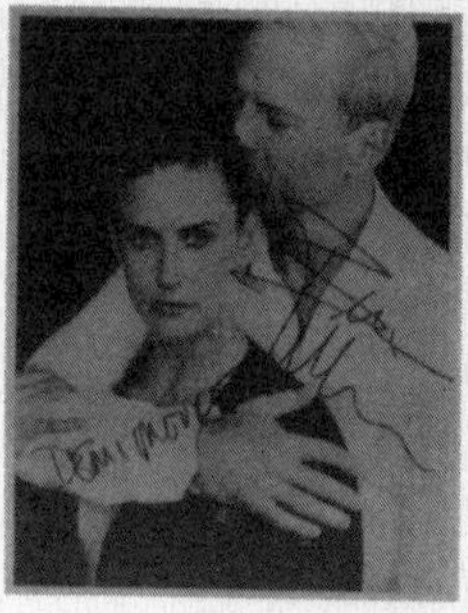

Moore & Willis, signed color 8 x 10, by both Demi Moore and Bruce Willis, head and shoulders with his arms around her.
(Vennett-Smith) $68

Laurel & Hardy, a good signed and inscribed 9 x 11, by both, full-length standing together in characteristic pose holding bowler hats, 16th May 1952, 13 x 18 overall.
(Vennett-Smith) $1,287

Jayne Mansfield, signed and inscribed 11 x 9.5 to white upper border of photographer's mount, half-length holding a microphone to her mouth and with one hand on the shoulder of a seated gentleman.
(Vennett-Smith) $170

Laurel & Hardy, theatre programme for Laurel and Hardy's appearance at the Palace Theatre, Manchester, 28th July 1947, signed by both to front cover.
(Vennett-Smith) $344

Cary Grant, signed and inscribed postcard, head and shoulders, early, Picturegoer 735a.
(Vennett-Smith) $197

Julia Roberts, signed color 8 x 10, half-length.
(Vennett-Smith) $86

Vivien Leigh, signed postcard, head and shoulders, partially in darker portion, though legible.
(Vennett-Smith) $139

A pair of French gilt bronze chenets, late 19th century, with standards modelled as lyres with crossed torchères, 18in. high.
(Christie's) $2,236

A pair of sheet and cast iron andirons, American, early 20th century, silhouettes, each in the form of a seated jockey on a galloping horse, 20in. high.
(Christie's) $2,760

A pair of silvered bronze andirons, late 19th century, with foliate clasped urn finials, the boldly cast scrolling bases with female masks and on claw feet, 22in. high.
(Christie's) $907

A pair of bronze and brass andirons, early 20th century, with foliate terminals above tapering reeded standards on splayed feet, 26½in. high.
(Christie's) $1,181

A pair of cast iron andirons, American, 19th century, each cast in the half-round in the form of a woman with hair pulled back, tightly corseted bodice and arms folded together, 12in. high.
(Christie's) $575

A pair of wrought iron andirons, late 19th century, the hexagonal shafts with beaded intersections on splayed feet, with billet bars to the rear, 42in. high.
(Christie's) $1,452

A pair of Louis XVI style gilt bronze chenets, late 19th century, with flambeau urn finials suspended with berried laurel swags, 16½in. high.
(Christie's) $12,355

A pair of Louis XVI style bronze chenets, late 19th or early century, the urn standards with cone terminals and satyr masks, 15¼in. high. (Christie's) $1,490

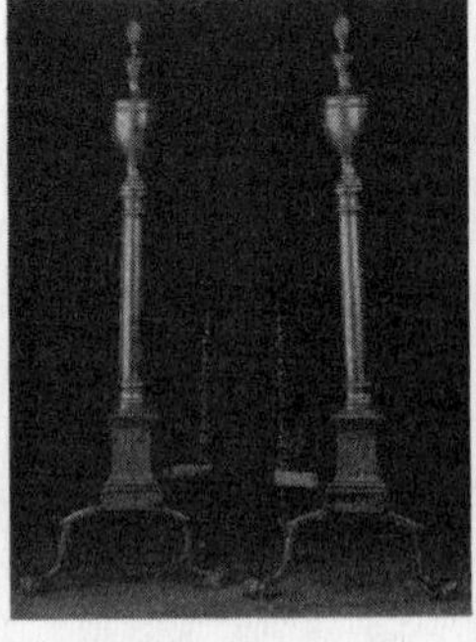

A pair of American brass andirons, late 19th century, the urn finials on tapering shafts with rectangular bases above splayed feet, 31in. high. (Christie's) $1,452

A cast iron and brass firegrate, early 20th century, the railed basket above a ribbon tied reeded X-frame on paw feet, 21in. wide.
(Christie's) $3,085

A steel and cast iron firegrate, early 20th century, the railed basket above a pierced frieze flanked by outset tapering standards with urn finials, 30in. wide.
(Christie's) $9,980

A cast iron firegrate, 19th century, the railed basket with twin scrolling handles with swags to the front, on a waisted socle, 22in. wide.
(Christie's) $2,722

A brass and steel basket grate of George III style, late 19th/early 20th century, of serpentine form with urn finials and a pierced and engraved frieze, 33¼in. wide.
(Christie's) $5,888

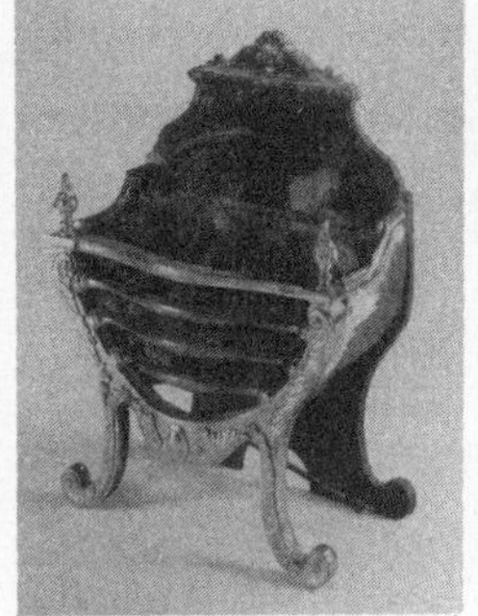

A steel and brass mounted fire grate, early 20th century, the tapering railed basket applied with foliate mounts, on scroll feet, 18½in. wide.
(Christie's) $525

A George III brass mounted wrought iron firegrate façade, circa 1800, the bowed railed front with urn-shaped finials, within a reed molded rectangular frame, 35½in. wide. (Christie's) $6,351

An American steel and brass firegrate, early 20th century, the railed basket with a scalloped frieze flanked by twin naturalistic standards with pierced disc terminals, 34in.
(Christie's) $3,266

A Victorian steel and brass mounted firegrate, of rectangular form, the bow fronted grate within an enclosed rectangular frame, applied with stiff-leaf cast border mounts, 34in. wide, overall.
(Christie's) $7,621

A brass and steel fire grate, early 20th century, the rectangular railed basket above a solid fret cast with running scrolls, the standards surmounted by twin handled urn finials, 34in. wide.
(Christie's) $1,218

A late William IV steel fire grate, circa 1835, the serpentine railed grate flanked by baluster knopped standards with mushroom shaped finials below the later associated arched backplate, 29in. wide.
(Christie's) $1,817

A Victorian cast iron fire grate, after the design by Alfred Stevens, the flared and bowed basket flanked by tall standards each modelled with Pluto and Proserpine supporting lobed shallow urns, 46in. wide.
(Christie's) $8,165

A steel and brass mounted dog grate, early 20th century, in the Adam taste, the serpentine railed basket above a solid steel apron applied with classical portrait medallions, 34½in. wide.
(Christie's) $3,997

A steel and brass mounted firegrate, 20th century, the serpentine fronted and railed basket flanked by flambeau torch standards modelled with entwined serpents below an arched plate, 21¼in. wide.
(Christie's) $1,180

A cast iron and brass mounted firegrate, circa 1900, the serpentine railed front on cabriole legs flanking the swept apron below baluster knopped finials, 21¼in. wide.
(Christie's) $1,180

A William IV steel and cast iron register grate, the arched frame applied with theatrical masks, palmettes and further foliate ornament enclosing the bowed and railed grate, 40¾in. wide.
(Christie's) $2,180

A steel fire grate, late 19th or early 20th century, in the George II style, the serpentine railed front above a lattice pierced fret, 29in. wide.
(Christie's) $1,996

A cast iron firegrate, late 19th/early 20th century, the bowed basket on scroll legs, the apron cast with husks and scrolls, surmounted with brass urn-shaped finials, 22in. wide. (Christie's) $872

A brass and cast iron firegrate, 20th century, the serpentine railed basket above a pierced fret flanked by square section standards, 22in. wide. (Christie's) $1,452

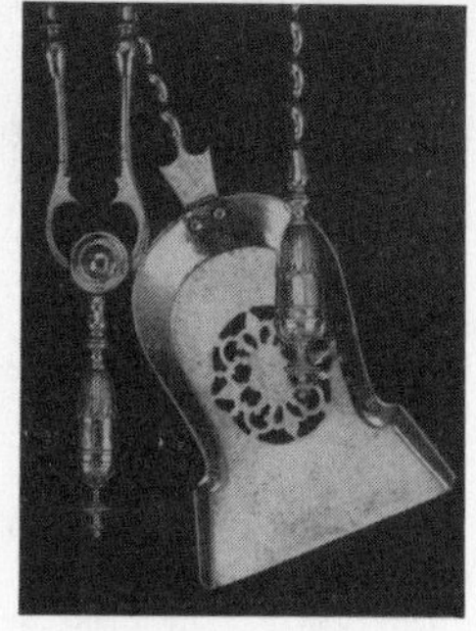

A set of three steel and brass fireirons, with spiral shafts and later lanceolate leaf clasped urn grips, the shovel 29in. long.
(Christie's) $1,723

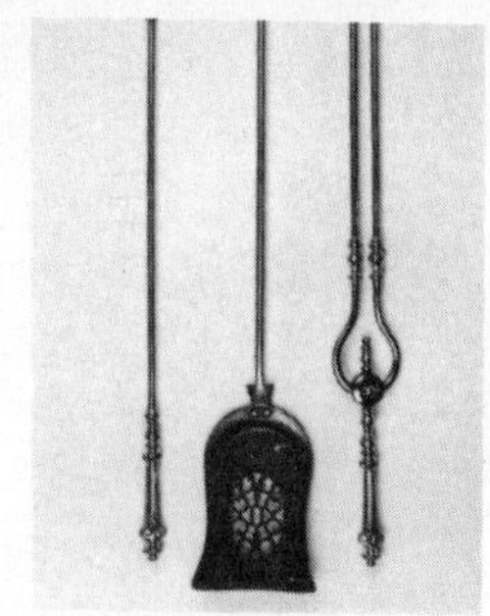

A set of three mid Victorian polished steel and brass fire irons, the tapering grips with stylized anthemions and Greek key ornament, 31½in.
(Christie's) $1,024

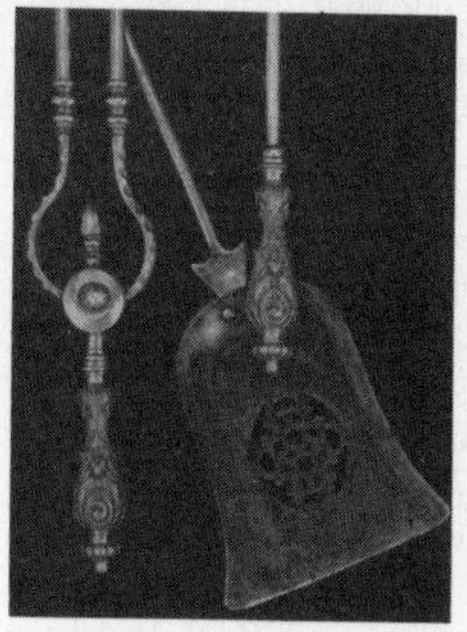

A set of three steel and gilt brass fire irons, 19th century, the plain cylindrical shafts with foliate cast grips, the shovel, 28¼in. long.
(Christie's) $907

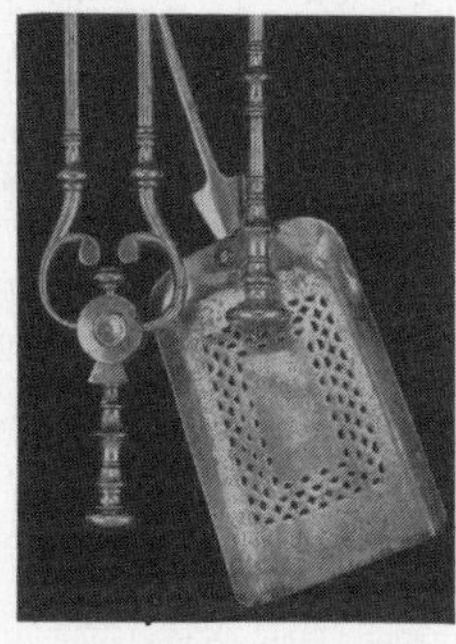

A set of three steel fire irons, mid 19th century, the plain shafts with knopped intersections, and multi-knopped grips, with pierced shovel, the shovel 30in. long.
(Christie's) $2,177

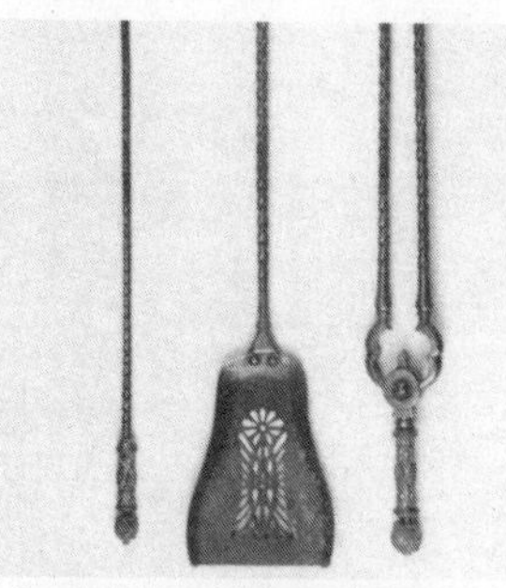

A set of three Victorian brass mounted polished steel fire irons, the writhen shafts with geometrically cast cylindrical grips and faceted pommels, each with date lozenge, shovel 30⅛in. long.
(Christie's) $459

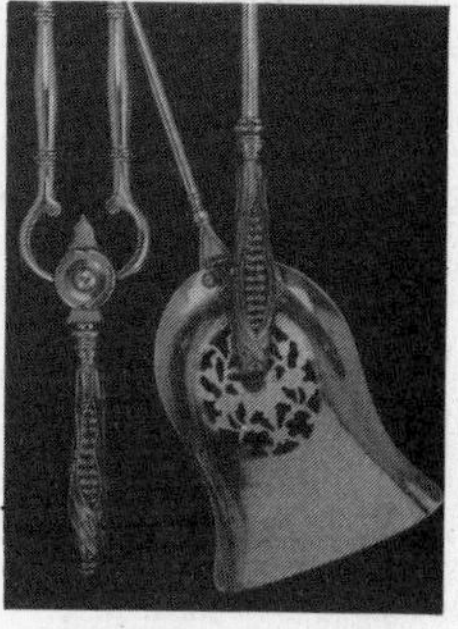

A set of three steel and brass fireirons, 19th century, with grips modelled as corn on plain cylindrical shafts, 31½in. long.
(Christie's) $2,359

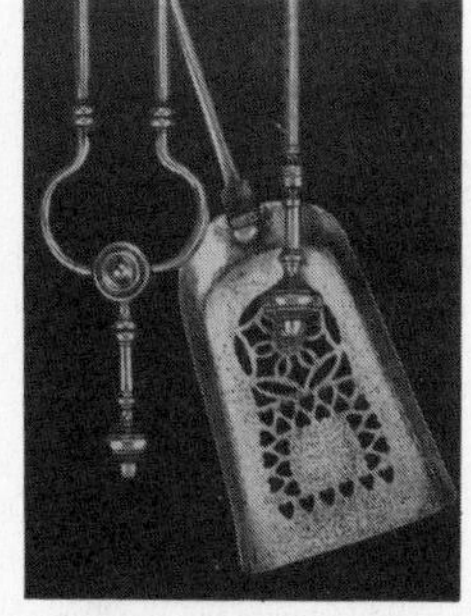

A set of three steel fireirons, 19th century, the plain cylindrical shafts with reeded intersections and pommels, the shovel, 29in. long.
(Christie's) $1,996

A set of three Victorian gilt bronze mounted polished steel fire irons, the writhen shafts mounted with associated scroll and cabochon cast grips, shovel 31½in. long.
(Christie's) $515

A set of three steel and brass fireirons, 19th century, with foliate cast grips and pommels on plain cylindrical shafts, 32in. long.
(Christie's) $2,722

Federal carved mantelpiece, possibly Samuel McIntyre, Salem, Massachusetts, circa 1800, the molded shaped cornice above a carved frieze centering a basket of flowers and fruit flanked by floral swags, 78½in. wide. (Skinner) $5,175

A late 19th century dark oak fire surround and overmantel, the overmantel with deep molded cornice and frieze boldly carved with mask and scrolled leafage, 84in. wide.
(Dreweatt Neate) $2,268

A green and white painted Federal fireplace surround, possibly New Jersey or Pennsylvania, circa 1800, the reverse-breakfronted mantel above a chip-carved frieze on molded stiles, 5ft. 10in. wide.
(Sotheby's) $3,450

A George III white painted carved pine chimneypiece, supplied to Aske Hall under the direction of John Carr of York, the molded rectangular breakfront shelf above a stepped molded cornice with ribbon and rosette and lappeted bands, 60 x 74in.
(Christie's) $26,404

A Louis XV style white marble chimneypiece, 20th century, with serpentine moulded shelf above conforming frieze with central stylised shell, the jambs with scroll tops above shaped pilasters, 52in. wide.
(Christie's) $8,176

Federal painted yellow pine fireplace mantel, Virginia, circa 1780, the molded cornice above a reeded and molded frieze, the recessed panel with flanking molded pilasters, 46½in. high.
(Skinner) $977

A Victorian walnut veneered and feather banded chimneypiece, circa 1890, the rectangular opening within a stiff-leaf molded frame, flanked by rebated jambs, below the bowed plain frieze, 61¼in. wide. (Christie's) $7,258

A Victorian pine and gesso chimneypiece, in the Adam Revival style, the fluted jambs with stiff-leaf caps flanking an inverted breakfront frieze, the central rectangular tablet modelled with a floral trophy, 69½in. wide. (Christie's) $8,165

A pine and gesso chimneypiece, 19th century, the panelled jambs applied with ribbon suspended sheaves below the stiff-leaf caps, the frieze decorated with flambeau urns and pine cones interlinked with foliate scrolls, 149cm. wide. (Christie's) $4,718

A Carrara marble chimneypiece, late 19th or early 20th century, the volute scroll jambs with scallop molded caps, flanking the conforming swept frieze, below a serpentine fronted shelf, 49in. wide. (Christie's) $12,701

A 19th century carved white and veined green marble chimneypiece, the broken shelf with molded edge above a frieze decorated with riband tied swags centered by an urn and flanked by classical female figures with musical instruments, 200cm. wide. (Phillips) $37,720

A George III carved white statuary marble chimneypiece, the rectangular shelf with egg and dart border, the frieze centered by a lion's mask head the jambs decorated with flowers on a block foot, 152cm. wide. (Phillips) $36,080

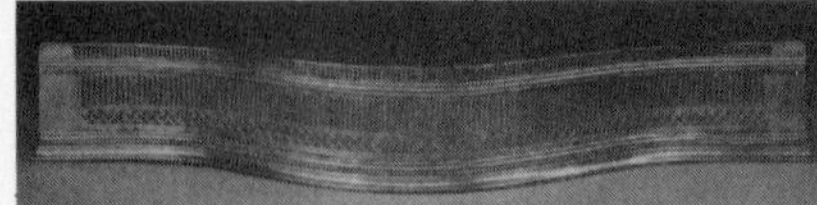

A Regency steel fender, early 19th century, of serpentine outline, the pierced frieze above a molded plinth, 46½in. wide. (Christie's) $544

A George III steel fender, circa 1780, of serpentine outline, the frieze pierced and engraved with scrolling foliate ornament, 48¼in. wide. (Christie's) $1,542

A Victorian pierced brass fender, mid 19th century, the frieze with two rows of concentric banding, on bun feet, 63in. wide. (Christie's) $3,629

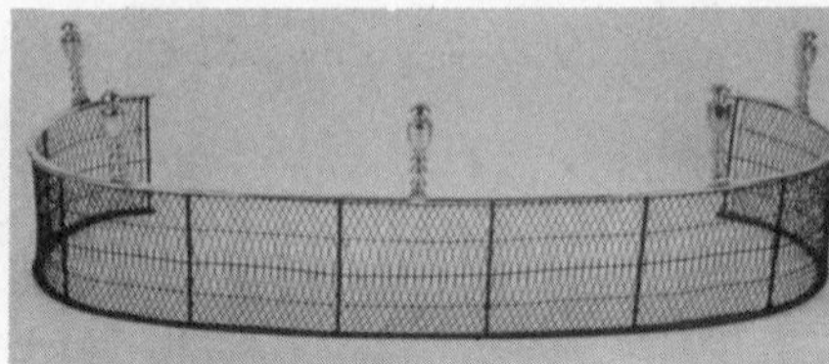

Brass and wire oval fire fender, 19th century, woven wire in a diamond pattern, brass top rim and five urn-form finials, 48in. long. (Skinner) $575

A French bronze fender, late 19th century, with ewer standards suspended with floral swags flanking a pierced and gadrooned rail with female mask, 52in. wide. (Christie's) $3,634

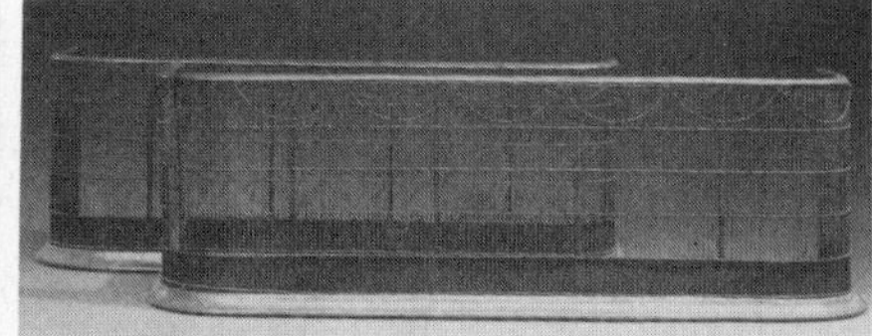

Two similar American wirework and brass fenders, 19th century, of curved rectangular form with writhen swags to the leading edge, 35in. wide. (Christie's) $1,748

A polished steel and brass club fender, early 20th century, with padded seats to the angles, on cylindrical supports above the pierced frieze and molded plinth, 54in. wide. (Christie's) $5,152

A steel club fender, early 20th century, the padded seat rail above an elaborate frieze of stylized scrolling foliage raised on a molded plinth, 56in. wide overall. (Christie's) $9,980

Brass and wire fender, America or England, late 18th/early 19th century, brass top rim, vertical wirework, iron base, 29¾in. long. (Skinner) $1,495

A Victorian gilt brass fender stool, the narrow brown button down leather seat with scroll ends, on supports joined by a turned stretcher and terminating in dual splayed legs, 83in. wide. (Christie's) $2,362

A Regency tôleware coal box, the cover painted to simulate wood within gilt bands of geometric motifs, 44cm. wide.
(Cheffins) $1,268

A gilt bronze and brass coal box, the shaped case with rococo style mounts, raised on scroll feet, 19¼in. high.
(Christie's) $999

A good 19th century brass coal bin of urn form, the circular domed lid with central handle, the body with twin applied mask handles, 35cm. diameter. (Bristol) $346

A sheet brass log bin, early 20th century, the cylindrical body with twin lion mask ring handles and foliate capped paw feet, 19½in. high. (Christie's) $1,996

A French folding firescreen, late 19th or early 20th century, the shaped rectangular frame with laurel cresting and floral swags, 51in. wide.
(Christie's) $1,817

A French bronze firescreen, late 19th century, the oval frame with pierced floral mount to the mesh ground, with outset tapering standards and on splayed feet, 34in. high.
(Christie's) $2,177

Unusual Art Nouveau period gilt metal framed fire screen, the central glass panel inset with stylized foliate design in colors, raised on splayed supports, 32in. high. (G A Key) $467

A Bronze and brass fan shaped firescreen, early 20th century, the nine pierced brass leaves radiating from the pierced foliate cast frame, 29½in. high.
(Christie's) $1,271

A Victorian black japanned and gilt decorated oval two-handled purdonium with cast iron leaf scroll handles and with conforming open footrim, 20in. x 17in. x 20in. high.
(Canterbury) $521

A J.S Sharpe 'Featherweight' #5, 7ft.6in. impregnated built cane Trout Fly Rod, two piece, 4oz., suction ferrule complete with stopper in maker's bag and in unused condition, built 1968. (Bonhams) $310

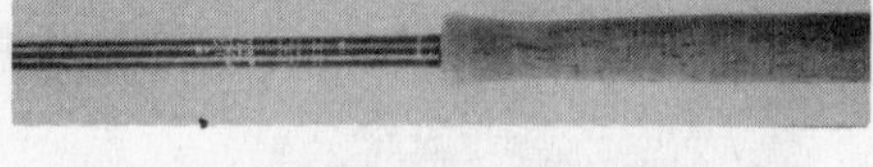

A Hardy 'Graphite Salmon Fly' #9, 13ft.9in. Salmon Rod, three piece complete in maker's bag together with a Hardy 'Favourite Graphite Salmon Fly' #9, 12½ft. salmon rod, three piece complete in maker's bag. (Bonhams) $293

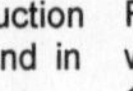

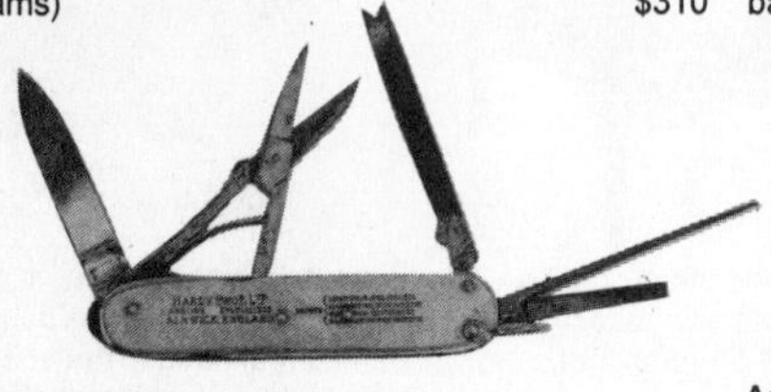

A Hardy's Angler's Knife No. 3, or the Dry Fly angler's knife, with large blade, scissors, file/discorger, screw driver, tweezers and stiletto. (Bonhams) $474

An unnamed 1⅝in. brass collar multiplying winch, with offset curved crank, brass rim stop lever, triple pillared cage and lyre screw to collar foot. (Bonhams) $359

An Illingworth No.3 fixed spool reel in very rare postal box, the reel with reciprocating spool, adjustable spool drag, finger pick-up flyer. (Bonhams) $897

A Hardy Neroda fly box, oxblood finish with chenille bars, 6¼ x 3¾in. x 1in., containing a quantity of assorted flies. (Bonhams) $237

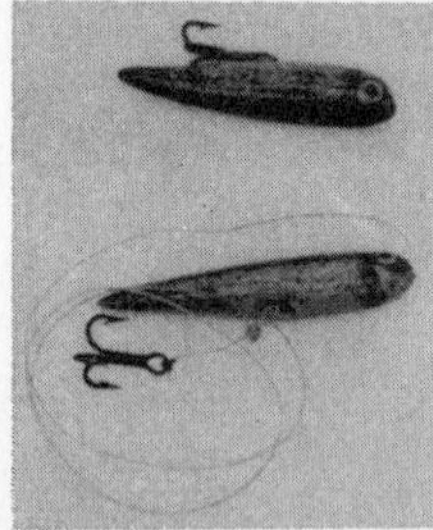

A pair of scarce Foreman's 'Flick-It' floating fly minnows, the 1⅛in. hand painted baits complete with traces in original box and complete with instruction and testimonial leaflets. (Bonhams) $221

A scarce japanned fly reservoir containing a large quantity of gut-eyed salmon and other flies, the reservoir with hinged front folding down to reveal six pull out trays. (Bonhams) $695

A Gregory glass-eyed Norwich spoon, the 1¼in. spoon stamped *Gregory* and retaining much original finish. (Bonhams) $237

A rare 3½in. nickel silver 'Superior Flexible Jointed Bait' attributed to Gregory, circa 1890, glass-eyed, stamped *Patent* to each fin. (Bonhams) $2,369

A fine cased bream, the 5lb. 4oz. fish 'Caught at South Mills, Blunham, July 19th 1910' and realistically presented. (Christie's) $953

A cased bream, the 5lb. 8oz. fish caught at 'Tuzzy Muzzy Meadow, St. Neot's, 1890' and realistically presented. (Christie's) $817

A fine chub attributed to Cooper, mounted against a green background *Chub. 5lbs. 1oz. 2drms. Caught by H.H Warwick. Wytham Stream. 31st December 1953.* Case 25 x 12½in. (Bonhams) $1,222

A 20lb stuffed pike in bow front case by J. Cooper & Sons, London, inscribed *Caught by William Mills Tollit, spinning with a small perch in Slapton Ley Devon, Sept. 6th 1906,* 118cm. (Bearne's) $1,056

A tench by W. F. Homer, mounted in a setting of reeds and grasses with red groundwork, gold inscription to case *Tench 5 lbs. 4 ozs. caught in 'Daventry Reservoir' by J. Parker. July 8th 1908*, case 25¾ x 14½in. (Bonhams) $1,222

A fine grayling by W. F. Homer, mounted in a setting of reeds and grasses against a typical reed painted background, in a gilt lined bowfront case, W.F. Homer label to case interior, case 21½ x 11 3/8in. (Bonhams) $896

Two perch, attributed to Cooper, mounted swimming in opposite directions, card to interior inscribed *Perch. Caught by Mr. J. Swain, Vice President of the Oldbury Piscatorials. October 13th 1903. Weights 3lbs. 13ozs. & 2lbs. 12ozs.* Case 37 3/8 x 18½in. (Bonhams) $3,260

A fine brown trout attributed to Hardy's, mounted in a setting of reeds against a green to blue reed painted background, *Caught on Doctor Barker's Water in the Don River. June 10th 1913 by W. M. Weight 5lbs.*, case 28½ x 14¾in. (Bonhams) $1,222

A Julius Vom Hofe B 'Ocean' 3/0 multiplier, black hard rubber with nickel silver fittings, counter-balanced serpentine crank.
(Bonhams) $316

A Hardy 'The Bougle' MK IV 3½in. trout fly reel, for left or right hand wind, being no. 68 of a limited edition of 500, triple raised pillars, wood handle.
(Bonhams) $237

An Otto Zwarg Model 600 'Maximo' 4/0 multiplier, black hard rubber with nickel silver fittings, free spool and optional check rim levers.
(Bonhams) $632

A Hardy 'The Perfect' 3in. brass trout fly reel (1896 version reproduction), being no. 309 of a limited edition of 1,000, with 1896 caliper check.
(Bonhams) $790

A rare unnamed Allcocks The 'Eared' 2½in. alloy trout fly reel, 1887-1914, with single central raised pillar with one brass roller pillar to either side and rosewood handle. (Bonhams) $253

A scarce Chevalier, Bowness & Bowness 2½in. brass crankwind reel, late 19th century, with raised constant check housing, ivory handle to curved crank.
(Bonhams) $221

A Hardy 'The Perfect' 3¾in. 1896 pattern brass fly reel, circa 1893/4, with four nickel silver pillars, early check, open ball race, dished drum with large perforations.
(Bonhams) $1,342

A rare Nottingham sidecasting reel, possibly by Fosters and of similar design to a Malloch's sidecasting reel with brass starback foot.
(Bonhams) $442

A Hardy 'The Bougle' 3in. alloy trout fly reel (1903 version reproduction) being no. 834 of a limited edition of 1,000, with triple raised pillars.
(Bonhams) $316

A rare Bond & Son 2¾in. folding handle crankwind winch, mid 19th century, folding ivory handle with corresponding rim cut-away. (Bonhams) $600

A Hardy 'The Sea Silex' 6in. duralumin sea centerpin reel, circa 1930s, three rim control model with ivorine rim brake. (Bonhams) $663

A Milwards 'The Overseas' 7in. frogback Nottingham reel, ventilated drum with brass flange, brass frogback foot with optional check. (Bonhams) $474

A rare Hardy 'Hercules' 2⅝in. Special Pattern brass fly reel, circa 1895, with ivorine handle, waisted foot, brass handleplate stamped with "Rod-in-Hand' logo. (Bonhams) $600

A scarce 2½in. brass Malloch's patent sidecasting reel retailed by Brown of Aberdeen, early model with non-reversible copper line guard. (Bonhams) $158

An unnamed 4in. brass and banded rosewood Perth reel, late 19th century, with quadruple pillared cage and rosewood handle. (Bonhams) $221

A Hardy 'The Perfect' 4¼in. alloy wide drum fly reel, with 1905-11 check, ivorine handle, central circular logo, bridged rim tension regulator with Turk's head locking nut. (Bonhams) $284

An Illingworth No. 3 fixed spool reel in box, the reel with reciprocating spool, adjustable spool drag and finger pick-up flyer. (Bonhams) $189

A Hardy 'The Uniqua' 3⅝in. 'Spitfire' finish alloy trout fly reel, circa 1940, with MK I check, backplate stamped *Duplicated Mark II*, grooved brass foot. (Bonhams) $237

An Italian carved and gilded auricular frame, early 17th century, the pierced, reverse profile, outer surround with cartilaginous and foliate motifs in high relief, 43.8 x 34.9 x 14.2cm.
(Christie's) $3,496

An Italian carved tabernacle frame, parts 16th century, the architrave with running recessed tongue motif; plain entablature with a block to either side, 39.6 x 27.3 x 8-15.5cm.
(Christie's) $1,615

A French Régence carved and gilded frame, concave outer edge; the cavetto with scallop-shells to the centers, strap-work on cross hatched ground to the sight edge, 78.8 x 62.5 x 11.4cm.
(Christie's) $7,535

An Italian painted and silvered molding frame, 18th century, the eared outer edge with silvered reverse moldings, the mottled red fascia with L-shaped incised recesses, 15½ x 10¼ x 4in.
(Christie's) $897

An Italian carved, pierced and gilded tabernacle frame in the Venetian Sansovino style, 17th century, the cresting to the top with scrolled broken pediment, 28.6 x 22.8 x 10.8cm.
(Christie's) $7,176

An Italian ebonized and painted cassetta frame, 17th century, the outer ovolo ebonized; the fascia painted to simulate tortoiseshell, 21¾ x 15 x 4½in.
(Christie's) $1,534

An English carved and gilded frame, late 17th century, with schematic foliate outer edge; raised course of fruit and foliage in high relief with acanthus to the corners, 125.4 x 100.6 x 12.1cm.
(Christie's) $2,870

A Northern European carved and painted frame, 17th century, some traces of gilding; two confronting cherubs bearing a central wreath, above a scallop-shell to the cresting, 12¾ x 10½ x 3¼in.
(Christie's) $1,345

A French Louis XIV carved and gilded frame, with dentilled outer edge; the raised corners of the ovolo with inverted scallop shells flanked by beaded acanthus, 8½ x 6¾ x 3½in.
(Christie's) $3,128

An important carved and gilded English frame, 18th century, with double-bead-and-bar course to the outer edge, outer cavetto, 124.3 x 98.4 x 8.6cm.
(Christie's) $31,280

A Spanish carved giltwood picture frame, 18th century, the circular aperture flanked by boldly carved scrolling foliage, inset with an oil on canvas of a saint, 22½in. high.
(Christie's) $1,280

A French carved and gilded arch-topped frame, 18th century, with bead-and-bar course to the outer edge, the raised torus with tied acanthus to the corners, 91.5 x 53.3 x 10.2cm. (Christie's) $1,104

An English carved and gilded Kentian frame, 18th century, eared, with carved, pierced and applied cresting to the top consisting of a central scallop-shell flanked by scrolling foliage, 74.6 x 61.6 x circa 12.7cm. (Christie's) $3,946

A European gilded Modernist molding frame, 20th century, with curvilinear splayed corners, 25 x 19 x 3¼in. (Christie's) $2,167

An Italian carved, painted and gilded cassetta frame in the 17th century style, 19th century, (parts possibly earlier) torus to the outer edge with imbricated leaves, tied at the centers, 37 x 27 x 5½.
(Christie's) $1,615

An Arts and Crafts enamelled picture of oblong form, depicting a landscape in a cushion molded and beaten copper frame, label verso inscribed *Harry Handley 1905 ESK*, 12¼ x 10½in.
(Andrew Hartley) $2,951

A Spanish carved and gilded frame, 17th century, with egg-and-dart outer edge, raised opposed scrolling foliate centers and corners, 12 x 9½ x 4¾in.
(Christie's) $3,588

An Italian ebonized cassetta frame, 17th century, with gilt astragal to the outer edge; the parcel-gilt fascia with incised flower heads and scrolled foliage, 16¾ x 13 x 4½in.
(Christie's) $1,625

Antique American pineapple-post bed, in mahogany and tiger maple, panelled head and footboard, 54in. across bolt holes.
(Eldred's) $660

A 17th century child's crib of good untouched color and patination with four turned simulated bedposts to the corners, 37in. long.
(Boardmans) $1,336

A Louis Philippe rosewood and boxwood lined lit en bateau, the panelled ends with cylindrical top-rails and panelled, flower and foliate carved stiles, 47in. wide.
(Christie's) $920

A mahogany four poster bed, late 19th century, the tester surmounted by pierced C-scroll and rock work carvings, the cluster column posts decorated with foliate carvings, 68in. wide.
(Christie's) $40,986

Renaissance style carved oak double bedstead, late 19th century, comprising headboard, footboard and rails, boldly carved with foliage and molded details.
(Skinner) $1,840

A 16th century-style carved and panelled oak tester bedstead, the headboard with two panels inlaid with stylized foliage above a reeded rail and two recessed panels, 163cm. wide.
(Bearne's) $12,898

Federal mahogany carved tall post bed, probably Southern, 19th century, the four reeded tapering tall posts with carved wrapped leafage above the stylized pineapple carving, 52¼in. wide.
(Skinner) $9,200

A late 19th century Louis XV style mahogany and caned bed, 159cm. wide. (Bonhams) $706

Birch tall pencil post bed, probably New England, early 19th century, the four octagonal tapering posts continuing to square legs, 51in. wide. (Skinner) $2,300

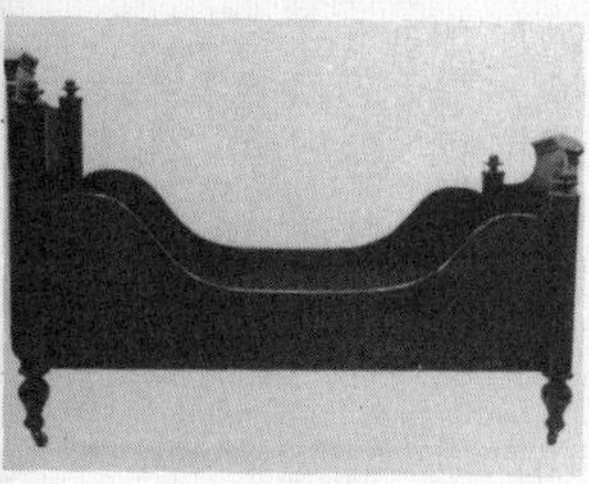

Victorian mahogany boat shaped single bed with bowed head and foot boards and shaped sides, on turned reeded legs, 46in.
(Ewbank) $1,107

An early 17th century style stained oak tester bed.
(Dockrees) $15,680

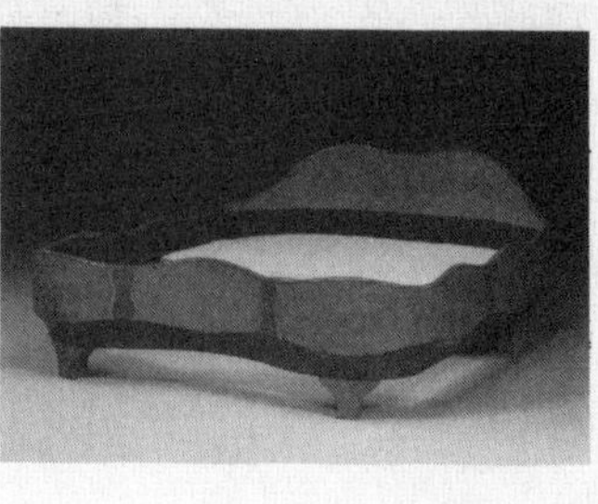

A veneered burr-ash double bed designed by Maurice Dufrêne, 1925, curvilinear shape with undulating sides, 87 x 67in.
(Christie's) $3,657

A kingwood, mahogany and gilt-bronze bed, Paris, circa 1890, the headboard veneered au soleil within a crossbanded border embellished with cast foliage, 159cm. wide.
(Sotheby's) $5,624

A Regency mahogany and polychrome-decorated four-post bed, the associated arched cornice with simulated patera cavetto molding above a foliate-decorated frieze, 72½in. wide.
(Christie's) $33,327

A Louis XVI style ormolu-mounted mahogany bed, third quarter 19th century, the rectangular headboard with egg and dart molding above an armorial trophy, 65in. wide.
(Christie's) $5,750

Eugène Printz, bed, 1930s, Brazilian rosewood headboard, footboard and side panels, the head and end each comprised of four panels in a semi-opened fan design, 57¾in. wide.
(Sotheby's) $5,382

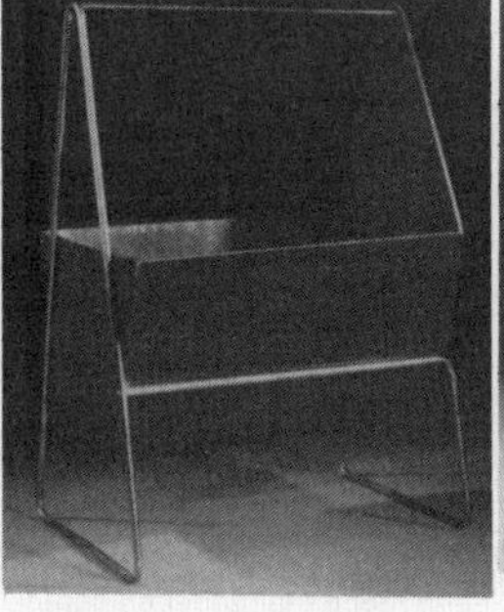

A chromed tubular steel and painted wood cradle, Dutch, circa 1930, the blue painted wood cradle with arched panel to one end on chromed tubular steel frame, 40in. wide. (Christie's) $992

An Indo Portuguese rosewood bed, 19th century, with bobbin and ring-turned uprights, with pierced foliate scroll cross rails, 45½in. wide.
(Christie's) $6,905

An Edwardian mahogany bookcase decorated throughout with boxwood lines and satinwood banding, 60in. wide. (Christie's) $3,667

A late Victorian mahogany bookcase, the upper part with a molded cornice, fitted with adjustable shelves and enclosed by four glazed panel doors, 130½in. wide. (Christie's) $14,899

A Victorian mahogany bookcase, the upper part with molded cornice above three arch glazed doors enclosing adjustable shelves, 72in. wide. (Peter Francis) $5,394

Gustav Stickley mahogany two-door bookcase, New York, circa 1904, design by Harvey Ellis, rectangular top with two square leaded, clear glass panels over two oak divided rectangular panels, 48in. wide. (Skinner) $21,850

A revolving bookcase, circa 1930, attributed to D.I.M., macassar, of almost cube form, each side with two square compartments with burrwood interiors, 15¾in. (Sotheby's) $2,024

George III mahogany and inlay breakfront bookcase, late 18th century, with broken reticulated swan-neck cresting over a carved and inlaid molding, above glazed mullioned doors, 101in. wide. (Skinner) $11,500

A mahogany open bookcase, early 19th century, with ebonized bandings, with three graduated tiers with shaped sides, 33¾in. wide extended.(Christie's) $7,631

A William IV mahogany breakfront library bookcase with molded cornice and four arched astragal glazed doors with anthemion decoration, 90in. wide. (Christie's) $11,040

A Victorian walnut bookcase with molded dentil cornice, three glazed doors enclosing adjustable shelving, flanked by guilloche carved pilasters, 80in. wide. (Andrew Hartley) $3,091

A composed Victorian mahogany bookcase, 92in. wide. (Dockrees) $1,664

A mid 19th century mahogany library bookcase, the lower part with six short panelled doors, 128in. wide. (Peter Francis) $5,190

A 19th century mahogany bookcase, 95in. wide, distressed. (Dockrees) $2,640

An early 19th century mahogany open bookcase, the three shelves on turned pillar supports, the base with a drawer, the flattened bun feet on casters, 28in. (Woolley & Wallis) $2,404

A pair of French mahogany and brass mounted bibliothèques, late 19th century, each fitted with a pair of glazed and panelled doors flanked by fluted column uprights, on turned feet, lacking finials, 56in. wide. (Christie's) $7,452

A mahogany, satinwood and tulipwood banded bookcase, 19th century, the molded cornice above a pair of astragal glazed doors enclosing three adjustable shelves, 49½in. wide. (Christie's) $5,870

Gustav Stickley two-door bookcase, New York, circa 1905-07, gallery top, each door with eight panes, V-shaped pulls, circular device paper label, 43in. wide. (Skinner) $6,900

Arts & Crafts oak breakfront bookcase, the center section with two leaded glazed doors with flowerheads, the base with six carved cupboard doors, 112in. (Ewbank) $3,509

A mahogany library bookcase, the base 19th century, with dentil-molded cornice and a pair of geometrical astragal glazed doors, 68½in. wide. (Christie's) $2,392

A George III crossbanded mahogany bureau bookcase, restorations, 108cm. wide.
(Bonhams) $3,888

A fine scarlet and gilt japanned George I bureau cabinet possibly attributable to John Belcher.
(Phillips) $530,400

A burr-walnut and parcel-gilt bureau-cabinet, the lower section 18th century and refitted, feather banded to the front, 42½in. wide.
(Christie's) $18,515

A Chinese Export ormolu mounted black and gilt-lacquer bureau-cabinet, mid 18th century, the molded pointed cornice with three turned finials above a wreath and arched panelled doors, 42½in. wide. (Christie's) $93,920

A mid 19th century German mahogany roll-top bureau cabinet, the galleried superstructure with an arrangement of four doors with shaped panels, 110cm. wide.
(Bearne's) $2,120

A George I red, black and gilt-japanned bureau-cabinet, decorated overall with raised japanned decoration of birds and foliage, with simulated trellis and foliate decoration, 41in. wide.
(Christie's) $159,795

An 18th century Dutch padouk desk-and-bookcase, in three parts,the bookcase having a shaped and scrolled cornice centered on a shell, 256cm.
(Tennants) $14,130

A Georgian walnut bureau bookcase, glazed upper section fitted with shelves, fitted interior to drop front, one long, two short and two long drawers on bracket feet.
(G.A. Key) $5,565

A walnut and burr-walnut bureau-cabinet, inlaid overall with feather-banding, the molded rectangular cornice above a pair of mirror-backed doors enclosing two adjustable shelves, 41½in. wide.
(Christie's) $14,536

A George I walnut and burr-walnut bureau-cabinet, by John Belcher, the front feather-banded and the sides crossbanded, 40¾in. wide. (Christie's) $55,545

A matched Queen Anne walnut bureau cabinet, 85 x 41in. (G. E. Sworder) $10,880

A mahogany bureau bookcase, associated, both parts 18th century, 105cm. wide. (Bonhams) $4,740

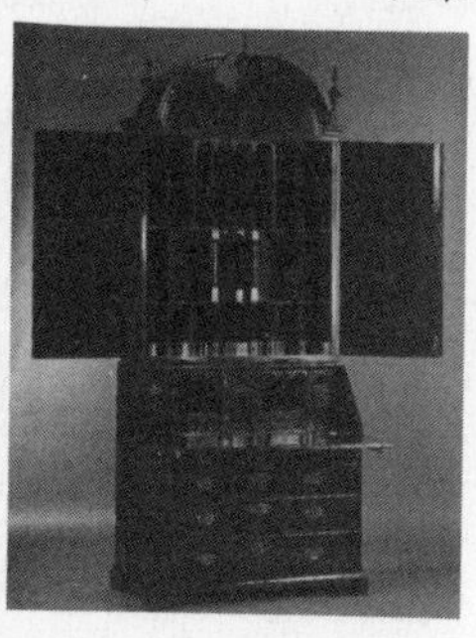

The Nathaniel Appleton carved silver-mounted plum-pudding mahogany dome-top secretary bookcase, attributed to Job Townsend, the mounts by Samuel Casey, Newport Rhode Island, 1730-50. (Sotheby's) $8,252,500

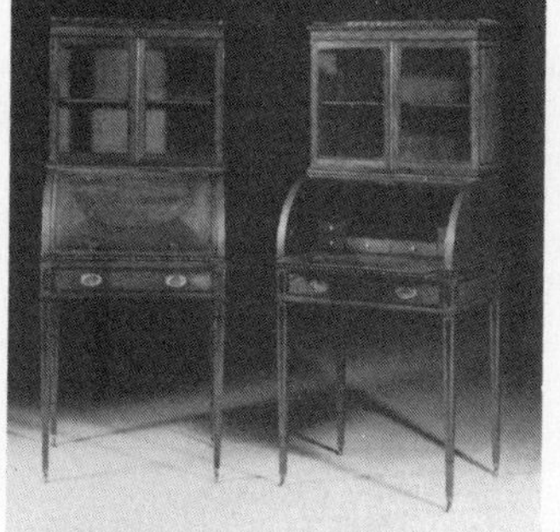

A pair of Edwardian satinwood and mahogany cylinder bureau-cabinets, by Edwards and Roberts, inlaid overall with ebonized lines, each with three-quarter pierced brass gallery above a geometrically-glazed frieze, 26¾in. wide. (Christie's) $25,438

A George III mahogany bureau-cabinet, the stepped rectangular cornice with dentilled molding above three mirror-backed doors enclosing seven adjustable shelves, 46¾in. wide. (Christie's) $27,050

A fine and rare transitional Federal inlaid cherrywood secretary bookcase, Southern, circa 1780, in two parts; the upper section with a broken swan's-neck pediment, 44in. wide. (Sotheby's) $37,375

A walnut and oak bureau bookcase, early 18th century, decorated with crossbanding, the molded cornice above a pair of bevelled mirrored doors enclosing adjustable shelves, 37in. wide. (Christie's) $12,110

A Queen Anne figured-walnut double-domed bureau-cabinet, cross and feather-banded overall, the double-domed molded cornice with three urn finials, 41¾in. wide. (Christie's) $18,170

A George III mahogany bureau with satinwood crossbanding and stringing, the fall front with oval marquetry panel depicting a musical trophy.
(Andrew Hartley) $1,902

A George III Provincial oak and mahogany crossbanded bureau, altered, 99cm. wide.
(Bonhams) $954

A late George III mahogany bureau, the fall flap reveals a fitted interior, oak back, on bracket feet, 3ft.7in. wide.
(Woolley & Wallis) $2,688

A Chippendale carved maple and cherrywood slant front desk, New England, probably New Hampshire, circa 1780, the hinged, molded lid opening to reveal a fitted interior, 35in. wide.
(Sotheby's) $6,900

An early 18th century oak bureau, the carcase applied with channel moldings, 91cm. wide, originally with upper section.
(Bearne's) $3,618

A Chippendale carved and figured maple slant front desk, Massachusetts, circa 1780, the hinged molded lid opening to a fitted interior, 38½in. wide.
(Sotheby's) $6,325

A Sheraton period faded mahogany bureau, the fall flap reveals a satinwood fitted interior, above four long graduated drawers, 3ft.6in.
(Woolley & Wallis) $1,960

Chippendale mahogany carved reverse serpentine slant lid desk, probably Massachusetts, circa 1780, the lid opening to a fitted interior, 40¾in. wide.
(Skinner) $2,875

An early George III mahogany bureau, of small proportions, the slope enclosing small cupboard, two pillar drawers, pigeon holes ar six small drawers, 29½in. wide.
(Canterbury) $7,79

George III oak bureau, the hinged ont enclosing pigeon holes and awers, fitted four long graduated awers below, 92cm. wide.
Vintertons) $3,053

A George III mahogany bureau, the sloping top enclosing a fitted interior above four graduated long drawers, 36¼in. wide.
(Christie's) $4,417

A George III walnut and inlaid bureau, the fall front enclosing a well, a series of drawers and pigeon holes, 101cm.
(Wintertons) $3,240

iladelphia Chippendale slant nt desk, circa 1770 to 1780, of lnut with architecturally fitted erior, entire compartment pulls t to reveal secret drawers behind, 3/16in. wide.
reeman) $22,400

A fine Chippendale carved and highly figured mahogany block-front slant-front desk, Boston Massachusetts, circa 1770, the hinged molded lid opening to a fitted interior, 41½in. wide.
(Sotheby's) $26,450

A Chippendale mahogany block-front slant-front desk, Boston or Salem, 1760-1790, case fitted with four blocked and graduated long drawers with cockbeaded surrounds, 40 1/8in. wide.
(Christie's) $28,750

George III mahogany tambour reau, enclosing a fitted interior th green leather writing surface, ove a pair of mahogany-lined eze drawers, 36¼in. wide.
hristie's) $4,048

Chippendale cherry carved slant lid desk, probably Virginia or North Carolina, circa 1780, the case of four thumbmolded graduated drawers, 39 7/8 wide.
(Skinner) $18,400

A fine kingwood, fruitwood, marquetry and parquetry gilt-bronze mounted bureau à cylindre, probably by Paul Sormani, Paris, circa 1900, 106cm. wide.
(Sotheby's) $54,689

A mahogany bureau, 75cm. wide.
(Bonhams) $174

A French kingwood, mahogany and ormolu-mounted serpentine tambour cylinder bureau, the marble top with a pierced three-quarter gallery, 34½in. wide.
(Christie's) $9,085

An oak bureau, 98cm. wide.
(Bonhams) $708

An antique burr-walnut and maple bureau in the early Georgian style, the feather banded fall enclosing well fitted interior with cupboard, secret drawers and pigeon holes, 2ft. 9in. wide. (Russell Baldwin & Bright) $3,139

A French Empire style mahogany and ormolu mounted bureau à cylindre, circa 1900, the gray veined marble top above a raised superstructure with three short drawers, 39in. wide.
(Christie's) $6,586

A Chippendale figured and carved mahogany reverse-serpentine sla front desk, Massachusetts, circa 1770, the rectangular molded lid opening to a fitted interior, 41½in. wide.
(Sotheby's) $11,50

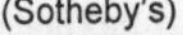

A George I walnut bureau, feather-banded overall, the bureau slope enclosing a fitted interior and well, 27in. wide.
(Christie's) $12,512

A parquetry and gilt-bronze bureau à cylindre, French, the gray marble top within a pierced gallery above a roll top veneered au soleil, 108cm. wide. (Sotheby's) $11,247

A George I walnut bureau, crossbanded overall, the slope enclosing a fitted interior above a fitted drawer and three graduated drawers, 30¼in. wide.
(Christie's) $26,68

An Anglo-Indian ivory inlaid padouk and rosewood cylinder bureau, 18th century, Vizagapatam, inlaid overall with foliate patterns, with brown leather lined cylinder, 38in. wide.
(Christie's) $14,720

An Edwardian mahogany and satinwood banded cylinder bureau, inlaid with lines, the superstructure with a three quarter pierced gallery and fitted with three drawers, 47in. wide. (Christie's) $5,451

A William and Mary style walnut bureau with feather banding, having fitted interior over three long drawers, on turned supports with flat cross stretcher, 2ft. 8in. wide.
(Russell Baldwin & Bright) $1,628

A George II mahogany and marquetry bureau, inlaid overall with chequer banding, the slope with a central starburst and enclosing a fitted interior, 37½in. wide.
(Christie's) $10,672

A French Empire Revival mahogany bureau à cylindre, late 19th century, applied with various classical gilt metal mounts, the associated rectangular green veined marble top with three drawers below, 47in. wide.
(Christie's) $10,247

A George II mahogany small bureau, the hinged slope enclosing a fitted interior with mahogany lined drawers around a cupboard and a well, above a secret drawer, 25½in. wide. (Christie's) $8,832

A Queen Anne scarlet and gilt-japanned bureau, decorated overall with raised chinoiserie scenes, the sloping top enclosing a fitted interior with pigeon-holes, drawers and a well, 36in. wide.
(Christie's) $12,512

A North European mahogany bureau à cylindre, second quarter 19th century, applied with gilt metal mounts, with a breche violette marble top, possibly German, 66½in. wide.
(Christie's) $9,688

A French kingwood and marquetry cylinder bureau, late 19th century, applied with gilt metal mounts, the rectangular mottled marble top fitted with a pierced brass three-quarter gallery, 26½in. wide.
(Christie's) $3,353

A George III oak bureau, with mahogany crossbanding, the fall front revealing shaped and stepped interior fitted with drawers and pigeon holes, 44½in. wide.
(Andrew Hartley) $661

A Queen Anne style figured maple child's desk on frame, in two parts; the upper section with a hinged lid opening to a block- and fan-carved interior, 25¾in. wide.
(Sotheby's) $6,900

Queen Anne style maple child's slant lid desk, New England, circa 1750, the lid opening to a compartmented interior, above two graduated drawers, 19¼in. wide.
(Skinner) $2,530

Federal cherry inlaid fall-front desk, Southeastern New England, fall front revealing a fitted interior above a case of four graduated drawers, 39½in. wide.
(Skinner) $2,185

Maple slant lid desk, Concord, Massachusetts, 1780-90, with inscription reading *the property of Merriam, the first settlers of Concord*, superstructure with three thumb-molded drawers, 35in. wide. (Skinner) $17,250

Transitional walnut slant front desk late 18th century, architecturally fitted interior, entire compartment pulls out to reveal secret compartments, 39¼in. wide.
(Freeman) $5,04

A George III mahogany bureau, crossbanded with string inlay, fall front revealing fitted interior with drawers and pigeon holes, 34in. wide.
(Andrew Hartley) $1,573

Chippendale maple slant lid desk, New England, late 18th/early 19th century, the lid opening to a two-tiered interior, 35in. wide.
(Skinner) $1,840

A French Provincial fruitwood bureau, late 18th/early 19th century, the sloping panelled fal enclosing a fitted interior on sho cabriole legs, 27½in. wide.
(Christie's) $4,87

Sheraton-style painted satinwood bowfront side cabinet, decorated with musical trophies, floral and husk swags, 64cm. wide.
(Bearne's) $2,202

A French kingwood dwarf side cabinet, early 19th century, applied with ormolu mounts and decorated with crossbanding, 40in. wide.
(Christie's) $3,726

A mid-16th century French walnut cabinet on stand, inset with marble panels and carved with masks, figures, scrolls and foliage, 116.5cm. wide.
(Bearne's) $6,921

A Regency mahogany glazed floorstanding cabinet, the architectural pediment with central brass finial, molded edge above double astragal glazed doors, 132cm. wide.
(Wintertons) $4,455

Alvar Aalto, a birch cocktail cabinet, designed 1936, manufactured for Artek, the rectangular top above a pair of panel doors, each of curly-birch faced plywood, 37½in. wide.
(Christie's) $2,888

A Chinese hardwood arched cabinet-on-stand, late 19th/early 20th century, the architectural interior profusely decorated with floral and foliate tendrils and with arcaded baluster galleries, 40in. wide. (Christie's) $2,544

A French Provincial fruitwood side cabinet, 18th century, the rounded rectangular top with a molded edge above a frieze centered by a ten-pointed star, 58½in. wide.
(Christie's) $1,184

A Scottish George III mahogany cabinet-on-chest, the molded rectangular dentilled top above a pair of mirror glazed doors, enclosing three shelves, 39¼in.
(Christie's) $3,312

A Napoleon III ebonized, scarlet-tortoiseshell, brass-inlaid and ormolu mounted side cabinet, the black marble top with canted corners, 48in. wide.
(Christie's) $1,184

A 19th century mahogany music cabinet with marquetry and stringing, the raised top with pierced brass gallery.
(Andrew Hartley) $1,664

A pair of Edwardian satinwood inlaid mahogany pedestal cabinets for the dining room, 36in. high.
(Michael J. Bowman) $2,542

Gustav Stickley oak music cabinet, New York, circa 1912, no. 70w, gallery top over rectangular panelled door, branded mark, 20in wide. (Skinner) $7,475

A late Victorian ebonized amboyna and parcel gilt side cabinet, the raised back with turned finials and spindles above rectangular mirror, 76cm. wide.
(Dreweatt Neate) $763

A pair of 19th century French pier side cabinets, veneered in figured walnut, the top brass and ebonized moldings with beading and having inlaid stringing, 30¼in. wide.
(Woolley & Wallis) $2,564

A small early 19th century penwork decorated cabinet, decorated with classical motifs and vines, the top with a cavetto cornice above pink interior with shelves, 25in.
(Woolley & Wallis) $4,042

A late 19th century mahogany music cabinet in the Art Nouveau style, the raised shaped oblong top on four supports with undershelf, 22in. wide.
(Andrew Hartley) $818

A William IV rosewood side cabinet, with a marble top above a reed and dart decorated frieze, 3ft.11in.
(Woolley & Wallis) $4,950

A well figured mahogany dentist's cabinet, English, mid 19th century, with carved scroll pediment, roll top revealing marble work surface and mirror surround, 75cm. high.
(Bonhams) $1,648

A Robert Thompson of Kilburn 'Mouseman' cabinet, executed 1934, dark stained oak, the square top above an open shelf with single cupboard door, 17¾in. square.
(Sotheby's) $1,435

A Regency brass inlaid rosewood table cabinet, early 19th century, with bands of foliate and line inlay overall, the top with crossbanding of rosewood and walnut, 15¾in. wide. (Christie's) $3,270

A 19th century French style oval walnut bijouterie cabinet, fitted galleried top with inset bevelled glass panel, fitted single door, 55cm. wide.
(Wintertons) $1,223

A Victorian ormolu mounted marquetry walnut side cabinet, the floral inlaid frieze over a pair of glazed doors enclosing velvet lined shelves, 51in. wide.
(Michael J. Bowman) $2,870

A rare burr walnut dentist's cabinet, English, mid 19th century, top doors revealing fitted shelving for bottles, below twelve graduated drawers, 175cm. high.
(Bonhams) $2,801

An oak free standing folio cabinet, the bolted carcase with pollarded oak veneer, the top on an adjustable ratchet with a rising folio rest, 4ft.2½in. wide.
(Woolley & Wallis) $3,200

One of a pair of Victorian marquetry inlaid walnut and gilt metal mounted pier cabinets, circa 1870, frieze inlaid with floral marquetry with conforming panelled cupboard door, 33¾in. wide.
(Christie's) (Two) $10,662

A 19th century rosewood pier cabinet with pierced brass gallery, crossbanded frieze with bead and reel edging over door, 30¼in. wide.
(Andrew Hartley) $3,775

A 19th century French kingwood, marquetry and brass mounted dwarf cabinet inset with yellow Breccia marble slab to top, 35in. wide. (Canterbury) $2,623

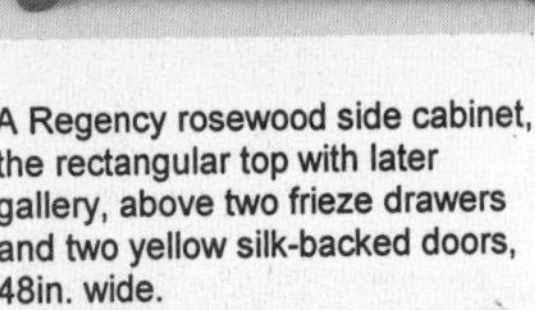

A Regency rosewood side cabinet, the rectangular top with later gallery, above two frieze drawers and two yellow silk-backed doors, 48in. wide.
(Christie's) $5,152

A pair of 19th century French walnut pier cabinets, of serpentine form with ormolu mounts, white marble tops on fluted column supports, 32½in. wide.
(Andrew Hartley) $5,104

A Victorian walnut, gilt-metal mounted and marquetry dwarf side cabinet, the front decorated with meandering floral and foliate stems, 60¾in. wide.
(Christie's) $6,359

A sycamore sewing cabinet, designed by Franz Messner, circa 1900, the top with two hinged doors opening to reveal the compartmentalized interior, 19¾in. wide. (Christie's) $5,796

Jean Prouvé and Charlotte Perriand, storage unit/room divider for the Maison du Mexique, Paris, 1953, pine and acacia frame, three sliding and two fixed aluminium doors, 182.5cm. wide.
(Sotheby's) $39,721

An ebonized and inlaid walnut and burrwood writing cabinet, the design attributed to Ernest Gimson circa 1930, the upper compartmen with burrwood fall-front inlaid with ebonized banding, 34in.
(Christie's) $5,589

A walnut side cabinet, 20th century, profusely carved with opposed C-scroll borders, flowerheads and scrolled foliage, gray marble top, probably Italian, 44½in. wide.
(Christie's) $2,812

A Swedish baroque apothecary's cabinet of painted oak, the upper section with graduated rows of drawers, 136cm. wide.
(Stockholms AV) $6,685

A Victorian walnut and marquetry side cabinet, the concave marquetry frieze above two doors with oval glazed panel centers in a burr walnut surround, 44in. wide.
(Boardmans) $2,50

A mid- Victorian walnut canterbury whatnot, the lower part with three sections and drawer under, distressed, 55.5cm. wide.
(Bonhams) $786

Late George III mahogany four division canterbury with turned corner supports and legs, one drawer, 20in.
(Ewbank) $2,441

A rosewood canterbury, 19th century, with lyre shaped end supports, incomplete and restored, 51cm. wide.
(Bonhams) $472

Late Victorian music canterbury in bird's eye maple, three divisions with turned spindle sides and drawer under, the top galleried shelf with turned supports.
(Jacobs & Hunt) $800

A George III mahogany four division canterbury, with slatted compartments and a carrying handle, on ring-turned supports, 16¼in. wide.
(Christie's) $4,124

A mid-Victorian burr walnut veneered combined canterbury and whatnot, of shaped oval form inlaid with boxwood lines, on toupie feet, 66cm. wide.
(Bearne's) $2,226

A Victorian rosewood canterbury, with three folio sections within turned and lotus carved corner posts, 53cm.
(Tennants) $3,768

A Regency mahogany canterbury, stamped *Gillows.Lancaster*, the rectangular top above four X-dividers and baluster supports, 19½in. wide.
(Christie's) $6,480

A William IV mahogany canterbury of rectangular form with nine spindle divides, above a frieze drawer, 22in. wide.
(Christie's) $4,784

An early 19th century rosewood music canterbury, dipped divisions, with a central hand grip, 19in. (Woolley & Wallis) $3,763

A walnut three division music canterbury on casters. (Academy Auctioneers) $1,840

A Victorian rosewood canterbury, with four carved scroll divisions and drawer below, on short turned supports with castors, 56.5cm. wide. (Bristol) $1,648

A Regency mahogany canterbury with dished slatted divisions over single drawers on turned tapering supports with brass toe caps and casters, 18in. wide. (Russell Baldwin & Bright) $2,343

A 19th century mahogany canterbury, the dished slatted divisions with loop handle, 19¾in. wide. (Andrew Hartley) $2,688

An early 19th century mahogany music canterbury, the 'X' frame with turned side stretchers, above a frieze drawer, 19in. (Woolley & Wallis) $1,960

A William IV faded rosewood music canterbury, the dipped divisions with a central grip handle, the turned block corner supports with finials, 20in. (Woolley & Wallis) $3,795

A Neo-Grec ebonized and gilt-incised canterbury, probably New York City, 1870-1890, the triple-welled case with scrolled and pierced sides. (Christie's) $1,840

A Regency mahogany four division canterbury, by Gillows, the curved slatted compartments with a central carrying handle above a drawer, 21½in. wide. (Christie's) $4,600

A Queen Anne walnut corner chair, possibly by Solomon Fussell, Philadelphia, 1740-60, the U-shaped back with shaped crest above vasiform splats.
(Sotheby's) $17,250

A Chippendale mahogany corner chair, Boston, 1760-1790, the shaped crest above a shaped armrail continuing to outscrolling handholds over column-turned supports.
(Christie's) $23,000

Walnut Queen Anne corner arm chair, circa 1740-1760, plain three piece crest rail terminating in volutes, solid vasiform back splats.
(Freeman) $20,160

A George III mahogany corner armchair, the shaped back with outswept arms above two pierced vertical splats.
(Cheffins) $954

Queen Anne walnut roundabout chair, Boston, 1752-60, the shaped crest continuing to scrolled hand holds above three vase and ring turned stiles.
(Skinner) $43,700

Chippendale walnut roundabout chair, Massachusetts, 1770-1800, the shaped crest on scrolled arms above shaped splats.
(Skinner) $10,350

A George II mahogany corner elbow-chair, the horse-shoe top-rail on turned uprights and solid splats.
(Christie's) $2,608

A George II mahogany corner chair, the curved toprail with scrolled ends above a pair of pierced interlaced splats.
(Christie's) $7,728

A mahogany corner armchair, George III, the seat carved with blind fretwork, on chamfered square legs. (Sotheby's) $1,536

One of a pair of early Victorian mahogany dining chairs.
(Bonhams) (Two) $219

Two of a set of four George III mahogany side chairs, the shaped panelled toprail above a pierced trellis splat with reeded fan.
(Christie's) (Four) $6,440

A fine Federal painted and parcel gilt side chair, attributed to Simon Gragg, Boston Massachusetts, circa 1810, the arched crest with projecting tablet.
(Sotheby's) $9,200

One of a set of four George III yellow and floral painted side chairs, decorated with floral swags, the pierced back above a drop-in seat covered in striped material.
(Christie's) (Four) $1,769

Two of a set of eight George III mahogany dining chairs, including two open armchairs, each with an arched top rail above a pierced, interlaced, vase shaped splat.

(Christie's)
(Eight) $16,560

Queen Anne/Chippendale Transition mahogany side chair, Philadelphia, circa 1740-1770, incised crest with carved shell and bold ears above a pierced vasiform splat. (Freeman) $5,040

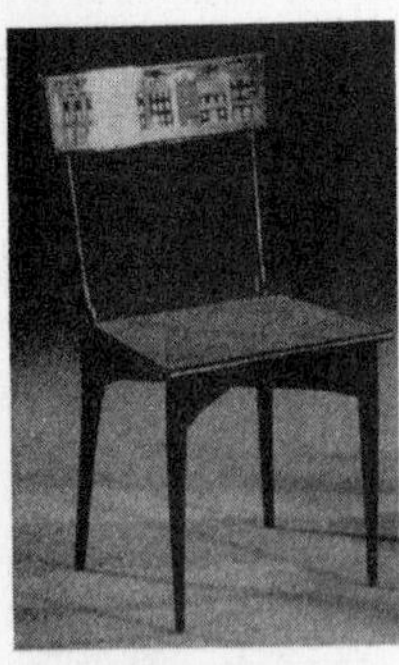

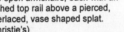

Piero Fornasetti, an ebonized side chair, designed circa 1955, the panel back with transfer decoration to both sides, above square cane seat, on tapering uprights.
(Christie's) $579

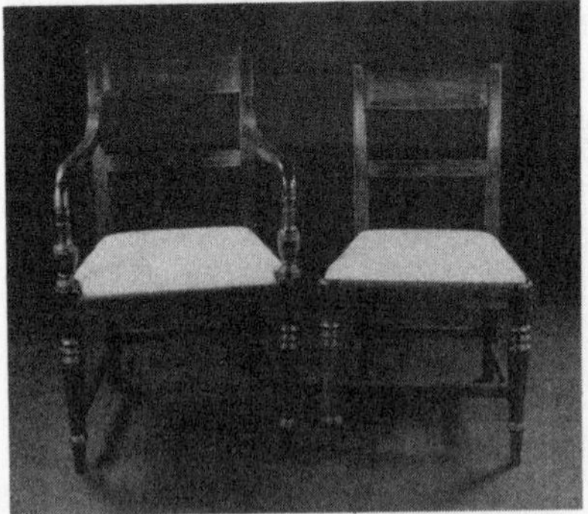

Two of a set of twelve Regency mahogany dining chairs, with curved bar backs and horizontal mid-rails between reeded uprights, by Gillows. (Tennants)
(Twelve) $13,345

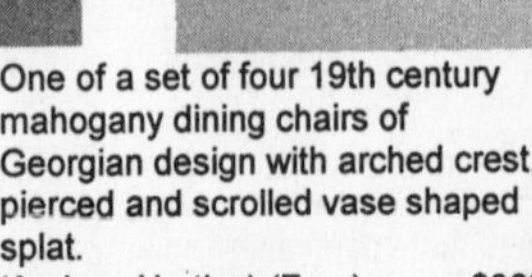

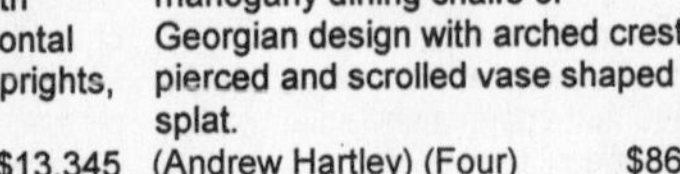

One of a set of four 19th century mahogany dining chairs of Georgian design with arched crest, pierced and scrolled vase shaped splat.
(Andrew Hartley) (Four) $862

One of a set of four Victorian mahogany dining chairs.
(Bonhams) (Four) $471

A pair of mid Victorian polychrome painted oak side chairs, designed by Henry Woodyer, made in 1861 by Harland and Fisher.
(Christie's) $5,520

A fine and rare Chippendale carved mahogany upholstered side chair, Philadelphia, circa 1765, the shaped C-scroll carved crest with central acanthus motif.
(Sotheby's) $156,500

A Queen Anne mahogany side-chair, Boston, circa 1750, the yoked crest with vasiform splat flanked by straight stiles above a balloon-shaped seat, 40in. high.
(Christie's) $7,475

Two of a set of ten late Victorian mahogany dining chairs, having scoop shaped backs with a central carved baluster splat.
(Tennants) (Ten) $2,512

One of a pair of bentwood side chairs, designed by Josef Hoffmann for the Grimenstein Sanatorium, Semmering, manufactured by J. & J. Kohn, circa 1905.
(Christie's) (Two) $5,409

Michael Thonet, a bentwood side chair, Model No. 4, designed circa 1848 for Thonet, with decorative bentwood back within arched toprail extending to form uprights.
(Christie's) $992

Two of a set of six early 19th century ash and elm chairs, the slightly splayed rectangular backs containing four ring turned spindles.
(Tennants) (Six) $1,250

An important Queen Anne figured maple side chair, labelled *William Savery*, Philadelphia, circa 1760, the serpentine incised crest with flared ears,
(Sotheby's) $134,500

A Victorian mahogany pair of hall chairs, the scroll shaped back with inset shield above turned supports.
(Bristol) $708

A pair of walnut and beech side chairs of late 17th century style, 19th/20th century, each with a serpentine crested rectangular padded high back.
(Christie's) $3,312

Two of a set of four 17th century walnut chairs, the padded back with pierced scrolled crest and turned finials on wrythen turned uprights.
(Andrew Hartley)
(Four) $2,393

A pair of early Victorian walnut hall chairs, the spoon shaped back with central oval splat molded with initials.
(Wintertons) $574

One of a pair of William IV mahogany side chairs, each with a deep curved bar top-rail decorated with scrolled cornucopiae.
(Christie's) (Two) $562

AUCTIONEER'S ADVICE

While Caveat Emptor is a good rule of thumb when buying at auctions, these are in fact covered by the Trades Descriptions Act and the auctioneer is duty bound to describe the goods offered in a fair and honest way. If in doubt before the sale, speak to the auctioneer. If you're still not happy, don't bid. Doubts after the sale are most simply addressed if raised before the vendor is paid out.

(Michael Bowman)

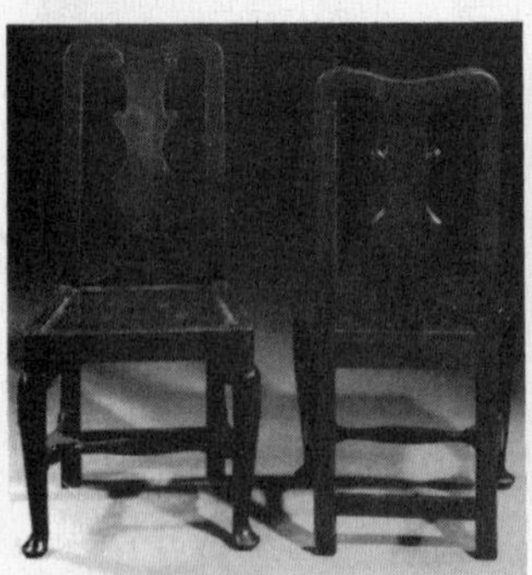

Two of a set of six oak chairs, English, mid 18th century, each with wavy scroll-carved top-rail and shaped vase splat.
(Christie's) (Six) $12,473

Pair of Thonet ebonized side chairs, late 19th century, reticulated back, caned seat, 38½in. high.
(Skinner) $575

Two of a set of eight single and two arm Hepplewhite style mahogany dining chairs, the shield shaped backs decorated with bell-flower molding. (Anderson & Garland)
(Ten) $5,688

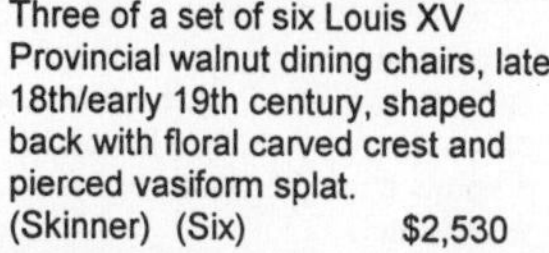

Three of a set of six Louis XV Provincial walnut dining chairs, late 18th/early 19th century, shaped back with floral carved crest and pierced vasiform splat.
(Skinner) (Six) $2,530

One of a set of six Victorian walnut balloon back dining chairs, each with interlaced scroll carved splat and serpentine fronted seat.
(Bearne's) (Six) $1,749

Two of a set of eight mahogany side chairs, in Adam style, the oval pierced splat backs centered with an oval patera. (Woolley & Wallis)
(Eight) $2,805

A pair of early George II walnut side chairs, the veneered shaped backs with carved scallop shell crests to the splats.
(Woolley & Wallis) $11,220

Queen Anne carved walnut side chair, Boston, 1740-65, the double arched crest with central carved shell above a vasiform splat over a balloon shaped over upholstered seat. (Skinner) $8,050

Two of a set of nine mahogany side chairs, with pierced splat backs, serpentine crests, seven late 18th century and a later pair to match.
(Woolley & Wallis)
(Nine) $4,290

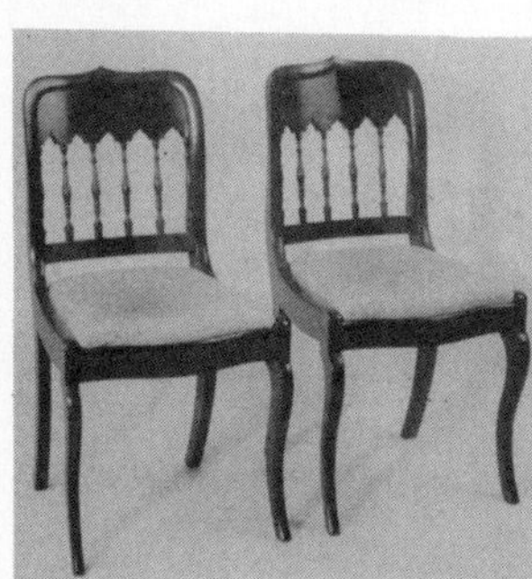

Two of a set of ten Empire style mahogany side chairs, mid 19th century, each with spindle inset backrests, serpentine slip-seat and angular cabriole legs.
(Skinner) (Ten) $1,380

The Morris family Chippendale carved mahogany side chair, Philadelphia, circa 1770, acanthus and C-scroll carved crest above an interlaced bellflower and C-scroll carved Gothic splat.
(Sotheby's) $68,500

Pair of black painted stencil decorated gilt and polychrome Hitchcock side chairs, Hitchcocks-ville, Connecticut, circa 1825-30, the turned crest rails above horizontal splats.
(Skinner) $1,150

A three legged low chair, Scottish Lowlands or English, second half 19th century, the base constructed of hawthorn branches, the front legs carved as stockings and boots, the left leg with a projecting point carved as a dog's head.
(Christie's) $5,851

A fine and rare pair of Queen Anne turned and figured cedar rush-seat side chairs, Bermuda, early 18th century, each with a yoke form crest above a vasiform splat.
(Sotheby's) $13,800

A late 19th century Chinese desk chair, in hardwood, the back with pierced carving of a dragon and dragons amongst clouds to the surmount.
(Woolley & Wallis) $120

A Queen Anne carved cherrywood compass-seat side chair, Massachusetts, 1730-50, the shaped crest with carved ears above a vasiform splat and shaped slip seat. (Sotheby's) $2,587

A pair of Shaker style stained maple and pine revolving desk chairs, 20th century, the concave crest above eight flaring spindles and a circular seat.
(Sotheby's) $632

Rare Philadelphia Queen Anne Transitional side chair, circa 1750-1760, of walnut with shell carved crest rail with double scrolled volutes.
(Freeman) $336,000

A late Regency painted metal chair, probably by Evans & Cartwright, circa 1820, the top rail with floral painted design, molded 'cane'seat with turned legs.
(Bonhams) $710

Two of a 'Reformed Gothic' set of six oak dining chairs, with bar backs, overstuffed seats and on chamfered square section supports, 90cm. (Bristol) (Six) $1,008

One of a set of six beechwood and elm kitchen chairs, Thames Valley, late 19th century, each with arched top-rail and turned horizontal splat with central tablet.
(Christie's) (Six) $1,189

One of a set of four Regency simulated rosewood and beechwood chairs with brass mounts, arched and reeded crest rail. (Andrew Hartley) (Four) $1,007

Two of a William IV mahogany set of seven bar back dining chairs, with drop-in seats, on turned lappeted supports. (Bristol) (Seven) $1,788

One of a set of thirteen Victorian oak boardroom chairs, including an armchair.(Bonhams) (Thirteen) $1,272

One of a set of six Victorian rosewood dining chairs, the waisted back with dished crest rail, pierced leaf and scroll carved splat and similar cross bar. (Andrew Hartley) (Six) $2,393

A pair of 18th century walnut side chairs with shaped top rails, solid figured splats and upholstered drop-in seats. (Russell Baldwin & Bright) $6,318

A George II mahogany hall chair, the shaped and waisted back above a dished seat, the apron carved with heart-shaped C-scrolls, 38¼in. high. (Christie's) $5,184

One of a set of six George III mahogany dining chairs, with arched crest, pierced and waisted splat with fluted base. (Andrew Hartley) (Six) $4,626

Two of a set of six George III elm chairs, the dished crest rail over pierced vase shaped splat with anthemion. (Andrew Hartley) (Six) $2,592

One of a set of eight antique mahogany dining chairs of Chippendale style, with gothic-pierced splats. (Russell Baldwin & Bright) (Eight) $1,333

A George IV mahogany bergère, the curved and scroll bar top-rail with carved lotus flowerheads and stems. (Christie's) $7,631

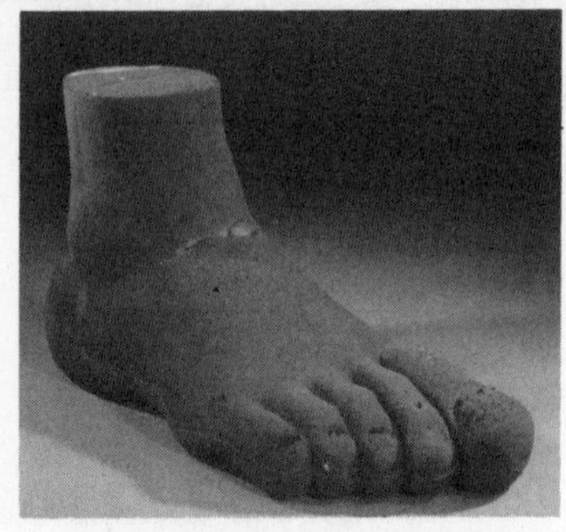

Gaetano Pesce, an Up-7 II Piede seat, this example believed to be a prototype, designed 1969, produced by B&B Italia, 63in. long. (Christie's) $5,427

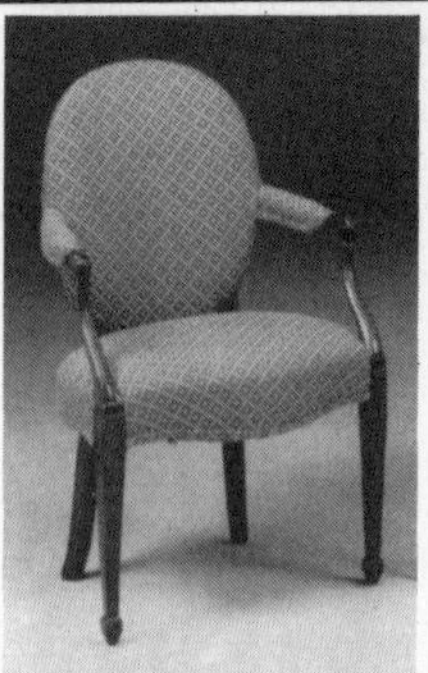

A George III mahogany open armchair, with a padded oval back, scroll arms and serpentine seat on square tapering gaitered legs. (Christie's) $1,453

One of a pair of cream and green painted armchairs, each with a padded oval back, molded arms and serpentine seat with a fluted frieze, possibly 18th century. (Christie's) (Two) $2,907

Verner Panton, Denmark, a rare early square cone chair, designed 1958, upholstered blue fabric with metal frame of pyramid form. (Bonhams) $6,292

A Gothic Revival carved mahogany armchair, possibly New York, 1840-1860, the pointed crest centering a leaf-carved crocket above a carved splat, 48in. high. (Christie's) $2,530

A mahogany open armchair, of Gainsborough type, with a padded back and rocaille carved downswept arms, 18th century. (Christie's) $3,634

Joe Colombo, an Elda lounge chair, designed 1963-65, for Comfort, the fibreglass shell with revolving pedestal. (Christie's) $4,341

Franco Albini and Franca Helg, a PL19 armchair, designed 1957 for Poggi, with red fabric upholstery o gray enamelled tubular frame. (Christie's) $904

A Victorian mahogany armchair, with a close nailed padded back and scroll arms with eagle's heads on husk uprights.
(Christie's) $2,725

An early 19th century easy chair, with scrolled over tub shaped back and arms, the seat raised on a sunken panelled front rail.
(Tennants) $2,198

An early Victorian maple chair, with a button-down scrolled back, downswept to S-scrolls and a serpentine seat.
(Christie's) $908

Chippendale carved mahogany lolling chair, Boston, Massachusetts, circa 1770, the serpentine crest above a padded back and arms on downswept, faceted, supports.
(Sotheby's) $43,125

Ferdinand Porsche, and Antropovarius lounge chair, designed 1984 for Poltrona Frau, green leather padded seat on adjustable and articulated black plastic and metal spine.
(Christie's) $2,894

A William IV rosewood and parcel-gilt open armchair, carved with scrolling acanthus, the padded cartouche shaped back with a foliate edge.
(Christie's) $8,176

A George III mahogany tub shaped armchair, with a padded arched back, outswept rounded arms and serpentine seat, on cabriole legs.
(Christie's) $1,998

Gaetano Pesce, a Sit-Down lounge chair, designed 1975 for Cassina, with quilted colored upholstery, over polyurethane foam base.
(Christie's) $1,266

A George I mahogany armchair on cabriole legs headed by foliage and pad feet, previously with castors, probably originally wider.
(Christie's) $8,887

Attributed to Michael Thonet, folding bentwood deck chair, Model No. 1, designed circa 1863-66 for Thonet, the pliable frame enclosing elliptical cane seat and back. (Christie's) $920

George Nelson, a fibreglass DAA desk chair, designed 1956 for Herman Miller, with yellow-white fibreglass seat elements connected by steel and rubber mounts. (Christie's) $2,166

A William IV rosewood bergère, the arm terminals carved with stylized foliage, on lotus-carved turned legs. (Christie's) $2,437

Erich Dieckmann, one of a pair of birch armchairs, designed circa 1930, probably manufactured by Weimar Bau- und Wohnungskunst, each with cane back and seat. (Christie's) (Two) $1,264

Hans Pieck, a laminated beech lounge chair, designed 1946-7, cut and folded from a single laminated sheet. (Christie's) $2,708

Alessandro Mendini for Alchimia, manufactured by Gavina SpA, 'Scivolando' mirror chair from the Collezione Oggetti senza Tempo, 1983, unique piece, wood, mirrored glass, 140cm. high. (Sotheby's) $18,400

An adjustable chair/ladder designed by Eileen Gray, 1932-34, aluminum modernist framework, textured surfaces, 24¾in. maximum height. (Christie's) $29,256

Gerrit Rietveld, a stained wood high-back armchair, designed 1924, later executed by G.A. van de Groenikan, plywood back and seat to linear open framework. (Christie's) $10,472

Marcel Breuer, a nickel plated tubular steel armchair, Model No. B34, designed 1929-30 for Gebrüder Thonet, the cantilever form with downswept wooden armrests. (Christie's) $1,379

Gerrit Rietveld, a stained pin Zig-Zag chair, designed 1934 for G.A. van de Groenikan, the geometric form with white stain finish, of butt-jointed construction.
(Christie's) $3,312

A painted wood and canvas folding side chair, probably French, circa 1925-30, the red painted hinged wooden frame with hook and eye catch to fasten.
(Christie's) $812

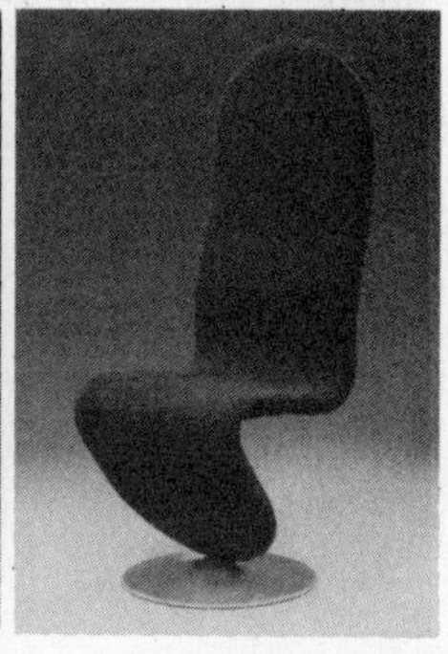

Verner Panton for Fritz Hansen Eftf, '1-2-3 Chair', 1973, fabric upholstered S-shaped metal frame with high back, on circular foot.
(Sotheby's) $515

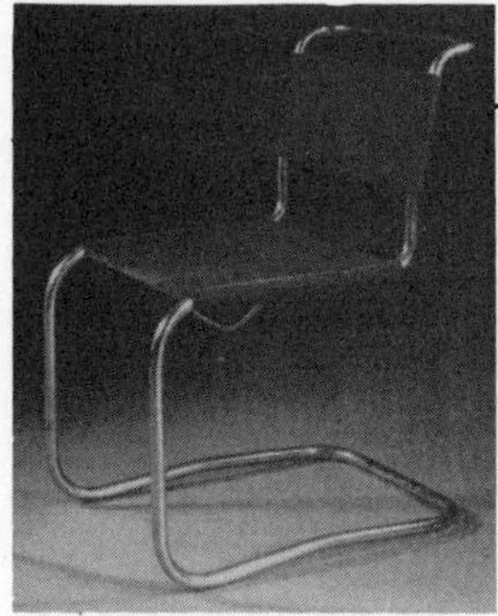

Mart Stam and Marcel Breuer, a nickel plated tubular steel side chair, Model No.B33, designed 1927-28, manufactured by both Thonet and Desta, with red canvas seat elements.
(Christie's) $1,353

Jean Prouvé, an oak and metal Visiteur lounge chair, designed 1942, executed by Ateliers Jean Prouvé, black fabric seat pads on sheet zinc and oak frame.
(Christie's) $12,277

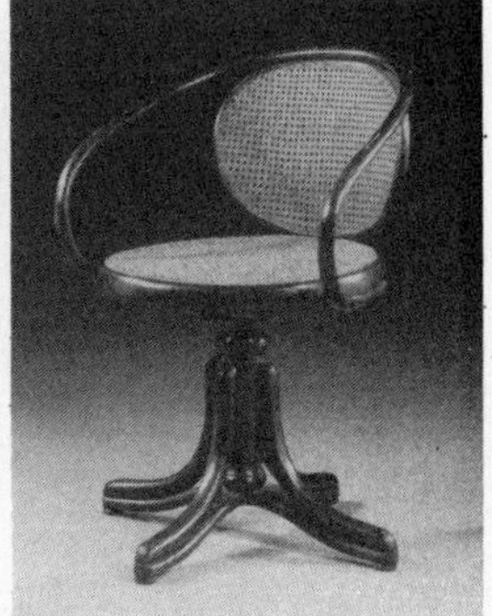

A Thonet bentwood desk chair, designed 1865-6, the elliptical cane back and seat within continuous line frame.
(Christie's) $1,840

Marcel Breuer for Thonet, lounge chair 'B35' designed 1928-9, this example manufactured circa 1930, chromium plated tubular steel frame.
(Sotheby's) $3,784

Marcel Breuer, an aluminum lounge chair, designed 1932-33, manufactured by Embru-Werke AG, for Stylclair, France.
(Christie's) $8,125

Claude Siclis, an enamelled tubular steel lounge chair, designed 1935-36, manufactured by Thonet Frères, Paris, for use in the Val d'Isère resorts, ebonized beech armrests.
(Christie's) $4,416

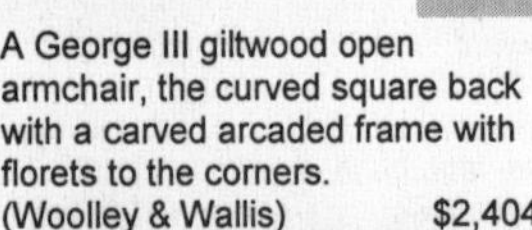

A George III giltwood open armchair, the curved square back with a carved arcaded frame with florets to the corners.
(Woolley & Wallis) $2,404

A pair of George III beech-framed open armchairs with fluted upholstered oval backs, padded arms on stop-fluted supports.
(Bearne's) $1,416

A Victorian upholstered mahogany showframe salon chair, in need of re-upholstery.
(Dockrees) $640

A Regency simulated rosewood bergère, the back with four turned spindles between a finial capped ring-turned frame.
(Christie's) $1,549

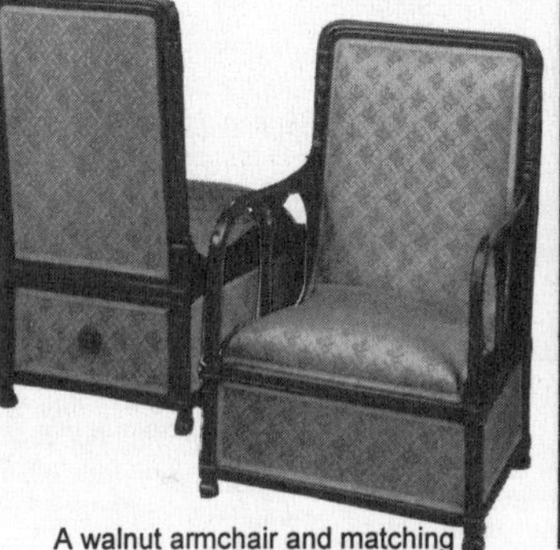

A walnut armchair and matching side chair, early 20th century, each upholstered in patterned green fabric, with a padded back and seat between spiral-turned uprights.
(Christie's) $1,396

A Louis XVI style giltwood tub bergère, circa 1900, the bowed top rail with outset corners, continuing to padded arms.
(Christie's) $1,411

Alessandro Mendini for Studio Alchimia, 'Poltrona de Proust' designed 1978 for the Bau.haus Collection, this example made 1987, carved wood frame.
(Sotheby's) $9,930

A Louis XV style walnut and parcel gilt salon suite, circa 1900, comprising a settee, four armchairs and a pair of side chairs.
(Christie's) $2,822

A 19th century French giltwood bergère armchair, with torch and quiver cresting with stylized acanthus and paterae decoration.
(Bristol) $471

A mahogany and caned library bergère, 19th century, the reeded toprail above a caned back with downswept channelled supports.
(Christie's) $2,552

Ron Arad, Israel, 'Rolling Volume', designed 1989, an important early hand welded and beaten mild steel single volume rocking armchair.
(Bonhams) $18,875

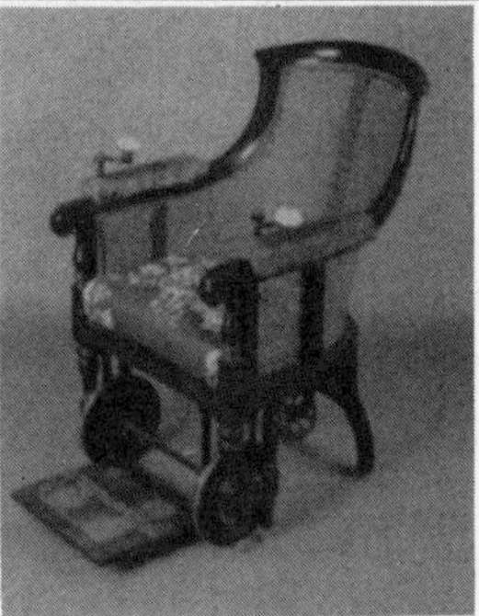

A Victorian caned mahogany patent invalid's chair.
(Bonhams) $1,100

Carlo Bugatti, Italy, a corner chair, designed circa 1902, the wooden frame of square design with turned supports, curved back rest with tassel frieze.
(Bonhams) $2,359

Joe Colombo, a plywood armchair, No. 4801, designed 1965 for Kartell, composed of three interlocking white enamelled wood sections.
(Christie's) $3,075

One of a pair of Louis XVI style giltwood fauteuils, late 19th century, each chair with an arched top rail centered by ribbon and leaf carving.
(Christie's) (Two) $1,882

A 19th century French walnut framed library chair, the upholstered adjustable back and seat with carved leaf scrolled crest centered by a mask.
(Andrew Hartley) $1,134

Benjamin Fletcher, U.K., a cane lounge chair, manufactured by Dryad, circa 1907, green painted canework frame of sweeping form, the back flaring to large arms with compartments on both sides.
(Bonhams) $865

An early Victorian mahogany and caned bergère, on lapetted turned tapering legs with brass and ceramic castors.
(Christie's) $5,287

A 17th century wainscot armchair with shaped top rail carved with dragons and scrolls, floral carved panel beneath with molded surround. (Russell Baldwin & Bright) $5,033

Paul Goldman, U.S.A., 'Cherner-Chair', designed 1956-7, manufactured by Plycraft Ltd. Laminated walnut veneered plywood, the seat of hourglass form. (Bonhams) $1,180

One of a set of four 19th century low back Windsor armchairs, yew with elm seats, with pierced splats, baluster turned front arm supports. (Andrew Hartley) (Four) $5,184

A yew-wood, walnut and elm Windsor armchair, North East, early 19th century, with central pierced splat, arms with ring-turned bulbous front supports and turned legs. (Christie's) $914

Sack-back Windsor chair, Massachusetts, 1780-95, the bowed crest above shaped arms, an incised seat and splayed legs joined by swelled stretchers. (Skinner) $345

A fruitwood, elm and inlaid Mendlesham armchair, East Anglia, mid 19th century, the rectangular tapered back with spindle and ball decoration and replaced central splat. (Christie's) $512

An ash and elm comb back Windsor arm chair, with arched crest, scrolled arm bow, shaped circular seat, possibly 18th century. (Andrew Hartley) $891

A Regency simulated rosewood bergère chair, the U shaped back with a broad curved and scrolled top rail over caned panels. (Tennants) $12,560

A George III mahogany elbow chair of Sheraton style, the straight molded edged crest rail on similar uprights, three turned reeded and leaf carved spindles. (Andrew Hartley) $713

An ash, fruitwood and elm Windsor armchair, Thames Valley, mid 19th century, with pierced wheel splat and outswept arms on inswept supports. (Christie's) $512

Adrien Claude, a steel and aluminum armchair, designed 1950, for Meubles Artistiques Modernes, Paris, with resilient scrolling perforated steel seat. (Christie's) $1,805

A late 17th century walnut elbow chair, the scrolled top rail centered by a crown with florettes, over a caned back panel with a scroll and flower carved surround. (Andrew Hartley) $1,308

A beechwood, oak and elm child's high chair, Thames Valley, late 19th century, with bar top-rail and tablet centered splat, ring-turned arms and supports, 35in. high. (Christie's) $475

A pair of stained maple splint-woven armchairs, American, late 19th century/20th century, each with projecting stiles and shaped arms on turned supports. (Sotheby's) $805

A yew-wood, elm and beechwood Windsor armchair, Thames Valley, early 19th century, the solid shaped central splat carved with roundel and pierced with two small motifs. (Christie's) $1,646

A brown-painted polychrome-decorated maple child's highback chair, New England, 1780-1810, the shaped crest with compass rose on back,flanked by downswept arms with peaked terminals. (Sotheby's) $632

Unusual 19th century oak captain's chair, short spindle back, joined by two dolphin molded arm rests, raised on acanthus leaf molded baluster supports. (G A Key) $534

A green-painted comb-back Windsor armchair, Pennsylvania, 1750–70, the serpentine crest with volute-carved ears above a concave stay rail pierced by seven flaring spindles. (Sotheby's) $16,100

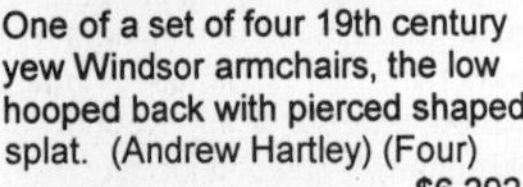

One of a set of four 19th century yew Windsor armchairs, the low hooped back with pierced shaped splat. (Andrew Hartley) (Four) $6,292

A pair of George III mahogany open armchairs, each channelled overall and with oval back centered by a scrolling anthemion.
(Christie's) $12,590

A 19th century yew high back Windsor armchair, the hooped back with shaped and pierced splat, baluster turned arm supports.
(Andrew Hartley) $1,652

One of two similar Italian walnut elbow chairs, 17th century, close nailed seat on square legs joined by sleigh feet.
(Christie's) (Two) $4,540

Charles Rennie Mackintosh, a low back armchair designed for the billiards and smoking rooms of the Argyle Street Tea Rooms, Glasgow, 1897.
(Bonhams) $56,624

A yew-wood and elm Windsor armchair, Thames Valley, early 19th century, with three pierced roundel centered vertical splats and arms with similar splats.
(Christie's) $5,503

A mahogany open armchair, 19th century, decorated with foliate carvings, with an undulating top-rail and pierced splat.
(Christie's) $2,236

A pair of oak elbow chairs by Thompson of Kilburn, the rectangular arched backs having three shaped vertical splats between posts with carved finials.
(Tennants) $6,629

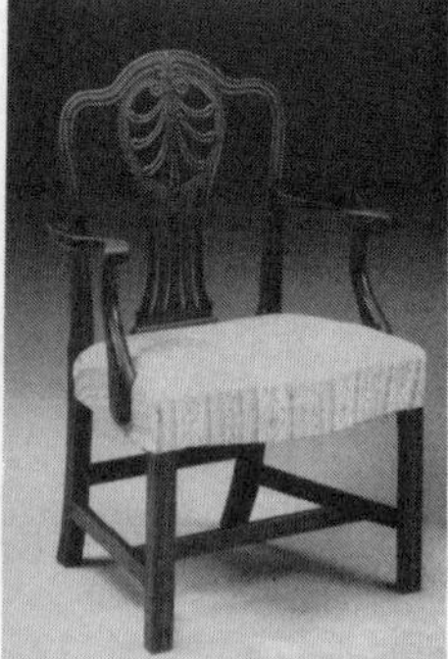

A George III mahogany armchair, the back with an undulating top-rail and anthemion and flowerhead carved pierced vase splat.
(Christie's) $1,000

A painted satinwood tub armchair, 20th century, decorated with floral sprays, ribbons and paterae.
(Christie's) $2,049

Marco Zanuso, a folding bridge armchair, designed 1951, for Arflex, the beechwood frame with tan vinyl upholstery and black vinyl armrests. (Christie's) $2,351

One of a set of eight George III style mahogany dining chairs.
(Bonhams) (Eight) $2,826

One of a pair of simulated bamboo armchairs, early 19th century, each oval back with interlaced splats and downswept arm supports, with caned saddle seats.
(Christie's) (Two) $5,589

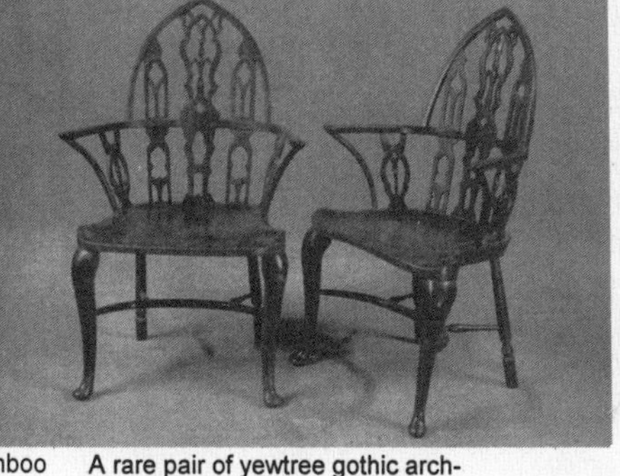

A rare pair of yewtree gothic archback Windsor chairs, the arched back with pierced gothic tracery and shaped arm supports, with elm saddle seats.
(Boardmans) $7,348

A 19th century yew Windsor chair, the low hooped back with pierced shaped splat, scrolled arms on turned supports.
(Andrew Hartley) $4,404

A George IV mahogany caned armchair, with rectangular back and sides, the shaped arms on reeded turned-baluster supports.
(Christie's) $5,925

Gerald Summers, armchair, designed 1933-34, manufactured by Makers of Simple Furniture Ltd. London, ply cut and formed plywood.
(Bonhams) $21,234

A mahogany open armchair, late 19th century, decorated with foliate carvings, with an undulating top-rail and pierced ribbon tied splat.
(Christie's) $3,167

Harden & Co., oak rocking chair, curved crest rail over four narrow and one wide vertical slat, open arm with two side corbels.
(Skinner) $517

A silvered grotto rocking chair, early 20th century, with a broad shell back and seat and crooked fish arms, on seahorse supports, 26¾in. wide.
(Christie's) $5,451

Arts and Crafts oak rocking chair, attributed to L. & J.G. Stickley, circa 1912, curved crest rail over five vertical slats, straight sides with spring cushion seat, arched seat rail. (Skinner) $373

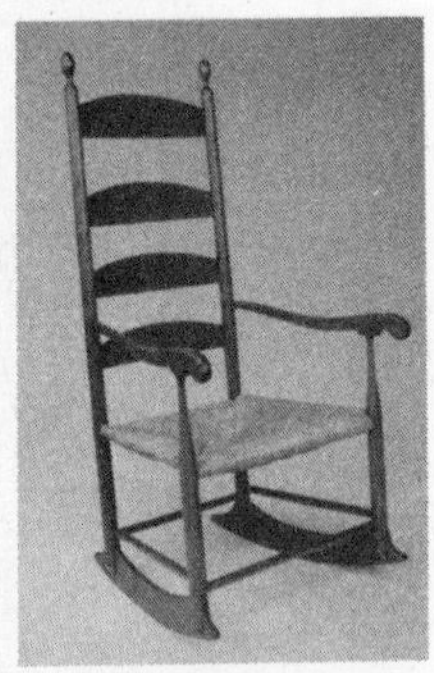

Shaker maple and birch armed rocker, probably Canterbury, New Hampshire, circa 1850, the four arched slats joining turned stiles to the scrolled arms.
(Skinner) $7,475

Child's rustic rocking chair, New York State, circa 1900, with bent elements intertwined above a solid splat and plank seat.
(Skinner) $230

A rocking chair, after 1851, after a design by R. W. Winfield & Co. for the Great Exhibition, 1851, silver painted metal serpentine frame.
(Sotheby's) $1,625

Comb back Windsor armchair, New England, circa 1810-15, the rectangular splat above six spindles and barrel crest rail with applied scrolled arms.
(Skinner) $1,380

A late Victorian cast brass rocking chair.
(Bonhams) $4,404

Shaker Production No. 3 armed rocker, Mount Lebanon, New York, 1875-80, the shawl bar above the shaped splats.
(Skinner) $460

Oak and leather platform rocker, late 19th century, all over geometric forms, square crest rail over trapezoid shaped back with leather insert. (Skinner) $862

A Cassina beechwood rocking chair, circa 1955, with accentuated wing-back, the open seat flanked by shaped armrests, on rockers. (Christie's) $1,356

Arts and Crafts oak rocker, circa 1912, curved crest rail over four vertical slats, flat open arms, spring cushion seat, unsigned. (Skinner) $373

Antique American combback Windsor rocker, with original stencilled grape and grapevine decoration on a black ground. (Eldred's) $330

Arts and Crafts armchair and rocker, circa 1907, straight crest rail, cutout back and side slats, flat arm with through tenons, spring cushion seat, unsigned. (Skinner) $230

A late Federal black-painted and polychrome-decorated rocking chair, American, circa 1815, the horizontal crest above an X-form brace inscribed *Liberty*. (Sotheby's) $1,275

Arts and Crafts oak rocker, attributed to J.M. Young, circa 1910, four curved horizontal crest rails, flat arm with short corbel supports, leather spring cushion seat. (Skinner) $230

Antique American ladderback armed rocker, with four-splat back, rush seat and bulbous front stretcher, converted to a rocker. (Eldred's) $137

L. & J.G. Stickley rocker, no. 451, circa 1912, concave crest rail over six vertical slats, shaped flat arm with corbels, over six vertical slats.(Skinner) $1,380

A good Chippendale mahogany easy chair, probably Philadelphia, circa 1780, the serpentine crest flanked by ogival wings and outscrolled supports.
(Sotheby's) $21,850

A George III mahogany buttoned wing armchair with camel back and scroll arms on square legs and castors. (Dee Atkinson & Harrison) $6,270

18th century wing back elbow chair, raised on short cabriole front supports, molded at the knees with scrolls.
(G.A. Key) $2,400

A walnut wing armchair, early 20th century in the Georgian style, the rectangular back with outscrolled arms above a bowed seat with loose cushion.
(Christie's) $954

A Queen Anne maple and turned birchwood easy chair, Massachusetts, 1740-60, the arched crest flanked by ogival wings and outscrolled arms on conical supports.
(Sotheby's) $46,000

A Queen Anne walnut and figured maple easy chair, Boston, Massachusetts, 1740-60, the arched overupholstered back flanked by ogival wings and outscrolling arms.
(Sotheby's) $11,500

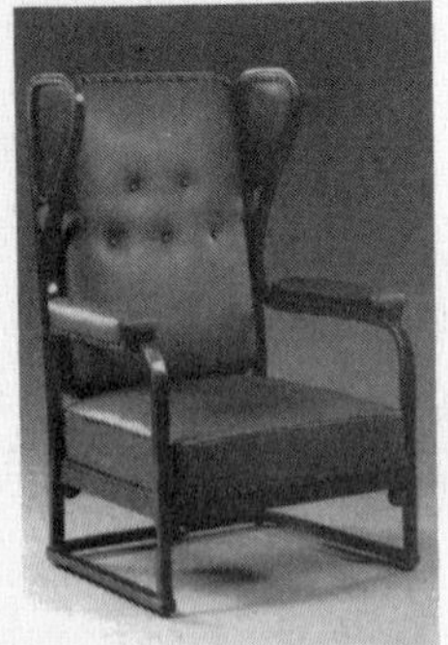

Josef Hoffmann for J.& J. Kohn, large wing chair, circa 1905, stained beech bentwood frame, re-upholstered in forest green leather.
(Sotheby's) $7,208

A Queen Anne maple easy chair, Massachusetts, 1730-50, the arched crest flanked by ogival wings and outscrolled arms on downswept supports.
(Sotheby's) $27,600

A fine Chippendale carved and figured mahogany wing armchair, New York, circa 1770, the serpentine upholstered crest flanked by ogival wings and conical arm supports.
(Sotheby's) $37,375

A Regency mahogany wing armchair, upholstered in close-nailed leather, with a barrel shaped padded back.
(Christie's) $3,726

An Irish George I walnut and oak reclining wing armchair, on cabriole legs, each headed by a shell.
(Christie's) $2,208

A Georgian mahogany wing back armchair, on carved cabriole ball-and-claw supports.
(Bristol) $1,312

hippendale-style upholstered wing air, late 19th/early 20th century, mahogany with claw and ball et.
ldred's) $770

A fine Queen Anne walnut leather-upholstered easy chair, Boston, Massachusetts, 1730-50, the arched crest flanked by ogival wings above conical outscrolled supports.
(Sotheby's) $43,700

A Queen Anne carved mahogany wing armchair, Massachusetts, circa 1760, the upholstered arched crest flanked by shaped ogival wings and outscrolled arms.
(Sotheby's) $9,775

Queen Anne turned walnut easy air, Boston, Massachusetts, 30-50, the arched crest flanked ogival wings and outscrolled ms on conical supports.
otheby's) $17,250

A Chippendale carved mahogany easy chair, Boston, Massachusetts, circa 1770, the arched crest flanked by ogival wings and outscrolled arms on conical supports.
(Sotheby's) $21,850

A 19th century Georgian style winged armchair with floral pattern upholstery on leafage carved cabriole legs and ball and claw feet.
(Russell Baldwin & Bright) $959

A 17th century oak boarded coffer, the hinged lid with iron hasps, the fascia with a possibly later carved winged beast flanked by tracery panels, 67½in. wide.
(Andrew Hartley) $2,219

A 17th century oak panelled coffer with hinged plank lid, the four arcaded panelled fascia with roundel carved frieze, 64in. wide x 29in. high.
(Andrew Hartley) $1,515

A leather and brass studded chest, English, mid 18th century, the hinged top with cabochon and stylised rosettes above similarly decorated sides, 115cm. wide.
(Sotheby's) $2,062

An oak panelled coffer with four panel hinged lid and guilloche frieze over three arcaded panels, 49in. wide, late 17th century.
(Andrew Hartley) $3,240

An oak chest, North European, late 17th century, profusely carved overall with trailing foliage and floral rosettes, initialled *H.A.S.* and dated below *1695*, 51in. wide.
(Christie's) $2,194

A joined oak chest, mid-17th century, the panelled lid above three panelled front carved with quatrefoil guilloche decoration, 54½in. wide.
(Bonhams) $1,040

Most unusual chart chest, 19th century, in oak and pine, door at either end, contains charts, 38in. wide. (Eldred's) $357

A small 17th century oak coffer, the hinged three panel lid with molded borders, the interior with a candlebox, the three panel front carved with a central flowerhead, 3ft.2½in.
(Woolley & Wallis) $1,410

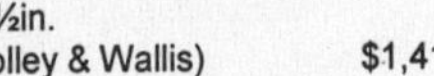

A Spanish walnut cassone, the hinged lid to a carved front depicting a cathedral, tubs of flowering shrubs and evergreens 5ft.7½in.
(Woolley & Wallis) $1,92

A blue-painted seaman's chest, American, 19th century, the hinge rectangular top opening to a well, the case fitted with rope carrying handles, 5ft. 2in. long.
(Sotheby's) $1,15

Silversmith's walnut tool chest, America, mid-19th century, dovetailed construction, with two removable trays above a locking drawer containing tools, 11 x 15 x 11in. (Skinner) $2,76

An 18th century oak sea captain's chest, with a domed hinged lid, applied contemporary pierced fre ironwork, 3ft. 6in.
(Woolley & Wallis) $1,56

An Adige cypress wood chest, 16th century, the incised and penwork lid and sides decorated with foliage and figures, 5ft. 6in. wide. (Sotheby's) $3,841

An oak panelled chest, possibly Dutch, late 17th/early 18th century, with molded four panel lid and foliate frieze, above three panels, the center panel with boss, 50½in. wide. (Christie's) $1,280

Antique Chinese camphor chest with brass banding and brass carrying handles, 40in. long. (Eldred's) $550

Gustav Stickley oak shirtwaist box, New York, circa 1912, rectangular form, cedar lined, hammered copper lift handles, 32in. wide. (Skinner) $9,775

An oak chest, English, early 17th century, the associated lid with gouged edges, above an interlocking rosette and bead-filled frieze, 43in. wide. (Christie's) $1,463

Bermudan mahogany and inlay chest on stand, late 19th century, rectangular molded lift top on a base with long drawers, 53in. wide. (Skinner) $1,380

A George II mahogany coffer on stand, the molded top above solid panel box, on two-drawer stand with four bracket supports, 119cm. wide. (Bristol) $1,217

1930s touring trunk with fitted luggage. (Christie's) $3,680

Pine chest over drawer, New England, 18th century, the molded hinged top lifting above a deep well and case of single drawer with turned pulls and cutout ends, 36¼in. wide. (Skinner) $1,265

A paint-decorated blanket chest, possibly Georgia, dated *1871*, case decorated with stylized foliate motifs in green and yellow on red and green grounds, 37¼in. wide. (Christie's) $9,775

Pine chest over drawer Massachusetts, early 18th century, molded top with pintle hinges above a single arch molded base centering a panel with carved initials, 42in. wide. (Skinner) $4,600

An antique Welsh oak mule chest with hinged lid over carved fruiting vine frieze and three floral carved panels fitted with two drawers, 4ft. 9in. wide. (Russell Baldwin & Bright) $2,281

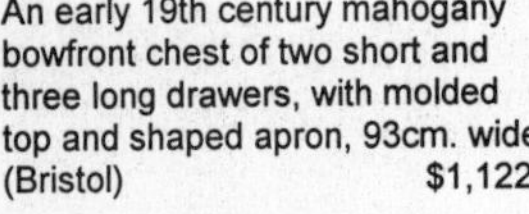

An early 19th century mahogany bowfront chest of two short and three long drawers, with molded top and shaped apron, 93cm. wide. (Bristol) $1,122

18th century oak country made chest, arched frieze over three ogee molded drawers, three full width graduated drawers below, on bracket feet, 31in. (G A Key) $1,080

A basically late 17th century oak chest of drawers, 43½in. wide. (Dockrees) $1,280

TOP TIPS

The positioning of valuable antiques in a house can be crucial. Direct sunlight has a lethal affect on wood, so keep your precious furniture well away from south or east facing windows.

The same goes for watercolors, which can also be seriously damaged by over exposure to the sun.

(Dee, Atkinson & Harrison)

Gustav Stickley oak chest of drawers, New York, circa 1912, no. 906, rectangular top over two short and four long drawers, hammered circular pulls, 41in. wide. (Skinner) $13,800

Maple and birch chest of drawers, New England, circa 1790, the rectangular overhanging top above a case of four drawers with incised beading and diamond inlaid escutcheons, 40in. wide. (Skinner) $2,185

A teak secrétaire military chest, the secrétaire drawer with two small drawers either side, with three drawers beneath, width 39in. (George Kidner) $3,846

Tiger maple chest of drawers, probably Pennsylvania, circa 1830, the scrolled backboard joining three plinths above the rectangular top, 46in. wide. (Skinner) $2,185

A mahogany early 19th century bow fronted chest of drawers, 36in. wide. (Dockrees) $1,056

fine and rare Queen Anne carved nd figured mahogany block-front hest of drawers, Boston lassachusetts, circa 1770, top 5½in. wide.
Sotheby's) $43,125

A small early George II faded Cuban mahogany chest, the moulded edge top above a slide and four long graduated drawers, 32in.
(Woolley & Wallis) $2,970

A walnut chest, French, early 17th century, carved with symmetrically displayed fabulous beasts and foliage, 6ft. wide.
(Sotheby's) $12,483

Queen Anne maple tall chest of awers, New England, 1740-60, e overhanging stepped cornice ove two short drawers and four aduated long drawers on straight acket feet, 39in. wide.
otheby's) $2,300

A Chippendale mahogany block-front chest of drawers, Boston, 1760-1790, the rectangular top with molded edge and blocked front above a conforming case fitted with four graduated and blocked long drawers, 37in. wide.
(Christie's) $33,350

A rare Chippendale cherrywood chest with serpentine top, Connecticut, circa 1780, the oblong shaped top with cove molded edge, above four graduated drawers, 41in. wide.
(Sotheby's) $6,325

eorge III mahogany serpentine ited chest, with inlaid canted ners, fitted with a brushing slide four long drawers, 39in. wide.
orge Kidner) $42,900

Classical tiger maple and cherry tall chest of drawers, Pennsylvania or Ohio, circa 1825, lower section with four graduated drawers, 42¾in. wide.
(Skinner) $2,760

A Regency mahogany chest, the rectangular top above a writing-slide and two short drawers and four graduated long drawers, 41in.
(Christie's) $5,520

Antique American Hepplewhite bowfront chest of drawers, New England, circa 1800, in tiger maple, four drawers with mahogany banding and cockbeaded fronts,
(Eldred's) $4,730

William and Mary walnut and burl walnut chest of drawers, 18th century, molded rectangular top, with two short over three long drawers, 37in. long.
(Skinner) $2,415

A late 17th/early 18th century yew chest, crossbanded with stringing, two short over three long drawers, 40in. wide.
(Andrew Hartley) $3,17

A George III mahogany chest of two short and three long graduated cockbeaded drawers, raised on bracket feet, 33in. wide.
(Peter Francis) $2,433

Federal chest of drawers, southeastern New England, circa 1800-10, the overhanging rectangular top above a case of four cockbeaded graduated drawers, 36¾in. wide.
(Skinner) $4,600

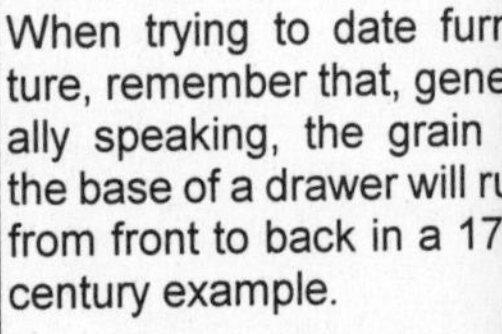

TOP TIPS

When trying to date furniture, remember that, generally speaking, the grain the base of a drawer will ru from front to back in a 17 century example.

Remember, too, that fro about 1850 cabinet make started introducing qua rant beading into the co struction of drawers, othe wise known as dust prote tors.

(Amersham Auction Rooms)

A walnut chest, the rounded oblong top quarter veneered with herring bone banding, two short over three long drawers, 39½in. wide, early 18th century.
(Andrew Hartley) $4,147

Italian Renaissance carved walnut chest of drawers, comprising antique elements, rectangular molded top over four drawers 39in. wide.
(Skinner) $4,025

A George III oak chest with mahogany crossbanding, molded edged top with rounded corners, two short over three long drawers 41¾in.wide.
(Andrew Hartley) $1,3

An early Victorian figured bow front chest of drawers having protruding corners with full round barley twist columns, 47in. wide.
(H.C. Chapman) $1,382

A 19th century mahogany chest, crossbanded with string inlay and parquetry banded frieze, 43in. wide.
(Andrew Hartley) $745

A George III mahogany chest, fitted with a slide with four long drawers below, on bracket feet, 34½in. wide. (Christie's) $3,270

An early 19th century bowfronted mahogany chest of two short and two long graduated cock beaded drawers, raised on bobbin turned feet, 36in. wide.
(Peter Francis) $2,676

An early Victorian walnut collector's chest, the molded edge top above eight graduated drawers with turned handles, 19in.
(Dreweatt Neate) $786

Mahogany brass bound camphorwood chest of drawers, China, mid-19th century, the rectangular two-part case of two half-drawers above three reverse graduated long drawers, 38¾in. wide. (Skinner) $4,025

A late 17th century walnut chest of drawers, the dentil molded top over four geometrically molded drawer fronts, 38in. wide.
(Michael J. Bowman) $4,264

A small George III mahogany chest, the molded edged top with cusped corners, brushing slide over four long drawers, 31in. wide.
(Andrew Hartley) $1,944

A William and Mary walnut and burr walnut-veneered chest of two short and three graduated long drawers, all outlined with feather banding, 100cm. wide.
(Bearne's) $16,515

A George III mahogany chest of two short and three long drawers, with molded edged top and base, 37½in. wide.
(Andrew Hartley) $1,347

Continental walnut bombé fronted commode chest, profusely inlaid throughout with panels of floral marquetry, raised on paw feet, 18th/19th century, 39in.
(G.A. Key) $4,770

A Queen Anne walnut chest of two short and three long drawers with feather banding on replaced bun feet, 3ft.4in. wide.
(G.A. Key) $3,339

A painted mirror-glass chest of drawers, designed by Gio Ponti, 1951, the painted panels by Edina Altara, made for the apartment of Gio Ponti, the top and front richly decorated with painted figures, 39½in. wide.
(Christie's) $55,890

Red painted pine chest over drawers, New England, late 18th century, the molded hinged top above a case of two false and four working thumbmolded graduated drawers, 36in. wide.
(Skinner) $4,887

A late 18th century Dutch mahogany chest of drawers, with serpentine molded top and shaped sides, having three long drawers, 115cm.
(Tennants) $2,512

A Swedish jacaranda, amaranth and plumwood veneered and ormolu mounted rococo chest of drawers, signed *E. Nygren*, with red marble top, late 18th century, 116cm. wide.
(Stockholms AV) $13,133

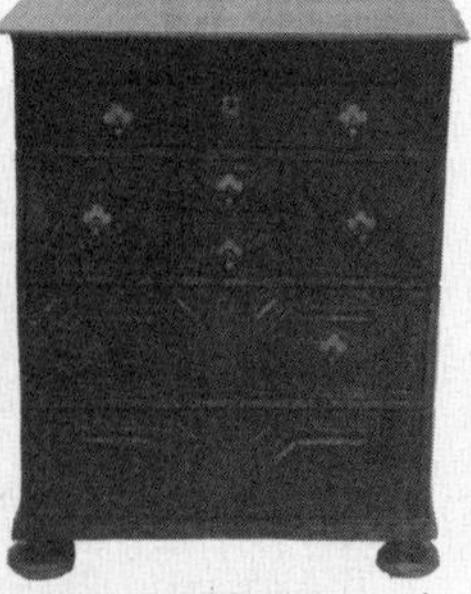

Late 17th/early 18th century oak chest, molded edge, full width drawer over two central short drawers, flanked on either side by two deeper drawers, two further full width graduated drawers below, 30in. (G.A. Key) $557

Art Deco mahogany three-drawer bureau, circa 1935, rectangular raised panel mahogany top over canted and zigzag drawer pulls an sides, 30½in. wide.
(Skinner) $1,84

A George III mahogany chest on chest, 19th century and associated, 111.5cm. wide.
(Bonhams) $1,422

A George III oak chest on chest with molded dentil cornice, blind fret frieze, 43in. wide.
(Andrew Hartley) $2,933

A George III mahogany chest on chest, extensive restorations, 107cm. wide.
(Bonhams) $1,296

A mahogany tallboy, 19th century, the dentil molded cornice above two short and three graduated long drawers, 42in. wide.
(Christie's) $1,986

A George I walnut chest on chest with crossbanding, herringbone stringing and sunburst inlay, 42in. wide x 68in. high.
(G. E. Sworder) $10,880

A George III mahogany tallboy, the molded rectangular cornice above a Gothic-arched frieze and two short drawers and three long graduated blue paper-lined drawers, 44in. wide.
(Christie's) $5,485

A George III mahogany chest on chest, the upper section with molded and dentil cornice over two short and three long drawers, 42in. wide.
(Andrew Hartley) $4,125

A late George III mahogany tallboy with molded cornice and plain frieze above two short and three long graduated drawers, 43½in. wide. (Christie's) $2,708

An oak tallboy, English, late 18th/early 19th century, with a Greek key molded cornice, above two short and six long drawers, 45in. wide.
(Christie's) $5,503

An early 18th century walnut chest on stand, with string inlay and burr yew crossbanding, pointed cabriole legs and pad feet, 37½in. wide.
(Andrew Hartley) $3,828

An 18th century walnut chest-on-stand, the drawer fronts crossbanded in walnut, the base fitted with three small drawers, 39ins wide.
(Canterbury) $2,067

A late 17th century oak chest on later stand, the molded rectangular top over four long panelled drawers, 109.5cm. wide.
(Phillips) $1,840

A Queen Anne figured maple flat-top high chest of drawers, Rhode Island, circa 1740, in two parts; the overhanging stepped cornice above two short and four graduated thumbmolded long drawers, 37in. wide. (Sotheby's) $10,925

Antique American chest-on-frame, in maple and tiger maple, molded cornice above four drawers. Lower drawer with faux front simulating three drawers, the central one fan-carved, 40½in. wide.
(Eldred's) $10,450

A Queen Anne carved maple flat-top high chest of drawers, New Hampshire, 1740–60, in two parts; the stepped cornice above three short drawers, the center one fan-carved, 39½in. wide.
(Sotheby's) $9,200

An early 18th century walnut chest on stand, the upper half with cyma cornice, two short and three graded long drawers, 38in.
(Dreweatt Neate) $6,480

A George I walnut and cross banded chest on stand, the upper section with concave cornice fitted with three short and three long graduated drawers, 42in. wide.
(George Kidner) $3,300

A George I walnut chest on stand with a flared cornice and canted sides, with three short drawers and three long graduated drawers, 43in. wide. (Anderson & Garland)
$15,180

A William IV faded rosewood chiffonier, the raised mirror back with a galleried shelf on open 'S' scroll volutes with carved tassel terminals, 4ft.
(Woolley & Wallis) $1,282

A Regency calamander chiffonier, the raised shelf panelled back above two frieze drawers and a central honeysuckle tablet, 137cm. wide. (Cheffins) $1,805

An early Victorian chiffonier, mahogany veneered, the top with a superstructure fitted with a shelf and a pediment, 3ft.1in.
(Woolley & Wallis) $1,192

AUCTIONEER'S ADVICE

It is good practice for an auctioneer to take bids from only two people at a time. If this is so, don't become frustrated if your frantic arm-waving is ignored. The auctioneer will concentrate on the existing parties until one drops out and then will look around to see if there are any other bidders. If you are then admitted to the bidding duel you will be afforded the same courtesy.

(Michael Bowman)

A William IV chiffonier, veneered in rosewood, the top with a marble slab and a superstructure shelf on doric columns, 4ft.
(Woolley & Wallis) $1,815

A Regency mahogany chiffonier, the raised shelved back with three quarter gallery and S scroll supports, the base with reeded edged hinged top, 36½in. wide.
(Andrew Hartley) $4,247

Victorian mahogany chiffionier, the pediment molded with 'C' scrolls and acanthus leaves, applied with a shelf, raised on linked 'C' scrolled supports, 42in.
(G A Key) $1,497

A Victorian chiffonier base, with marble top, circa 1870, serpentine, lacking original back, 50in. wide.
(Dockrees) $608

Roycroft mahogany chiffonier, East Aurora, New York, circa 1910, backsplash with shaped ends, rectangular top, two short drawers over four long drawers, 45⅝ in. wide. (Skinner) $1,840

A Regency mahogany chiffionier outlined throughout with ebonized lines, 69.5cm. wide.
(Bearne's) $5,662

A Victorian oak chiffonier, alterations, 101cm. wide.
(Bonhams) $616

A late Victorian burr walnut and marble topped chiffonier, 109cm. wide. (Bonhams) $948

A George IV mahogany chiffonier, the raised back with foliate scrolls and a shelf, the long frieze drawer above two panelled doors flanked by freestanding columns and on a plinth base, 143cm. high x 112cm. wide. (Bearne's) $1,884

A Victorian mahogany chiffonier base, 89cm. wide.
(Bonhams) $346

A black-lacquer, chinoiserie decorated and gilt-metal mounted chiffonier, early 19th century, decorated with figures in lakeside landscapes, 33in. wide.
(Christie's) $2,54

A Regency rosewood chiffonier, the shelf with three-quarter gallery, beaded edge and on columnar supports, 97cm. wide.
(Bearne's) $2,831

A William IV rosewood chiffonier, the scrolled and shelved top rail supported by turned and carved columns, set on an inverted breakfront top, 130cm. wide.
(Bonhams) $3,240

A rosewood and brass inlaid secrétaire chiffonier, 19th century, decorated with husk and foliate patterns and lines, 36in. wide.
(Christie's) $6,56

A French 19th century marble topped commode, 120cm. wide.
(Bonhams) $2,844

A Biedermeier walnut commode, 110.5cm. wide.
(Bonhams) $778

A Dutch marquetry bombé shaped commode, 35½in. wide.
(Bonhams) $3,160

A Transitional style walnut and marquetry petit commode, late 19th century, with later replacement top, 78.5cm. wide.
(Bonhams) $1,296

A late 18th century Dutch walnut marquetry bombé commode inlaid throughout with floral bouquets, trailing flowers and scrolling foliage, 91cm. wide.
(Bearne's) $4,553

A George III style small mahogany and boxwood inlaid serpentine commode, circa 1900, 71cm. wide.
(Bonhams) $480

A Transitional style kingwood and gilt metal mounted petit commode with marble top, 62cm. wide.
(Bonhams) $632

A French ormolu-mounted kingwood commode, in the Louis XV style, circa 1880, the gray brèche marble top of serpentine outline, above a pair of drawers inlaid sans travers, 48in. wide.
(Christie's) $3,611

A Louis XV style walnut commode with gilt metal mounts 56.5cm. wide. (Bonhams) $711

A Dutch mahogany and marquetry bombé commode, 19th century, interlaced with checker lines and decorated with floral sprays with foliate scrolls, 41½in. wide. (Christie's) $5,814

An Italian fruitwood serpentine commode, early 19th century, fitted with two drawers between rounded angles above a shaped apron, 53in. wide. (Christie's) $7,825

A late 18th century Italian commode in kingwood, having all over marquetry decoration with frieze of scrolls and central floral medallion in satinwood, 4ft. 3in. wide. (Russell Baldwin & Bright) $33,210

A kingwood and tulipwood inlaid petit commode, late 19th century, decorated with lines and crossbanding, the mottled marble top with projecting corners, 25in. wide. (Christie's) $1,030

A French kingwood serpentine commode, 18th century, applied with gilt-metal mounts, decorated with crossbanding, 46½in. wide. (Christie's) $3,374

An Italian ebonized walnut and marquetry commode, decorated with ripple moldings, of tapering form, fitted with five drawers, 26½in. wide. (Christie's) $3,374

A French kingwood and marquetry bombé commode, late 19th/early 20th century, applied with gilt-metal mounts and decorated with meandering floral vines and crossbanding, 37¾in. wide. (Christie's) $5,436

An Italian walnut commode, 18th century, of broken outline, decorated with crossbanding and lines, fitted with four drawers, 26½in. wide. (Christie's) $10,805

A kingwood and gilt-bronze commode, Paris, circa 1890, of bombé form, with a shaped, molded brocatelle marble top above two drawers sans travers 99cm wide. (Sotheby's) $7,12

A marquetry and gilt-bronze commode, Paris, circa 1880, with a Spanish brocatelle shaped marble top above a frieze drawer applied with foliate scrolls, 137cm. wide.
(Sotheby's) $14,996

A French kingwood, tulipwood and marquetry commode, late 18th century, decorated with lines and crossbanding, later mottled rouge marble top, 50¼in. wide.
(Christie's) $4,124

A gilt-bronze mounted marquetry commode by Paul Sormani, Paris, circa 1880, in Louis XV style, the serpentine brêche violet marble top above a guilloche and patera inlaid frieze drawer, 153cm. wide.
(Sotheby's) $18,745

A kingwood, marquetry and gilt-bronze commode, French, circa 1890, of bombé form, with a molded marble top above a pair of drawers with sprays of foliage, sans travers, 134cm. wide.
(Sotheby's) $13,122

A pair of Italian walnut and fruitwood commodes, 18th century, decorated with crossbanding, lines and ebonized borders, each with a shaped projecting front fitted with six drawers, 19½in. wide.
(Christie's) $35,397

An Italian walnut and parquetry commode, late 18th/early 19th century, decorated with crossbanding, checker borders and panels, 38¾in. wide.
(Christie's) $5,624

A late Empire mahogany commode, with a variegated marble top and three overhanging frieze drawers, three long drawers below, 40¼in. wide. (Christie's) $3,452

Anon, French, commode, circa 1930, demi-lune, green galuchat, the side panels, front and top with sunburst motif, 105cm. wide.
(Sotheby's) $62,400

A French Provincial gray painted serpentine commode, late 18th/early 19th century, with a simulated marble top above three long drawers between rounded angles, 45½in. wide.
(Christie's) $7,079

A Victorian mahogany commode, 70cm. wide.
(Bonhams) $315

A George III mahogany bedside cabinet with pierced and shaped rectangular tray top, 56cm. wide.
(Bearne's) $2,123

George III mahogany tray top night commode, 24in. wide.
(Jacobs & Hunt) $2,080

A George III mahogany tray top commode, the undulating gallery with pierced carrying handles, fitted with a shallow drawer, on square legs, 23in. wide.
(Christie's) $5,814

A mid 19th century Continental rosewood night commode, the molded square top surmounted by a gallery rail, above a panelled cabinet door, 52cm. wide.
(Bonhams) $1,361

A mahogany tray-top bedside commode, late 18th century, with an undulating gallery pierced with carrying handles above a pair of doors decorated with lines, 21½in. wide. (Christie's) $1,593

A mahogany tray-top bedside commode, late 18th century, with an undulating gallery pierced with carrying handles, above a drawer and two doors, 21¾in. wide.
(Christie's) $1,875

A George III mahogany bedside commode, the rectangular galleried top above a hinged sliding flap enclosing a plain interior, 22in. wide. (Christie's) $2,576

A George III mahogany commode, with a ledge back and hinged top on downswept sides, the hinged seat enclosing a circular recess, 22½in. wide.
(Christie's) $3,997

A painted pine corner cabinet, 57cm. wide.
(Bonhams) $1,399

An oak corner cupboard on stand, part 18th century, 113cm. wide.
(Bonhams) $405

A George III mahogany corner cabinet with dentil cornice, blind fret-carved gothic frieze, two ogee-arched fielded panel doors, 117cm. wide. (Bearne's) $10,205

A green-painted poplar architectural corner cupboard, Chester County, Pennsylvania, circa 1780, in two parts; the stepped dentil-molded cornice above a similarly molded arched tympanum, 4ft. wide.
(Sotheby's) $12,650

A fine pair of gilt-bronze and marquetry encoignures, French, in Louis XV style, mid 19th century, each of bombé form, with a rouge royale molded marble top, 89cm. wide.
(Sotheby's) $124,369

An oak mirror fronted corner cabinet, English, 18th century, the mirror door surrounded by mirror panels opening to a two-shelf interior, 10 x 4¼in.
(Bonhams) $789

Figured oak and mahogany inlaid quarter circular corner cupboard with brass 'H' shaped hinges and escutcheons.
(Whitworths) $1,080

A Louis XV kingwood and marquetry inlaid ormolu mounted encoignure with a breche d'Alep marble top, mid 18th century, 68.5cm. wide.
(Bonhams) $3,657

A George III mahogany corner cupboard, crossbanded with string inlay, molded cornice over fluted frieze, 31in. wide.
(Andrew Hartley) $724

An early 19th century mahogany hanging bow front corner cupboard, with acorn and drop head molded cornice, 33in.
(Dreweatt Neate) $1,022

A Chippendale carved pine architectural corner cupboard, New Jersey, circa 1790, in two parts, the overhanging dentil molded cornice above a carved frieze, 4ft. 8in. wide. (Sotheby's) $10,350

Pine glazed corner cupboard, New England, circa 1800, glazed door opening to two shaped shelves above a cupboard door, 48in. wide.
(Skinner) $3,450

A Chippendale figured mahogany corner cupboard, probably Mid-Atlantic States, circa 1780, in three parts; with removable pitched pediment, 47½in. wide.
(Sotheby's) $13,800

A pair of 19th century French walnut corner cupboards, serpentine fronted doors, having floral trophy inlay and gilt mounts, 2ft. 4in. wide. (Russell Baldwin & Bright) $3,077

Federal walnut carved glazed corner cupboard, probably New Jersey, early 19th century, the top with flat cove molded cornice with tiger maple frieze, 44in. wide.
(Skinner) $8,625

An adzed oak corner cupboard by Robert Thompson, Kilburn, the single panelled door with wrought iron hinges and latch enclosing shelving, panelled canted sides, 27in. wide, 38in. high.
(Andrew Hartley) $1,914

A George III oak bow fronted corner cupboard, with molded and dentil cornice, two doors enclosing shelving under a pierced fretwork frieze, fluted pilasters and molded base, 32in. wide x 42¾in. high.
(Andrew Hartley) $2,712

Pennsylvania cherry corner cupboard, circa 1800, overhanging cornice with applied ebonized gadroon molding over twin double arched glazed doors, 49in. wide.
(Freeman) $6,440

An early 19th century oak corner display cabinet with canted corners, two glazed doors with curved lozenge astragals, 113cm. wide. (Bearne's) $743

A George III oak corner cupboard, with mahogany crossbanding, the inverted breakfront with molded cornice, single panelled door with inlaid arch, 35¾in.wide. (Andrew Hartley) $1,555

Georgian style mahogany and inlay corner display cabinet, late 19th century, molded cornice over mullioned doors and sides, 54⅝in. wide. (Skinner) $2,185

A Federal green-painted pine corner cupboard, Pennsylvania or New Jersey, circa 1800, in two parts; the upper section with cavetto molding, 45in. wide. (Sotheby's) $11,500

Two near matching Georgian mahogany hanging corner cupboards, each with a dentil cornice above a pair of astragal doors enclosing shelves, 27in. and 27½in. wide. (Anderson & Garland) $2,356

A George III oak standing corner cupboard with molded dentil cornice, four doors with fielded panels enclosing shaped shelving, 44½in. wide. (Andrew Hartley) $3,078

A George III mahogany corner cupboard, crossbanded with string inlay, two panelled doors each with oval marquetry panel depicting Britannia, 33in. wide. (Andrew Hartley) $1,184

Pine glazed corner cupboard, New England, early 19th century, flat molded cornice above case with glazed door opening to three shelves, 57in. wide. (Skinner) $1,725

A George III mahogany bow front hanging corner cupboard, with dentil cornice, and three interior shelves, 43¼in. high. (Dreweatt Neate) $1,022

A 16th century-style oak cupboard with molded cornice, two 'Romayne' panel doors flanking a central carved panel, 147cm. wide. (Bearne's) $1,887

An oak tridarn, North Wales, early 18th century, the upper section with molded cornice and turned column front supports with panelled sides, 52½in. wide. (Christie's) $7,680

A 16th century-style oak aumbry with an arrangement of three doors depicting figure subjects, 143cm. wide. (Bearne's) $3,932

A Shaker stained cupboard with drawers, New England, late 19th century, the rectangular molded top above a conforming case fitted with a framed door, 26in. wide. (Christie's) $2,760

A 16th century-style carved and panelled oak aumbry with an arrangement of two central doors carved with tracery, 133cm. wide. (Bearne's) $1,652

A George III mahogany pedestal cupboard, decorated with lines and crossbanding, with a twin-flap hinged top, 19in. wide. (Christie's) $1,593

A good green-painted pine and walnut cupboard, possibly New Jersey, 1800-50, in two parts, the canted upper section with three reeded shelves, 4ft. 2in. wide. (Sotheby's) $5,175

An 18th century oak court cupboard with fleur-de-lys pattern frieze above turned pilasters and a pair of arched panel doors, 56in. wide. (Anderson & Garland) $3,088

An oak architectural housekeeper's cupboard, Yorkshire, late 18th/early 19th century, with Greek key molded cornice and lattice blind fret frieze, above a pair of doors, each with four lobed panels, 71½in. wide. (Christie's) $10,057

A Victorian rosewood davenport 66cm. wide.
(Bonhams) $1,570

A mid Victorian walnut and walnut grained serpentine davenport 55.5cm. wide.
(Bonhams) $1,944

A Victorian walnut and inlaid davenport, 53cm. wide.
(Bonhams) $1,185

A pollard oak and tulipwood-banded davenport, 19th century and later, the galleried rectangular hinged compartment enclosing a fitted interior, with hinged curved fall enclosing three drawers, the carcase 19th century; 22½in. wide.
(Christie's) $1,806

An early Victorian mahogany davenport, the sliding desk with leather lined slope enclosing a fitted interior, 55cm.
(Tennants) $2,198

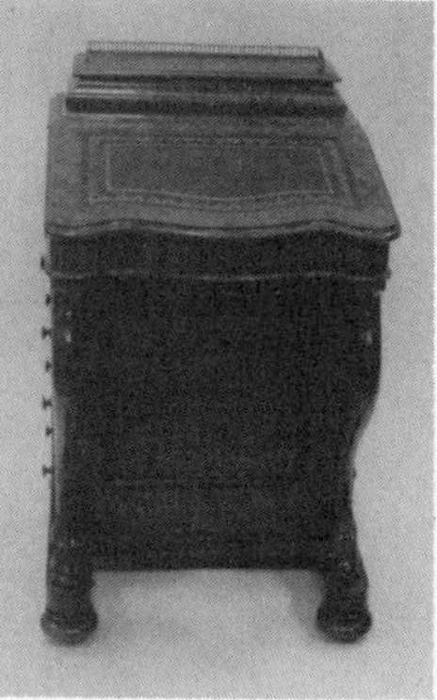

Late 19th century walnut davenport, the top with concealed stationery compartment and pen trays, slope front with leather inset, 22in. wide.
(Ewbank) $1,201

A William IV rosewood davenport, attributed to Gillows, the sliding top with a pierced brass three-quarter gallery and a sloping fall, 20½in. wide. (Christie's) $6,561

A Victorian burr walnut davenport desk with raised cabinet of pigeon holes, wreath inlaid door and two drawers, 27in. wide.
(Russell Baldwin & Bright) $5,273

A William IV mahogany davenport, the sliding top with a pierced foliate gallery and panel sloping fall, 22¼in. wide.
(Christie's) $5,087

A late Victorian mahogany display cabinet, with an overhanging bowed cornice and foliate-carved frieze, 54in. wide.
(Christie's) $1,379

A French kingwood serpentine vitrine cabinet, late 19th century, applied with gilt-metal mounts and decorated with foliate marquetry panels, 46in. wide.
(Christie's) $8,942

An Edwardian mahogany display cabinet, the twin glazed doors with applied arch-top glazing bars, flanked by fluted columns, 83cm. wide. (Bristol) $640

A late 19th century mahogany china cabinet, with floral marquetry and line inlay, broken swan neck pediment, 3ft.¼in.
(Woolley & Wallis) $4,290

A pair of Victorian walnut display cabinets, each with projecting rounded angles and trompe l'oeil and dentil parquetry frieze, 44½in. wide. (Christie's) $11,265

An Edwardian mahogany display cabinet on stand, with satinwood stringing, scrolled flower carved pediment, 43in. wide.
(Andrew Hartley) $2,430

A fine Edwardian satinwood veneered crossbanded and inlaid cabinet with two arched glazed doors, flanking a bow front niche with mirrored back, 47½in. wide.
(David Lay) $2,441

A good Edwardian mahogany and line inlaid display cabinet, the shaped top over central drawer and paterae inlaid door flanked by glazed doors, 137.5cm. wide.
(Bristol) $2,219

A French mahogany veneered Vernis Martin display cabinet with gilt bronze rococo mounts, single door with over painted panels on cabriole legs, 49½in. wide.
(David Lay) $1,490

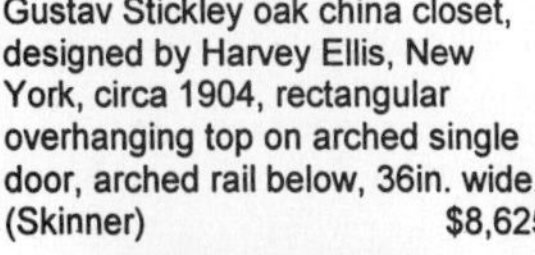

Gustav Stickley oak china closet, designed by Harvey Ellis, New York, circa 1904, rectangular overhanging top on arched single door, arched rail below, 36in. wide. (Skinner) $8,625

A Victorian walnut breakfront display cabinet, inlaid floral and scroll designs, ormolu mounted fitted central glazed door flanked by single glazed doors, 5ft.4in. (G.A. Key) $2,465

A Dutch walnut-veneered and marquetry vitrine, inlaid overall with trailing flowers and foliage, 127cm. wide. (Bearne's) $3,932

A Louis XV-style mahogany vitrine applied throughout with gilt-brass foliate moldings and mounts, 126cm. wide. (Bearne's) $5,662

A carved mirrored vitrine, French, circa 1900, the central glazed twin-door cabinet with bracket shelf above, flanked by asymmetrical glazed cabinets, 94½in. maximum width. (Christie's) $11,178

A mahogany and cameo glass vitrine, designed by Jacques Gruber, circa 1900, the upper shelf surmounted by rounded back panel inset with mauve and white cameo glass landscape, 41¼in. wide. (Christie's) $18,630

An Edwardian mahogany display cabinet, the whole inlaid with floral and ribbon swags and Neo Classical ornament within satinwood bandings, 52in. wide. (Canterbury) $1,908

A carved oak vitrine 'Modèle Chicorée, designed by Louis Majorelle, circa 1905, the twin-door cabinet inlaid with flowering hydrangea below frieze drawers, 89½in. maximum width. (Christie's) $20,493

An Edwardian mahogany display cabinet, the mirror back with floral marquetry, above bowfront frieze drawer and door flanked by two glazed doors, 133cm. wide. (Bristol) $951

A late 19th century pine dresser, with planked back and three open shelves, 155cm. wide.
(Bonhams) $551

An adzed oak enclosed dresser by Robert Thompson, Kilburn, with ledge back on molded edged top with canted corners, two small over three long central drawers, 60½in. wide.
(Andrew Hartley) $4,785

A late George III oak dresser, and a rack, with molded cornice above three open shelves, 153cm.
(Tennants) $7,536

A George III oak dresser, the raised open rack with molded cornice, the base fitted with three drawers, 58in. wide.
(George Kidner) $6,089

An antique oak dresser, the breakfront rack fitted with a pair of glazed and panelled doors, flanking further pair of fielded panelled doors, 6ft. 9in. wide.
(Russell Baldwin & Bright) $4,466

An oak dresser, the upper section with molded cornice and shaped frieze and an arrangement of open shelves, 157cm. wide, the base mid-18th century.
(Bearne's) $3,146

18th century oak North Wales dresser, the base with three large and three small drawers, on chamfered square legs with pot shelf under, 57in.
(Ewbank) $3,828

A Georgian oak dresser with open shelves above base fitted with three frieze drawers on square tapering legs, 6ft. 6in. wide.
(Russell Baldwin & Bright) $5,128

A late 18th century oak South Wales dresser, fitted with three frieze drawers, four tapering pillar legs to the front, 5ft.10in. wide.
(Russell Baldwin & Bright) $5,427

An oak dresser, English, 18th century, the associated architectural plate rack with later backboards and two open shelves, 75in. wide.
(Christie's) $9,143

A Georgian oak dresser and shelves with shaped frieze, the base fitted with three drawers, with shaped frieze on square supports, 7ft. long. (Russell Baldwin & Bright) $6,156

An oak and inlaid dresser, Staffordshire, late 19th century, the boarded plate-rack with molded cornice and shaped frieze above three shelves, 71½in. wide.
(Christie's) $4,361

An 18th century oak dresser, the delft rack with molded cornice, serpentine frieze, shaped sides, and three molded edged shelves 57½in. wide.
(Andrew Hartley) $8,294

An oak dresser, West Midlands, late 18th/early 19th century, the open plate rack with later cornice, fret-carved frieze above three shelves, 79in. wide.
(Christie's) $3,634

A French chestnut and brass-mounted dresser, 18th century, the superstructure with a molded cornice and undulating frieze with stylized flowerheads and meandering stems, 56in. wide.
(Christie's) $6,541

An oak dresser, South Wales, late 18th/early 19th century, the later boarded plate rack with molded cornice, wavy frieze and three shelves, 64in. wide.
(Christie's) $6,400

An oak and inlaid dresser, probably West Midlands, early 19th century, the upper section with a molded cornice and two central shelves flanked by twin panelled cupboard doors, 79in. wide.
(Christie's) $11,040

An oak dresser, Cardiganshire, late 19th century, the inverted breakfront upper section with molded cornice and three central open shelves flanked by arched astragal glazed doors, 61in. wide.
(Christie's) $6,948

An 18th century oak dresser, with three raised open shelves to the back, the base fitted with three drawers and two panelled doors, 65½in. wide.
(George Kidner) $2,970

18th century oak dresser, the associated top with three plate racks applied with fluted moldings with similar uprights, 81½in.
(G.A. Key) $6,360

An 18th century oak dresser base with later rack to top, molded cornice fitted with three shelves and two small cupboards, 71in. wide.
(Canterbury) $4,418

A 19th century oak dresser, the stepped and dentil molded cornice above two shelves and a panelled back carved with lozenges and thistles, 200cm. wide.
(Cheffins) $1,982

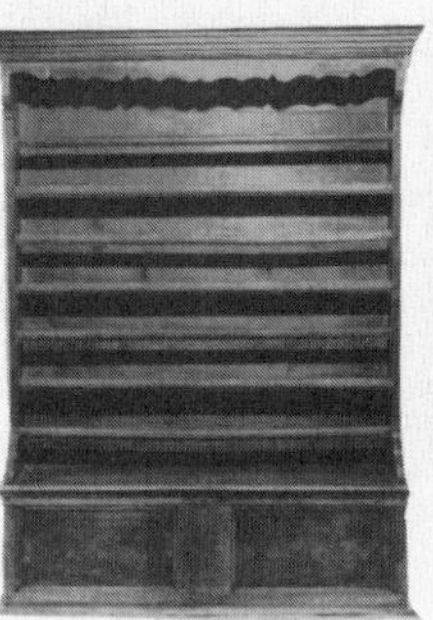

Provincial walnut and fruitwood wall rack with molded cornice above a scalloped frieze and four plate shelves, cupboard under, 19th century, 41in. wide.
(Eldred's) $1,265

An oak dresser, South Wales, early 19th century, the plate rack with molded cornice and frieze with cup hooks, above two divided shelves, 70½in. wide.
(Christie's) $7,314

An 18th century style oak Welsh dresser, the three-shelf shaped back on base with three central drawers flanked by twin panelled doors, 183cm. wide.
(Bristol) $1,072

An oak dresser, West Midlands, late 18th century, with associated 19th century plate rack and two open shelves flanked by three smaller shelves, 73in. wide.
(Christie's) $5,088

A late 18th early 19th century oak and mahogany banded dresser, the plate rack with molded cornice and wavy edge surround with three shelves, 173cm. wide.
(Wintertons) $3,726

A late Regency mahogany dumb waiter, the two circular tiers with a molded edge and three turned brass columns, 27in. diameter.
(Woolley & Wallis) $2,324

A mahogany two tier dumb waiter, altered, 65cm. wide.
(Bonhams) $954

A mid-18th century mahogany dumb waiter with three graduated circular tiers on a tripod base, 108cm. high.
(Bearne's) $1,573

A Regency mahogany dumb waiter, the circular galleried top on ring-turned splayed legs joined by concave sided undertier, 14in. diameter. (Christie's) $7,498

A matched pair of George IV mahogany dwarf two-tier dumb waiters attributed to Gillows, each with a circular dished top on a gadrooned and ring-turned baluster column above a lower dished tier, 28½in. high.
(Christie's) $10,971

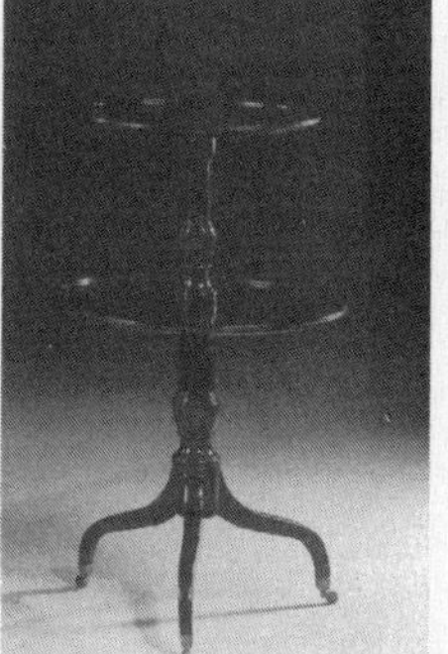

A mahogany two-tier dumb waiter, early 19th century, with two graduated revolving circular tiers, on a turned column, 22¾in. diameter.
(Christie's) $2,062

A George III mahogany three tier dumb waiter, with three graduated hinged platforms on a turned vase column and splayed tripod supports, 23¼in. diameter.
(Christie's) $4,542

An early Victorian mahogany metamorphic three tier dumb waiter, the top with a moulded edge, on a quatrefoil platform and bun feet with castors, 41½in. wide.
(Christie's) $1,840

A mahogany and gilt-bronze dumb waiter, Paris, circa 1870, with two revolving graduated tiers and a further tier, all cross-banded and veneered au soleil with pierced galleries, 72.5cm.
(Sotheby's) $14,720

A fine and rare Queen Anne bonnet-top maple high chest of drawers, Connecticut, 1750-60, in two parts, the upper section with broken swan's neck pediment, 41½in. wide.
(Sotheby's) $34,500

A French mahogany chest of drawers, 70cm. wide.
(Bonhams) $474

Chippendale walnut scroll top carved high chest, Massachusetts, 1760-80, the molded scrolled pediment above three small drawers, lower case 40in. wide.
(Skinner) $90,500

A Queen Anne figured maple flat-top highboy, coastal Connecticut, probably Stonington area, circa 1760, in two parts, the upper section with molded cornice fitted with a secret drawer, 39in. wide.
(Sotheby's) $26,450

A Queen Anne cherrywood and poplar stepped high chest of drawers, Connecticut or Massachusetts, 1730-1750, in three sections: the crown, with three graduated and stepped shelves with double-beaded molded edges, 41in. wide.
(Christie's) $68,500

A Chippendale inlaid walnut tall chest-of-drawers, Berks County, Pennsylvania, dated 1790, the molded and dentilled cornice above a conforming case fitted with three thumbmolded short drawers, 43¾in. wide.
(Christie's) $74,000

Queen Anne walnut and walnut veneer high chest of drawers, probably Boston or Essex County, 1730-50, the top section with flat deep molded cornice with concealed linen drawer, 38½in. wide. (Skinner) $33,350

A walnut harlequin bachelor's chest, late 20th century, incorporating some earlier elements, feather-banded to the top and front, 28¾in. wide.
(Christie's) $14,262

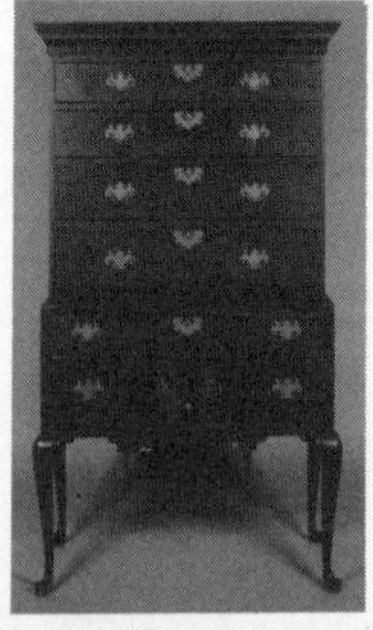

New England Queen Anne cherry flat top highboy, circa 1740-1760, step molded overhanging cornice over four wide graduated drawers, later butterfly brasses, 40in. wide.
(Freeman) $16,800

A Victorian walnut pedestal desk, circa 1850, 121cm. wide. (Bonhams) $3,950

Anon, French, desk and armchair, circa 1930, macassar ebony, rectangular section desk with two banks of four drawers, centered by frieze drawer covered with galuchat, desk 55in. wide. (Sotheby's) $15,249

A late Victorian oak cylinder bureau, circa 1900, 53in. wide. (Bonhams) $2,370

A George III mahogany kneehole dressing table with long frieze drawer, an apron drawer and six short drawers around the recess cupboard, on shaped bracket feet, 78cm. high x 93cm. wide, some restoration.(Bearne's) $1,884

A Sheraton Revival mahogany and inlaid dressing table, having a rectangular mirror with scrolled pediment between jewelry drawers to each side, 143cm. wide. (Tennants) $2,736

A George II mahogany kneehole desk or dressing table, with an ovolo molded top over seven drawers about the kneehole cupboard, 75cm. (Tennants) $4,396

A large late 19th century oak roll top desk by John Guy & Sons London, 137cm. wide. (Bonhams) $1,134

A mid Victorian mahogany pedestal desk, the rectangular top fitted with two corner drawer sets, central sloping fall front, which opens to reveal a fitted satinwood interior, 136cm. wide. (Bonhams) $2,187

An early 20th century oak tambour front desk, 122cm. wide. (Bonhams) $680

A mid Victorian mahogany partner's desk, the leather inset top with arrangement of nine drawers opposed by three drawers and two doors, the top 154 x 98cm.
(Bristol) $4,800

A walnut and inlaid desk by Whytock and Reid, Edinburgh, the semi-bowed rectangular top crossbanded and inlaid with burr panels, 155cm. wide.
(Phillips) $2,720

George III mahogany twin pedestal desk, the molded and leather inset top over two frieze drawers simulated as three. 4ft.3in.
(Lawrences) $4,508

A Victorian mahogany partner's desk, the rectangular top with molded edge and rounded corners above three frieze drawers to each side, 155cm. wide.
(Phillips) $4,640

A 19th century Continental kingwood pedestal desk, with gilt metal mounts crossbanded with string inlay, 50½in. wide.
(Andrew Hartley) $1,560

Art Nouveau oak desk, flat top with rounded corners over center drawer, two open-side bookshelves, 47¼in. wide.
(Skinner) $517

D.I.M. (Décoration Intérieure Moderne), desk, circa 1935, brazilwood, rounded rectangular top, above twin pedestals each with three drawers, 47½in. wide.
(Sotheby's) $8,073

A Victorian oak kneehole writing desk, 47in. wide.
(Dockrees) $704

A George III mahogany partner's pedestal desk, the top inset with a panel of tooled leather, the frieze fitted with one long and two short drawers to either side, 55¼in. wide.
(Christie's) $8,384

A George III mahogany pedestal desk, the top inset with a panel of green tooled leather and with a foliate edge, 58in. wide.
(Christie's) $29,072

A mahogany kidney-shaped pedestal desk, early 20th century, decorated with boxwood lines, the leather-lined top above a frieze fitted with three drawers, 80in. wide. (Christie's) $6,707

A Victorian burr walnut pedestal desk, the molded edged rounded oblong top with leather writing surface, 48in. wide.
(Andrew Hartley) $2,016

A Regency mahogany pedestal desk, the regular green leather-lined top above three frieze drawers and a kneehole, 72¼in. wide.
(Christie's) $31,395

Grain painted pine merchant's kneehole desk, New England, first half 19th century, the rectangular drop-leaf top above two rectangular cabinets, 48in. wide.
(Skinner) $460

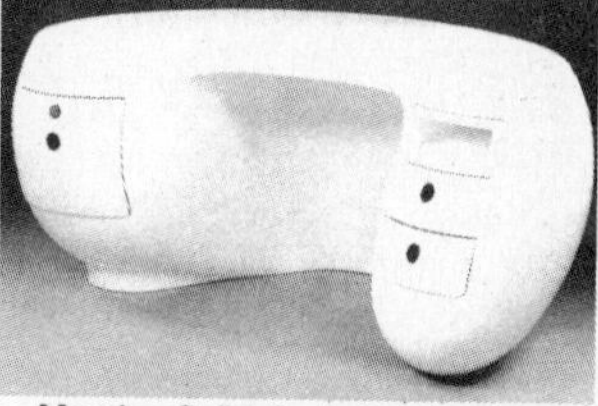

Maurice Calka for Leheu Deshays, 'Boomerang' desk, designed 1969, white painted fibreglass, 74in. wide.
(Sotheby's) $14,531

A mid-Victorian mahogany partner's pedestal desk, the rounded rectangular green leather-lined top above a slightly recessed mahogany-lined frieze drawer, 78in. wide. (Christie's) $18,745

A matching mahogany and gilt-bronze desk, French, circa 1890, in Empire style, the rectangular top above a frieze applied with classical emblems, 164cm. wide.
(Sotheby's) $18,975

A mahogany pedestal desk, 19th century, probably German, the round rectangular leather-lined top with molded edge and three frieze drawers to either side, 73½in. wide.
(Christie's) $8,832

An Edwardian mahogany kneehole desk of unusual 18th century design, the whole inlaid with bellflower swags, Classical urns and acanthus leaves and with green leather inset to top, 45in.
(Canterbury) $1,988

A George III mahogany desk, crossbanded overall, including the reverse, the sloping ratcheted top covered in black simulated leather, 48in. wide.
(Christie's) $3,680

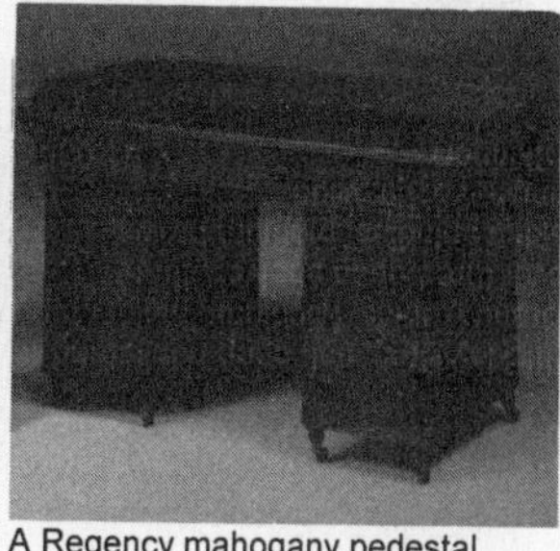

A Regency mahogany pedestal writing table, the top with a three-quarter gallery and inset panel, fitted with three frieze drawers and three drawers to each pedestal, 52½in. wide.
(Christie's) $3,997

Heywood Wakefield maple desk, circa 1955, rectangular top over long drawer flanked by four side drawers, with shaped wooden pulls, 42in. wide.
(Skinner) $431

An adzed oak partner's desk by Robert 'Mouseman' Thompson, with carved wave banded frieze, panelled sides, 65 x 39in.
(Andrew Hartley) $14,584

One of a pair of late 19th century oak pedestal desks, each with leather inset top, three-drawer frieze, 106cm. wide.
(Bristol) (Two) $1,815

TOP TIPS

Central heating can have a drastic effect on furniture, causing furniture to split. To minimise such damage it is necessary to ensure the ambient air is not too dry. The solution is to purchase a humidifier which can be hung on a radiator and topped up with water on a regular basis. Even a small bowl of water placed in a room will help.
(Dee, Atkinson & Harrison)

An English linen press, circa 1899, limed oak, two sliding panelled doors flanking a central panelled section, 59in. wide.
(Sotheby's) $903

A good Federal eagle-inlaid mahogany linen press, New York, circa 1810, in two parts; the upper section with a swan-neck pediment centering an acorn finial, 46¼in. wide. (Sotheby's) $12,650

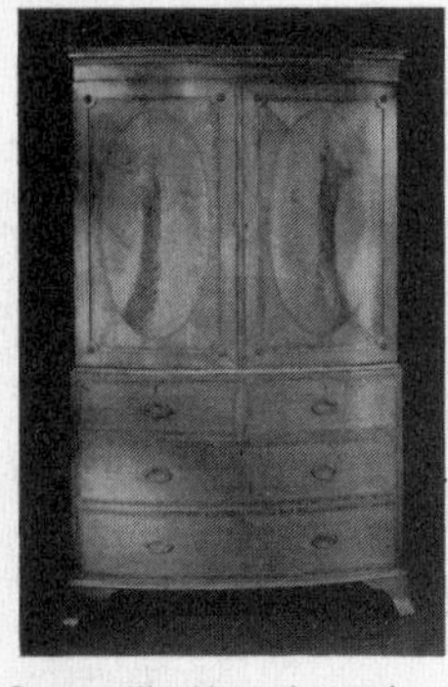

A George III style satinwood and mahogany bowfront linen press, circa 1900, with a pair of panelled cupboard doors enclosing shelves, 51¼in. wide.
(Christie's) $5,331

A Chippendale figured gumwood linen press, probably New Jersey, circa 1785, in two parts, the upper part with stepped molded cornice above shaped panelled cupboard doors, 47½in. wide.
(Sotheby's) $6,900

A George III style cream and foliate painted linen press, the stepped cornice above a pair of grilled silk pleated doors enclosing six slides, late 19th century, 139cm. wide.
(Cheffins) $5,707

A late 19th century Georgian style mahogany linen press, the dentil cornice above twin panelled doors, on a four-drawer base, 127cm. wide. (Bristol) $1,980

A small Regency mahogany and cedar linen press, with reeded edge to the top over two panelled doors enclosing trays, 53cm.
(Tennants) $2,826

A Regency mahogany linen press, the flame grain doors enclosing slides above two short and two long drawers, 130cm. wide.
(Bristol) $3,636

A walnut lowboy, decorated with crossbanding, the rectangular top above three drawers with a shaped apron below, 28½in. wide.
(Christie's) $1,769

A George I walnut lowboy, the rounded rectangular top above two drawers and three drawers, above a shaped apron, 29½in. wide.
(Christie's) $11,040

An oak lowboy, mid 18th century, the top with a molded edge, fitted with a short and two deep drawers, 32in. wide.
(Christie's) $3,270

An early George III mahogany lowboy, the top with a molded edge and re-entrant corners, fitted with a short drawer in the arched apron, 30in. wide.
(Christie's) $2,725

Philadelphia Queen Anne lowboy, circa 1750-1760, attributed to William Savery, possibly owned by Benjamin Franklin, two piece curly maple top with notched corners on maple case, 35½in. wide.
(Freeman) $392,000

An early Georgian walnut lowboy, feather-banded to the top and front, the quarter veneered rectangular top above one long and three short drawers, 30¼in. wide.
(Christie's) $12,880

An early Georgian style lowboy in old walnut with checkered banding and molded edge to the top, three drawers over shaped arch, 32in.
(Russell Baldwin & Bright) $1,523

A George I walnut lowboy, the crossbanded quarter-veneered rectangular top above one long and two short drawers, flanking a shaped kneehole, 28½in. wide.
(Christie's) $8,832

A George III oak lowboy, with a molded round cornered top over three drawers, the arched kneehole embellished with pierced frets, 79cm. (Tennants) $3,925

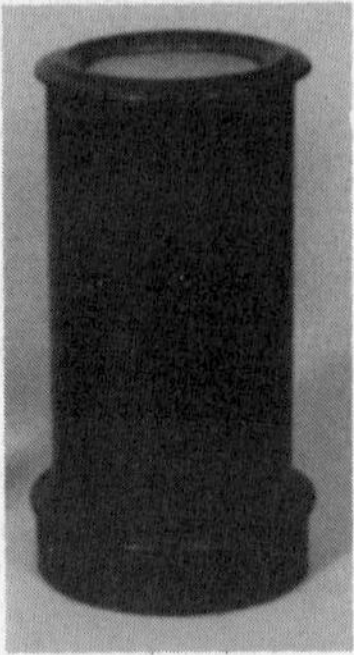

A Victorian mahogany pillar box bedside cabinet with inset marble top, single door cupboard and plinth base, 29in. high.
(John Maxwell) $600

A mahogany bedside cabinet, 62cm. wide.
(Bonhams) $439

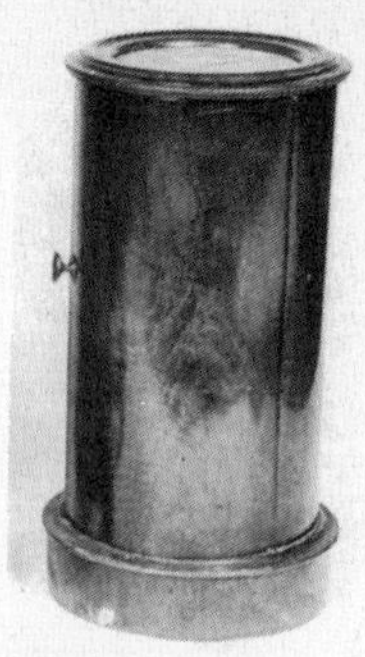

A 19th century mahogany cylindrical pot cupboard, with inset marble top, on plinth base, 38in. diameter. (Bristol) $736

A Regency mahogany tray-top pot cupboard, the top with pierced carrying handles, enclosed by a crossbanded panel door, 14in. wide. (Christie's) $2,362

A pair of mahogany pedestal cupboards, Danish, circa 1860, each in the form of a column with a bowed door on a molded fluted base, 50cm. diameter.
(Sotheby's) $11,247

A late Victorian satinwood and tulipwood-banded pot cupboard, the marble top with a molded edge above a banded frieze and conformingly inlaid cupboard door, 14½in. (Christie's) $589

A George III mahogany pot cupboard, the raised compartmentalised gallery above a frieze drawer and a pair of cupboard doors, 20¾in. wide.
(Christie's) $1,288

Federal carved mahogany veneer chamber stand, north shore Massachusetts, circa 1815–25, the shaped splashboard above the top and veneered cabinet door, 21½in. wide. (Skinner) $2,300

A mahogany Classical Revival tray top bedside table, painted with figures and garlands of flowers, on square tapering legs, 39 x 33cm.
(Dreweatt Neate) $1,102

A George II mahogany clothes press, with a pair of doors with C-scroll molding, enclosing three later shelves, 50in. wide.
(Christie's) $14,812

An oak deuddarn, North Wales, early 18th century, the upper section with a pair of doors flanking a central door with arcaded panel, 55in. wide.(Christie's) $3,997

A Regency mahogany clothes press, the key molded cornice with pendants to the satinwood veneered frieze, 4ft.8in.
(Woolley & Wallis) $7,920

A 17th century style oak press cupboard in two stages, the canopied upper part having cornice and molded frieze with turned angle pendants above a pair of doors, 48in. wide.
(Peter Francis) $2,212

An oak press cupboard, English, 17th century and later, carved overall, with molded cornice and scroll-carved frieze, above three recessed geometrically molded cupboards, 76in. wide.
(Christie's) $5,486

A Regency mahogany clothes press, the figured veneered front with an arcaded cornice, inlaid with an elongated star in ebony stringing and satinwood banded end panels, 4ft. wide.
(Woolley & Wallis) $3,205

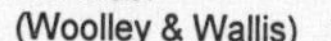

A carved oak press cupboard, the upper section with molded cornice over lunette frieze, foliate cup and cover turned supports, basically 17th century, 59in. wide.
(Andrew Hartley) $3,190

An oak press cupboard, Lake District, early 18th century, with a guilloche carved frieze centered with a rosette, initialled and dated *R.F. 1717* and with drop pendants, 67½in. wide.
(Christie's) $3,657

Late 17th/early 18th century oak press cupboard, molded pediment over two arched panelled doors enclosing cupboard, 63in.
(G.A. Key) $2,385

An oak press cupboard, English, late 17th century, the overhanging frieze carved with foliate strap-work, centered with and flanked by corbels carved with heraldic devices, 77in. long.
(Christie's) $3,997

A George II mahogany press, the upper section fitted with four short drawers above a projecting base, 49½in. wide.
(Christie's) $5,623

An oak press cupboard, North Country, late 17th century, with later molded cornice above a rosette filled guilloche frieze raised on turned columns, 55in. wide.
(Christie's) $8,228

A Victorian burr-walnut press cupboard, fitted with two frieze drawers, with two panelled doors below enclosing three sliding trays, 48in. wide.
(Christie's) $2,812

A Georgian mahogany press cupboard, upper section fitted with slides enclosed by pair of oval panelled doors with crossbanding and ebony stringing, 4ft. wide.
(G.A. Key) $5,168

An oak press cupboard, Lake District/Yorkshire, early 18th century, with molded cornice and foliate scrolling frieze centered with initials *W.H.A.* and supported by turned column uprights, 73in. wide.
(Christie's) $6,970

A joined oak press cupboard, the canopy having a carved frieze on bulbous carved supports over two bevelled panel doors, 167cm. wide.
(Tennants) $1,884

An oak press cupboard, possibly Welsh, late 17th century, the upper section with dentil molded cornice and drop pendants above a central arcaded panel flanked by geometrically molded doors, 61in. wide. (Christie's) $5,486

An oak press cupboard, North Country, late 17th century, profusely carved overall with rosettes and stiff leaves, the upper section with a molded front cornice, 74in. wide.
(Christie's) $10,057

A 19th century four fold screen, the panels painted after Uccello, The Battle of San Romano, 7ft. high.
(Russell Baldwin & Bright) $4,225

A French bronze firescreen, late 19th/early 20th century, the foliate capped frame with loop handle and on splayed feet, 32½in. high.
(Christie's) $1,363

Alvar Aalto, 'Screen no. 100, 1935-6, executed circa 1945, rolled pine wood slats strung with wire, 130cm. high x 250cm. wide.
(Sotheby's) $5,520

A lacquered four fold screen designed by Paule Leleu, manufactured by Sain & Tambute for Jules Leleu, circa 1950, decorated with a stylized gilt and silvered landscape, 67in. high.
(Christie's) $10,971

A French bronze and mesh firescreen, late 19th/early 20th century, the rectangular frame with flambeau standards on foliate capped hoof feet, 29¾in. wide.
(Christie's) $2,362

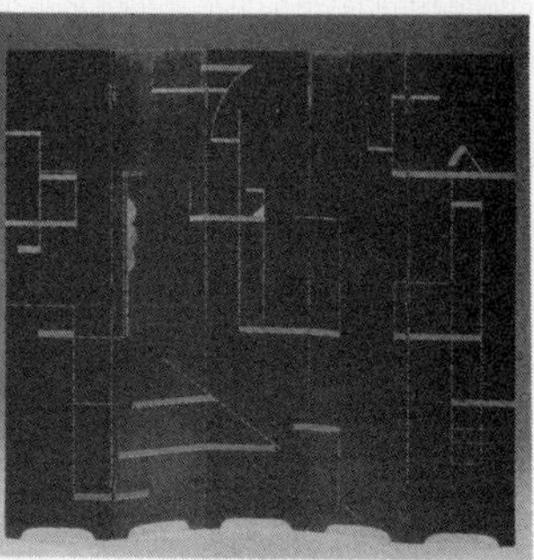

Eileen Gray, five panel screen, circa 1922-25, natural, brown/black oriental lacquer on wood, incised and decorated with gilt with abstract geometric motifs, 12½in. wide each panel.
(Sotheby's) $171,720

Paul Etienne Saïn, four panel abstract screen, circa 1930, each panel with silver leaf decoration on a black background, 68¾ x 17¾in. each panel.
(Sotheby's) $11,661

A George III mahogany firescreen, the elevating ratcheted arched panel inset with a needlework in silk heightened gros and petit point needlework, 25in. wide.
(Christie's) $1,543

Robert Mallet-Stevens, five panel screen, 1930s, nickel-plated metal five rectangular panels inset with mirrored glass, ball feet, 30cm. wide each panel.
(Sotheby's) $13,455

A George III mahogany secrétaire with rounded edged molded oblong top, fall front, on later bracket feet, 50¾in. wide.
(Andrew Hartley) $2,871

An 18th century oak secrétaire with molded edged top, fall front secrétaire drawer, three graduated drawers below, 37½in. wide.
(Andrew Hartley) $1,015

Federal mahogany inlaid butler's desk, probably New York, circa 1790-1800, the rectangular top with string inlaid edge above a case of a deep drawer with two inlaid ovals set in mitred panels, 46in. wide.
(Skinner) $2,530

Classical carved mahogany and mahogany veneer secrétaire à abattant, Boston, 1820–25, with marble top above a cove molding and mahogany veneer façade, 35in. wide. (Skinner) $16,100

American four-drawer Empire bureau, 19th century, in cherry and tiger maple, mahogany veneered drawer fronts, 44in. wide.
(Eldred's) $660

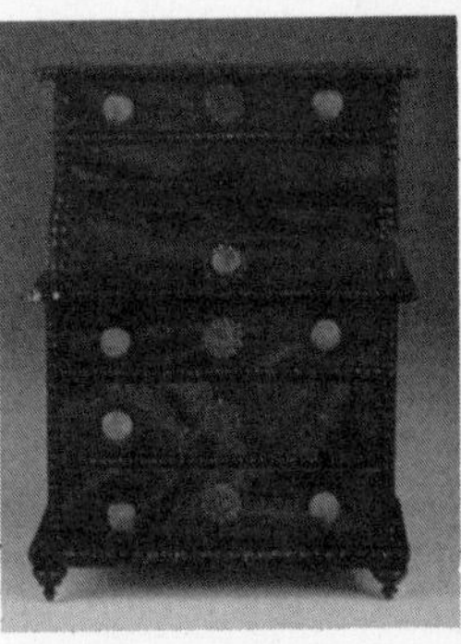

A faux walnut Continental bureau, German, 19th century, the three drawer base and roll desk front revealing four drawer compartments and letter hole, 6in. high. (Bonhams) $1,183

A fine Federal inlaid mahogany tambour lady's secretary, Boston, Massachusetts, circa 1800, in two parts; the upper section with an inlaid edge above a prospect door, 37in. wide.
(Sotheby's) $17,250

A late Victorian campaign mahogany secrétaire chest in two parts, the upper with two short and one long drawer above a shallow secrétaire drawer, 39in.
(Dreweatt Neate) $4,455

A 17th century Spanish walnut vargueño, the plain exterior enclosing tortoiseshell and ebony veneered interior in the Northern European style, 34½in.
(Canterbury) $2,800

An Art Nouveau period oak secrétaire writing desk, 38in. wide.
(Dockrees) $576

19th century mahogany secrétaire chest, the top with drawer fall front enclosing a fitted interior of drawers and pigeon holes, over two panelled doors enclosing cupboard, plinth base, 46½in.
(G A Key) $2,080

A 19th century mahogany brass bound military secrétaire chest, fitted with four short drawers either side of the fall flap, 40in. wide.
(Anderson & Garland) $1,333

A Regency mahogany secrétaire à abattant, the galleried rectangular top with a molded edge above a frieze flap revealing eight pigeon holes, 3ft.4¾in. overall.
(Woolley & Wallis) $4,327

A Renaissance Revival walnut and ebonised patent desk, stamped by the Wooton Desk Company, Indianapolis, Indiana, circa 1874, the scroll-carved crest with turned finial flanked by similar ornament above a shaped and veneered gallery, 42½in. wide.
(Christie's) $21,850

English Aesthetic Movement mahogany and inlay tall chest/desk, last quarter 19th century, rectangular top over a cabinet door enclosing sliding shelves to the left, 42½in. wide.
(Skinner) $6,900

Camphorwood brass bound two-part campaign desk, China, 19th century, the top drawer containing a fold-down writing surface and compartmented, multidrawer interior, 36in. wide.
(Skinner) $4,025

An early 18th century walnut secrétaire, the upper part with molded cornice above cushion fronted frieze drawer, 41in. wide.
(Canterbury) $7,235

Classical carved and mahogany veneer butler's desk, possibly New England, circa 1825, case of three recessed long drawers with flanking freestanding columns, 45in. wide.
(Skinner) $920

A stained wooden secrétaire, English, 19th century, the drop-leaf front with six drawers and pigeon-hole, 6 x 4¾in. (Bonhams) $252

A late 18th century mahogany secrétaire chest, having satinwood stringing, the secrétaire drawer fitted with drawers and pigeon holes, 3ft. 4in. wide. (Russell Baldwin & Bright) $2,114

A Biedermeier mahogany secrétaire à abattant, with gray marble top, a long frieze drawer, fall front, 91.5cm. (Bearne's) $1,65

A late George III mahogany, satinbirch and polychrome papier mâché bureau-bookcase, with molded cornice and plain frieze above panelled papier mâché doors, 51¾in. wide. (Christie's) $23,000

A pair of Louis XVI style gilt-metal mounted marquetry, parquetry, bird's eye maple and mahogany secrétaires à abattant, third quarter 19th century, each with inset eared rectangular marble top, 31¼in. wide. (Christie's) $7,475

An Art Nouveau mahogany and inlaid secrétaire à abattant, with a pierced three-quarter gallery, the frieze inlaid with abalone with stylized interlaced stems with flowers, 27in. wide. (Christie's) $6,178

A Georgian mahogany secrétaire tallboy chest of two short and six long drawers flanked by fluted quarter round pilasters on ogee bracket feet, 4ft. wide. (Russell Baldwin & Bright) $4,212

A walnut escritoire, early 18th century, decorated with feather-banding, the molded cornice above a cushion molded long drawer, 46in. wide. (Christie's) $10,247

A German mahogany and ormolu mounted secrétaire à abattant, late 18th century, with canted angles, top with a pierced scrolling foliate three-quarter gallery, 38½in. wide. (Christie's) $5,451

A George III mahogany secrétaire bookcase, with molded dentil cornice, two astragal glazed doors enclosing adjustable shelving, 43in.
(Andrew Hartley) $3,190

A George III mahogany secrétaire bookcase.
(G. E. Sworder) $6,400

A George III mahogany secrétaire bookcase, the upper part with dentil molded cornice above a pair of astragal glazed doors, 43in. wide.
(Peter Francis) $5,056

Federal cherry and mahogany inlaid desk and bookcase, New Hampshire, circa 1820, flat top with quarter round molding above a case with inlaid panel frieze, 37¾in. wide. (Skinner) $5,462

A Federal rosewood and birchwood-inlaid mahogany lady's writing desk, North Shore, Massachusetts, circa 1810, in two parts; the upper section arched glazed cupboard, 39¾in. wide.
(Sotheby's) $14,950

A George III, mahogany and satinwood strung secrétaire bookcase, the molded cornice above a pendant frieze and a pair of five pane glazed doors, 114cm. wide. (Cheffins) $5,073

A Victorian mahogany secrétaire bookcase, the molded cornice over twin panelled doors, the base crossbanded and with fitted interior, 109cm. wide.
(Bristol) $1,300

A late George III mahogany bookcase-on-chest, with molded cornice and a pair of astragal glazed doors, the chest with checker-strung frieze, 51in. wide.
(Christie's) $1,840

A George IV mahogany and satinwood secrétaire bookcase/display cabinet, outlined with stringing and crossbanding, 114cm. wide.
(Bearne's) $4,293

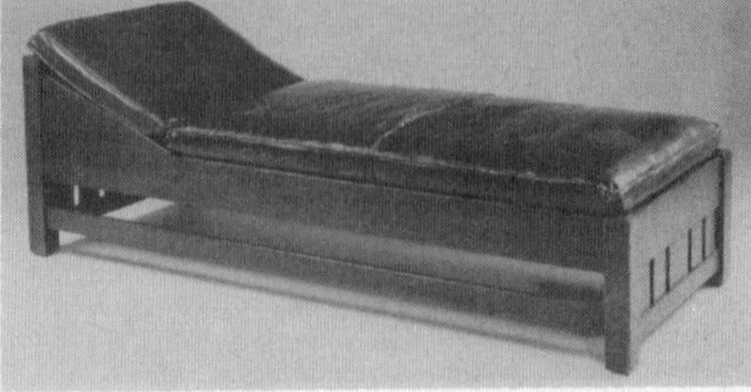

L. & J.G. Stickley couch, Fayetteville, New York, circa 1910, no. 295, slanted head rest, headboard and footboard with four horizontal slats centered by a single wider slat, 72½in. long. (Skinner) $1,150

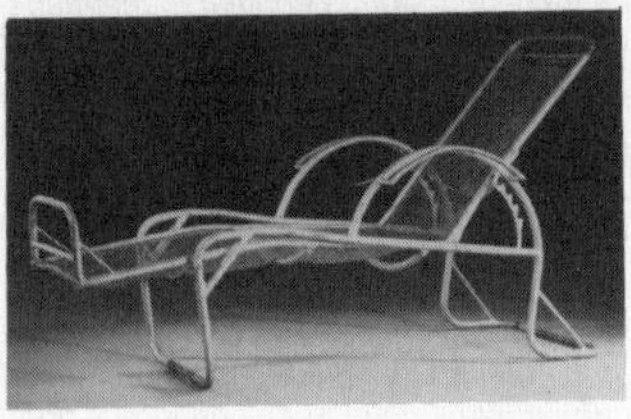

Alvar Aalto, a painted tubular steel sun chair, designed 1932, specifically for use in the Paimio Sanatorium, silver painted tubular steel frame with hinged backrest, 79in. long.
(Christie's) $7,222

A fine classical carved mahogany settee, probably New York, circa 1825, the upholstered double shield-shaped back surmounted by a wing-spread eagle carved in the round, 6ft. long overall.
(Sotheby's) $6,325

Renaissance Revival rosewood, bronze and parcel-gilt settee, third quarter 19th century, tripartite back with crest depicting Leda and the Swan, 72in. long.
(Skinner) $6,900

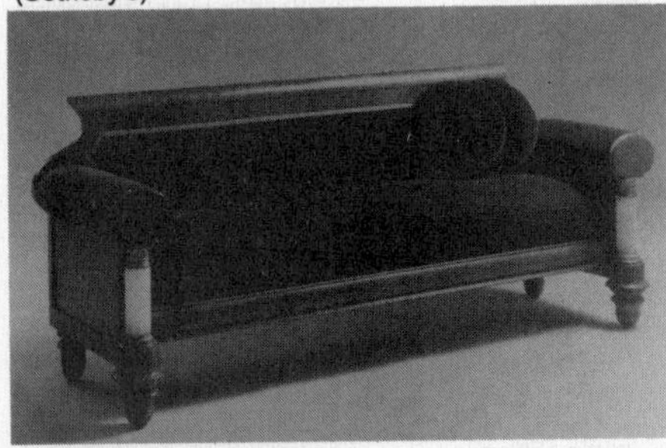

A fine Empire figured mahogany, marble and brass-mounted sofa, Boston, Massachusetts, circa 1830, with a reverse scrolling crest above a padded back and semi-overupholstered seat flanked by ovoid arms on free-standing brass-mounted marble columnar supports, 7ft. long overall. (Sotheby's) $4,600

A Classical inlaid and carved mahogany sofa, New York, circa 1825, the horizontal panelled crest flanked by cornucopia carved arms on leaf, volute and flower carved legs, 5ft. 8in. long overall.
(Sotheby's) $5,175

British Colonial carved and inlaid teakwood caned sofa, circa 1840 with S-scroll back and arms and molded seat rail, 93in. long.
(Skinner) $9,775

Classical carved and veneered mahogany sofa Baltimore or Philadelphia areas, 1825-35, with reede crest rail above scrolled arms with applied frontal she carving, 84in. long. (Skinner) $690

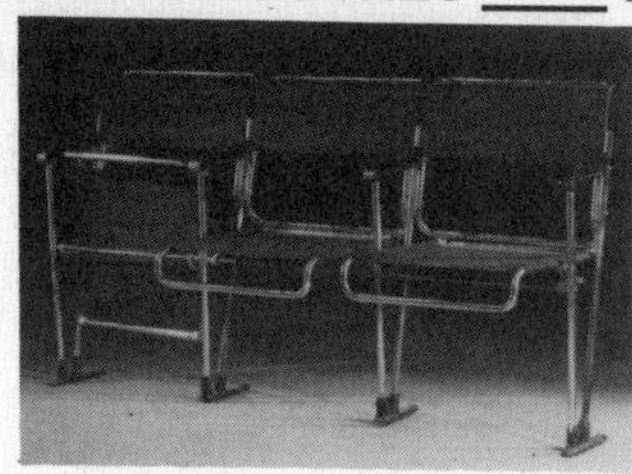

Marcel Breuer, a chromed tubular steel theater seat Model No. B70, designed 1926-30, manufactured by Thonet, each seat section with black canvas seat elements, flanked by ebonized wood armrests, the seats hinged, 69in. wide. (Christie's) $9,389

19th century Empire style mahogany framed scroll end sofa, the frieze applied with gilt metal bird of prey mounts, supported on scrolled feet, upholstered throughout in green Regency stripe, 73in. (G.A. Key) $1,420

A stained beechwood and upholstered sofa, 20th century, of large size, the rectangular back above two squab cushions and outswept arms, on square tapering legs with brass caps and castors, 87in. wide. (Christie's) $2,005

Gustav Stickley even arm settle, No. 205, back with five wide slats, sides with one wide slat, spring cushion seat, side rails with through tenons, 56in. wide. (Skinner) $3,737

A Federal mahogany inlaid sofa, probably Massachusetts, circa 1810-1815, the slightly arched crest continuing to downward sloping sides and reeded arms on swelled vase and ring turned reeded posts on bird's eye maple and string inlaid panels, 78in. wide. (Skinner) $8,625

Antique American mammy's bench, with grain-painted and stencilled decoration, 48in. long. (Eldred's) $660

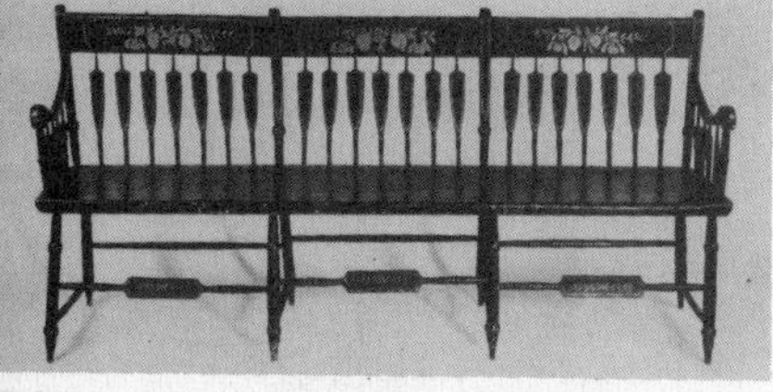

Painted and decorated arrow-back settle, Pennsylvania, 1820-30, the gilt-decorated three panel crest above the arrow-back splats, outlined in gilt striping above an incised plank seat, on ring-turned tapering legs, 78in. long. (Skinner) $1,092

Small Classical mahogany carved recamier, Boston, circa 1825, the molded and shaped crest rail continuing to a leaf-carved scroll, above the scrolled panelled arms, 65¹/8in. long. (Skinner) $8,625

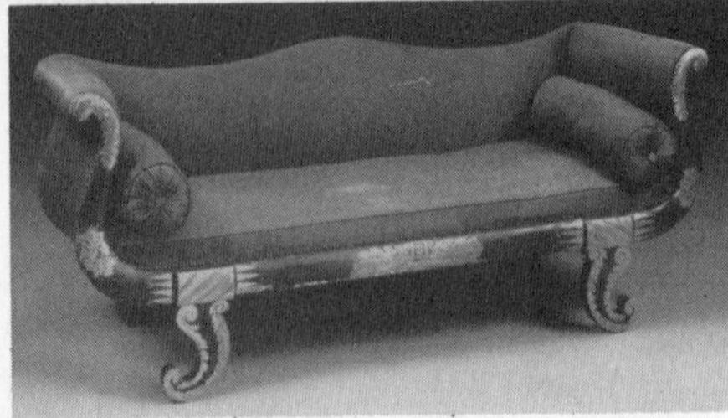

A Regency simulated rosewood sofa, decorated with parcel-gilt foliage, the hump back between outswept ends, on outswept legs, 82in. wide.
(Christie's) $4,099

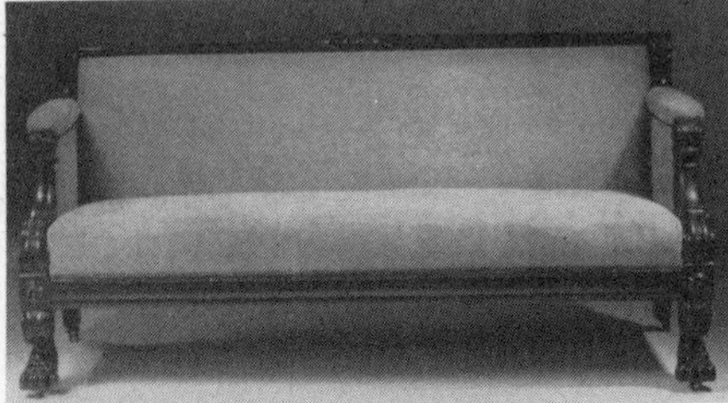

A William IV mahogany sofa, with turned baluster toprail above a rectangular padded back, sides and seat, on downswept arm-supports carved with foliage and lion legs with sunk brass castors, 80¾in. wide.
(Christie's) $8,332

A Regency mahogany sofa, reeded overall, with rectangular padded back, sides, seat and three seat cushions, on ring-turned tapering legs with brass associated castors, 72in. wide.
(Christie's) $3,703

Gerrit Rietveld, a Parana pine and metal pew, designed 1960-63, for use in the Dutch Reformed Church of Uithoorn, with long rectangular panel back, the reverse with enamelled metal hymnal brackets, 85in. long. (Christie's) $4,514

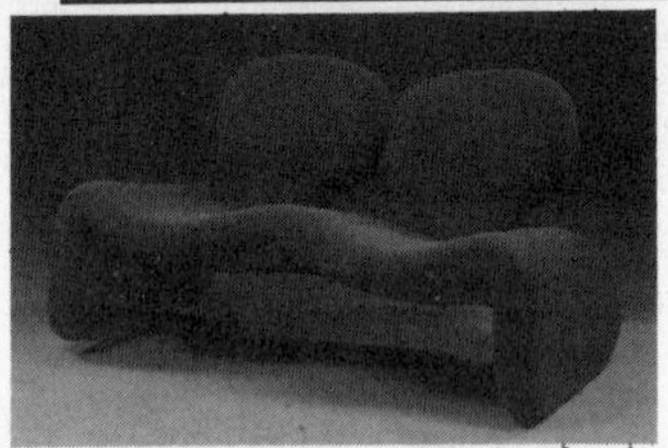

Olivier Mourgue for Airborne, 'Djinn' sofa, designed 1965, purple fabric, steel and urethane foam upholstered frame, 24¾in.
(Sotheby's) $1,379

A late Regency simulated rosewood and brass inlaid sofa, decorated with scrolling foliate inlaid panels and reeded lines, the padded back surmounted by a pediment top-rail, on turned legs terminating in brass caps and castors, the caps stamped *B.S. & P. Patent*, 80in. wide. (Christie's) $2,437

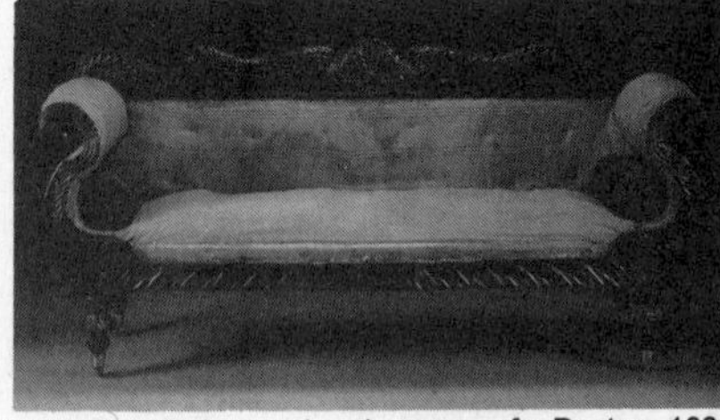

A late Classical carved mahogany sofa, Boston, 1830-1860, the scrolled crestrail centering a carved anthemion flanked by scrolled leaf carving above an upholstered back flanked by S-curved upholstered arms with reeded and leaf-carved supports, 83in wide. (Christie's) $4,02

A giltwood canapé, 19th century, with a channelle frame decorated with ribbon, reel and stiff-le moldings, with an oval padded back and sides, 85in wide. (Christie's) $5,24

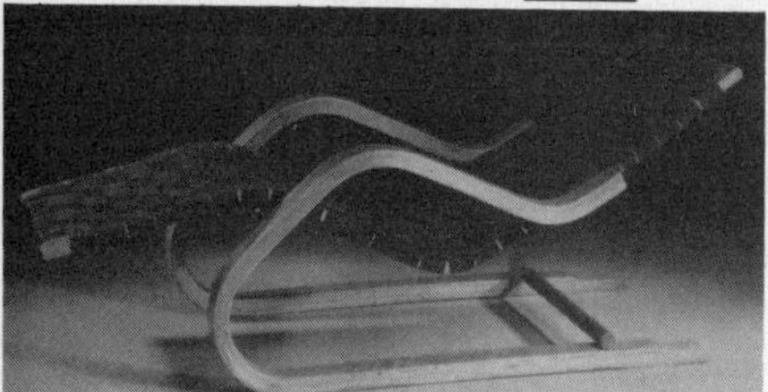
Alvar Aalto, a birch chaise longue, Model No. 39, designed 1936, with plaited webbing seat on cantilever frame, joined by a dowel stretcher, 65½in. long. (Christie's) $10,833

Dominique for the Lanvin Villa, sofa, 1932, rosewood base and side panels, with chromium-plated metal strip, 90½in. wide. (Sotheby's) $8,252

A Regency mahogany sofa, the rectangular padded back, sides and squab covered in dark-red foliate damask, with scrolled ends carved with foliage, above a foliage-carved apron, 84in. wide. (Christie's) $8,887

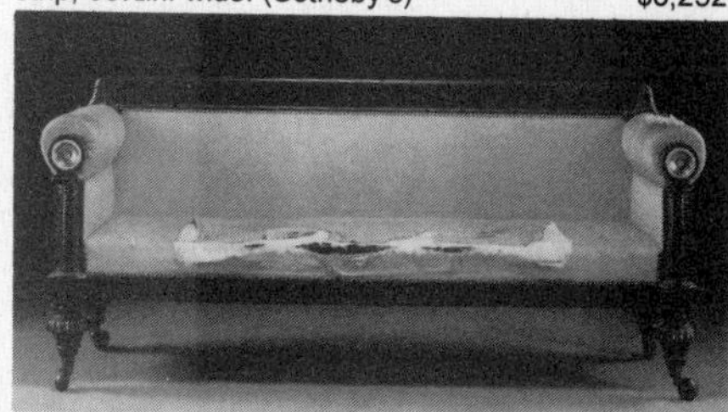
A Classical mahogany carved and veneered sofa, possibly Boston, 1820-1840, the half-round crestrail above a veneered frieze flanked by carved stylized leaves and downscrolling motifs over an upholstered back, 81¼in. wide.(Christie's) $4,830

A William IV mahogany-framed sofa inlaid with panels of cut brass motifs, with shaped foliate-carved back, outscrolled arms, two seat squabs and two bolsters and on turned legs, 200cm. wide. (Bearne's) $1,730

A late Regency rosewood sofa, the shaped padded back surmounted by a reeded cresting, the outswept padded arms with foliate acanthus-carved terminals, on outswept legs, 70in. wide. (Christie's) $4,124

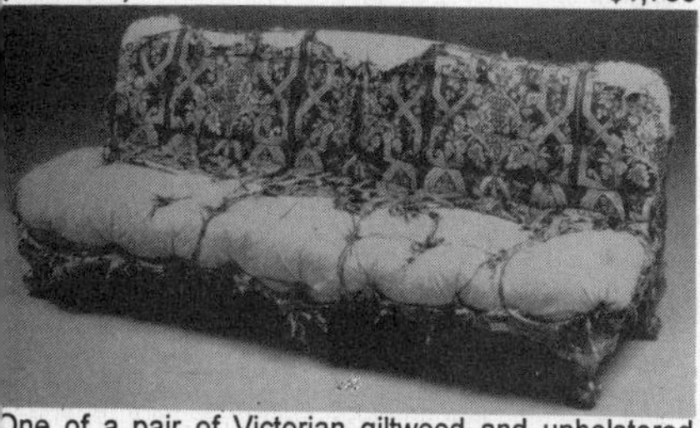
One of a pair of Victorian giltwood and upholstered banquettes, each arched buttoned upholstered back covered in a crimson damask with serpentine fronted upholstered seats, on squat foliate-carved cabriole legs, 84in. wide. (Christie's) (Two) $8,021

An early 19th century Anglo Indian mahogany and cane chaise longue, the reeded frame with trellis back, overscrolled ends carved with flower-heads and on reeded inverted baluster legs, 180cm. wide. (Bearne's) $1,652

An Ernest Gimson beechwood hanging shelf, the shaped top rail above two open shelves 24in. wide and an open bookshelf with two open shelves, 33in. wide. (Christie's) $2,243

A pair of Austrian polychrome decorated and parcel-gilt wall-brackets, each with a shaped and molded top with bead-and-reel band above a female mask, 10¼in. high. (Christie's) $2,290

Alvar Aalto, shelf model No. 111 designed 1935-1936, polished and ebonized birch laminated frame with three shelves. (Bonhams) $6,921

Stickley Bros. oak open bookstand, Grand Rapids, Michigan, gallery top over three open shelves, three-sided spindles, medium brown finish, 26¾in. wide. (Skinner) $1,035

A pair of Victorian mahogany three tier hanging shelves, the upper tier with turned finials supported on baluster-turned finials supported on baluster-turned column supports, 32¾in. wide. (Christie's) $920

Painted pine hanging spoon rack, probably Europe, late 18th century, the lid with cotter pin hinges, 24¾in. high; together with six pewter spoons. (Skinner) $920

A Victorian mahogany three-tier twin-sided book wagon, with carved foliate and scroll decoration, on plinth base, 96cm. wide. (Bristol) $5,115

A pair of Spanish mahogany bowfront corner shelves, 19th century, inlaid with ebonized lines, each with an arcaded frieze, 25½in. wide. (Christie's) $2,981

Gustav Stickley book rack, New York, V-shaped side panels with through pegged tenons and D-shaped cut-out handles, 29¾in. wide. (Skinner) $1,840

A fine Federal carved and figured mahogany bowfront sideboard, attributed to William Hook, Salem, Massachusetts, circa 1810, 47in. wide.
(Sotheby's) $24,150

Alessandro Mendini and Bruno Gregori for Nuova Alchimia, 'Cantaride' cocktail bar/sideboard, 1984, prototype, polychrome lacquered and veneered wood, 57¾in. wide.
(Sotheby's) $3,312

Limbert sideboard, Grand Rapids and Holland, Michigan, circa 1907, rectangular plate rack over central mirror on conforming rectangular top, 48in. wide.
(Skinner) $2,185

A good 19th century oak Puginesque sideboard, the back with graduated open shelves before chevron planking with shaped pierced ends and ring turned column supports, 84in. wide.
(David Lay) $1,568

Grain painted sideboard or locker, Shaftsbury area, Vermont, 1825-40, the rectangular top above two short and one long drawer, projecting over two recessed panel cupboard doors, 46¾in. wide.
(Skinner) $1,840

An oak Arts and Crafts sideboard, the raised back having a bowed glazed and leaded cupboard set with embossed round copper panels, Waring & Gillow, Manchester, 169cm.
(Tennants) $3,454

A late 19th century mahogany and checkered inlaid break front sideboard with two center drawers and side cellaret cupboards and brass back rail, 66in. wide.
(Dreweatt Neate) $1,328

A late 19th century mahogany sideboard, in French style, having marquetry and parquetry inlay and brass moldings, 5ft.5in. wide.
(Woolley & Wallis) $2,038

A small adzed oak sideboard by Robert 'Mouseman' Thompson, with ledge back, the fascia with two short and three long drawers, 42in. wide.
(Andrew Hartley) $2,853

An early 19th century pedestal sideboard in mahogany inlaid with Sheraton style medallions and satinwood stringing, fitted with three frieze drawers to the bow front, 8ft. wide. (Russell Baldwin & Bright) $2,398

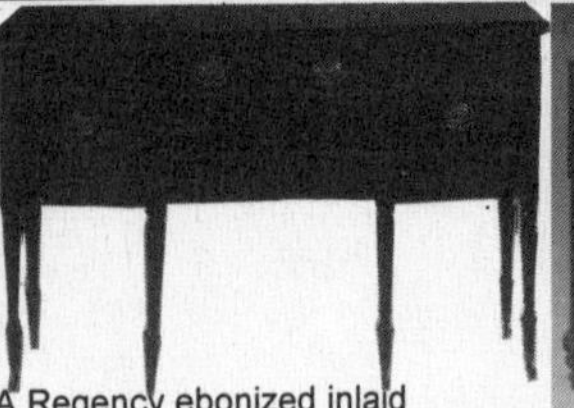
A Regency ebonized inlaid mahogany bowfront sideboard, the crossbanded top above a drawer and an arch with a tambour door, 58in. wide.
(Christie's) $4,416

A George IV mahogany pedestal sideboard outlined with beaded edge moldings, satinwood banding and boxwood and ebony stringing, 190cm. wide.
(Bearne's) $3,498

A George III bowfront mahogany sideboard, inlaid overall with boxwood and ebonized lines and crossbanded in satinwood, 72¼in. wide. (Christie's) $8,832

Late 19th century Sheraton Revival mahogany and satinwood banded and boxwood line inlaid breakfront sideboard with a central drawer flanked by cupboards, 62in. wide.
(Ewbank) $1,109

A George III mahogany bowfront sideboard, crossbanded in tulipwood and inlaid with lines, fitted with a frieze drawer, 55¼in. wide.
(Christie's) $7,268

A mid Victorian mirrorbacked mahogany sideboard, 184cm. wide.
(Bonhams) $2,226

A George III mahogany bowfront sideboard, basically late 18th century, banded to the front in tulipwood and wengewood, 63¼in. wide. (Christie's) $11,109

Antique American sideboard, in pine, three drawers over two panelled doors, top 24¾ x 46½in.
(Eldred's) $1,760

An American mahogany sideboard, New York, early 19th century, the rectangular top above two frieze drawers and three crossbanded cupboard doors, 58in. wide.
(Christie's) $2,734

George III Irish mahogany and boxwood inlay sideboard, early 19th century, shaped reeded top over drawers, 56in. long.
(Skinner) $4,600

An Edwardian mahogany pedestal sideboard, carved with interlaced scrolling foliage with rocaille, strap-work and cabochon decoration, 32in. wide.
(Christie's) $4,542

A late Georgian mahogany bowfront sideboard with a wide central drawer flanked by two drawers, cellaret and cupboard, 7ft. wide. (Russell Baldwin & Bright) $3.136

German Art Deco veneered sideboard, Oriental-style gallery over a rounded rectangular body of parquet-style exotic woods veneer, 87in. wide.(Skinner) $460

A mahogany, satinwood-banded and marquetry sideboard, 19th century, of breakfront D-shaped outline, inlaid with lines and banded in tulipwood, 90in. wide. (Christie's) $9,085

An adzed oak sideboard by Robert 'Mouseman' Thompson, with carved wave banded frieze, central panelled door flanked on either side by a frieze drawer over a panelled door, 81 x 38½in. (Andrew Hartley) $8,243

A William IV rosewood sideboard, with a raised back, fitted with a brass inlaid frieze drawer with a foliate-carved shaped arched drawer below, 73½in. wide. (Christie's) $3,997

A Scottish Regency mahogany sideboard, the galleried top with central shell motif, above two short frieze drawers centered by a shell and above a pair of panelled doors, 79in. wide. (Christie's) $3,312

Paul Dupré-Lafon, sideboard, circa 1940, rosewood, rectangular, the central section with two sets of vellum covered cupboard doors, 81¾in. wide. (Sotheby's) $19,734

A mahogany breakfront pedestal sideboard, decorated with lines with a brass gallery with urn finials, the top with rounded projecting ends, 95½in. wide. (Christie's) $7,498

Alessandro Mendini and Bruno Gregori for Nuova Alchimia, 'Meligete' sideboard, 1984, prototype, composed of two pieces in blue and pink lacquered wood, 48½in. wide. (Sotheby's) $1,840

A Regency mahogany sideboard, the bowfront rectangular top above a small fitted drawer and a further deep drawer, 48in. wide. (Christie's) $5,888

A Regency mahogany pedestal sideboard, the raised panelled shaped back carved with scrolling foliage above a concave fronted top, 86¼in. wide. (Christie's) $2,999

A William IV mahogany breakfront sideboard, the small raised back decorated with carved shell motif with acanthus leaf scrolls, 90in. wide. (Anderson & Garland) $2,763

Gustav Stickley single-drawer stand, New York, circa 1912, square top, single drawer with circular wooden pull, lower median shelf, branded mark, 16in. wide. (Skinner) $575

A pair of Regency mahogany stands, each with a rectangular top with a molded edge, on dual ring-turned splayed end supports, 16in. wide. (Christie's) $1,453

Unusual Pontipool two-section umbrella stand, 19th century, copper colored with gold highlights surrounding landscape reserves, 26in. high. (Eldred's) $385

AUCTIONEER'S ADVICE

Try to decide for yourself how much a particular lot is worth to you if you intend bidding, and then stick to it! Writing the figure down clearly and keeping it in front of you may be a good way of reminding yourself. A good auction works its magic if passions rise, and we are all only human. There is always that teasing possibility that your next bid just might be the clincher!

(Michael Bowman)

A mahogany five division book trough raised on turned supports and club legs united by an X-shaped stretcher, 93cm. wide. (Cheffins) $1,510

A walnut folio stand on turned supports and stretchers, second half 19th century, 108 x 75 x 61cm. (Finarte) $2,897

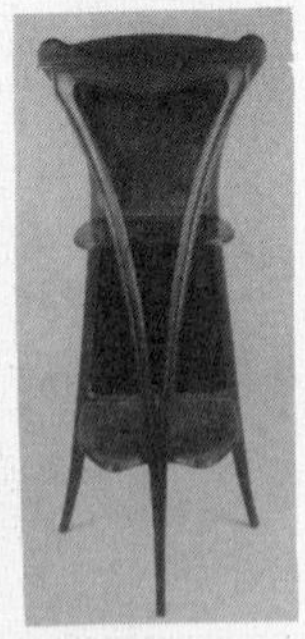

Majorelle fruitwood and marquetry three-tier stand, France, circa 1900, two rear legs with conjoined front support, two open shelves in stylized floral designs, 21½in. wide. (Skinner) $3,737

A pair of 19th century Burmese carved hardwood jardinière stands, of circular form with foldover rim, tapering sides and tin liners, 31½in. high. (Andrew Hartley) $4,307

Arts and Crafts oak magazine rack, circa 1916, square top over four shelves joined by cutout sides flaring to base, 42in. high. (Skinner) $460

Federal cherry tilt-top stand, New England, 1780, the octagonal top with molded edge tilts above the swelled and ring-turned pedestal, 24in. wide. (Skinner) $1,610

A Federal birchwood and cherrywood candlestand, New England, circa 1800, the square cockbeaded top above a gadrooned urn-form support, 16¾in. wide. (Sotheby's) $2,300

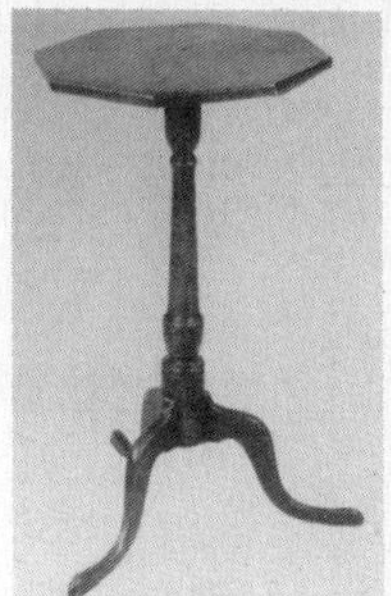

Federal maple candlestand, New England, circa 1790, the octagonal top on a vase and ring turned post and tripod cabriole leg base, 15in. wide. (Skinner) $1,610

Federal mahogany tilt-top candlestand, probably Massachusetts, circa 1800, the serpentine top with square corners on a vase and ring turned post and tripod cabriole leg base, 19in. wide. (Skinner) $2,300

A Queen Anne turned mahogany dishtop candlestand, Philadelphia, Pennsylvania, circa 1750, the circular hinged top revolving and tilting above a birdcage support, 23¼in. diameter. (Sotheby's) $8,050

Federal cherry candlestand with drawer, probably Connecticut, circa 1815-20, the rectangular top above a single drawer and straight sides, 19in. wide. (Skinner) $747

Federal mahogany tilt-top candlestand, Massachusetts, circa 1790, the oval top on a vase and ring-turned post and tripod cabriole legs, 17in. wide. (Skinner) $2,415

A Chippendale carved and figured walnut and mahogany candlestand, New York, circa 1770, the circular top tilting above a flaring standard and an urn-form support, 20½in. diameter. (Sotheby's) $5,175

A rare Federal carved cherrywood candlestand, Connecticut, circa 1800, the oval molded top tilting above a short drawer, 21in. wide. (Sotheby's) $34,500

A set of early Victorian mahogany bedsteps, with three tiers inset with green leather, the top two hinged, 18½in. wide.
(Christie's) $1,312

Set of modern Gothic walnut metamorphic library steps, third quarter 19th century, of typical chair form, horizontal slats to back.
(Skinner) $1,265

A set of mahogany three tread bedsteps, 19th century, each step with fleurs de lys centered black leather lining and with ebonized line inlay, 32½in. long.
(Christie's) $2,528

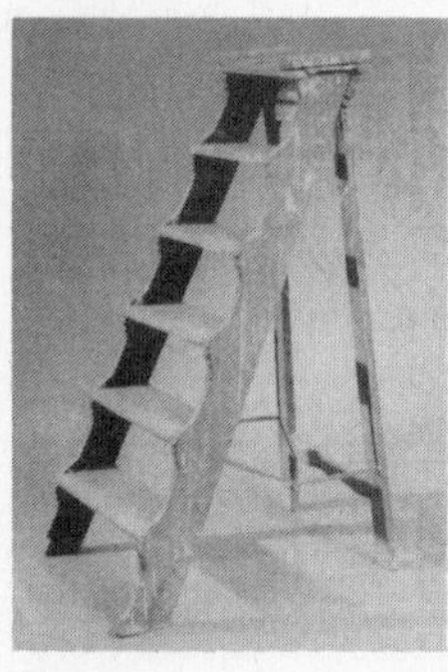

A set of George III bleached mahogany steps, the six treads within a shaped tapering frame with orginal ironwork hinged braces.
(Woolley & Wallis) $693

An early Victorian oak Gothic Revival metamorphic library armchair, with lancet open panels, the back with foliage finials, hinged to make library steps.
(Woolley & Wallis) $8,792

A set of limed oak library steps designed by Jean-Michel Frank, circa 1929, seven shallow steps, double uprights on shaped runners, 78½in. high.
(Christie's) $38,399

A set of pine library steps with four treads, turned supports and a turned handrail with painted banding. (David Lay) $925

A Regency oak set of metamorphic library steps/whatnot, the bottom shelf pulling out to form two red leather-lined steps, 23in. wide, closed. (Christie's) $3,840

A set of late Victorian oak library steps, circa 1880, 50cm. wide.
(Bonhams) $2,511

A pair of late Victorian oak, brown oak and ebonized stools, on ring-turned fluted tapering legs headed by S-scrolled angles, 73in. wide. (Christie's) $59,096

Classical carved mahogany veneer window bench, Boston, 1835–45, with upholstered seat above a veneered rail on leaf-carved cyma curved ends joined by a ring-turned medial stretcher, 48in. wide. (Skinner) $2,185

Régence style walnut banquette, late 19th century, serpentine top upholstered in green striped silk over a foliate carved frieze, 45½in. wide. (Skinner) $1,840

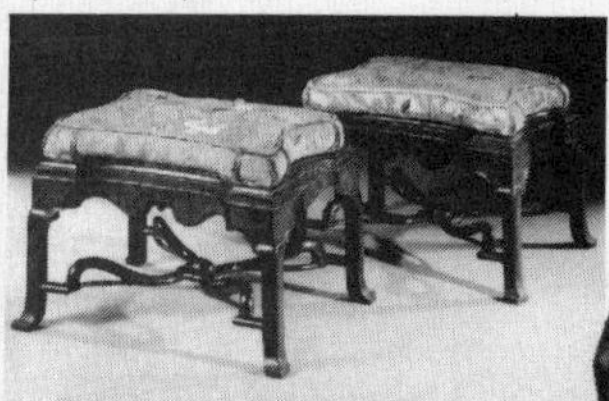

A pair of Queen Anne black and gilt-japanned stools, possibly by Philip Guibert, the stool decorated overall with foliage, with a waved apron and square legs joined by a waved X-shaped stretcher, 28½in. wide. (Christie's) $191,880

A William IV mahogany rectangular stool on decorative carved splay legs. (Dee Atkinson & Harrison) $2,062

A pair of George IV rosewood stools, in the manner of Gillows, each with a dished rectangular padded seat, on channelled X-frame scrolled supports, 20¼in. wide. (Christie's) $26,404

Classical mahogany and mahogany veneer footstool, probably Boston, circa 1835, the rectangular concave over-upholstered top on conforming veneered frame, 25in. wide. (Skinner) $1,380

A Victorian walnut revolving adjustable piano stool on carved tripod support. (Dreweatt Neate) $302

An early 19th century oak hall seat, in the manner of John Loudon, the turned rail lifts on rondel and block capped turned tapering legs, 3ft.7in. (Woolley & Wallis) $4,547

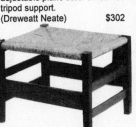

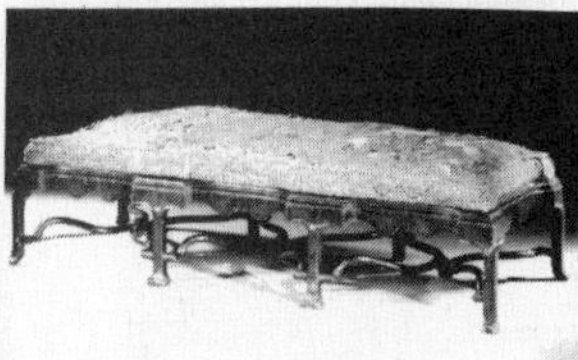

A Queen Anne black and gilt-japanned long stool, possibly by Philip Guibert, the rectangular padded drop-in-seat with eared corners and triple concave cut front, 79½in. wide. (Christie's) $83,640

Gustav Stickley footstool, rush cover, brand mark, original finish, 19½in. wide. (Skinner) $546

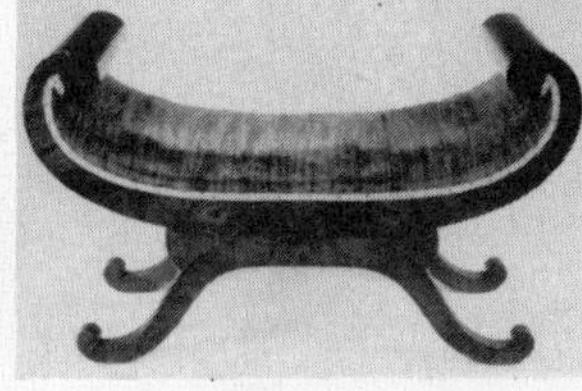

Classical mahogany veneer window bench, 1815–25, New York, the curving upholstered seat flanked by scrolled ends above a scrolled base, 39½in. wide. (Skinner) $3,450

A Regency rosewood X-framed stool, by Gillows, the padded rectangular later seat on X-frame legs with paterae, 19in. wide. (Christie's) $6,992

A Queen Anne walnut stool with waved apron and cabriole legs joined by a waved H-shaped stretcher, unupholstered, 24in. wide. (Christie's) $4,073

A Classical carved mahogany piano stool, New York City, 1810-1825, the ring-turned crest centering a leaf-carved raised tablet flanked by fish-tail stiles continuing to dolphin-carved seatrails, 26in. high. (Christie's) $2,185

Le Corbusier, pair of stools from the Maison du Brésil à la Cité Universitaire de Paris, 1957-9, oak, two sides with carrying hole, 43cm. wide. (Sotheby's) $7,208

A George I walnut stool, with a floral gros point needlework drop-in seat, on hipped cabriole legs with rocaille decoration and terminating in pad feet, 22in. wide. (Christie's) $3,452

A George II mahogany stool, the rounded rectangular drop-in seat covered in gros point floral needlework, above an apron to the front and reverse centered by a shell, 21in. wide. (Christie's) $5,555

A pair of early Victorian simulated-rosewood and parcel-gilt stools, the scrolled sides and foliate apron on cabriole legs, 18¼in. wide.
(Christie's) $10,183

A mahogany stool, part 18th century, the rectangular padded seat above a blind gothic fretwork apron, on later conforming square legs, 18¼in. wide.
(Christie's) $2,392

A pair of Swedish Gustavian white painted and gilt stools. (Stockholms AV) $3,581

A George II mahogany commode stool, the floral upholstered padded drop-in seat above a shaped apron, possibly Irish, 20½in. wide.
(Christie's) $1,490

A George III mahogany stool, the slatted dipped seat on square tapering legs joined by stretchers, 18in. wide. (Christie's) $1,312

Attributed to Charles Rennie Mackintosh, a pair of beech stools, designed for the Queen Margaret Medical College, Glasgow, 1894-96. Solid circular seat, raised on three outstretched legs.
(Bonhams) $1,887

An early Victorian rosewood X-frame stool, the rectangular padded seat fitted with a floral needlework panel, 21½in. wide.
(Christie's) $1,097

An oak boarded stool, English, 16th century, the top with moulded edges, the aprons with shaped chamfered overhang and centred with a pointed ogee-arched open panel, 24in. wide.
(Christie's) $26,738

A mahogany rectangular stool, 19th century, on turned reeded baluster legs, 32¾in. wide.
(Christie's) $3,312

A George III giltwood window seat, the frame molded overall, the waved seatrail centered by flowerheads, 45in. wide.
(Christie's) $6,440

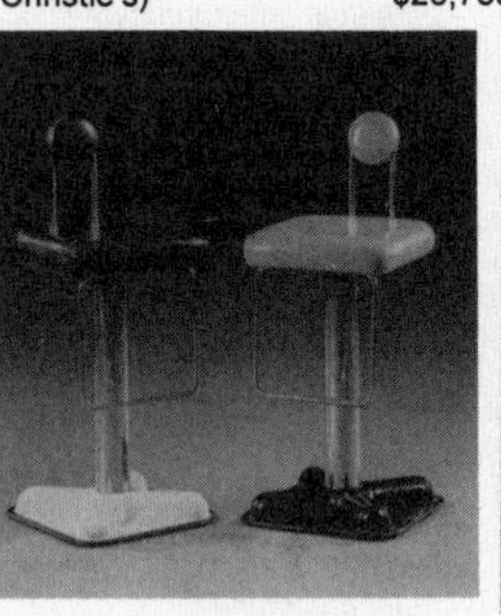

Joe Colombo for Zanotta, two 'Birillo' stools, designed 1970, red or yellow plastic upholstered seats and back on steel leg, white or black fibreglass bases, 105cm. high. (Sotheby's) $1,104

A good early Victorian carved mahogany stool, with tapestry drop-in seat and gadrooned border above rosette applied frieze, 50cm. width. (Bristol) $680

A Regency rosewood-framed dressing stool applied with pressed brass flowerheads and lion masks, 55cm. wide.
(Bearne's) $2,202

A pair of pictorial needlework footstools, 19th century, each of square form, on foliate cast gilt-metal claw and ball feet, 14in. wide.
(Christie's) $1,840

A walnut stool on faceted legs and hoof feet, joined by a stretcher, the legs probably 18th century, 20½in. wide. (Christie's) $4,048

Art Deco thuya and rosewood dining table and six chairs, Europe, circa 1938, rectangular-top table with cut corners in veneer over eight panelled cone-shaped pedestal, waisted pedestal above flared panel base, together with six side chairs with dropped crest rail over tapered angled back splat, table 59in. long. (Skinner) $4,600

A definitive 1950s Ercol dining room suite comprising: a circular top drop leaf **dining table**, together with four standard chairs having *Festival of Britain 1950* across the splats, and a sideboard, fitted center cupboard enclosed by two twin panelled doors, 127cm. (Locke & England) $412

A suite of late Victorian Louis XVI style giltwood chairs, comprising a canapé and a pair of fauteuils, the frames molded and carved with husks and leaves, open arms with elbow rests and acanthus scrolled terminals. (Phillips) $2,560

A giltwood three-piece suite, early 20th century, in the Louis XV style, comprising: a pair of fauteuils, each with a shell and foliate-carved top-rail and a deep buttoned padded back, open arms and a serpentine seat, on channelled cabriole legs; and a small canape to match, 63in. wide.
(Christie's) $920

A suite of Louis XV style giltwood seat furniture, late 19th century, comprising four fauteuils and a canapé, each with arched rectangular padded back and seat, within a channelled and foliate-carved frame, on cabriole legs and scroll feet, the canapé 59½in.
(Christie's) $34,500

N.K., Scandinavia, three piece salon, 1930s, comprising sofa, pair of deep armchairs, pale honey oak frames with dark conker brown seats and backs, the sofa with three panel back, sofa 64¼in. wide.
(Sotheby's) $11,713

An Art Deco period figured walnut dining suite with wide satin birch crossbanding comprising; dining table, length 66in., a set of six dining chairs, double cupboard on plinth, serving/cutlery table, length 42in.
(John Maxwell) $1,104

Art Deco maple dinette set, National Chair Co., Boston, Massachusetts, circa 1938, cut-corner table on U-shaped fluted base with extension leaves, accompanied by four stepped panel-back chairs with plank seats, table 42in. wide. (Skinner) $345

Olivier Mourgue for Airborne, 'Djinn' sofa, two armchairs and table, designed 1965, olive green fabric, steel and urethane foam upholstered frame, white painted wood table with steel runners, sofa 48½in. wide. (Sotheby's) $5,512

A French mahogany matched three piece suite, mid 19th century, each with a gadrooned gently arched top-rail with scroll cresting and padded back with a needlework panel with flowers and trophies, the canape 70½in. wide. (Christie's) $3,997

Anon, Austrian, dining room table and eight chairs, circa 1910, the chairs veneered with ebonized and honey colored wood in a zebra pattern the table similarly veneered in checker pattern, 201cm. long. (Sotheby's) $17,940

Marcel Louis Baugniet, Modernist dining table and eight chairs, circa 1930, the circular table veneered in sycamore with central chromium plated metal disk and raised on eight cylindrical chromium plated metal legs, 58¾in. diameter. (Sotheby's) $32,436

A rococo carved mahogany suite, American, mid-19th century, comprising: a settee and two armchairs, each with deeply carved and bowed crestrail centering a cabochon cartouche in a shell-carved and acanthus C-scrolled surround flanked by rampant griffins above a tufted black-leather upholstered back, the settee 61in. wide. (Christie's) $7,478

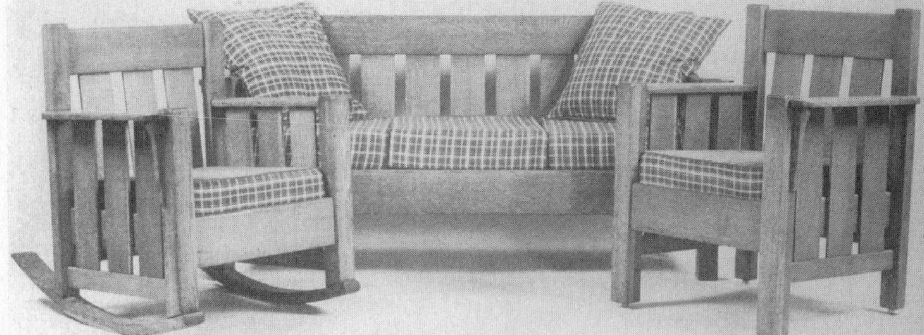

Suite of Arts and Crafts furniture, circa 1912, including a drop arm settle, armchair and rocking chair, the settle with wide crest rail over nine vertical slats, all having flat arms, short corbel supports, through tenons over three wide vertical slats. (Skinner) $3,105

An Art Deco dining room suite, circa 1930, comprising: table, six chairs, sideboard and serving table, burrwood veneer, the rectangular table with shaped end supports, the cloud-backed chairs upholstered in tan leather, table: 71¼in. wide. (Sotheby's) $4,048

An Egyptian Revival ivory-inlaid, ebonized and parcel-gilt suite of seat furniture, circa 1880, comprising a canapé and two armchairs, each with outscrolled pierced crestrail above a padded back and seat flanked by Egyptian term figure arm supports, on paw feet, the canapé 72in. wide. (Christie's) $14,950

A burr-birch six piece suite, central European, 19th century, comprising a settee, a pair of fauteuils, a pair of chaises and a center table of a later date, the chairs with scroll uprights and bar backs, the settee 71in. wide. (Christie's) $2,907

A suite of Louis XVI style giltwood seat furniture comprising a canapé and four fauteuils, the canapé with arched rectangular padded back carved with ribbon-tied garlands flanked by foliate carved padded arms, the canapé 71¼in. wide. (Christie's) $23,000

A Regency rosewood breakfast table, the circular top above a gadrooned molding, on three foliate-scrolled supports, 54in. diameter.
(Christie's) $18,400

A George IV brown oak and marquetry breakfast table, the circular tilt-top inlaid with a stylized foliate band, 51in. diameter.
(Christie's) $16,560

A Regency mahogany breakfast table, the oval tilt-top crossbanded in tulipwood, on a turned baluster column and single reeded downswept legs, 58in. wide.
(Christie's) $4,048

A Regency rosewood breakfast table, the inlaid brass stringing having scrolled corner designs, with rounded rectangular tip-up top, 5ft. long. (Russell Baldwin & Bright)
$9,588

An early Victorian rosewood breakfast table, the circular tilt top on a faceted column and concave sided platform base, 53½in. wide.
(Christie's) $5,589

A Regency mahogany breakfast table, the rounded rectangular tilt top on a ring-turned column and downswept legs, 60in. wide.
(Christie's) $3,562

Federal mahogany and kingwood inlaid breakfast table, Charleston, South Carolina, 1790-1800, the top with a large oval veneered central reserve banded in kingwood veneer and stringing, 31¼in. wide.
(Skinner) $266,500

A George III rosewood, satinwood and thuya breakfast table, the canted rectangular tilt-top crossbanded in sycamore and inlaid with a central canted rectangle, 47½in. wide.
(Christie's) $4,600

A black and gilt japanned circular breakfast table, 19th century, decorated with geometric and meandering floral borders, the circular tilt top decorated with a floral spray, 42in. diameter.
(Christie's) $16,767

A Regency rosewood D-shaped card table, decorated with bead moldings, the hinged swivel top opening to reveal a green baize playing surface, 36½in. wide.
(Christie's) $3,749

A late Victorian mahogany envelope folding card table, the baize lined top with leather trim and copper counter wells, 21½in. wide.
(Andrew Hartley) $1,007

A Regency kingwood and brass-inlaid D-shaped card table, the crossbanded hinged top opening to reveal a green baize lined playing surface, 36in. wide.
(Christie's) $4,311

A George II style mahogany folding top games table, English, 19th century, the table opening to a green fabric covered top, supported by four tapering legs with ball feet, 3½ x 3½in. (Bonhams) $1,420

A Regency brass-inlaid and mounted rosewood-veneered card table, with kingwood-crossbanded D-shaped top, 73cm. wide.
(Bearne's) $3,454

A kingwood, marquetry and gilt-bronze card table, French, circa 1890, the shaped rectangular folding top with small flower marquetry and within a gilt-bronze border, 72cm. wide.
(Sotheby's) $5,624

A George II mahogany tea table, the hinged top with projecting angles, fitted with a frieze drawer, 31½in. wide.
(Christie's) $2,362

A French mahogany and brass-inlaid envelope card table, late 19th century, the hinged top opening to reveal a green baize lined playing surface, 23in. wide.
(Christie's) $2,624

Mahogany and brass-inlaid card table, early 19th century, decorated with lines and applied with gilt-metal mounts, 36in. wide.
(Christie's) $5,623

A good classical and figured dolphin-base mahogany games table, New York, circa 1820, the hinged crossbanded rectangular top with canted corners, 37in. wide, open. (Sotheby's) $17,250

An unusual Edwardian walnut card table, the rectangular fold-over top with inset plated mounts to the corners, 91cm. wide. (Bearne's) $2,983

A Victorian Gothic Revival oak table, the molded rectangular top with outset corners, over a sunk panel frieze molded with gothic tracery, 105cm. (Tennants) $1,962

A Regency mahogany tea table, of D-shaped outline, with a hinged top on a ring-turned baluster column, 35½in. wide. (Christie's) $3,634

A mahogany card table, decorated with checker lines, the hinged top crossbanded in rosewood with projecting rounded corners, 34in. wide. (Christie's) $4,124

A walnut demi-lune tea table, early 18th century, the later double hinged top concealing a compartment, 29¾in. wide. (Christie's) $3,270

A George IV rosewood-veneered card table with rounded rectangular fold-over top, bead and reel edge to the frieze, 91cm. wide. (Bearne's) $707

A George III mahogany serpentine tea-table, the hinged top above a serpentine frieze, on scrolled channelled cabriole legs, 36¼in. wide. (Christie's) $6,992

One of the Bradford-Dewolf family pair of Federal inlaid mahogany card tables, labelled by John Townsend (1732-1809), Newport, dated 1794, 34½in. wide. (Christie's) (Two) $420,500

A Regency rosewood center table, with a rectangular top, on roundel-decorated dual S-scroll end supports, 30¼in. wide.
(Christie's) $3,452

A walnut center table, French, circa 1930, circular top with inlaid sunburst design on octagonal column, 60¼in. diameter.
(Christie's) $10,246

A 19th century French center table having oval central inlaid panel of flowers, crossbanded in kingwood on cabriole supports, 3ft.9in.
(G.A. Key) $2,226

A Chinese export brass and mother of pearl inlaid padouk and rosewood center table, late 18th/early 19th century, the reeded circular top inlaid with lines and foliage, 49½in. diameter.
(Christie's) $14,812

A Dutch floral marquetry and mahogany center table, 19th century, decorated with meandering floral sprays, lines and birds, 29½in. wide.
(Christie's) $3,912

A specimen marble topped, ebonized and parcel-gilt center table, late 20th century, the circular radically veneered top within a brass border, 37in. diameter.
(Christie's) $8,435

A rectangular center table with plain hardwood top supported by two First World War French laminated hardwood four-bladed propellers, probably by Renault, 60 x 35in.
(Canterbury) $5,977

A walnut octagonal centre table in the 17th century Italian manner, the top with eight small red tortoiseshell and ivory panels, 95cm. wide.
(Bearne's) $1,494

A William & Mary laburnum oyster and marquetry center table, the fine quality top of bird-infested floral marquetry center in an oyster surround, 37in. wide.
(Boardmans) $17,535

A German maple and gilt-metal mounted oval center table, 19th century, with an anthemion and flowerhead mounted frieze, 44½in. wide. (Christie's) $2,907

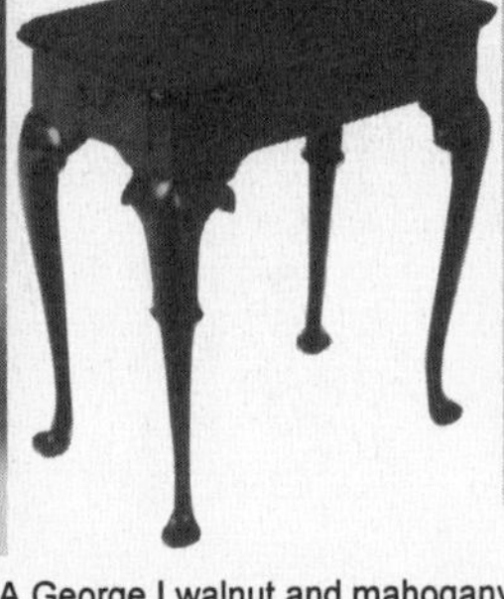

A George I walnut and mahogany table with a molded edge and 'broken' corners to the rounded rectangular top, 68.5cm. wide. (Bearne's) $4,561

A mid-Victorian burr walnut-veneered and inlaid center table of serpentine outline and applied with gilt-brass foliate mounts, 128cm. wide. (Bearne's) $2,674

A carved giltwood center table French, circa 1890, in Louis XV style, with a shaped molded verde antico marble top above a pierced frieze, 126cm. wide. (Sotheby's) $10,310

A marquetry table, designed by Gallé, circa 1900, with shaped quatrefoil top inlaid with irises, on tapering carved legs, 28¾in. high. (Christie's) $3,353

A walnut and marquetry center table, Victorian, circa 1860, with a circular top crossbanded, quarter-veneered hinged top, centered by spray of flowers, 136cm. wide. (Sotheby's) $22,49

A fine Victorian marquetry inlaid sycamore, amboyna and ormolu mounted center table, in the manner of Edward Holmes Baldock, circa 1840, 54 in. diameter. (Christie's) $29,792

A Louis XVI style kingwood and marquetry drop-leaf occasional table, the square top with four D-shaped drop leaves all inlaid with scrolling foliage. (Bearne's) $1,988

A Victorian mahogany center table, English, 1856, the circular top on a turned shaft with triple splayed base on three ball feet, 3 x 3¼in. (Bonhams) $379

A Victorian rosewood serpentine fronted console table, the shaped top with a molded edge above a shell-carved S-scroll frieze, 69in. wide. (Christie's) $2,188

One of a pair of Louis XV style giltwood console tables with carrara marble tops, 106cm. (Bonhams) (Two) $1,884

A plaster and marble console table, designed by Emilio Terry, circa 1927, the rectangular off-white and pale gray mottled marble top raised on a pedestal plaster base, 49¾in. wide. (Christie's) $70,146

A French fruitwood console table, early 19th century, with an associated rectangular top above a frieze drawer with lion mask handles, 31½in. wide. (Christie's) $1,276

Gerrit Rietveld, executed by G.A. van der Goenekan, extending console table, 1927, extension later, wood, centrally hinged circular top raised on three cylindrical column legs, 47¼in. diameter. (Sotheby's) $14,777

A carved giltwood console table Paris, circa 1900, after the celebrated model by Jacob, with a shaped green marble top above a guilloche frieze, 89cm. wide. (Sotheby's) $11,247

A Louis Philippe mahogany console table, the mottled gray marble top above a molded frieze fitted with a drawer, 40½in. wide. (Christie's) $3,912

A 19th century mahogany console table carved with scrolling leaves, scallops and faces. (Academy) $1,840

A carved oak console table, early 19th century, with a brêche marble top, above a scrolled frieze on a monopodia support, 24¾in. wide. (Christie's) $1,312

Raymond Subes, console table, circa 1925, polished metal base with scroll supports, thick rectangular textured glass top with rounded corners, 58½in. wide. (Sotheby's) $9,373

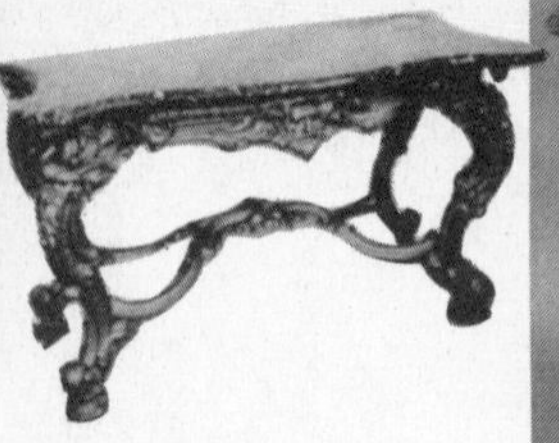

A 19th century gilded cast iron serpentine console table, with mottled black and white marble top over an ornate frieze, 58in. wide. (Dee Atkinson & Harrison) $9,075

A Victorian oak and marble topped console table, alterations. (Bonhams) $648

Gilbert Poillerat, console table, circa 1935, dark patinated wrought iron with gilt details, rectangular streaked cream top above elaborate scrolling base, 102cm. wide. (Sotheby's) $11,178

A Louis Philippe burr-elm console table, with a rounded rectangular top and cushion molded frieze drawer, on sabre legs, 26½in. wide. (Christie's) $2,236

A Regency giltwood console table, the Siena marble veneered top above a lappeted molding and a plain frieze, above a twisted foliage molding supported by a pair of winged dragons, 33½in. wide. (Christie's) $6,948

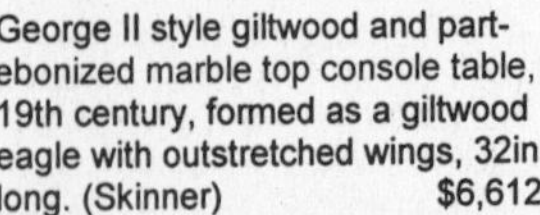

George II style giltwood and part-ebonized marble top console table, 19th century, formed as a giltwood eagle with outstretched wings, 32in. long. (Skinner) $6,612

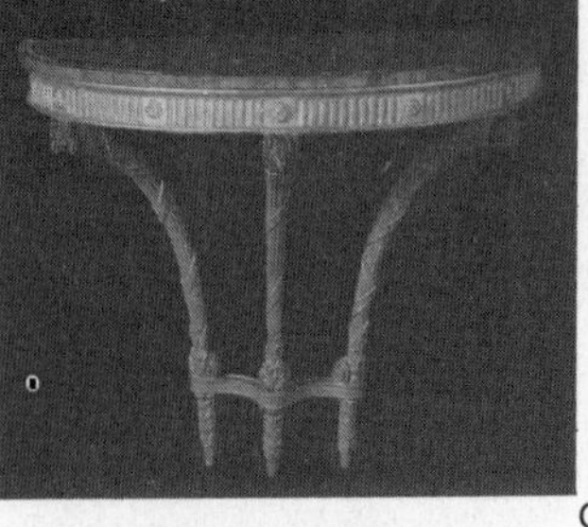

A George III satinwood, marquetry and parcel-gilt console table, attributed to Mayhew & Ince, the semi-circular crossbanded top inlaid with floral swags, 40¾in. wide. (Christie's) $51,520

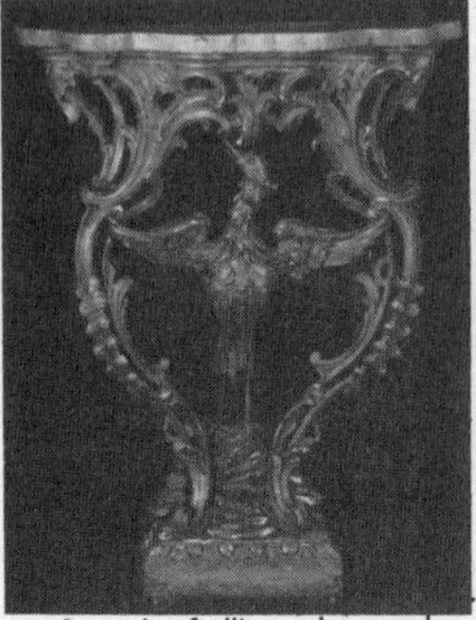

One of a pair of giltwood console tables, probably German, 19th century, each with shaped green and white serpentine marble above a pierced scrolling foliate frieze, 27¼in. wide. (Christie's) (Two) $11,040

A good mahogany extending dining table in the Gillows style with two leaves, 50 x 63in.
(G. E. Sworder) $9,600

Gustav Stickley dining table, no. 634, New York, circa 1910, round table top above center square pedestal joined to four square post legs by flared cross stretchers, with six leaves, extending to 10ft.
(Skinner) $6,900

A substantial Victorian oak extending dining table, with three leaves, on four turned carved supports with ceramic castors, 302 x 122cm. extended.
(Bristol) $1,201

A mid 19th century loo table, veneered in faded rosewood, the circular tilt top inlaid with a band of burr elm with a crossbanded edge and frieze, 4ft.4in. diameter.
(Woolley & Wallis) $4,290

A Victorian mahogany extending dining table, with three leaves, on four lobed inverted baluster supports with brass castors, 237 x 119cm. extended.
(Bristol) $2,766

A Victorian walnut loo table, with molded edged quarter veneered burr walnut top on fluted and gadrooned turned baluster stem, 42 x 32½in.
(Andrew Hartley) $2,268

Tiger maple dining table, New England, circa 1825, the rectangular overhanging drop-leaf top above six ring-turned legs, 56½in. wide, open.
(Skinner) $3,325

Irish George III mahogany tilt-top tripod table, late 18th century, piecrust top on a plain and reeded support, on cabriole legs, ending in foliate carved pad feet, 26¾ diameter. (Skinner) $4,025

Oak pedestal base dining table, American, late 19th century, round table top raised on square pedestal with fleur-de-lis cut-outs, 48in. diameter. (Skinner) $805

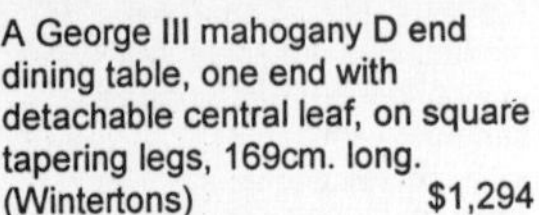

A George III mahogany D end dining table, one end with detachable central leaf, on square tapering legs, 169cm. long.
(Wintertons) $1,294

Regency tilt-top dining table in cross-banded mahogany with rosewood inlay, square column on four splayed and fluted legs with brass capped feet and castors.
(Jacobs & Hunt) $5,120

An Anglo-Indian rosewood table, 19th century, the circular top with floral molding, above a frieze, on spirally turned tapering legs, 70in. diameter.
(Christie's) $10,120

A mid Victorian walnut loo table, the molded oval quarter veneered top, set on a tripod base with a turned pedestal and carved scrolled legs, 136cm. wide.
(Bonhams) $2,015

A mahogany Cumberland action drop-leaf dining table, 19th century, on four reeded tapered columns joined by stretchers and molded splayed legs, 60½in. extended.
(Christie's) $10,900

An Edwardian walnut extending dining table with one extra leaf, 148cm. wide extended.
(Bonhams) $64

A Victorian mahogany extending dining table with rounded rectangular top and on lotus-carved tapering turned legs with brass castors, 258cm., including two extension leaves.
(Bearne's) $4,082

William IV period circular tilt-top dining table in rosewood on rounded pillar and triform base with carved claw feet, 54in. diameter.
(Jacobs & Hunt) $2,160

A Victorian mahogany extending dining table, with a deep molded edge to the rounded rectangular top, 254cm., including two extension leaves.
(Bearne's) $3,925

A French giltwood bijouterie table, in the Louis XV style, circa 1890, of serpentine outline, with an ormolu-mounted glazed hinged top and sides, 29¼in. wide. (Christie's) $3,972

An Edwardian walnut display table, 53cm. wide. (Bonhams) $453

A late 19th century French gilt brass-mounted mahogany table vitrine, applied throughout with foliate edge moldings, 75cm. wide. (Bearne's) $4,719

A mahogany, marquetry and gilt-bronze vitrine table, French, circa 1900, the hinged glazed trefoil top with a floral marquetry border, 57cm. diameter. (Sotheby's) $2,734

A French ormolu-mounted mahogany vitrine table, in the Louis XVI style, by Henry Dasson & Cie, Paris, dated *1893*, the rectangular glazed top with engraved surround, above four glazed sides, 26¾in. wide. (Christie's) $12,638

A rosewood and kingwood serpentine bijouterie table, late 19th century, applied with gilt-metal mounts, the glazed hinged top above glazed sides, 28in. wide. (Christie's) $5,962

A mahogany and gilt-bronze table vitrine, French, circa 1890, the shaped oval top with a bevelled glass insert above a glazed door, 59cm. wide. (Sotheby's) $6,927

A French style kingwood and glazed display table with ormolu mounts raised on cabriole legs. (Academy) $1,504

A boulle table vitrine, French, circa 1860, the glazed hinged rectangular top above the frieze inlaid with stylized scrolling foliate designs, 65cm. wide. (Sotheby's) $4,550

A Queen Anne figured walnut dressing table, Pennsylvania, 1730-50, the rectangular molded top with notched corners above four short drawers, 36½in. wide.
(Sotheby's) $6,900

A late Regency mahogany dressing table, the rectangular top above two drawers and side pull-out slides, 72cm. wide.
(Cheffins) $1,823

An early 19th century mahogany kneehole dressing table with three-quarter gallery and beaded edge to the rectangular top, 98.5cm. wide.
(Bearne's) $2,393

Classical mahogany and mahogany veneer stencil decorated dressing chest, possibly New York, circa 1825, with rectangular black painted and foliate stencil decorated framed mirror, 36½in. wide. (Skinner) $2,990

A pair of Regency mahogany dressing tables, each with deep three-quarter galleried top above a panelled frieze, 38½in. wide.
(Christie's) $4,600

Paul McCobb two-drawer stand with mirror, Massachusetts, two-drawer night stand, maple with medium brown finish, supported by a matching platform stand, 24in. wide. (Skinner) $230

Queen Anne walnut dressing table, Boston, 1730-50, the thumbmolded top with shaped front corners overhanging a case with one long drawer over three small, 30½in. wide.
(Skinner) $10,350

Mahogany high boy chest with mirror in wishbone holder, Chippendale Queen Anne style with Rococo ornamentation, 39in. wide, circa 1910-1920.
(Jackson's) $935

Queen Anne walnut carved dressing table, Massachusetts, circa 1750-60, the molded overhanging top with shaped corners, 29¾in. wide.
(Skinner) $24,150

A George III mahogany bowfront dressing-table, with hinged central section enclosing a ratcheted hinged mirror, above circular holes for pots. (Christie's) $8,228

A Chippendale mahogany dressing-table, probably Virginia, 1760–1780, the rectangular top with an applied molded edge above a conforming case, 32¼in. wide. (Christie's) $5,750

Post war mirrored vanity, manufactured by Heywood Wakefield, circa 1955, champagne finish, semi-circular bank of drawers, next to arched mirror, 50in. wide. (Skinner) $345

A French kingwood and walnut dressing table/poudreuse of Transitional style, the top with three quartered veneered rectangular panels, 32in. (Canterbury) $693

A Queen Anne walnut veneered diminutive dressing table, Boston, Massachusetts, 1720-30, the herringbone inlaid quarter-veneered rectangular top above one long and two short drawers, top 27½in. wide. (Sotheby's) $12,650

Gustav Stickley oak dresser with mirror, New York, circa 1912, no. 905, swivel mirror on rectangular top, two short drawers over three long drawers, large hammered brass ring pulls, 48in. wide. (Skinner) $9,775

A Victorian white-painted and parcel-gilt dressing table, the tiles Minton, circa 1860, decorated overall to simulate bamboo, with a superstructure inset with tiles, 39¾in. wide. (Christie's) $17,807

Early 20th century mahogany dressing table with cabriole legs, oval mirror attached, 33in. wide. (Eldred's) $385

A Queen Anne maple and pine dressing table, New England 1740-60, the rectangular molded top above three short drawers, 30in. wide. (Sotheby's) $3,737

Federal mahogany carved drop-leaf table, New England, circa 1825, the rectangular top with shaped leaves on a straight skirt, 19in. wide. (Skinner) $690

Chippendale mahogany carved dining table, Massachusetts, circa 1770, the overhanging rectangular drop-leaf top with rounded corners and molded edge, 46in. deep, open. (Skinner) $2,415

Chippendale walnut carved dining table, Massachusetts, circa 1780, the rectangular hanging drop-leaf top on four cabriole legs ending in claw and ball feet, 47½in. wide. (Skinner) $2,070

A Chippendale carved mahogany drop-leaf table, Massachusetts, circa 1770, the oblong top flanked by rectangular leaves, 42in. wide, open. (Sotheby's) $3,737

Chippendale mahogany carved dining table, Massachusetts, circa 1770, the circular overhanging drop-leaf table above a scrolled skirt joining four cabriole legs, 47in. wide. (Skinner) $4,600

A Federal green-painted birchwood drop-leaf table, New England, circa 1805, the oblong top flanked by rectangular leaves on square tapering legs. (Sotheby's) $1,265

TRICKS OF THE TRADE

When dealing with ordinary scratches on French polish sand lightly to equalise the surface and try to soften the old polish with spirit. If it dissolves and goes tacky spread it out with a pad on which you've placed a little fresh polish. Proceed as with normal polishing but avoid overloading the frontier of the sanded area. Sand lightly between coats.
(Hobbs Parker)

A rare Queen Anne C-scroll carved mahogany drop-leaf dining table, Boston, Massachusetts, 1735-50, the oblong top with hinged D-shaped leaves, 46½in. wide, extended. (Sotheby's) $46,000

Post-war walnut dining table, designed by Hans Wegner, Denmark, circa 1950, rectangular top, semi-circular drop leaves, wide rectangular drop-leaf insert. (Skinner) $862

Queen Anne mahogany dining table, New England, late 18th century, the square overhanging drop leaf on four cabriole legs with arris knees, 47in. wide.
(Skinner) $2,760

A Shaker turned maple drop-leaf work table, American, early 19th century, the rectangular top backed by a single hinged leaf, 48½ wide.
(Sotheby's) $6,900

A George I red walnut drop flap dining table, with molded top above frieze drawer, on four cabriole supports, 106.5cm. wide.
(Bristol) $1,106

A good Queen Anne carved and figured walnut drop-leaf dining table, Pennsylvania circa 1750, the oblong top flanked by rectangular leaves with a shaped apron, length open 4ft. 2½in.
(Sotheby's) $4,887

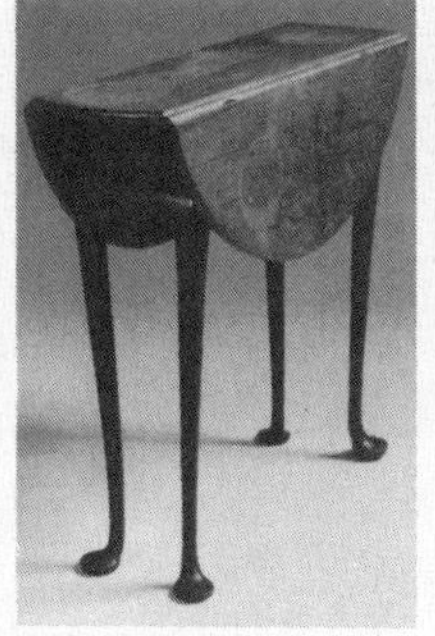

The John Hancock Queen Anne walnut drop-leaf diminutive dining table, Boston, Massachusetts, 1740-60, the oblong top with two D-shaped leaves, 29in. wide, extended.
(Sotheby's) $63,000

A good Chippendale carved mahogany drop-leaf table, North Shore, Massachusetts, circa 1770, the oblong top with bowed ends flanked by D-shaped leaves, 48in. wide, open.
(Sotheby's) $9,200

Grain painted classical table, Maine, 1830-40, the hinged rectangular leaves with rounded corners fall over a straight skirt, 42in. wide.
(Skinner) $690

George III mahogany drop leaf table, with one drawer on square straight legs with shaped undershelf, on castors, 29 x 32in. maximum.
(Ewbank) $616

An early George III mahogany dining table, the well figured faded rectangular drop leaf top on end friezes, the plain turned legs to outswept carved claw and ball feet, 3ft.6in. x 5ft.
(Woolley & Wallis) $676

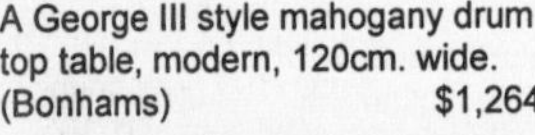

A George III style mahogany drum top table, modern, 120cm. wide.
(Bonhams) $1,264

A good George III mahogany drum table, the leather inset top above four shallow drawers interspaced by four dummy drawers with Bramah locks. 51in. diameter.
(Boardmans) $11,356

A Regency mahogany drum top table, 54in. diameter.
(Bonhams) $6,320

An early Victorian mahogany drum table, the top inlaid with a black leather writing surface above four drawers and four dummy drawers, 41½in. diameter.
(Christie's) $4,333

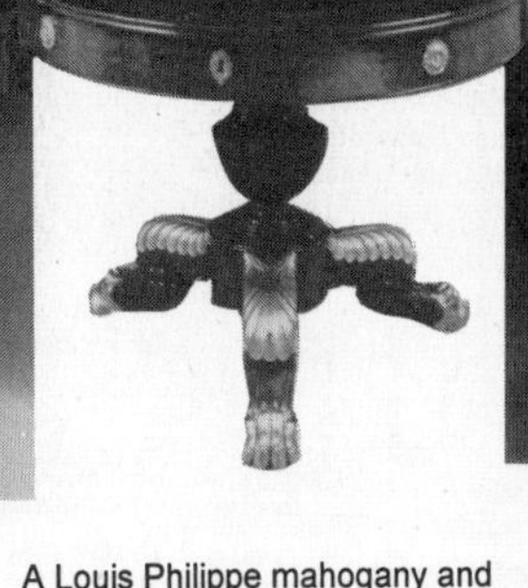

A Louis Philippe mahogany and parcel-gilt drum table, the circular top inset with a black leather writing surface above a frieze fitted with four drawers, 39in. diameter.
(Christie's) $6,334

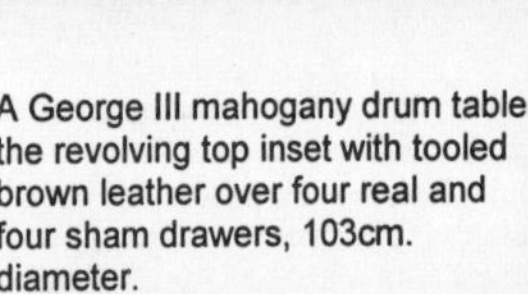

A George III mahogany drum table, the revolving top inset with tooled brown leather over four real and four sham drawers, 103cm. diameter.
(Tennants) $11,304

A mahogany pedestal library table, the octagonal top with tooled leather insert, the frieze with four fitted drawers and four false drawers, 127cm. diameter, 19th century and later.
(Bearne's) $2,512

A Regency mahogany drum table, with a leather lined top over four real and four sham frieze drawers, raised on a reeded baluster, 119cm. diameter.
(Tennants) $6,080

An early 19th century mahogany drum table, the top inset with tooled green leather over four sham and four real drawers, one is stamped *GILLOWS*LANCASTER.*
(Tennants) $9,734

An early 18th century oak gateleg table with oval top, and on turned legs joined by molded square stretchers, 126cm. wide.
(Bearne's) $472

An oak gateleg table, part 18th century, 86cm. wide.
(Bonhams) $421

A walnut gate-leg table, English, late 17th/early 18th century, with oval top and frieze drawer to each end above dentil molded arches, 65in. extended.
(Christie's) $10,971

A George II mahogany gate-leg table, with an oval hinged top on turned columnar supports joined by stretchers and terminating in outswept feet, 29in. wide extended.
(Christie's) $6,359

A mahogany serpentine spider leg table, the twin-flap hinged top carved with a foliate and ribbon border with a drawer to one end, 35½in. wide.
(Christie's) $2,624

A very rare William and Mary maple 'butterfly' table, New England, probably Massachusetts, 1720-60, the oblong top with bowed ends flanked by D-shaped leaves, 29¼in. wide, open.
(Sotheby's) $57,500

An 18th century oak oval gateleg dining table, fitted with a drawer to both ends, and on turned supports, 174cm. (Tennants) $7,065

A mahogany spider-leg table, 18th century and later, with a rectangular hinged top on ring-turned legs and feet, 24¾in. wide extended.
(Christie's) $1,090

A William and Mary turned pine gate-leg table, 1730-60, the oblong top flanked by rectangular leaves centering a frieze drawer, width open 5ft 9in.
(Sotheby's) $5,462

A chestnut refectory table, Spanish, late 17th/early 18th century, with rectangular one piece top, on square chamfered legs joined by end stretchers and with later twin wrought iron central stretchers, 101½in. long. (Christie's) $4,571

An elm and oak six leg refectory table, English, the base 17th century, the top 18th century, the rectangular top with a one piece slab of elm, above molded friezes and ring-turned bulbous legs joined by square section stretchers, 128in. long. (Christie's) $20,114

A beechwood refectory table, English, the top 18th century, with cleated four flank top, on oak standard end supports with arched sleigh feet joined by a central stretcher, 110½in. long.
(Christie's) $6,400

A mahogany three-pedestal dining table of George III style, late 19th/early 20th century, comprising three tilt-top sections, the rectangular top on turned spreading columns with square tapering downswept legs, 159in. long, fully extended.
(Christie's) $12,880

An oak six leg refectory table, English, late 17th century, with a cleated plank top, the front and side friezes carved with scrolling stylized foliate decoration and scroll spandrels, on baluster legs, 116in. long.
(Christie's) $13,757

A Regency mahogany twin pedestal dining table inlaid with ebonized lines, comprising two tilt-top pedestal end-sections and two leaves, the rounded rectangular top on turned columns and hipped square tapering legs, 109½in. long, fully extended.
(Christie's) $7,360

A Regency mahogany extending dining table, the rounded rectangular top extending to enclose two further leaves, on four baluster columns and a rectangular platform with reeded downswept legs 123½in. long, fully extended.
(Christie's) $55,200

An 18th century (and later) oak and elm refectory table, triple planked rectangular top, half moon leaf carved frieze, fitted drawer to each end, on barley twist turned legs linked by block stretchers, width 87.5cm. x 199cm. long.
(Wintertons) $4,04

An early 19th century mahogany extending dining table with molded edge, on five carved and octagonal tapering legs, four leaves, together with a storage rack, 137cm. wide x 387cm. long. (Wintertons) $6,794

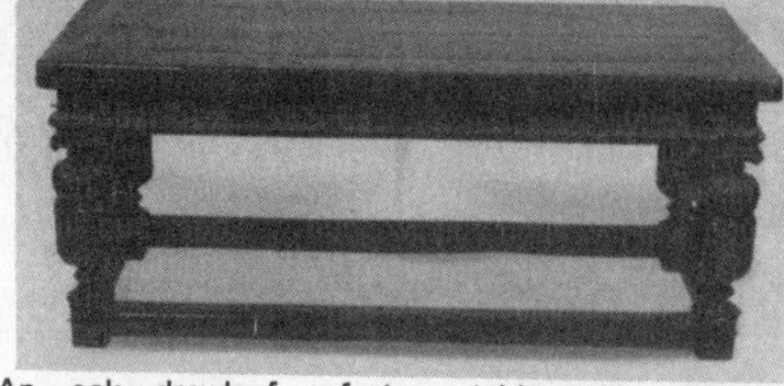

An oak drawleaf refectory table with cleated rectangular top, parquetry-inlaid and gadrooned frieze, 213cm., late 16th/early 17th century and later. (Bearne's) $5,505

A French mahogany drop-leaf extending dining table, early 19th century, the oval hinged top extending with four later leaves, on ring-turned legs, 123in. wide extended. (Christie's) $5,087

A mahogany three pillar dining table, 19th century, including two extra leaves, the top with a reeded edge on ring-turned columns and splayed tripod supports, 150in. long extended. (Christie's) $10,538

An oak folding top refectory table, Lake District, late 17th century, the hinged plank top metal bound and with lopers to the reverse frieze, the facing frieze carved with foliate lunettes, stylized foliage and dated *1667*, 49in. wide. (Christie's) $7,314

A Victorian oak extending dining table by Gillows of Lancaster, including seven extra leaves, the top with a molded edge on turned, petal molded and fluted legs, 240in. extended. (Christie's) $12,719

A fine and rare carved walnut tavern table, Pennsylvania, 1740-60, the removable rectangular cleated top above a central frieze drawers flanked by opposing drawers, 5ft. 9in. long. (Sotheby's) $33,350

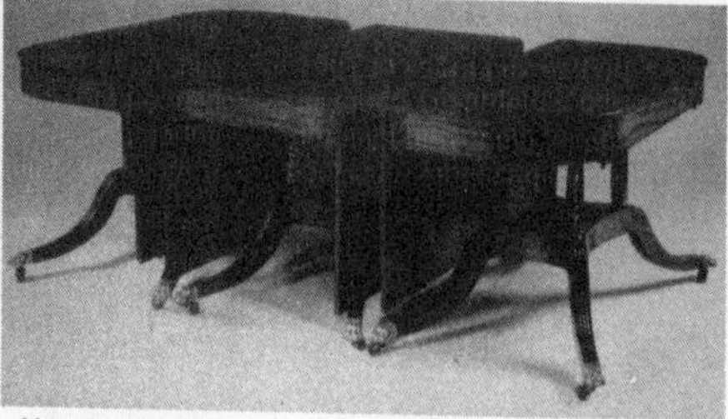

Neoclassical mahogany three-part pedestal dining table, New York, circa 1805, the center section with two hinged leaves which drop to flank the shaped veneered platform, 163½in. long. (Skinner) $68,500

Antique English papier mâché tip-top table, with mother of pearl inlay and painted decoration, shaped top 23 x 28in. (Eldred's) $660

George III style satinwood and inlay supper table, late 19th/20th century, rectangular top with flaps, above a frieze fitted with a drawer, 27¼in. wide.
(Skinner) $11,500

Federal mahogany inlaid tilt-top table, probably Massachusetts, circa 1800, the octagonal top bordered with inlaid geometric stringing and crossbanding, 23¼in. wide. (Skinner) $2,990

A George II Virginian walnut reading table, the pivoted rectangular cleated border top with a book rest, on an adjustable square stem with metal shaft, 26in.
(Woolley & Wallis) $6,731

A George IV mahogany folio table, inlaid mahogany with bands of cocus wood, 34in.
(Woolley & Wallis) $330

Federal tiger maple table, New England, circa 1800-1810, overhanging square top with ovolo corners above a straight skirt with drawer, top 19¾ x 19½in.
(Skinner) $4,312

TOP TIPS

Burns are wounds of a mechanical order, rather than stains, and no natural or artificial chemical can ever remove the discoloration of wood caused by a hot iron carelessly put down or by a forgotten cigarette or cigar.

Only by scraping or sanding can such marks be mitigated and removed.

(Hobbs Parker)

Alvar Aalto, a laminated beech and plywood table , Model No. 915, deisgned 1931-32, manufactured by Oy. Huonekalu-ja Rakennustyötehdas for use in the Paimio Sanatorium, 24in. wide.
(Christie's) $4,514

A Victorian walnut occasional table, the oval top with a pierced wavy gallery raised on four tapering bobbin turned legs, 48cm. wide.
(Cheffins) $666

Post war beech expansion table designed by Bruno Matheson, Sweden, 1907-88, of veneered beechwood, deep drop leaves fitted with a top leaf during closure, 104in. wide, open.
(Skinner) $920

Pennsylvania German slate topped table, circa 1790, maple framed slate top on splayed block and spool turned legs, top 39 x 33in.
(Freeman) $2,464

A George III sycamore, tulipwood and marquetry chevet table, the three-quarter gallery above a crossbanded rectangular top, 19½in. wide.
(Christie's) $5,888

A Continental Renaissance style ormolu and malachite-veneered low table, late 19th century, by E. Cornu, with a circular black marble top centrally inlaid with butterflies and flowering branch, 29in. diameter.(Christie's) $6,900

An oak chair-table, Dutch, late 17th century, with oval top swivelling up on bolts, square section arms raised on bulbous supports, solid plank seat, 46½in. high, open.
(Christie's) $6,774

Diego Giacometti for Jean Michel Frank, table, after 1933, wrought iron, circular top set in decorative border, openwork pedestal base with four splayed legs, 32¼in. diameter.
(Sotheby's) $14,352

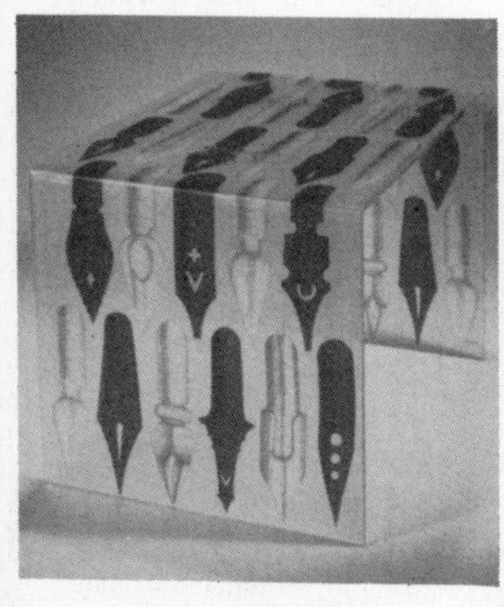

Piero Fornasetti, an acrylic occasional table, designed circa 1970, of folded rectangular form, with internal transfer decoration, 25in. wide. (Christie's) $1,537

A pair of satinwood and floral painted occasional tables, late 20th century, decorated with ribbon-tied swags, paterae and lines, 30in. wide.
(Christie's) $5,962

An early 19th century mahogany reading/games table, the top crossbanded in rosewood, rising and sliding, fitted with two drawers, 23in. (Russell Baldwin & Bright) $634

A George III Gonçalo-Alves and mahogany tripod table, crossbanded overall in calamander, the rounded rectangular tilt-top on a baluster support and tapering cabriole legs, 29in. wide.
(Christie's) $8,832

A mahogany silver table, late 19th century, the rectangular top with a pierced fret gallery and blind fret-carved frieze, 42½in. wide.
(Christie's) $3,634

A George II brass-inlaid padouk and mahogany tripod table, the galleried octagonal tilt-top centered by a foliage cartouche and with a strapwork border, 20in. diameter.
(Christie's) $117,530

An inlaid mahogany circular games table, 19th century, the tilt top decorated with cribbage and checkerboards, on a faceted column on a concave sided cast-iron platform, 24½in. diameter.
(Christie's) $2,624

Jean Prouvé, an enamelled steel Cafétéria table, designed 1950, executed until 1954 by Ateliers Jean Prouvé, circular green linoleum top with anodized aluminum edge.
(Christie's) $8,666

A carved gilt composition and porcelain guéridon, German, circa 1900, the circular top with a central inset porcelain plaque depicting two classical maidens, 55cm. diameter.
(Sotheby's) $5,469

North Italian carved wood occasional table, late 19th century, the rectangular silvered shell shaped top on scroll legs, 35½in. wide. (Christie's) $29,980

A George III mahogany tripod table, the top and base associated, the molded piecrust top above a birdcage support, 27¾in. diameter.
(Christie's) $5,520

A George IV mahogany games table, the reversible sliding top inlaid with a chess board with backgammon box beneath, 2ft. wide, closed. (Russell Baldwin & Bright) $2,106

A very rare brown and green painted Windsor tripod table, Pennsylvania, probably Philadelphia, third quarter 18th century, 23in. diameter.
(Sotheby's) $101,500

A small Regency pollard oak occasional table or vide poche, the rectangular top with flared rim raised on slender supports, 32cm.
(Tennants) $3,611

A mahogany tripod table of George II style, 19th/20th century, the molded circular pie-crust top above a birdcage support, 24in. diameter.
(Christie's) $7,728

A Dutch and floral marquetry oak table, 19th century, decorated with floral sprays and lines, the rectangular top above a frieze drawer, 31½in. wide.
(Christie's) $2,608

Marcel Breuer, a chromed tubular steel table Model No. B18, designed 1928 for Gebrüder Thonet, the rounded rectangular glass top with bevelled edge, 30in. long. (Christie's) $3,128

Burmese profusely carved rosewood round table, the top with a band of animals, buildings and foliage, the pierced frieze with similar decoration, 30in.
(Ewbank) $957

A Victorian mahogany coaching table, the folding rectangular top above a chamfered X-shaped stand joined by turned baluster supports, 29½in. wide.
(Christie's) $2,208

A pair of French kingwood oval guéridons, early 20th century, each decorated with lines, with a breche violette marble top with a pierced three-quarter brass gallery, 20½in. wide. (Christie's) $5,403

A Regency rosewood and polychrome decorated pedestal table, the canted rectangular top decorated with flowers and foliate border, 25½in. wide.
(Christie's) $6,440

A Regency mahogany pedestal table in the manner of Duncan Phyfe, one of the two dropleaves with rosewood banding and reeded edge and a drawer at either end, opening to 47 x 41in.
(Boardmans) $2,171

Small George III mahogany oval Pembroke table.
(Jacobs & Hunt) $1,600

A Regency satinwood and painted Pembroke table, the rectangular cut-cornered top centered by an octagonal panel painted en grisaille with infants leading a lion, 110cm. (extended) by 72cm.
(Tennants) $15,700

A satinwood Pembroke table, 20th century, crossbanded and inlaid with lines, the swivel hinged top with canted angles, 32¼in. wide extended.
(Christie's) $2,543

A fine and rare Federal inlaid mahogany Pembroke table, New York, circa 1795, the oblong top with bowed ends flanked by D-shaped leaves above one false and one real drawer, 21in. wide, open.
(Sotheby's) $34,500

A good Federal inlaid mahogany Pembroke table, Philadelphia or Baltimore, circa 1795, the rectangular top flanked by serpentine leaves above a frieze drawer, 45in. wide, open.
(Sotheby's) $5,175

A mid Georgian mahogany Pembroke table with butterfly-wing top, drawer to one end and molded squared legs fitted with undertray, 34 x 38in., open.
(Russell Baldwin & Bright) $1,786

A George III amboyna Pembroke table, crossbanded overall in rosewood and inlaid overall with boxwood and ebonized lines, 40¾in. wide, open.
(Christie's) $9,568

A Chippendale figured mahogany Pembroke table, probably Mid-Atlantic States circa 1780, the oblong top with bowed ends flanked by shaped leaves, width closed 20½in. (Sotheby's) $8,050

An important Chippendale figured mahogany serpentine-front marble top pier table, Boston, Massachusetts, 1755-75, the original gray-veined marble top with outset corners, 4ft. 7in. long.
(Sotheby's) $882,500

A classical marbleized, grained and stencilled pier table, decoration attributed to Hugh Finlay (1781-1831), Baltimore, the rectangular marbleized top above a conforming frame centered by a gilt-stencilled laurel wreath, 48in. wide.
(Christie's) $46,000

A Classical mahogany marble-top pier table, New York City, 1815-1830, the rectangular marble top with canted corners above a conforming pulvinated frieze over marble columns, 42¾in. wide.
(Christie's) $7,475

Classical mahogany and mahogany veneer pier table, probably Boston, circa 1825, the rectangular marble top above an ogee molded frieze on two scrolled supports, 40¼in. wide. (Skinner) $2,070

Charles X mahogany and rosewood inlay pier table, second quarter 19th century, rectangular polished stone top over a plain frieze raised on square cabriole legs, 35¾in. wide.
(Skinner) $2,990

A fine Classical stencil and paint decorated ormolu mounted carved and gilt figured maple marble top pier table, New York, circa 1820, 42¼in. wide.
(Sotheby's) $28,750

SERVING TABLES

A Federal brass-mounted figured mahogany diminutive serving table, New York, circa 1800, the rectangular top above two short drawers on turned flaring supports, 32in. wide.
(Sotheby's) $4,600

Classical mahogany carved and mahogany veneer server, probably New York, circa 1825, the rectangular top above a case of two cockbeaded short drawers and long drawer, 30in. wide.
(Skinner) $2,070

A Federal brass-and rosewood-inlaid carved mahogany serving table, New York, circa 1820, the rectangular top above two short and one long cockbeaded drawer, 36in. wide. (Sotheby's) $10,350

A pair of North Italian green-painted and parcel-gilt tables, late 18th/early 19th century, each with a rectangular jasper marble top above a frieze centered by a rectangular panel, 30in. wide. (Christie's) $13,363

Charles Rennie Mackintosh, a rare stained oak side table, designed for the Billiards Room of the Argyle Street Tea Rooms, Glasgow. 600mm² x 700mm. high. (Bonhams) $70,781

A pair of mahogany and gilt-bronze side tables, French, circa 1890, each with a hinged shaped top within a molded border, above a frieze with a pair of drawers, 41cm. wide. (Sotheby's) $7,498

A pair of satinwood and black japanned side tables, Edwardian, circa 1900, each in Chinese style, with fret and pierced sections painted with foliage, 30cm. wide. (Sotheby's) $1,875

A pair of satinwood and polychrome-painted giltwood side tables, each with a shaped rectangular top crossbanded in tulipwood with a ribbon-twist and pearled border, 48in. wide. (Christie's) $17,181

A late 18th century Dutch semi-circular side table in walnut and marquetry of various woods depicting floral/leafage branches, on oak carcass, 2ft.7in. (G.A. Key) $1,399

A small George IV faded mahogany sofa table, the rectangular top inlaid ebony stringing and gothic crosses, 31½in.
(Woolley & Wallis) $4,704

A Regency calamander and burr-yew sofa table, inlaid overall in boxwood and ebony banding, on flared square supports, 61¾in. wide.(Christie's) $22,218

A Regency rosewood and brass inlaid sofa table, the hinged top with a band of stylized foliate scroll in contra-partie, the top 179 x 71cm. extended.
(Phillips) $26,240

A mahogany sofa table, the rounded rectangular twin flap top decorated with crossbanding and lines, 58in. wide.
(Christie's) $5,030

A George III satinwood, rosewood crossbanded and inlaid sofa table, the hinged top with rounded corners, crossbanding and stringing, the top 150 x 66cm.
(Phillips) $8,528

A Regency rosewood sofa table with satinwood stringing fitted with two drawers on lyre shaped column, 4ft.3in. fully extended.
(G.A. Key) $3,895

A Regency rosewood-veneered pedestal sofa table with canted corners and parquetry banding to the crossbanded top, 149cm. wide.
(Bearne's) $3,932

Classical mahogany and mahogany veneer sofa table, probably Boston, circa 1825, the rectangular overhanging top with rounded leaves above a straight skirt, 257¼in. wide.
(Skinner) $1,840

A George III mahogany sofa table, decorated with lines, the rounded rectangular twin-flap crossbanded top above a frieze fitted with two drawers, 67in. wide.
(Christie's) $8,998

A late Victorian mahogany two-tier Sutherland table, 90cm. wide. (Bonhams) $472

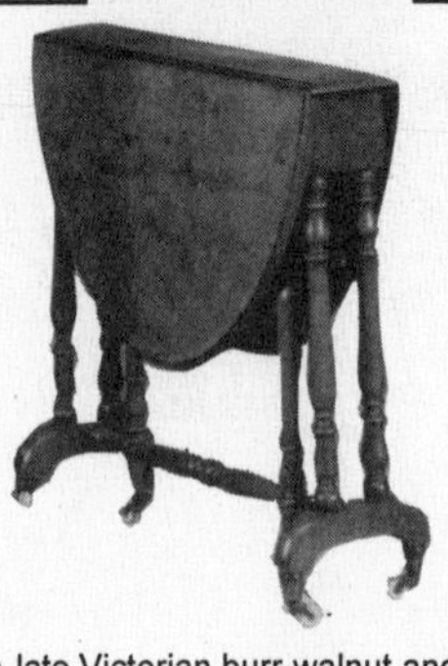

A late Victorian burr-walnut and walnut Sutherland table, the oval top with tulipwood crossbanding, on twin end column supports, 39in. extended. (Christie's) $736

An Edwardian mahogany Sutherland table, 77cm. wide. (Bonhams) $445

An Edwardian mahogany and satinwood banded Sutherland table, the hinged top with fan inlaid motif, on turned legs and stretchers, width 24¾in. (George Kidner) $641

A Victorian burr-walnut Sutherland table of shaped outline, the quartered veneered top with plain edge-moldings, 36in. x 42in. (Canterbury) $1,357

A mid-Victorian burr walnut veneered Sutherland table with shaped oval top and on pierced and carved shaped end supports, 128cm. wide. (Bearne's) $1,463

A Victorian walnut-veneered Sutherland table with shaped oval top and on four foliate S-scroll supports, 117cm. wide. (Bearne's) $1,730

An Edwardian mahogany and satinwood crossbanded two tier Sutherland table, 59cm. wide. (Bonhams) $790

A walnut Sutherland table 61cm. wide. (Bonhams) $942

A turned walnut tavern table, probably Pennsylvania, 1740-70, the rectangular top above a molded frieze drawer on turned tapering legs, 4ft. 6in. long.
(Sotheby's) $8,050

A rare William and Mary pine and birchwood tavern table, New England, 1700-30, of diminutive size, the oval top above a frieze drawer on splayed vase-turned legs, 25½in. wide.
(Sotheby's) $12,650

A turned maple, birchwood, and pine tavern table, New England, 1750-80, the rectangular cleated top above a molded frieze on ring-turned legs, 47in. wide.
(Sotheby's) $4,887

TEA TABLES

A Queen Anne carved and figured walnut piecrust tilt-top tea table, Irish, 1740-50, the piecrust top tilting and revolving on a birdcage support.
(Sotheby's) $25,875

A rare Queen Anne figured mahogany diminutive tray-top tea table, Connecticut or Massachusetts, 1740-60, rectangular molded top above a conformingly shaped frieze, 25in. wide. (Sotheby's) $28,750

A Federal mahogany tea table, Massachusetts, circa 1780, the shaped top tilting and turning above a bird-cage support over a ring and urn-turned pedestal, 33in. wide.
(Christie's) $2,760

A fruitwood, marquetry and micro mosaic veneered tilt-top table with a central panel of a dancing couple, on tripod base, Italy, mid 19th century, 84cm. diameter.
(Lempertz) $4,448

An Irish George II mahogany tea-table, the semi-circular hinged top enclosing a well, 30in. wide.
(Christie's) $14,812

A Queen Anne turned walnut dishtop tea table, Pennsylvania, circa 1750, the circular hinged top revolving and tilting above a birdcage support, 25½in. diameter.
(Sotheby's) $6,900

Queen Anne maple tea table, the oval overhanging top on four block turned tapering legs ending in pad feet, 32½in.
(Skinner) $3,220

A George II mahogany and walnut semi-circular tea table with hinged fold over top enclosing a well, 67.5cm. wide.
(Bearne's) $2,558

Dunbar occasional table, Berne, Indiana, rectangular top above single drawer with leather covered drawer pulls, 19in. wide.
(Skinner) $201

A late Victorian rosewood tea table, the circular top with central marquetry roundel, four round stands revolving on the ring turned cylindrical legs, 51cm. diameter.
(Dreweatt Neate) $1,264

Queen Anne maple tea table, new England, late 18th century, the overhanging oval top on four block turned tapering legs ending in pad feet, 32¾in. wide.
(Skinner) $5,462

Continental brass and painted porcelain folding tea table, third quarter 19th century, the two porcelain plaque shelves depicting birds and lovers, 25in. wide.
(Skinner) $8,337

Maple and tiger maple tilt-top tea table, New England, late 18th century, the round two-board top tilting above the ring-turned pedestal, 30in. diameter.
(Skinner) $2,530

A mahogany, parquetry and gilt-bronze low coffee table, French, circa 1890, the rectangular shaped parquetry top within a gilt-bronze border and flanked by foliate handles, 90.5cm. wide.
(Sotheby's) $5,249

Chippendale cherry tilt-top tea table, New England, late 18th century, the circular top on a vase and ring turned post and tripod cabriole leg base, 34¾in. diameter,
(Skinner) $2,185

Alvar Aalto, a birch tea trolley, Model No. 90, designed 1936-37, the rectangular top with yellow linoleum surface, on laminated birch frame, 36in. wide.
(Christie's) $6,861

Alvar Aalto for Artek, tea trolley '98', designed 1935-36, this example manufactured late 1930s, laminated birch frame, white painted wheels, cream linoleum tray surfaces, 35¼in. long.
(Sotheby's) $2,522

Alvar Aalto, Finland, tea trolley model No. 98, designed 1936-37, laminated frame of ribbon form supporting two birch veneered shelves. (Bonhams) $2,674

A chromed tubular steel tea cart, circa 1930-35, the frame of two hoops joined by stretchers supporting rectangular glass shelves, 28in. high.
(Christie's) $1,379

Ettore Sottsass, a beechwood serving trolley designed circa late 1950s, the angular beechwood frame with bronze-colored metal fittings.
(Christie's) $3,979

An early Victorian mahogany three tier buffet, 89cm. wide.
(Bonhams) $1,416

An early Victorian mahogany three-tier dinner wagon, with lobed finials, angle ledge gallery, on turned tapering uprights, 110cm. wide.
(Bristol) $2,113

A brass tea trolley with black trays, by Josef Frank for Svenskt Tenn, 70cm. high, 88cm. long.
(Stockholms AV) $418

Alvar Aalto for Artek, tea trolley, 1930s, blondewood on castors, 65cm. wide.
(Sotheby's) $1,472

A Regency rosewood work table, the rectangular top and sides decorated with inlaid floral scrolls, 22in. wide. (Anderson & Garland) $2,763

An early 19th century sewing table, veneered, in Brazilian rosewood, the rectangular stepped hinged lidded top with molded edges, 21in. (Woolley & Wallis) $909

A Victorian walnut games/work table, the top inlaid with a chessboard within crossbanded borders, 24in., wide. (Canterbury) $1,337

A 19th century French work table with rectangular marquetry top decorated with birds, insects, acanthus leaf scrolls, bellflowers and other foliage, 25in. wide. (Anderson & Garland) $2,356

Classical mahogany carved and mahogany veneer work table, probably Massachusetts, circa 1825, the rectangular top with rounded drop leaves above two drawers, 19in. wide. (Skinner) $1,610

An early Victorian mahogany work table, the faded flame rectangular top, with a molded edge, above a frieze drawer to a pierced and carved foliage apron, 24½in. (Woolley & Wallis) $1,923

An European figured mahogany musical work table with concave fronted hinged lid enclosing a fitted interior of lidded compartments and hinged pin cushion enclosing a musical movement, 21½in. wide. (Christie's) $2,208

Classical mahogany veneer workstand, Massachusetts, 1840s, the square top with hinged drop leaves flanking two veneered concave drawers, 17¾in. wide. (Skinner) $230

A Chinese export black and gold lacquer rectangular work table, the shallow container with hinged lid, opening to reveal an arrangement of covered compartments, circa 1860, 23¾in. wide. (Christie's) $1,256

A George IV mahogany dropleaf work table fitted with two real and two dummy drawers, on turned and reeded legs, 23½ x 32in. (Canterbury) $2,123

A Louis Philippe walnut work table, the mottled gray marble top above a frieze fitted with two drawers, on lyre-shaped end standards, 30in. high. (Christie's) $1,210

A Victorian walnut games/work table with string inlay, the folding swivel top with floral marquetry center opening to reveal inlaid game boards, 22in. wide. (Andrew Hartley) $3,828

A French brass inlaid rosewood serpentine work table, circa 1870, the hinged top enclosing a fitted interior above a work box, 21½in. wide. (Christie's) $1,716

Classical mahogany and mahogany veneer work table, possibly New York, circa 1815-25, the rectangular top inlaid with sections centering a circular panel with ovolo corners, 20in. wide. (Skinner) $1,265

A mid-Victorian walnut and burr-walnut and burr-walnut serpentine work table with eared figured top enclosing a fitted interior with fret-carved lidded compartments, 27in. wide. Christie's) $1,840

Classical mahogany carved and mahogany veneer work table, possibly New York State, circa 1825, the rectangular top with rounded leaves above two drawers, 19¼in. wide. (Skinner) $1,265

Federal mahogany carved and mahogany veneer astragal end work table, New York or Philadelphia, circa 1815, on vase and ring-turned legs, 24½in. wide. (Skinner) $2,530

Tiger maple and bird's eye maple work table, probably New York, circa 1825, the rectangular top with rounded drop leaves above two drawers, 17in. wide. (Skinner) $805

A French 19th century rosewood writing table, the rectangular top inlaid with a marquetry panel in ivory, bronze and brass of The Sirens, 3ft.9½in.
(Woolley & Wallis) $4,808

A Victorian walnut writing desk, the superstructure surmounted by a pierced brass three-quarter gallery with three central drawers below, 45in. wide.
(Christie's) $3,374

An Edwardian Louis XV style kingwood and tulipwood crossbanded bureau plat, with gilt brass mounts, the shaped rectangular top of arc-en-arbalette profile, 131cm. wide.
(Phillips) $5,280

Painted desk/cupboard, in pine with yellow and red floral decoration on a blue ground, signed *Whorf,* 20th century, 24in. wide.
(Eldred's) $1,100

Dutch rococo style mahogany and floral marquetry lady's slant-lid desk, third quarter 19th century, 29½in. wide, with a Dutch Neoclassical style mahogany and floral marquetry side chair.
(Skinner) $1,840

BUYER BEWARE

When buying a pedestal desk or writing table, take a closer look. Has it been adapted from a dressing table, many of which are still being bought by the trade with this purpose in mind?

Have a look at the back to check for holes where a mirror might once have been attached.

(Clarke Gammon)

An Edwardian inlaid mahogany lady's writing desk, the raised back fitted with two short and two long drawers flanked by a pair of cupboards, 2ft.6in. wide.
(G.A. Key) $3,530

Victorian carved oak architect's desk and stool, late 19th century, divided hinged writing slope enclosing a fitted interior, 49½in. wide. (Skinner) $2,300

Limbert desk, Michigan, circa 1912, central pen tray flanked by letter holders over two drawers with 'V' pulls, 36in. wide.
(Skinner) $1,092

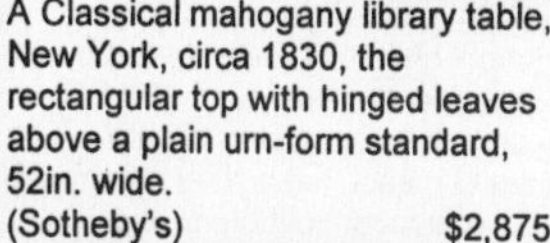

A Classical mahogany library table, New York, circa 1830, the rectangular top with hinged leaves above a plain urn-form standard, 52in. wide.
(Sotheby's) $2,875

Small Spanish Baroque walnut writing table, 18th century, rectangular top over two carved drawers and secret drawers, 41¼in. wide. (Skinner) $2,645

Oak library table, 'The Arnold 3-in-1', manufactured by the Auglaize furniture Co., New Bremen, Ohio, rectangular top over single door with square wooden pulls, 41in. wide. (Skinner) $230

\ George III mahogany lady's vriting-table, after a design by Thomas Sheraton, inlaid overall vith boxwood lines, the rectangular op with concave-cut front and reen leather-lined writing-surface, 29½in. wide.
Christie's) $7,776

A Louis XV style marquetry inlaid bureau mazarin, mid 19th century, the inverted breakfront top profusely inlaid with floral swags, garlands and putti, 41½in. wide.
(Christie's) $4,704

A Chinese carved hardwood desk, the cleated rectangular top with a detachable superstructure, the galleried frieze of pierced berries, 3ft.6½in. overall, circa 1900.
(Woolley & Wallis) $481

\ Regency mahogany and bonized Carlton House desk, with hree-quarter gallery above five nahogany-lined drawers around a reen leather-lined writing-surface, 9in. wide.
Christie's) $55,545

Shaker butternut and chestnut sewing desk, 1860s, Canterbury, New Hampshire community, the gallery is divided into thirds by a frame and panel construction door, the base containing four drawers on the right side, 29in. wide.
(Skinner) $17,250

A 19th century kingwood crossbanded burr walnut and gilt metal mounted lady's writing table, the pierced gallery over a bank of five molded front drawers above the serpentine writing surface, 42in. wide. (G.A. Key) $5,644

George Nelson, U.S.A., an early desk model No. 4658, designed 1946, manufactured by Herman Miller. The rectangular wooden work surface with tan leather covering.
(Bonhams) $9,437

Edwardian lady's rosewood bonheur du jour, the back with serpentine shaped shelf above an inlaid panel of scrolling faliage, 20in. wide.
(Ewbank) $770

Louis Majorelle, bureau de dame 'Aux Nenuphars', circa 1900, various fruitwoods and exotic woods, each leg with elaborate gilt bronze mounts, 121cm. wide.
(Sotheby's) $74,412

A good Federal inlaid and figured mahogany tambour writing desk, Boston, Massachusetts, circa 1795, in two parts, the upper section with two frieze drawers above tambour slides, 40½in. wide.
(Sotheby's) $46,000

Attributed to Josef Hoffmann, probably manufactured by J. &. J. Kohn, desk, circa 1905, wood, single upper shelf above two frieze drawers, 43in. wide.
(Sotheby's) $14,416

A French tulipwood and gilt-metal mounted bonheur du jour, mid 20th century, crossbanded and inlaid with lines, the shaped arched superstructure with a pierced three-quarter gallery, 26¼in. wide.
(Christie's) $3,634

A Regency mahogany writing table, the rectangular top with three-quarter gallery above a frieze fitted with two drawers, 35in. wide.
(Christie's) $2,608

An Edwardian lady's mahogany desk of shaped outline, the whole inlaid with satinwood bandings, the top inset with red leather to the writing surface, 42in. wide.
(Canterbury) $2,226

A good blue-painted birchwood magistrate's desk, New England, circa 1800, in two parts, the upper section with hinged lid, the lower section fitted with thumbmolded long drawer, 40in. wide.
(Sotheby's) $4,88

An Empire style yew wood bonheur du jour, 107cm. wide. (Bonhams) $715

An early 19th century dropleaf writing table with molded edge to the rounded rectangular top, 96cm. wide. (Bearne's) $1,730

A mid-Victorian oak writing-table, the gadrooned molded top inlaid with ebony lines, above two foliate and shell-carved drawers, 56in. wide. (Christie's) $5,555

A French rosewood, tulipwood-banded and gilt-metal mounted serpentine bonheur du jour, mid 20th century, the superstructure with an undulating ledge back inset with an oval Sèvres style plaquette, 30¾in. wide. (Christie's) $5,451

An Edwardian mahogany Carlton House type desk, decorated with lines and satinwood crossbanding, 54½in. wide. (Christie's) $11,247

A Louis XVI tulipwood and purplewood bonheur du jour, inlaid with lines and checker-banding, the superstructure with a marble top, 26in. wide. (Christie's) $3,089

A French kingwood and parquetry bonheur du jour, late 19th/early 20th century, decorated with lines and crossbanding, 28¾in. wide. (Christie's) $3,353

A mahogany and gilt-bronze bureau plat, Paris, circa 1880, in Louis XVI style, with a felt-inset rectangular top above a frieze drawer cast with putti in relief, 135cm. wide. (Sotheby's) $13,122

A George III mahogany bonheur du jour, the superstructure with a molded three-quarter gallery with an open compartment, 30in. wide. (Christie's) $4,360

A Regency rosewood teapoy, the rectangular top with a molded edge enclosing a fitted interior above a tapered body, 16in. wide. (Christie's) $942

A William IV mahogany teapoy with fitted interior, circa 1835, 48.5cm. wide. (Bonhams) $1,422

19th century mahogany teapoy, bead molded borders and raised on ring turned cylindrical shaft, terminating in quadruped base, 16in. (G.A. Key) $800

An early Victorian burr walnut and walnut teapoy, the circular top hinged to reveal a four section interior, the molded border above a turned and lobed pedestal, diameter 44cm. (Wintertons) $2,587

A Victorian burr walnut teapoy with ten sided hinged top enclosing vacant compartments, on turned column and tripod base, 16in. diameter. (Russell Baldwin & Bright) $820

A William IV bird's-eye maple and rosewood teapoy, with sarcophagus-shaped top, on an octagonal baluster support and circular platform with four scrolled legs with later bun feet, 17½in. wide. (Christie's) $2,907

A William IV mahogany teapoy, decorated with reeded moldings, with a hinged top enclosing a fitted interior, 11½in. wide. (Christie's) $1,024

A Regency tortoiseshell inlaid teapoy, circa 1815, 36cm. wide. (Bonhams) $1,590

An early Victorian rosewood teapoy, the sarcophagus shaped top with hinged lid enclosing a fitted interior, 16½in. wide. (Christie's) $1,173

A Peter Waals calamander wardrobe, with rectangular top above a pair of cushioned panel doors, on shaped feet, 47in. wide. (Christie's) $17,250

19th century mahogany inverted breakfront wardrobe, the central section with a cupboard above two short and three long drawers, 89½in. (Ewbank) $1,495

A French fruitwood and burr-elm armoire, 19th century, the arched molded cornice above a pair of fielded panelled doors enclosing a shelf, 64in. wide. (Christie's) $4,658

A Flemish oak armoire with a pair of full length panelled doors surmounted by a carved basket of flowers in relief, 53in. wide. (Anderson & Garland) $845

A large Adam Revival satinwood and painted wardrobe, of serpentine breakfront form, with an arched cornice over two central doors, 212cm. wide. (Tennants) $7,986

Louis XVI Provincial oak armoire, late 18th/early 19th century, rectangular form, doors with molded detail, raised on plain feet, 44½in. wide. (Skinner) $4,025

An Art Nouveau mahogany wardrobe, the cornice with pierced convex brackets and set with hammered pewter roundels, 69¼in. (Dreweatt Neate) $1,749

A good 18th century oak wardrobe, 77in. wide. (Dockrees) $7,520

A French Provincial walnut armoire, early 19th century, with a molded cornice above a pair of doors with molded shaped panels. (Christie's) $2,201

An early Victorian mahogany triple section wardrobe, 233cm. wide.
(Bonhams) $1,416

An early 20th century chinoiserie decorated two-door wardrobe, 130cm. wide.
(Bonhams) $1,337

A George III mahogany breakfront wardrobe, the broken pediment with acanthus leaves above a pair of small doors and a pair of long panelled doors, 96½in. wide.
(Christie's) $16,560

An Art Nouveau wardrobe circa 1900, inspired by Edward Colonna, fruitwood, the mirrored glass door enclosing two adjustable shelves, 57¼in. wide.
(Sotheby's) $1,325

An Edwardian mahogany and satinwood-banded breakfront wardrobe, inlaid with lines, the upper part with a molded cornice and fitted with sliding trays, 101in. wide. (Christie's) $6,541

A Louis XV oak armoire, the two doors each with moldings of shells and foliage, on incurved sabot feet, Liège, 19th century.
(Galerie Moderne) $2,889

An early Victorian mahogany breakfront wardrobe, the molded cornice with four arched panelled doors below and central drawers, 90in. wide.
(Christie's) $5,962

A Louis Philippe mahogany armoire with a stepped molded and shaped cornice, enclosed by a pair of mirror panel doors, 47½in. wide.
(Christie's) $1,635

A Dutch walnut and figured walnut secrétaire armoire, late 18th/early 19th century, decorated with lines, the arched molded cornice centered with a floral carving abov a pair of panelled doors, 76in. wid
(Christie's) $9,74

A Scottish George II mahogany washstand, the hinged twin-flap top with one large and two small circular holes, 12½in. square. (Christie's) $5,888

A George III mahogany, satinwood and tulipwood banded enclosed washstand, circa 1795, 75.5cm. wide. (Bonhams) $2,226

A George III mahogany corner washstand, decorated with lines, the raised shelved back with circular incisions, 23in. wide. (Christie's) $1,024

Federal mahogany chamber stand, possibly Connecticut, circa 1800, the square top with circular molded opening surrounded by an applied scrolled decorative element, 16in. wide. (Skinner) $690

A late Victorian mahogany wash stand, 123cm. wide. (Bonhams) $282

A George III mahogany enclosed washstand, inlaid with lines, the hinged top enclosing circular recesses, 14in. wide. (Christie's) $2,180

George III mahogany bowfront washstand with raised back, having shaped hand holds and shell motif inlay, 2ft. 3in. wide. (Russell Baldwin & Bright) $4,550

A George III mahogany and boxwood strung gentleman's washstand, the hinged lid enclosing a mirror and lidded compartments over a writing slide, 28in. (George Kidner) $3,525

Victorian enamelled oval pedestal basin with 'hot' and 'cold' taps and waste plunger, on fluted tapering pedestal and round base, 33in. (Ewbank) $308

Classical paint decorated and gilt stencilled chamber stand, possibly Vermont, circa 1825-35, the scrolled splashboard above a pierced top with bowfront, 18½in. wide. (Skinner) $2,300

A late Regency mahogany washstand, the rectangular top with a three-quarter gallery, a pierced bowl ring and a later cover, 30in. wide. (Christie's) $827

Federal mahogany and mahogany veneer chamber stand, probably Massachusetts, circa 1810, the shaped splashboard centering a quarter round shelf above the pierced top, 22¾in. wide. (Skinner) $690

A 19th century mahogany washstand, the molded circular top with bowl aperture raised on baluster turned supports, the triangular center section with two drawers, 12½in. wide. (Andrew Hartley) $638

A Federal green- and yellow-painted pine washstand and a similar dressing table, New England, circa 1810, the pierced top with shaped three-quarter gallery, the washstand 18in. wide. (Sotheby's) $2,300

A 19th century mahogany washstand, the rectangular and bowfronted top surmounted by three-quarter gallery rail, with associated basin and pail, 80cm. wide. (Bristol) $244

An early 19th century mahogany corner washstand, the top pierced for a bowl, flanked by wooden soap dishes, with shaped raised back, 23¼in. (Woolley & Wallis) $1,570

Paint decorated chamber stand, England, circa 1830, grain painted to simulate mahogany with the exception of the top which simulates gray marble, 36in. wide. (Skinner) $862

Federal mahogany chamber stand, probably Massachusetts, circa 1815, the shaped splashboard with two quarter-round shelves above a pierced rectangular top, 20in. wide (Skinner) $690

A Victorian rosewood whatnot, 56cm. wide.
(Bonhams) $874

A mahogany four-tier whatnot, 19th century, fitted with three serpentine tiers, above a square tier fitted with a drawer, 18½in. wide.
(Christie's) $2,437

A Victorian mahogany three tier whatnot, 75cm. wide.
(Bonhams) $440

A George III mahogany four-tier whatnot, fitted with a drawer, on ring-turned supports terminating in brass castors, 18½in. wide.
(Christie's) $3,167

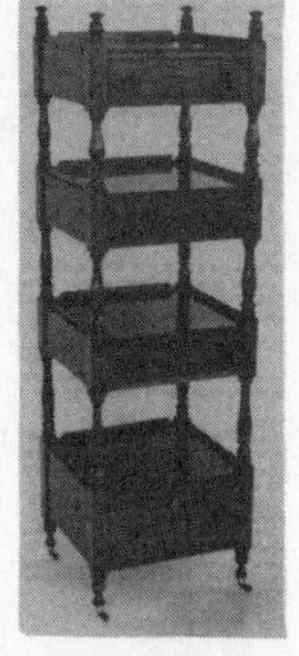

Victorian mahogany four tier tray top whatnot, each tier fitted with a full width frieze drawer, the whole raised on ring turned tulip baluster supports, 21in. wide, 67in. high.
(G.A. Key) $2,160

A William IV mahogany four-tier whatnot, the rounded rectangular top with turned finials and supports above a shelf, a mahogany lined drawer and a further shelf, 19in. wide. (Christie's)
$2,944

A George IV mahogany whatnot, the rectangular molded top with three-quarter pierced gallery above three shelves supported by ring-turned balusters, 21in. wide.
(Christie's) $7,776

A satinwood and polychrome decorated whatnot, early 20th century, the rectangular top with pierced shaped gallery and further shaped apron, 18in. wide.
(Christie's) $1,823

A walnut and brass three-tier étagère, late 19th century, the top tier fitted with a pierced brass gallery with turned supports and brass castors, 21½in. wide.
(Christie's) $5,589

A George IV rosewood three-tier whatnot, the rectangular top with brass gallery and gadrooned finials, 25in. wide.
(Christie's) $2,552

A Regency mahogany four-tier whatnot, the three-quarter top with a hinged ratcheted slope, two tiers below, 18in. wide.
(Christie's) $3,270

A Sinhalese rosewood étagère, 19th century, the three tiers with elaborate lotus-leaf supports, carved overall with pierced foliage, 44in. wide. (Christie's)
$10,120

A mahogany sarcophagus shape wine cellaret, the front panel carved in relief and a vase issuing foliage, 28¼in.
(Woolley & Wallis) $1,771

An early Victorian mahogany wine cooler, with liner, 40cm. wide.
(Bonhams) $708

A late Regency mahogany wine cooler, the sarcophagus body inlaid with ebony lines, 79cm. wide.
(Bearne's) $2,960

Arts and Crafts oak cellaret, circa 1905, drop front inlaid with copper, interior with racks and porcelain cylinder, 21¾in. wide.
(Skinner) $546

A George III brass bound wine cooler, late 18th century, the cover hinged to either side over twin cylindrical liners, 10¼in. high.
(Christie's) $8,175

A George III mahogany and brass-bound hexagonal cellaret, the hinged top above brass carrying handles to the sides, on square tapering splayed legs, 18½in. wide.
(Christie's) $2,608

A rare Federal inlaid cherrywood cellaret on stand, probably North Carolina, circa 1800, in two parts, the upper with a rectangular molded lip opening to a divided interior, 33½in. wide.
(Sotheby's) $13,800

A Chinese export lac burgauté cellaret, early 19th century, the hinged canted rectangular top inlaid with a landscape scene with figures, 19in. wide.
(Christie's) $5,485

A George III brass bound mahogany octagonal cellaret on stand, the crossbanded and line inlaid top enclosing fitted interior, with three brass bands and carrying handles, 56.5cm. wide.
(Bristol) $3,789

A late Victorian mahogany wine-cooler, Adam Revival, of oval shape, with copper liner, the gadrooned rim with four ram-masks, 24½in. wide.
(Christie's) $11,960

A George III mahogany and brass bound oval wine cooler on stand, circa 1780, 69cm. wide.
(Bonhams) $2,067

A George III mahogany wine cooler on stand, circa 1770, with painted tin liner, reeded and acanthus clasp carved edge, continuing to over scrolled acanthus handles.
(Bonhams) $35,200

A George IV mahogany brass bound cylindrical cellaret, the hinged top disclosing a lead lined interior with brass tap below, brass ring handles, raised on turned legs, 24cm. diameter.
(Bonhams) $1,975

A Regency cellaret, mahogany veneered, crossbanded and inlaid diamond stringing with a bead to each corner of the domed lid, 19½in.
(Woolley & Wallis) $1,603

A George III mahogany wine cooler, the brass bound oval body with a hinged lid enclosing an interior converted to a cellaret, 58cm. (Tennants) $4,710

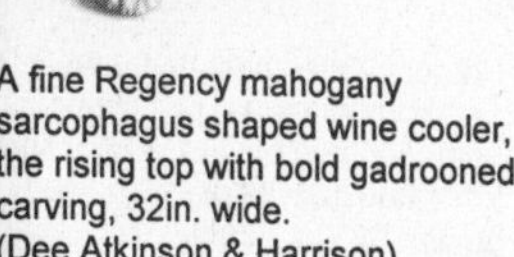

A fine Regency mahogany sarcophagus shaped wine cooler, the rising top with bold gadrooned carving, 32in. wide.
(Dee Atkinson & Harrison) $7,040

A George III mahogany and brass bound oval wine cooler-on-stand, fitted with a liner, with a carrying handle to either side, 24in. wide.
(Christie's) $2,725

A late Regency mahogany wine cooler of sarcophagus form, the hinged lid with beaded and gadrooned decoration with a panelled front, 87cm. wide.
(Phillips) $3,936

An early 19th century painted iron garden seat with reeded scroll-filled back and downswept arms, 168cm. wide. (Bearne's) $3,135

A mid Victorian sandstone sundial, surmounted by a cast iron calibrated plate and scrolled gnomen, the tapered octagonal pedestal carved with foliate garlands, 49in. high. (Bonhams) $4,640

A George III lead water-butt, the front panel with molded decoration and inscribed *S H* and dated *1775*, 50in. wide. (Christie's) $8,176

A painted cast-iron garden bench, late 19th century, the rectangular back continuing to scrolled arms and fitted with three allegorical figural panels, 5ft. 6in. long. (Sotheby's) $4,600

A Netherlandish terracotta figure of a river god, circa 1650, attributed to the workshop of Artus Quellinus, reclining, his head wreathed with foliage he rests his left elbow on a rockwork base, 25in. long. (Sotheby's) $90,400

One of a pair of carved stone sphinxes, French or Flemish, late 17th or early 18th century, each wearing a jewelled head-band and tasseled head-dress; each on an integrally carved rectangular plinth, 49in. long. (Christie's) (Two) $81,600

Two of a set of four Victorian cast iron garden chairs, each with rocaille cresting above a foliate scrolled pierced waisted back and pierced circular foliate cast seat. (Christie's) (Four) $1,650

An early Victorian carved limestone pedestal, in three parts, the circular top with an egg and dart rim on a baluster column carved with ribbon tied leopard masks, 35in. high. (Bonhams) $3,840

Pair of painted cast-iron stag garden ornaments, possibly manufactured by J.W. Fiske, New York, late 19th century, painted brown, 62¼in. high. (Skinner) $6,900

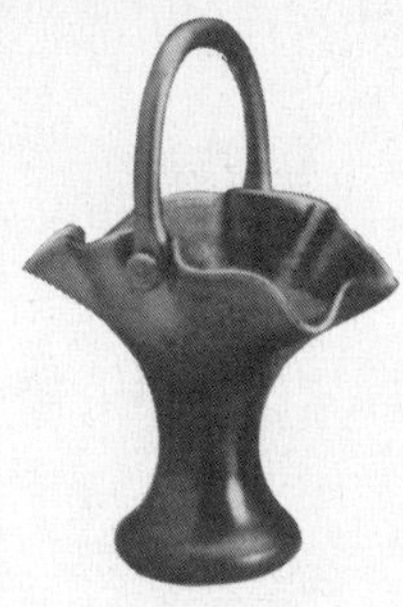

Carder Steuben blue Aurene basket, ruffled form with strong blue luster, total 7in. high.
(Skinner) $862

A Clichy latticinio basket with pinched sides, decorated with alternate stripes of green and white spiral threads, mid 19th century, 14cm. wide. (Christie's) $327

A Wiener Werkstätte style silvered metal and glass basket and cover, the clear glass within frame pierced with bands of squares, with swing handle, 18.2.cm. high.
(Christie's) $960

BOTTLES

A sealed and dated onion wine bottle of olive-green tint with string rim, the seal inscribed *B. Greive* and dated *1727*, 15cm. high.
(Christie's) $1,454

Rare American one-quart cabin-form bottle, in amber, inscribed *E.C. Booz's Old Cabin Whiskey 120 Walnut St. Philadelphia 1840.*
(Eldred's) $550

Unusual skull-form cobalt blue glass poison bottle, late 19th century, U.S. Patent Office design patent number 23,399 granted to Carlton H. Lee of Boston, Mass., June 26, 1894, 4½in. high.
(Eldred's) $935

BOWLS

Carder Steuben amethyst quartz cintra applied and etched bowl, scalloped rim on mottled and crackled pink, blue, and frosted colorless glass body, 6in. high.
(Skinner) $1,150

Unusual Art Deco period punch set, comprising: cylindrical covered punch bowl and matching ladle; pair of glasses etched with twining foliate design and decorated with abstract green glass prunts, tube lined detail.
(G A Key) $112

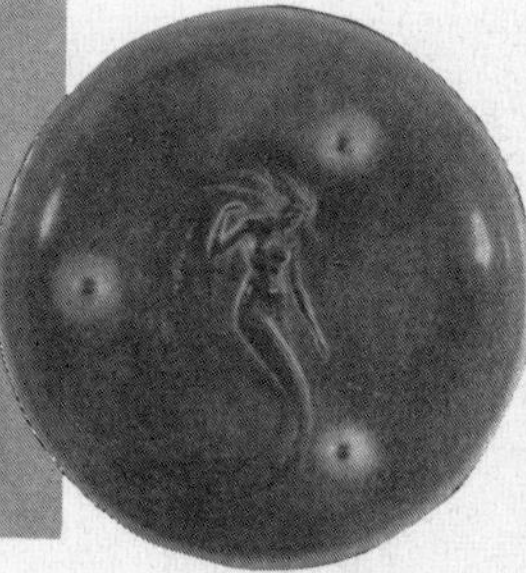

'Sirenes' No.376 a clear, frosted and sepia-stained bowl, on three feet, molded mark *R.Lalique*, 37cm. wide.
(Christie's) $5,417

A cameo glass bowl by Daum, circa 1910, the gray glass internally mottled with yellow and amethyst towards base, overlaid in brown, 22cm. diameter.
(Christie's) $1,539

'Lys' No.382 a clear, frosted and opalescent bowl, wheel engraved *R.Lalique France*, 23.7cm. diameter. (Christie's) $1,444

A cut two-handled cylindrical bowl with serrated rim above a diamond band, the body cut with rectangular panels and fan-cut handles, circa 1825, 18.5cm. wide.
(Christie's) $1,003

A Barovier & Toso ' Intarsio' bowl, designed by Ercole Barovier, 1961, the colorless glass decorated with an arrangement of smoky brown triangles, 12in. wide.
(Christie's) $1,447

An early punch-bowl, circa 1690, the circular bowl with in-curving rim, the lower part molded with 'nipt diamond waies', the domed and folded foot molded with a canopy of 'nipt diamond waies', 9in. diameter.
(Christie's) $19,078

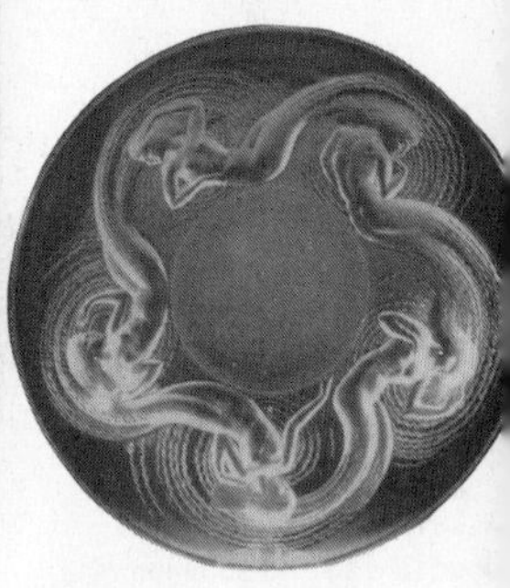

'Calypso' No.413, a clear and frosted glass bowl, the everted rim molded on underside in low relief with five sea sprites, incised *Lalique France,* 36cm. diameter.
(Christie's) $3,312

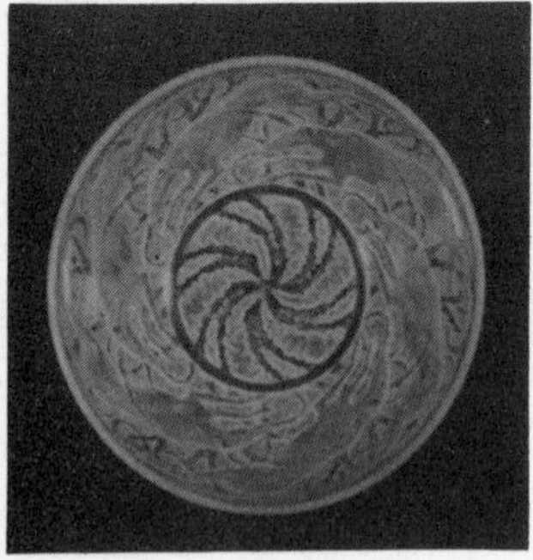

'Chiens No.1' No.3214 a clear and frosted bowl, molded mark *Verrerie D'Alsace France,* 23.5cm. diameter. (Christie's) $378

A Bohemian green and white overlay center bowl with gilt-line ogee crenellated rim above a band of oval panels, one painted with bust length portrait of a woman, circa 1860, 26cm. high.
(Christie's) $1,362

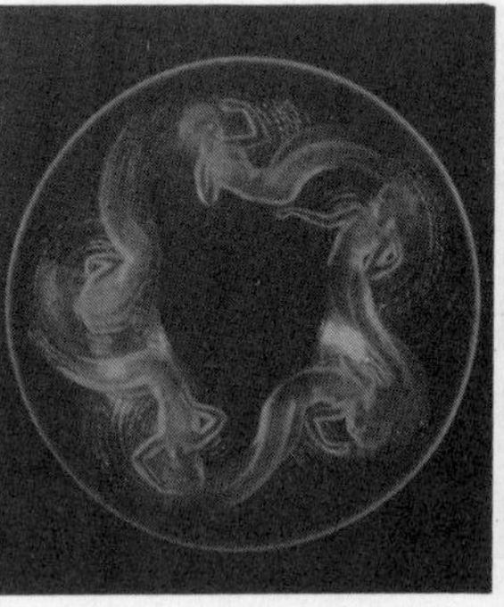

'Calypso' No.413 a clear, frosted and opalescent bowl, stencil mark *R. Lalique France*, 36.6cm. diameter. (Christie's) $5,055

A Gabriel Argy-Rousseau box and cover 'Hortensias', 1921, pâte de verre, gray glass decorated in shades of dark pink/red, white and black with flowerheads, 7.4cm. (Sotheby's) $3,611

G. Argy Rousseau pâte de verre flower and foliage covered box, France, circa 1923, cylindrical form of muted purple decorated with central red flower, amber and purple leaves, 5¼in. diameter. (Skinner) $4,312

A cameo glass box and cover by Daum, circa 1900, the circular box and cover acid-etched and carved with a twilight lakeside view, 14cm. diameter. (Christie's) $1,449

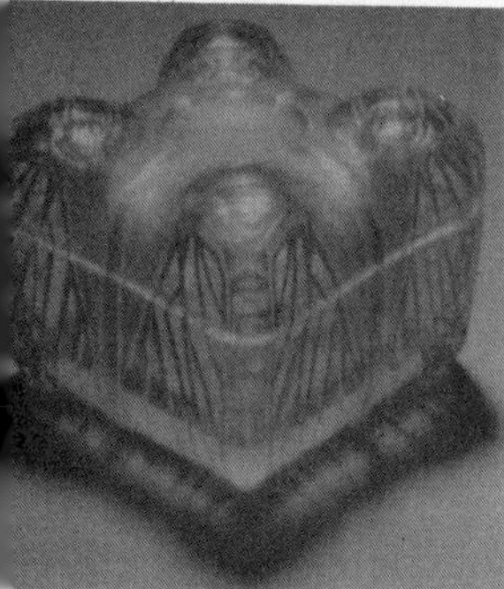

'Cigalia' a clear and gray-stained box and cover, 7.2cm. diameter. (Christie's) $992

A Bohemian ruby-flashed gilt-metal-mounted rectangular box and cover with canted corners, the cover engraved with a panel of a castle, titled *Le vieux Château de Sade*, mid 19th century, 11cm. wide. (Christie's) $911

A cameo glass box and cover by Gallé, circa 1900, the frosted gray glass internally mottled with inky blue, overlaid in amber, the cover acid-etched and carved with a dragonfly, 12cm. diameter. (Christie's) $1,358

CANDLESTICKS

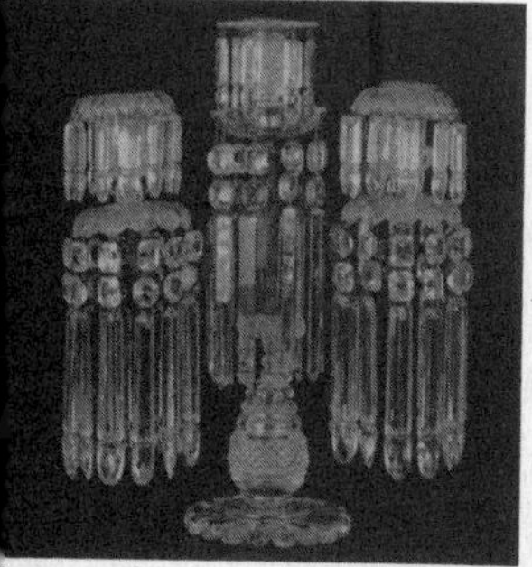

One of a pair of Regency cut glass candelabra, each with three branches with everted drip pans hung with spear drops, 43cm. (Tennants) (Two) $1,520

A pair of cut candlestick lustres of baluster form, the flared sconces cut with horizontal flutes and serrated rim suspending drop lusters, late 19th century, 20.5cm. high. (Christie's) $1,188

A pair of Regency style gilt-bronze mounted cut-glass candelabra, early 20th century, the foliate cast scroll branches supporting faceted nozzles and petal dish-pans hung with pendants, 17¼in. high. (Christie's) $2,725

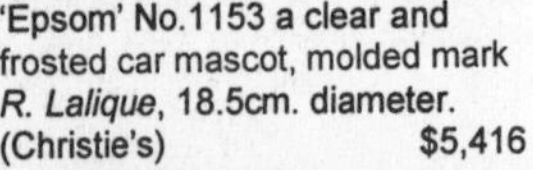

'Epsom' No.1153 a clear and frosted car mascot, molded mark *R. Lalique*, 18.5cm. diameter. (Christie's) $5,416

'Vitesse' No.1160 a frosted car mascot on a circular base, molded marks *R.Lalique France*, 18cm. high. (Christie's) $2,347

'Perche' No.1158 a clear, frosted and opalescent car mascot, wheel-cut *R. Lalique France*, 10cm. high. (Christie's) $2,347

'Chrysis' No.1183, a Lalique clear and frosted car mascot, modelled as a reclining female figure with windswept hair, stencil mark, 13.5cm. high. (Christie's) $4,416

'Tête d'Epervier' No.1139 a clear and frosted car mascot with a silvered mount, molded mark *Lalique France*, 6.7cm. high. (Christie's) $1,173

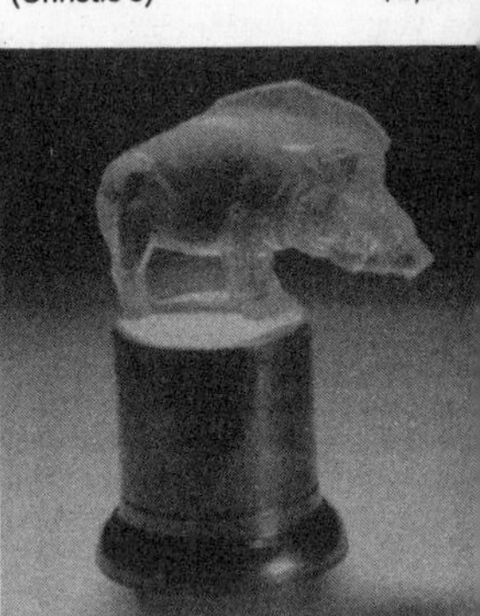

'Sanglier' No.1157 a clear and frosted car mascot, fixed in a metal base, molded mark *R.Lalique France*, 12.5cm. high. (Christie's) $1,173

'Tête d'Aigle' No.1138 a clear and frosted car mascot, molded mark *R.Lalique*, 11cm. high. (Christie's) $1,986

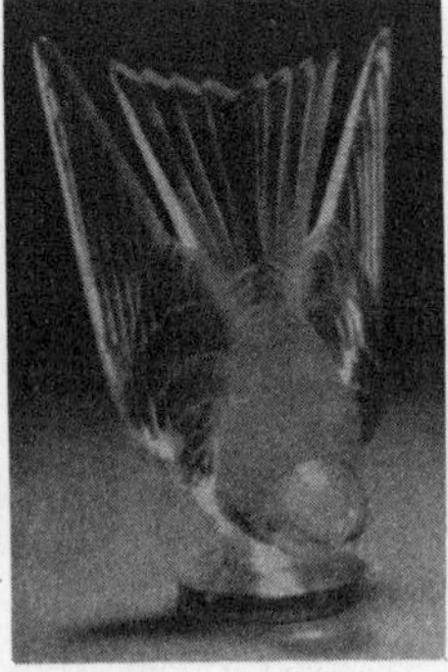

'Hirondelle' No.1143 a clear and frosted car mascot, molded mark *R. Lalique France*, 14.5cm. high. (Christie's) $1,625

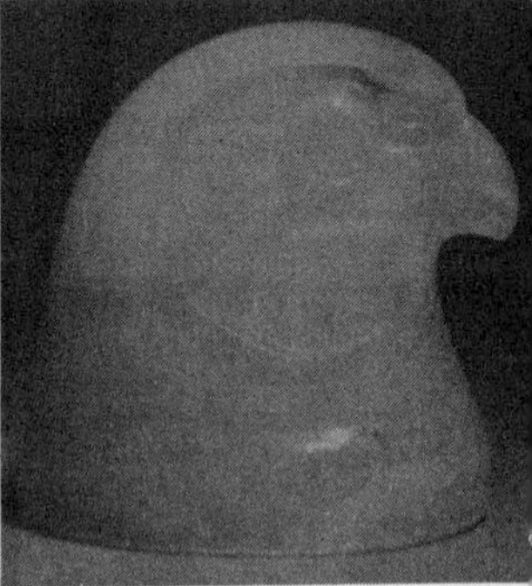

'Tête D'Épervier' No.1139 a clear, frosted and opalescent car mascot, engraved *R. Lalique*, 6.7cm. high. (Christie's) $722

A late Victorian or Edwardian glass and ormolu centerpiece, late 19th or early 20th century, possibly by Osler, 12½in. high. (Christie's) $1,363

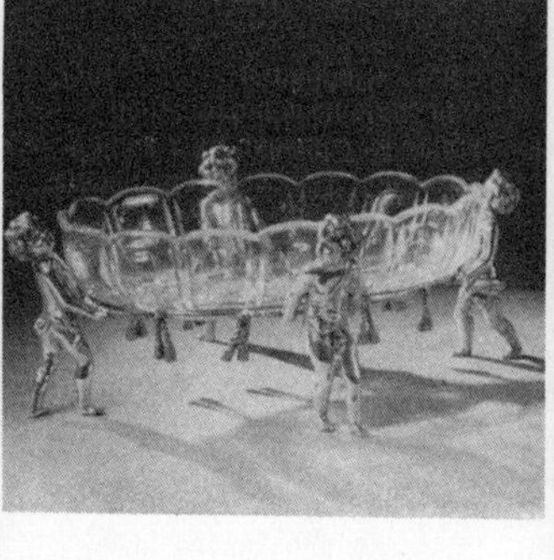

A silvered, bronze and cut-glass centerpiece by Christofle, Paris, circa 1890, of oval form with a lobed glass dish, upheld in a framework by four putti, 51cm. wide. (Sotheby's) $21,557

A Belgian silver oil and vinegar cruet, Louvain, 1781, maker's mark, probably for Jan-Baptist Walgraeve, the stand with two bottle-holders and on six scroll feet, the sides chased with foliage and flowers, 10¾in. high., 27oz. (Christie's) $2,944

COUPES

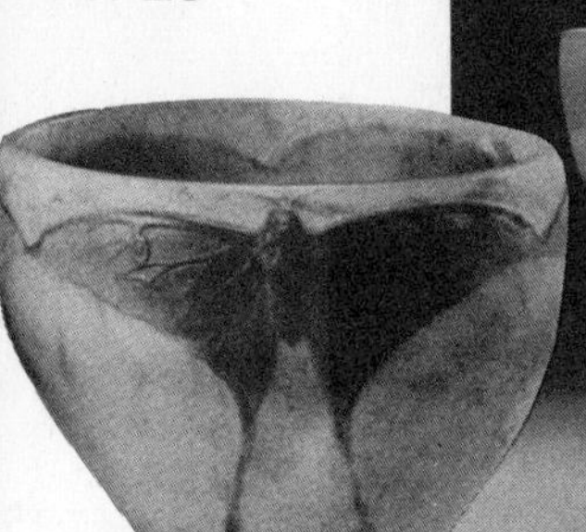

A Gabriel Argy-Rousseau coupe 'Papillons', 1915, pâte de verre, clear glass decorated in shades of purple, green and red, 3in. (Sotheby's) $5,778

A cameo glass coupe, by Gallé, circa 1900, the yellow and turquoise opalescent body overlaid in white and brown, with etched and carved decoration of seagulls, 22.5cm. high. (Christie's) $27,945

A Gabriel Argy-Rousseau coupe 'Anémones', 1920, pâte de verre, gray glass decorated in shades of blue, brown and black, 3in. (Sotheby's) $5,055

A Gallé maple leaf coupe, circa 1900, hexagonal, gray glass internally decorated with red towards the base and at the rim, 7.3cm. (Sotheby's) $1,444

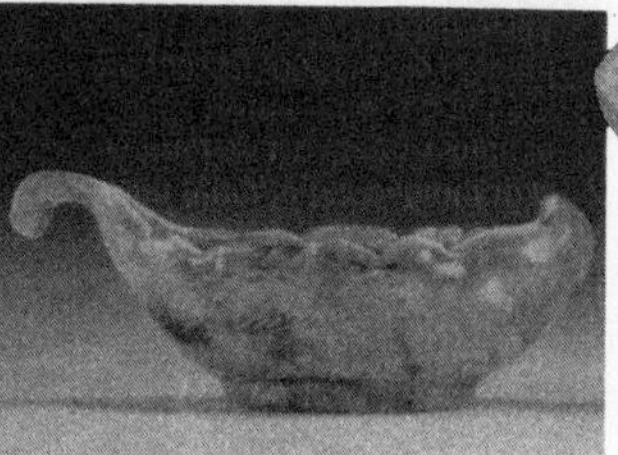

Emile Gallé, coupe, circa 1900, clear glass internally decorated with gold foil inclusions and random splashes of sunflower yellow, green and chocolate brown, 3in. high. (Sotheby's) $17,808

A Schneider tazza, the clear glass bowl internally mottled with white, blue and amethyst, on knopped stem with mottled amethyst foot, 20.2cm. diameter. (Christie's) $640

An engraved decanter and stopper, early 19th century, perhaps Irish, of club shape with hammered flutes to the lower part, engraved with a sailing ship, 10¾in. high.
(Christie's) $596

A pair of German mounted clear-glass liqueur decanters and stoppers, with pull-off pierced bases, decorated with putti and festoons, by Nereshseimer of Hanau, 24.5cm. high, 4oz weighable silver.
(Christie's) $1,186

An early Victorian three bottle silver plated tantalus, tri-part base containing three wine bottles in Bristol blue, purple and yellow, circa1840, 17in.
(Dee Atkinson & Harrison) $1,040

An early 19th century cut decanter, with triple ring neck, and a mushroom stopper.
(Bristol) $148

A 19th century inlaid rosewood tantulus box, containing a two tier lift-out stand with a pair of liquor decanters and six glasses.
(Academy) $464

Unusual cut glass hour-glass decanter with embossed acorn and oak leaf banding and hallmarked silver collar/pourer, 10in. high, Birmingham, 1905.
(G.A. Key) $96

A pair of Victorian silver-necked cut-glass decanters, the tapering square section glass bodies with plain silver four-spout mounts, 23cm. high overall, Heath and Middleton, Birmingham 1896.
(Bearne's) $472

Art Deco chrome and glass decanter set, Krome Kraft, Faber Bros., New York, circa 1935, chrome metal fitted holder with locking mechanism and black resin handle, 12in. wide.
(Skinner) $230

A pair of 'Bristol' blue decanters with lozenge stoppers, each decorated in gold, one inscribed *Hollands* the other *Brandy*, 24cm. high, 19th century.
(Bearne's) $676

A late 19th century oak tantalus, having three crystal bottles, cigar and playing card provision, 36cm. (Locke & England) $422

A pair of mallet shaped cut-glass decanters and lozenge shaped stoppers, circa 1820, each with a faceted triple-ring neck, 9½in. (Sotheby's) $269

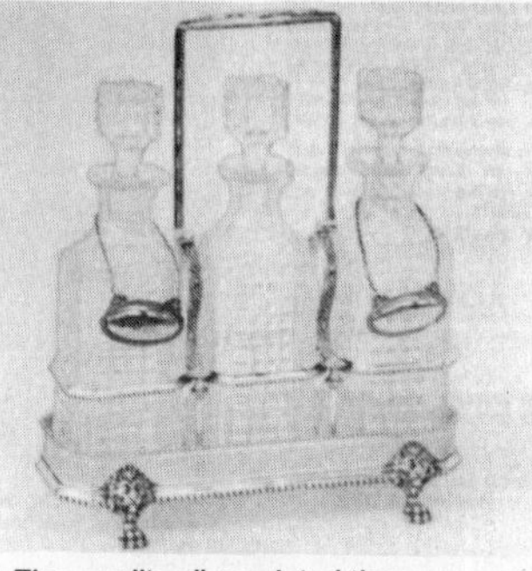

Fine quality silver-plated three bottle tantalus, rectangular shaped with canted corners, having a beaded slot pierced gallery, late 19th century. (G.A. Key) $640

A late Victorian mounted cut-glass liqueur decanter with an elongated, barrel-shaped body cut with bands of reeding, maker's mark G.W, Sheffield 1895, 26cm. high. (Christie's) $730

A set of four cut-glass decanters, and stoppers, first quarter 19th century, of Prussian shape, the faceted triple-ring necks and cylindrical body cut with hobnails, 9in. (Sotheby's) $4,033

A Barovier & Toso decanter and stopper of tapering cylindrical form with elongated neck and everted rim, with multi-colored vertical stripes cased in clear, 15in. high. (Christie's) $440

A pair of magnum decanters and stoppers, with tall faceted necks and spherical bodies engraved with bands of stylized leaves to the shoulders, late 19th century, 13in. (Woolley & Wallis) $1,988

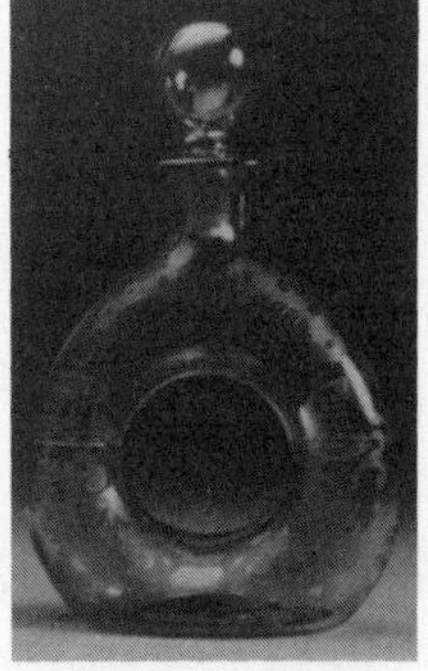

Green etched glass decanter, attributed to Pairpoint, etched Chinese junks, gazebos and stylised flowers, 9in. high. (Skinner) $190

A pair of late Regency decanters, (to hold three bottles) each with a diamond cut mushroom stopper, the octagonal section tapering necks cut with steps, circa 1820, 12in. (Woolley & Wallis) $4,869

A pâte de verre vide-poches by Alméric Walter, after a model by Henri Berge, circa 1920, molded with large deep blue and green speckled fish with aquamarine fins, 6½in. wide.
(Christie's) $6,583

A carved glass dish by Gallé, circa 1900, the aqua-green glass internally mottled with blue, ocher and beige with random airbubbles, molded and carved with a large fish to one side, 25.7cm. diameter.
(Christie's) $1,720

A pâte de verre vide-poches by Alméric Walter, after a model by Henri Berge, circa 1920, modelled with a reddish-brown dragonfly, 8in. diameter.(Christie's) $9,687

ÉPERGNES

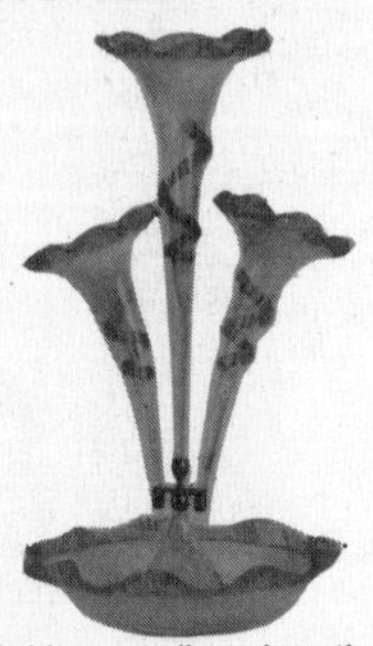

A Stourbridge vaseline-glass three-trumpet épergne with crimped rims and trailed ornament, late 19th century, 56.5cm. high.
(Christie's) $547

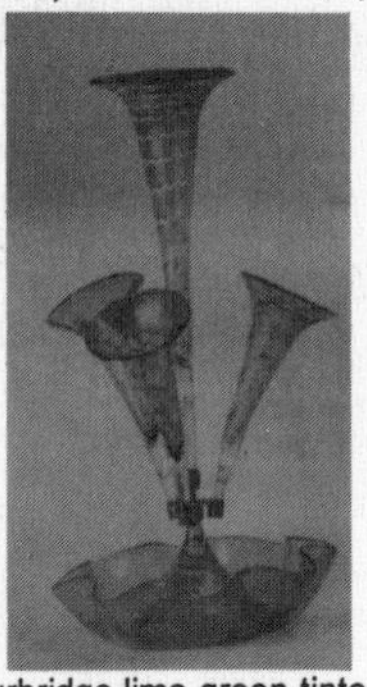

A Stourbridge lime-green-tinted four trumpet épergne with opaque-white trailed decoration, on crimped base, late 19th century, 51cm. high.
(Christie's) $639

A Stourbridge vaseline-glass three trumpet épergne with two clear rope-twist arms suspending floriform baskets, on crimped rim base, pale-pink through green, late 19th century, 56cm. high.
(Christie's) $821

EWERS

Mary Gregory cranberry ewer of tulip baluster form, crimped rim, clear glass looped handle, painted in cream, scene of a young girl carrying a hamper in a woodland landscape, 19th century, 7½in.
(G A Key) $401

A Glasgow School ewer, clear glass with three applied swirl motifs of green trail and purple spot decoration, with strap handle and drop in stopper.
(Bonhams) $629

A Continental ruby ewer, late 19th century, enamelled and gilt with stylized flowers and foliate meanders, 25.5cm.
(Bonhams) $542

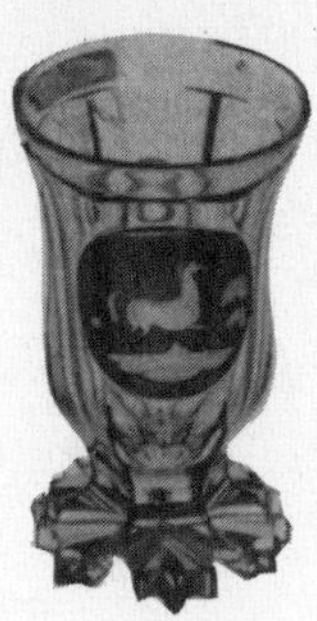

A Bohemian engraved blue-flash goblet, with raised oval boss engraved with a horse, on shaped foot, circa 1875, 13cm. high. (Christie's) $457

A mammoth early goblet, the ovoid bowl with gadrooned lower part supported on a hollow stem with a cushion knop above an inverted baluster section, 17th century. (Christie's) $11,849

A Silesian engraved goblet, the fluted ogee bowl engraved with a continuous scene of a boar and a stag hunt, circa 1740, 20.5cm. high. (Christie's) $693

A Bohemian pale-pink and white opalescent overlay goblet cut with oval panels with central oval bosses within enamelled bands of foliage, circa 1860, 12cm. high. (Christie's) $581

A 'Bijou' glass goblet by Schneider, 1920s, the clear glass internally mottled with orange with inky blue towards rim, the lower half of the stem of mottled amethyst, 20.5cm. high. (Christie's) $2,536

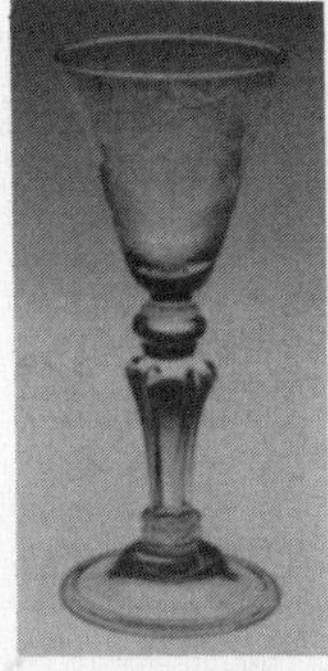

A Dutch-engraved pedestal-stemmed goblet, the funnel bowl engraved with a man-o'-war and inscribed *SALUS PATRIÆ*, circa 1750, 19.5cm. high. (Christie's) $1,458

A Bohemian engraved amber-flashed goblet, the generous bowl cut with raised oval panels, engraved with figures at a hunt meet before an inn, circa 1860, 25.5cm. high. (Christie's) $875

A Dutch engraved goblet, the round funnel bowl with man-o'-war within a C-scroll cartouche and inscribed *WELVAREN VAN DE VROUWANNA MARIA*, circa 1770, 13.5cm. high. (Christie's) $1,733

A Bohemian engraved and flashed spa goblet, the ovoid bowl cut with four raised oval bosses engraved with titled spa scenes and alternately flashed with pale-pink and blue grounds, circa 1860, 15.5cm. high.(Christie's) $545

Antique millefiori inkwell bottle, close pack millefiori canes at base of dome-shaped bottle, stopper in the form of a paperweight, total height 6¼in.
(Skinner) $546

Daum, inkwell , liner and cover, circa 1900, gray glass internally mottled with pink and apricot, overlaid with spring green and yellow, 3½in.
(Sotheby's) $4,485

Attractive Victorian glass ink well, circular shaped with hobnail cut base, having a pierced and embossed overlaid silver collar and hinged lid, 3½in. tall, London 1895.
(G A Key) $342

JARS

Mount Washington Crown Milano biscuit jar, 19th century, handpainted floral and gold enamel decoration, signed *CM*, 6¾in. high.
(Skinner) $747

Durand 'King Tut' covered jar, ginger jar form in green glass with iridized gold 'King Tut' decoration, applied amber glass decoration on cover, 7¼in.
(Skinner) $3,105

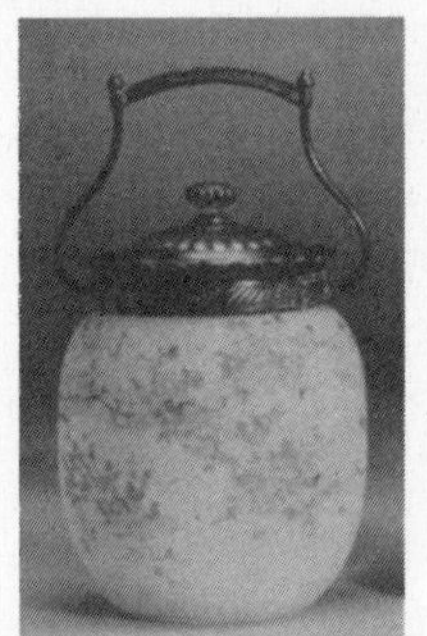

Pairpoint Mount Washington decorated biscuit jar, New England, late 19th century, swollen form of shaded pink and creamy white glass, decorated with delicate blue flowering branches, 7in. high.
(Skinner) $345

JUGS

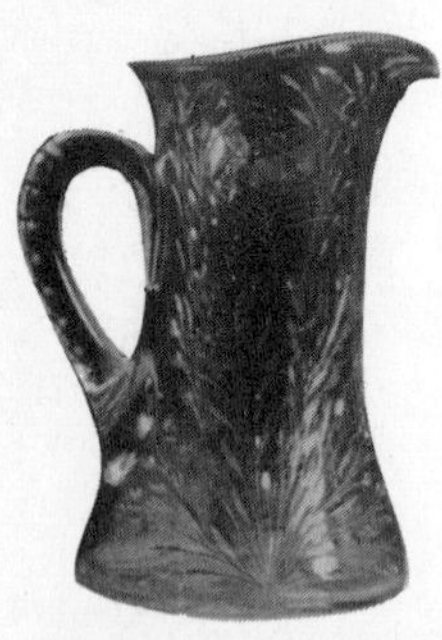

Five-piece jug and tumbler set, attributed to Pairpoint, etched butterflies, cut floral and leaf sprays, spider webs, pitcher height 9¼in. (Skinner) $287

A 'Seasons' jug with autumnal decoration in white, yellow, gold and blue, with broad spout and opaque glass handle, Daum, Nancy, 1900-1910, 14.3cm. high.
(Lempertz) $1,830

A late Victorian mounted cut-glass claret jug, the squat circular body cut with swirling and with floral bosses in the center, J. Grinsell & Sons, 1898, 25cm. high.
(Christie's) $1,931

A Stourbridge frosted baluster water jug, perhaps Richardson, with trefoil rim, gilt and enamelled in ocher with a field of four pointed stars, mid 19th century, 22cm. high. (Christie's) $328

A dated engraved baluster jug, 1811, engraved with a ship in full sail and an anchor flanked by foliage sprays, 8¼in. high. (Christie's) $930

A cut oviform water jug cut with a flowerhead medallion on a band of swags between a diamond pattern bands and flutes, circa 1810, 16cm. high. (Christie's) $512

LUSTERS

A pair of white overlay green glass luster vases, each decorated with flowers and foliage in enamel colors and gold, 26cm. high. (Bearne's) $1,828

A pair of 19th century Bohemian green and white opaque overlay glass luster vases, the flared rims with shaped edge enamelled with six vignettes, 13in. high. (Canterbury) $975

Pair of cobalt blue and clear cased glass garnitures, second half 19th century, decorated with gilded leaf tips, lappets and crosshatched designs, 13½in. high. (Skinner) $1,495

Pair of Victorian green glass large lusters, foliate molded spreading rims, decorated below with panels of stylized berries and flowers, 13½in. (G A Key) $602

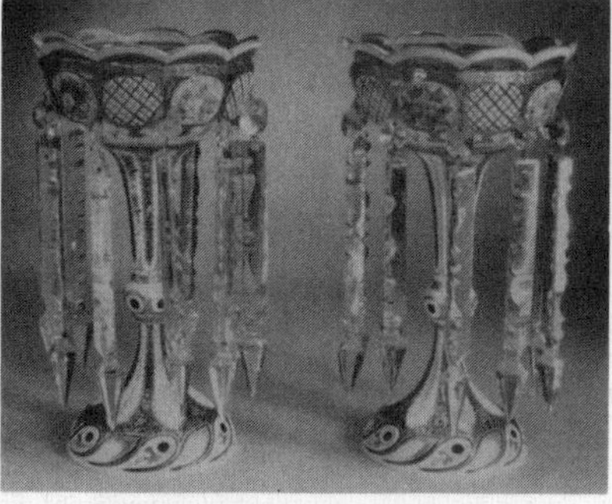

Pair of white overlay green glass lusters, circa 1880-1900, each with scalloped top, tapered stem and circular foot painted with multicolored foliage, 12½in. high. (Skinner) $2,300

A pair of Victorian glass lusters, with prism cut drops, raised on star cut bases, 24cm. high. (Cheffins) $571

A pâte de verre ashtray by Alméric Walter, after a model by Henri Berge, circa 1920, in deep orange, modelled with two small wriggling lizards on either side, 4½in. diameter.
(Christie's) $3,657

'Tête d'Aigle' No.1138, a clear and frosted bookend, modelled as an eagle's head, on black rectangular glass base, molded mark, 14cm. high. (Christie's) $2,760

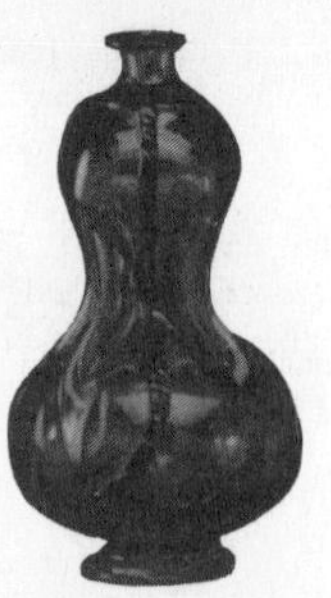

Clear glass flask applied with amethyst trails, 19th century, Swedish, 21cm. high.
(Stockholms AV) $477

'Le Jour et La Nuit' a gray and frosted clock surround, engraved *R.Lalique France*, 37cm. high.
(Christie's) $10,472

An engraved and dated baluster loving cup applied with a band of stringing beneath the rim and two incised loop handles, inscribed with initials *B E E E* and dated *1771*, 11cm. high.
(Christie's) $1,635

'Dahlias' No.2459 a clear and frosted plafonnier, engraved *R.Lalique France,* 30cm. diameter.
(Christie's) $1,353

'Inséparables' No.765 a clear, frosted and opalescent clock, molded mark R.Lalique, 11cm. high. (Christie's) $2,256

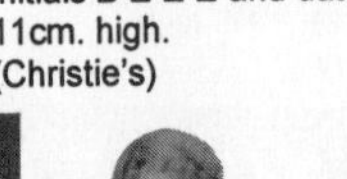

A pair of silver mounted liqueur flasks, with helical glass bodies and glass stoppers, Mappin & Webb, Birmingham, 1911/12, 27cm. high.
(Finarte) $1,286

'Fleurs d'Amour' a metallic powder box, made for Roger et Gallet, marked *Lalique*, 7.5cm. diameter.
(Christie's) $325

A pair of fantastic animal glass ornaments, with contrasting black forelegs, designed by Toni Zuccheri for Barovier & Toso, Murano, circa 1970, 27.5cm. high.
(Finarte) $4,729

Muller Frères and Chapelle, snail lamp, 1920s, wrought iron armature cast as a snail with four horns, the body blown with clear glass internally decorated with bright red and dark blue, 15.5cm.
(Sotheby's) $11,122

A figure of a bull in the style of Barbini, in standing stance, the clear glass with green acid-treated finish, 15½in. wide.
(Christie's) $1,447

René Lalique, statuette 'Suzanne Au Bain', after 1925, richly opalescent glass, molded as a standing female poised on one leg, 22.5cm.(Sotheby's) $15,249

'Perdix Inquiète' No.1241 a clear and frosted statue, molded mark *Lalique France,* 14.5cm. high.
(Christie's) $505

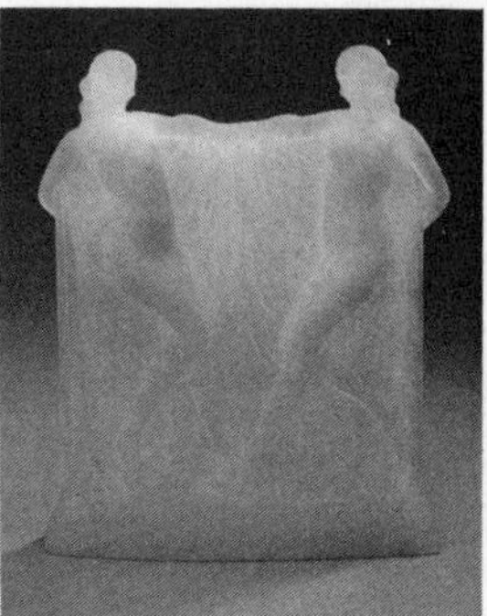

Marius-Ernest Sabino, statuette 'Double Suzanne', 1930s, opalescent, frosted glass, modelled as two dancing female figures draped in a large veil, 21.9cm.
(Sotheby's) $5,023

Lalique 'Printemps surtout Quatre Saisons', No.839bis, a frosted and blue stained statue, modelled as a naked classical female kneeling and surrounded by flowers, 19.5cm. high. (Christie's) $2,024

A pâte de verre sculpture, by Decorchement, circa 1920, stylized chameleon in shades of aubergine/purple with splashes of bright blue, 5¾in. maximum width.
(Christie's) $3,091

'Tête De Diane', a pâte de verre mask by Henry Cros, circa 1895, high-relief laurel-crowned head in naturalistic colors, 7¼in. high.
(Christie's) $7,314

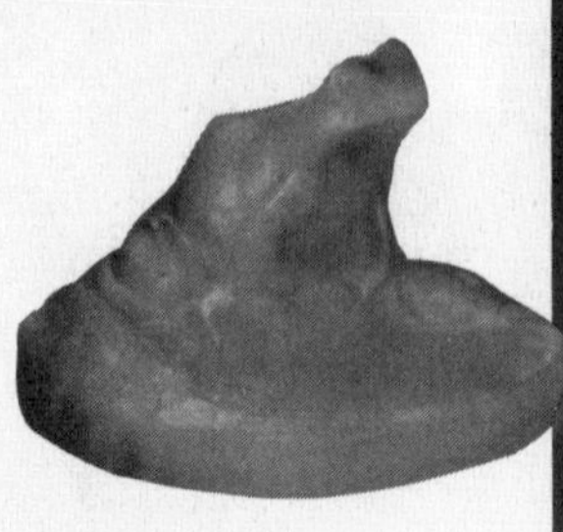

A pâte de verre paperweight by Daum, circa 1910, modelled with a frog seated on a rock amongst leaves and a snail, 3¼in. high. (Christie's) $2,194

Rare Frederick Carder cire perdue sculpture head of 'Ophelia', delicate form in opaque pink-beige glass with a sculpted marble quality, 4in. high. (Skinner) $6,900

'Moineau Moqueur' No.1167, a clear and frosted paperweight modelled as a sparrow, stencil mark *R. Lalique*, 8cm. high. (Christie's) $883

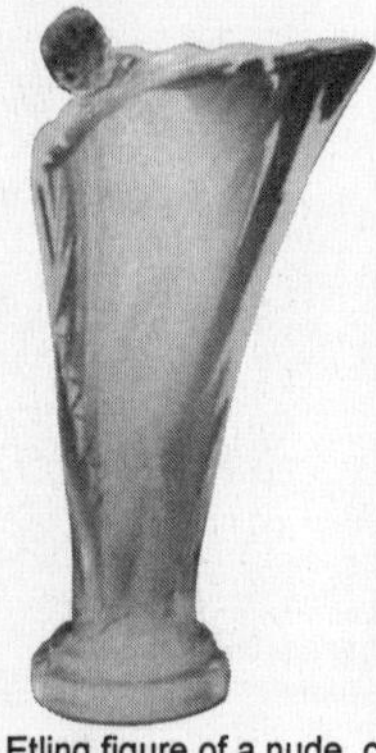

An Etling figure of a nude, circa 1925, opalescent glass modelled as a naked woman with her left arm outstretched backwards, 8in. (Sotheby's) $1,625

Pair of Steuben crystal fish, stylized version of angel fish, design by Frederick Carder and Sidney Waugh, 10½in. (Skinner) $1,495

Lalique figural group, two dancing female nude figures in frosted colorless glass on a textured colorless glass base, 10in. high. (Skinner) $546

A Lalique opalescent figure of Suzanne, modelled as a young woman with a large drape suspended from her arms, 8¾in. (Woolley & Wallis) $1,192

Loredano Rosin glass figure, of a kneeling nude female, agate-like effect in yellow, green, blue and brown glass, signed, 5¾in. high. (Skinner) $920

A Lalique post-war clear glass figure modelled as bust of a stylized horse, on a circular black glass base, etched marks, 48cm. high. (Christie's) $1,747

A small Baccarat pansy weight, mid-19th century, the purple and yellow flower with pink and white star center, with three green leaves showing behind, 2in. diameter.
(Christie's) $384

An English footed weight with badge of the King's Royal Rifle Corps with Battle Honours, 19th century, 11cm. high.
(Christie's) $158

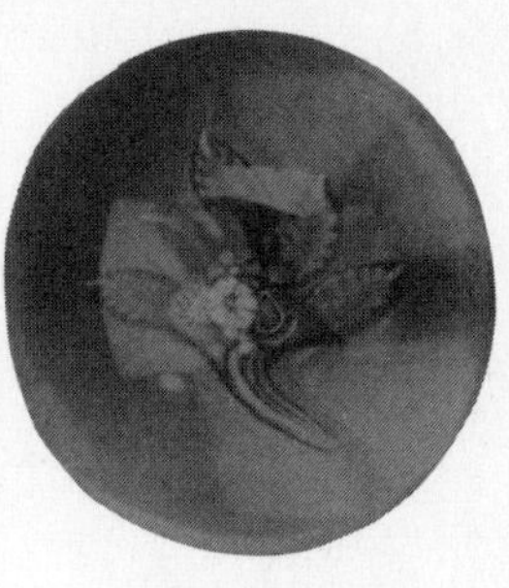

A St Louis clear ground posy weight, mid 19th century, set with four cane clusters set on five leaves with serrated edges joined by a thick stalk, 8.5cm.
(Bonhams) $248

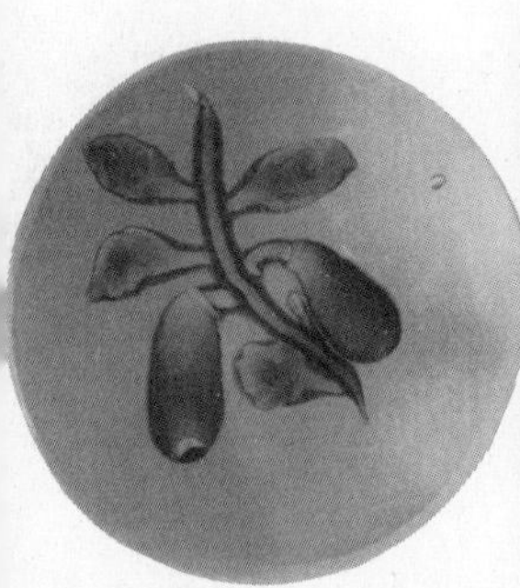

A Saint Louis pear weight, the clear glass set with two russet colored fruit growing from a long curved green branch, 6.6cm. diameter.
(Christie's) $2,530

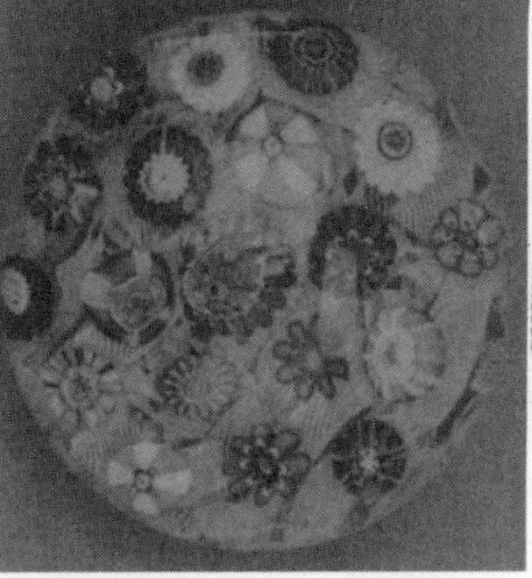

A Clichy millefiori on muslin ground weight, mid 19th century, the clear glass set with an assortment of brightly colored canes including a pink and green rose cane, 6.4cm.
(Bonhams) $744

A Baccarat pansy weight, mid-19th century, the purple and yellow flower with pink and white star centre, 2¾in. diameter.
(Christie's) $864

A St Louis pansy muslin ground weight dated *1980*, the flower formed with two upper violet and three lower yellow petals, 8.2cm.
(Bonhams) $310

A Baccarat flower weight, with a central white flower and bud with green leaves, within a ring of red and white canes, 2¾in.
(Woolley & Wallis) $1,192

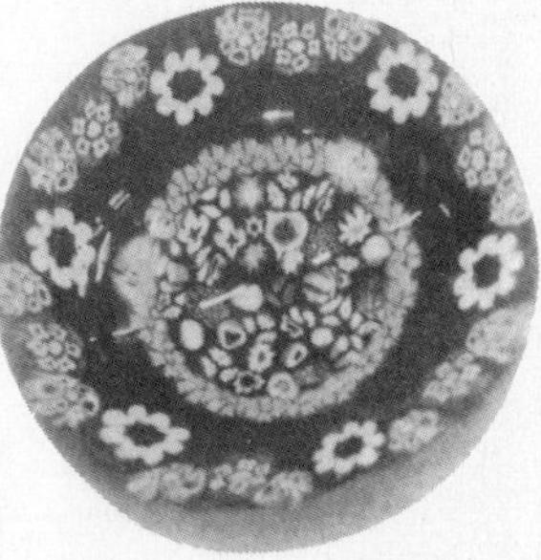

Large globular paperweight, the floating airdrop inset with colored cane circlets, the base below decorated with three radiating circlets of canes in blue, red and white, 2½in. (G.A. Key) $64

A Clichy pink flower weight, mid 19th century, the flower with five rounded pink petals with green sepals, 7.3cm. diameter. (Christie's) $2,180

A Baccarat garlanded butterfly weight, mid 19th century, the insect with a purple body, turquoise eyes and marbled wings, 6cm. diameter. (Christie's) $1,453

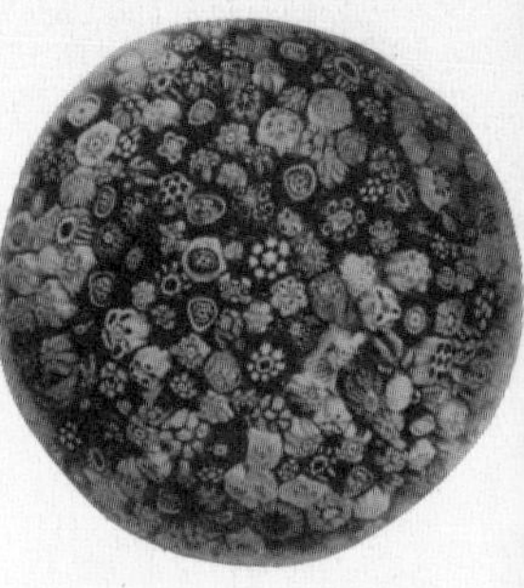

A Baccarat dated close millefiori weight, 1846, the closely packed brightly colored canes including one inscribed *B 1846*, 8cm. diameter. (Christie's) $1,543

A St. Louis faceted aventurine-ground flat bouquet weight, mid 19th century, the bouquet comprising a loose arrangement of flowers, 2¾in. diameter. (Christie's) $12,355

A Clichy three-color swirl weight, mid 19th century, the turquoise, pink and white staves radiating from a large central red white and blue cane, 3in. diameter. (Christie's) $1,308

A Bacchus close millefiori weight, mid 19th century, the closely packed large canes in predominant shades of white, blue and pink, 3½in. diameter. (Christie's) $2,725

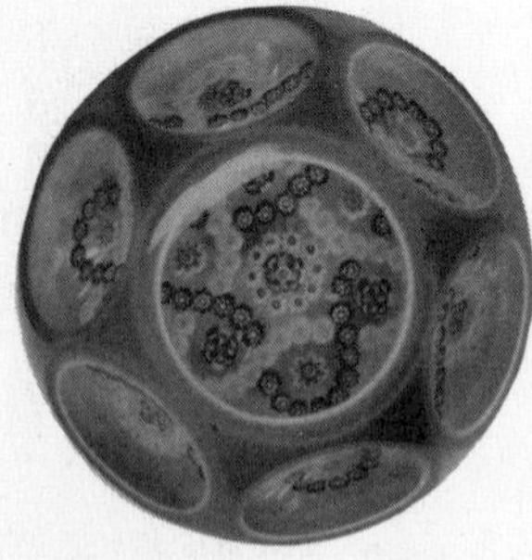

A Baccarat faceted double-overlay patterned millefiori weight, circa 1848, the central red, white and blue arrow's head setup within a circle of pink and white canes, 8cm. diameter. (Christie's) $3,088

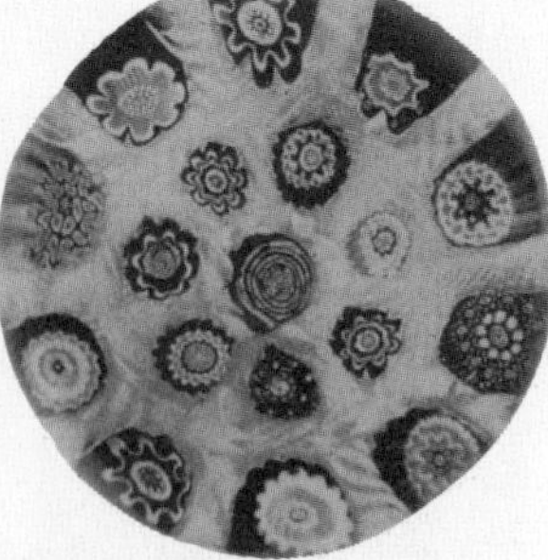

A Clichy spaced concentric millefiori checker weight, mid 19th century, the central pink rose within two circles of spaced brightly colored canes, 8cm. diameter. (Christie's) $1,453

A St. Louis faceted amber-flash posy weight, mid 19th century, the posy of five florettes in shades of salmon-pink, blue, orange and white, 7.3cm. diameter. (Christie's) $399

PITCHERS

Floret satin glass pitcher, possibly Mt. Washington, a cased glass pitcher of pink glass to a frosty colorless exterior, 6¾in. high.
(Skinner) $143

A cut gilt-metal-mounted ewer with shaped everted rim above fluted shoulder and diamond band, the tapering body cut with a broad spiral band, circa 1810, 26cm. high.
(Christie's) $1,641

Amberina pitcher, late 19th century, ovoid vessel of amber glass with inverted thumbprint decoration, shading to red at raised neck, 9in.
(Skinner) $115

PLATES

Lalique 'Poissons No.1' No.3056 a clear, frosted and opalescent plate, 31cm. diameter.
(Christie's) $686

Ten Lalique black alga plates and serving tray designed by Mark Lalique, France, circa 1950, black satin polished crystal with aquatic plant motif, tray 11in. diameter.
(Skinner) $632

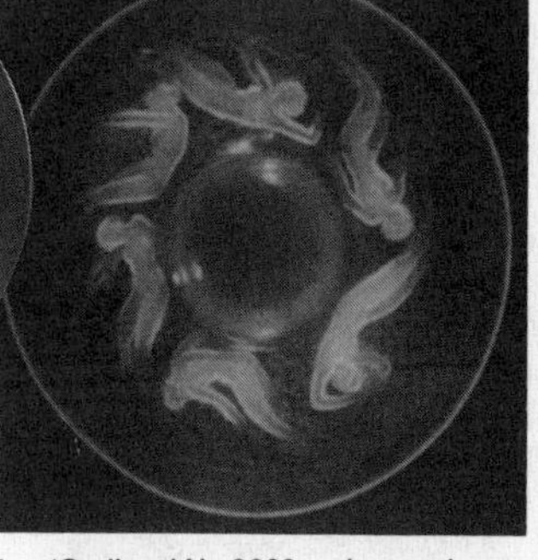

'Ondines' No.3003 a clear and opalescent plate, wheel-engraved *R.Lalique France*, 27.3cm. diameter. (Christie's) $2,166

SAND GLASSES

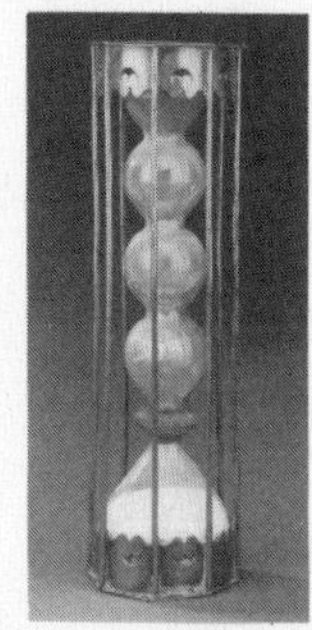

A rare 17th century five-bulb brass-cased sand glass, with one large and four interconnected smaller bulbs bound at the stem with waxed cord, 21.3cm. high.
(Christie's) $9,994

A rare 17th-century four double-bulb sand glass, the gilt-brass frame of rectangular polygonal form and finely engraved with strapwork, foliate decoration, 9in. wide.
(Christie's) $14,536

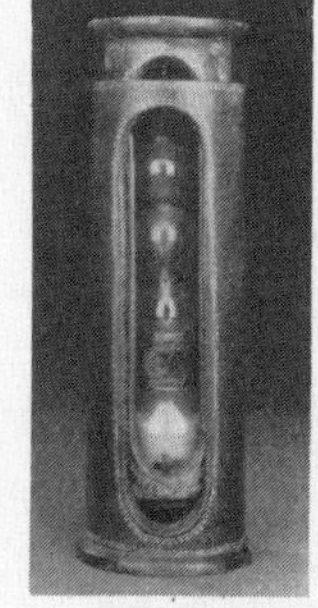

A rare late 17th century five-bulb hour glass, contained in a leather-covered wood sliding cylinder within an outer cylinder, 11¼in. high.
(Christie's) $12,719

A Victorian ruby tinted glass and silver mounted double-ended scent bottle, the bulbous covers embossed and chased with floral and leaf scroll ornament, 5in. (Canterbury) $442

An Apsley Pellatt sulphide scent-bottle and a stopper, circa 1830, of flattened oviform set with a sulphide portrait of King George IV, 5¼in. high. (Christie's) $2,543

A Victorian gold colored metal mounted white opaline glass scent bottle of waisted form, the oval panels decorated in gilt, 3¾in. high. (Canterbury) $694

A late Victorian silver topped scent bottle, the green flashed glass oval flattened body cut with palmettes and floral ornament, 5¼in. high, London 1897. (Canterbury) $536

A Lalique glass scent bottle of rectangular form with a molded pattern of ferns radiating from a central medallion decorated with the head of a woman smelling a flower, 10cm. high. (Bearne's) $1,416

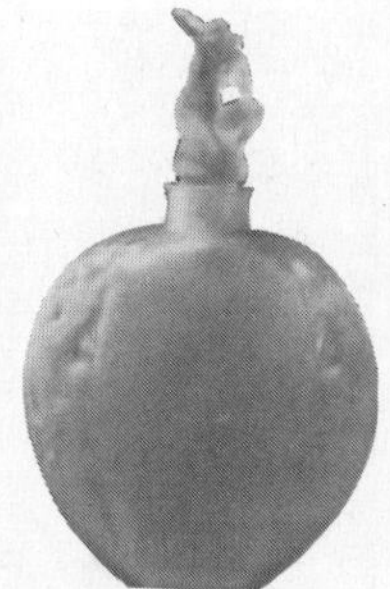

A Lalique flask vase and stopper 'Sirènes avec Bouchon Figurine', after 1920, frosted glass, the shoulders and sides of the flask molded with female nudes, 13¼in. (Sotheby's) $1,840

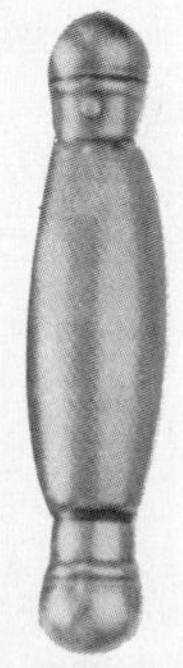

A good Victorian silver double-ended scent bottle with slightly bulbous body, one with folding cover, 5in., by T.J., London 1866. (Canterbury) $473

A pair of French green scent-bottles and stoppers, mid 19th century, the globular bodies gilt with scattered stars between gilt lines, 6½in. high. (Christie's) $399

A Victorian clear glass and silver-gilt mounted double-ended scent bottle with slice-cut cylindrical body, 5½in., by Samuel Mordan & Co. (Canterbury) $253

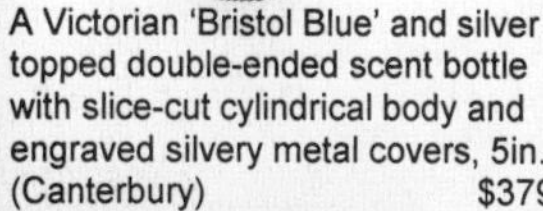

A Victorian 'Bristol Blue' and silver topped double-ended scent bottle with slice-cut cylindrical body and engraved silvery metal covers, 5in. (Canterbury) $379

A pair of Bohemian pale-green opaque cased scent bottles and stoppers of fluted bell-shaped form, cased in clear glass and gilt with bands of scrolls, circa 1860, 19.5cm. high. (Christie's) $911

A Victorian green tinted glass and gilt brass mounted double-ended scent bottle with slice-cut cylindrical body and plain gilt screw-on covers, 5in. (Canterbury) $189

An etched and enamelled glass perfume bottle and stopper, by Daum, circa 1900, the body in sky blue mottled glass etched and enamelled with a naturalistic landscape, 10.5cm. high. (Christie's) $3,477

A good Victorian silver-gilt topped double-ended scent bottle with heavy slice-cut clear glass cylindrical body, with one folding end, inset with turquoise, 5¼in. (Canterbury) $694

A Victorian silver mounted cut-glass scent bottle, with smoothed cut-glass body and silver hinged cover, 16.5cm. high, J. Gloster and Sons, Birmingham 1891. (Bearne's) $346

A Victorian gilt base mounted double-ended scent bottle with slice-cut bodies in ruby tinted glass and clear glass, 5¼in. (Canterbury) $457

'Naiades', a clear, frosted and sepia stained handbag scent bottle and stopper, of circular form with a molded design of maidens emerging from foliate tendrils, molded mark *Lalique*, 5.8cm. high. (Christie's) $920

A Victorian pale green tinted glass and gilt brass mounted double-ended scent bottle with slice-cut cylindrical body and plain folding covers, 5in.(Canterbury) $189

A Schuco monkey perfume bottle, German, circa 1920, metal framed bright green mohair monkey with brown felt ears, hands and feet, head lifts of to reveal glass bottle, 3½in. tall. (Bonhams) $869

A graduated set of three early 20th century French gilt metalware mounted scent or toilet water bottles, circa 1900, the largest 15cm. high. (Christie's) $922

A Victorian silver parcel-gilt and enamel scent bottle, the oval cylindrical base with two lidded compartments, 4½in. high, by E.S., London 1883. (Canterbury) $1,814

Lalique L'Air du Temps display bottle, France, model created 1947, spiral-ribbed bottle of colorless glass supporting a pair of doves in flight on stopper, total height 12¼in. (Skinner) $402

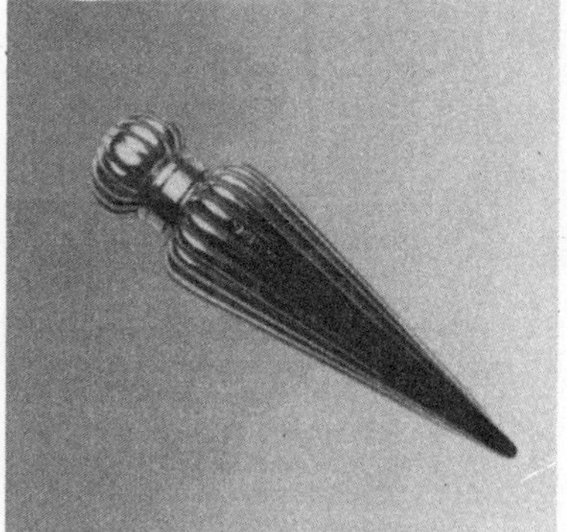

A Victorian scent bottle of tapering reeded form, with detachable stopper, Birmingham 1884, 8cm. long, in fitted case. (Bearne's) $396

A French silver and enamel mounted glass scent bottle, circa 1880, marks indistinct, baluster-shaped, the applied mounts cast and chased with shells, cartouches and putti, 4½in. long. (Christie's) $1,463

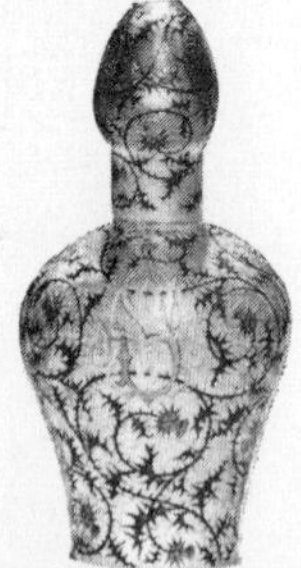

An enamelled glass scent bottle, stopper and cover, by Daum, circa 1900, the textured clear glass enamelled in red, black and gilt with allover design of thistles, 17cm. high. (Christie's) $905

Miss Dior, a Baccarat clear scent bottle, for Christian Dior, sealed with contents in presentation carton. (Bonhams) $480

Baccarat for Elizabeth Arden 'It's you', 1935, modelled in the form of a frosted hand with blue enamel ring, 6¼in. high. (Bonhams) $1,120

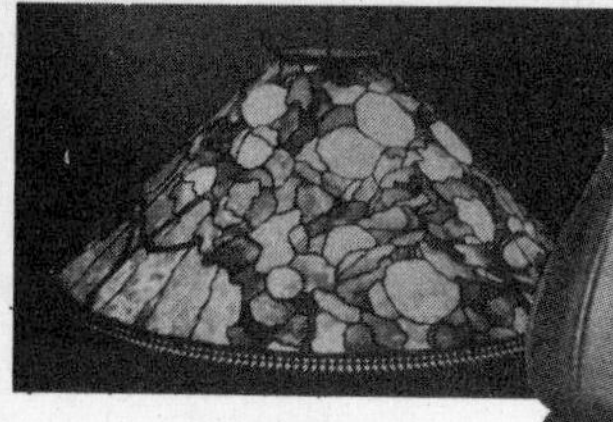

Tiffany 'Hydrangea' leaded glass and bronze chandelier shade, wide conical shade featuring abundant white mottled blossoms amongst variegated leaves, 11in.high. (Skinner) $68,500

Four Steuben Art Glass shades, gold aurene, shaped bell form with ten ribs, rims marked *Steuben*, 4½in. high. (Skinner) $747

Art Glass chandelier shade, America, early 20th century, patinated metal shade with radiating panels of progressive tiles, border panels with diamond motif and dropped apron, 13in. high. (Skinner) $2,300

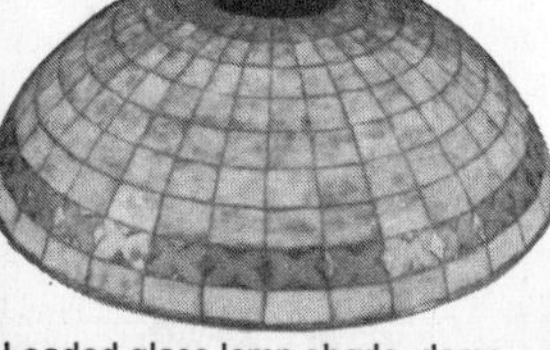

Leaded glass lamp shade, dome shade of mottled butterscotch and creamy slag glass segments with a border of butterscotch X's, 6¾in. high. (Skinner) $1,150

Tiffany bronze and amber linenfold glass shade, twelve-sided flared shade with amber glass panels bordered by rectangular matching drapery glass, 7¼in. high. (Skinner) $8,625

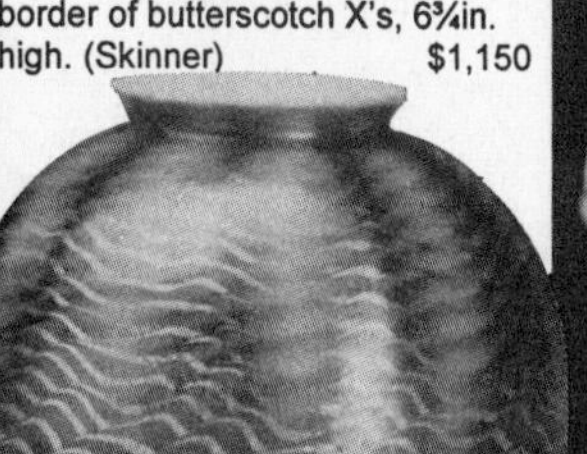

Tiffany favrile green optic rib shade, a ten-ribbed dome shade of white exterior decorated with green swirls highlighted with trailing gold iridescent ribbons, 7in. diameter. (Skinner) $3,737

'Champs-Elysees' No.2467, a Lalique frosted glass plafonnier, of spherical form, moulded in low relief with stylised foliage, 43cm. high. (Christie's) $1,656

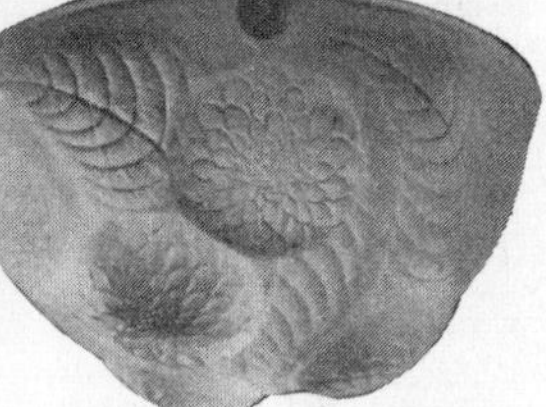

A Lalique plafonnier, 'Dahlia' design, circular and moulded in relief with flowers and foliage, 11¾in. (Woolley & Wallis) $880

Leaded glass chandelier, America, early 20th century, domed shade with scalloped crown of caramel slag glass, depicting Geishas crossing a bridge with swans on water, 15½in. high. (Skinner) $747

A cameo glass table lamp, by Gallé, circa 1900, the frosted grey glass internally mottled with yellow and overlaid in amethyst, 24cm. high. (Christie's) $5,797

Contemporary leaded glass sunflower chandelier, by Bauer Kopel, cone-shaped shade with undulating border, designed as sunflowers in naturalistic golds, yellows, and tans, signed, diameter 26in. (Skinner) $3,105

An engraved light baluster sweetmeat glass, the flared bowl with a border of stylized foliage, the stem with beaded knop, mid 18th century, 13cm. high. (Christie's) $727

A flat-cut sweetmeat glass, the ogee bowl and scalloped rim above diamond band and scale-cut lower section, mid 18th century, 15cm. high. (Christie's) $272

An engraved pedestal-stemmed sweetmeat glass, the flared bowl with a border of stylized foliage, above a compressed beaded knop and short octagonally-molded tapering stem, mid 18th century, 12cm. high. (Christie's) $763

TUMBLERS

A Baccarat cut cylindrical tumbler, mid 19th century, enamelled in colors on gilt foil with a flower-spray, 3¾in. high. (Christie's) $763

A bell-shaped mug, third quarter of the 18th century, with applied S-scroll ribbed handle, trailed decoration to the everted rim , 5½in. high. (Christie's) $199

An inscribed tumbler, circa 1785, of flared form and inscribed *R * Warton.* above closed lock gates, 12cm. high. (Christie's) $363

A Baccarat cut sulphide cylindrical tumbler, mid 19th century, the cylindrical sides set with a sulphide portrait of Louis Philippe, 3¾in. hide. (Christie's) $453

A Bohemian white overlay tumbler and stand, cut with gilt-line shaped panels and painted with sprays of flowers, gilt-line rims, circa 1880. (Christie's) $766

An early 19th century Sunderland tumbler engraved with a sailing ship passing beneath Sunderland Bridge, 4½in. high. (Christie's) $740

Emile Gallé, marqueterie-sur-verre vase, circa 1900, clear glass internally decorated with dichroic pale green/gray at the top, 3½in.
(Sotheby's) $13,496

A Lalique brown stained amber glass vase, catalogued 'Formosa', the globular body molded overall with carp, 16.5cm. high.
(Bearne's) $2,782

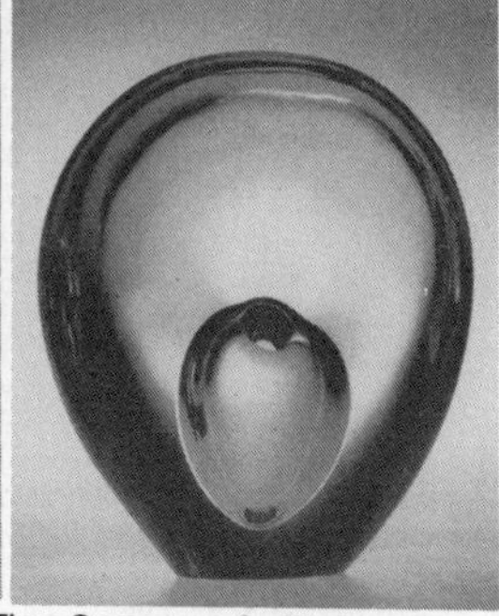

Timo Sarpaneva for Iittala, vase, 1950s, clear crystal with central aperture, 17cm.
(Sotheby's) $1,656

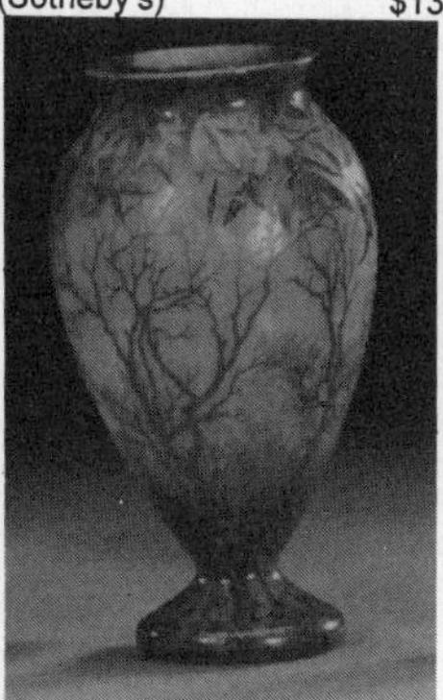

An etched and enamelled glass vase by Daum, circa 1900, the milky yellow glass streaked with dark violet and mottled amber, 8¼in. high.
(Christie's) $5,410

A pair of mounted glass vases, French, circa 1900, gourd-shaped, the iridescent glass surrounded by bronze mounts formed as cyclamen flowers, 12in. high.
(Christie's) $3,478

Daum, geometric vase, 1920s, gray glass internally mottled with orange and speckled with brown, overlaid with bright tangerine, mottled charcoal and chocolate brown, 13¾in. (Sotheby's) $7,176

A rare 'Penguin' cameo glass vase, by Gallé, circa 1925, the sky blue glass overlaid in white and matt black etched with penguins on an ice floe, 8½in. high.
(Christie's) $52,164

Loetz, iridescent vase, circa 1900, pink glass washed with pink/gold iridescence and decorated with green iridescent stripes and roundels, 15cm.
(Sotheby's) $2,153

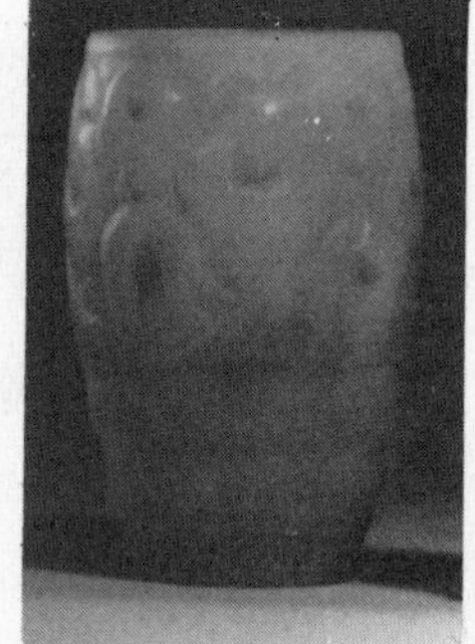

A pâte de verre vase by Alméric Walter and Jacques Adnet, circa 1920, in green molded with stylized flowers in yellow with a deep blue center, 6¼in. high.
(Christie's) $5,410

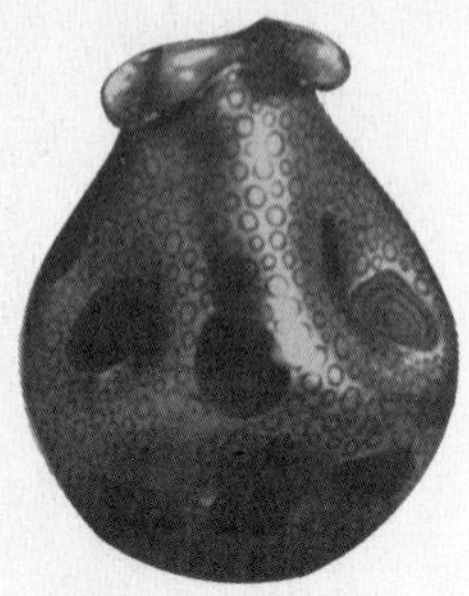

Austrian Art Glass vase, attributed to Koloman Moser for Loetz, colorless glass oval with tricorn ruffled rim and dimpled sides, 5in. (Christie's) $575

Steuben pink Cluthra vase, flared rim on broad oval body of rose, white and colorless surround. 10½in. high. (Skinner) $1,380

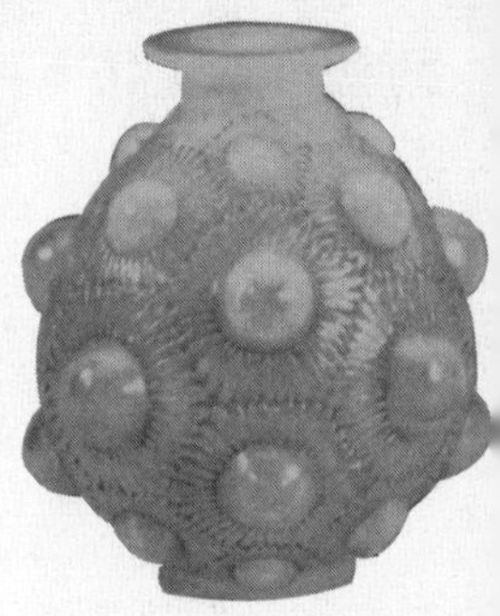

Réné Lalique opalescent daisy vase, mold blown vessel, floral surface with blue patina, 4¾in. high. (Skinner) $1,092

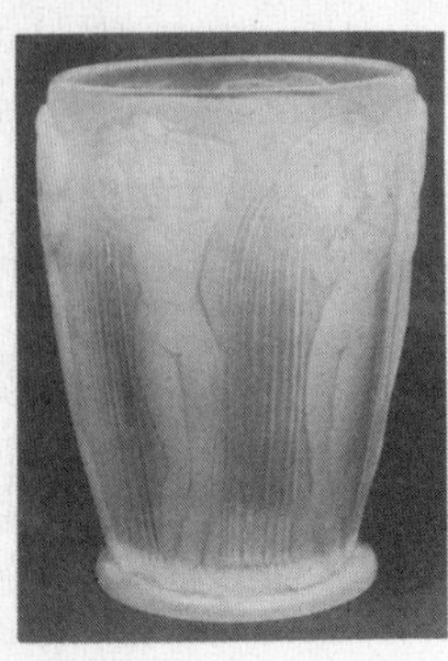

'Danaïdes'. A Lalique opalescent vase, the exterior molded with six naked young maidens with urns to the shoulders issuing water, 18.2cm. (Bristol) $1,544

René Lalique brilliant blue Perruches parrot vase, France, mold-blown as fourteen pairs of lovebirds perched on flowering branches, 10in. high. (Skinner) $8,050

Durand gold luster beehive vase, New Jersey, 1925, shape 1978, stepped form of amber glass with gold iridescent surface, 13in. high (Skinner) $920

Daum reticulated glass vase, mottled amber to dark orange glass blown in to Majorelle wrought iron armature, 12½in. high. (Skinner) $1,610

Rare Carder Steuben blue Aurene on yellow jade vase, broad oval body of yellow jade cameo etched with overall 'blanket of flowers' decoration.(Skinner) $9,775

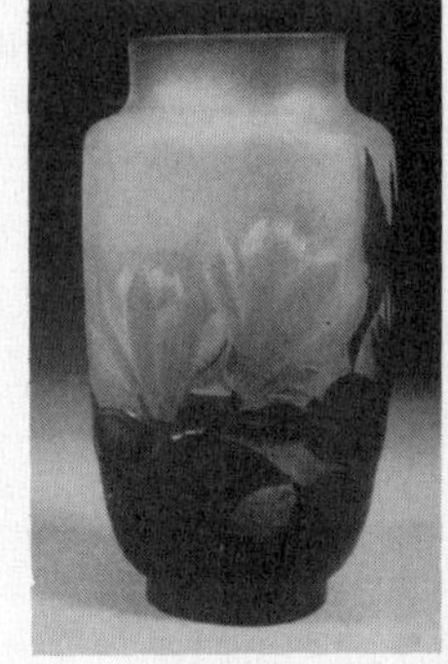

Gallé mold blown waterlily vase, frosted colorless oval shaded to teal, overlaid and molded with lime green, brown, and white, 10in. (Skinner) $12,65

New England Glass Company Pomona footed planter-form vase, blue cornflower and gold leaf border on etched first ground surface, 5½in. high.
(Skinner) $546

Daum, vase, circa 1905, gray glass internally mottled towards the base, overlaid with green, white, yellow and pink and with white flowering stems, 5¾in.
(Sotheby's) $4,485

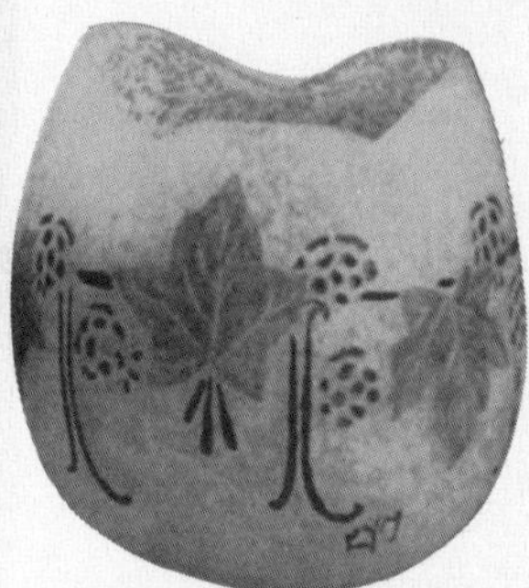

Legras Art Glass vase, cameo-etched mottled white and colorless broad vase with enamelled stylized grape arbor border, signed, 6in. high. (Skinner) $287

Art Glass vase, attributed to Durand, wide flared rim on oval body of iridescent blue glass with silvery blue threaded spider glass overlay, 7¼in. high.
(Skinner) $632

An Almeric Walter pâte-de-verre vase of trumpet form modelled by Henri Bergé, blue lower body and green upper, the latter decorated by a band of fir cones and leaves, 4in. high. (H.C. Chapman) $1,145

A Lalique vase 'Eucalyptus', after 1925, opalescent glass, molded with leaves, the seeds extending to form feet, 6¼in.
(Sotheby's) $1,534

A 19th century Daum pink glass vase, of oblong form, painted with a sepia winter landscape depicting figures by a lake, with gilt embellishment, 9¾in. high.
(Andrew Hartley) $1,134

A large cameo glass 'Hydrangea' vase, by Gallé circa 1900, creamy white body overlaid in shades of blue and deep indigo, finely etched with flowering hydrangea, 20in. high. (Christie's) $25,116

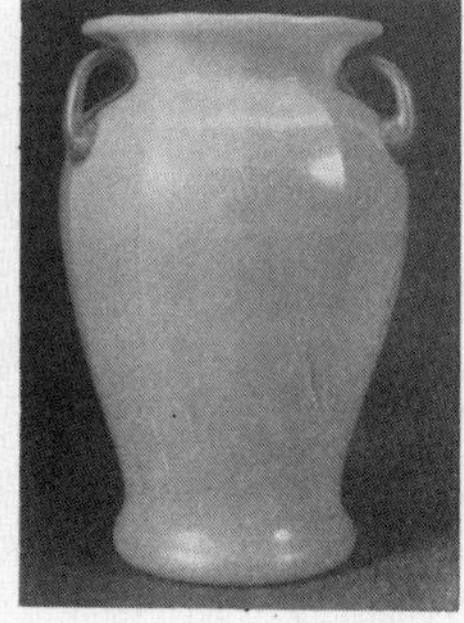

Carder Steuben Ivrene handled vase, ribbed urn-form body of lightly iridized ivrene glass with three applied aqua cintra handles, 11¼in. high. (Skinner) $1,380

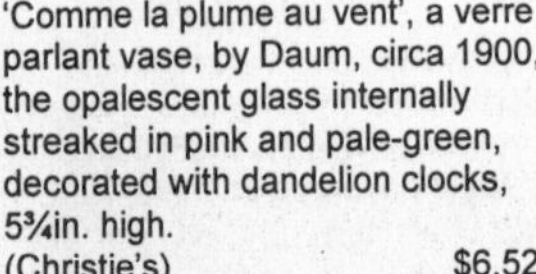

'Comme la plume au vent', a verre parlant vase, by Daum, circa 1900, the opalescent glass internally streaked in pink and pale-green, decorated with dandelion clocks, 5¾in. high.
(Christie's) $6,520

A cameo and carved glass vase by Daum, circa 1900, the gray glass internally mottled with yellow, overlaid in pinkish red, 13.6cm. diameter. (Christie's) $2,718

A Bohemian pale-ruby shell-shaped vase, possibly Moser, of lobed form, enamelled with panels of flowers and foliage reserved on a gilt ground, late 19th century, 17.5cm. high.
(Christie's) $729

'Marignane' No.10-895 a clear and frosted glass vase, stencil mark *R.Lalique France*, 23.5cm. high.
(Christie's) $3,250

A cameo glass vase by Schneider, circa 1925, the gray glass internally mottled with green and patches of yellow, overlaid in speckled reddish brown, 16.5cm. high.
(Christie's) $1,268

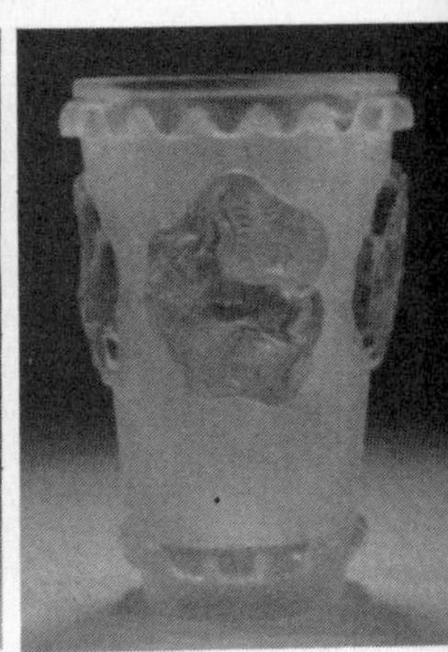

'Camargue' No.10-937 a clear, frosted and sepia-stained vase, stencil mark *R.Lalique France*, 28.5cm. high.
(Christie's) $4,333

A cameo 'Verre de Pekin' glass vase by Gallé circa 1900, of double gourd form, the opaque white glass overlaid in sealing wax red, 12cm. high. (Christie's) $2,899

'Soucis' No.1039 a clear, frosted and sepia-stained vase, engraved *R.Lalique France*, 15.8cm. high.
(Christie's) $1,264

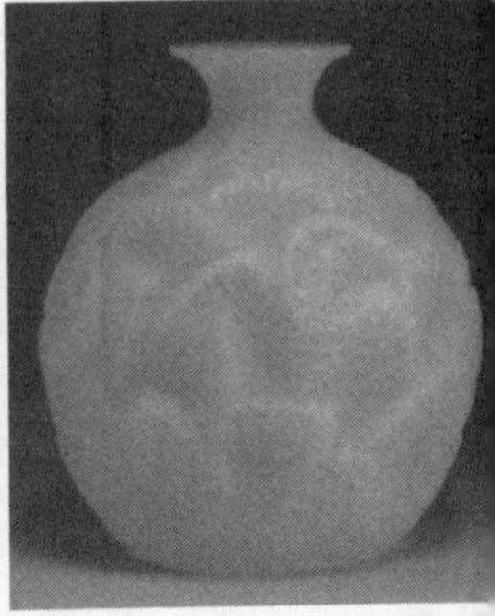

'Ormeaux' No.984 a cased opalescent vase, engraved *R.Lalique France No.984*, 17cm high. (Christie's) $1,083

An enamelled glass vase by Daum, circa 1910, the clear glass internally mottled with orange graduating to yellow towards base, etched and enamelled with a continuous winter landscape, 10cm. diameter.
(Christie's) $1,539

A pair of pale-amethyst enamelled and gilt two-handled vases, painted and gilt with birds, putti and stylized foliage, 62cm. high.
(Christie's) $3,646

A cameo glass vase by Gallé, circa 1900, the frosted gray glass overlaid in green and brown, acid-etched and carved with a continuous river landscape, 12.5cm. high.
(Christie's) $2,536

'aies' No.894 a clear, frosted and ue-stained vase, intaglio-molded *Lalique*, 26.5cm. high.
(Christie's) $5,055

'Sauterelles' No.888 an electric blue clear and frosted vase, engraved *R. Lalique*, 27cm. high.
(Christie's) $10,833

A cameo glass vase by Gallé, circa 1900, the frosted gray glass internally mottled with yellow and overlaid in cherry red, 7.5cm. high.
(Christie's) $996

ac De Come', a cameo glass se by Gallé, circa 1900, the sted gray glass internally mottled th yellow towards neck and base, erlaid in amethyst and blue, cm. high.
hristie's) $11,776

An enamelled glass vase by Daum, circa 1905, each side etched and enamelled in green and pinkish red with sprays of aquilegia and foliage, 15cm. high.
(Christie's) $4,892

A cameo 'peacock feather' glass vase by Daum, circa 1900, the aqua blue glass internally mottled with aubergine towards base, overlaid in green with patches of turquoise and indigo, 18.3cm. high.
(Christie's) $4,529

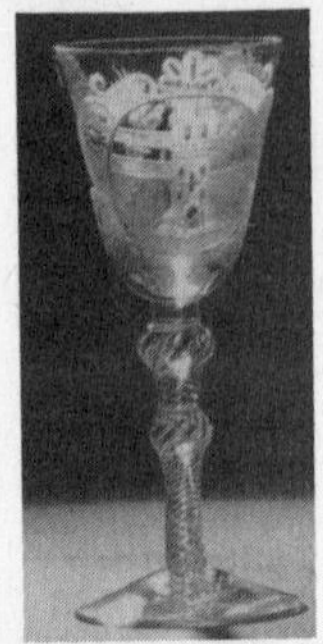

A Jacobite armorial airtwist goblet, mid 18th century, the funnel bowl engraved and polished with a coat-of-arms within a foliate-scroll cartouche, 7¼in. high.
(Christie's) $2,907

A baluster wine-glass, circa 1720, the flared funnel bowl with a solid lower part supported on a knop, 5¼in. high. (Christie's) $581

Josef Hoffmann for J. & L. Lobmeyer, drinking glass, 1912, clear glass, 18.8cm. (Sotheby's) $5,766

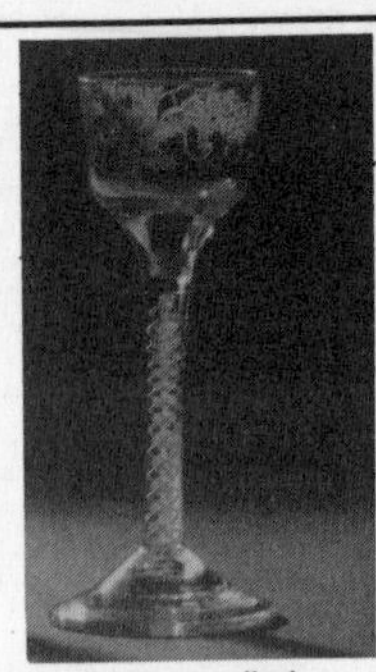

A Beilby enamelled opaque-twist wineglass, circa 1765, the stem with gauze corkscrew core enclosed within two spiral threads, 5½in. high.
(Christie's) $2,90

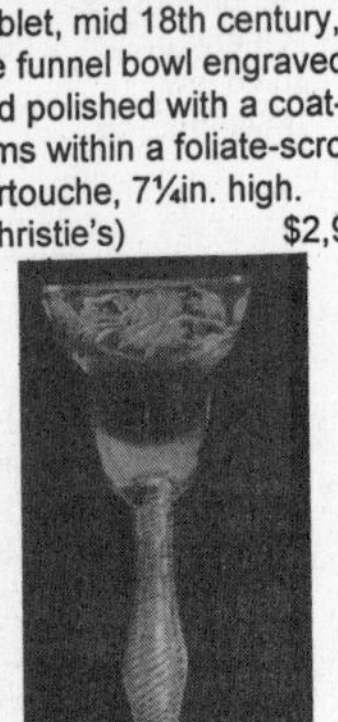

A Jacobite airtwist wineglass, circa 1750, the pan-topped bowl engraved with a border of flowers including a half-opened rose and two buds, 6¼in. high.
(Christie's) $1,543

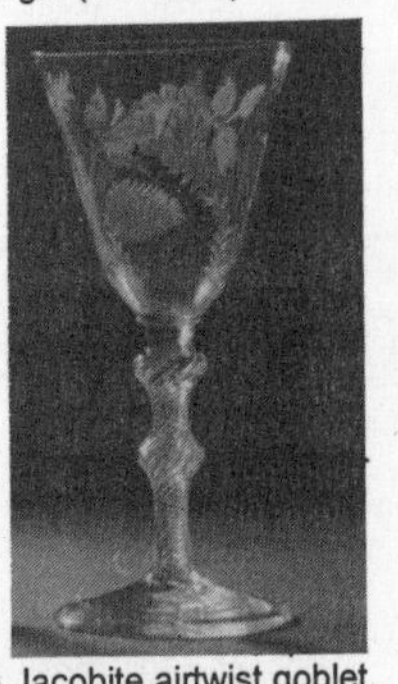

A Jacobite airtwist goblet, the glass circa 1750, the engraving later, the funnel bowl engraved and cut with a rose-spray, including a flower in profile and a bud, 7¼in. high.
(Christie's) $763

The Ogilvy of Inshewan 'Amen' glass, circa 1745, the bowl engraved in diamond point with the Crown, *JR* cipher, and with the first two verses of the Jacobite anthem.
(Christie's) $56,248

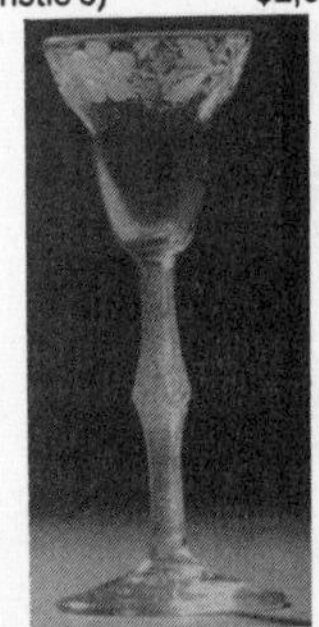

An engraved airtwist pan topped wineglass, circa 1750, the pan-topped bo engraved with a border c honeysuckle, carnation, sunflowers and fruiting-vine, 6¼in. high.
(Christie's) $5

An engraved facet-stemmed wineglass, circa 1785, the funnel bowl engraved and polished with a border of fruiting-vine and flowerheads, 5½in. high.
(Christie's) $399

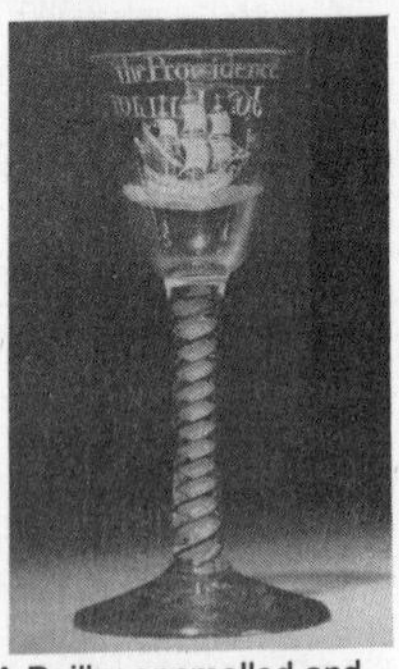

A Beilby enamelled and dated 'Privateer' color-twist wineglass, 1767, the funnel bowl enamelled in white with a three masted ship in full sail, 6¼in. high.
(Christie's) $47,242

A baluster wine-glass, circa 1725, the bell bowl with a solid lower part, supported on an angular knop and true baluster knop, 6in. high.
(Christie's) $1,362

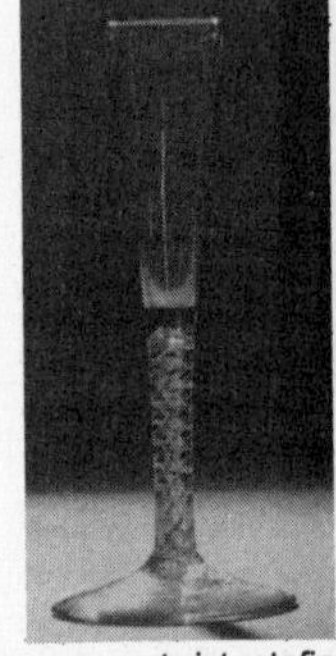

An opaque-twist ratafia-glass, circa 1765, the slender funnel bowl supported on stem with entwined double ribbon core 16.3cm. high.
(Christie's) $2,1

A composite-stemmed wine-glass, circa 1740, of drawn form, the slender bell bowl on a plain stem terminating in a basal knop, 6½in. high.
(Christie's) $908

An engraved color-twist wineglass, circa 1760, the ovoid bowl with a schematic flower-spray and a bird in flight, 5in. high.
(Christie's) $2,362

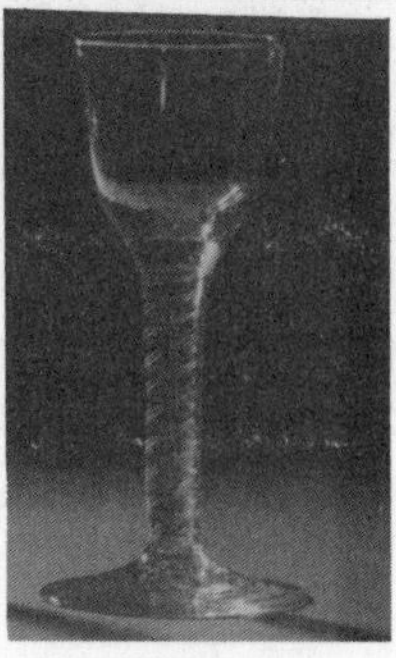

A color-twist wineglass, circa 1765, the stem with a single opaque thread core within a reddish-brown six ply spiral, 5¼in. high.
(Christie's) $1,817

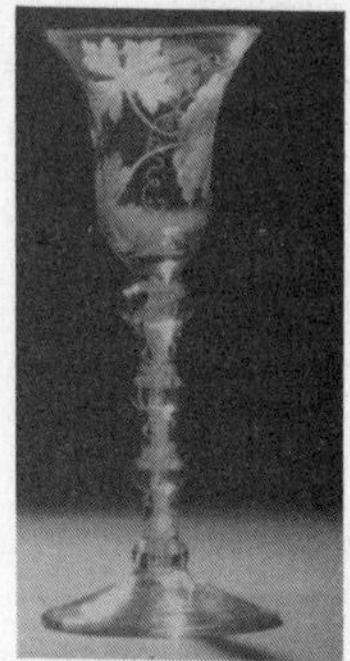

An engraved quadruple-knopped opaque-twist wineglass, circa 1765, the bell bowl with a branch of fruiting-vine and a bird in flight, 6¾in. high.
(Christie's) $2,180

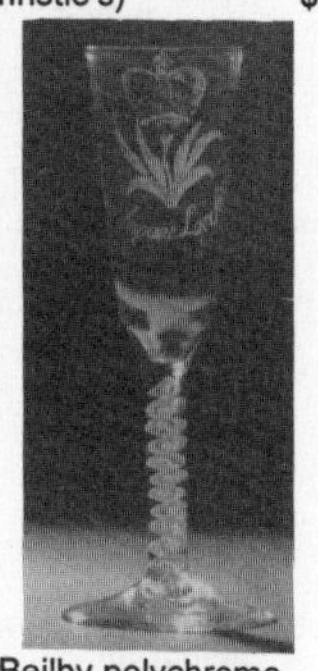

A Beilby polychrome enamelled opaque-twist ale-flute, circa 1765, enamelled in colors with flowering Scotch thistle beneath a Royal Crown, 19.5cm. high. (Christie's)
$19,078

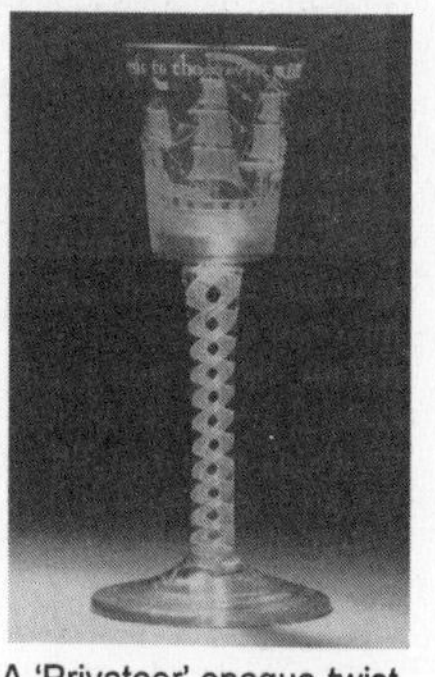

A 'Privateer' opaque-twist wine-glass, circa 1760, the slightly flared bucket bowl engraved with a ship in full sail and inscribed above *Succefs to the DEFIANCE Privateer*, 6in. high.
(Christie's) $13,627

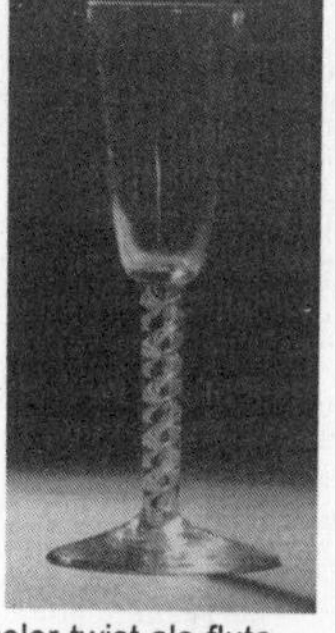

A color-twist ale-flute, circa 1765, the slender funnel bowl set on a stem enclosing an opaque flat ribbon spiral edged in translucent bright-red, 19cm. high.
(Christie's) $2,725

A color-twist pan-topped wineglass, circa 1765, the stem with a twisted opaque-white solid core enclosed within two entwined translucent sky-blue threads, 15.5cm. high.
(Christie's) $7,631

A Dutch-engraved light baluster goblet, circa 1760, the funnel bowl engraved with a rearing horse flanked by foliage-sprays, 7½in. high.
(Christie's) $1,543

A baluster goblet, circa 1710, the straight-sided flared funnel bowl with a solid lower part set on an inverted baluster stem, 17.5cm. high.
(Christie's) $2,725

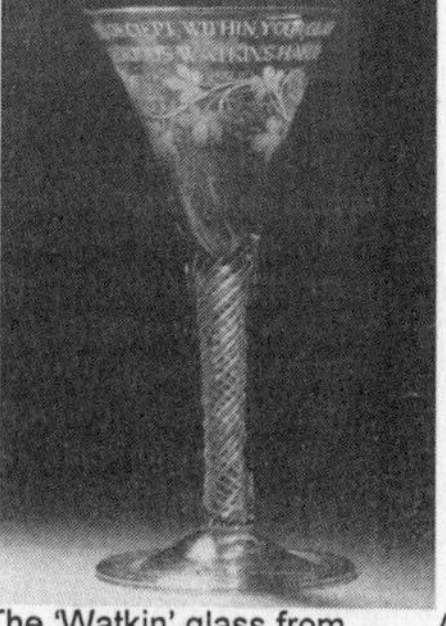

The 'Watkin' glass from Oxburgh Hall: an engraved airtwist goblet of Jacobite significance, circa 1750, the stem filled with spiral threads, 7½in. high.
(Christie's) $34,570

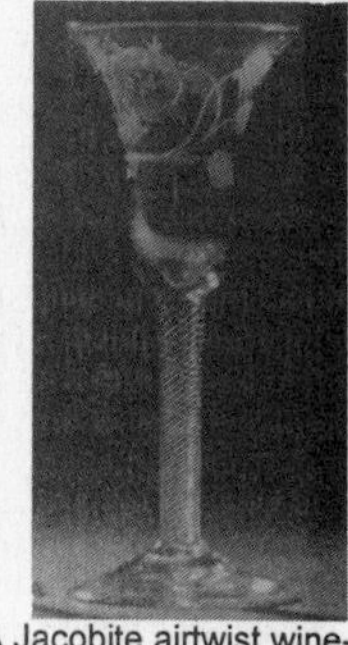

A Jacobite airtwist wine-glass, circa 1750, the generous bell bowl engraved with a rose and two buds, the reverse with a moth, 7in. high.
(Christie's) $1,053

G. Thomas, Paris, circa 1930, a 5in. diameter terrestrial table globe made up of twelve chromo-lithographed gores and two polar calottes, 11in. high. (Christie's) $515

Malby, London, 1844, a 3¼in., diameter miniature terrestrial globe, in a turned fruitwood case with domed lid, 4in. high. (Christie's) $2,576

John & William Cary, London, 1800, a 12in. diameter terrestrial table globe, raised on four mahogany quadrant supports, 25in. high. (Christie's) $4,784

Gabriel Wright, (1740-1803) and William Bardin, (1740-1798), London, a 12in. diameter celestial globe, on four mahogany supports to carved and turned pillar, 24in. high. (Christie's) $8,832

A pair of George III 18in. globes on mahogany stands in their George III display-cases, by George Adams Senior, circa 1765, the globes: 32½in. high. (Christie's) $321,195

A 7in. diameter brass Indo-Persian celestial globe, with two engraved quadrant supports and engraved horizon ring raised on four baluster turned legs to cruciform base, 10¾in. high. (Christie's) $1,011

Forest J. Paris, circa 1890, a 3in. diameter miniature brass terrestrial globe, the interior of the sphere half-filled with coarse stuffing, resting on a baluster turned fruitwood stand, 5¼in. high. (Christie's) $552

Newton & Son, London, 1851/2, a 12in. diameter terrestrial table globe made up of twelve hand-colored engraved gores and two polar calottes, raised on three baluster turned fruitwood legs, 18½in. high. (Christie's) $6,992

Gerard Valk, Amsterdam, 1707, 15in. diameter terrestrial table globe made up of two sets of eighteen hand-colored engraved gores, on a Dutch-style mahogany stand, 24in. high (Christie's) $21,160

Heinrich Kiepert, Berlin, an 8in. diameter terrestrial table globe made up of twelve colored printed paper gores, raised on an ebonized tripod stand, 18½in. high.
(Christie's) $2,760

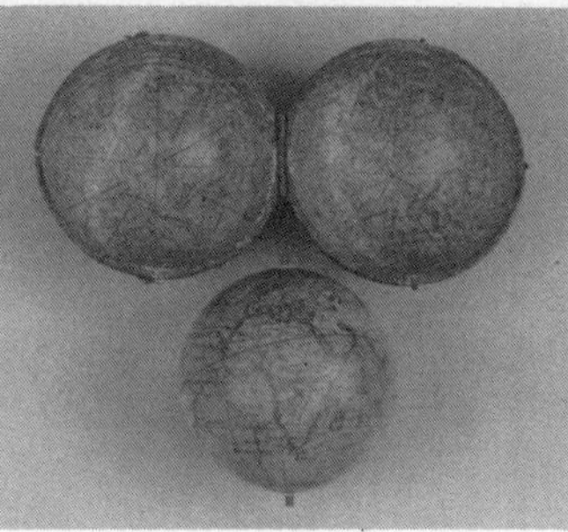

Joseph and James Cox, London, 1835, a 3in. diameter terrestrial pocket globe made up of twelve hand-colored engraved gores and one polar calotte.
(Christie's) $5,888

Jan Felkl & Son, Rostok, circa 1888, a 13in. diameter terrestrial table globe, raised on ebonized wire support and turned ebonized column, 22in. high.
(Christie's) $643

Faustino Paluzie Mir, Barcelona, circa 1924, an unusual 15¾in. diameter Spanish terrestrial library globe, the fruitwood horizon ring with two moving catches to hold the globe, 32in. high.
(Christie's) $4,600

John & William Newton, London, 1824, a pair of 12in. diameter terrestrial and celestial table globes, supported by three ebonized baluster turned legs united by stretchers, 18½in. high.
(Christie's) $13,800

C. Abel-Klinger, Nuremburg, a 6in. diameter terrestrial globe made up of twelve colored printed gores, on a baluster turned fruitwood column and plinth base, 12½in. high, circa 1905.
(Christie's) $736

C. Abel-Klinger, Nuremburg, a 4in. diameter miniature terrestrial globe made up of twelve chromolithographed paper gores and two polar calottes, 8in. high, circa 1860. (Christie's) $1,195

Shibukawa Harumi (1639-1715), a terrestrial globe, the image of the world painted on leather over a wooden base, diameter 55cm., the earliest dated Japanese globe, 1670.
(Christie's) $358,830

Gunnar Saitz, Stockholm, a 13in. diameter terrestrial table globe made up of twelve color printed paper gores and two polar calottes,19in. high.
(Christie's) $1,472

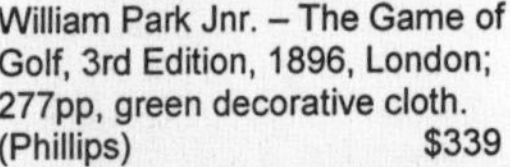

William Park Jnr. – The Game of Golf, 3rd Edition, 1896, London; 277pp, green decorative cloth.
(Phillips) $339

An Edwardian four piece egg cruet, the central dimple golf ball rising above a cylindrical column over a circular base.
(Phillips) $216

Francis Bowler Keene, Lyrics of The Links; Poetry, Sentiment and Humor of Golf, 1st Edition, New York, 1923. 126pp, decorative cloth. (Phillips) $370

Horace Hutchinson (Ed) – British Golf Links: A Short Account of The Leading Golf Links in the United Kingdom; 1st Trade Edition, London, 1897.
(Phillips) $1,385

A Life Association of Scotland Calendar for 1905, showing the Amateur Golf Championship at Sandwich 1904.
(Phillips) $554

Unknown artist (circa 1925), Gleneagles: The Golfing Girl, a fine London Midland & Scottish Railway poster, entitled 'On the Hinny Mune', lithograph printed in colors, 39¾ x 29¾in.
(Sotheby's) $5,741

Bernard Darwin, The Golf Courses of The British Isles, 1st Edition, London, 1910, 254pp (uncut) green cloth, gilt, illustrations by Harry Rountree. (Phillips) $770

Horace G. Hutchinson, The Badminton Library, Golf, 1st Edition, London 1890, 463pp, brown decorative cloth.
(Phillips) $277

A photographic print of Old Tom Morris, by James Patrick, Edinburgh, showing Old Tom in traditional pose at St. Andrews, published by Geo. Stewart & Co., 13 x 10in.(Sotheby's) $986

Harold Simpson, The 7 Stages of Golf and Other Golf Stories in Picture and Verse, first American edition, colored illustrations by G.E. Shepheard, 1909.
(Sotheby's) $1,165

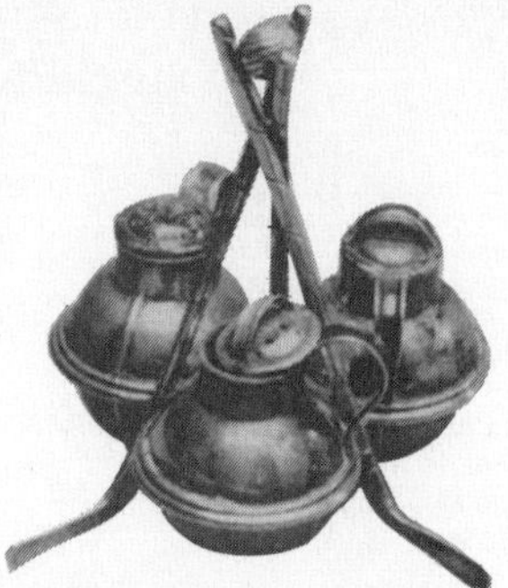

A late Victorian silver condiment set, in the form of mesh gutty balls, the handles as crossed clubs united by a ball, by Walker and Hall, Birmingham 1899.
(Phillips) $231

W.W. Tulloch, The Life of Tom Morris, With Glimpses of St. Andrews and its Golfing Celebrities, 1st Edition, London, 1908, 334pp.
(Phillips) $1,771

Robert Clark, Golf: A Royal and Ancient Game, 1st (Trade) Edition (Small paper), Edinburgh 1875; Green decorative cloth, gilt; 284pp *Presented to Jack Westland, United States Amateur Champion.*
(Phillips) $924

A fully autographed British Ryder Cup team photograph, 1937, together with and unsigned photograph of the United States team, 8 x 10in.
(Sotheby's) $1,435

Unknown artist (circa 1925), Gleneagles: The 'Bogey' Man, a fine London Midland & Scottish Railway poster, entitled 'On the Kittle Kink' lithograph printed in colors, 39¾ x 29¾in.
(Sotheby's) $5,023

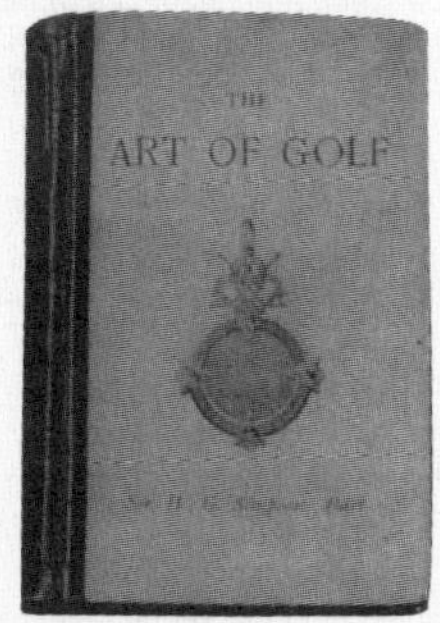

Sir W.G. Simpson – The Art of Golf, 2nd Edition (Revised), 1892; Quarter green calf, cream illustrated boards.
(Phillips) $524

Robert K. Risk – Songs of The Links, 2nd (First Illustrated) Edition, London, 1919 (Illustrated by H.M. Bateman); 78pp, green cloth.
(Phillips) $123

Gene Sarazen – Thirty Years of Championship Golf: The Life and Times of Gene Sarazen; 1st Edition, New York, 1950, 276pp, cloth, signed.
(Phillips) $400

After Allen C. Sealy, A Crucial Putt, Pau, 1893, a rare photogravure, signed in pencil on mount, 11¼ x 17in. (Sotheby's) $2,512

A Chambers patent golf ball marker circa 1910, patent no. 18712, in good working order. (Sotheby's) $787

After Allen C. Sealy, The First Tee, Pau, 1893, a rare photogravure, signed in pencil on the mount, 11¼ x 17in. (Sotheby's) $2,512

A Bobby Jones stereoscopic 3D viewer, circa 1930, with nine monochrome stereographic photograph viewcards of Jones in various stages of swings. (Sotheby's) $897

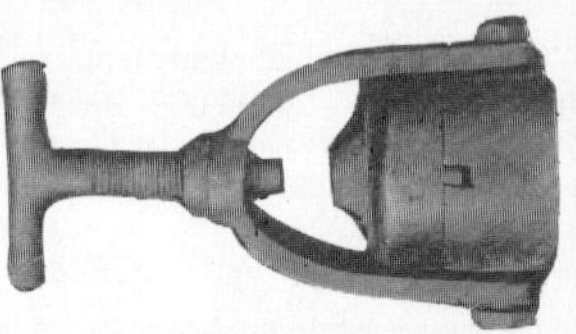

A mesh gutty ball press with side clamps, stamped *Patent No.11917*, John White & Co., Edinburgh. (Phillips) $2,464

A rare photograph of professional golfers, circa 1860, with Old Tom and young Tom Morris, Willie Park, Charles Hunter, Walter MacDonald and David Strath, the image 7 x 9in. (Christie's) $9,840

BALLS

A Tom Morris feather ball, circa 1850, marked *T. Morris*, approximately 42mm. diameter. (Sotheby's) $19,734

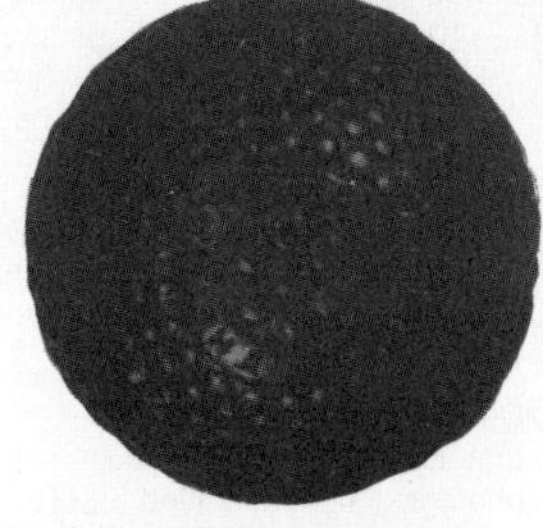

The Opresto 27½ gutty ball circa 1901, by Bridgestone Gun & Instrument Company, Conn., unpainted. (Sotheby's) $843

A rare John Sharp feather ball, circa 1850, marked *J. Sharp 30*, approximately 46mm. diameter. (Sotheby's) $19,734

An Allan Robertson feather ball, circa 1840, marked *Allan 29*, approximately 44mm. diameter. (Sotheby's) $10,764

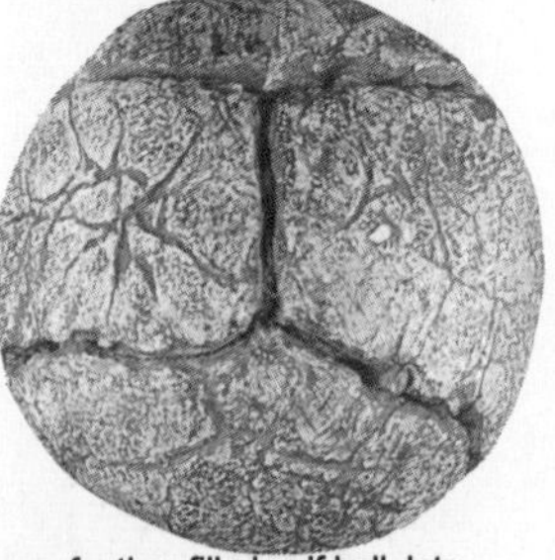

A rare feather-filled golf ball, late 18th/early 19th century, with stitched seams and painted cover, with one small hole to the leather cover, 2½in. diameter. (Christie's) $14,760

A Spalding Tour Edition Shark ball, used by Greg Norman to hole out to win the Open Championship, Turnberry, 1986 and signed by him. (Sotheby's) $2,332

A Tom Morris, St. Andrews, long nosed putter, circa 1890, with stained beech head and hickory shaft. (Sotheby's) $1,615

An unnamed long nosed driver, circa 1870, the boxwood head with no horn, hickory shaft. (Sotheby's) $986

An R. Forgan scared head mallet putter, circa 1895, the dogwood head stamped with Prince of Wales feathers. (Sotheby's) $574

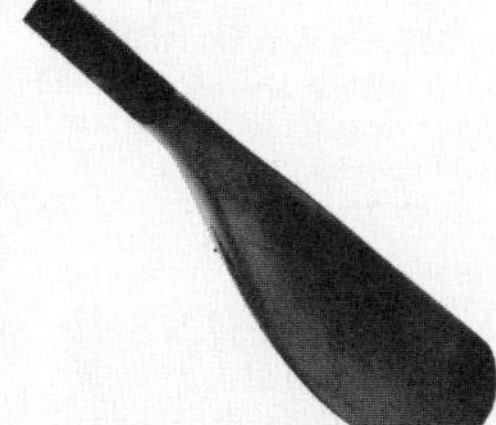

A Lunn & Co. long nosed putter, circa 1890, with beech head and hickory shaft. (Sotheby's) $610

An Urquhart's Patent adjustable iron, circa 1905, No. 1836, with hickory shaft. (Sotheby's) $1,524

A fine early putter, circa 1800, possibly by McEwan, with large thorn head and hickory shaft. (Sotheby's) $17,043

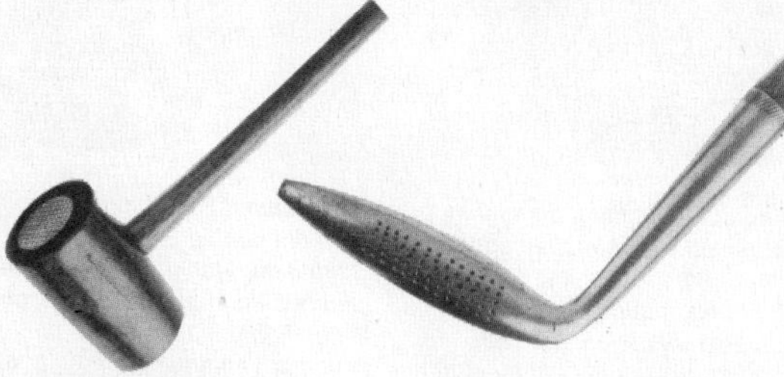

An unusual cylindrical putter, the shaped cylindrical head stamped *A. McQuaker*, with horn face insert, with hickory shaft. (Sotheby's) $1,524

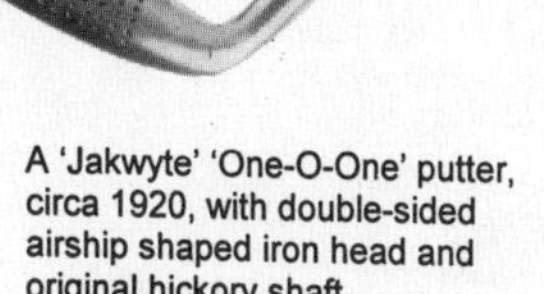

A 'Jakwyte' 'One-O-One' putter, circa 1920, with double-sided airship shaped iron head and original hickory shaft. (Sotheby's) $3,947

A Lillywhite's wooden faced putter, by Spence & Gourlay, St. Andrews, circa 1920, with wry neck and hickory shaft, with square cross-section grip. (Sotheby's) $807

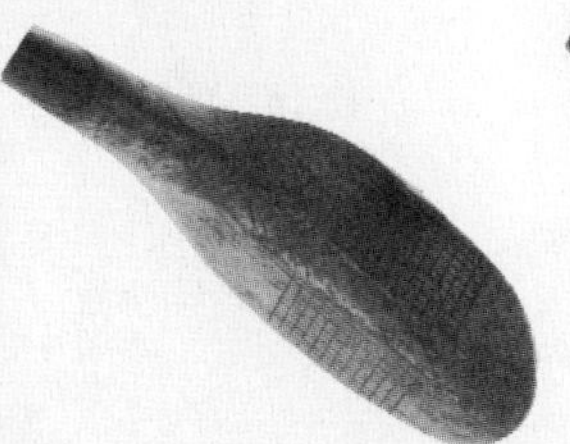

A Standard Golf Company of Sunderland Patent Duplex 'iron', circa 1920, RL2 model, with aluminum head and hickory shaft. (Sotheby's) $431

An unnamed 'ball' putter, circa 1912, the aluminum head and hickory shaft, stamped *Murray Lurcock, Maidstone Special.* (Sotheby's) $627

A Strath, St. Andrews long nosed putter, also stamped *Beveridge*, circa 1875, with thorn head and hickory shaft. (Sotheby's) $6,458

A Columbia Graphophone mahogany table gramophone, with original soundbox and screw-in mahogany horn.
(Auction Team Köln) $1,875

A horn gramophone with gold decorated red horn, circa 1910.
(Auction Team Köln) $669

The 20th Century Columbia Graphophone, large model with outsize sound box and 121cm. long brass horn, circa 1905.
(Auction Team Köln) $3,215

An HMV Model 460 Diaphragm Lumière with Plissée-paper membrane table gramophone, rare model produced for only 18 months. Few of the paper speakers have survived. 1924.
(Auction Team Köln) $2,143

A good 1930s Ginn mahogany veneered table top gramophone with Collaro motor and patent no. 18771 reproducer arm, with massive papier mâché horn.
(David Lay) $977

A miniature Trumpf portable gramophone by Biedermann & Czarnikow, Berlin, brown leather covered wooden case, with original Bing 'Pigmynette' disc.
(Auction Team Köln) $147

A Gramophone & Typewriter Ltd. gramophone, English, circa 1910, with 24cm. turntable, 'W' soundbox and green flower petal horn.
(Bonhams) $461

A Soviet miniature Cameraphon gramophone, in the form of a folding camera, after the Thorens 'Excelda', tin case with textured green paint. (Auction Team Köln)
$214

An HMV Model 194 re-entrant tone chamber gramophone with four-spring motor No. 34 and 5a soundbox, in mahogany case, 44½in. high, 1928.
(Christie's) $1,655

A Columbia disk graphophone, Type BH ('Champion'), with green flower horn, needle-clamp soundbox, single spring motor and oak case.
(Christie's) $1,104

An Edison Bell Discaphone with unusually placed tin horn, painted as imitation wood, two doors at front for sound regulation, circa 1920.
(Auction Team Köln) $1,004

An HMV Monarch gramophone, 1911 model, with double-spring motor, oak case and fluted oak horn. (Christie's) $2,024

An Edison Bell Electron cabinet gramophone, with Electrotone Super soundbox, gilt fittings, internal horn enclosed by doors and chinoiserie lacquer finish, 45in. high, circa 1928.
(Christie's) $1,379

An E.M. Ginn Expert Junior gramophone, with papier mâché horn and four-spring Expert soundbox, in oak case, the horn 24in. diameter.
(Christie's) $2,024

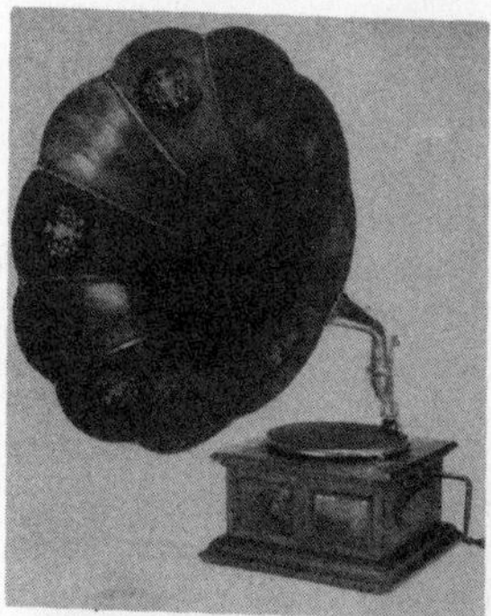

A horn gramophone with large petalled wood horn, the case adapted from an HMV Model VI hornless gramophone, now with Paillard motor and Phoenix soundbox, the horn 28½in. diameter. (Christie's) $994

A very rare Hutschachtel ('hat box') table gramophone by the Gramophone & Typewriter Co., London, with folding tin cover and integral wooden speaker, circa 1920.
(Auction Team Köln) $301

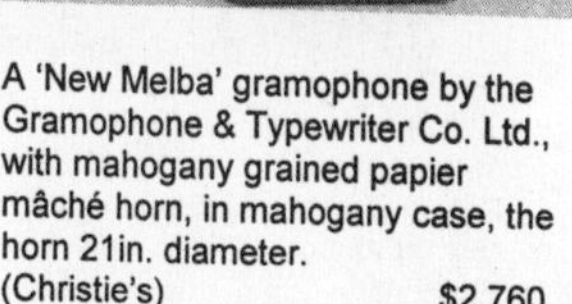

A 'New Melba' gramophone by the Gramophone & Typewriter Co. Ltd., with mahogany grained papier mâché horn, in mahogany case, the horn 21in. diameter.
(Christie's) $2,760

A Russian miniature table gramophone, linen lined wood case, with 11 25cm. Russian shellac disks, in wood carrying case. (Auction Team Köln)
$200

The Mother of God of Tenderness, called Korsun, Russia, Moscow School, 15th century, shown half-length in sombre colors, 31.2 x 25.1cm.
(Christie's) $19,205

Russian icon of the Mother of God Kazanskaya, 19th century, Moscow School, 12¼in. high.
(Skinner) $172

Saints John the Evangelist and Prokhor, Russia, 15th century, the Evangelist seated looking behind him dictates his Gospel to Prokhor, 49 x 36.5cm.
(Christie's) $14,404

Northern Greek icon of St. Philippos, probably from the top of an iconostasis, late 17th century, 17in. high.
(Skinner) $2,530

Mother of God 'of the Playful Child', Russia, Moscow School, 16th century, the Mother of God in a dark brown gilt highlighted maphorion with green lining, 13 x 10½in.
(Christie's) $9,218

Saint Nicholas the Wonderworker, Russia, Moscow School, 16th century, shown shoulder-length, painted in bright colors on gilt ground, 15 x 12.5cm.
(Christie's) $13,444

The Pokrov and Eight Chosen Saints, North Russia, 16th century, the Feast of the Protecting Veil of the Mother of God surrounded by saints, 11 x 9½in.
(Christie's) $8,642

Russian icon of Pokrov, late 18th/early 19th century, Moscow School, Hymn of Exultation to the Mother of God, 12¼in. high.
(Skinner) $632

The Mother of God of the Sign, Russia, early 19th century, the Mother of God shown half-length with her hands raised in prayer, 62 x 53.3cm.
(Christie's) $4,225

A three-case inro, signed *Masanari*, late 18th/early 19th century, with black lacquer ground; decoration in gold and silver, with a wolf prowling behind susuki, 2½in. long. (Christie's) $3,947

A four-case lacquer inro, signed *Kajikawa Yoshinobu Saku*, Edo Period (late 18th century), decorated with a temple overlooking a lake in front of Mt Fuji, the inro 3¼in. high. (Christie's) $2,608

A four-case inro, signed *Koma Koryu Saku,* Edo Period (18th century), decorated with two karashishi in takamakie, 3³/8in. high. (Christie's) $3,726

A three-case inro, signed *Koma Kyuhaku*, late 18th/early 19th century, with black lacquer ground almost entirely covered in decoration of red, gold and silver hiramaki-e and takamaki-e with gold foil mosaic, 3¼in. long. (Christie's) $39,468

A two-case inro, signed *Koma Kansai*, Edo Period (mid-19th century), of exceptionally large size and circular form; black lacquer ground; decoration in gold, silver and colored hiramaki-e and togidashi-e, Kansai, 4in. long. (Christie's) $46,644

A four-case inro, unsigned, 19th century, with gold kinji lacquer ground; decoration in gold and silver hiramaki-e and takamaki-e, on one side a group of Chinese musicians playing on the back of a caparisoned elephant, 8.4cm. long. (Christie's) $8,970

A fine three-case inro shaped as a wooden barrel, signed *Kakosai* and *Nakayama*, Edo Period, (19th century), the togidashi ground simulating wood grain, inlaid in Shibyama style with Shoki seated, 2⁷/8in. (Christie's) $13,972

A three-case inro, signed *Masanari*, late 18th/19th century, with gold lacquer ground; decoration in black and polychrome togidashi-e, with a herdboy sleeping on his basket by a recumbent ox, 3¼in. long. (Christie's) $10,764

A three-case inro, signed *Kajikawa Saku* and *Chu*..., Meiji Period (late 19th century), decorated in Shibayama style and gold hiramakie, takamakie, togidashi and kirikane, with three figures. (Christie's) $5,962

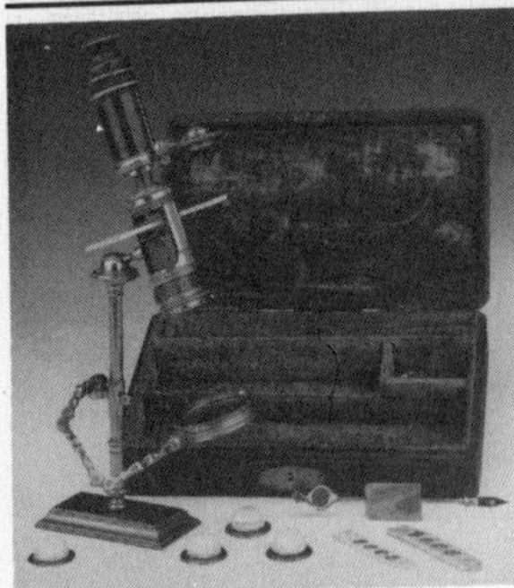

An early 18th century brass and stained ivory Culpeper-pattern screw-barrel microscope, unsigned, the screw-barrel section with sprung slide holder, 22cm. wide. (Christie's) $9,993

A rare 17th century gilt brass and silver nocturnal and calendar, in the manner of Johann Wolfgang Hager (1643-1705) of Wolfenbüttel, unsigned, the gilded arm with engraved rose at the centre, 4½in. long. (Christie's) $27,255

A 19th century lacquered-brass dip circle, signed on the vernier index arm *Troughton & Simms, LONDON*, the 6in. diameter casing mounted with a bubble level, 12½in. high. (Christie's) $4,361

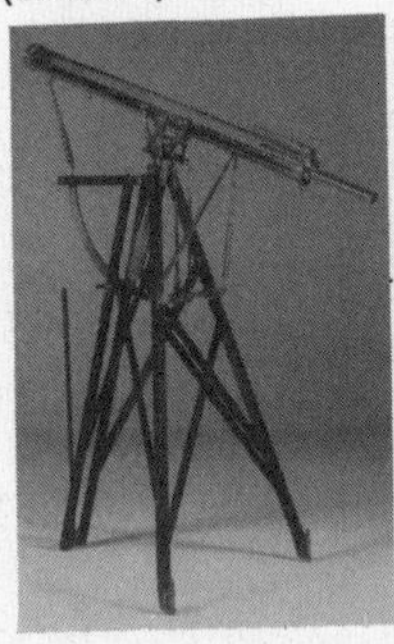

A rare 19th century lacquered-brass 4-inch refracting telescope, signed *Dolland London*, the 59½in. long body-tube with starfinder telescope, supported on twin columns, 66in. wide. (Christie's) $89,270

A late 18th century lacquered and silvered-brass equinoctial compass sundial, signed on the hour ring *DOLLAND, LONDON*, the spring-loaded gnomon with scroll support, 14.4cm. wide. (Christie's) $3,634

A late 18th-century lacquered brass compound monocular microscope, signed on the stage *ADAMS LONDON*, the tapering and waisted-section body-tube mounted on an adjustable arm and pinion for fore and aft motion, 44.1cm. wide. (Christie's) $13,627

A finely engineered mid 19th century probably instrument maker's brass and ferrous metal model of a single cylinder vertical reversing stationary engine, with cylinder ¾in. bore x 1in. stroke, 8¾ x 5in. (Christie's) $3,271

A finely engineered 1/5 scale museum display quality model of the 10nhp Atkinson Patent Cycle single cylinder gas engine originally built by The British Gas Engineering Co. Ltd. and modelled by A. Walshaw, 26 x 31½in. (Christie's) $5,814

A 19th century Italian wood polychrome decorated polyhedral sundial, unsigned, the seventeen dials painted in gilt with floral reserves in red, green, blue and brown, 9in. high. (Christie's) $6,905

An early 18th century ivory screw-barrel microscope, the shaped brass arm stamped on one side *I*, the other *W* (James Wilson), the screw-barrel with sprung-loaded brass stage and slide holder, 18.7cm. wide.
(Christie's) $14,536

An 18th century brass universal equinoctial ring dial, signed on the meridian ring *Shuttleworth LONDON*, further engraved with two quadrants, the other side with declination scale, 6in. diameter.
(Christie's) $3,634

An 18th century monocular, signed on the green-stained vellum draw-tube H. Pyefinch London, the draw-tube further decorated with scrolls and flowers in silver, 5in. long extended.(Christie's) $1,725

A rare 19th century lacquered-brass air-flow meter, signed on one of two cross bars *Biram's Patent Anemometer Davis Derby No. 63,* overall height 9in.
(Christie's) $4,724

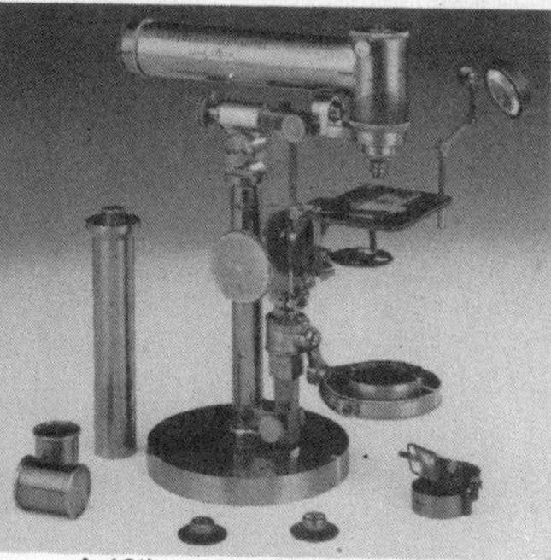

A 19th century lacquered brass compound monocular horizontal microscope, signed on the body-tube *Microscope Achromatique Universel Inventé par CHARLES CHEVALIER INGÉNIEUR Palais Royal, 158, à Paris.*
(Christie's) $15,444

A magnificent 19th century lacquered-brass repeating circle, signed *Gambey à Paris*, the primary telescope with graduated bubble level, fore and aft sights, 19¾in. high. (Christie's) $47,242

An important Renaissance universal astronomical ring dial, unsigned, undated, Louvain, circa 1550, brass, outer diameter 15.5cm., inner diameter 12.7cm.
(Christie's) $32,706

A fine museum display quality 1/5 scale model of the Atkinson Patent Differential Gas Engine originally built by the British Gas Engineering Co. Ltd, London, circa 1885, 18 x 17in. (Christie's) $6,905

An early 19th century mother of pearl drawing protractor, engraved on the base rule with scrolling foliage and the initials *MV*, 4¾in. wide. (Christie's) $1,000

A black painted brass theodolite by W. Gregory, London, circa 1900, telescope 31cm. long, compass diameter 10cm., incomplete.
(Auction Team Köln) $619

A late Georgian silver and hardstone magnifier, English, early 19th century, in swivel case between two polished agate hardstones, 7.5cm. wide.
(Bonhams) $264

A Marion's pencil cutter and sharpener, of brass with adjustable steel blade, instruction sheet (in French and English) and maker's carton, marked *Registered 5th September 1851*.
(Christie's) $542

A mahogany cased compass, English, mid 19th century, with blued steel needle, printed compass rose in a mahogany case with hinged cover, 12cm. wide.
(Bonhams) $214

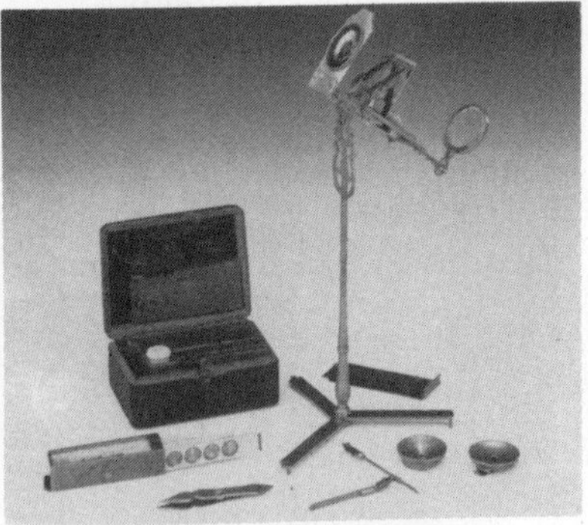

A rare mid 18th Century brass simple microscope, signed on a silver plate *Geo' Lindsay Inv & Fec.,* when dismantled all contained in the original plush-lined and fitted fishskin-covered case, 8cm. wide.
(Christie's) $23,621

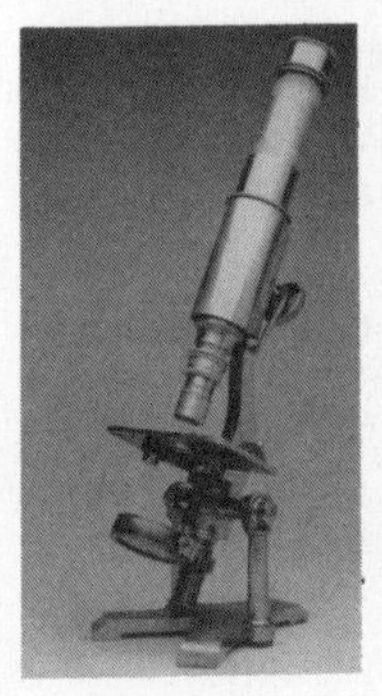

A rare Dancer lacquered brass microscope, English, 1850s, signed *Dancer,* Manchester with Y-shaped claw foot,30cm. high.
(Bonhams) $956

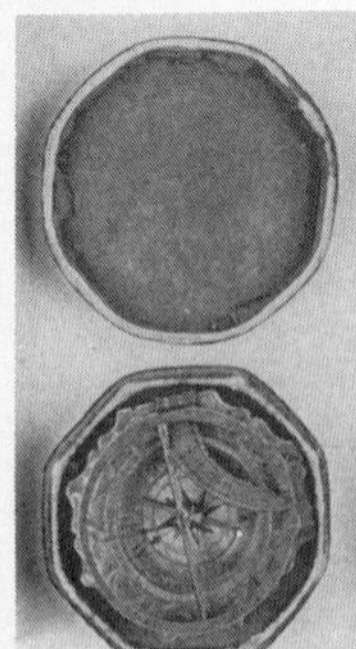

An Andreas Vogler brass universal equinoctial dial, Augsburg, circa 1780, the scalloped octagonal dial with engraved scroll decoration and inset compass well, 5.5cm.
(Bonhams) $527

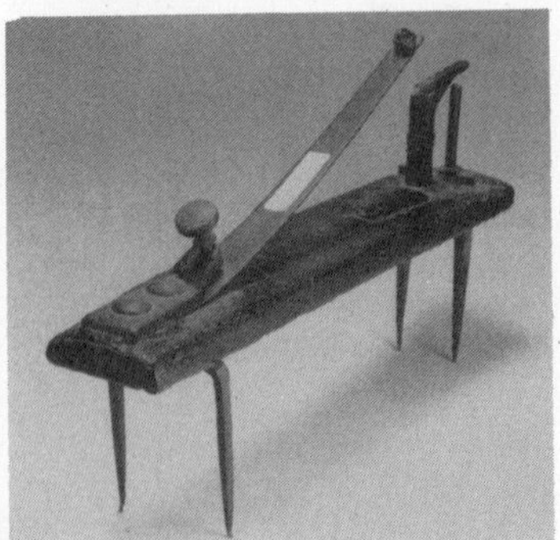

A knurr and spell ball launcher, English, 19th century, the oak rectangular launcher supported by four tapering iron feet, 26in. long.
(Sotheby's) $861

A NEMA enciphering machine by Zellweger AG, Type T-D No. 565 with ten rotors, three bank keyboard, lamp panel, dated *1947*, declassified 1992.
(Christie's) $920

An oak cased barograph, English, early 20th century, with seven aneroid bellows, lacquered brass mechanism and clockwork recording drum, 38cm. wide.
(Bonhams) $956

A French giltwood and gesso barometer, mid 19th century, the rectangular shaped dial with glazed and painted dial, 36in. high.
(Christie's) $2,624

An oak cased barograph, English, 1920s, with eight aneroid bellows, lacquered and blackened brass mechanism and barometer, 37cm.
(Bonhams) $1,318

A rare 18th century French brass horizontal and inclining compass sundial, signed on the upper face *Inventé par Julien Le Roy de La Societé des Arts*, the hour dial engraved in Roman and Arabic figures, 3¼in. long.
(Christie's) $6,905

A 16th century German ivory diptych dial, dated *ANNO 1566* and signed *HIERONIMUS REINMAN NORENBERGE FACIEBAT*, upper leaf, outer face: universal equinoctial dial in green and red with large sun face at the center, 3¾in. long.
(Christie's) $7,268

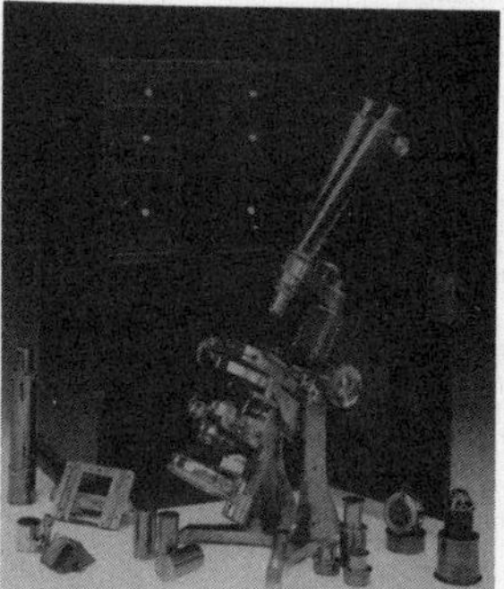

A 19th century lacquered-brass compound binocular microscope, signed on the stand *A. Ross London 1706*, with rack and pinion coarse and micrometer fine focusing, 23½in. high.
(Christie's) $4,543

A rare Federal engraved brass and poplar theodolite, Goldsmith Chandlee, Winchester, Virginia, circa 1780, ovoid poplar case, 15in. long (Sotheby's) $24,150

A fruitwood mortar and pestle, early 18th century, the mortar with reeded banding and waisted foot, 6⅝in. high, the pestle 12in. long.
(Christie's) $2,194

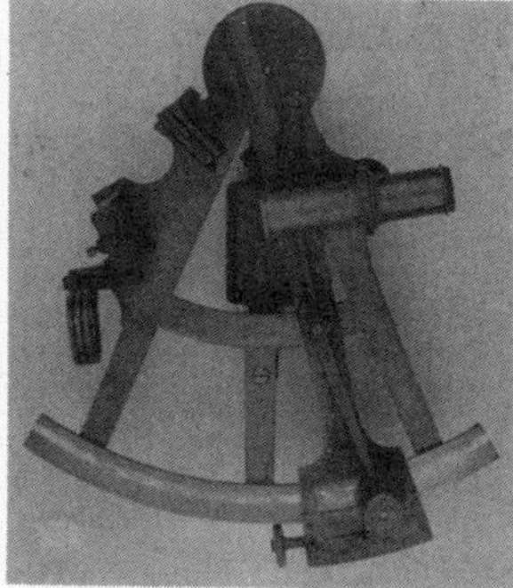

A D. McGregor & Co. brass octant, Scottish, last half of the 19th century, signed on the silvered scale *D.Mc Gregor & Co. Glasgow S. Greenock.*
(Bonhams) $362

An Umetada School tsuba, signed *Ittoshi Umetada Naritoshi* and *Kao*, the circular shakudo nanako plate decorated with a man riding a deer under a pine, 2¾in.
(Christie's) $4,124

A cast iron egg-laying hen chocolate egg sales dispenser, an early German machine by MUM-Automaten, Niedersedlitz/Dresden, circa 1920.
(Auction Team Köln) $3,543

A Mokkogata Aoi tsuba, Edo Period (Late 18th/early 19th century), decorated in shakudo depicting two gilt takazogan dragons in a turbulent sea, 3⅛in.
(Christie's) $2,437

Cast iron doorstop, 'The Warrior', in the form of a gnome, 13½in. high.
(Eldred's) $374

A fine and very rare molded cast iron fire mark, The Associated Fireman's Insurance Company, probably Baltimore, circa 1850, and two others.
(Sotheby's) $575

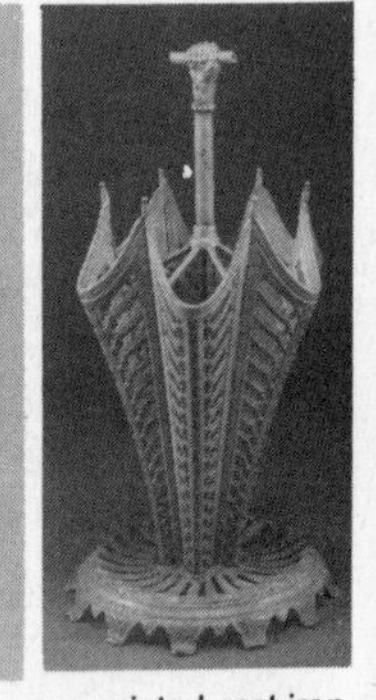

A Victorian green painted cast iron walking stick stand, third quarter 19th century, in the form of an umbrella, on a pierced circular base, 29¼in. high.
(Christie's) $2,725

A Clement Garret & Co. cast iron 'Bijou Gold Changer' with slots for one pound and half pound coins, made by Slater & Co.
(Academy) $512

A wrought iron casket, the design attributed to Edgar Brandt, circa 1925, hemispherical lid edged with beading, square handles, 11in. maximum height.
(Christie's) $4,571

A French polychromed cast-iron figure of a Geisha, third quarter 19th century, cast after a model by Charles Masse, wearing traditional costume with both hands raised, 60¼in. high.
(Christie's) $8,050

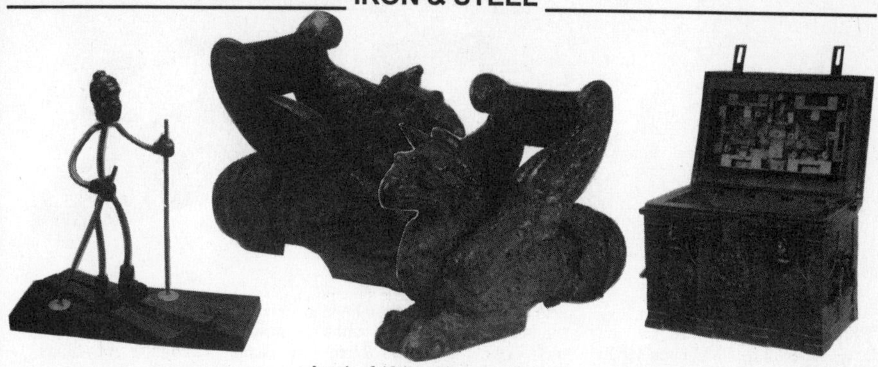

A model of a skier, of metal form on wooden skis with rectangular wooden base, 10in. high. (Christie's) $181

A pair of 19th century cast iron bootscrapers in the form of gryphons, with cannon barrel bases. (Russell Baldwin & Bright) $1,333

An 18th century war chest, with armorials in relief and 12 locks, lacking lockplate and keys, 49 x 74 x 47cm. (Arnold) $958

Cast iron painted figure of a black boy, second half 19th century, the standing figure wearing hat, scarf and vest, his right arm outstretched to hold a flag, 24½in. high. (Skinner) $805

Pair of Arts and Crafts wrought iron and brass fire dogs, America, early 20th century, obelisk-form with crossbar, decorative belting, and scrollwork studded, 35in. long. (Skinner) $1,955

A Nestle chocolate dispenser, with red painted cast metal case with gold decoration, attractive Art Nouveau style, circa 1920, 105cm. high. (Auction Team Köln) $2,143

A German wrought iron armada chest, 17th century, the rectangular box with bands of strapwork, twin loop handles and pierced false lockplate, 18½in. wide. (Christie's) $2,726

A Coalbrookdale cast iron, glazed and mirrored wall cabinet, of architectural design, the central recessed niche with a circular convex mirror within spandrel plates, circa 1902, 143cm. x 75cm. (Tennants) $1,976

A barrel shaped forged iron war chest, the upper part as a detachable lid containing lock, the lower bound with bands, German, 17th/18th century, 38cm. diameter. (Lempertz) $7,325

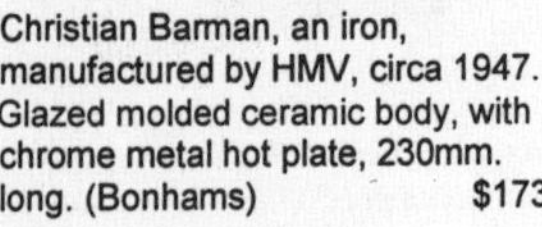

Christian Barman, an iron, manufactured by HMV, circa 1947. Glazed molded ceramic body, with chrome metal hot plate, 230mm. long. (Bonhams) $173

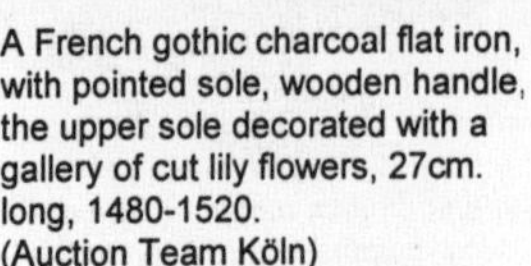

A French gothic charcoal flat iron, with pointed sole, wooden handle, the upper sole decorated with a gallery of cut lily flowers, 27cm. long, 1480-1520.
(Auction Team Köln) $11,886

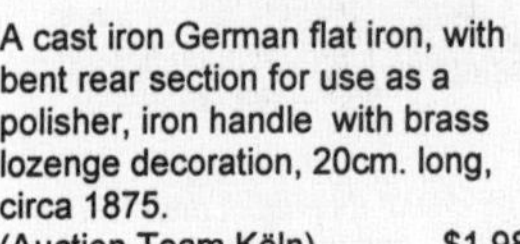

A cast iron German flat iron, with bent rear section for use as a polisher, iron handle with brass lozenge decoration, 20cm. long, circa 1875.
(Auction Team Köln) $1,980

A German 'Swiss' charcoal iron, cast iron with ash handle on dolphin posts, pointed sole 21cm., front latch with man's head decoration, circa 1900.
(Auction Team Köln) $119

A wrought iron French slug iron, rear loading, pointed sole, walnut handle on two outwardly bowed posts, circa 1780, 16.5cm. long.
(Auction Team Köln) $264

A cast iron 'Swiss' charcoal iron, semicircular beech handle on front post with griffin finial, rear damper, Austro-Hungarian, circa 1880, 21cm. long.
(Auction Team Köln) $184

A French box type wrought iron slug iron with boxwood handle between two dolphin supports, ornamented upper plate with coat of arms, circa 1800, 15.5cm. long.
(Auction Team Köln) $4,953

A chromed cast iron miniature slug iron with rounded sole, rear loading, beechwood handle on a single baluster post, Belgian, circa 1890, 8cm. long. (Auction Team Köln)
$231

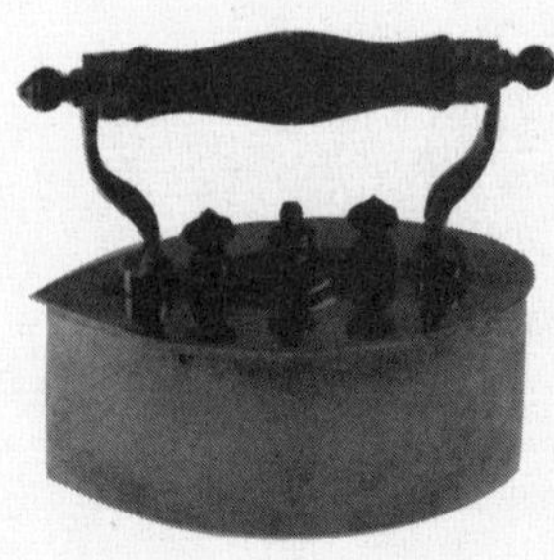

A Scottish cast iron and nickel plated box form slug iron, with almond shaped sole, turned wood handle and movable upper plate, 17cm. long, circa 1900.
(Auction Team Köln) $990

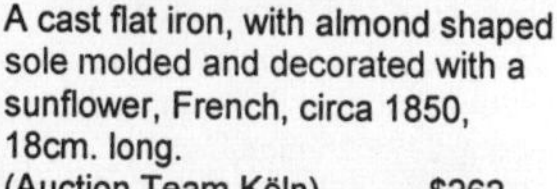

A cast flat iron, with almond shaped sole molded and decorated with a sunflower, French, circa 1850, 18cm. long.
(Auction Team Köln) $262

Alessandro Mendini, for Alchimia, iron from the series' L'Oggetto Banale', 1980, iron redesigned with colored plastic cutouts.
(Sotheby's) $184

A brass flat iron, with hinged cover to the interior, inscribed to the top *AMOD S* and dated *1759*, 6½in. long.
(Christie's) $1,000

A cast iron and engraved and pierced brass slug iron, with foliate brass upper plate and pointed sole, hornbeam handle, French, circa 1750, 13.5cm.
(Auction Team Köln) $5,613

A French charcoal iron, the body of sheet steel with unheated tip for ironing delicate materials, ventilation holes in the form of Jacobin caps, 1789.
(Auction Team Köln) $297

A brass box type slug iron, with walnut handle on S-form supports, upper plate with foliate decoration and dated *1875*, German, 17.5cm. long.
(Auction Team Köln) $561

A chrome Omega spirit iron with transverse reservoir, with wooden handle and hand protector, old wooden carrying case with brass handle, circa 1900, sole 18cm.
(Auction Team Köln) $131

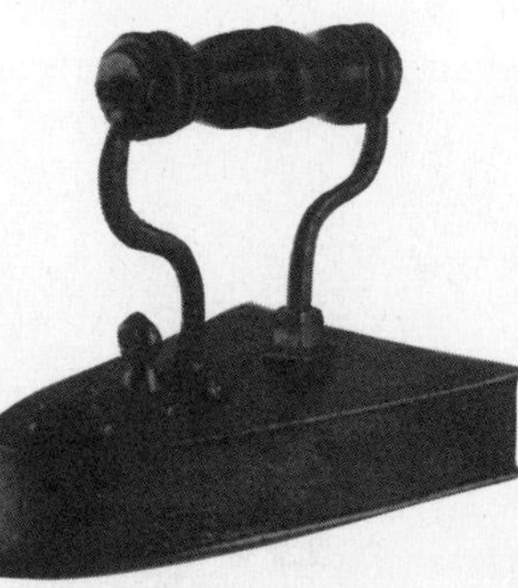

A forged wrought iron slug iron with beechwood handle, the sole with short unheated tip, rear loading, French, circa 1780, 17cm. long.
(Auction Team Köln) $462

A wrought iron box type slug iron, with pointed sole and walnut handle, straight front post and rear post of stirrup form, French, circa 1800, 18cm. long.
(Auction Team Köln) $363

TOP TIP
Can you tell the difference between bone, ivory and walrus ivory, which can greatly affect the price? All will feel cold against the cheek - if warm the item is probably plastic. Bone has small brown flecks which appear naturally. Ivory has natural striations which fade and reappear as the item is twisted under a light. Walrus ivory is often used for larger pieces and will have natural crystalline patches.
(Clarke Gammon)

Six ivory sculptures of musicians, on barrel shaped wooden bases, circa 1900, circa 18cm. high.
(Arnold) $1,276

A carved ivory tankard, German, late 19th century, the cylindrical body carved with a frieze of maenads, satyrs and putti above four mask supports, 39cm. high.
(Sotheby's) $14,876

A set of seven Austrian carved ivory figures of musicians, late 19th or early 20th century, shown standing on turned fruitwood barrels, 6in. high.
(Christie's) $5,087

A fine and rare carved and turned ivory Prisoner of War spinning lady mechanical toy, early 19th century, in the form of a stylized woman wearing a bonnet holding a spindle with thread, 5in. high.
(Sotheby's) $3,737

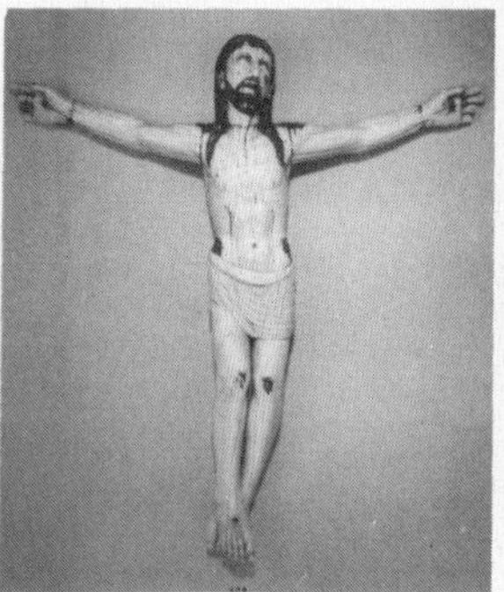

A Goanese polychrome ivory Corpus figure, 18th century, with painted hair about His shoulders, the perizonium tied to His right, 20¾in. high.
(Christie's) $13,714

An Art Deco ivory figure modelled as a partially nude female figure holding a gilt and silvered robe, 15¾in. high.
(Andrew Hartley) $8,773

'The Draughts Players', and unusual carved ivory group with jeweled silver-gilt mounts, apparently unmarked, Austro-Hungarian, late 19th century, 9½in. wide. (Sotheby's) $12,761

A gilt metal mounted ivory trinket box, 19th century, with relief carved portrait of a gentleman to the domed and hinged cover, 6¼in. high. (Christie's) $637

Continental carved ivory figure of an 18th century soldier on horseback, late 19th century, the horse leaping over a cannon, 5½in. high. (Skinner) $2,990

A large Azorian white bone model of a boat, early 20th century, the gaff-rigged mast and booms with stitched linen main sail, 36in. high. (Christie's) $5,486

TRICKS OF THE TRADE

When a piece of elaborately carved ivory has become encrusted with dust or tenacious dirt, give it a bath for a few hours in fresh milk (not boiled or pasteurized).

Then brush it with a stiff brush and rub it with a soft cloth until it is perfectly dry.

(Hobbs Parker)

A Japanese ivory okimono of a birdcatcher kneeling beside an open cage and feeding the bird within, signed *MORITOSHI*, Meiji, 11cm. (Bearne's) $1,227

A set of seven German or Austrian boxwood and ivory musician figures, late 19th century, each standing on a satin birch barrel, the conductor 7¼in. high. (Christie's) $12,747

A German carved ivory tankard, late 19th century, the body carved in relief with a bacchic procession, 9½in. high. (Christie's) $5,087

'Gamine' a silvered, cold-painted bronze and ivory figure, cast and carved from a model by Ferdinand Preiss, base with incised signature and stamped foundry seal to back of figure, 23.5cm. high. (Christie's) $11,736

A gilt bronze and ivory figure cast and carved from a model by Orlandini, of a dancer, signed in the bronze, 29.5cm. high. (Christie's) $5,416

'Sonny Boy' a cold-painted bronze and ivory figure, cast and carved from a model by Ferdinand Preiss, base with incised signature and stamped foundry seal to back of figure, 20.5cm. high. (Christie's) $6,319

A Singhalese padouk tripod jardinière, 19th century, the pierced folliate vase on a waisted foliate column and supported by three bird monopodia, 25in. diameter.
(Christie's) $5,184

A luster glazed earthenware jardinière, by Clement Massier, circa 1900, the body decorated with branches, leaves and flowers in deep ruby and gold luster glaze, 12¾in. high.
(Christie's) $7,079

A turquoise ceramic jardinière by Clement Massier, France, circa 1905, with two stylized wing handles, on hipped tripod support 110cm. high overall.
(Finarte) $2,523

One of a pair of terracotta jardinières of recent manufacture, the reeded and acanthus and ribbon-twist edge above flower decoration, 43in. diameter.
(Christie's) (Two) $1,823

A French spelter and painted figural jardinière, late 19th century, cast as an Algerian girl holding a tambourine, standing before an ovoid jardinière, 50in. high.
(Christie's) $5,018

One of two Japanese jardinières on stands, 19th century, each with a rectangular bronze bowl with a handle to either end, 39½in. wide.
(Christie's) (Two) $10,538

A Linthorpe Pottery jardinière green glazed, the fluted rim with raised corners having Egyptian motifs molded in low relief, 11¼in. wide.
(Andrew Hartley) $135

A carved pine jardinière modelled as a swan, late 19th or early 20th century, the body inset with a liner between the wings, on oval base, restoration to neck, 31in. high.
(Christie's) $3,634

One of two terracotta garden urns, designed by Archibald Knox, made for Liberty & Co., circa 1904, each with broad central entrelac design and low loop handles, 19¾in. and 19¼in. high.
(Christie's) (Two) $8,38

A Crown Ducal pottery jardinière by Charlotte Rhead, tube lined with a band of stylized flowers in green, yellow, orange and blue on a trellis ground.(Andrew Hartley) $285

A French champlevé enamel jardinière in the form of a miniature commode, third quarter 19th century, of bombé form, with panels of flowers and foliage, with satyr masks to the foliate capped paw feet, 5¾in. wide. (Christie's) $1,104

Decorative Torquay Ware jardinière of circular baluster form with crimped rim, the border inscribed with verse, decorated with scrolling foliate designs on a green ground, 7½in. (G A Key) $168

A Black Forest carved and stained wood jardinière, early 20th century, naturalistically modelled as a basket, on baluster and leaf carved column, 34½in. high. (Christie's) $1,363

A pair of French tôle peinte jardinières, second quarter 19th century, with pierced frieze and twin lion mask ring handles, 8¼in. high. (Christie's) $3,452

A wrought iron jardinière, designed by Richard Riemerschmid, circa 1897/98, the three-legged frame on foliate feet, the stretchers described as tendrils, rising to create interlacing strapwork, 41½in. maximum height. (Christie's) $18,630

A 19th century Continental kingwood and rosewood shaped jardinière, brass mounts and hand painted inset porcelain plaques, on cabriole legs, overall width 58cm. (Wintertons) $4,155

A pair of ebonized bentwood jardinières designed by Josef Hoffmann, manufactured by J. & J. Kohn, circa 1905, oval top pierced with a double row of checkers, 31½in. wide. (Christie's) $6,182

A Louis XV style parquetry inlaid kingwood and ormolu mounted jardinière, circa 1890, the loose crossbanded top within a pierced gallery. (Christie's) $2,038

TOP TIPS

It's amazing how many people soldier on with things which would be transformed just by a good clean. Jewelry is a case in in point - buy a proprietary cleaner and follow instructions and you'll be amazed at the result.

The same goes for oil paintings. The removal of years of grime and dirt will restore the work to its original beauty and freshness.

(Dee, Atkinson & Harrison)

BUYER BEWARE

Larger caratage diamonds, say one carat plus as solitaires or mounted in other styles always command a premium. The larger the caratage, all else being equal, the higher the price per carat.

We are now at the stage that real man-made diamonds are being produced. A process exists whereby the natural ingredients, principally carbon, fused together under great pressure as in the natural environment, produce diamonds in every way as good as the real thing. While the cost of the equipment to do this is astronomic, no doubt capital will be found for such a project, and the effect of such diamonds entering the normal commercial market could be very interesting indeed.

While the science is still in its infancy, some examples are said to be already out there. Let the buyer therefore beware!

(David Dockree)

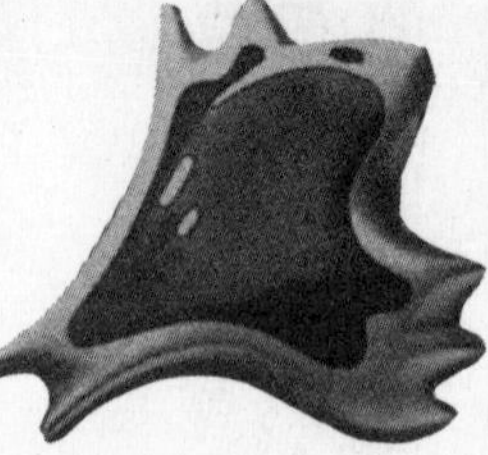

Henning Koppel for Georg Jensen, brooch, 1960s, silver colored metal, enamel, with designer's monogram.
(Sotheby's) $552

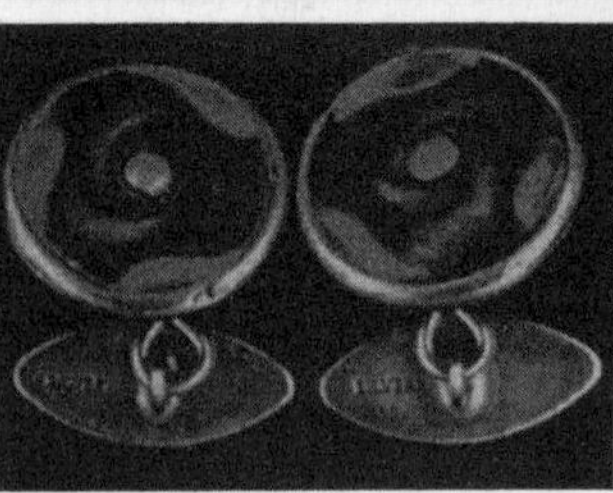

A pair of silver and enamel cufflinks by Liberty, Birmingham, 1900.
(Bonhams) $288

A solitaire ring, the brilliant cut stone measuring approximately 7.5 x 4.25mm, calculated as weighing approximately 1.47ct.
(Wintertons) $3,509

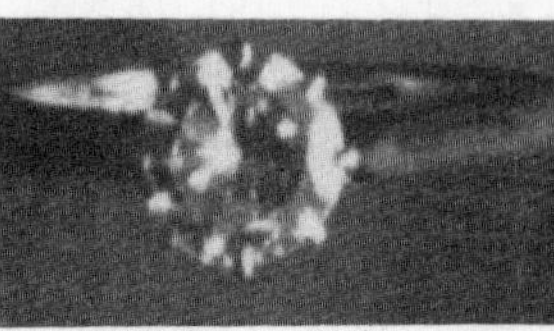

A solitaire diamond ring, the brilliant cut stone measuring approximately 6.8 x 3.5mm., calculated as weighing approximately 0.98ct, stamped *18ct platinum.*
(Wintertons) $1,848

Koloman Moser for the Wiener Werkstätte, brooch, 1912, metal, square, enamelled in black and white with a chess-board pattern against a gold-colored background, 2.8cm. square.
(Sotheby's) $3,784

A diamond and seed pearl cluster marquise ring, the navette shaped cluster with three central brilliant cut diamonds and pearl surround.
(Anderson & Garland) $569

Danish sterling silver kingfisher brooch, rectangular frame, decorated as a kingfisher perched on a leafy branch, 1¾in. diameter.
(Skinner) $460

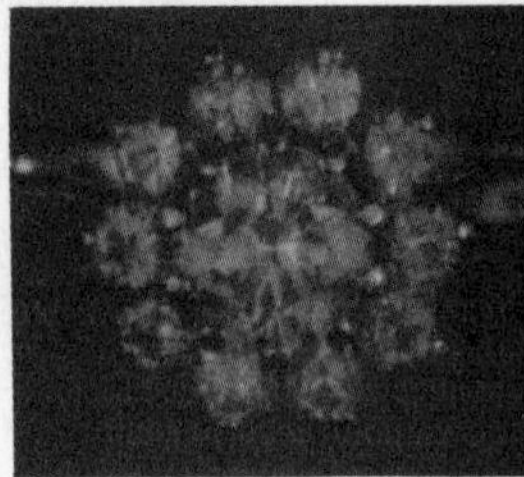

A modern cluster ring set with brilliant cut diamonds, the center stone weighting approximately 0.83ct. (Wintertons) $1,600

An Art Deco cluster ring set with diamonds.
(Wintertons) $798

An Art Deco clip, with aquamarines of tapering and baguette shape and baguette and brilliant cut diamonds mounted in white gold.
(Tennants) $2,747

A cluster ring set with center step cut emerald surrounded by brilliant cut diamonds, stamped *18ct.*
(Wintertons) $1,237

A single stone ring, the brilliant cut diamond measuring 6.9 x 4.3mm, calculated as weighing approximately 1.21ct, stamped *PLAT*. (Wintertons) $2,227

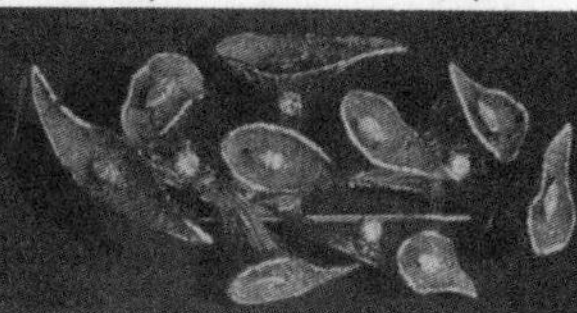

A diamond mounted brooch of textured and stylized floral design with circular and marquise-shaped diamonds in claw setting.
(Bearne's) $1,073

A solitaire diamond ring, the brilliant cut stone measuring approximately 6.8 x 3.7mm, calculated as weighing approximately 1.04ct.
(Wintertons) $2,313

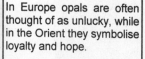

A turquoise and diamond cluster ring, the oval turquoise surrounded by twelve old cut brilliants, approximately 2.00ct total.
(Wintertons) $1,499

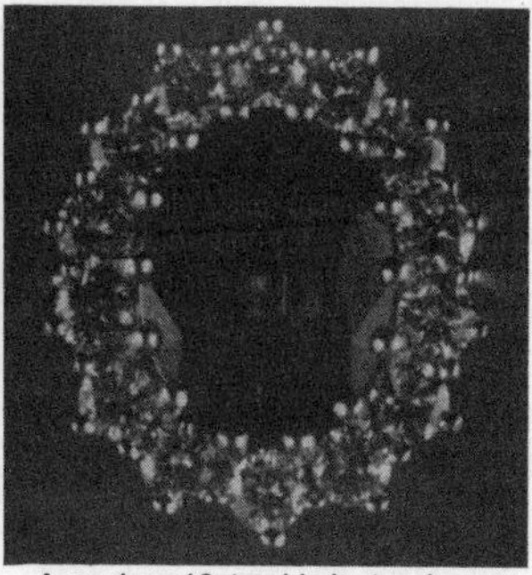

A modern 18ct gold cluster ring set with a single oval blue sapphire surrounded by brilliant cut diamonds weighing approximately 1.50ct. (Wintertons) $3,240

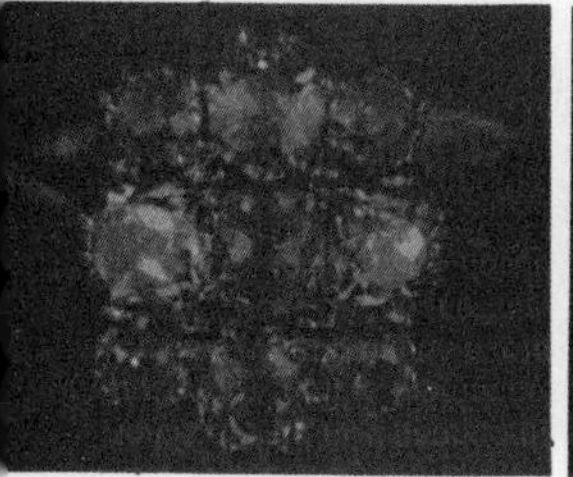

A cluster ring set with nine old cut diamonds, weighing approximately 3.50cts total, in modern shank, stamped *18ct*.
(Wintertons) $4,000

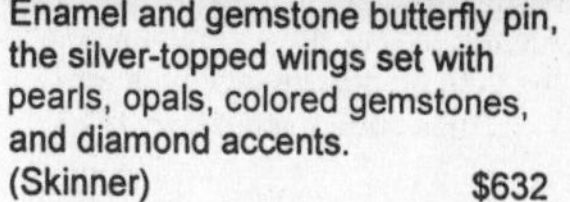

Enamel and gemstone butterfly pin, the silver-topped wings set with pearls, opals, colored gemstones, and diamond accents.
(Skinner) $632

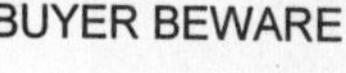

BUYER BEWARE

In Europe opals are often thought of as unlucky, while in the Orient they symbolise loyalty and hope.

It is thought that the association with bad luck may stem from the fact that opal is sensitive to pressure and knocks, can absorb water and therefore can crack and the opalescence diminish.

Very thin pieces of opal are sometimes mounted on a piece of common opal or onyx, termed opal doublets. Triplets are also found, where the top layer may consist of rock crystal.

Fakes can also be found where duller opals are colored to liven up the fire within the stone.

(Cotswold Auction Co.)

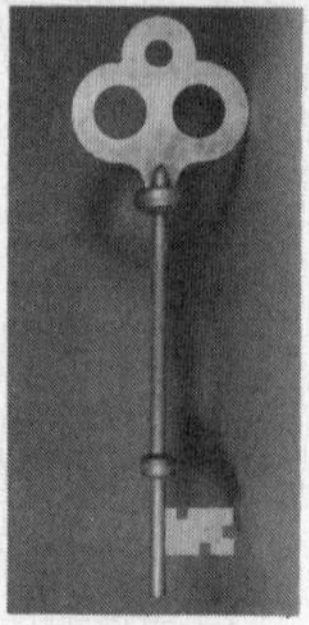

A carved and gilded wood trade sign, American, early 20th century, in the form of a key, with rectangular notched front, cylindrical collared shaft and pierced clover terminus, 149½in. long. (Christie's) $1,495

A cast iron lock and key, the spring lock with three bars, tapering trapezoidal plate with dragon heads at the corners, Italian, probably South Tirol, 16th century, 17cm. long. (Lempertz) $888

A secret dual key, the bow unscrewing from the shank to reveal an inner shank with folding bit of different pattern, 6in. long, probably early 19th century. (Christie's) $470

A gilt bronze treasury key, the large head with the arms of Bavaria under a crown, Bavaria, 1886-1912, 16.2cm. long. (Lempertz) $418

A group of nickeled-metal and brass door handles and lock plates, Walter Gropius for S.S. Loewy, Wilhelm Wagenfeld for Bauhochschule Weimar and Ferdinand Kramer for Bergisch-Märkisches Eisenwerk, circa 1920s, each mounted on a wooden stand. (Christie's) $4,830

A gilt bronze treasury key, the pierced head with the initials *MJ* under a crown, Bavaria, early 19th century, 15.2cm. long. (Lempertz) $523

A pair of Imperial gilt-bronze 'Dragon' chest locks and keys, cast Qianlong six-character marks and of the period, each of broad U-shape and decorated in repoussé, 11¼in. long. (Christie's) $36,800

An iron lock and key, 18th century, the pierced square lockplate with *VOC* monogram and dated *1723*, 8¾ x 9¾in. (Christie's) $768

A forged iron gate lock and key, German, 17th century, mounted on wood, 22cm. long. (Lempertz) $1,570

A rare gold lacquer and nashiji kodansu, decorated in hiramakie, takamakie and okibirame with panels depicting coastal villages, Meiji Period, 8¼ x 4¾ x 4¾in. (Christie's) $2,512

A pair of lacquer kogo, signed *Toyo saku*, Meiji Period (late 19th century), modelled as oshidori [mandarin ducks] similarly decorated in red, gold, silver and black hiramakie, 11cm. and 9.8cm. long. (Christie's) $7,079

A kogo in the form of the Takarabune, Meiji Period (late 19th/early 20th century), the top of the cover decorated with the takaramono [attributes of the Seven Gods of Good Fortune] 4.9 x 17.2 x 11cm. (Christie's) $4,657

A 19th century Persian black lacquered book cover decorated to front & reverse with people and animals in landscape, the inside covers painted with a medallion, 15 x 10½in. (Michael J. Bowman) $508

A fine gold lacquer suzuribako, Meiji-Taisho Period (late 19th/20th century), the kinji and e-nashiji ground decorated with a small pavilion amongst pine and mountains, 5.3 x 24.8 x 27.4cm. (Christie's) $12,109

A small tebako in Rimpa style, Meiji Period (late 19th century), the dark brown lacquer ground sparsely sprinkled with large-flaked nashiji, over which are scattered many dragonflies, 12 x 17.5 x 22.9cm. (Christie's) $2,608

A Chinese black and gold incised lacquer screen, the twelve panels with a panoramic view of noble women and attendants in a summer palace garden, 8ft. high. (Woolley & Wallis) $5,449

A gold Imperial lacquer silver-rimmed tebako, Meiji Period (late 19th/20th century), the cover and sides decorated with peach trees by a rocky shore and a crane flying, 6 x 9½ x 11½in. (Christie's) $8,384

19th century Japanese lacquered panel of three ladies in a garden landscape, raised decoration with ivory inserts within a root frame, 23 x 21in. (Christie's) $479

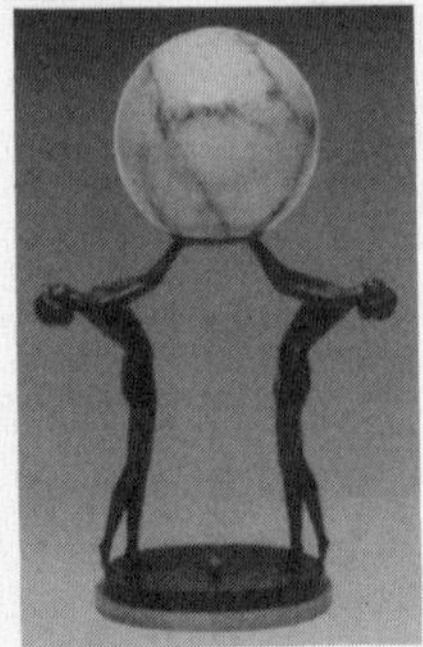

An Art Deco style bronzed metal table lamp with two girls holding aloft the smoked glass spherical shade, on alabaster base, 51cm. high. (Bearne's) $986

A pair of bronze colza pier lamps, mid 19th century, each with waisted urn-shaped reservoir with twin arm fitting below, 18¼in. high. (Christie's) $3,266

Pairpoint puffy grape lamp, blown out, reverse painted shade with multicolored grapes and leaves, signed on rim, total height 19½in. (Skinner) $20,700

Art glass table lamp, America, early 20th century domed textured cased green to white glass shade embellished around the rim with repeating foliate cartouches, 23in. high. (Skinner) $4,887

A pair of mounted alabaster table lamps, French, circa 1925, the cylindrical alabaster shades supported by highly formalised leaping horses, 13½in. high. (Christie's) $6,706

Fenton decorated Burmese hurricane lamp, Williamstown, Wes Virginia, 1974, shade with a ruffled rim decorated with a mountainous landscape, matching glass base, total height 19½in. (Skinner) $51

A George III bronze and cobalt blue glass lamp base, probably by William Parker, 1780, of waisted square section, heightened in gilt with festoons of husks with guilloche borders, 10¾in. high. (Christie's) $2,451

A pair of mounted glass table lamps, in the style of Jacques Adnet, 1930s, faceted glass squares pivoting on a central brass stem, 9½in. high. (Christie's) $3,353

An Art Deco patinated spelter figural table lamp, modelled as a naked dancer poised on tiptoe, within open arch composed of mottled white bakelite and zigzag metal vertical bands, 50cm. high. (Christie's) $957

Tiffany bronze table lamp base, spun bronze tobacco leaf and ribbed base with inserted electrified oil-lamp, total height 18½in. (Skinner) $6,325

An Art Deco style bronzed metal table lamp in the form of a reclining Egyptian lady supporting a spherical frosted glass shade, 36cm. (Bearne's) $715

McKenny and Waterbury Co. boudoir lamp, domed shade with reverse painted daffodils on an amber ground, 13¾in. high. (Skinner) $1,150

Marcel Louis Baugniet and E. van Tonderen, lamp, before 1930, black painted wood, cylindrical body on stepped base with rectangular aperture with semi-circular opaque white glass shade, 28.8cm. (Sotheby's) $3,244

Pair of Tiffany gilt bronze and gold linen-fold glass table lamps, twelve-sided shade of favrile fabrique golden amber glass arranged in panel configuration, 24in. high. (Skinner) $24,150

An English Art Nouveau table lamp, circa 1880, in the style of W.A.S. Benson, brass, the triform base extending to form a curved upright support, 28.3cm. (Sotheby's) $812

Decorative 1950s painted metal standard lamp in the form of a palm tree with six branches suspending glass shades, 71in. high. (Ewbank) $739

Ettore Sottsass for Stilnovo, 'Valigia' table lamp, designed 1977, black and red metal, black rubber, 55cm. (Sotheby's) $773

Tiffany bronze table lamp base, trumpet formed base cast with artichoke leaves raised on twelve flattened ball feet, 27in. high. (Skinner) $54,625

Reverse painted scenic boudoir lamp, attributed to the Pittsburgh Lamp Company, domical shade in sand finished glass, 15½in. high. (Skinner) $1,092

Loetz Art Glass desk lamp, double socket lamp with raised gold iridescent festoons on linen-fold style shades, 17¼in. high. (Skinner) $1,495

Handel tropical overlay desk lamp, hexagonal shade with metal overlay in a tropical palm tree over sunset colored slag glass, 14½in. high. (Skinner) $2,300

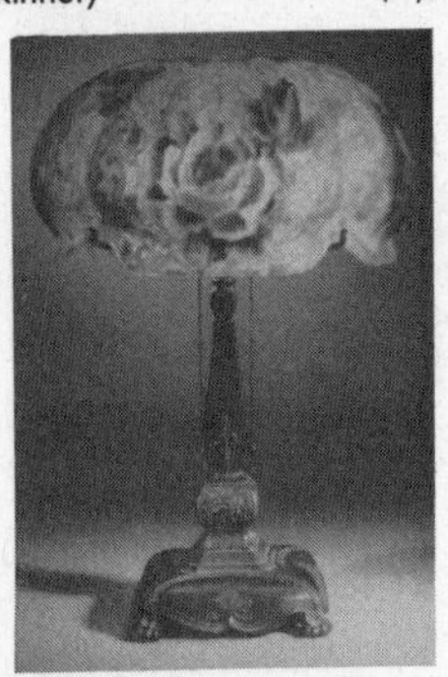

Pairpoint rose tapestry table lamp, New Bedford, Massachusetts, reverse-painted decoration, ribbed rust background, scrolling leaf and flowers on a Venice shade with closed top, 20in. high. (Skinner) $6,325

Quezal Art glass shade on desk lamp, America, early 20th century, bulbous ribbed iridescent amber shade with flared rim supported on single-socket patinated metal fixture, 12¼in. high. (Skinner) $402

Pairpoint Puffy rose bouquet lamp, New Bedford, Massachusetts, early 20th century, reverse-painted shade with open top, decorated with blossoms in colors of creamy white and pink, 21in. high. (Skinner) $4,025

Steuben bell harp desk lamp, America, early 20th century, patinated verdigris finish on adjustable bell-shape harp over oval domed base, 15¼in. (Skinner) $1,495

Bradley and Hubbard table lamp, Connecticut, early 20th century, domed bent panel glass shade, green and amber shaded and ribbed surface, 21½in. high. (Skinner) $977

Slag glass floriform table lamp, America, early 20th century, comprising blossoming flower shade and bud with striated green and white slag glass petals, 13½in. high. (Skinner) $345

Tiffany intaglio carved and favrile glass boudoir lamp, dome shade on a restored oviform base, both of iridescent gold glass, total height 15½in. (Skinner) $9,775

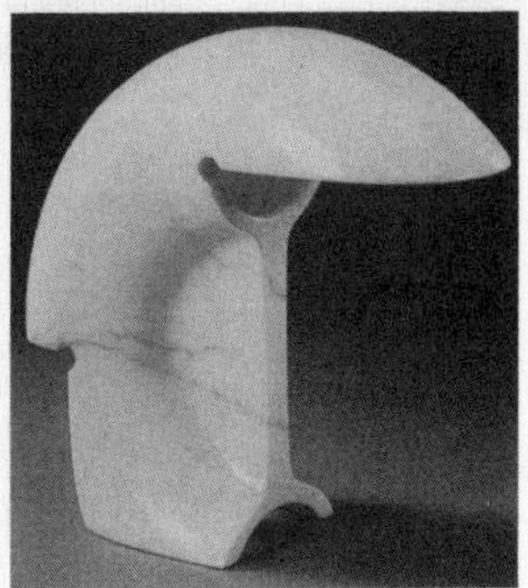

Tobia Scarpa for Flos, 'Biaggio' table lamp, designed in 1968, white marble, 13¾in. (Sotheby's) $1,288

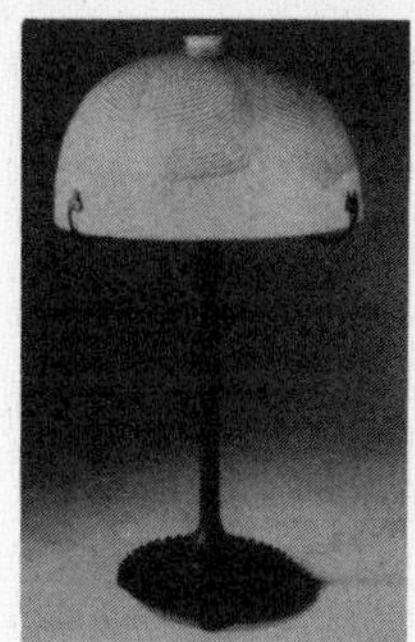

Quezal Art Glass and bronze desk lamp, heavy walled half-round shade of opal glass, lined with brilliant iridescent gold, 19in. hgh. (Skinner) $1,725

Table lamp with reverse-painted shade, America, early 20th century, domed shade with painted interior depicting cottage by the sea with mountains in the distance, 24in. high. (Skinner) $1,725

Large leaded glass table lamp, possibly Seuss Ornamental Glass Co., Chicago, Illinois, early 20th century, domed shade with drop apron and undulating rim, shade composed of tulips, honeysuckle, and entwining leaves, 25½in. high. (Skinner) $9,200

Reverse-painted water lily table lamp, America, early 20th century, ribbed panels with leafy scroll devices between reverse-painted panels of water lilies in the foreground, 24in. high. (Skinner) $1,380

Bradley and Hubbard slag glass and metal boudoir lamp, square bent-panel striated green slag glass shade with dark patinated metal riveted strapwork, 18½in. high. (Skinner) $1,035

Seuss leaded glass table lamp, early 20th century, parasol shade with open top, radiating panels of caramel and soft green colored glass segments, 21½in. (Skinner) $2,990

Moe Bridges reverse-painted scenic lamp, Milwaukee, textured shade reverse-painted with trees by a lake in naturalistic colors, total height 20½in. (Skinner) $2,300

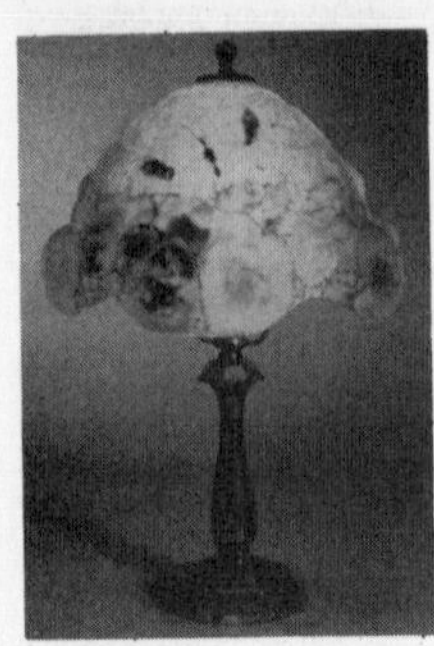

Pairpoint puffy boudoir lamp, blown out rose tree shade, signed, with two butterflies above a border of pink and yellow roses, total height 14in. (Skinner) $4,140

A pair of Empire style gilt bronze bouillotte lamps, late 19th century, the branches modelled as swans supporting nozzles with anthemions banding, 23in. high.
(Christie's) $3,992

Handel leaded glass table lamp, domed shade with lapped-petal design in amber and cream slag glass, 26in. high.
(Skinner) $3,335

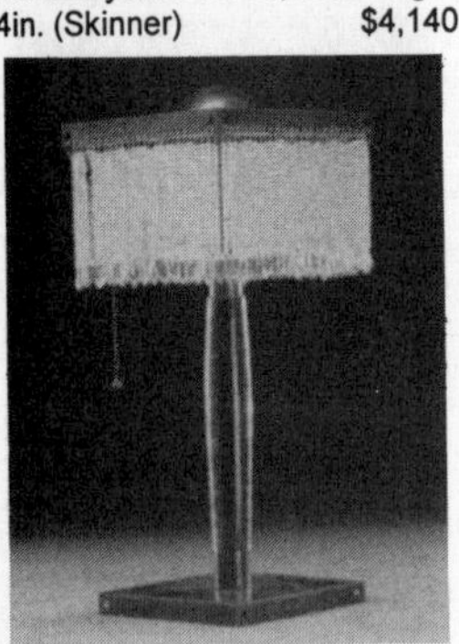

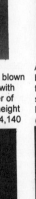

A table lamp, designed by Hans Ofner, circa 1905, the lamp on square foot with pierced corner details, the stem of clear glass, 19¼in. high.
(Christie's) $6,520

A Phonolamp Capital Model EA Art Nouveau style table gramophone by the Burus-Pollock Electric Mfg. Co., Indiana Harbor, the speaker in the copper base, on three brass claw feet, 1919.
(Auction Team Köln) $3,937

Tiffany Studios nasturtium lamp, broad shade with a curved apron of intricately leaded glass in the design of trailing nasturtium blossoms in red, yellow, and orange, total height 31½in.
(Skinner) $63,000

Tiffany Favrile three-part electrolier candlestick, swirled rib gold iridescent holder fitted with gilt-metal and favrile glass 'candle', total height 12in.
(Skinner) $1,150

A pair of German patent oil lamps, by Wild & Wesson, late 19th century, in the neo-classical taste, the boat-shaped reservoirs cast in relief with panels of grotesque masks and foliate scrolls, 21in. high. (Christie's) $4,149

Pittsburgh painted scenic table lamp, handpainted domed shade depicting an evening tree-lined shore in tones of amber, rust and green, 9¼in. high.
(Skinner) $1,150

Triangular form painted tin barn lantern, mid-19th century, brown paint with black highlights, two glass panels, 19in. high.
(Skinner) $345

A glass and metal ceiling lamp, manufactured circa 1932 by Sistrah Licht GmbH, with domed white glass upper shade above stepped lower shade of clear glass, 15½in. diameter. (Christie's) $812

A 19th century brass hall lantern of hexagonal form, each corner with a turned column, suspended from double C scroll supports, 31½in. high.
(Andrew Hartley) $1,652

A copper hall lantern, circa 1900, of architectural outline, the glazing panels of trefoil shape below the sloping top with dormer-shaped protrudences, 32in. high.
(Christie's) $1,360

A German porcelain and brass hall lantern, early 20th century, of square outline, the glazing bars modelled with pseudo armorial devices, the scrolled crestings centered by grotesque masks, 19½in. high.
(Christie's) $2,722

A French gilt-bronze hall lantern, early 20th century, of lobed pentagonal form, with foliate cast scroll frame and conforming corona, 23½in. high.
(Christie's) $1,814

Nautical beaded bull's-eye round fixed globe lantern in a pierced brass frame with two tie-down rings, America, mid-19th century, 11½in. high.
(Skinner) $2,300

C.J. Weinstein, luster, 1930s, gilt bronze chain and cage mount, inset with twenty-six clear glass spikes in various sizes, 47¼in. approximate drop. (Sotheby's) $17,940

Fixed etched globe and painted tin lantern, probably England, late 19th century, brass trademark label, bronze ring handle, 19½in. high,
(Skinner) $460

Alvar Aalto for Artek, 'A 331' lamp, 1951, white painted aluminum with perforated brass rings, 12in. high. (Sotheby's) $920

Ingo Maurer, Germany, 'Bulb', circa 1980. Giant bulb shaped hanging lamp in yellow black and white plastic, 610mm. high. (Bonhams) $551

A Victorian gilt brass and leaded glass hall lantern, circa 1880, of hexagonal form with three colored glass raised bosses to the angles, 32in. high. (Christie's) $2,981

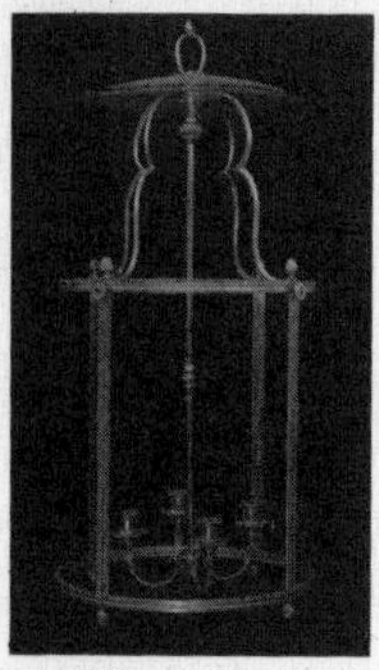

A Louis XVI style glazed bronze cylindrical hall lantern, early 20th century, the fluted uprights with foliate clasped cone finials, 27in. high. (Christie's) $2,422

A pair of Victorian tôle hexagonal lanterns, circa 1870, the glazed frames with tapering undersides and domed covers, 42in. high. (Christie's) $5,814

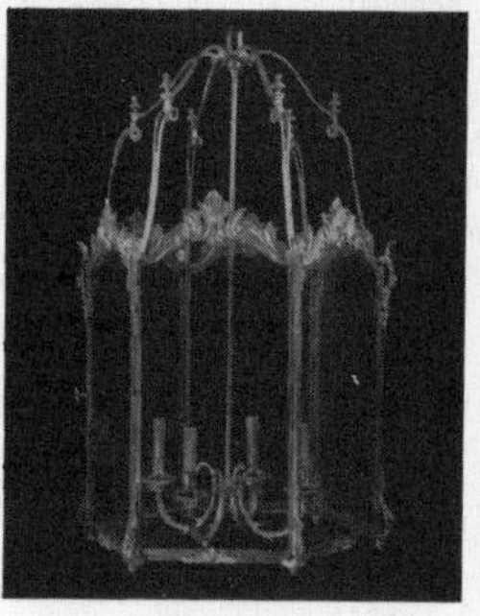

A late Victorian gilt brass hall lantern, late 19th century, of hexagonal outline, the arched panels to the sides with leafy crestings, 40½in. high. (Christie's) $5,451

One of a pair of large polished brass hall lanterns, 20th century, the cylindrical frames with ribbon tied reeded borders and cone finials to the openwork corona, 48in. high. (Christie's) (Two) $7,498

A gilt-bronze pentagonal hall lantern, late 19th century, the serpentine panels with bell-flowers to the angles and floral swags, 21in. high. (Christie's) $1,405

A gilt bronze and brass glazed hall lantern, late 19th or early 20th century , the rectangular frame with pierced cabochon friezes and outset spiral columns, 36in. high. (Christie's) $1,863

A gilt-bronze hall lantern, Paris, circa 1890, of cylindrical form with four bowed panels divided by four pilasters, 100cm. high.
(Sotheby's) $7,498

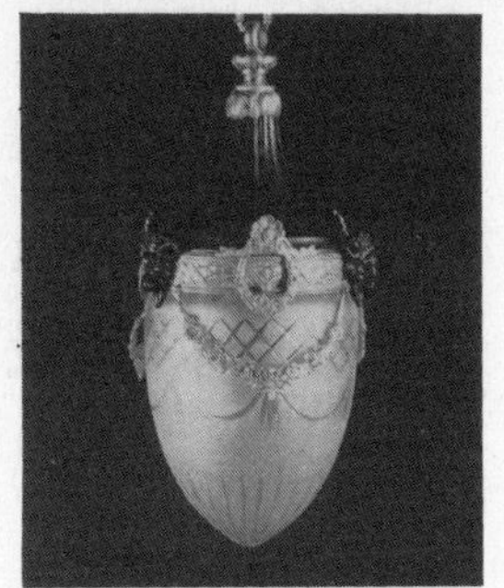

One of a pair of frosted glass hall lanterns, early 20th century, of ovoid form, the shades cut with swagged, lattice starburst ornament, 20in. high.
(Christie's) (Two) $2,624

A Victorian gilt bronze and brass sanctuary lantern, late 19th century, in the Gothic Revival style, of hexagonal form with outset spires, 34in. high. (Christie's) $1,304

A set of four silvered copper hall lanterns, 20th century, of tapering hexagonal form, the domed covers with embossed cartouche crestings and flambeau finials, 29in. high.
(Christie's) $3,353

One of a pair of glazed gilt-bronze hall lanterns, early 20th century, each with eight concave glazed panels within a stylized foliate frame, 15¼in. diameter.
(Christie's) (Two) $4,124

A Victorian brass gas hall lantern, last quarter 19th century, of cylindrical outline, the frame with scroll terminal and conforming openwork suspension, 40in. high.
(Christie's) $1,875

A large bronze and ruby tinted glass cylindrical gas hall lantern, early 20th century, the lattice frame with floral rosettes to the angles, 61in. overall.
(Christie's) $8,435

A Regency hexagonal hall lantern, first quarter 19th century, the glazed frame with anthemion crestings and scroll suspension to the corona, 28in. high.
(Christie's) $5,249

Alvar Aalto, manufactured by Valaisintyö, hanging lamp, prototype version for the Kaufmann Rooms, 1950s, brass, white enamelled metal, 21¼in.
(Sotheby's) $1,840

A leather cartridge magazine by Thomas Horsley & Son, for approximately 300 cartridges. (Bonhams) $596

A brass-bound oak and leather cartridge magazine by Holland & Holland, for approximately 500 cartridges. (Bonhams) $832

An Edwardian silver and leather mounted stationery box and blotter folder, the sectioned letter box with curved flip-top mounted with a pierced, fluted mount embossed with flowers and scrolls, H. Matthews, Birmingham, 1906, 30.5 x 22.5cm. (Christie's) $973

An 'erotic' spectacle case, Spanish, mid 19th century, painted pressed leather panels decorated with a young lady at her toilet, 11cm. wide. (Bonhams) $280

A pair of late 19th century mounted leather mugs with 'stitched' scroll handles in the style of black jacks with copper interiors and applied shield cartouches, probably American, circa 1900, 16cm. high. (Christie's) $883

A leather jug, 17th century style, with later silvered metal rim, the body with entwined foliage and integral handle, 13½in. high. (Christie's) $402

A brass mounted leather dog collar, late 18th/early 19th century, with padlock clasp, applied with initials *JN HR* flanked by shaped symbols, 4¼in. diameter. (Christie's) $2,377

The Ancient Order of the Boot, English, 1908, the leather boot with one penny stamp on toe and tri-color grosgrain ribbon bow ties, below a faded type-written letter dated *Nov. 14th 1908*, 61cm. high. (Bonhams) $659

A Regency brass-mounted black-leather covered camphor trunk, covered overall in studded black leather, enclosing a pink paper-lined interior with two removable trays, 45½in. wide. (Christie's) $4,388

Henri Weigele, French, 1858-1927, Diana, a bust, signed, white marble, on a mottled green marble socle, 33½in.
(Sotheby's) $17,077

A fine 19th century white marble head and shoulders bust of a classical female with fleur-de-pêche marble drapery, on socle base, 69cm. (Bearne's) $11,010

An ormolu mounted Breccia marble wall fountain, 19th century, the lobed basin issuing from a rectangular back plate with mask cresting and molded borders, 13in. wide.
(Christie's) $5,888

Hiram Powers, American 1805-1873, Proserpine, a bust signed, white marble, in overall weathered condition, 22½in.
(Sotheby's) $14,231

A pair of ormolu mounted cream and green veined solid vases, each with a fruiting finial above a waisted neck, 18½in. high.
(Christie's) $3,312

William Ordway Partridge, American, 1861-1930, an ideal head of a woman, signed, white marble, 27½in.
(Sotheby's) $11,385

A white marble bust of a peasant girl, on turned marble socle, second half 19th century, 57cm. high.
(Finarte) $2,269

An Italian white marble jardinière, circa 1880, the sides each centered with a shield-enclosed coat of arms, on a pair of double acanthus-carved scrolled volute supports, 39½in. wide.
(Christie's) $4,025

A black marble plaque decorated with a micromosaic polychrome bouquet, in giltwood frame, 19th century, 31.5 x 24cm. overall.
(Finarte) $2,365

An Italian sculpted white marble group of Cupid and Psyche, late 19th century, after Antonio Canova, 27¾in. wide.
(Christie's) $3,374

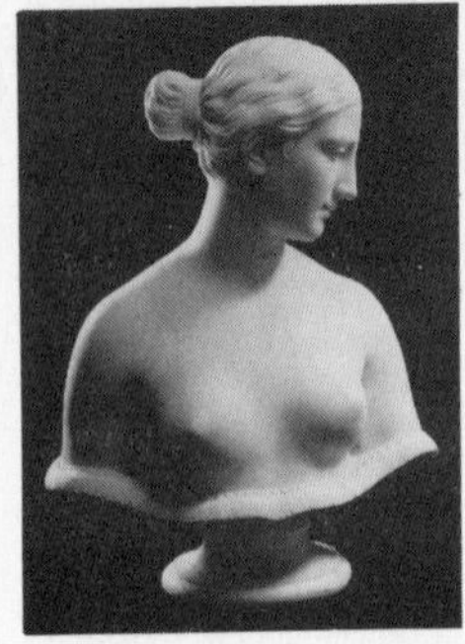

Hiram Powers, American (1805-1873), The Greek Slave, a bust, signed, white marble, 23¾in.
(Sotheby's) $54,689

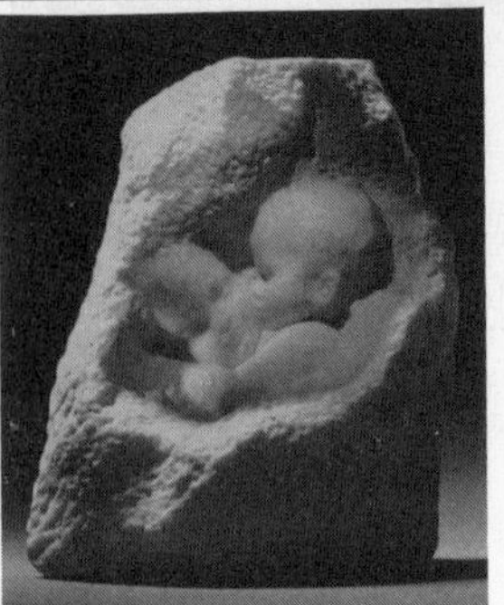

Alfred Boucher, French (1850-1934), Two children embracing, signed, white marble, 12¾in.
(Sotheby's) $7,292

A carved marble relief hand sign, American, late 19th century, the octagonal plaque carved in relief with a pointing hand with a checked cuff, 6½in. long.
(Sotheby's) $1,495

Two early 19th century Ottoman carved white marble gravestones with differing tops, the front panels each with five and six lines of Arabic script, 36in. and 37in. high.
(Canterbury) $1,357

A late 19th century colored marble sweet meat dish, comprising shallow circular red marble bowl with applied gilt metal rim embossed with foliage and studded with gem stones, 4in. high.
(Andrew Hartley) $356

A fine marble bust of a young woman by Marcel Leduc (b.1876), signed. 46.5cm. high.
(Bristol) $2,616

Raymond Germain, French (b. 1881), Narcissus, signed, white marble, 54¼ x 50 x 30¼in.
(Sotheby's) $51,043

Edoardo Rossi, Italian, (b. 1867), a bust of a lady with a butterfly in her hair, signed and inscribed, white marble, 28¼in. high.
(Sotheby's) $11,302

Bernhard Hoetger, German (1874-1949), Portrait of a Man, granular white marble, 14in.
(Sotheby's) $5,104

Large Italian carved carrara marble font, late 19th century, carved in high relief and depicting frolicking infant bacchantes, grape bunches and masks, 42in. wide.
(Skinner) $21,850

Italian, late 19th century, after Canova, a white marble bust of Paris, 22in. high.
(Sotheby's) $10,026

A statuary marble bust of a young lady, with her head inclined to sinister and her hair tied in a bun, on a circular socle, 52.5cm. high.
(Christie's) $1,098

An Italian statuary marble figure of a seated lady by A. Cataldi, late 19th/early 20th century, the naked lady with her arms in her lap and head resting on her right knee, 15½in. high.
(Christie's) $2,509

A white marble bust of a young woman, her bowed head looking to the left, long ribbon tied hair plait, unsigned, 19th century, 20½in. high.

(Andrew Hartley) $2,753

A 19th century marble statue of Apollo, with damage, 41in. high.
(Dockrees) $3,840

Charles Vital-Cornu, French (1851-1927), a white marble group of a mother and her young child, 43cm.
(Sotheby's) $14,584

A 19th century marble study of Cupid, slight damage, 46in. high.
(Dockrees) $61,600

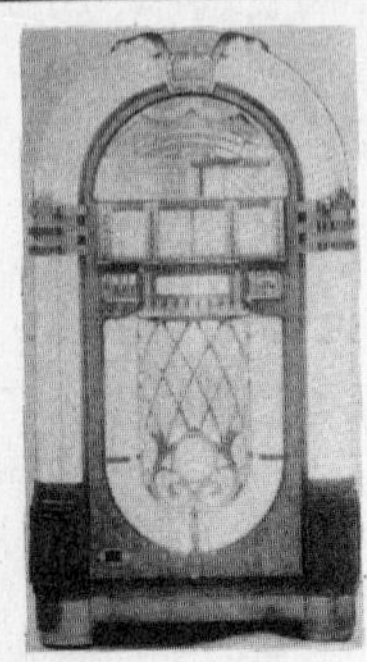

A Wurlitzer 1015 juke box, with 8 bubble tubes and four-colored spinning cylinders, with 24 disks, 1946, 155cm. high.
(Auction Team Köln) $9,044

A cabinet roller organ twenty-note organette in gilt-stencilled case with instructions in swell-flap, 1887 patent date and fourteen cobs, 17in. (Christie's) $807

A German Klingsor oak-cased table gramophone with built-in zither arrangement at front supposedly to improve sound quality, stained glass front doors, 1913.
(Auction Team Köln) $1,071

An Imhof & Mukle 'Drawing-Room' barrel piano with fifty-four-note action, in rosewood case with fretted front panel, the base containing one spare barrel, 47½in. wide, with four further barrels.
(Christie's) $3,229

A rare coin-slot musical stereoscope, with 18 French stereocards on a conveyor, in walnut case with ground-glass panel in lid, 50cm. high, circa 1890.
(Christie's) $4,600

An Austrian musical clock, with musical movement in base playing two airs, three train grand sonnerie clock striking hours and quarters, 19¾in. high.
(Christie's) $1,288

A 27-note portable barrel piano by Henry Distin, in typical rosewood-veneered upright piano form case, 37¾in. high.
(Christie's) $2,208

A Mignon 32-note organette in japanned case with gilt stencils to front and rear and label of Ph. Hakker Jr., 92 Weste, Wagenstraat, Amsterdam, 23½in. wide, with fourteen rolls.
(Christie's) $827

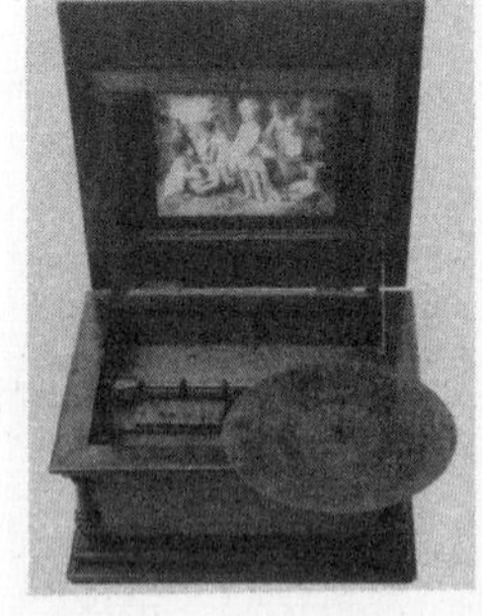

A $13\frac{5}{8}$ in. Symphonion with two combs, glass inner lid and walnut case, 22in. wide, with ten disks.
(Christie's) $2,024

A gold musical fob seal, with typical barillet movement in oval base with répoussé floriate frieze, winding shaft with modern watch-winder cap. (Christie's) $1,379

A 20-note portable street barrel organ by Gebrüder Bruder, Waldkirch, playing ten tunes, with three stops, in fruitwood case with inlaid and arcaded front, 21½in. wide. (Christie's) $6,440

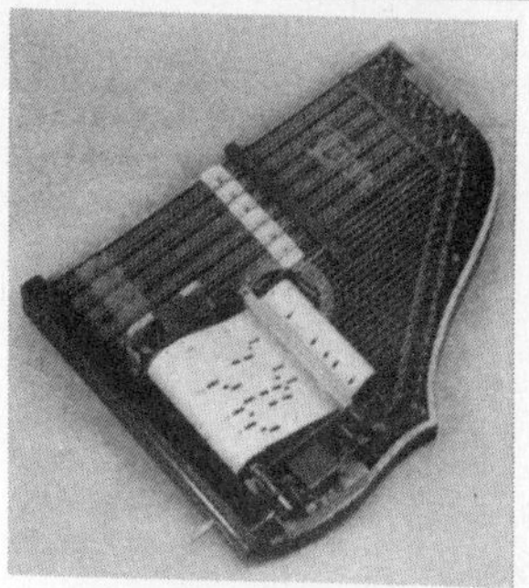

A Triola zither with twenty-five-note roll-played section and six chords for hand accompaniment, and one roll. (Christie's) $1,472

A Swiss musical chair, with movement playing The Wedding March and two other tunes when the seat is in use, Geo. Baker Musical Box Manufacturer, Geneva, circa 1900.
(Christie's) $1,840

A Salon Pathéphone with cream-painted flower horn, Pathé soundbox on vertical/lateral neck and motor with accelerating start, in walnut case, 32in. high.
(Christie's) $3,128

A chamber barrel organ by George Astor & Company, London, with divided key-frame, mahogany case with sliding front panel of simulated pipes, 76½in. high.
(Christie's) $8,280

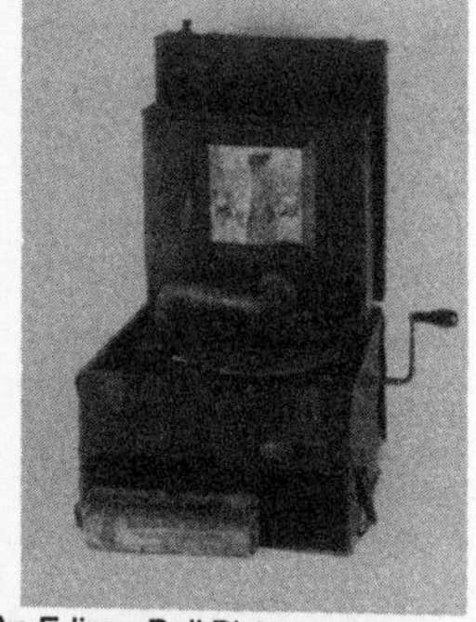

An Edison Bell Picturegram with turntable-driven panoramic picture device stored in base, Era soundbox, 8in. turntable and black cloth covered case, 12¾in. wide.
(Christie's) $736

A portable barrel organ by J. Thibouville-Lamy, with 17-key action playing six airs for the British market, each controlled by a stop, 20in. wide.
(Christie's) $4,126

A 19th century cabinet barrel organ with two interchangeable wood cylinders each playing ten airs, Joseph W. Walker, London, 57cm. wide. (Bearne's) $2,475

An early Victorian rosewood medicine cabinet, the twin doors enclosing an arrangement of pigeon holes and two drawers, 27cm. (Bearne's) $660

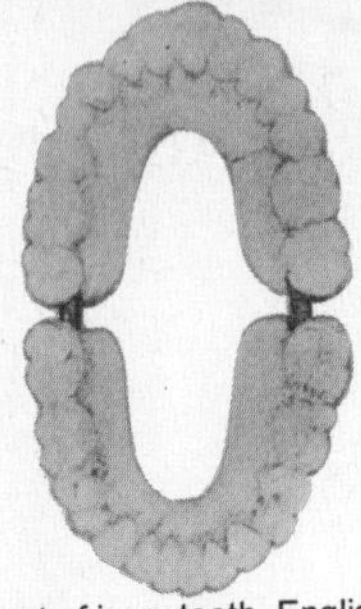

A small set of ivory teeth, English, early 19th century, finely carved with teeth of maxillary and mandibular jaws, metal pins, each jaw approximately 3cm. (Bonhams) $362

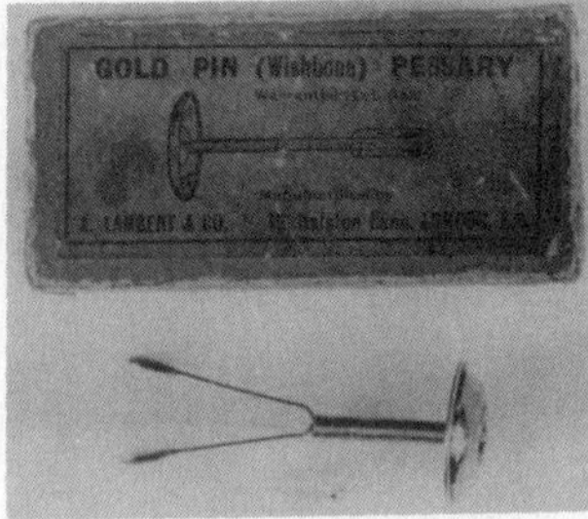

A rare gold pin 'wishbone' pessary contraceptive device, English, early 20th century, in original case, together with a Graftenberg intrauterine ring, 6cm. long. (Bonhams) $379

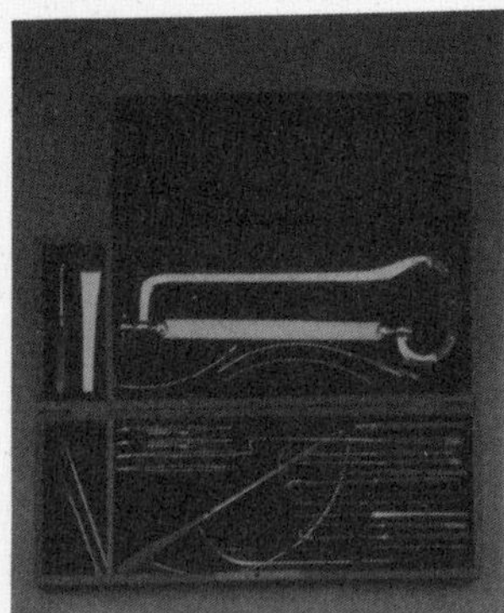

A late 19th century part set of surgical instruments, by J. Stöpler, Greifswald, in purple plush-lined leatherette-covered case, the case 18½in. wide. (Christie's) $1,379

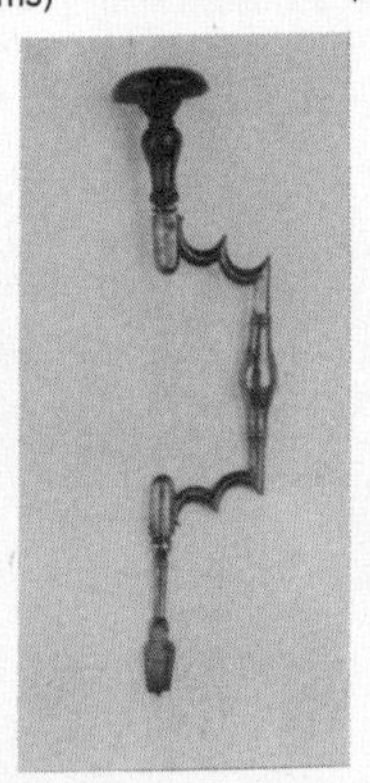

An 18th century burnished-steel trepanning brace, unsigned, with turned fruitwood handle and double-bladed bit with spade end, 11in. long. (Christie's) $552

A fine 19th century surgeon's medical set, by Stodart, the bone-saw with fruitwood handle, the bone-brush with ivory handle, brass-bound mahogany case, 16½in. wide. (Christie's) $7,728

An early Victorian travelling medicine chest, rosewood veneered and brass bound, the hinged lid with an inset shaped rectangular brass plaque. (Woolley & Wallis) $881

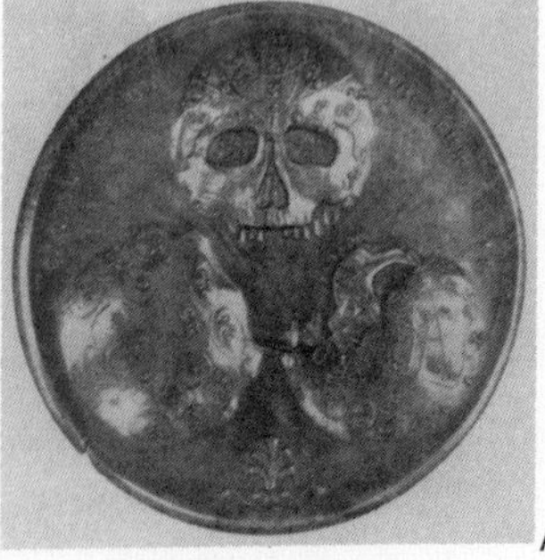

A phrenology patch box 'Cranologie du Doctor Gall', French, mid 19th century, the circular fruitwood case predded in relief, 8cm. (Bonhams) $1,285

A 19th century walnut domestic medicine chest by James Epps and Co, London, the hinged lid fitted internally with leather plaster pockets and containing fifty glass bottles, 10¼in. wide. (Andrew Hartley) $960

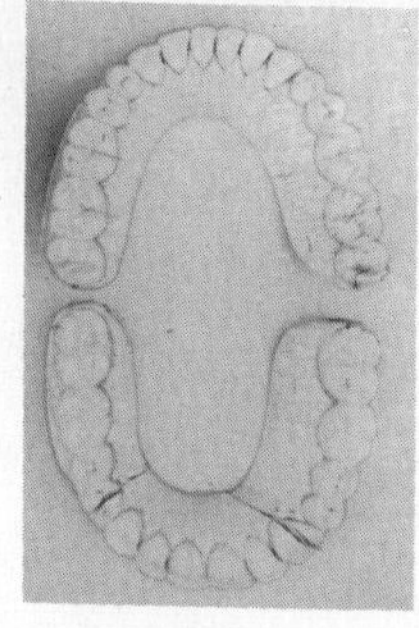

A set of bone false teeth, English, early 19th century, upper and lower jaw, together with a bone maxillary plate. (Bonhams) $313

A collection of teeth extracted from 19th century royalty & other worthies including Queen Victoria and Florence Nightingale, in a red morocco box. (Bonhams) $2,636

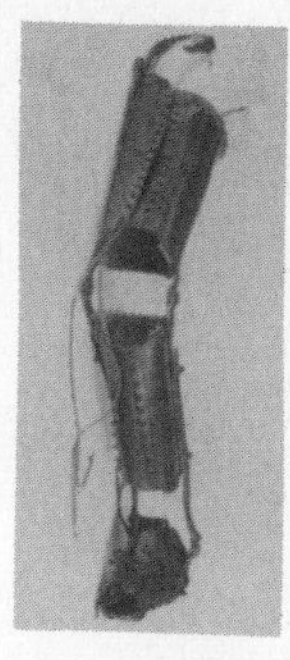

A late 19th-century iron, leather and canvas artificial leg, unsigned, the iron bracings copper-riveted to the leather, with waist strap, 38in. long. overall. (Christie's) $368

A 19th century mahogany medicine chest, the hinged lid with brass loop handle, the split fascia hinged to reveal a fitted interior with square clear glass bottles, 9in. wide. (Andrew Hartley) $840

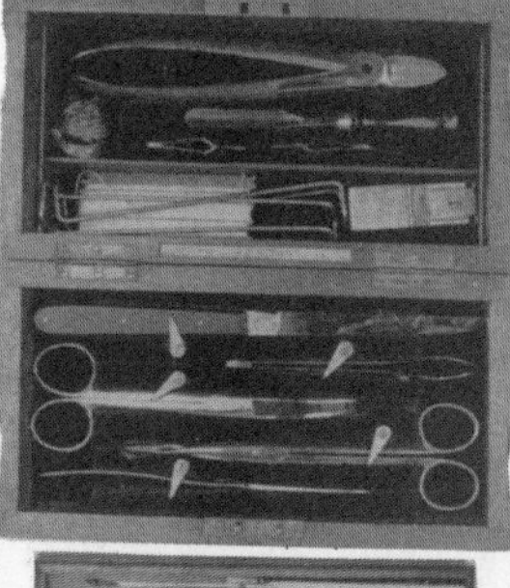

A C. Wright & Co. mahogany set of surgical instruments, English, circa 1860, a two tiered full set, in a rectangular mahogany case. (Bonhams) $1,021

A 19th century mahogany domestic medicine chest, compartments for eight bottles, the drawer below containing a tray for a steel balance and weights, and compartments, 11¾in. wide. (Christie's) $1,011

A 19th century mahogany medicine box with satinwood banding and string inlay, 6¼ x 6in. high. (Andrew Hartley) $144

A painted pine apothecary chest, American, 19th century, the rectangular molding above an arrangement of 42 graduated short drawers, 5ft.8in. wide. (Sotheby's) $19,550

A Weiss mahogany and brass bound cased amputation set, English, circa 1830, all in a velvet lined brass bound air tight case, 37.5cm. (Bonhams) $4,119

A Coca Cola miniature painted tin refrigerator, 13.5cm. high, with removable ice tray and two miniature bottles, circa 1970.
(Auction Team Köln) $120

A Biedermeier cherrywood miniature chest, fitted with two drawers, on square tapering legs, 16¾in. wide.
(Christie's) $581

19th century mahogany small apprentice's chest of two short and two long cockbeaded drawers, splayed feet, circa 1820, 10in.
(G A Key) $190

A Regency miniature mahogany chest, the rectangular top above two short and three graduated long drawers, 14¼in. wide.
(Christie's) $2,222

An unusual miniature tall case clock, probably English, 19th century, composed of various veneered woods, 18½in. high.
(Sotheby's) $2,300

A Georgian miniature oak bureau, the fall-front over a shallow drawer flanked by pull-out slides and a further drawer beneath, 18in. wide.
(Boardmans) $802

Dutch baroque beechwood miniature chest of drawers, scrolled case and three drawers, claw and ball feet, 17 x 9 x 10in.
(Skinner) $431

A fine wooden miniature dressing mirror, English, 19th century, the mirror supported by finely-turned wooden frame with inlay surround, 4½in. high. (Bonhams) $868

16in. miniature Georgian chest of five drawers, 15.5in. high.
(Jacobs & Hunt) $1,152

A George III rosewood square piano, English, early 19th century, the eight key piano with hinged top opens to reveal the internal workings, 3¼ x 5in.
(Bonhams) $1,499

A panbone candlestand, having a circular top with thumb-molded edge above a turned and incised baluster support continuing to three arched legs, 5¾in. high.
(Sotheby's) $690

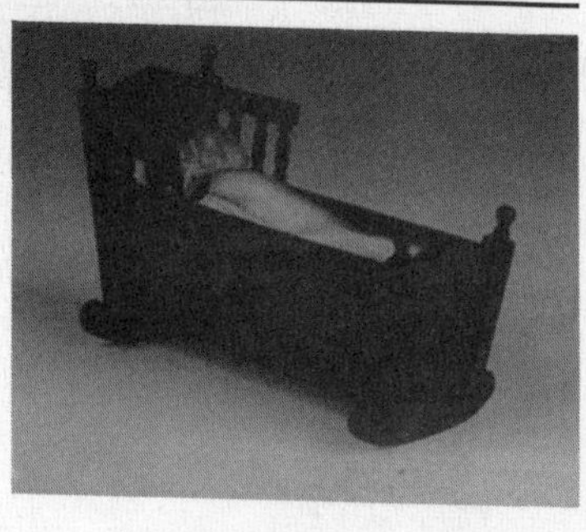

A miniature mahogany cradle, probably English, early 19th century, with shaped rocker supports, 'ball' finial decoration to sides and ends, 2¾ x 4in.
(Bonhams) $1,026

An alabaster ornament table, English, circa 1840, with tassel braiding to edge and detachable top, molded plates with napkins, food and drink, 5 x 4in.
(Bonhams) $442

A 19th century satinwood miniature chest of three graduated drawers with stained ivory handles and bun feet, 28cm. wide.
(Bearne's) $2,120

A miniature grain-painted chest of drawers, American, mid-19th century, with three drawers and a hinged top opening to a rectangular well, 42.6cm. wide.
(Sotheby's) $6,900

A Victorian mahogany miniature sideboard, the raised mirror back with molded surround and leaf and fruit carved terminals, 46cm.
(Tennants) $1,368

A miniature cast iron laundry stove with two chambers, one drawer for ashes, with five small cast iron irons held on a ledge, 20cm. high, circa 1900, salesman's model.
(Auction Team Köln) $1,716

A mahogany 'Thunder Box', English, 19th century, the portable closet with hinged lid revealing a basin with dummy porcelain knob, 1½ x 4in. (Bonhams) $868

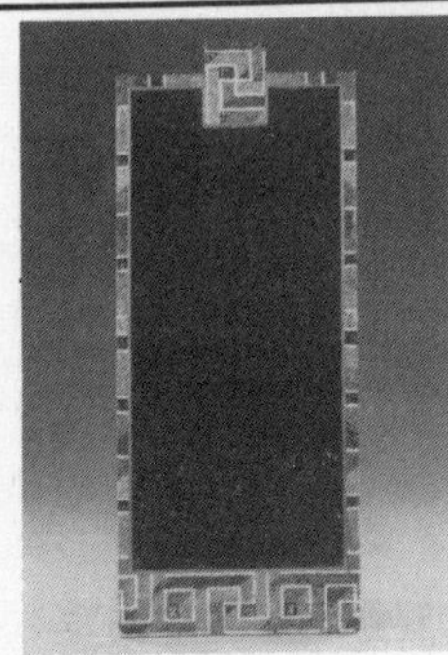

Alessandro Guerriero for Alchimia, mirror, 1986, rectangular mirrored glass, the metal frame composed of colored glass mosaic, 200cm. high. (Sotheby's) $1,747

A giltwood and gesso convex mirror, 19th century, decorated with stiff-leaf moldings, with a central panel of scrolling and meandering foliage, 62in. diameter. (Christie's) $6,521

A walnut crossbanded and oyster-veneered cushion frame wall mirror, late 17th century, the rectangular plate with a molded edge, 32in. wide. (Christie's) $8,721

A Regency brass-mounted mahogany cheval mirror, the rectangular plate in an ebonized slip and crossbanded frame flanked by ring-turned baluster trestle end-supports, 28½in. wide. (Christie's) $3,312

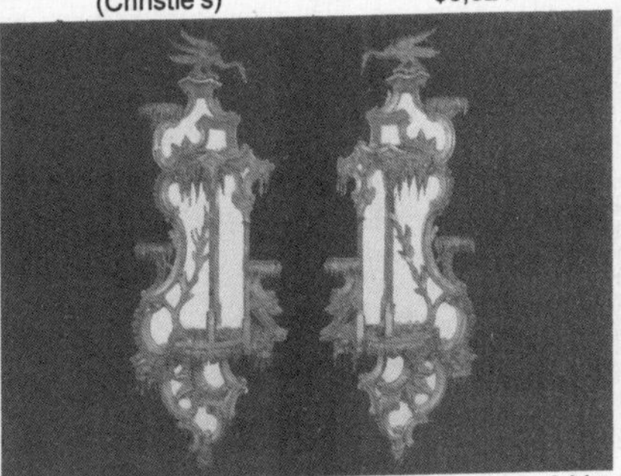

A pair of Victorian giltwood mirrors, each with asymmetrical plates within opposed C-scroll and rock-work frames and with four projecting shelves, 20in. wide. (Christie's) $8,998

A Venetian carved and painted mirror, late 19th/early 20th century, decorated with floral sprays, the cartouche shaped plate within a scrolling foliate and rock-work frame, 54in. wide. (Christie's) $5,624

C.F.A. Voysey, dressing table mirror, 1906, oak, the rectangular swivel mirror with gently arched top flanked by tapering H-form supports, 67.5cm. wide. (Sotheby's) $5,406

A 19th century large gilt wood framed circular wall mirror carved frieze of interlaced fruiting vine and wheatears, 3ft. 6in. diameter. (Russell Baldwin & Bright) $6,278

A giltwood, composition Venetian marginal plate mirror, 19th century, the ribbon-twist cresting above foliate etched marginal plates within a stiff-leaf surround, 52½in. high. (Christie's) $2,188

A rare Chippendale mahogany shaving mirror, Philadelphia, circa 1780, the shaped crest with scrolled ears on a canted trestle-form support, 26in. high.
(Sotheby's) $9,775

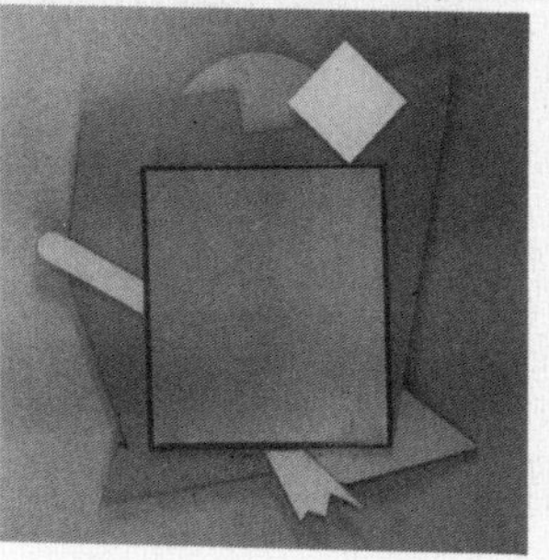

Alessandro Mendini for Studio Alchimia, 'Kandissa' mirror for the Bau.haus Art Collection, 1979, polychrome lacquered wood, 41in. high. (Sotheby's) $2,208

A George III giltwood mirror, possibly Scottish, the later rectangular plate within a C-scroll and rockwork frame, 49in. high.
(Christie's) $1,687

Lacloche Frères, mirror, circa 1930, stepped architectural caramel/opal onyx frame with slide-in rectangular mirror, 20cm.
(Sotheby's) $13,894

A pair of 19th century Venetian giltwood wall mirrors of molded cartouche form with molded floral cresting and C and shell scroll border, 42in. x 23in. overall.
(Canterbury) $4,611

A cut glass mirror, late 20th century, the rectangular plate engraved from the reverse with a stylised lady ski jumping across an alpine landscape, 69 x 56in.
(Christie's) $3,611

A giltwood oval mirror, 18th century, with a central oval plate bordered by a marginal plate, with pierced meandering floral border, 39in. high.
(Christie's) $5,249

Neoclassical carved giltwood girandole mirror, England, circa 1790, the circular convex mirror surrounded by delicately executed ornaments and flanked by double candlearms, 63in. wide, overall.
(Skinner) $26,450

A George III satinwood-veneered and rosewood-crossbanded dressing mirror, with later oval glass plate, 35.5cm. wide.
(Bearne's) $1,730

A gilt composition pier mirror, early 19th century with a beaded and ball encrusted cornice above a verre eglomise frieze, 21½in. wide. (Christie's) $825

Queen Anne mirror, probably New England, 18th century, the black painted arched frame enclosing a glass with bevelled edge, 16in. high. (Skinner) $690

Louis XVI giltwood mirror, late 18th/early 19th century, ribbon-tied husk crest over a rectangular mirror plate within a carved surround, 49½in. high. (Skinner) $2,645

A mid-Victorian polychrome-decorated and parcel-gilt overmantel, the broken pediment carved with acanthus and egg-and-dart moldings, 71¼ x 68¼in. (Christie's) $9,258

A Louis Majorelle mahogany framed triple-panel cheval mirror, the central section with an interwoven arched top carved in high relief with clematis and foliage, 211cm. x 152cm. (Tennants) $2,280

Art Nouveau giltwood mirror, Continental, early 20th century, half-round bevelled mirror mounted on giltwood frame, the lower half decorated with carved scroll silvered and gilt reeded border, 22in. wide. (Skinner) $575

Hammered copper and enamelled mirror, circa 1916, rectangular form of hammered copper accented by enamelled circular ornament in shades of green and blue, 35 x 18¾in. (Skinner) $1,955

A George IV giltwood convex mirror, the circular plate in an ebonized reeded slip and concave frame with spheres and ribbon-tied reeled edge, 36½in. diameter. (Christie's) $5,152

Baltic Neoclassical-style maple and inlay mirror, late 19th century, molded rectangular cornice above a conforming frame, flanked by stylized columns, 71in. high. (Skinner) $1,265

Arts and Crafts oak wall mirror, early 20th century, rectangular oak frame, unsigned, 40 in. high.
(Skinner) $172

An early 19th century gilt convex mirror, 95cm. diameter.
(Bonhams) $4,710

An Edwardian pierced silver mirror 16.5in., London 1901.
(Dockrees) $368

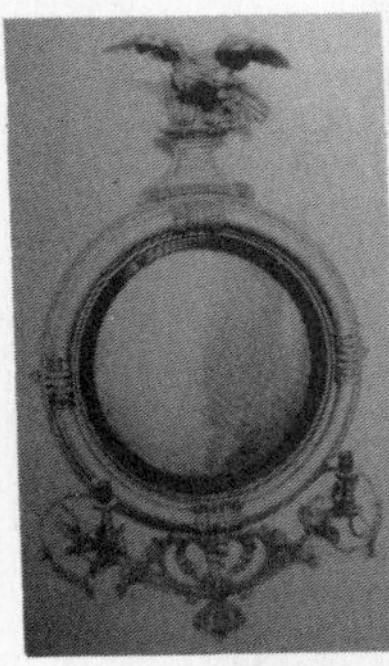

A Regency gilt framed convex mirror with carved eagle finial, molded ebony slip and twin candle sockets on acorn scroll branches, 39in. high.
(David Lay) $1,675

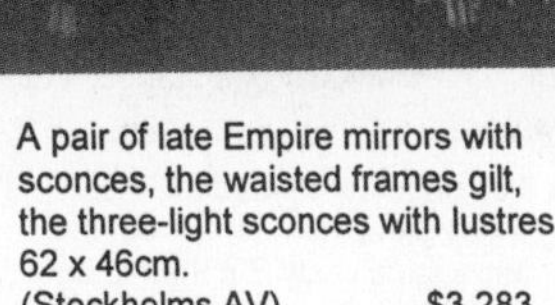

A pair of late Empire mirrors with sconces, the waisted frames gilt, the three-light sconces with lustres, 62 x 46cm.
(Stockholms AV) $3,283

Mirror timepiece, attributed to Benjamin Morill, Boscawen, New Hampshire, circa 1830, the rectangular case with hinged split baluster framed gilt and black painted door, 14in wide.
(Skinner) $5,175

TOP TIP

The condition and thickness of the actual mirror plate are often the best pointers for dating a mirror. Old mirrors usually show signs of wear, sometimes flaking. Pre-1820s plates often look like dull silver from the tin or mercury backing and the reflection is soft. Older plates are also thinner, while post-1820 plates often show a pink or maroonish color and a somewhat harsher reflection.

(Cotswold Auction Co.)

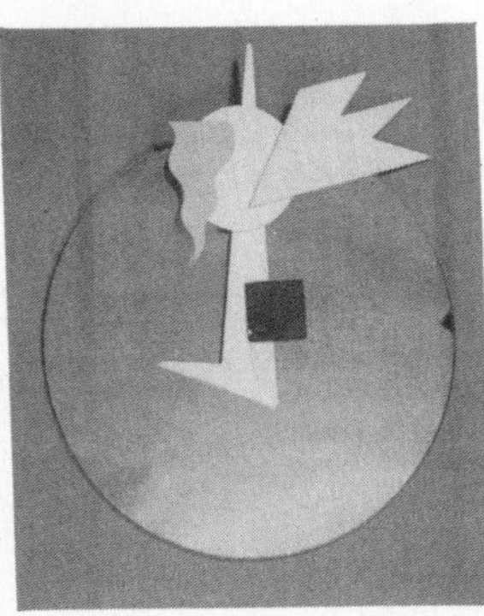

Alessandro Mendini for Alchimia, circular mirror, 1981, with colored plastic elements, 50.5cm. diameter.
(Sotheby's) $331

A George III giltwood marginal mirror, the rectangular plate with beaded molding bordered by divided plates, 35in. wide.
(Christie's) $843

A well engineered 1/5 scale model of a Gnome 9-cylinder monosoupape rotary aeroplane engine, built by L.C. Lowe with finned cylinders, pushrod and rocker operated exhaust valves, 22 x 10in. (Christie's) $8,280

A horizontal one-cylinder model steam engine motor, with brass regulator, outer cylinder diameter 40mm.
(Auction Team Köln) $603

A well engineered and presented 1in.:1ft scale model of a Sanderson 12hp beam pumping engine, built by E. Lofthouse with brass bound wood lagged cylinder 7/8.in. bore x 2½in. stroke, 16 x 17¾in.
(Christie's) $1,104

A well engineered model Rider Ericsson hot air driven feed pump, built by E. Lofthouse with table mounted water jacketed concentric cylinders, the working cylinder 2in. bore x 2in. stroke, 20½ x 18½in.
(Christie's) $1,120

A well engineered model single cylinder six column tank mounted beam engine Lady Stephanie, built by E. Lofthouse with wood lagged cylinder ½in. bore x 1in. stroke, main stop and governor valves, parallel motion, 9 x 13½in.
(Christie's) $1,011

A fine and detailed scale model of the single cylinder three pillar vertical reversing stationary engine, originally built for Booths Shoe Factory, Farsley, Leeds, and modelled by J. Webster, Farsley, 1906, 14¼ x 13½in.
(Christie's) $2,760

A finely engineered single cylinder horizontal reversing stationary engine, with blued-steel clad cylinder 1in. bore x 1in. stroke, inlet and exhaust pipes with flanged joints, 4½ x 9¼in.
(Christie's) $1,747

A Maxwell Hemmens model locomotive steam engine, adapted for coal firing, 56cm. high.
(Auction Team Köln) $5,359

A well engineered model 'Major' single cylinder center pillar beam engine, with brass bound mahogany lagged cylinder 1¾ x 3¾in. stroke, cylinder head oiler, studded stuffing boxes, 19½ x 26¼in. (Christie's) $2,576

Bing clockwork gunboat 'Möve, 54cm. single screw, painted in red lined gray, 1906.
(Christie's) $3,270

Fleischmann clockwork 34cm. liner, painted in red, ivory, black and tan, 1950. (Christie's) $909

Cased detailed model of the lightship 'Nantucket', built by William Hitchcock, well detailed and mounted in an inlaid case, model length 9in.
(Eldred's) $825

French ivory 'prisoner of war' ship model, 19th century, three-masted, fully rigged and with cannon, on a wooden base, 15½in. long.
(Skinner) $2,990

Cased sailor-made model of a full-rigged ship, late 19th, early 20th century, fully rigged, with hull painted black, case length 53in. long. (Eldred's) $1,320

Cased model of the American steam tug 'Brooklyn', planked basswood deck carries a red deckhouse and mahogany wheelhouse, mounted in an inlaid mahogany case, model length 25in.
(Eldred's) $1,650

A Bassett Lowke 0 gauge live steam 2-6-0 Mogul, refinished overall black, with 6 wheel tender Southern in gold, RN 890, spirit fired cab controls for regulator and whistle, in original box.
(Wallis & Wallis) $272

A beautifully detailed fully working live steam 1/8 scale model of the Baldwin-built variant of the classic 'American' style 4-4-0 of circa 1870, offered in fully decorated deep red livery, extensively embellished, as UPRR No. 7. (Christie's) $36,340

A Bassett Lowke 0 gauge live steam 4-4-0 Enterprise, finished overall maroon and black with yellow lining *RN6285* in gold/red shadow lettering to 6 wheel tender, three wick spirit burner, cab whistle control only, in original box. (Wallis & Wallis) $272

A 3½in. gauge L.M.S Stanier 2-6-0 locomotive and tender No 2979, English, 20th century, with a tubed copper boiler, back head fittings include pressure gauge, water gauge and more, chassis details include twin outside cylinders with valve gear, fluted connecting rods, all finished in black livery, engine 28½in., tender 17¼in. long.
(Bonhams) $1,501

A late 19th century engineered model of the 2–4–0 railway locomotive and tender 'Rover', with coal-fired boiler, outside cylinders and all normal working parts, in a mahogany framed glazed display case, 99 x 39cm. (Bearne's) $10,048

An early 1930s Hornby 0 gauge No 2 mixed goods set, containing clockwork 4-4-2 special tank loco in black, with Shell Motor Spirit tanker, 3 LMS wagons, cattle truck, open wagon and brake van, all finished in light green and gray, and an oval of track.
(Wallis & Wallis) $240

A 5½in. gauge 4-4-0 'North Eastern' locomotive and tender, English, first quarter 20th century, with a copper tubed boiler, backhead fittings include pressure gauge, twin water levels, shut off cocks and more, the engine and tender finished in green 'North Eastern' livery, engine 30½in. long.
(Bonhams) $3,476

A J & E Stevens Co. 'Two Frogs' bank, cast-iron frog with baby frog lying on back, $8^{7}/_{16}$in. long. (Christie's) $273

A painted cast iron 'Uncle Sam' mechanical bank, American, third quarter 19th century, by Shepard Hardware Co. designed by Charles Shepard and Peter Adams, 11½in. high. (Sotheby's) $1,150

A replica eagle and eaglets mechanical bank by J. & E. Stevens Co., USA, designed by Charles M. Henn, coin is placed in eagle's beak and on pulling the lever it feeds its young. (Auction Team Köln) $119

A painted cast iron 'Tammany' mechanical bank, American, third quarter 19th century, by J. & E. Stevens, designed by John D. Hall, cast in the form of a rotund politician seated in a filigree chair, 6¼in. high. (Sotheby's) $517

A Shepard Hardware Co. 'Speaking Dog Bank', maroon and yellow painted cast-iron, with seated girl dressed in red and seated dog, 7in. high, late 19th century. (Christie's) $817

A painted cast iron still 'Magic' bank, American, late 19th century, by J. & E. Stevens, designed by Henry W. Prouty, the bank with a brown-painted roof and green painted sides, 5½in. high. (Sotheby's) $2,587

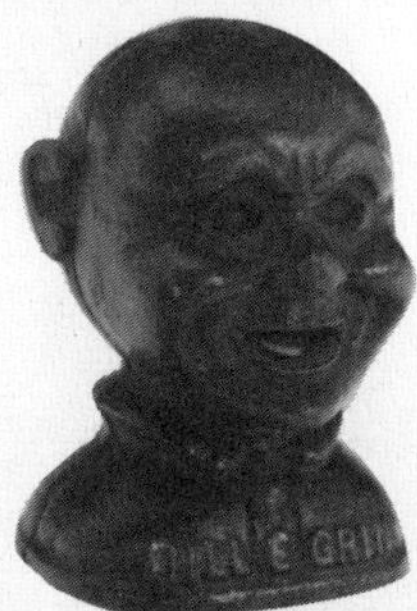

A Bill E Grin cast mechanical bank by the J. & E. Stevens Co., Cromwell CT, on inserting coin eyes roll and tongue comes out, 8.7 x 11 x 8.5cm., circa 1900. (Auction Team Köln) $788

A Calamity Bank (Football) mechanical bank by J. & E. Stevens, Cromwell, CT., cast iron, with original paint, 18cm. high, post 1905. (Auction Team Köln) $561

A Dinah mechanical savings bank by John Harper & Co., Willenhall, England, long-sleeve version, 17cm. high, 1911. (Auction Team Köln) $628

1927 Raleigh Sport 500sv, well finished sports model ready for use in original restored condition. (Tennants) $4,256

1923 A.J.S. 350cc 'Big Port' Motorcycle Reg. No. DN7088, the only 350cc machine to ever win a Senior T.T. race. This machine is a very early example of the model; it is complete and to original specification. The V5 Registration Document does not appear to belong to the machine. (Tennants) $6,080

1914 Eclipse 4 h.p. Motorcycle Reg. No U1818, this machine is the only known example of the Eclipse: fitted with their own 499cc engine and a four-speed gear box and kick starter. It is of very advanced design and with some re-commissioning will provide a useable veteran machine. Includes various spares and history file. (Tennants) $8,360

1935 B.S.A. Blue Star 350cc BKT 793, ready for the road with a full history file including brown log book. (Tennants) $3,648

1950 AJS 497cc Model 18S, VDY 601, an early example featuring the 'candlestick' rear suspension, comes with V5. (Tennants) $3,648

1951 Norton 500T 490cc FBA 266, with brown log book and V5. Taxed, believed genuine mileage of 5817. History file including a letter from the original owner. Formerly the property of Norton Factory rider, Dougie Connet. Comes with a letter of authenticity from the Norton Owner's Club.
(Tennants) $4,256

1930 Scott Sprint Special Reg. No.WX4053 Frame No.17 Engine No.PY3237, introduced for the 1930 season, and developed from the Speedway model it had a single down seat tube, the long stroke engine was specially tuned by the competition department. This machine won a silver medal in the 1930 Scottish Six Days Trial in the hands of Miss E. Stuart. (Tennants) $16,720

1951 B.S.A. B33 OSU 203, restored ready to use, first time starter, full handbooks.
(Tennants) $2,280

1919 Rover 498cc X9157, three speed foot clutch, very nicely presented with original North East registration. (Tennants) $6,080

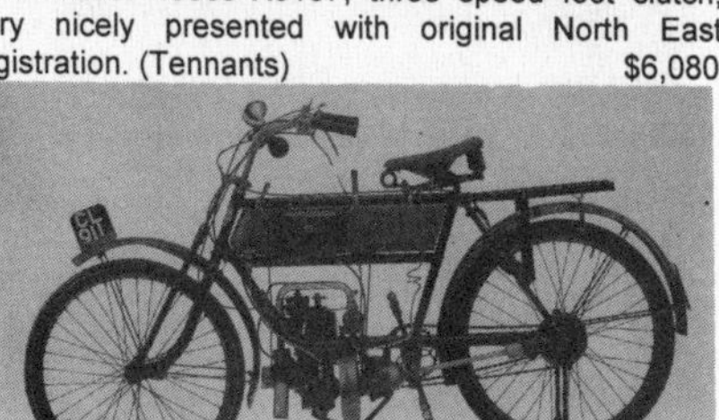

1911 F.N. 2½ h.p. single cylinder motorcycle Reg. No. CL 911, introduced in 1909, the single cylinder lightweight machine was very popular and gained a reputation for reliability and build quality.
(Tennants) $9,880

1906 FN 363cc Four Cylinder Motorcyle Reg. No. 0 49, the famous Belgian company, 'La Fabrique Nationale D'Armes de Guerre' was founded in 1889 to produce arms at their Herstal factory. They diverted to bicycle production in the 1890s and produced their first motorcycle in 1901. F.N.'s Chief Designer Paul Kelecom produced his innovative four cylinder machine during 1904;.1920s A.M.A.C. carburettor fitted. (Tennants) $19,152

1949 B.S.A. A10 Gold Flash Rigid Teles, very early example, handbook and VMCC dated.
(Tennants) $3,952

Rudge Special 500cc, converted to swinging arm after the war in an effort to stay modern.
(Tennants) $3,140

1926 Rex-Acme 348cc Motorcyle Reg. No. DN 5117 The Rex Motor Manufacturing Co. of Coventry was one of the first British manufacturers, producing their first machine in November 1900. The motorcycle is an older restoration but in very sound condition and still carries the name of its local suppliers, Shearsmiths of York. (Tennants) $5,776

1918 Norton 633cc Big 4 Combination VY 2961, in original livery with original lighting set. A model reputedly made for World War I then released onto the civilian market. (Tennants) $9,120

1925 Scott 498cc Motorcyle Reg. No. HN 3808, a very sound example of the mid twenties two speeder. It was restored some years ago by Jim Noble who used it in vintage events. (Tennants) $5,320

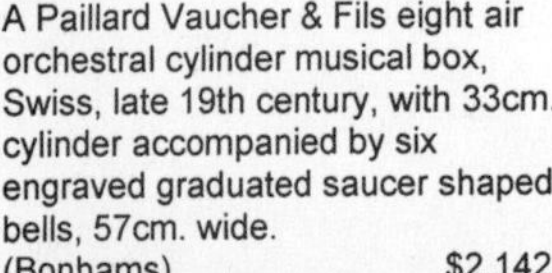

A Paillard Vaucher & Fils eight air orchestral cylinder musical box, Swiss, late 19th century, with 33cm. cylinder accompanied by six engraved graduated saucer shaped bells, 57cm. wide.
(Bonhams) $2,142

An organ box by Bendon, playing six Moody and Sankey hymns, in burr walnut case with crossbanding and printed tune-sheet, 21½in. wide. (Christie's) $1,195

A Nicole Frères grand format four air musical box, Swiss, circa 1875, 42cm. cylinder, silver songsheet plaque in the lid of the pewter and brass inlay ebonized case, 78cm. wide. (Bonhams) $11,533

An orchestral musical box playing ten operatic and other airs, accompanied by twenty-note organ, inlaid and crossbanded rosewood front and lid, 26¾in. wide.
(Christie's) $4,784

A drum and bells musical box by P.V.F., No. 5456, playing 12 airs, walnut case with brass and mother of pearl inlay, 25½in. wide, the cylinder 13in.
(Christie's) $2,576

A Britannia 'smoker's cabinet', 9in. disk musical box with two combs, walnut-veneered cabinet with crossbanded doors, 20¼in. high, with 12 disks.
(Christie's) $1,747

A drum and bells musical box playing eight airs accompanied by drums and six bells, crossbanded and inlaid rosewood veneered case, 23in. wide.
(Christie's) $1,656

An upright 9-inch Britannia disk musical box, with two combs and front-wind enclosed motor, in corner cabinet with bevelled miror panels to door, 19¼in. high, with 13 disks. (Christie's) $1,379

A George Bendon eight air bells in view musical box, Swiss, 1870s, with 33cm. cylinder, three piece comb, six graduated saucer shaped bells, 61cm. wide.
(Bonhams) $2,636

French brass and painted wood parade drum, painted rim in blue and white and red, 19th century, 20in. diameter, 15in. high.
(Eldred's) $385

Classical mahogany carved and mahogany veneer piano, C.F.L. Albrecht, Philadelphia, circa 1825, the cabinet with gilt scroll and foliate designs, 68in. wide.
(Skinner) $345

A good Royal Air Force band side drum, brass body decorated with royal coat of arms and Royal Air Force Band.
(Wallis & Wallis) $370

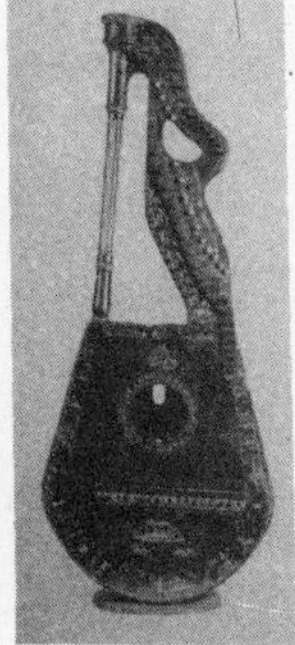

An early 19th century freestanding Dital harp by Edward Light, chinoiserie decorated body, 86cm. high in a fitted case.
(Phillips) $1,443

A Classical paint decorated curly maple veneered ormolu mounted mahogany pianoforte, signed *Charles Albrecht, Philadelphia*, circa 1825, the case fitted with three drawers, on circular reeded legs, with Federal mahogany piano stool, pianoforte 5ft. 9in. long. (Sotheby's) $2,587

A guitar, French, circa 1830, the one-piece back and the ribs of mahogany, in case, 17½in. high.
(Sotheby's) $960

Classical mahogany and mahogany veneer harmonica, probably New England, 1830s, the rectangular hinged top with rounded corners banded in veneer, 41in. wide.
(Skinner) $2,300

Civil War snare drum by A.H. White, Boston, second quarter 19th century, wooden rim, metal body engraved with band of five pointed stars centering a reserve with the Massachusetts State Seal, 12½in. high.
(Skinner) $977

A Georgian broad shaped bass drum, painted with post-1837 Royal Arms and supporters, with long feather flourishes at the top.
(Wallis & Wallis) $560

'Miss Frivolity', an original mutoscope sign with hand-tinted photographic motif, 35 x 55.cm.
(Auction Team Köln) $529

An Edison Projecting Kinetoscope, early model with original label *Patented by Thomas Edison*, with original lead, 1897.
(Auction Team Köln) $3,233

A four-color original mutoscope poster 'Patience', with hand-tinted photograph, graphics by Ralph Miele, 35.5 x 56cm.
(Auction Team Köln) $353

An original 'Sweetie' mutoscope arcade sign, 4-color, red, beige, blue and green, with hand-tinted photograph, *Approved by New York Censors*, 35 x 55.5cm.
(Auction Team Köln) $470

A four-color original mutoscope or stereo viewer poster sign 'An Adorable Savage - She Won't Scalp You', hand-tinted photograph, 35.5 x 55.5cm.
(Auction Team Köln) $469

Three-colored blue, red and black 'The Shady Lady' mutoscope sign, with hand tinted photograph, marked *Passed by New York Censor*, 35 x 55.5cm
(Auction Team Köln) $499

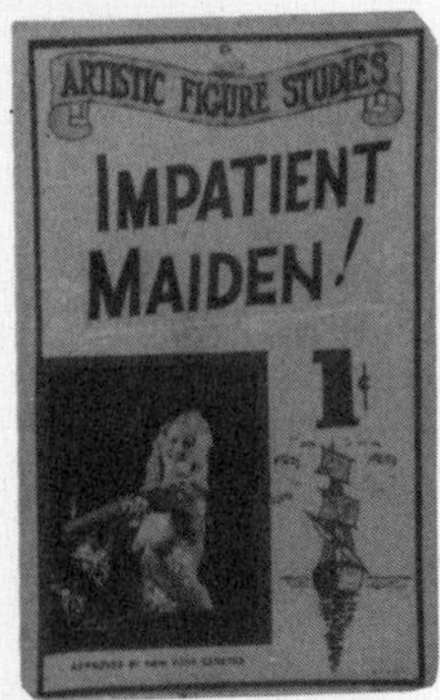

An original mutoscope sign, 'Impatient Maiden'', blue and red with hand-tinted photograph, 35 x 54.5cm.
(Auction Team Köln) $559

A decorative original poster for mutoscopes and viewers, 'Phylis of the Follies', four-color, with hand-tinted photograph, 35.5 x 56cm.
(Auction Team Köln) $353

A rare original mutoscope sign 'Give me That Veil', four-color, with sepia toned photograph, 27 x 50cm.
(Auction Team Köln) $469

An ivory netsuke, signed *Hojitsu,* Edo Period (19th century), of the sanju, 4.1cm. wide.
(Christie's) $13,041

An ivory netsuke, signed *Sekitomi,* Edo Period (late 18th century), of a Portuguese representing Fernandez Mendes Pinto, 7.4cm. high. (Christie's) $2,608

A coral and iron netsuke, Edo Period (19th century), of an iron Myochin School fly resting on a coral branch, 5.3cm. long.
(Christie's) $1,583

An ivory and lacquer netsuke, Edo Period (19th century), of a shojo kneeling and tightly holding the sleeves of its kimono, 4.7cm. high.
(Christie's) $1,490

A wood netsuke, signed *Masakuni, Edo* period (late 18th century), of an octopus in a tsubo with its tentacles stretched around it, eyes inlaid in horn, 1½in. high.
(Christie's) $3,284

A lacquered yellow willow wood netsuke, signed *Shuzan*, Edo Period (late 18th/early 19th century), of Hagoromo Hakuryo standing, spreading his arms, 4.9cm. high.
(Christie's) $559

A dark stained wood netsuke, signed with a kao, Edo Period (late 18th century), of Daruma coming to life from a kakemono, 5.6cm. high.
(Christie's) $838

A wood netsuke, signed *Jugyoku,* Edo Period (19th century), of a cheerful and smiling mermaid, her tail curled back to her body, 1¾in. long. (Christie's) $5,710

A lacquer netsuke, signed *Gyokkei*, Edo Period (19th century), of a Noh actor in the role of Shojo decorated in gold, silver and iroe hiramakie, 4.1cm. (Christie's) $2,795

An ivory netsuke, signed *Okakoto*, Edo Period, late 18th/early 19th century, of a wolf leaning over to chew on a deer's leg, 4.5cm. long. (Christie's) $8,611

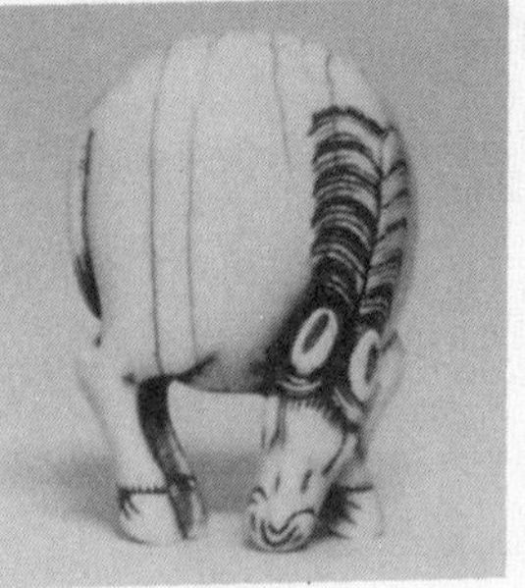

An ivory netsuke, Edo Period (18th century), of a grazing horse with its tail swept over its back, age cracks, 1¾in. (Christie's) $1,396

An ivory netsuke, signed *Garaku (Osaka)*, 18th century, of a seated monkey, his right hand on his right leg, looking down at his left leg, 1½in. (Christie's) $7,535

A wood netsuke signed *Minko*, Edo Period, of a powerfully modelled tiger, its head turned back to the right as it licks its back, wood with eyes inlaid in gilt metal with pupils in dark horn, 4cm. high. (Christie's) $4,664

An ivory netsuke, signed *Kaigyokusai Masatsugu*, Edo/Meiji Period, of a monkey grooming one of her young while another baby scrambles on her back and pulls its sibling's tail, the eyes inlaid in horn, 1½in. high. (Christie's) $25,116

An ivory netsuke, signed *katomo(kyoto)*, Edo Period, of a puppy playing with an awabi shell, katabori, ivory with staining, eyes inlaid in horn, 3.5cm. long. (Christie's) $4,485

A marine ivory netsuke, signed *Chogetsu*, 19th century, of a kappa clambering on an elaborately carved volcanic rock, its arms and legs covered in scales, 4.2cm. long. (Christie's) $5,382

An ivory netsuke, Edo Period (mid 18th century) of a Dutchman holding in his hand a trumpet with tassels and carrying a karako, 2¾in. high. (Christie's) $2,608

An ivory netsuke, signed *Jugyoku*, 19th century, of a kappa sitting by a large cucumber next to an infant kappa which clasps its parent by the right arm, 4cm. long. (Christie's) $3,050

A Safe-Guard Model S American cheque writer for dollar amounts, 1918.
(Auction Team Köln) $111

A metal cased office clock by Julius Pintsch, Berlin, with classic dial and Roman numerals, circa 1910.
(Auction Team Köln) $164

A cast iron steam copying press, possibly by Alexanderwerk, Berlin, platen size 25 x 28cm., circa 1880.
(Auction Team Köln) $185

A safe by the Victor Safe & Lock Co., Cincinnati, Ohio, with number combination lock, on castors 34 x 53 x 39cm., circa 1905.
(Auction Team Köln) $622

A Gestetner Rotary Cyclostyle No. 6 copier, with two wax plate cylinders, with original metal cover, circa 1920.
(Auction Team Köln) $217

A rare Hughes Typograph, the circular index mechanism with lever-operated plungers for each letter, connected via ratchet and pawl to spirally-grooved guide-rod, 15in. deep.
(Christie's) $23,322

The Lightning Checkwriter F & E, an American check writer by Hedman Mfg. Co., Chicago.
(Auction Team Köln) $215

The Excelsior, a cast iron hand printing press by Kelsey, Meriden CT, USA, lacking cylinders, 18.5 x 11cm. format, circa 1880.
(Auction Team Köln) $459

A Peerless Senior check writer, an obsolete design by the Peerless Check Protecting Co., Rochester, NY. (Auction Team Köln) $111

Le Photo-Éclair no. 1227, J F Fetter, France; 38 x 38mm. metal body, internal five-plate holder, and lens. (Christie's) $2,222

A light wood graphoscope with 10 stereo cards, with black painted carved exterior, 9.5cm. diameter of largest lens.
(Auction Team Köln) $247

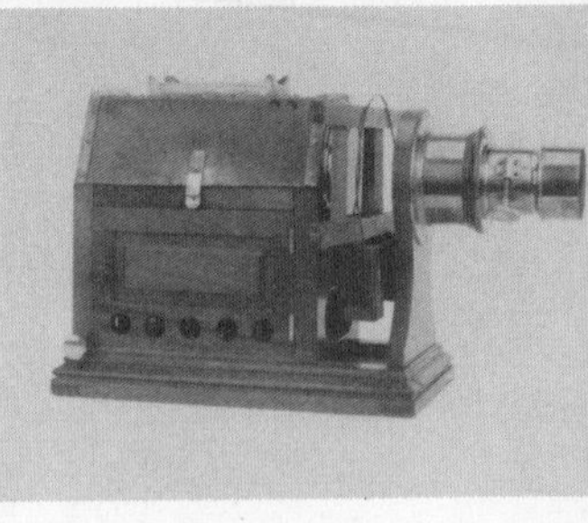

Magic lantern, American-style; shaped wood body, metal top, brass lens mount, an EA (Edward Anthony) brass bound lens with rack and pinion focusing.
(Christie's) $407

Choreutoscope slide, wood-mounted slide with hand-wound Maltese Cross movement operating a painted mica disk depicting a dancing skeleton.
(Christie's) $2,812

A Victorian walnut table top stereoscopic viewer by Smith, Beck & Beck, the walnut case with a brass inset carrying handle, overall height 18in.
(David Lay) $1,302

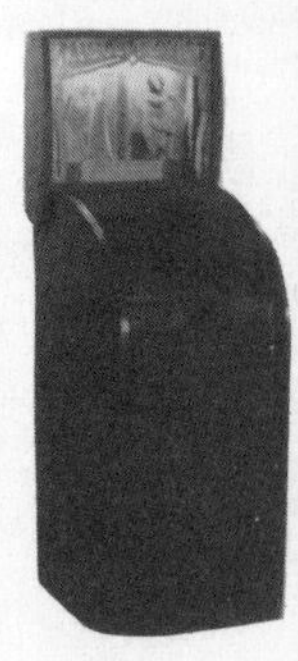

A Midget Movies coin operated 16mm. film projector on endless spool, for 25 ore pieces which give circa 3 minutes viewing time, circa 1960.
(Auction Team Köln)

$1,79

A Smith Beck & Beck table top stereo viewer, English, circa 1860, with rack adjustment to the eyepieces, with hinged top with mirrored insides.
(Bonhams) $577

The Monarch Ethopticon biunial lantern, Riley Bros, Bradford; mahogany body, black japanned metal chimney, lacquered brass fittings and lens mounts, two condensing lenses.
(Christie's) $8,887

Achromatic stereoscope no. 288, R & J Beck, London, polished wood body, brass fittings, with a pair of focusing lenses, the stereoscope inverting into mahogany box.
(Christie's) $555

Magic lantern, mahogany body, brass fittings, brass lens mount, lens, chimney and four-wick burner. (Christie's) $592

A B.M. & Biograph Co. Ltd Kinora viewer, English, circa 1900, bevelled glass viewer and crank standing on a cast iron Corinthian column, 34cm. high. (Bonhams) $1,977

Photosphere no. 1304, Cie. Française, Paris; 8 x 9cm. metal body, double darkslide and lens. (Christie's) $1,481

Le Praxinoscope by Emile Reynaud, Paris, an improved version of the zoetrope by use of a drum mirror allowing the pictures to be shown without dark flashes, post 1878. (Auction Team Köln) $1,038

Reflex camera obscura, wood body, with sliding box front section, hinged top, 7 x 10cm. viewing screen and lens. (Christie's) $1,296

A Victorian box stereoscope, veneered in burr walnut, the hinged covers revealing mirrors, revolving slide holders to turned wood knob side handles, 17¾in. high, with quantity of cards. (Woolley & Wallis) $737

Cylinder lantern, Jean Schoener, Germany, metal body with lens, chimney and integral illuminant and a quantity of circular and strip transfer slides. (Christie's) $444

Magic lantern, McIntosh Battery & Optical Co., Chicago; metal lamphouse, nickelled metal fittings, brass lens mount, a Carlot, Paris, lens. (Christie's) $203

Magic lantern, Queen & Co., Philadelphia, USA, metal lamphouse, wood base, chimney, spirit illuminant and a Queen & Co. brass bound lens, in wood box. (Christie's) $314

A Medaillon magic lantern by Lapierre Borthers, France, with colored white tin case, for 6cm. strips, with handle at rear, 33cm. high, 1880.
(Auction Team Köln) $272

Achromatic stereoscope no. 601, Smith, Beck & Beck, London, hand model, wood body, brass fittings, with a pair of focusing lenses, in maker's box.
(Christie's) $407

A 'Le Taxiphote' walnut and nickel mounted table top stereo viewer by Richard Paris, for 45 x 107mm. slides, with 9 magazines, 1910.
(Auction Team Köln) $1,814

A Taxiphote desk top stereo viewer by Richard Frères, Paris for 4.5 x 10cm. glass stereo slides, 25 slide capacity, with 17 slides of nudes.
(Auction Team Köln) $1,255

A magic lantern by Jean Schoenner, Nürnberg, for round disks, with red painted case and black chimney, complete, 29.5cm. high, circa 1880.
(Auction Team Köln) $282

A Verascope wooden stereoscope by Richard, Paris for 45 x 107mm. slides, with 49 slides, 43cm. high.
(Auction Team Köln) $665

A Czech magic lantern by Josef Razin, mahogany projector with metal lamp house and extending bellows, 59 x 22.5 x 45cm.
(Auction Team Köln) $328

A complete Zeiss Ikon/Ernemann II film system with left and right hand projectors, enabling one man to operate them from a central point, circa 1928.
(Auction Team Köln) $3,345

A Newton mahogany magic lanterr with brass mountings and slides, with two lenses, lacking burner, circa 1870.
(Auction Team Köln) $3,01

Jennens & Bettridge rectangular large papier-mâche tray, decorated with a central medallion bordered by elaborate flowering foliage, green and red detail on a gilded ground, 30½in.
(G A Key) $1,376

A Victorian black papier mâché watch stand, with gilt and mother of pearl inlaid foliage, shaped borders and base, 8¼in.
(Woolley & Wallis) $148

Rare papier mâché mechanical bulldog pull-toy, circa 1900, tan with brown and black spots, squeezing a wire leader to neck activates mouth to open with a growl, 27in. long.
(Eldred's) $1,980

Papier mâché frog, circa 1900, painted green with wide open mouth, on a wooden wheeled platform, possibly a carnival balltoss game, 19in. high.
(Eldred's) $330

A painted papier mâché lacquer cigar box by the Lukutin Factory, Moscow, 1880-1, the hinged cover painted with an Italianate scene with two young women and a man listening to a balalaika player, 20cm. long.
(Christie's) $5,377

A black and gilt papier-mâché tray, 19th century, decorated with foliage and butterflies, on a modern ebonised and gilt-decorated simulated bamboo stand, the tray 31½in. wide.
(Christie's) $1,312

A Regency papier mâché oblong tray with leopards, tigers, floral and leafage designs, on a later stand of simulated bamboo 24 x 18in.
(G.A. Key) $1,844

A Victorian papier mâché tray on stand, 78.5cm. wide.
(Bonhams) $405

A papier mâché lacquer snuff box by the Lukutin Factory, Moscow, 1841-1863, the hinged cover painted with a portrait of Nicholas I after Kruger, 3½in. long.
(Christie's) $8,066

Parker, a First Year Jotter Demonstrator ballpen, with a brushed stainless steel CT cap and a ridged nylon barrel, American, 1954. (Bonhams) $161

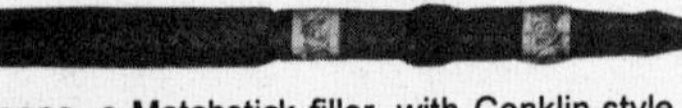

Keene, a Matchstick filler, with Conklin-style guard in black chased hard rubber with decorated gold-plated bands and a warranted 14ct 4 nib, American, 1915-1920. (Bonhams) $195

Waterman's, a 412 white metal filigree overlay Eyedropper, with no. 2 nib, clip marked *Sterling,* American, circa 1918. (Bonhams) $354

Waterman's, a silver taper cap Eyedropper, with stunning Art Nouveau decoration of bold flowers and leaves on a matted ground, with 2 nib in a period Waterman's presentation box, London hallmark, 1903. (Bonhams) $4,830

Pilot, an Art Craft Silvern Fuyu Kodachi ('Clump'), marked *Sterling Silver* with Pilot nib, Japanese, 1970s. (Bonhams) $402

Waterman's, a 9ct gold overlaid 94 Blue Ripple pen and pencil set, with barley decoration and 4-size nib, English, London hallmarks for 1929 and 1933. (Bonhams) $580

Parker, a gold filled 'Giraffe' Eyedropper, with panels of raised decoration surrounded by a textured engraved ground, with Lucky Curve Pen 3 nib, American, circa 1910. The Parker 'Giraffe' is so rare it is not even illustrated in the company's catalogues of the period. (Bonhams) $28,980

Sailor (?), an ivory and red lacquer pen decorated with Daoist Paradise, with figures beside trees in mountainous lakeside, with Kokusai 15 nib, Japanese 1930-35. (Bonhams) $1,288

Waterman's, a 403 basket weave filigree pen and pencil set, with 'coffin' clips and 2 nib, in a Waterman's presentation box, American, circa 1936. (Bonhams) $515

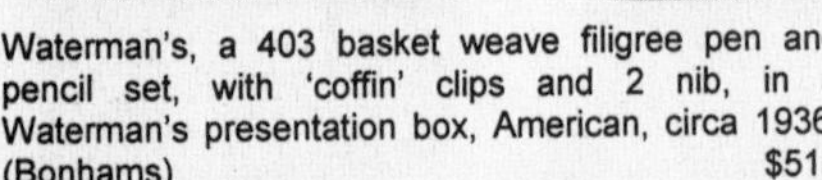

Waterman, a chased black hard rubber 18S safety pen, with No. 8 Waterman nib, American, circa 1915. (Bonhams) $1,600

Unic, a black 'Duocolor' Zerollo double pen, with Uni nibs, Italian for the French market, 1930s (Bonhams) $1,12

Waterman's, a black hard rubber 56 with broad band, Waterman's Manifold 6 nib and cloth covered box, American, 1920s. (Bonhams) $45

Aiken Lambert, a 'Mercantile' light green mottle leve filler, with a 14ct. gold nib, American, circa 192 (Bonhams) $16

M.I., a 'Rastrum' music stave writing pen, with bowl shaped reservoir and ink channels to the fine writin points, brass bound wooden handle and screw-ou terminal with cleaning blade, English, early 19t century. (Bonhams) $16

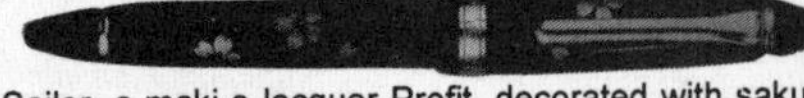

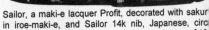

Sailor, a maki-e lacquer Profit, decorated with sakur in iroe-maki-e, and Sailor 14k nib, Japanese, circ 1990. (Bonhams) $48

Conklin, a Nozac-style faceted lever-filler, in a black/gold reticulated pattern with a 14k gold Cushion Point fine nib, American, circa 1932. (Bonhams) $242

D.D. Zerollo, a gold plated Zerollo double pen, wit chevron design and D.D. Zerollo nibs, Italian, 1930s There are very few other recorded examples c overlaid Zerollo's such as this, which are the rares versions of this already rare and unusual pen (Bonhams) $1,93

Kaweco, a decorated gold-plated overlay hexagona safety pen, with alternating floral and wavy line panels, a floral band circling mid-cap, and a 14ct. gol 202 nib, German, circa 1920. (Bonhams) $290

Platinum, a maki-e lacquer pen decorated with nightingale in a plum tree, in iroe-hira-maki-e inlai with aogai, with (replaced) Pilot 2 nib, Japanese, circ 1930-35. (Bonhams) $1,04

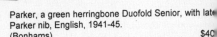

Parker, a green herringbone Duofold Senior, with lat Parker nib, English, 1941-45. (Bonhams) $40

Conklin, a black and pearl Ensemble Pen/Pencil, pen a lever-filler with Toledo nib, rotary pencil, American, circa 1930. (Bonhams) $402

Dunhill-Namiki, a maki-e lacquer 6 size balance decorated with a fighting goldfish, in iroe-hira-maki-e, on a roiro-nuri ground with Dunhill-Namiki 6 nib, Japanese, 1930s. (Bonhams) $644

Unic, a white metal basketweave filigree baby safety, with French control marks and warranted nib, French, 1920s. (Bonhams) $209

Mordan, a silver butterknife novelty pencil, with telescopic mechanism by extending the pistol-butt handle and registered design mark for 3rd August 1882, English 1880s/1890s.
(Bonhams) $563

Montblanc, a black-veined Pearl A III-Series, with 'a' nib, German, circa 1932-34.
(Bonhams) $612

Parker, an anodised aluminium No. 11 taper cup, with engraved foliate design spiralling around the barrel and overfed nib, American, circa 1903.
(Bonhams) $1,207

Namiki for Cartier, a maki-e lacquer pen decorated with a beauty dancing under a cherry tree, the green ground rendered iridescent through the use of shell in a maki-e raden style, numbered on the side of the lever and 18K Cartier 3 nib, Japanese, circa 1926.
(Bonhams) $12,880

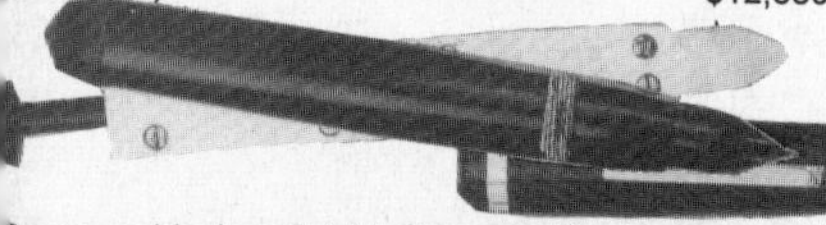

Omas, a black celluloid Colorado Double pen, with 'scissor' mechanism, two pump-filling reservoirs and Omas nibs, Italian, circa 1945.
(Bonhams) $2,093

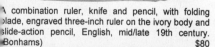

A combination ruler, knife and pencil, with folding blade, engraved three-inch ruler on the ivory body and slide-action pencil, English, mid/late 19th century.
(Bonhams) $80

Mont Blanc, a limited edition Octavian No. 2377/4810, marked *925*, with Sterling spider's web overlay and Spider nib, German, 1993. (Bonhams) $2,600

Parker, a 51 Vacumatic Demonstrator, with Classic cap and a fine nib, Canadian, 1950s.
(Bonhams) $290

A rosewood and white metal cabletwist penholder, marked *Solid Silver* and Fairchild 5 nib, possibly American. 20th century.
(Bonhams) $290

Bucherer, a white metal and enamel watch pencil, with jeweled Swiss lever movement and signed black dial, Swiss, 1930s. (Bonhams) $177

Henry Charles Simpole, a limited edition Gold Snake pen No. 001, the hard-rubber button-filling pen with 18ct gold overlay of two naturalistic textured snakes each set with emerald eyes, London Millennium hallmark for 1999/2000. (Bonhams) $4,830

Aiken Lambert, a gold filled basket weave Filigree Eyedropper, with ALCo nib, American, circa 1905-10.
(Bonhams) $161

Mordan, a silver and porcupine quill double pencil, marked *S. Mordan & Co* with side-action mechanism, English, 1880s/1890s.
(Bonhams) $258

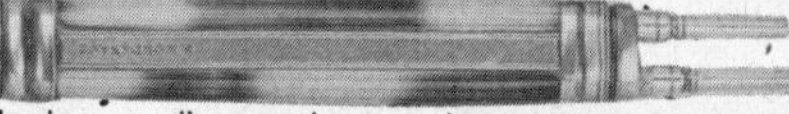

Dunhill-Namiki, a maki-e lacquer pen decorated with the Hakone Pass and Lake Biwa, tree-clad rocks framing a view of the lake with reeds and a red-sailed boat, with Dunhill Namiki 2 nib, card sales box and instructions, Japanese, circa 1930.
(Bonhams) $8,859

Mordan, a silver and enamel three-color drop action pencil, marked *S.Mordan & Co Patt 18435-89* with spiral lines of red, black and blue enamel, English, 1890s. (Bonhams) $515

Montblanc, a yellow metal 35 Meisterstück, marked *585*, with milled yellow metal clip and 18ct gold 35 nib, German, circa 1930.
(Bonhams) $8,520

Waterman's, a white metal 472½V EXT 'Extension End' Eyedropper, and 2 nib, American, circa 1917-25.
(Bonhams) $483

Two Swiss or German pewter copies of Guild flagons, 19th century, the covers mounted with shields, one supported by a lion, the other a hound, 14 x 12½in. high respectively.
(Christie's) $1,745

Four-piece pewter coffee and tea set, American, 19th century, by Roswell Gleason, consisting of a coffee pot and a teapot, both with wooden handles, a two-handled sugar and creamer, height of coffee pot, 12½in. (Eldred's) $467

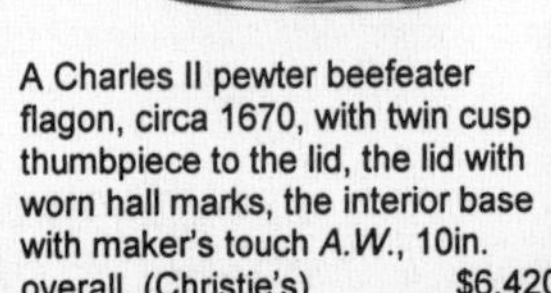

A Charles II pewter beefeater flagon, circa 1670, with twin cusp thumbpiece to the lid, the lid with worn hall marks, the interior base with maker's touch *A.W.*, 10in. overall. (Christie's) $6,420

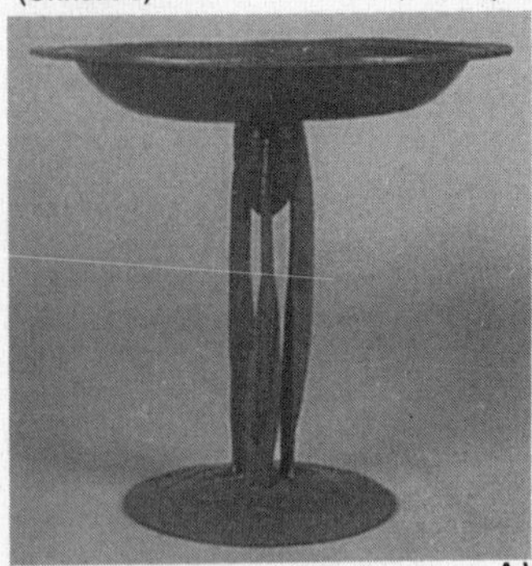

An English pewter tazza, possibly designed by Archibald Knox, of circular form, cast with spiralling tendrils and leaves, 24.5cm.
(Bonhams) $352

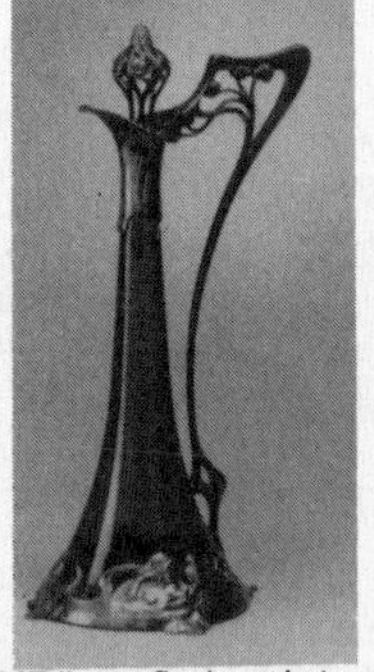

A WMF liquor flask and stopper, tapering green glass form with Britannia metal mounts, the base with the figure of a girl, Germany, early 20th century, 39cm. high.
(Stockholms AV) $656

Erik Herløw for Anton Michelsen, teapot, 1948, silver colored metal, wicker covered handle, ivory finial, 6½in. high.
(Sotheby's) $6,487

A Liberty Tudric pewter strut clock by Archibald Knox, the silvered dial within a molded Art Nouveau foliate surround in low relief with inset blue enamel leaves, 4in. wide.
(Andrew Hartley) $960

A pair of W.M.F. silvered metal candelabra, each with four sconces supported on whiplash scroll arms, the central stem of bulbous form tapering to triangular section base, 38cm. high.
(Christie's) $3,312

A French triple reeded pewter charger, later wriggle decorated in commemoration of the wedding of Charles II to Catherine of Braganza, the king shown astride his steed to the center, 19¾in. diameter. (Christie's) $2,889

A W.M.F. silvered metal tazza, modelled as a winged nymph, standing before large flowering lily pads, stroking a dove in her arms, 20.5cm. high.
(Christie's) $2,208

A W.M.F. silvered metal teaset, comprising teapot and cover, coffee pot and cover, milk jug, sugar bowl and cover, with stylized linear and square motifs, coffee pot 22cm. high. (Christie's) $460

An Art Nouveau silvered metal mirror, of shaped rectangular form, on side casting in relief with scantily clad maiden stretching upwards towards scrolling irises, 1902, 50cm. high.
(Christie's) $2,392

A George I leather-covered pewter tankard with silver-mounts and cover, Benjamin Pyne, London, 1717, the body applied with a silver cartouche chased with a portrait bust of Queen Anne, shells and scrolls. (Christie's) $3,680

Pentti Sarpaneva; Finland, a pair of white metal candlesticks designed circa 1970, each with pierced well and shaft, the circular foot molded to resemble a tree shaft, both stamped *P. Sarpaneva, ALP*, 6½in. high. (Christie's) $515

Swiss pewter tankard, top dated *1605* and stamped *Zanon…Antoine*, with cylindrical body and shaped spout, 8¼in. high.
(Skinner) $747

Tudric pewter dish stand with green glass liner.
(Jacobs & Hunt) $672

A German white metal kettle on stand, circular form, embossed foliate decoration, domed hinged cover with a foliate handle.
(Bonhams) $550

A Continental pewter alms dish, 18th century, with raised gadrooned boss to the center and with conforming ornament to the rim, 36cm. diameter.
(Christie's) $368

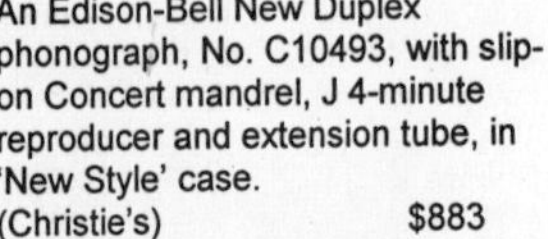

An Edison-Bell New Duplex phonograph, No. C10493, with slip-on Concert mandrel, J 4-minute reproducer and extension tube, in 'New Style' case.
(Christie's) $883

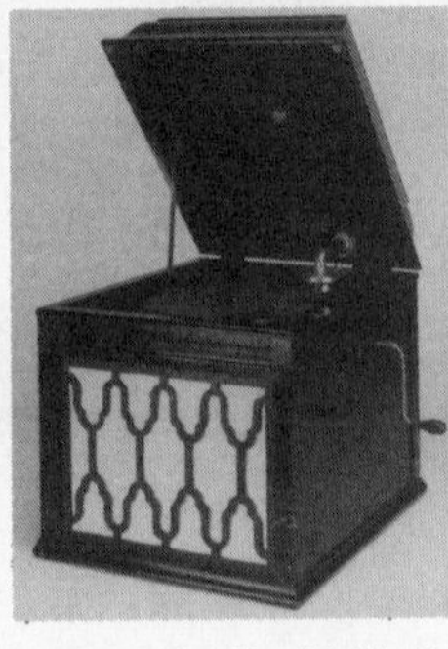

An Edison London No. 1 table disc phonograph No. 2863, with nickel-plated reproducer and mahogany case.
(Christie's) $294

A rare Edison Parlor tinfoil phonograph, by The Edison Speaking Phonograph Company, New York, the black japanned iron base with cream lines, the mandrel with groove for foil-ends, 1878, 13in. long.
(Christie's) $50,232

An Edison Concert phonograph, Model A 'New Style', now with standard mandrel and low carrier arm, Diamond B reproducer and oak-grained No. 11 Cygnet horn, oak case.
(Christie's) $1,656

A rare mahogany Edison home phonograph, Model A No. 127747, now with combination pulley, Model O reproducer, 25 x 19in.
(Christie's) $1,011

An Amberola V phonograph No. 563, with Diamond B reproducer, brown mechanism with auto-stop and mahogany case, and mahogany East-Light record cabinet. (Christie's) $827

A Beethoven Edisonic disc phonograph No. BN22929, with bronze finish Edisonic reproducer, in console cabinet with crossbanded and figured mahogany doors, 44½in. high.
(Christie's) $1,011

A Schubert Edisonic disc phonograph, No. CLT 5653, with bronze finish Edisonic reproducer, cloth-backed fret, panelled doors and turned legs, 41in. high.
(Christie's) $920

An Edison William and Mary console disc phonograph, Type W&MC33, No.116, with bronze finished reproducer, mahogany case, 43½in. wide.
(Christie's) $312

An Edison Amberola A-1 phonograph No. SM496, with traversing mandrel, Model M 2/4-minute reproducer, and mahogany case, 49in. high.
(Christie's) $2,392

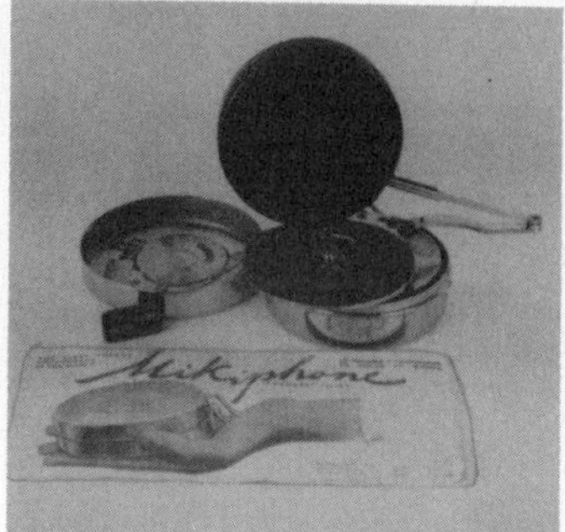

A Mikiphone pocket phonograph, with Mikiphone soundbox, nickel-plated pocket-watch form case with red and blue lettering, in mahogany box, 4½in. high.
(Christie's) $1,011

An Edison B80 table disc phonograph, with belt-drive motor, small internal horn raised an lowered by knurled knob at rear, mahogany case with replacement fret. (Christie's) $515

An Edison Amberola C VI table phonograph, with Diamond B reproducer, fixed internal horn, brown bedplate, Fireside-pattern mechanism and mahogany case with metal grille.
(Christie's) $736

A Syrena Puck phonograph with green flower horn, the base cast with a mermaid.
(Christie's) $736

A rare Amberola 60 phonograph No.1080, with Diamond D reproducer, double-spring motor, fixed motor board and mahogany case, with replacement fret.
(Christie's) $589

An Edison Triumph phonograph, Model B No. 45984, now with Combination attachment, C and H reproducers, shaver and replica witch's hat horn.
(Christie's) $1,011

A Pathé Le Gaulois phonograph with original 25cm. diameter glass horn, red painted metal case with gold decoration, 1900-1903.
(Auction Team Köln) $5,024

An Edison Standard phonograph, Model D No. 820178, with combination gearing, ICS attachment, Model R reproducer and No. 11 Cygnet horn.
(Christie's) $827

August Sander, Radio Secretary, Cologne, 1930, gelatin silver print, printed 1972, 32.6 x 21cm.
(Lempertz) $2,340

A fine framed and glazed photograph of the M.C.C. team to Australia 1911/12, in good condition, 16 x 22in.
(Sotheby's) $487

Robert Lebeck, Alfred Hitchcock in Hamburg, 1960, later gelatin silver print, 36.7 x 24.7cm., signed, titled and stamped on reverse.
(Lempertz) $1,064

Stefan Moses, Tram Conductresses, Cologne 1963, gelatin silver print, 34.3 x 26.5cm., signed, titled and dated on reverse.
(Lempertz) $505

Leni Riefenstahl, Jesse Owens, 1936, old gelatin silver print, 20.3 x 20.8cm., stamped on reverse.
(Lempertz) $4,044

Andreas Feininger, Jewish Shop on the Lower Eastside, 1949, later gelatin silver print, 31.7 x 26cm., signed in felt on reverse.
(Lempertz) $904

Robert Lebeck, Midday Prayers in an Orphanage in Surabaya, India, 1971, later gelatin silver print 37.3 x 25.4cm., signed, titled and dated on reverse.
(Lempertz) $479

A photograph of a scantily clad girl smoking, by P.C., Paris, circa 1920, with folding case, 23 x 18cm.
(Auction Team Köln) $218

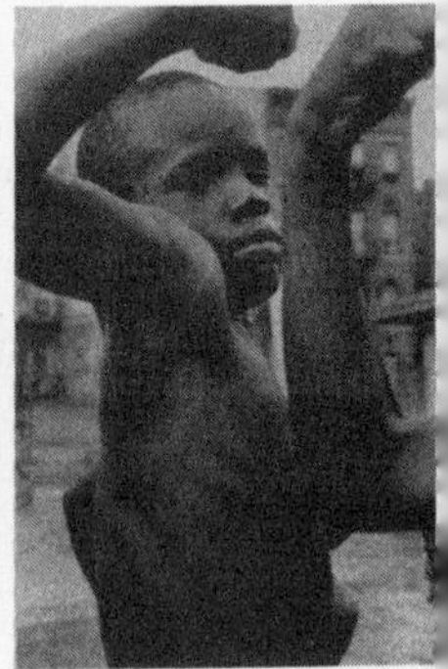

Leonard Freed, Harlem, New York 1963, later gelatin silver print, 30.2 x 20.3cm. signed, dated and titled in pencil on reverse.
(Lempertz) $586

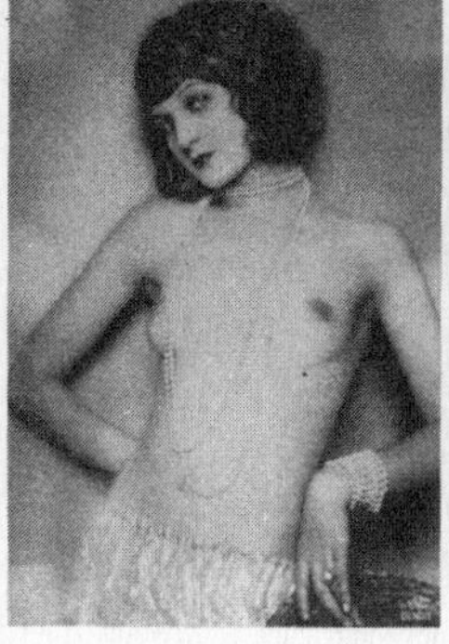

Studio d'Ora/Benda, Nude, circa 1935, gelatin silver print on board 21.5 x 15.5cm., studio stamp in the negative. (Lempertz) $586

Robert Doisneau, Pierrette d'Orient, rue Tiquetonne, 1952, gelatin silver print, 18.2 x 24cm. (Lempertz) $3,193

Gisèle Freund, Walter Benjamin, 1938, color photograph, 1980s Kodak color print, 30 x 20.3cm. signed in corner. (Lempertz) $1,064

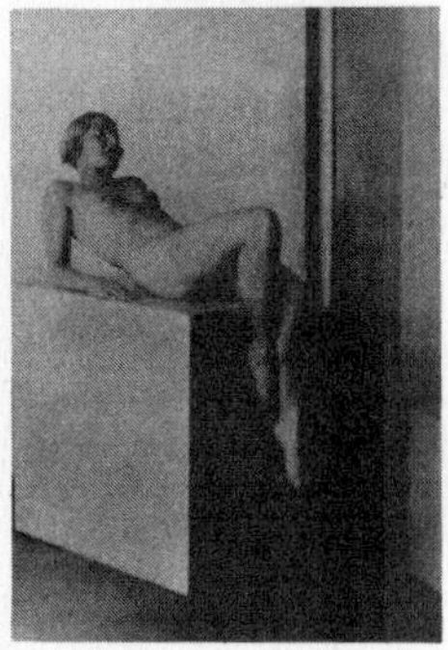

Josef Pécsi, Nude, circa 1930,old gelatin silver print, 22.6 x 16.2cm., stamped lower left and on reverse. (Lempertz) $1,595

Abe Frajndlich, Jack Lemmon, 1996, Cibachrome color print, 38.1 x 38cm., signed in pencil, dated and titled on reverse. (Lempertz) $690

Philippe Halsman, Marilyn (Dancing), 1950s, later gelatin print, 32.4 x 25cm. stamped on reverse. (Lempertz) $958

Lewis Carroll [Charles Lutwidge Dodgson] (1832-98), 'Evelyn S. Dubourg, August 1873, albumen print, mounted as a carte-de-visite, titled, dated and inscribed in ink on verso. (Christie's) $1,218

Anonymous, portraits of two sisters at different ages, 1850s, two half-plate daguerreotypes, mounted together with gilt-metal surrounds in double folding case. (Christie's) $1,312

Male nude photograph of a sportsman, anonymous, stamped on reverse *Collection Athlétique Prof. Desbonnet, Paris*, circa 1890, 15 x 23cm. in folding case. (Auction Team Köln) $314

Nan Goldin, Misty and Joey at Hornstrasse, Berlin, 1992, color photograph, Cibachrome print, 33.1 x 49.5cm., signed, titled and dated on reverse. (Lempertz) $2,340

Norman Parkinson, Montgomery Clift, New York 1951, printed later, gelatin silver print, 13½ x 11¼in., signed on the reverse. (Christie's) $1,490

Mary Ellen Mark (American b.1940), 'Ram Prahash Singh with his elephant Shyama at the Golden Circus, Ahmedabad, India, 1990', platinum print, 10 x 10in., matted, framed, titled, dated.
(Christie's) $465

Sean Scully, Lone Lewis Shack, 1990, color photograph, 50.7 x 60.5cm., signed dated, numbered and titled in biro on reverse.
(Lempertz) $1,011

Anthony Crickmay (b.1937) Mikhail Baryshnikov, 1985, printed later, gelatin silver print, 16⅞ x 23¼in., initialled on the reverse.
(Christie's) $484

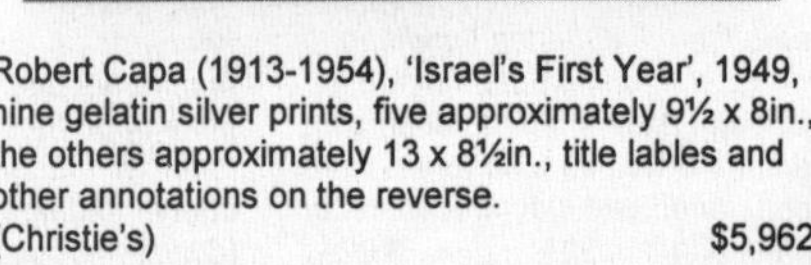

Robert Capa (1913-1954), 'Israel's First Year', 1949, nine gelatin silver prints, five approximately 9½ x 8in., the others approximately 13 x 8½in., title lables and other annotations on the reverse.
(Christie's) $5,962

Cecil Beaton (1904-1980), Andy Warhol and Candy Darling, 1969, gelatin silver print, 9½ x $9\frac{5}{8}$in., photographer's ink credit stamp.
(Christie's) $1,396

Max Scheler, Paris, circa 1960, old gelatin silver print, 19 x 28.4cm., stamped on reverse.
(Lempertz) $532

Henri Cartier-Bresson, 'Brussels',1955, printed later, gelatin silver print, image size 9½ x 14¼in., signed in ink and with photographer's blindstamp in margin.
(Christie's) $1,863

Dorothy Wilding (1893-1976) Frieze, 1923, warm-toned gelatin silver print, $9\frac{5}{8}$ x $9\frac{7}{8}$in., mounted on card, signed in pencil on mount.
(Christie's) $465

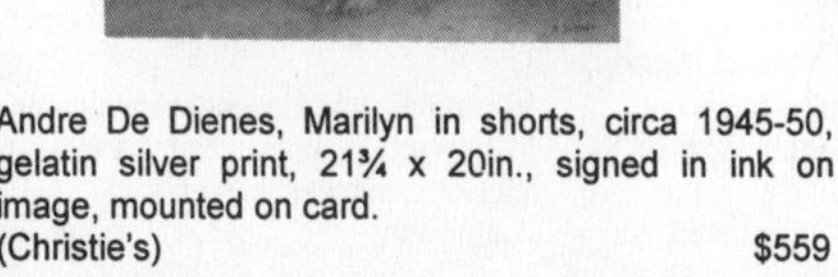

Andre De Dienes, Marilyn in shorts, circa 1945-50, gelatin silver print, 21¾ x 20in., signed in ink on image, mounted on card.
(Christie's) $559

Henri Cartier-Bresson (b.1908), 'On the Banks of the Marne, France', 1938, printed late 1970s/early 1980s, gelatin silver print, image size 9½ x 14¼in. signed in ink in margin, matted.
(Christie's) $3,353

Anon, Portrait of a mother and her two pretty daughters, mid 1850s, full plate daguerreotype with hand coloring, 28 x 23.5cm.
(Bonhams) $4,284

American photographer, 'General Tom Thumb in his 20th year', three stereo cards mounted on card with printed titles including one of the General with Barnum, and two others, related, 8.5 x 18cm.
(Bonhams) $115

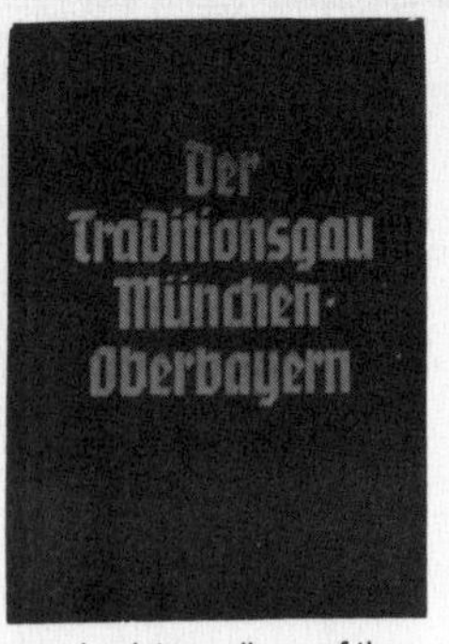

Panoramic picture album of the Munich and Upper Bavarian region, by Hitler's press photographer Heinrich Hoffmann, circa 1939.
(Auction Team Köln) $2,586

Bull, Hurrell, Harriet Louise, Greta Garbo, 1930s, six gelatin silver prints, each approximately 12¼ x 9½in., photographers' blindstamp credits in margins.
(Christie's) $1,863

Michael Roberts, 'Boy with flowers', 1988, gelatin silver print, 13⅛ x 10⅜in., signed on the reverse, matted, framed.
(Christie's) $522

Richard Avedon (b.1923), 'Marlene Dietrich/Turban by Dior/The Ritz, Paris August 1955', printed 1978, gelatin silver print, 18 x 14⅜in., signed and numbered *[?3]0/75* in pencil. (Christie's) $6,334

Berenice Abbot (1898-1991), 'James Joyce, Paris, 1928', printed circa 1990, platinum print, 13 x 10in., matted, framed, titled, dated.
(Christie's) $1,304

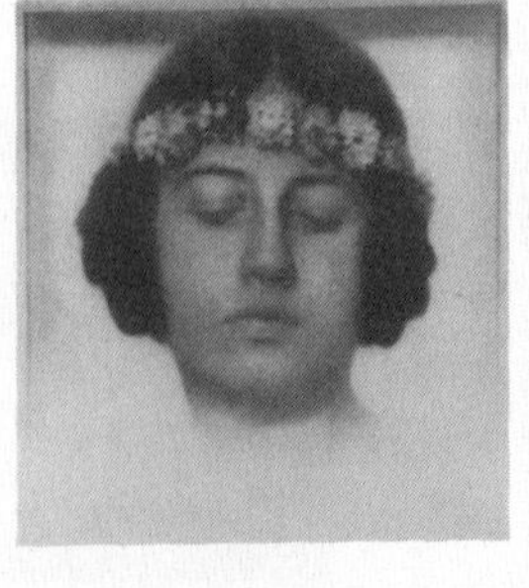

Rudolf Koppitz, Girl's Head (Spring) 1914-18, old bromoil transfer on thin card, 28.5 x 26.8cm., signed in corner.
(Lempertz) $5,756

Yousuf Karsh, Ernest Hemingway, 1957, gelatin silver print, 31.6 x 25.5cm., signed lower left.
(Lempertz) $1,915

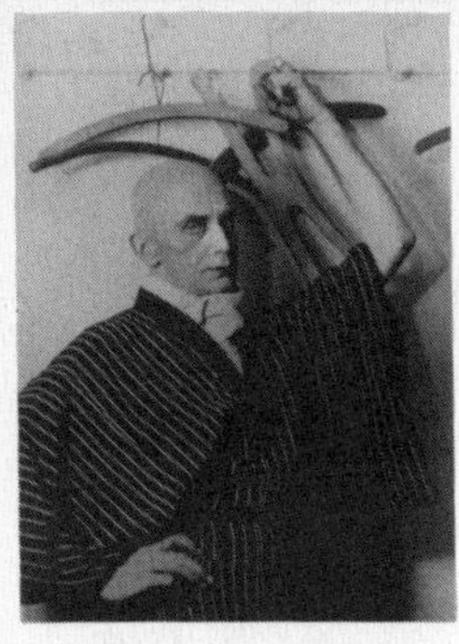

Harald Kreutzberg, 2 original gelatin silver prints, circa 23.5 x 17.7cm., one with stamp on reverse. (Lempertz) $1,064

A large collection of Fuhrmann's Kaiser-Panorama hand-tinted stereoscopic slides, in ten probably original boxes, covering such events as the Paris World Fair, 1900, and the Dreyfuss case. (Auction Team Köln) $16,457

Herbert List, Rome, 1950s, old gelatin silver print, 29.3 x 23.5cm. (Lempertz) $1,171

Regina Relang, Jacques Griffe Evening Dress, 1952, later gelatin silver print, 23.9 x 20.6cm., with monogram lower right and stamped and dated on reverse. (Lempertz) $1,064

Richard Beard, casual portrait of a gentleman wearing a hat and scarf, circa 1850s, half-plate daguerreotype, mounted as oval, paper-taped at edges, in folding morocco case. (Christie's) $6,110

Philippe Halsman, Sammy Davis, Jr. 1965, gelatin silver print, 13½ x 10¾in., titled and dated in pencil and with photographer's ink copyright and address stamps *33 West 67 Street/New York 10023* on the reverse. (Christie's) $1,118

Herbert Ponting, a grotto in an iceberg, circa 1910-12, gelatin silver print, 12 x 9in., matted, framed. (Christie's) $749

Julia Margaret Cameron, The Kiss of Peace, 1869, albumen print laid down on original card, 34.2 x 26.7cm. (Lempertz) $21,288

'Maria Paudler' by Manassé, 8 x 14cm., signed in the negative, with large folding case, circa 1935. (Auction Team Köln) $122

Thomas Robinson, 1803, a Gentleman, possibly a self-portrait, wearing red coat with black collar and gold trim, signed with initials, oval, 2½in. high.
(Bonhams) $942

Henry Edridge, circa 1790, Elizabeth Francis, with blue bandeau in her powdered hair, wearing blue dress, gold frame with plaited hair reverse, oval, 2¾in. high. (Bonhams) $2,041

English School, circa 1790, a Gentleman, with powered hair, wearing blue coat with red collar, white waistcoat and tied stock, gold frame with blue glass reverse, oval, 2½in. high. (Bonhams) $628

English School, circa 1790, a lady, wearing white bonnet and green dress and black ribbon choker, gilt-metal frame, the hinged reverse glazed to reveal locks of hair, oval, 65mm. high.
(Bonhams) $392

Henry Bone, 1830, after John Russell, Caroline Anne East, wearing pink dress, her arm around her younger brother Henry, who wears yellow dress, enamel, signed on obverse, 123mm. high.
(Bonhams) $2,355

Archibald Skirving, circa 1790, a Lady of the Cheesment-Severn family, wearing white dress and fichu with turquoise waistband and white turban, gold frame with plaited hair reverse oval, 3in. high.
(Bonhams) $1,570

James Millar, circa 1800, one of a pair of portraits of Elizabeth and Philip Francis: she with upswept brown hair wears white dress; he with gray hair and side whiskers wears blue coat, ovals, 3in. high.
(Bonhams) (Two) $1,884

Emilie Lachaud de Loqueyssie-Hebenstreit, 1821, a pair of portraits of a husband and wife: he, with side-whiskers, wears black coat, she wears black dress, signed, 67mm. high.
(Bonhams) (Two) $1,178

Abraham Seaman, circa 1730, a Gentleman, with full-bottomed wig, wearing white cravat, tan colored coat and blue waistcoat with gold figured yellow trim, enamel, gilt-mounted rectangular papier-mâché frame, oval, 1¾in. high.
(Bonhams) $1,100

Attributed to John Thomas Barber Beaumont, circa 1790, a Gentleman, with powdered hair, wearing black coat and waistcoat, gold frame, oval, 2¾in. high.
(Bonhams) $706

Samuel Hoffmann, circa 1645, a Gentleman, with brown hair and moustache, wearing black cloak and white collar, on vellum, ornate molded ormolu frame, oval, 3¼in. high. (Bonhams) $5,809

Attributed to Karl von Saar, circa 1835, a lady, wearing décolleté pale blue dress with black belt, green stained, turned wood frame, oval, 72mm. high.
(Bonhams) $1,209

Charles Hardy, 1806, a Gentleman, wearing brown coat with velvet collar, white waistcoat and cravat, signed on reverse and dated, oval, 2¾in. high. (Bonhams) $706

P. Benazzi, 19th century, an oval portrait miniature, bust of a girl wearing striped blue dress with lace collar, 2in. oval, signed.
(G.A. Key) $1,081

James Scouler, 1761, a young girl wearing décolleté blue dress, slashed to reveal white and decorated with pearls, signed and dated, oval, 1½in. high.
(Bonhams) $1,020

Anglo-Dutch School, circa 1700, a fine portrait of a young boy, with full-bottomed wig, wearing brown doublet, white jabot and red cape, oil on copper, oval, 3¼in. high.
(Bonhams) $4,553

Attributed to James Miller, circa 1800, a fine portrait of a young Lady, with powdered hair, wearing décolleté white dress with blue waistband and black ribbon choker, oval, 3in. high.
(Bonhams) $2,198

Circle of Michael Dahl, circa 1690, a Girl, her blonde hair falling in curls on her left shoulder, wearing white dress, oil on copper, oval, 3¼in.
(Bonhams) $628

George Engleheart, 1801, a fine portrait of Mr. Bogle, wearing black coat, white waistcoat, tied stock and frilled cravat, signed, gold frame, the reverse with locks of hair, oval, 93mm. high.
(Bonhams) $8,164

American School, 19th century, miniature portraits of a young couple, signed on reverse, *drawn by Peter Louise, Taken June 12th 1824*, watercolors on paper, 3¼ x 2⅝ and 2¾in.
(Skinner) $3,105

W. Thicke, circa 1800, a Naval Officer, wearing coat with blue collar and white facings, gold frame, oval, 68mm. high.
(Bonhams) $706

Thomas Hull, circa 1790, a gentleman, believed to be Richard Brinsley Sheridan, his powdered hair en queue, wearing black coat, oval, 1¾in. high.
(Bonhams) $706

American School, early 19th century, miniature portrait of a gentleman, unsigned, watercolor on ivory 3⅝ x 3in.
(Skinner) $575

Attributed to Thomas Peat, circa 1810, a gentleman, wearing blue coat with black collar and gold buttons, oval, 2½in. high.
(Bonhams) $597

French School, early 19th century, a young Lady, wearing décolleté white dress with coral-colored ribbon waistband, in landscape with waterfall, bearing signature *J.B. Isabey* and date *1810,* oval, 2¾in. high. (Bonhams) $1,256

American School, 19th century, miniature portrait of a naval officer, unsigned, watercolor on ivory, 3¼ x 2⅝in., in period frame.
(Skinner) $517

Walter Stephens Lethbridge, circa 1810, a Lady, wearing décolleté blue dress with white lace underslip, set in red leather travelling case, oval, 79mm. high.
(Bonhams) $502

An oval bust portrait miniature of a woman, in ornate case with scroll frieze blue and white enamel back, 2 x 1½in. (Russell Baldwin & Bright) $644

Jane Hay, circa 1870, 'Dressing Up'; The Hay Thorburn children, Alison, Priscilla and William, dressed in elaborate and colorful costumes, rectangular, 3¾in. high. (Bonhams) $1,413

Circle of Andrew Robertson, circa 1810, a young Gentleman, wearing blue coat with black collar, white stock and cravat, gold frame, oval, 62mm. high. (Bonhams) $707

Sir William Charles Ross, R.A., 1857, Mrs Howard of Brereton Hall, seated in a red upholstered chair, wearing spectacles, signed on reverse and dated, oval, 2¾in. high. (Bonhams) $1,020

B.D., circa 1830, a young Lady, her hair in ringlets with black ribbon and gold ornament at her center-parting, wearing blue dress, signed with initials, oval, 3in. high. (Bonhams) $864

Charles Robertson, circa 1800, a gentleman, three-quarter length, with powdered hat, wearing blue coat, white waistcoat and cravat, gold frame, oval, 63mm. high. (Bonhams) $1,178

English school, circa 1690, a Nobleman with full-bottomed wig, wearing gilt studded breastplate and white jabot, oil on copper, oval, 4¼in. high. (Bonhams) $706

Charles Dixon, circa 1760, a scholar wearing mortarboard over his powdered bag wig, oval, 1¾in. high. (Bonhams) $283

Emmanuel Flavien Chabanne, 1837, a Lady, wearing black dress with tied lace collar, gold drop earrings and pocket watch on chain, oval, 3¾in. high. (Bonhams) $2,198

The Rage of Paris, 1938, Universal, U.S. one-sheet, 41 x 27in., linen-backed. (Christie's) $181

Dead of Night, 1945, Ealing, British quad, 30 x 40in., unfolded, art by Leslie Hurry. (Christie's) $7,944

Blue Skies, 1946, Paramount, U.S. one-sheet, 41 x 27in., linen-backed (Christie's) $758

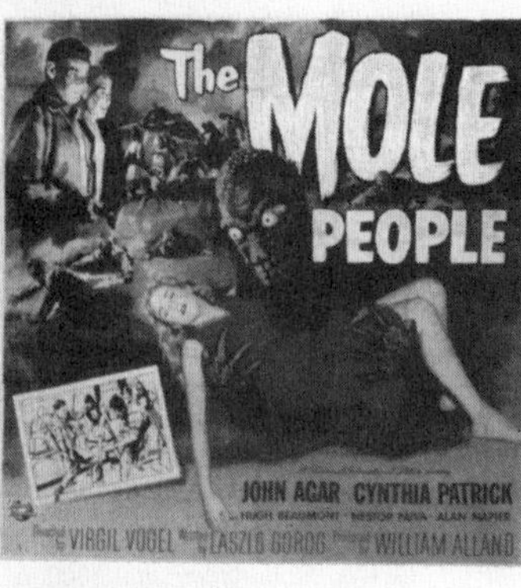

The Mole People, 1956, Universal, U.S. six-sheet, 81 x 81in., linen-backed, art by Reynold Brown. (Christie's) $722

The Killers/I Gangsters, 1946, Universal, Italian two-foglio, 55 x 39in., linen-backed. (Christie's) $2,556

Magnum Force, 1973, Warner Bros., U.S. six-sheet, 81 x 81in., linen-backed. (Christie's) $1,534

The African Queen/La Reine Africaine, 1951, Romulus, Belgian, 18¼ x 14in., linen-backed. (Christie's) $631

The Titfield Thunderbolt, 1953, Ealing, British quad, 30 x 40in., paper-backed, art by Edward Bawden. (Christie's) $1,534

Double Indemnity/Assurance sur la Mort, 1944, Paramount, French, 63 x 47in., linen-backed, art by Roger Soubie (b.1898), (Christie's) $2,889

Key Largo, 1948, Warner Bros., French, 31 x 24in., linen-backed. (Christie's) $1,714

Kid Galahad, 1937, Warner Bros., U.S. title card, 11 x 14in. (Christie's) $451

The Big Steal, 1949, R.K.O., U.S. one-sheet, 41 x 27in., linen-backed. (Christie's) $361

River of no Return/ Rivière sans Retour, 1955, Twentieth Century Fox, French, 63 x 47in., linen-backed, art by Roger Soubie (b. 1898) (Christie's) $1,264

Duck Soup, 1933, Paramount, U.S. lobby card, 11 x 14in.. (Christie's) $2,167

The Miniver Story/Addio Signora Miniver, 1950, MGM, Italian four-foglio, 79 x 55in., linen-backed, art by Ercole Brini, (Christie's) $643

The Elusive Pimpernel, 1950, Archers, British three-sheet, 79 x 40in., signed by Michael Powell. (Christie's) $758

Johnny Guitar, 1953, Republic, British quad, 30 x 40in., linen-backed, art by Eric Pulford. (Christie's) $469

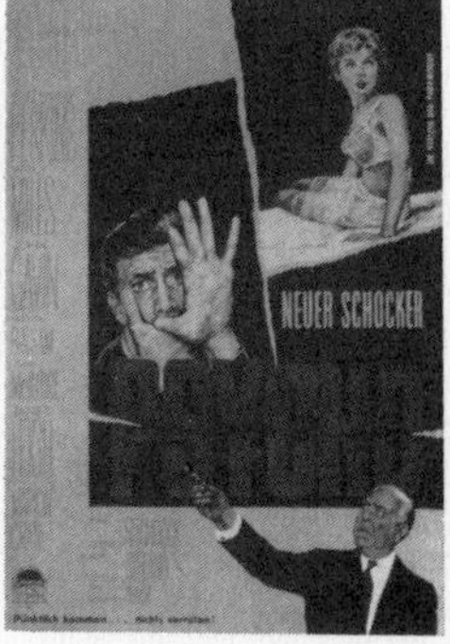

Psycho, 1960, Paramount, German, 33 x 23in., linen-backed, art by Rolf Goertz. (Christie's) $722

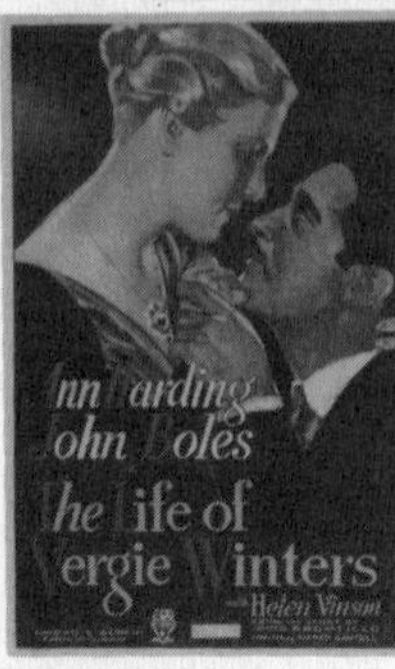

The Life of Vergie Winters, 1934, R.K.O., U.S. one-sheet, 41 x 27in., linen-backed.
(Christie's) $812

Bambi, 1942, Disney/R.K.O, U.S. six-sheet, 81 x 81in., linen-backed.
(Christie's) $1,625

Alfred Hitchcock, Rebecca, 1940, Selznick, U.S. one-sheet, 41 x 27in., linen-backed.
(Christie's) $1,625

The Invasion of the Body Snatchers/Invasione degli Ultracorpi, 1956, Allied Artists, Italian two-foglio, 55 x 39in., linen-backed, art by Antonio Biffignandi.
(Christie's) $722

The First Kiss, 1928, Paramount, U.S. half-sheet, 22 x 28in.
(Christie's) $361

Wuthering Heights/Cumbres Borrascosas, 1939, Goldwyn, Argentinian, 43 x 29in., linen-backed, art by Osvaldo Venturi (1900-89).
(Christie's) $361

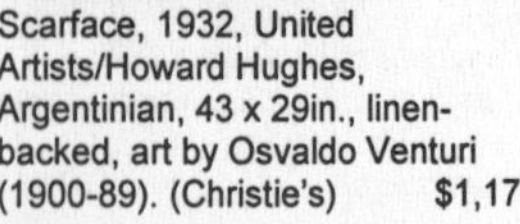
Scarface, 1932, United Artists/Howard Hughes, Argentinian, 43 x 29in., linen-backed, art by Osvaldo Venturi (1900-89). (Christie's) $1,173

The Halfway House, 1944, Ealing, British quad, 30 x 40in., paper-backed, art by Matvyn Wright.
(Christie's) $812

Black Narcissus/ Narciso Nero, 1946, Archers, Italian four foglio, 79 x 55in., linen-backed, art by Anselmo Ballester (1897-1989)
(Christie's) $3,250

Joe Louis vs Joe Walcott, 1948, R.K.O., Italian two-foglio, 55 x 39in., linen-backed.
(Christie's) $722

Thunderbirds Are Go, 1967, MGM, British quad, 30 x 40in., framed.
(Christie's) $631

James Cagney, circa 1930, French publicity portrait, Warner Bros., 39 x 26in., art by Jacques Bonneaud.
(Christie's) $722

The Adventures of Sherlock Holmes/Sherlock Holmes, 1939, Twentieth Century Fox, French, 46 x 30in., linen-backed, art by Jacques Bonneaud.
(Christie's) $1,174

The Trail of the Lonesome Pine/ La Fille du Bois Maudit, 1935, Paramount, French four-panel, 94 x 126in., art by Jacques Bonneaud.
(Christie's) $631

All Quiet on the Western Front/A l'Ouest Rien de Nouveau, 1930, Universal, French, 15½ x 11⅞in., linen-backed, art by Joseph Koutachy.
(Christie's) $686

Lost Horizon, 1937, Columbia, U.S. one-sheet, 41 x 27in., linen-backed, art by James Montgomery Flagg (1887-1960).
(Christie's) $5,416

Psycho, 1960, Paramount, U.S. lobby card, no. 3, 11 x 14in.
(Christie's) $758

My Darling Clementine, 1946, Twentieth Century Fox, U.S. one-sheet, 41 x 27in., linen-backed, art by art by Sergio Gargiulo.
(Christie's) $1,173

Raw Deal, 1948, Reliance, U.S. one-sheet, 41 x 27in., linen-backed. (Christie's) $1,264

Get Carter, 1971, M.G.M., British quad, 30 x 40in., linen-backed, art by Peltzer. (Christie's) $1,090

Gilda, 1946, Columbia, Belgian, 18½ x 14in., linen-backed. (Christie's) $922

The Black Cat, 1934, Universal, U.S. leader press one-sheet, 41 x 27in., linen-backed. (Christie's) $4,724

Reservoir Dogs, 1991, Dog Eat Dog Productions/Rank, British quad, 30 x 40in., unfolded, signed in different colored felt pens by Quentin Tarantino, Harvey Keitel and Tim Roth. (Christie's) $2,362

Sleepers West, 1941, Twentieth Century Fox, U.S. one-sheet, 41 x 27in., linen-backed. (Christie's) $325

An American in Paris/Un Americain à Paris, 1951, MGM, style A, French, 62 x 45in., linen-backed. (Christie's) $1,625

The Big Sleep, 1946, Warner Bros., U.S. half-sheet, 22 x 28in., paper-backed. (Christie's) $998

Planet of the Apes/ La Planète des Singes, 1967, Twentieth Century Fox, French, 63 x 47in. art by Jean Mascii. (Christie's) $361

Stagecoach, 1948, United Artists, U.S. one-sheet, 41 x 27in. (Christie's) $992

Angels With Dirty Faces, 1938, Warner Bros., U.S. title card, 11 x 14in. (Christie's) $2,362

Texas Bad Man, 1932, Universal, U.S. one-sheet, 41 x 27in. (Christie's) $2,528

Breakfast at Tiffany's/Diamants sur Canapé, 1961, Paramount, French, 63 x 47in., linen-backed, art by D. Vinin. (Christie's) $1,264

Singin' In The Rain, 1952, M.G.M., U.S. six-sheet, 81 x 81in., linen-backed, framed. (Christie's) $9,993

Shanghai Express, 1932, Paramount, French, 31 x 24in., linen-backed, art by Roger Soubie (b.1898). (Christie's) $12,719

The Big Shot/Le Caïd, 1942, Warner Bros., French, 63 x 47in., linen-backed, art by Boris Grinsson (b. 1907). (Christie's) $2,528

Champagne Charlie, 1944, Ealing, British quad, 28½ x 39in., paper-backed, art by S. John Woods. (Christie's) $722

La Belle et la Bête, 1946, Discina, French, 63 x 47in., linen-backed, art by Jean-Denis Malcles (b. 1912). (Christie's) $3,250

The Gold Rush, 1925, United Artists, U.S. window card, 22 x 14in., framed.
(Christie's) $5,451

Breakfast At Tiffany's, 1961, Paramount, British quad, 30 x 40in.
(Christie's) $1,999

Dark Victory, 1939, Warner Bros., U.S. insert, 36 x 14in.
(Christie's) $7,631

It Happened One Night, 1934, Columbia, U.S. one-sheet, 41 x 27in., linen-backed, framed.
(Christie's) $14,536

The Lavender Hill Mob, 1951, Ealing, British quad, 30 x 40in. paper-backed, art by Ronald Searle. (Christie's) $1,272

Sullivan's Travels, 1941, Paramount, U.S. three-sheet, 81 x 41in., linen-backed.
(Christie's) $7,268

Mysterious Lady/Den Mystiska Kvinnan, 1928, M.G.M., Swedish, 39½ x 27in., art by Eric Rohman (1891-1949)
(Christie's) $1,271

Dial M For Murder, 1954, Warner Bros., British quad, 30 x 40in., linen-backed, framed.
(Christie's) $4,360

Casablanca, 1961 re-release, Warner Bros., Italian four-foglio, 79 x 55in., linen-backed, art by Campeggi Silvano [Nano] (b.1923.)
(Christie's) $5,451

Lifeboat, 1943, T.C.F., U.S. one-sheet, 41 x 27in., linen-backed.
(Christie's) $2,180

Goldfinger, 1964, United Artists, British quad, 30 x 40in., style A, linen-backed.
(Christie's) $3,271

Casablanca, 1942, Warner Bros., U.S. one-sheet, 41 x 27in.
(Christie's) $11,810

King Kong, 1933, R.K.O., Swedish, 47 x 25in., paper-backed.
(Christie's) $19,078

Rope, 1950s re-release, Transatlantic, British quad, 30 x 40in., linen backed.
(Christie's) $509

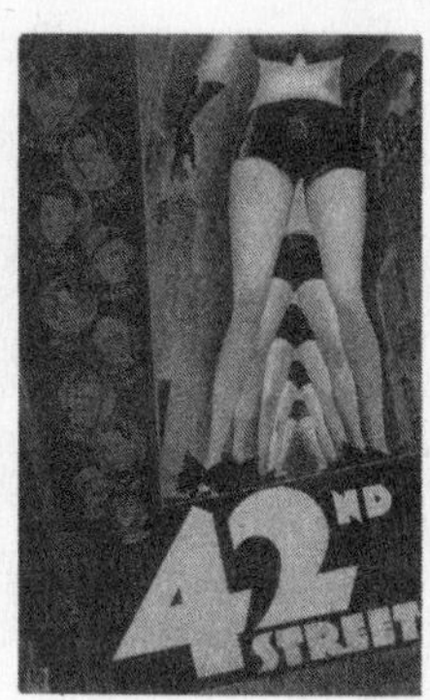

42nd Street, 1933, Warner Bros., U.S. one-sheet, 41 x 27in. linen-backed, framed.
(Christie's) $27,255

Beau Geste, 1939, Paramount, U.S. one-sheet, 41 x 27in., style B linen-backed.
(Christie's) $6,905

Wings In The Dark, 1934, Paramount, U.S. half-sheet, 22 x 28in., unfolded.
(Christie's) $581

La Sirene des Tropiques/Fresterskan Fran Tropikerna, 1927, Filmdepoten, Swedish, 35½ x 24in.
(Christie's) $12,719

Walter Koch, Davos, lithograph in colors, circa 1905, printed by J.E. Wolfensberger, Zürich, backed on japan 41 x 28½in.
(Christie's) $2,889

Emil Cardinaux (1877-1936), Davos, lithograph in colors, 1918, printed by Wolfsberg, Zürich, backed on linen, 50½ x 36½in.
(Christie's) $7,222

Jules Abel Faivre, Sports d'Hiver, Chamonix, lithograph in colors, 1905, printed by J. Barreau, Paris 42½ x 30in.
(Christie's) $8,66

Roger Broders, Sports d'Hiver, Au Col de Voza Voza, PLM, lithograph in colors, circa 1930, printed by L.Serre & Cie., Paris, backed on linen, 39½ x 25½in.
(Christie's) $3,611

Albert Muret (1874-1955), Chemin-de-Fer, Martigny-Orsieres, lithograph in colors, 1913, printed by Sonor, Genève, backed on linen, 39½ x 28in.
(Christie's) $3,069

Eric de Coulon (1888-1956) Alpes & Jura, lithograph in colors, circa 1935, printed by Le Novsteur, Paris, 39 x 24in.
(Christie's) $1,806

Paul Aigner, Winter Sports in Austria, offset lithograph in colors, circa 1950, printed by Brüder Rosenbaum, Vienna, 37½ x 25in.
(Christie's) $686

Paul Ordner, Mont Revard, lithograph in colors, circa 1930, printed by M. Déchaux, Paris, backed on linen 39 x 24½in.
(Christie's) $633

Carlo Pellegrini, (1866-1937) Les Avants, lithograph in colors, 1904, printed by A. Trüb & Cie., Lausanne, backed on japan, 44 x 20in. (Christie's) $1,62

Anonymous, L'Hiver en Norvège, lithograph in colors, 1909, printed by Kristen Petersen, backed on japan, 38 x 27in. (Christie's) $1,534

Roger Broders, Chamonix, lithograph in colors, 1930, printed by Lucien Serre & Cie., Paris, 39 x 24½in. (Christie's) $2,528

Sabi, Dolomiti offset lithograph in colors, 1947, printed by Trevisan, backed on linen, 39½ x 27½in. (Christie's) $1,806

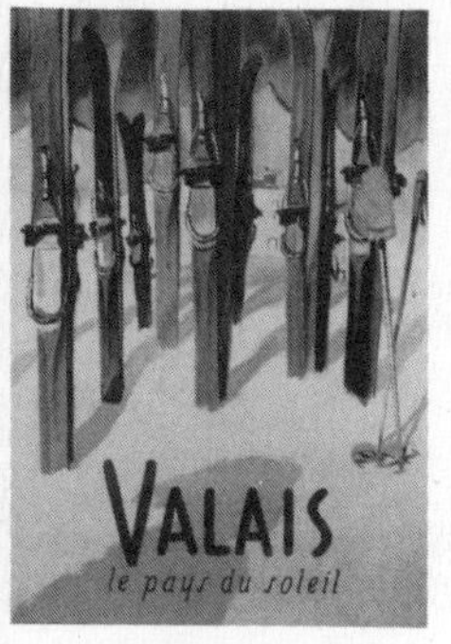

Herbert Libiszewski (1897-1985), Valais, lithograph in colors, 1949, printed by Säuberlin & Pfeiffer S.A., Vevey, backed on linen, 50½ x 36in. (Christie's) $13,541

Francisco Tamagno, Chamonix, Mont-Blanc, PLM, lithograph in colors, circa 1900, printed by Emile Pecaud & Cie., Paris, backed on linen, framed, 42 x 30in. (Christie's) $19,860

Gaston Gorde, St. Nizier, lithograph in colors, circa 1955, printed by Édition Gaston Gorde, Grenoble, 39 x 24½in. (Christie's) $89

Walter Herdeg, St. Moritz, FIS, lithograph in colors, 1933, printed by Orell Füssle, Zürich, backed on japan, 50 x 35½in. (Christie's) $5,417

Alex Walter Diggelmann, St. Moritz Sportwoche, lithograph in colors 1929, printed by Wolfsberg, Zürich, 50 x 35½in. (Christie's) $1,714

Eric de Coulon, Jeunes Gens..., lithograph in colors, circa 1925, printed by Money, Paris, backed on linen, 46½ x 31cm. (Christie's) $505

Anonymous, Wengen, lithograph in colors, circa 1925, printed by A. Trüb & Cie., Aarau, 40 x 25in. (Christie's) $15,640

Carl Kunst (1884-1912), Bilgeri-Ski-Ausrüstung, lithograph in colors, circa 1910, printed by Reichold & Lang, München, backed on linen, 20 x 30in. (Christie's) $1,444

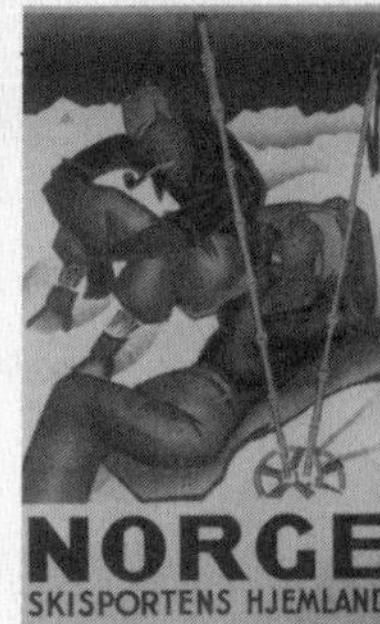

J-E, Norge, Skisportens Hjemland, lithograph in colors, 1936, printed by Norsk Lith. Officin, Oslo, 39½ x 24½in. (Christie's) $1,35

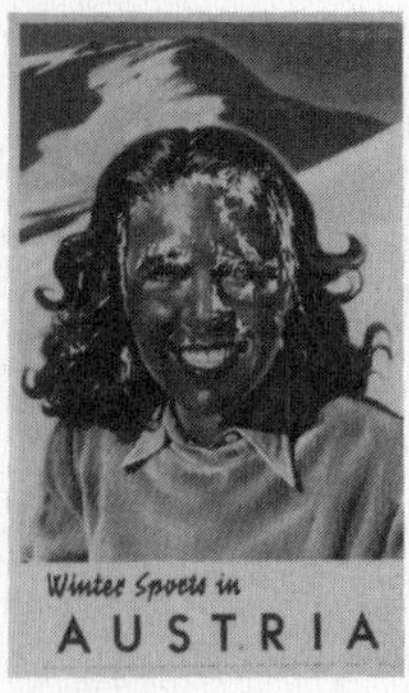

Paul Aigner, Winter Sports in Austria, offset lithograph in colors, circa 1950, printed by F. Adametz, Vienna, 37 x 25in. (Christie's) $451

Anonymous, Maloja, Hotels Schweizerhaus & Belvedere, lithograph in colors, circa 1910, printed by A. Trüb & Cie., Aarau, backed on japan, 31½ x 39½in. (Christie's) $4,694

Schettler, Mürren, lithograph in colors, 1937, printed by Orell Füssli, Zürich, backed on japan, 4 x 25in. (Christie's) $1,53

Anonymous, Wengen, lithograph in colors, circa 1920, printed by A. Trüb & Cie., Aarau, backed on japan, 40 x 24½in. (Christie's) $3,972

Knittel, Kreuzeckbahn, lithograph in colors, circa 1950, printed by Dr. Köhler & Co., München, backed on linen, 23½ x 34in. (Christie's) $451

Pellegrini, Andermatt, lithograph in colors, 1909, printed by J.E. Wolfensberger, Zürich, backed on japan, 43 x 26in. (Christie's) $2,52

Ludwig Howlwein, Winter In Deutschland, lithograph in colors, 1935, printed by Herm. Sonntag, 29 x 19½in. (Christie's) $397

Walter Koch, Davos, lithograph in colors, 1905, printed by Wolf, Basel, backed on japan, 35½ x 25½in. (Christie's) $4,694

Herbert Bayer (1900-1985), Ski In Aspen Colorado, photography and lithography, circa 1950, 40 x 30in. (Christie's) $5,777

Walter Schnackenberg (1880-1961), Hedemaria Scholz in 'Die Rodelhexe', lithograph in colors, 1912, printed by Oscar Consée, München, 49 x 35½in. (Christie's) $9,028

Burkhard Mangold (1873-1950), Confection Kehl, PKZ, lithograph in colors, 1909, printed by J.E. Wolfensberger, Zürich, backed on japan, 49 x 37½in. (Christie's) $1,625

Ludwig Hohlwein (1874-1949), Allemagne 1936, lithograph in colors, 1936, printed by Reichsbahnzentrale für den Deutschen Reiseverkehr, Berlin, on linen, framed, 40 x 25in. (Christie's) $2,708

Carl Moos (1878-1959), Kemm & Cie, lithograph in colors, 1916, printed by Fretz Frères, Zürich, backed on japan, 50 x 35½in. (Christie's) $1,806

Johannes Emil Muller, Vallorbe-Le Pont-Brassus, lithograph in colors, 1927, printed by Simplon, Lausanne, 36½ x 27½in. (Christie's) $2,528

Armando Testa (1917-), Cervinia, lithograph in colors, circa 1965, printed by Stig, Torino, backed on linen, 39½ x 28in. (Christie's) $686

Louis Icart, Golden Veil, etching and aquatint, printed in colors, signed in pencil, artist's blindstamp, copyright mark, numbered *181* and framed, 38 x 48cm. (Christie's) $1,656

Currier and Ives, publishers (American 1857-1907); Louis Maurer, lithographer (German/American 1832-1932) 'Life in the Woods, Starting Out', 1860, lithograph with hand coloring on paper, 22½ x 30in., framed. (Skinner) $1,495

Robert Havell, View of the City of Boston from Dorchester Heights, hand colored aquatint, published by W.A. Coleman, New York, 1841, printed by William Neale, colored by Havell and Spearing, image 309 x 447mm. (Sotheby's) $19,550

Nathaniel Currier, publisher, after Arthur Fitzwilliam Tait (American 1819-1905), Catching a Trout, 1854, lithograph with hand-coloring on paper, sheet size 20¼ x 25¾in. (Skinner) $1,150

Louis Icart, Attic Window, etching, printed in colors, signed in pencil, artist's blindstamp, copyright mark, numbered *196*, framed, 36 x 42cm. (Christie's) $1,560

Henry Bainbridge and George W. Casilear (Publishers), View of San Francisco, taken from the Western Hill at the foot of Telegraph Hill, looking toward Rincon Point and Mission Valley, hand colored lithograph, with touches of gum arabic, 1851, image 529 x 879mm. (Sotheby's) $5,750

Utamaro (1754-1806), oban tate-e, 38.3 x 24.5cm., from the series Twelve types of women's handicraft.
(Christie's) $15,835

Utamaro (1754-1806), oban tate-e, 38.1 x 25.4cm., a bijin arranging her make-up holding a mirror in her arm. (Christie's) $7,825

Utamaro (1754-1806), oban tate-e, 38.5 x 25.4cm., a bust portrait of Hitomoto of the Daimonjiro, reclining slightly.
(Christie's) $10,246

Harunobu (1724-1770): a large and rare oban tate-e, 38.7 x 26.1cm.; a female dancer performing a lion dance with a headdress resembling fans, signed.
(Christie's) $11,178

Harunobu (1724-1770): chuban 27.8 x 21cm., a scene in a tea house, with a gentleman leaving a room, a courtesan at his feet, signed.
(Christie's) $10,805

Harunobu (1724-1770): chuban, 28.5 x 21.1cm. ; a young woman in an elaborate kimono seated beneath a crescent moon and a tree watching the flight of a cuckoo.
(Christie's) $7,079

Toyokuni (1769-1825): oban tate-e, 38.9 x 24.7cm.; three bijin dressed up as sanbaso dancers, signed Toyokuni ga.
(Christie's) $2,049

Toyokuni (1769-1825), oban tate-e, 38.5 x 26.6cm., a posthumous bust portrait of the actor Sawamura Sojuro III in the role of Satsuma Gengobei.
(Christie's) $7,452

Utamaro (1754-1806), oban tate-e 38 x 25.5cm., half length and bust portrait of the courtesan Usumizu of the Amatsuruya.
(Christie's) $20,493

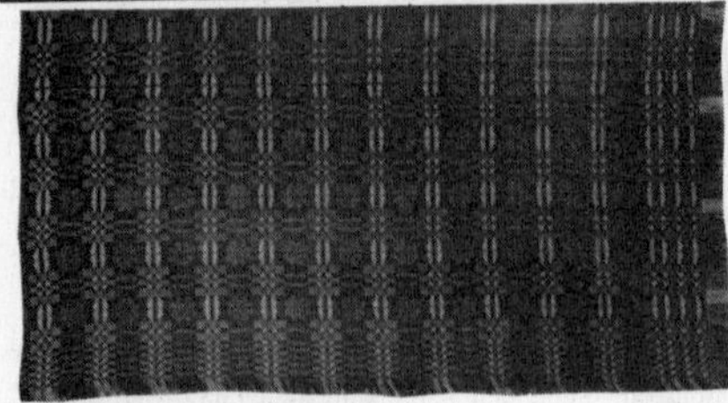

A red, green and slate-blue overshot woven coverlet, probably Pennsylvania, 19th century, in two panels sewn together woven with cloverleaf and checkerboards, has fringed border, approximately 74 x 68in. (Christie's) $460

A fine pieced and appliqued Baltimore album quilt, probably Baltimore, Maryland, circa 1860, composed of various printed and solid red, green, yellow and blue fabrics into a pattern of twenty-five squares, approximately 60 x 60in. (Sotheby's) $8,050

A pieced red white and blue cotton American flag with central medallion 'Civil War' quilt, American, circa 1865, composed of brightly colored red, white and blue patches, the red and white stripes with star-filled central medallion, approximately 88in. x 88in. (Sotheby's) $12,650

A pieced and appliquéd red, white and blue cotton 'Union' quilt, probably Pennsylvania, circa 1915, composed of brilliantly colored patches with four spread-winged American eagles and shields, 76in. square approximately. (Sotheby's) $8,050

A pieced cotton Star of Bethlehem quilt, American, late 19th/early 20th century, with central star medallion and patterned diamonds of green, pink, blue, yellow and beige with six-pointed stars of corresponding colors throughout, 98 x 96in. approx. (Sotheby's) $2,300

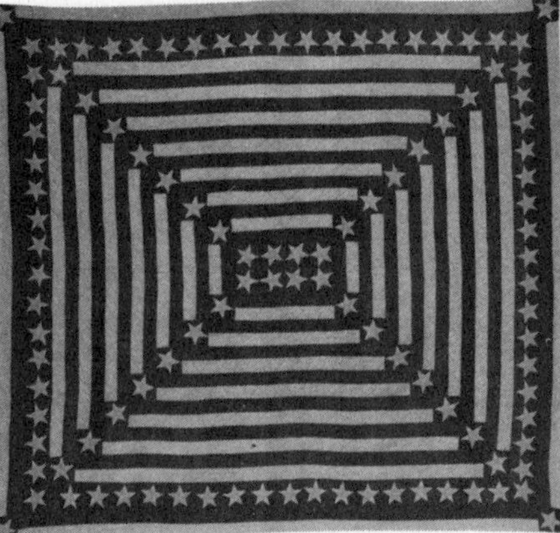

An unusual pieced and appliquéd red, white and blue 'Concentric Bars and Stars' quilt, American, circa 1915, composed of brilliantly colored red, white and blue patches arranged in concentric squares centring a block of stars, approximately 88in. x 76in. (Sotheby's) $7,475

A pieced cotton 'baby block' child's quilt, American, late 19th/20th century, composed of spruce-green, light brown and blue patches, the field with herringbone and outline quilting, 35½ x 44in. (Christie's) $172

A rare and unusual pieced and stuffed cotton Turtle Quilt, Southern, probably Georgia, late 19th/early 20th century, in an unusual variation of the Robbing Peter to Pay Paul pattern, in red and pale yellow patches, 76 x 64in. (Sotheby's) $12,650

A fine pieced and appliqued calico quilt, American, mid-19th century, composed of brightly colored red, green and yellow printed fabrics arranged in an oak reel pattern, 88 x 88in. (Sotheby's) $3,450

An Amish pieced 'Diamond in the Square' quilt, probably Pennsylvania, early 20th century, composed of green beige and burgundy wool and synthetic patches, 78 x 76in. (Sotheby's) $1,725

An extremely fine and rare, appliqued and embroidered Baltimore-style album quilt, signed *Mary Foster and Elizabeth Holland*, mid 19th century, composed of various printed and solid red, green, yellow, beige and blue fabrics in a pattern of twenty five squares, 99 x 99in. (Sotheby's) $8,625

An unusual pieced and appliquéd printed cotton 'Kerchief' quilt, American, circa 1876, composed of a variety of patriotic printed kerchiefs including depictions of George Washington, American eagles, flags and shields, 101 x 92in. approximately. (Sotheby's) $9,200

A Siemens three-valve Type 53 WL loudspeaker, bakelite case with doors, 1935. (Auction Team Köln) $234

A Westinghouse Model H124 Little Jewel bakelite portable radio. (Auction Team Köln) $254

A New Zealand 5 valve Sheffield radio, with Konvolut replacement parts. (Auction Team Köln) $220

A Philips Super Inductance Type 634 A radio with four tuning buttons, circa 1932, in working order.
(Auction Team Köln) $360

A Marconiphone Type 81 receiver No. S/V 1503, with eight valves, six condensers, two stud tuners, sloping panel enclosed by panelled flap, 25½in. wide, circa 1925.
(Christie's) $1,717

A very rare Kramolin Model RDV 40 Pentatron radio with original TKD triple valves VT 139, circa 1926.
(Auction Team Köln) $2,179

A Mark III short wave tuner, by W/T Factory, W.D. Southgate, with cat's whisker, perikon and carborundum detectors, 14in. wide, circa 1917.
(Christie's) $3,612

A novelty Ponti radio in the form of an urn, also called the Rondo 'Magic Box', 1949.
(Auction Team Köln) $1,453

Walter Maria Kersting, a bakelite Kleinempfanger receiver, designed 1938, manufactured by Hornyphon, the square brown bakelite case with circular cloth speaker grille, 9¾in. high. (Christie's) $631

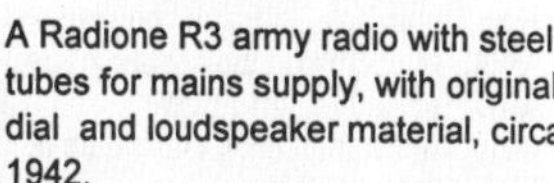

A Radione R3 army radio with steel tubes for mains supply, with original dial and loudspeaker material, circa 1942.
(Auction Team Köln) $335

A radio lamp, by Radio Lamp Company of America, Chicago, of bronzed metal with baluster stem, five-valve chassis in base, 25in. high. (Christie's) $686

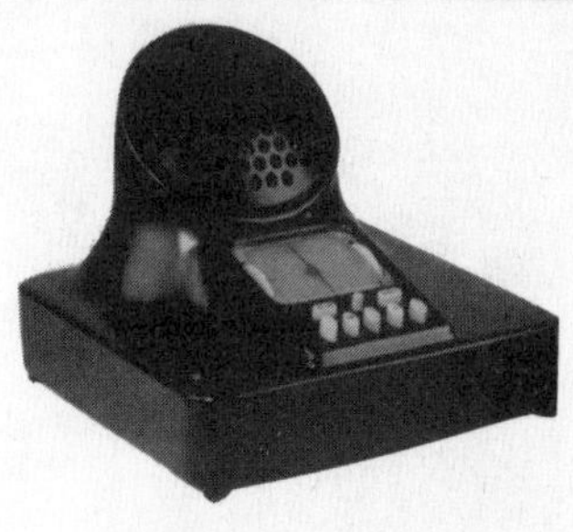

Luigi Caccia Dominioni & Livio & Pier Giacomo Castiglioni, Italy, radio model No. 547, for Phonola, 1938-39.(Bonhams) $1,730

A Pye Type 250AC mains receiver, with oval sloping control panel, walnut case with removable back and two Cosmos Short Path valves, 14in. wide. (Christie's) $397

A Radio Polar twin 2-valve set with special Radio Micro Bivolt tubes, metal case, circa 1922, possibly New Zealand. (Auction Team Köln) $669

A transmitter variometer, Type S1610, by Radio Communication Co. Ltd. London, with revolving copper helix within two outer helices, in plywood frame, 9in. wide. (Christie's) $217

A Burndept Ethophone V four-valve receiver with two condensers, swinging coil and black front panel, in oak case, 21¾in. wide, circa 1925, and a Burndept Ethovox horn speaker. (Christie's) $994

A British Marconi Type V2.A 2-valve radio, with accessories, lacking fascia, 1922.
(Auction Team Köln) $1,090

An HMV Model 800 autoradiogram, No. 220424, with counterbalanced pick-up, in walnut case with ebonized plinth, 35½in. wide, circa 1935. (Christie's) $552

Bob Dylan, signed and inscribed album record sleeve, to front cover, Nashville Skyline, record still present, rare.
(Vennett-Smith) $256

Jimi Hendrix, signed single record, to central label, Purple Haze, track record, Polydor, 1967, with plain sleeve, rare.
(Vennett-Smith) $558

Bob Dylan's autograph, probably 1966, in pencil on an album page with inscription, and other autographs including Sam Cooke, The Who and Nirvana.
(Sotheby's) $1,288

John Lennon, signed card, with an original red ink doodle, a self-caricature of himself and Yoko Ono, also incorporating a black ink sketch of a box at the head with the words Here You Are on the sides, 1971.(Vennett-Smith) $1,209

John Lennnon's Gallotone 'Champion' acoustic guitar Dutch, late 1950s, restored, the guitar that John is pictured playing with the Quarry Men at the St. Peter's Church fête, Woolton, 6th July 1957, the day of his historic first meeting with Paul McCartney.
(Sotheby's) $245,690

Bob Dylan's black leather jacket from his 1989 World Tour, biker-style with quilted lining, front embroidered in red *BD Bob Dylan*, the back with logo, with statement of provenance.
(Sotheby's) $1,817

Bob Dylan, signed 8 x 10, head and shoulders wearing sunglasses, with letter of authenticity from Nelson Deedle. (Vennett-Smith) $726

The Rolling Stones, signed 10 x 8, by Jagger, Richards, Wood and Watts, all in gold, full-length seated.
(Vennett-Smith) $310

Paul McCartney, signed color 8 x 10, full-length seated on white porch step.
(Vennett-Smith) $192

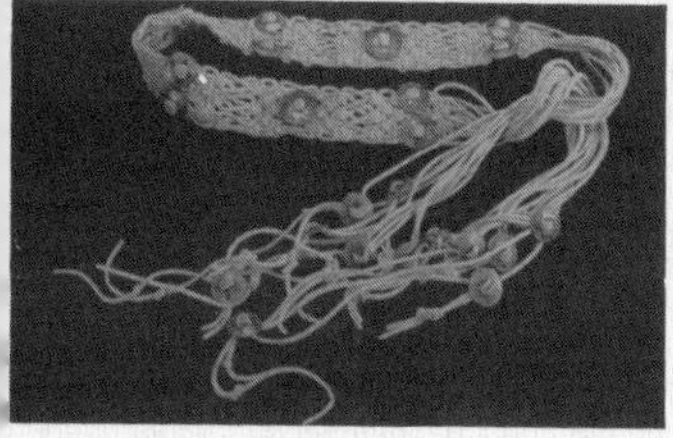

A belt worn by Elvis Presley circa 1970, decoratively knotted tan colored leather strips, the ends left long to fasten and hang as a fringe, threaded with Indian-style silver colored metal disks, 94in. long.
(Sotheby's) $10,902

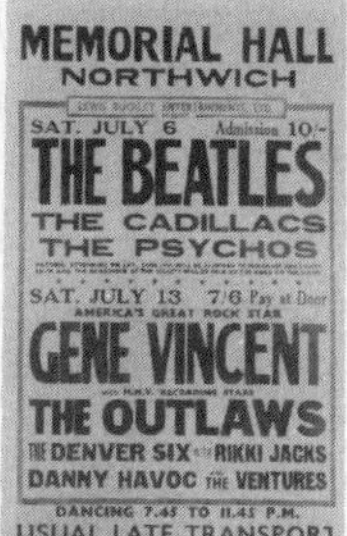

A concert poster for The Beatles and Gene Vincent at the Memorial Hall, Northwich, July 13th, 1963, printed in black and red on yellow paper, 18 x 30in.
(Sotheby's) $3,634

Presley And Perkins, printed sheet music for 'Blue Suede Shoes', the illustrated cover signed in blue ballpoint pen *Best Wishes, Elvis Presley and Carl Perkins.*
(Christie's) $2,392

The Beatles, an excellent set of signatures on a 5 x 6 white sheet by all four Beatles individually, 10 x 8 photo of the Fab Four.
(Vennett-Smith) $2,080

The Beatles, signed album record sleeve, by George Harrison John Lennon, Paul McCartney and Ringo Starr, to front cover Abbey Road, record still present.
(Vennett-Smith) $2,686

A self-portrait cartoon of John and Yoko, 1969, in black marker on a scrap of lined paper, signed by John, 4 x 4¾in.
(Sotheby's) $3,452

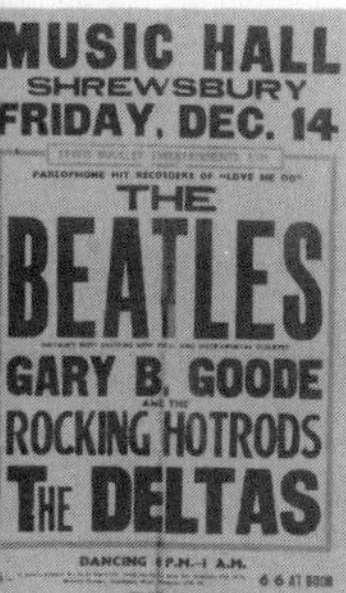

A poster for The Beatles at the Music Hall, Shrewsbury, December 14th 1962, printed in red and black on yellow, 20 x 30in.
(Sotheby's) $5,814

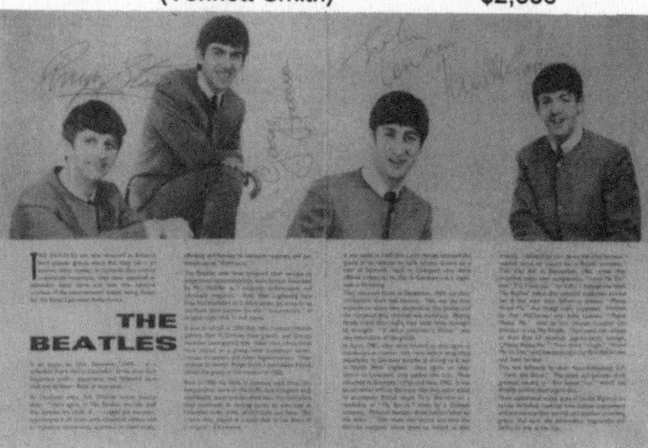

The Beatles, signed concert program by John Lennon, Paul McCartney, Ringo Starr and George Harrison to inside photo page, The Beatles Show 1963.
(Vennett-Smith) $2,133

The Beatles, signed 6 x 8 to reverse, by all four individually, with address of recipient in another hand to top edge.
(Vennett-Smith) $1,600

A Track Records promotional poster for 'Let Me Light Your Fire'/ 'The Burning Of The Midnight Lamp' November 1969, black on blue paper, 13 x 19¾in.
(Sotheby's) $908

The Rolling Stones, signed color 8 x 10, by Jagger, Richards, Wood and Watts, half-length, in silver.
(Vennett-Smith) $411

An autographed publicity photograph of The Rolling Stones, circa 1964, signed and dedicated *Love & Sincere Wishes* in blue ink and felt pen, 5½ x 7in.
(Sotheby's) $1,635

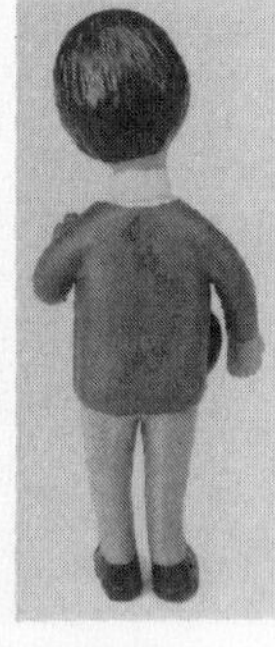

The Beatles, a foam Bendy doll circa 1964, modelled as a Beatle, signed on the back in black ballpoint pen by *Paul McCartney* and *John Lennon*, on the legs in blue ballpoint pen by *George Harrison* and *Ringo Starr*, 10½in. high. (Christie's) $1,747

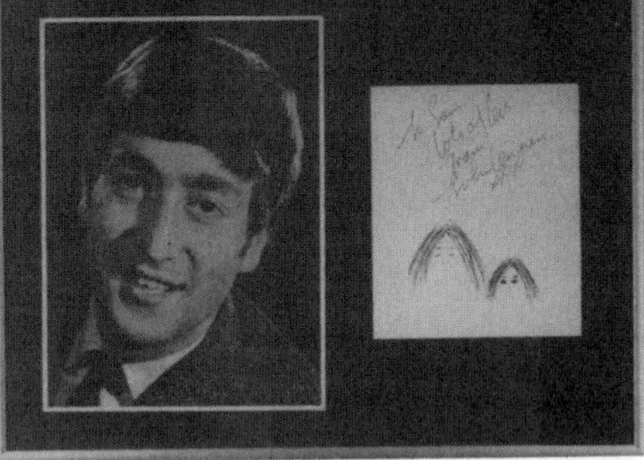

John Lennon, original signed and inscribed ink sketch of him and Yoko Ono, on 5.5 x 6 sheet of white paper, overmounted in black alongside 8 x 10 photo.
(Vennett-Smith) $885

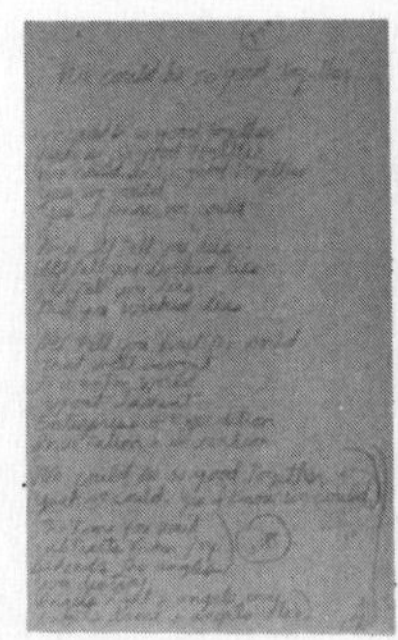

Jim Morrison's handwritten lyrics for 'Moonlight Drive' and 'We Could Be So Good Together' in pencil on both sides of a sheet of yellow, lined stationery with red felt pen annotations, 8 x 12½in.
(Sotheby's) $34,160

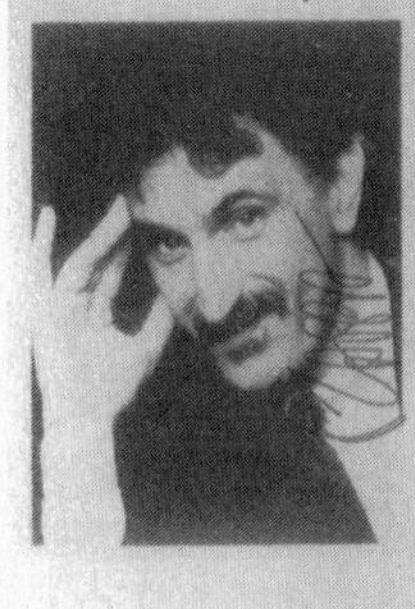

Frank Zappa, signed 8 x 10 head and shoulders with one hand raised to his head.
(Vennett-Smith) $110

Elvis Presley, signed piece, very slight ink bleeding and minor adhesion marks to reverse.
(Vennett-Smith) $403

Michael Jackson, signed 8 x 10, half-length in cardigan.
(Vennett-Smith) $112

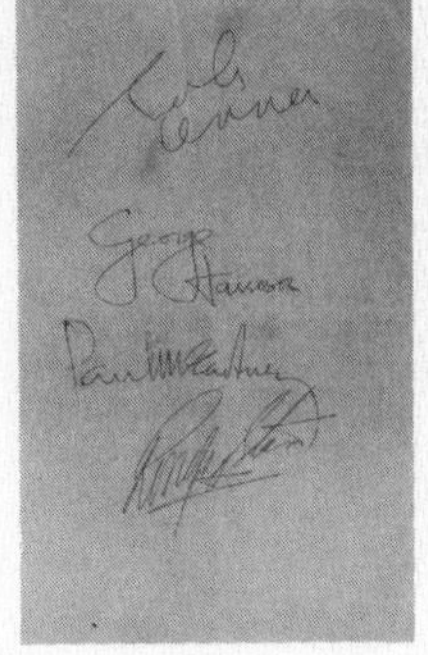

A good set of Beatles autographs 1963/64, in black ballpoint on a piece of paper, 5 x 8in. (Sotheby's) $3,634

Little Richard, signed 10 x 8, full-length performing with band in background. (Vennett-Smith) $120

Paul McCartney, signed 8 x 10, half-length, 1999. (Vennett-Smith) $276

Elvis Presley, signed 6 x 4 blue magazine photo, head and shoulders corners clipped and creased, not affecting signature. (Vennett-Smith) $377

Elvis Presley, signed 10 x 8, full-length dancing in a scene from one of his films, surrounded by girls in bikinis, in red, with two letters giving extensive provenance. (Vennett-Smith) $1,088

An early Pink Floyd concert poster, in blue on pink paper, for 'The Barn', 25th May 1967, as organised by the Gwent Constabulary, 37 x 50cm. (Sotheby's) $1,090

Newton John & Travolta, signed 8 x 10, embracing each other, from Grease. (Vennett-Smith) $208

The Eagles, signed color 8 x 10, by all five, half-length in group pose. (Vennett-Smith) $126

Bruce Springsteen, signed color 8 x 10, half-length performing, in silver. (Vennett-Smith) $79

Elvis Presley, a souvenir Folio Concert Edition, Volume Six, circa mid 1970s signed on the cover in black felt pen by subject, 16¼ x 13¼in. framed.
(Christie's) $291

Jimi Hendrix, a black and white half-length portrait photograph by Dezo Hoffmann, circa 1967, signed on the mount by photographer in silver felt pen, 11½ x 15½in.
(Christie's) $690

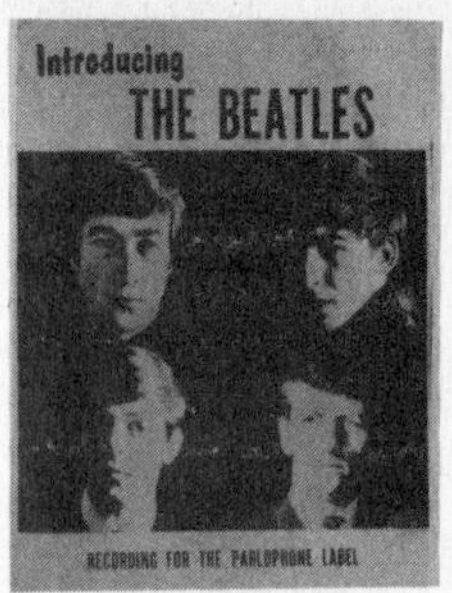

The Beatles, a rare press release Introducing The Beatles, 1962, four pages of information including background information on all four Beatles, the release date of their first single and a review by Tony Barrow. (Christie's) $999

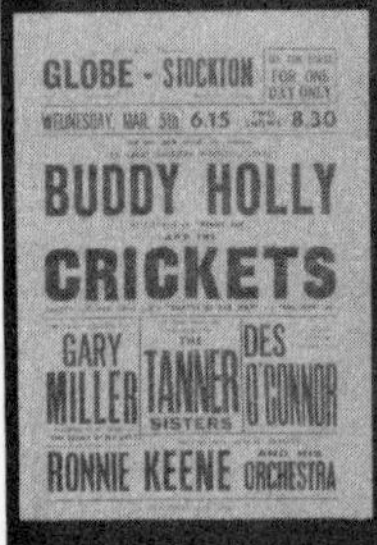

Buddy Holly And The Crickets, a concert handbill, The Great American Recording Stars Buddy Holly And The Crickets, Globe Theater, Stockton, 5th March, 1957, 8 x 6in.
(Christie's) $727

Elvis Presley, a rare page of lyrics in Presley's hand including a verse composed by Presley himself, the lyrics for Message to my Mother, circa 1959, in common mount with two black and white machine-print photographs of Presley with his mother. (Christie's) $10,902

Rock 'n' Roll, an original poster for the 1972 London Rock 'n' Roll Show at Wembley 5th August 1972 featuring Little Richard, Chuck Berry, Jerry Lee Lewis and others, 20 x 29in. (Bonhams) $300

The Beatles, The Beatles, (White Album), stereo Apple PCS 7067, 1968 No. 0000001, with fold out lyric sheet and portrait cards of each band member.
(Bonhams) $13,430

The Beatles, the front half of a single sleeve *I Saw Her Standing There/I Want To Hold Your Hand*, 1963, Capitol Records, signed in blue ballpoint pen by all four members of the group.
(Christie's) $9,085

Jimi Hendrix Experience, three pieces of paper, one signed by Jimi Hendrix, one signed and inscribed *Cheers Noel* [Redding] and the other signed in blue ballpoint pen by Mitch Mitchell, 12 x 13in.
(Christie's) $817

John Lennon, a black and white machine-print photograph of The Beatles, circa 1964, signed and inscribed in blue ink *To Jean love from the Beatles John Lennon xx*, 7¼ x 7¼in. (Christie's) $872

The Beatles, a poster advertising die Rock 'n' Twist-Parade 1962 on the opening night of the Star-Club, Hamburg on Friday 13th April, 16½ x 23in. (Bonhams) $5,530

Keith Richards, a 'pirate-style' shirt of white muslin slashed to the waist and fastening with wrap-around ties, worn by Richards on tour in America and Europe in the mid to late 1970s.(Christie's) $1,362

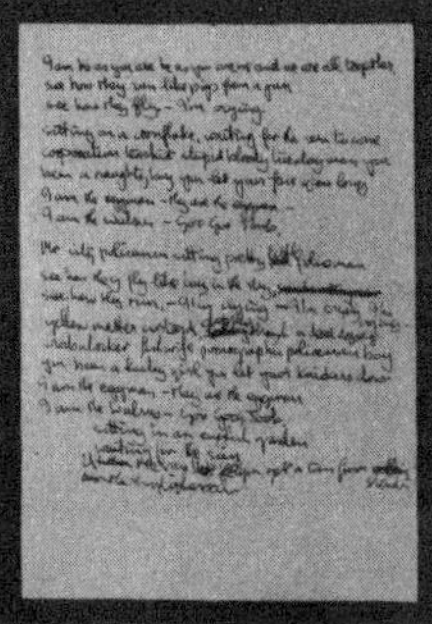

John Lennon, a rare page of lyrics in John Lennon's hand for I Am The Walrus, 1967, the twenty lines in black ink incomplete, omitting the concluding section of the final recorded version but showing deletions and alterations. (Christie's) $124,030

Elvis Presley, a stage-shirt of black voile printed in ivory and brown with floral pattern, the shirt with high collar and ruched sleeves and cuffs, made for Elvis in the 1970 MGM film Elvis, That's The Way It Is. (Christie's) $30,889

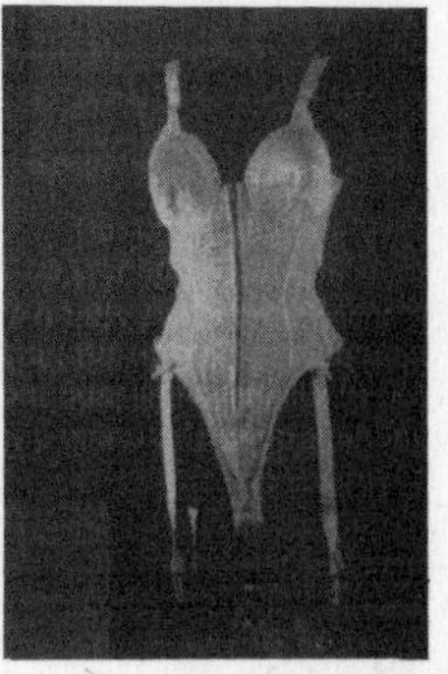

Madonna, a couture corset of rose pink lycra, labelled inside *Jean Paul Gaultier, Paris*, worn by Madonna in concert while performing Express Yourself during the Blonde Ambition Tour, Barcelona, August, 1990. (Christie's) $19,987

Elvis Presley, a blouson jacket of black rayon with pink collar, inscribed on the front in blue ballpoint pen *My best to you Elvis Presley*, in common mount with a black and white machine-print publicity photograph of subject, 11 x 8in. (Christie's) $6,360

John Lennon, a black and white half-length portrait photograph by Bob Gruen, the famous portrait of subject in New York, 1974, signed by photographer, 13½ x 10½in. (Christie's) $363

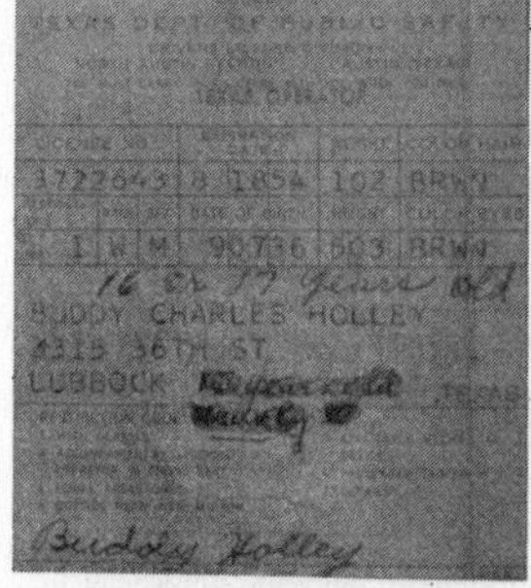

Buddy Holly, Buddy Holly's first driving licence issued by Texas Department of Public Safety, printed with his name and address Buddy Charles Holley, signed in blue ballpoint pen *Buddy Holley*. (Bonhams) $5,215

Shirvan prayer rug, East Caucasus, last quarter 19th century, rows of hooked diamonds, on the midnight blue field, 4ft.9in. x 3ft.6in. (Skinner) $1,380

Sultanabad Vagireh, West Persia, late 19th century, palmettes, rosettes, and blossoming vines, on the ivory field, 3ft.2 x 3ft.2in. (Skinner) $1,610

Kuba rug, Northwest Caucasus, last quarter 19th century, elongated 'keyhole' medallion inset with six large octagons on the red field, 5ft.5 x 3ft.10in. (Skinner) $2,530

A Karachopt Kazak rug, Southwest Caucasus, last quarter 19th century, oxidized browns, missing end guard stripes, approximately 7ft 1in. x 6ft. 1in. (Sotheby's) $5,462

Kurd Bagface, Northwest Persia, early 20th century, staggered rows of palmette motifs in red, royal blue, gold, tan, ivory, and red-brown on the midnight blue field, 1ft.9in. x 1ft.8in. (Skinner) $1,265

Kazak rug, Southwest Caucasus, last quarter 19th century, three concentric hooked hexagonal medallions and scattered small motifs on the red field, 6ft.8in. x 4ft.6in. (Skinner) $920

Afshar rug, South Persia, late 19th century, stepped diamond lattice with rosettes and small floral motifs, royal blue rosette and vine border, 6ft.x 4ft.5in. (Skinner) $1,265

A Kuba prayer rug, Northeast Caucasus, circa 1880, original macramé ends, partially oxidized browns, approximately 4ft. 1in. x 4ft. (Sotheby's) $6,900

Kitty Fischer, a wool runner, circa 1930, the elongated carpet with colored horizontal handhooked bands, 231in. long. (Christie's) $1,563

Baluch rug, Northeast Persia, early 20th century, overall design of palmettes and blossoming vines on the ivory field, 5ft. x 3ft.2in. (Skinner) $978

Afshar rug, South Persia, late 19th century, rows of alternating 'cat face' palmettes and leaf motifs on the ivory field, 5ft.10in. x 5ft. (Skinner) $1,725

Yomud chuval, West Turkestan, late 19th century, nine chuval guls on the rust-aubergine field, red stepped polygon border, plain elem, 4ft. x 2ft.10. (Skinner) $489

Kurd rug, Northwest Persia, early 20th century, four gabled square medallions surrounded by human and animal motifs on the midnight blue field, 8ft.8 x 5ft. (Skinner) $1,265

Daghestan prayer rug, Northeast Caucusus, late 19th century, serrated diamond lattice with blossoming plants on the ivory field, 4ft.4in. x 3ft.8in. (Skinner) $4,312

Baluch Balischt, Northeast Persia, late 19th century, single plant with branches of triangular leaves on the camel field, red diamond and triangle border, 3ft.2in. x 2ft. (Skinner) $1,840

Tekke Ensi, West Turkestan, last quarter 19th century, rust garden plan field with plant motifs, 'pole tree' border, 5ft. x 4ft. (Skinner) $2,645

Fereghan mat, West Persia, late 19th/early 20th century, stepped diamond medallion and Herati design on the rust field, floral meander border, 2ft.7in. x 2ft.2in. (Skinner) $402

Shirvan rug, East Caucasus, last quarter 19th century, narrow diagonal stripes, ivory hooked square border, 5ft.2in. x 3ft.9in. (Skinner) $2,300

Kurd flatweave cover, Northwest Persia, late 19th century, diamond lattice with small hooked diamonds on the plainweave red field, 6ft.4in. x 4ft.10in. (Skinner) $1,380

A pictorial Grenfell hooked rug, circa 1920, worked in tones of brown, blue, red, green, and black fabric on a burlap ground, 25¾ x 38½in. (Sotheby's) $4,600

Baluch Balischt, Northeast Persia, last quarter 19th century, staggered rows of hooked diamonds on the camel field, 3ft.2 x 1ft.8in. (Skinner) $172

Malayer rug, Northwest Persia, late 19th/early 20th century, overall Herati design in red, royal blue, ivory, dark red-brown, and blue-green on the midnight blue field, 6ft.2in. x 4ft.2in. (Skinner) $1,150

Noah's Ark hooked rug, America, 20th century, depicting Noah seated with his scroll and several pairs of animals en route to the ark, 52 x 33in. (Skinner) $1,380

Bakhtiari rug, West Persia, second quarter 20th century, large 'shield' medallion surrounded by palmettes and rosettes in red, navy blue, rose gold, red-brown, and olive on the midnight blue field, 6ft.6 x 4ft.5in. (Skinner) $920

A Sennah Kurd rug, red diamond shape center medallion with mid-blue inner medallion and spandrels filled with rows of flowering plants; 6ft.7in. x 4ft.6in. (Woolley & Wallis) $2,271

Noah's Ark hooked rug, American, 20th century, depicting Noah and his wife and pairs of animals disembarking from the ark, 54 x 30in. (Skinner) $1,380

Eagle Karabagh rug, South Caucasus, late 19th century, two and a half 'sunburst' medallions, on the rust-red field, narrow ivory 'crab' border, 7ft.6in. x 4ft.5in. (Skinner) $5,175

Bordjalou Kazak rug, Southwest Caucasus, last quarter 19th century, 6ft.4in. x 4ft.6in.
(Skinner) $5,175

Hooked rug, 2ft5in. x 3ft.8in., The Three Bears carrying steaming porridge, early to mid-20th century.
(Eldred's) $660

Caucasian rug, last quarter 19th century, overall scattered diamonds, rosettes, and stars on the red field, 6ft.8in. x 3ft.10in.
(Skinner) $1,035

TOP TIP

Eastern rugs are currently considered as very good purchases, especially if they date from before the 1940s.

Woollen and silk rugs always wear unreasonably on the floor. The true collector will more often hang them on the wall, or perhaps keep them rolled up to view from time to time simply for his pleasure - in any case untrodden!

(David Dockree)

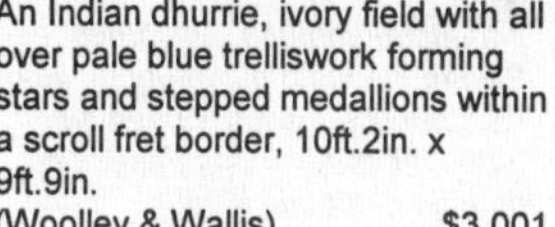

An Indian dhurrie, ivory field with all over pale blue trelliswork forming stars and stepped medallions within a scroll fret border, 10ft.2in. x 9ft.9in.
(Woolley & Wallis) $3,001

Kazak rug, Southwest Caucasus, last quarter 19th century, two gabled rectangular medallions surrounded by small bird and animal motifs, on the blue-green field, 5ft.2in. x 3ft.6in.
(Skinner) $863

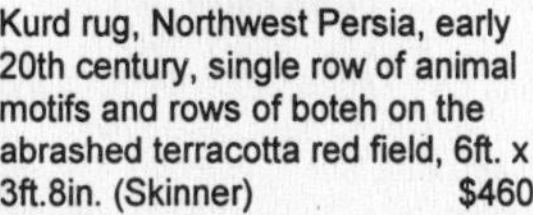

Kurd rug, Northwest Persia, early 20th century, single row of animal motifs and rows of boteh on the abrashed terracotta red field, 6ft. x 3ft.8in. (Skinner) $460

Yomud Asmalyk, West Turkestan, last quarter 19th century, hexagonal lattice with concentric ashik guls , ivory syrga border, 3ft.3 x 2ft.5in.
(Skinner) $920

Makri rug, Southwest Anatolia, last quarter 19th century, three flowering plants in red, gold, and aubergine on the navy blue field, 4ft.9 x 3ft (Skinner) $518

Karapinar rug, Central Anatolia, late 19th century, large stepped hexagonal medallion with pendants on the red-brown field, 5ft.5 x 4ft. (Skinner) $978

Kurd bagface, Northwest Persia, early 20th century, single palmette motif surrounded by small geometric motifs on the camel field, 2 x 2ft. (Skinner) $1,610

Shirvan prayer rug, East Caucasus, last quarter 19th century, serrated hexagonal lattice with flowering plants on the ivory field, 4ft.7 x 3ft.5in. (Skinner) $402

Moghan rug, Southeast Caucasus, late 19th century, 'keyhole' medallion inset with three octagons in navy blue, red, gold, and tan on the ivory field, 4ft.7 x 2ft.10in. (Skinner) $460

Khamseh bagface, Southwest Persia, early 20th century, rows of radiating hexagons flanked by palmette motifs, on the midnight blue field, 2ft.2in. x 2ft. (Skinner) $575

Karabagh rug, South Caucasus, late 19th century, large diamond medallion, matching spandrels, and paired animal heads on the rust-red field, 7ft.2 x 5ft.10in. (Skinner) $2,415

Kazak rug, Southwest Caucasus, early 20th century, three stepped hexagonal medallions and small hooked diamonds on the red field, 6ft.8 x 4ft.4in. (Skinner) $1,955

West Anatolian bagface, last quarter 19th century, large stepped hexagonal medallion and small geometric motifs on the navy blue field, 3ft.4in. x 3ft.2in. (Skinner) $920

Afshar rug, South Persia, late 19th/early 20th century, overall Mina Khani floral lattice on the ivory field, red floral meander border, 5ft.4in. x 3ft.10in. (Skinner) $575

Sarouk rug, West Persia, early 20th century, quatrefoil center and corner floral sprays on the midnight blue field, 5ft x 3ft.4in.
(Skinner) $1,265

Chinese mat, 18th century, circular navy blue fretwork medallion and matching spandrels on the tan-gold field, 3ft x 2ft.10in.
(Skinner) $14,950

Shirvan Kelim, East Caucasus, late 19th century, staggered rows of stepped diamonds in midnight and sky blue on the ivory field, 8ft.10in. x 6ft. (Skinner) $1,495

Anatolian Yastik, late 19th century, stepped hexagonal medallion with 'arrowhead' pendants in blue, gold, and olive on the abrashed red field, 2ft.4in. x 2ft.8in.
(Skinner) $345

Pair of Baluch bags, Northeast Persia, last quarter 19th century, rows of alternating square rosettes and hexagons in aubergine, ivory, and red on the navy blue field, 2ft. 10 x 2ft.5in.
(Skinner) $1,380

Shirvan kelim, East Caucasus, late 19th century, ivory horizontal bands of hooked and stepped diamonds, alternate with narrow red and blue plain bands, 9ft.9 x 5ft.3in.
(Skinner) $518

Qashqai bag, Southwest Persia, early 20th century, large hooked diamond medallion and four 'Memling' gul motifs on the midnight blue field, 2ft.6 x 2ft.2in.
(Skinner) $690

Northwest Persian rug, early 20th century, staggered Turkoman-style shaped medallions and small diamonds on the midnight blue field, 4ft.6 x 4ft.2in.
(Skinner) $2,530

Kuba mat, Northeast Caucasus, last quarter 19th century, central rosette medallion surrounded by angular serrated vine motifs on the navy blue field, 2ft.8 x 2ft.3in.
(Skinner) $2,185

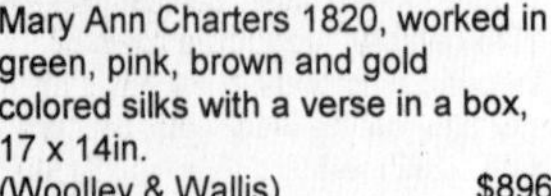

Mary Ann Charters 1820, worked in green, pink, brown and gold colored silks with a verse in a box, 17 x 14in.
(Woolley & Wallis) $896

A George III needlework sampler inscribed *Done by Me Jean Watson in my 7 Years of age Montrose 1783*, worked in brightly colored silks, 31. x 32.5cm.
(Bearne's) $6,449

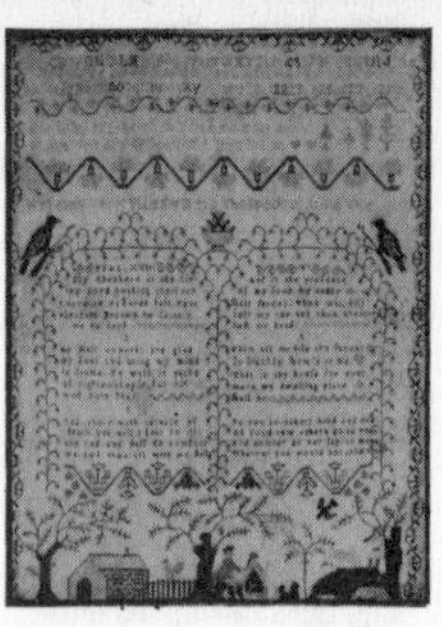

An early 19th century alphabet sampler in colored silks on wool, of Psalm XXIII framed by birds and foliage, 16 x 12in.
(Woolley & Wallis) $631

An 18th century sampler worked bands of letters interspersed with bands of pattern, *Mary felby her work finished May 5 177*, framed and glazed.
(Woolley & Wallis) $551

A very fine needlework sampler, signed *Diana Paine Age 9 Stockbridge, Mary Cooper Instructress*, dated *1826*, executed in a variety of greens, blue, yellow, tan and brown silk stitches, 16¼ x 17¼in.
(Sotheby's) $25,300

A George III cross sampler by Jane Bonny embroidered with an alphabet and verse 'The Twining Jasmine and the blushing Rose.....', 1790.
(Dreweatt Neate) $1,166

A Victorian woolwork pictorial sampler with silk highlights, worked with a spaniel, *Sarah Bray's work Aged 11 Year*, 11½ x 11in.
(Woolley & Wallis) $424

Mary Mitchell's 1833 worked in green, gold and brown colored silks with a list of brothers and sisters births and deaths, 16 x 12in.
(Woolley & Wallis) $382

Ure family 1810 worked in cream, brown and green silk with a large house, the roof line with two birds and crosses, 16in. x 16in.
(Woolley & Wallis) $896

A Victorian needlework sampler by Lydia Briggs dated *1844*, worked with a verse, floral swags, butterflies, animals, birds and a vase of flowers, 39 x 31cm.
(Bearne's) $629

Maria Louisa Ford 1817, worked in green, gold and cream silk on wool ground, depicting Adam and Eve under an apple tree, 12½ x 12¾in.
(Woolley & Wallis) $465

Caroline Mackenzie 1841, worked in green, brown and gold colored silks, the top third with a house flanked by fruit trees and dogs, 18 x 13¼in.
(Woolley & Wallis) $996

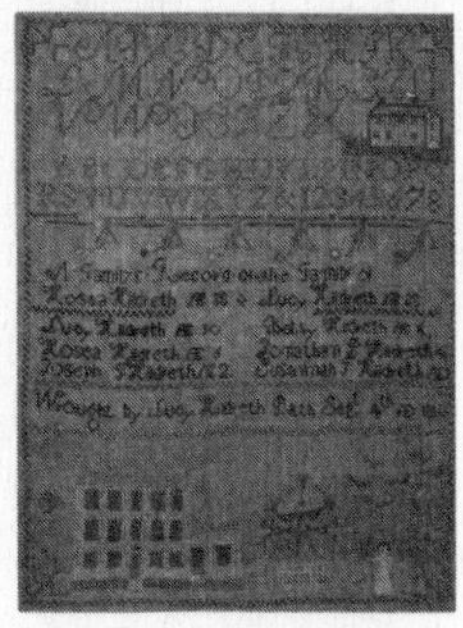

Needlework sampler/family register *Wrought by Lucy Hildreth Bath Sept 4th AD 1810*, central register below an alphabet panel with a Federal house, 15¾ x 12¼in.
(Skinner) $1,610

A needlework sampler, Philura Barton, Chatham, Connecticut, dated *September 1829*, executed in a variety of blue, white, brown and green stitches on a linen ground, 15¾ x 15¾in.
(Sotheby's) $19,550

A band sampler by Ann Anlaby 1775 worked in silks with bands of alphabets, stylized carnations, strawberries, and other similar motifs, 9 x 13¾in.
(Christie's) $436

Needlework sampler, early 19th century, *W* and *1822* enclosed in a flowering wreath, beneath alphabet panels, 22 x 17¼in.
(Skinner) $862

Sarah Anne Carey 1861, worked in wool cross stitch with silk highlights in various colors, 19½ x 20in.
(Woolley & Wallis) $415

An early 19th century sampler, worked in cross stitch in colored silks depicting Adam and Eve, *Margaret Humphrys, her work aged 10years 1827*, 23¾ x 18½in.
(Woolley & Wallis) $1,193

A fine needlework sampler, signed *Esther P. Payne, Miss Cornwall's School, Glastonbury, Connecticut*, dated 1828, executed in blue, green, yellow and white silk stitches on a linen ground, 18 x 24in.
(Sotheby's) $19,550

Needlework sampler, *Rizpah Farmer born Sept the 26 1797 aged 13 years*, three alphabet panels above a pious verse, 18½ x 17¾in. (Skinner) $1,955

Adam and Eve solidly stitched needlework sampler, early 19th century *Ann Maria Tius(?) her work aged I(?) January the 3 1823*, depicting Adam and Eve, 20 x 15in.
(Skinner) $7,475

A Georgian needlework sampler, worked in linen, depicting a country house within a floral surround, signed *Mary Greenhalgh* and dated *October 1821*, 12in. square.
(Andrew Hartley) $1,120

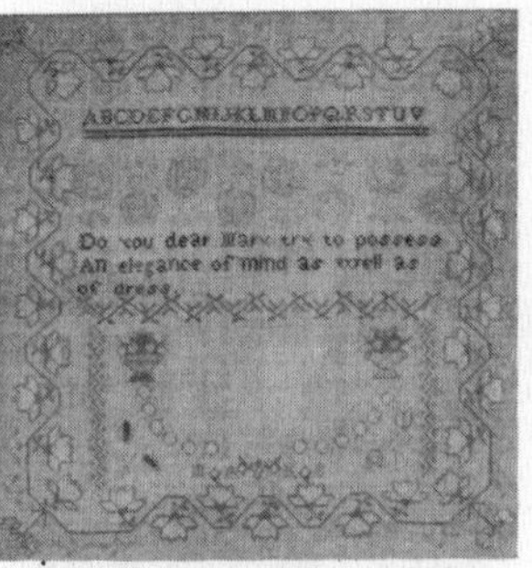

A silk on linen needlework sampler signed *Mary A. Duty, Granville County, North Carolina*, dated *1836*, inscribed *Do you dear Mary try to possess/An elegance of mind as well as/of dress*, centering the initials *MAKB*, 17 x 17in.
(Christie's) $6,325

An early 19th century alphabet sampler worked silk on linen, in mainly green and gold, embroidered *Elizabeth Ann Baldwin*, undated and unfinished, 12in. square.
(Woolley & Wallis) $178

A 19th century woolwork sampler worked by Ann Wade and dated *1849*, featuring a stanza with country house below, 24 x 23½in.
(Andrew Hartley) $638

Needlework family register, *'Amaziah Phillips born Jan 15 1785 Lucy Bates born Aug 14 1789'*, probably Beverly, Massachusetts area, 25 x 17in.
(Skinner) $4,600

A sampler by A.K [?]. Barnard, finely embroidered in colored silks with the central verse *Next unto God, Dear Parents...*, 14¾ x 16in., 1840s.(Christie's) $1,727

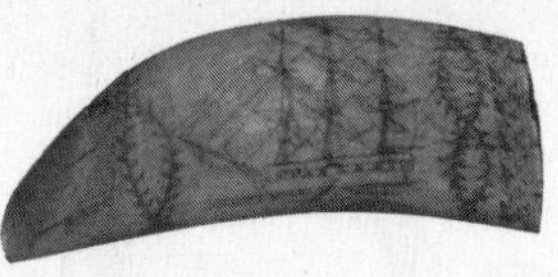

Engraved whale's tooth, 19th century, obverse with an English ship under full sail, geometric border around the base, 6 7/8 in. long. (Skinner) $1,265

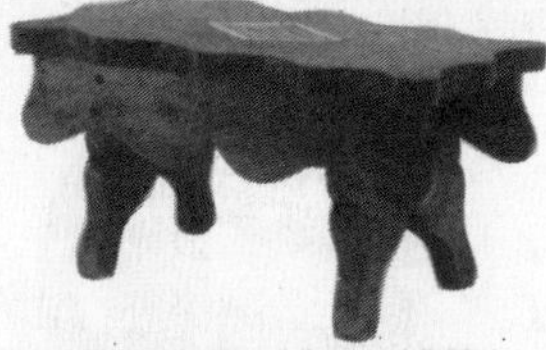

Rare scrimshaw cricket, mid-19th century, in walnut with whalebone and wood diamond and star-form inlays, length 12in. (Eldred's) $1,760

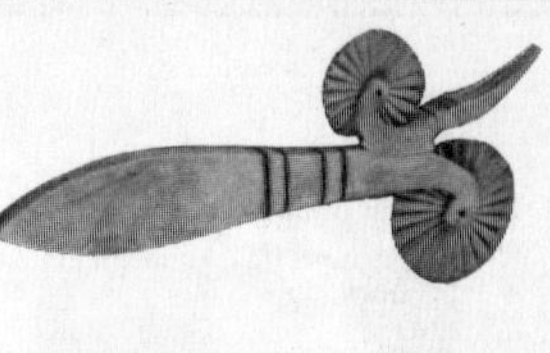

Whale bone and walrus tusk double jagging wheel, 19th century, with three tined crimper, baleen spacers, 7¾in. long. (Skinner) $1,840

Engraved whale's tooth, 19th century, depicting a square rigger under sail, 6in. long. (Skinner) $977

Engraved dolphin jawbone, 19th century, decorated by two different artists, one side with a whaling scene, the other with two whaleships, 16in. long. (Skinner) $1,610

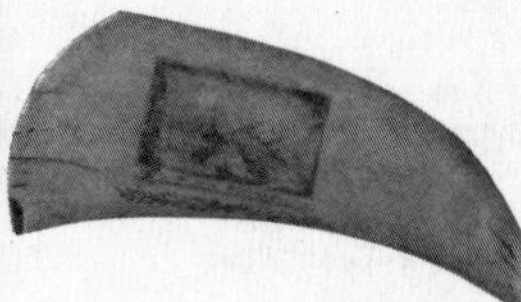

Engraved whale's tooth, 19th century, obverse depicting a ship under sail, reverse with a framed scene, 8¾in. long. (Skinner) $2,300

A fine engraved and scrimshawed whale tooth American, 19th century, engraved with a depiction of Lady Liberty holding an American eagle and an American flag, 6¼in. high. (Sotheby's) $1,380

Engraved polychrome decorated whale's tooth, 19th century, obverse depicting a bosun blowing his whistle, 8in. long. (Skinner) $12,650

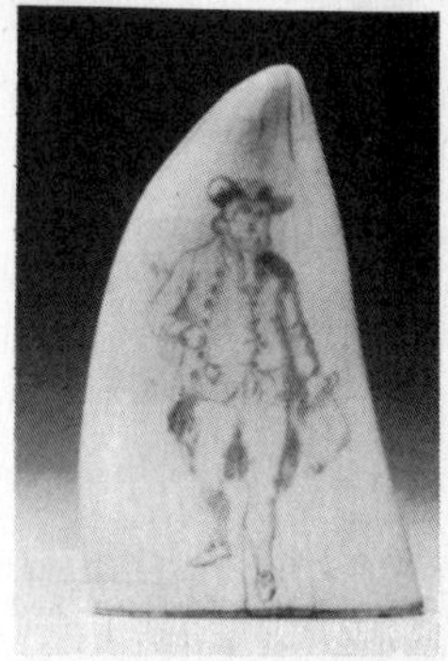

A fine engraved scrimshawed sperm whale's tooth, probably American, mid 19th century, engraved with a depiction of Benjamin Franklin, 5½in. high. (Sotheby's) $805

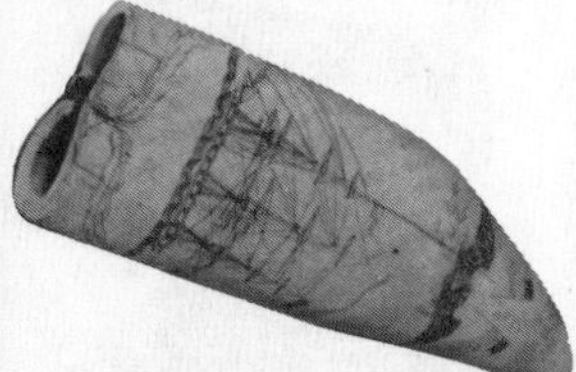

A fine engraved and scrimshawed sperm whale's tooth, American, early 19th century, engraved with a whaling ship at anchor below a spread-winged American eagle with two American flags. (Sotheby's) $7,475

Whalebone eight-finger oval ditty box, 19th century, wooden top and base, brass tack decoration, 8¼in. long. (Skinner) $3,105

Engraved whale's tooth, 19th century, obverse decorated with a ship, reverse depicting a ship under sail, 7½in. long. (Skinner) $1,035

An early American New England type domestic sewing machine, by Nettleton & Raymond, incomplete, circa 1859.
(Auction Team Köln) $250

A small American Raymond New England chainstitch domestic sewing machine, on heavy cast base and with retail label *Lacour y Lesage*, circa 1872.
(Auction Team Köln) $294

An Osborn A, the head of a very rare American domestic sewing machine, lacking shuttle, shuttle cover and foot, circa 1875.
(Auction Team Köln) $197

A child's wooden standard American Girl chainstitch sewing machine, on heavy wood base, American, circa 1935.
(Auction Team Köln) $1,087

The Challenge, a British transverse shuttle machine by the Imperial Sewing Machine Co., with chiselled stitch plate, cast iron base plate, in original mahogany case, circa 1872.
(Auction Team Köln) $635

An American Howe domestic sewing machine, cast frame, wooden cover, with shuttle, circa 1880.
(Auction Team Köln) $98

A Müller Nr. 15 cast iron child's chainstitch sewing machine by F.W. Müller, Berlin, lacks thread tension.
(Auction Team Köln) $262

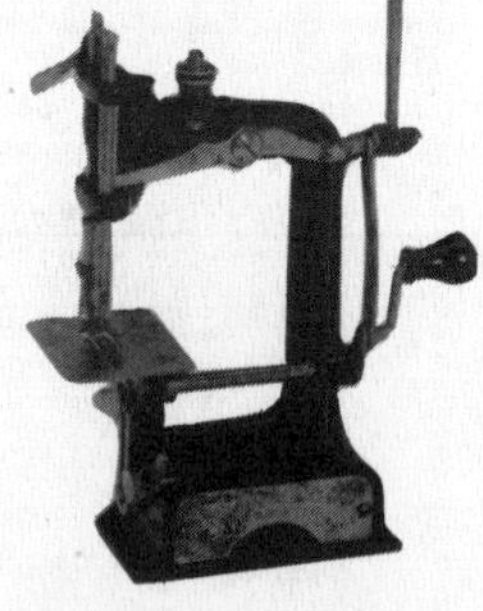

A Smith & Egge Automatic child's chainstitch machine, with original wooden case and table clamp, lacking cover, 1901.
(Auction Team Köln) $360

A Casige No. 0/1German chainstitch child's sewing machine.
(Auction Team Köln) $100

A Jones British hand sewing machine on a decorative cast base, circa 1880.
(Auction Team Köln) $250

A Foliage chain-stitch sewing machine by D.W. Clark, cast in brass with foliate fixed and moving arms, 6in. wide, circa 1859.
(Christie's) $4,048

A Jones British domestic transverse shuttle machine, some restoration, circa 1875.
(Auction Team Köln) $184

A Grant Brothers early American domestic sewing machine, chain stitch type similar to the New England, but drive under foot, circa 1870.
(Auction Team Köln) $262

A Singer Sewhandy Model No. 20, chainstitch machine, original box with sewing table and clamp.
(Auction Team Köln) $104

A Shaw & Clark 'Skinny pillar' American chainstitch machine by Shaw & Clark Sewing Machine Co., Biddeford, Maine, technically complete, circa 1864.
(Auction Team Köln) $7,245

A Bremer & Brückmann Kolibri German chainstitch hand sewing machine, in original box, sold as a domestic or child's machine, circa 1890.
(Auction Team Köln) $426

The Dorman, a swing shuttle machine by the Patents Manufacturing Co., Northampton & London, with original shuttle, circa 1885. (Auction Team Köln) $1,123

A French Avrial Legat domestic sewing machine with unusual pump drive, with shuttle, circa 1885.
(Auction Team Köln) $2,296

John Miers, 1811, Mr. M. Nichen, profile to the right, wearing robes and mortarboard, oval 3¼in. high, and two others by Miers.
(Bonhams) $942

Eight hollow-cut silhouettes, probably Pennsylvania, with cutwork background, unsigned, together in a common period frame. American School, 19th century, 7⅛ x 9⅛in. (Skinner) $575

G. Walker, circa 1840, Miss H. Grayson, aged 18, profile to the right, her hair in a bun and ringlets, cut-out on card with painted details in gold and coral, oval, 3½in. high.
(Bonhams) $392

Stephen O'Driscoll, 1843, a comic caricature of a Gentleman standing full-length, profile to the right, weighing his cat, watercolor, watercolor background, signed, rectangular, 11½in. high.
(Bonhams) $1,491

William Wellings, 1782, Captain Peyton, full-length, profile to the right, his powdered hair en queue, wearing Naval uniform, painted on card, signed and dated, rectangular, 248mm. high.
(Bonhams) $2,669

Royal Victoria Gallery, attributed to H.A. Frith, 1840, a Gentleman, standing full-length, profile to the right, wearing top hat, cut-out and bronzed, signed *Frith* and dated, rectangular, 10¼in.
(Bonhams) $502

J. Neville, 1823, Mr. J.T. Waitley, profile to the right, wearing coat, striped waistcoat and black stock, painted on card and bronzed, signed on the reverse and dated *March 4th, 1823.*
(Bonhams) $298

Mrs. Mary Lightfoot, circa 1790, an Officer, profile to the right, wearing coat, frilled cravat and fantail hat, painted on plaster, unbroken trade label on reverse, hammered brass frame, oval, 3½in. high.
(Bonhams) $1,256

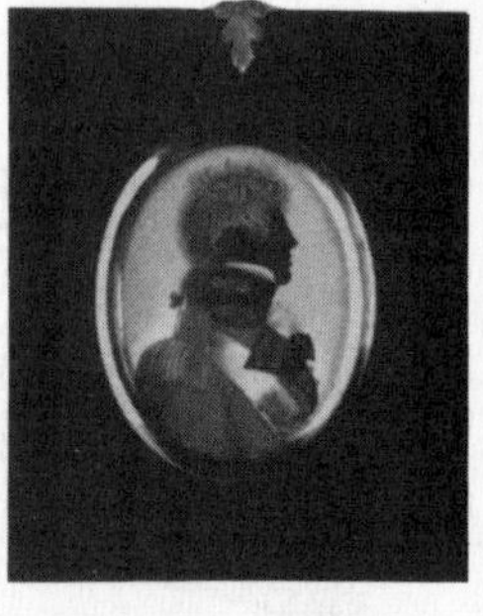

John Buncombe, circa 1790, General Gates, profile to the right, his hair en queue, wearing the uniform of the 1st Foot (Royal Scots), painted on card, inscribed on the reverse, oval, 73mm. high.
(Bonhams) $2,983

Mrs. Jane Read, circa 1805, a Lady, profile to the left, wearing indoor bonnet with frilled band, painted on convex glass backed with wax, oval, 73mm. high. (Bonhams) $597

Joshua Trewinnard, 1813, Mr. Matthew Simpson (1761-1824), profile to the left, his hair en queue, painted on card in shades of gray 86mm. high. (Bonhams) $392

John Miers, circa 1785-86, Frances Holden, profile to the left, wearing dress with buffon, painted on plaster, hammered brass frame oval, 3½in. high. (Christie's) $706

Mr. Raper, circa 1840, a Lady, seated full-length at a table with a sewing box, painted in black and embellished with brown, blue and Chinese white on paper, rectangular, about 10in. high. (Bonhams) $942

John Dempsey, circa 1834, Dr. Raffles of Liverpool, preaching from a pulpit, cut-out and heightened with watercolor, signed with initials, rectangular, 11¼in. high. (Bonhams) $392

Attibuted to Merryweather, circa 1840, a Child, standing full-length, profile to the left, holding a riding crop, cut-out on card and bronzed on black and gray watercolor base, rectangular, 7in. high. (Bonhams) $816

John Field, circa 1835, John Ward (d.1846), profile to the right, wearing coat and tied black stock, painted on card and heightened with blended yellow and white, signed, oval, 3¼in. high. (Bonhams) $596

Attributed to Mrs. L M. Lane Kelfe, circa 1785, Mrs. Walker of Tiverton, profile to the left, with banging chignon, wearing lace cap and buffon, inscribed on reverse, hammered brass frame oval, 4in. high. (Bonhams) $251

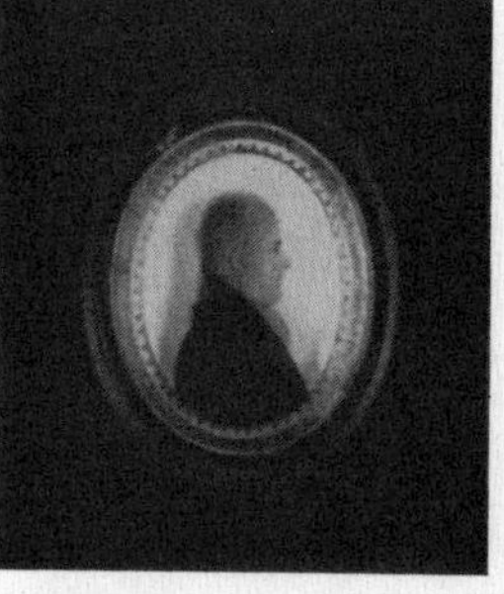

Arthur Lea, circa 1790, a Gentleman, profile to the right, wearing coat with dark collar, painted on convex glass in line against a stippled base, oval, 3⅜in. high. (Bonhams) $1,492

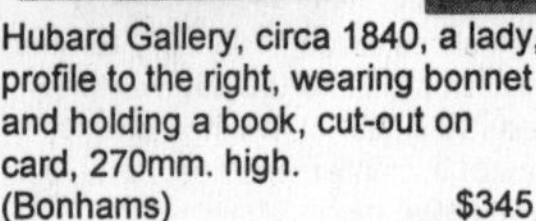

Hubard Gallery, circa 1840, a lady, profile to the right, wearing bonnet and holding a book, cut-out on card, 270mm. high.
(Bonhams) $345

Manner of W. H. Beaumont, circa 1840, 'The Sunday Stroll': Husband and wife, profile to the left, their son, daughter and dog, profile the right, cut-outs on card, painted on a sepia base color, rectangular, 11¼in. high. (Bonhams) $942

T. Lewis, 1840, a young girl, full-length, profile to the left, wearing bonnet and patterned dress, carrying a hoop and crop, rectangular, 6¾in. high.
(Bonhams) $502

August Edouart (French 1789–1861), miniature full length cut silhouette of Lt. Edward M. Yard *U. S. Navy Boston 1st March 1842 on John Adams Sloop of War*, 11¾ x 5¼in, framed. (Skinner) $748

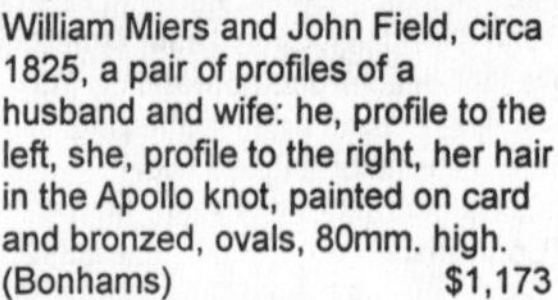

William Miers and John Field, circa 1825, a pair of profiles of a husband and wife: he, profile to the left, she, profile to the right, her hair in the Apollo knot, painted on card and bronzed, ovals, 80mm. high.
(Bonhams) $1,173

Attributed to Samuel Metford, circa 1835, a pair of full-length silhouettes: a nobleman holding a cane and a lady holding a shawl and fan, rectangular, 11¾in. high.
(Bonhams) $345

Augustin Edouart, circa 1830, a full-length profile of William Frederick, Duke of Gloucester (1776-1834), standing holding a book, cut-out against lithographed interior and balcony scene, signed, rectangular, 10½in. high. (Bonhams) $628

Lady Louisa Kerr, 1846, The Earl of Hillsborough, Lord William Hill and Lady Alice Hill, as children, playing with their dog in the garden, cut-outs on card, watercolor background, rectangular, 8¾in. high.
(Bonhams) $863

Attributed to the Royal Victoria Gallery, circa 1840, probably by H.A. Frith, a charming profile of a young boy, standing full-length, holding a whip, rosewood frame, rectangular, 7½in. high.
(Bonhams) $471

A Tiffany and Co. silver colored metal oval bread basket, chased and pierced with ribbon-tied festoons and fronds, 33cm. long. (Bearne's) $610

A shaped oval swing handled cake basket, with applied Art Nouveau relief decorated rim, 11¾in., 23oz., by Fattorini & Sons, Birmingham 1909. (George Kidner) $721

A George III two-handled basket with wirework sides and ball feet, probably by John Watson, Sheffield 1809, 39cm. long, 20oz. (Christie's) $1,440

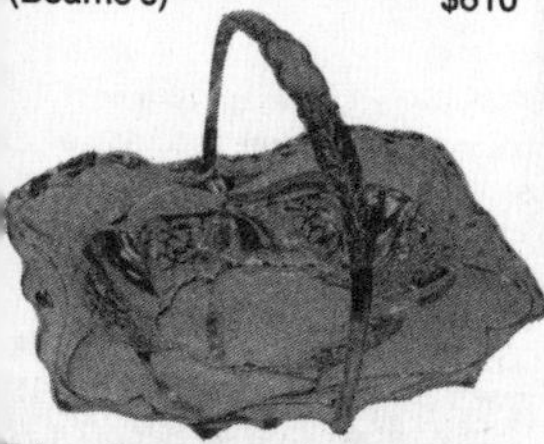
Edwardian silver cake basket of shaped rectangular design with folded rim, the center pierced with panels of foliate design, 11 x 8in., Birmingham 1903. (G.A. Key) $477

An Edwardian bon bon basket of shaped oval form with cast borders of masks, scrolls and husks, by Carrington & Co., 1909, 24cm. long, 16oz. (Christie's) $647

A George III oval cake basket with pierced sides, bead borders and a reeded swing handle, by Burrage Davenport, 1778, 34.5cm. long, 27oz. (Christie's) $3,864

A mid 18th century Dutch brazier, decorated with piercing and a cast border of scallop shells and scrolls, by Reynier de Haan, the Hague, 1741, 16.5cm. wide, 8oz. (Christie's) $1,733

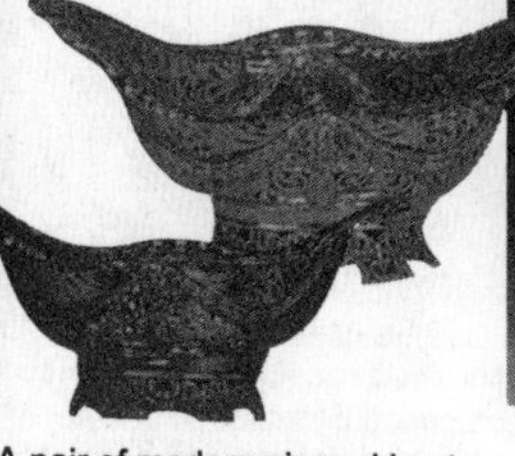
A pair of modern pierced boat shaped baskets, embossed with festoons with a cast border of roses and foliage, G. Nathan & R. Hayes, Chester 1913, 27.25cm. wide, 32.5oz. (Christie's) $2,024

Wm. B. Durgin Co. sterling cake basket, 20th century, retailed by Bigelow, Kennard & Co. on stepped foot, shaped circular body stamped with scrolls and shells, 8¼in. high., 23 troy oz. approximately. (Skinner) $690

Victorian silver cake basket, Sheffield, 1864–65, C. & Co. maker, molded round form, applied scroll and floral rim, 13in. diameter, approximately 29 troy oz. (Skinner) $747

Victorian silver fruit/cake basket, pierced and engraved with scrolls and foliate designs, presentation inscription to center, date 1868, London 1850 by William K Reid, 18oz. (G.A. Key) $541

A George IV cake basket of shaped circular outline with a cast, openwork swing handle, by Messrs Lias, 1828, 33.5cm. diameter, 40oz. (Christie's) $2,392

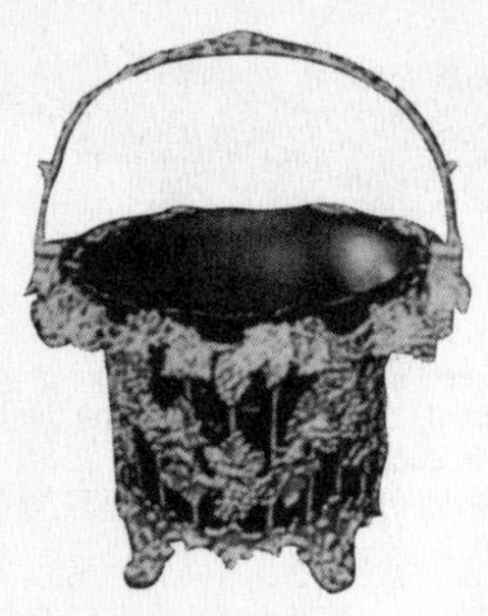

A sugar basket, of tapering shape with wirework applied with fruiting vines, E & J Barnard, 1856, 9½oz., 15cm. diameter.
(Tennants) $596

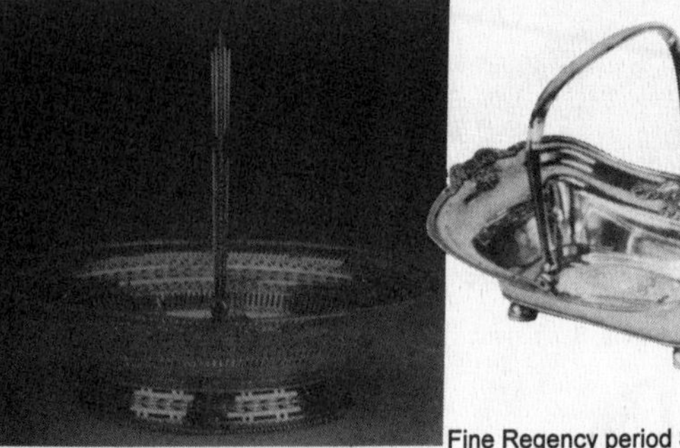

A George III pierced oval basket with bead borders and swing handle, by Burrage Davenport, 1781, 32cm. long, 20.5oz.
(Christie's) $2,944

Fine Regency period Sheffield plated cake basket, rectangular shaped with rounded corners, having an applied straight gadrooned and foliate edge, 11 x 7in., circa 1830.
(G.A. Key) $288

BUYER BEWARE

It is quite common practice to find good pieces of 20th century silver modelled in the 18th century manner. Typical examples would be beer mugs, tea services and swing handled cake baskets, and as 20th century items they are well sought after.

Equally, the 18th and 19th century pieces they emulate are also valuable. A George III cake basket would sell for a premium; a late 18th century beer mug or four piece tea service would be similarly prized.

The practice of removing the late 18th century assay from a battered teaspoon and reapplying it to a 20th century copy to enhance the value is, unfortunately, not unknown.

Watch out for transposed assays and buy from reputable and professionally qualified retail or auctioneering businesses.

(David Dockree)

A George IV swing-handled basket of shaped circular outline, pierced, embossed and chased with baskets of fruit and flowers, I.E. Terry, 1825, 34cm. diameter, 40.5oz.
(Christie's) $1,196

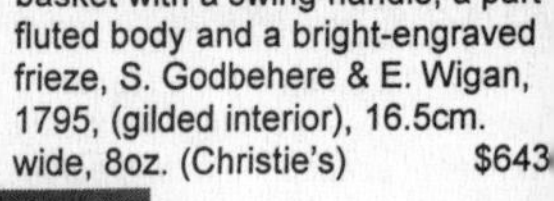

A George III boat shaped sugar basket with a swing handle, a part fluted body and a bright-engraved frieze, S. Godbehere & E. Wigan, 1795, (gilded interior), 16.5cm. wide, 8oz. (Christie's) $643

A George II sweetmeat basket, of shaped oval form with a swing handle and wirework sides, by Arthur Annesley, 1759, 14.25cm. long, 4oz. (Christie's) $1,368

Early George III silver sugar basket, circular shaped to a spreading circular foot, pierced with geometric designs, London 1771, probably by Edward Aldridge.
(G A Key) $634

A parcel gilt stopa, marked with the cyrillic initials of Nikifor Timofev, Moscow, circa 1732, the body repoussé, chased and engraved with scrolling acanthus leaves, 7¼in. high, 438gm.
(Christie's) $2,881

A late 17th/early 18th century German silver-gilt beaker, embossed with a row of opposing vertically arranged stylized pine cones, B? LANGE, Danzig, circa 1700, 9cm. high, 5oz.
(Christie's) $2,479

A silver gilt niello beaker, marked with the cyrillic initials of Pavel Ovchinnikov, Moscow, 1867, the body with wide band of nielloed floral and foliate scrolls, 3½in. high, 86gm.
(Christie's) $768

BELLS

An Edwardian silver mounted table or reception bell in the form of a tortoise, realistically modelled with silver shell and metal workings and frame, maker's mark *Gy & C, Chester*, 1910,15cm. long.
(Christie's) $1,327

A modern cast table bell with a part-reeded baluster handle and applied masks, flowers and shell motifs, by Richard Comyns, 1927, 12cm. high, 9oz.
(Christie's) $840

A gemset bell-push in the form of a rabbit, marked *K. Fabergé*, 1896-1908, the red cabochon eyes as pushpieces, 6in. long, 536gm. gross.
(Christie's) $160,487

BISCUIT BOXES

Fenton Brothers Sheffield, a Victorian triform biscuit box, the shell fluted downwards hinged covers with laurel ring handles, 10in.
(Woolley & Wallis) $758

Rare solid silver biscuit barrel of plain cylindrical form with slightly spreading båse with reed and tie edge and rim, 4½in. tall, London 1909, 19oz.
(G A Key) $761

A Victorian electro-plated mounted cut-glass biscuit box, of oblong form with a lift-off cover, pierced ropework mounts and a swing handle, 17cm. high x 18cm. long.
(Christie's) $673

A Henry VIII mazer bowl, the silver gilt mount with molded bands and scallop lower edge, engraved *Elizabeth Wood* and small later Earl's crest, 5¾in. diameter, London 1527. (Woolley & Wallis) $323,900

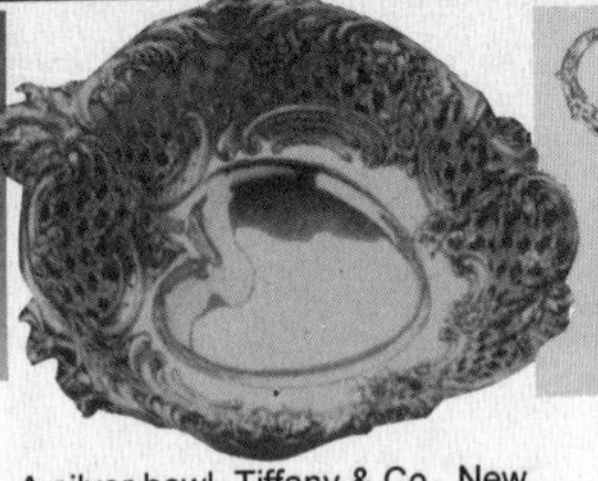

A silver bowl, Tiffany & Co., New York, 1891, heart-shaped on three scroll feet headed by acanthus, the sides repoussé and chased with scrolls and flowers under pierced trellis-work, 10¼in., 18oz. (Christie's) $2,990

A presentation rose bowl by Mappin and Webb, the body embossed with cartouches within floral surrounds, 18in. wide, Sheffield 1918, 72oz. 10dwts. (Andrew Hartley) $4,360

A Mappin & Webb salad bowl, with pierced fretwork foliage, the oval fluted rim and spreading foot with pendants of flowers, 8½in. diameter, London 1926, 20.5oz. (Woolley & Wallis) $773

Heavy hallmarked silver rose bowl, octagonal shaped with applied scroll and shell rim, strapwork scrolled handles, 8in. diameter, Birmingham 1927, 32oz. (G.A. Key) $581

A German silver bowl, Philipp Friedrich Bruglocher, Augsburg, 1789-1791, on spreading foot, with two plain drop-ring handles, 19.5cm. long, 17oz. (Christie's) $4,609

A late George III sugar bowl, the flared sides engraved with a band of oak leaves and acorns, Solomon Hougham, London 1805, 4.5oz. (Woolley & Wallis) $628

Large modern silver rose bowl, circular shaped with fluting at intervals, castellated rim, 8in. diameter, complete with grill, Sheffield 1974, 22oz. (G A Key) $440

Small hallmarked silver fruit bowl, tapering circular design to a flattened circular foot, the top pierced with floral and foliate designs and having a wavy edge, 8in. diameter, Sheffield 1934, 16oz. (G A Key) $425

A Victorian oval two-handled punch bowl floral and leafage embossed and chased, Sheffield 1897, 80oz by Mappin & Webb, 17in. (Russell Baldwin & Bright) $2,673

American Sterling silver punch bowl, by Arthur Stone, with bands of alternating lappets enclosing leaves, monogramed *C.*, diameter 11in. (Eldred's) $2,530

A Dutch 19th century Friesland bowl, with two cast scroll handles with mask terminals, engraved with initials and the date *1787*, Groninger. (Christie's) $1,344

A modern fruit bowl of low circular form with a collet foot and a frieze of fruiting vines, Mappin & Webb, 1934, 28.5cm. diameter, 57oz. (Christie's) $1,697

A silver centerpiece bowl, Whiting Mfg. Co., New York, circa 1885, Japanesque, circular on four scroll feet with stylized clouds, 10in. diameter, 23oz. (Christie's) $2,990

A modern bowl on three cast lion supports with three cast handles each in the form of a pair of lions and a pair of serpents, Mappin & Webb, 1915, 31cm. diameter, 65oz. (Christie's) $1,472

Large silver two handled punch bowl with applied leaf and stylized detail to a domed foot, hallmarked for London 1931 and bearing the Garrard and Co. maker's mark. (G.A. Key) $1,494

An Edward VII circular fruit bowl with plain everted rim on four pierced scrolling supports, 27cm. diameter, W. & S. Sissons, Sheffield 1909, 14.4oz. (Bearne's) $393

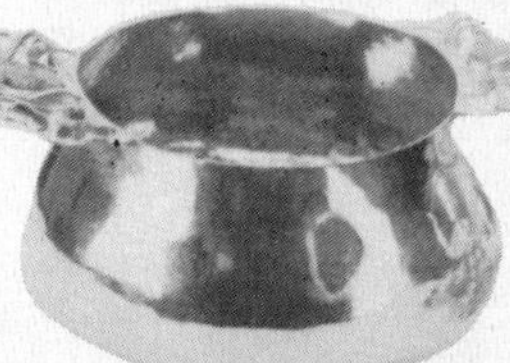

An Edwardian Arts & Crafts two handled bowl, on four ball feet of tapering circular form, by G.L. Connell, 1903, 17.5cm. wide, 11oz. (Christie's) $920

A Victorian sugar bowl, with molded rim, the sides embossed with scrolling foliage centered by a crested cartouche, on foot, 5½in. wide, Birmingham 1898, 8oz. 2dwt. (Andrew Hartley) $399

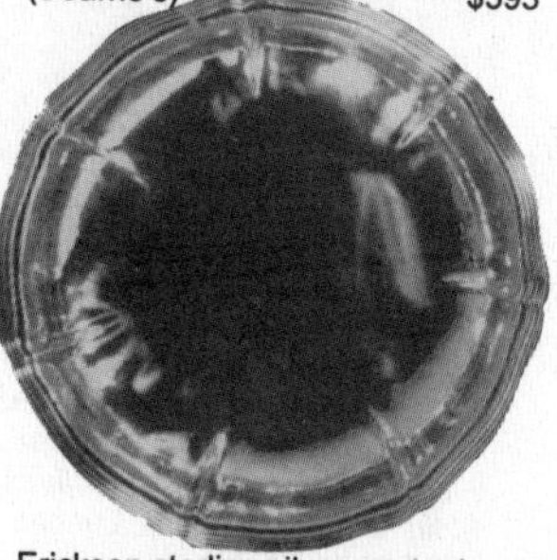

Erickson sterling silver center bowl, Herbert W. Glendenning, circa 1970, fluted bowl with seven ribs, flattened ribbed rim, 12¼in. approximately 43 troy oz. (Skinner) $1,035

Set of six American Sterling silver bowls, in the style of Paul Storr, with shell and gadroon rims and engraved coat of arms, marked *Sterling*, diameter 10½in. (Eldred's) $2,420

A large Edwardian two-handled bowl with embossed decoration below a pierced rim, by Ackroyd Rhodes, 1902, 44cm. wide, 86oz. (Christie's) $4,968

Omar Ramsden circular silver bowl of segmented circular design with beaded and applied scrolled edge, raised sectional dividers, 4½in. diameter, London 1937, 6½oz. (G A Key) $974

A Walker and Hall silver plated sugar bowl and scoop by Christopher Dresser, No.1995A. (Academy Auctioneers) $200

An Edwardian circular rose bowl, with a part-fluted lower body and a cast rim with masks and floral scrolls, by Walker & Hall, Chester, 1906, 26cm. diameter, 32oz. (Christie's) $937

Good quality Victorian silver plated presentation fruit bowl of pedestal type, circular shaped with applied scrolled and shell edge, pierced swing handle, 10in. diameter, circa 1840/60. (G.A. Key) $159

A rose bowl, part swirl ribbed, on a molded collet foot, 8in. diameter, by Nathan & Hayes, Chester 1910, 14oz. (Woolley & Wallis) $440

A late Victorian silver wine cooler/jardinière, London 1900, maker's mark of Charles Stuart Harris, of upright cylindrical form, with wavy edge border applied with masks and shells, approximate weight 30oz. (Bonhams) $1,570

Fine Arts and Crafts period silver pedestal bowl, the top embossed with continuous frieze of trailing foliage with heart shaped leaves, 5½in. diameter, 5ft. tall, London 1907, maker A J H , 13oz. (G A Key) $602

Sterling silver hexagonal punch bowl, by Gorham, engraved floral and foliate decoration, engraved *Clayton & Phyllis, 1932-1957*, diameter 13¼in., 45 troy oz. (Eldred's) $1,210

A George II silver punch bowl, Henry Brind, London, 1748, engraved with a coat-of-arms within a rococo cartouche, 10in. diameter, 53oz. (Christie's) $30,728

A silver-gilt sugar bowl and cover, embossed with foliate festoons and a calyx of stiff leaves, by Charles Stuart Harris, 1899, 14.5cm. high. 10.5oz. (Christie's) $686

A Victorian circular rosebowl with vacant circular panels within a reeded band, Edward Hutton, London 1887, 26cm. diameter, 36.6oz. (Bearne's) $1,073

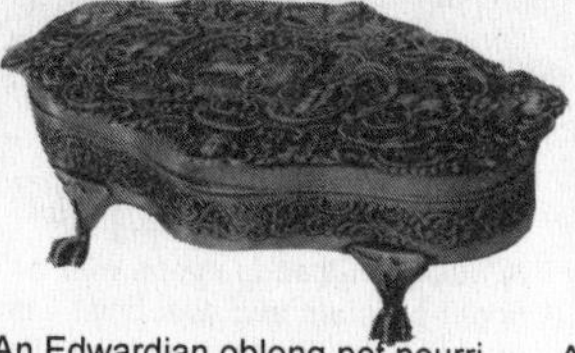

An Edwardian oblong pot pourri box, the serpentine shape body with an embossed foliage band, William Comyns, 7½in. London 1903, 8.75oz.
(Woolley & Wallis) $720

A late 19th century Continental silver oval box, the hinged cover pierced with a chinoiserie scene, backed with mother of pearl, 2in., import marks for London 1896.
(Woolley & Wallis) $128

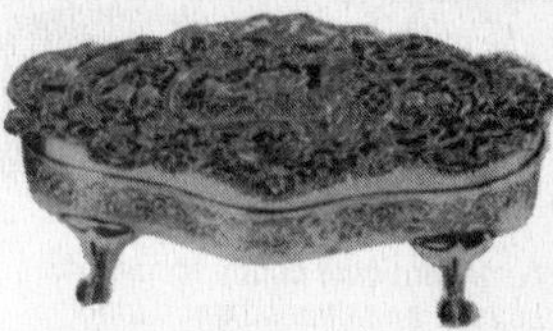

An Edward VII shaped oval trinket box, the hinged cover pierced and embossed with horse, carriage, bells, flowers and scrolls, London 1903, 7½in. (Russell Baldwin & Bright) $564

A late 19th century Dutch rectangular box, the hinged cover embossed with a scene of The Holy Family on the road to Egypt, 2⅞in. Import Marks for Berthold Muller, Chester 1901.
(Woolley & Wallis) $152

A good 19th century Continental silvery metal and enamel rectangular 'Singing Bird' box, oval lid opening to reveal small feathered automaton singing bird with pierced gilt grilles, 3¾in.
(Canterbury) $3,520

An Edwardian rectangular dressing table box, with ogee sides, embossed weave design and Art Nouveau motifs, 2.75in., Walker & Hall, Sheffield 1903.
(Woolley & Wallis) $128

Good quality large solid silver dressing table box of cylindrical form, the lid with garland applied edge, 3½ diameter, London 1905, by Mappin and Webb, 8oz.
(G.A. Key) $192

A late Victorian heart shaped dressing table box, relief decorated with 'C' scroll and floral decoration, width 2¼in. by H. Matthews, Birmingham 1899.
(George Kidner) $136

Continental silver repoussé box, late 19th century, shaped oval, the sides with scrolls and foliate, the front with monogramed cartouche, 2½in. high, approximately 13 troy oz.
(Skinner) $690

Victorian trinket box, of trefoil form, foliate embossed with hinged lid, 3¼in. wide, Birmingham 1888, oz 13dwt.
(Andrew Hartley) $380

A 19th century Dutch silver colored metal scallop shape box, the base with an embossed scene of shepherd and shepherdess, 2.25in. (Woolley & Wallis) $88

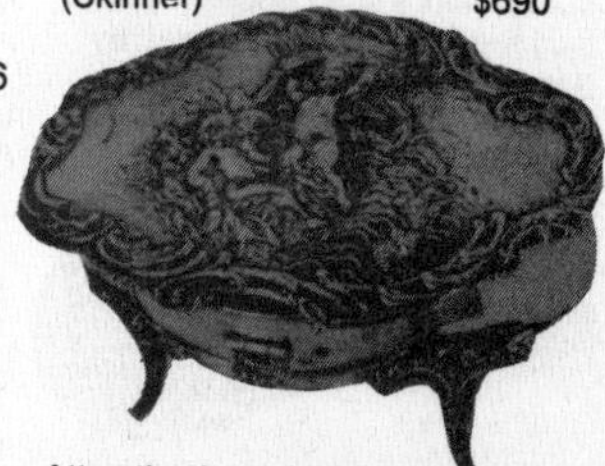

Attractive large hallmarked silver jewel box in the form of a decorative table, the lid well chased and embossed with cherubs, 6 x 4in., Chester 1902.
(G A Key) $558

A modern cast caddy spoon with incised and chased geometric patterns, by Liberty & Co, Birmingham 1913, 9.25cm. long. (Christie's) $690

A George III bright-engraved caddy spoon, with a fluted oval bowl by Hester Bateman, 1785, 10cm. long. (Christie's) $545

A George III caddy spoon with a bright-cut stem and oval bowl, inset with an oval filigree panel, initialled, by Samuel Pemberton, Birmingham 1802. (Christie's) $1,973

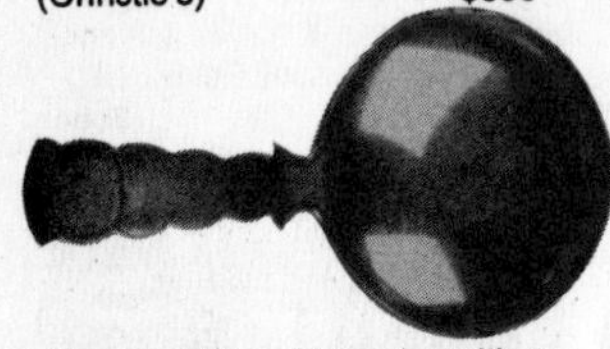

A George III caddy spoon with a round bowl and a graduated wavy stem decorated with 'pricked' border engraving, initialled, by Thomas James, 1811, 8.5cm. long. (Christie's) $635

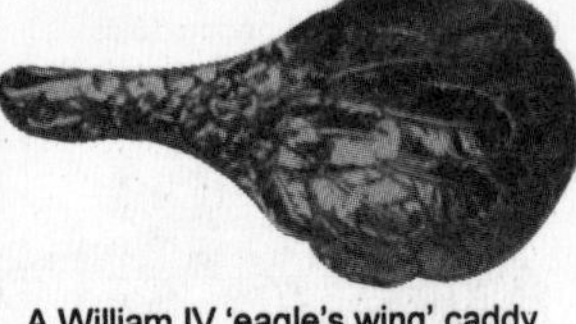

A William IV 'eagle's wing' caddy spoon, stamped in low relief with textured plumage, beak and eye detail, by Joseph Wilmore, Birmingham 1832, 8cm. long. (Christie's) $1,444

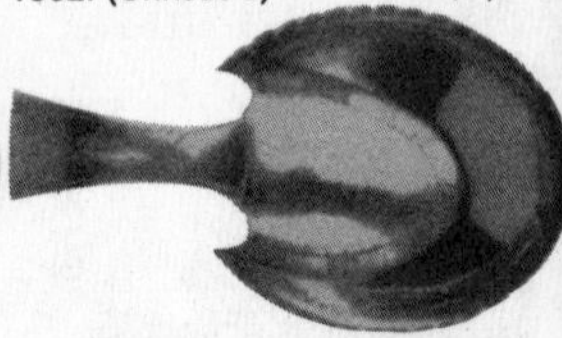

A George III 'pastern hoof' caddy spoon, with a pierced gallery around the bowl and 'pricked' borderwork, by Cocks & Bettridge, Birmingham 1807, 6.5cm. long. (Christie's) $690

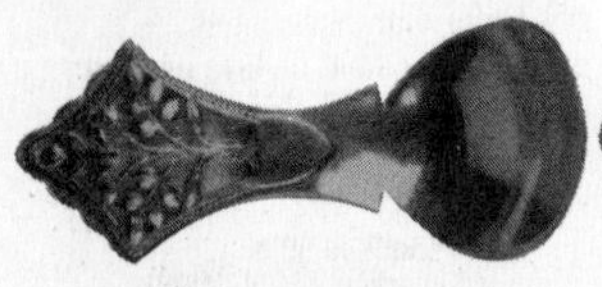

A modern caddy spoon, with an openwork shaped terminal, depicting the Tree of Life by Henry George Murphy, 1934, 9.5cm. long. (Christie's) $727

A George III caddy spoon, in the form of a right hand with a pricked and shaped cuff, by Josiah Snatt, 1808, 6.5cm. long. (Christie's) $1,272

A modern cast caddy spoon with a drop shaped bowl and an openwork cinquefoil handle, by Omar Ramsden, 1935, 9.75cm. long, 1.5oz. (Christie's) $1,632

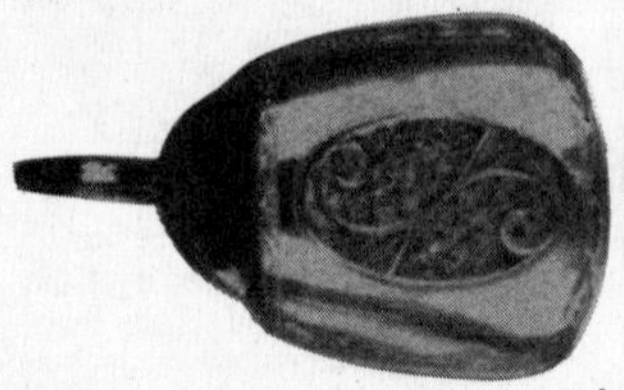

A George III engraved caddy shovel with a ring handle and an oval filigree panel in the bowl, by Samuel Pemberton, Birmingham 1804, 6cm. long. (Christie's) $344

A modern caddy spoon, with a heart-shaped bowl and a round lug handle decorated in the center with blue/green enamelled boss flanked by fine beading, by Liberty & Co., Birmingham 1911, 7cm. long. (Christie's) $1,999

A George III 'jockey cap' caddy spoon, decorated with alternating plain and reeded stripes radiating from the center, lion passant and duty mark only, circa 1800, 5.5cm long. (Christie's) $363

A Victorian cast caddy spoon, decorated with rocaille ornament berries and foliage, the gilt bowl 'hatched' in the center, by George Adams, 1848, 9.25cm. long. (Christie's) $909

A George III caddy spoon, in the form of an acorn with a bifurcated stem and canted square terminal, by Hart & Co., Birmingham 1806, 9.75cm. long. (Christie's) $1,543

A large George III caddy spoon, with wave-like sides and an amoeba-like motif engraved in the center, initialled, by Edward Fairbrother 1812, 11.25cm. long. (Christie's) $817

A pair of French silver-plated five-light candelabra, 19th century, after an 18th century model by Louis-Joseph Lenhendrick, on shaped circular base with ovolo and foliate border, 22in. high.
(Christie's) $9,142

A pair of modern three-light candelabra with shaped square bases, knopped baluster columns and reeded scroll branches, Turner Bradbury, 1918, 45cm. high.
(Christie's) $3,680

A pair of 19th century old Sheffield plated candelabra, with flamed finial on reeded turned tapering stem, 21in. high.
(Andrew Hartley) $874

A Victorian gilt-metal candelabrum centerpiece, unmarked, late 19th century, with detachable entwined palm-tree stem with three scroll branches each terminating in a vase-shaped socket, 21¾in. high.
(Christie's) $1,463

A pair of Victorian electroplated cast twin-light candelabra, on shaped triform bases with scroll decoration, by Elkington & Co., 29cm. high.
(Christie's) $1,055

An Edwardian five-light candelabrum with leafy scroll branches, by Hawkesworth, Eyre & Co., Sheffield, 1905, 49cm. high, 37cm. span of branches; loaded base; weight of branches 57.25oz.
(Christie's) $1,771

A pair of Continental three-light candelabra, probably Italian, 19th century, unmarked, the candlesticks each on shaped circular and lobed base, 13½in. high, 57oz.
(Christie's) $4,715

An important pair of French silver candelabra, François-Désiré Froment-Meurice, Paris, stamped *1853*, the stem shaped as two finely cast and chased guardian angels back to back, 34½in. high, gross 818oz.
(Christie's) $89,835

A pair of early 19th century Old Sheffield two branch three light candelabra, with fluted and leafage stems and octafoil lobed bases, by Waterhouse, Hatfield & Co, circa 1830, 46.5cm.
(Tennants) $2,905

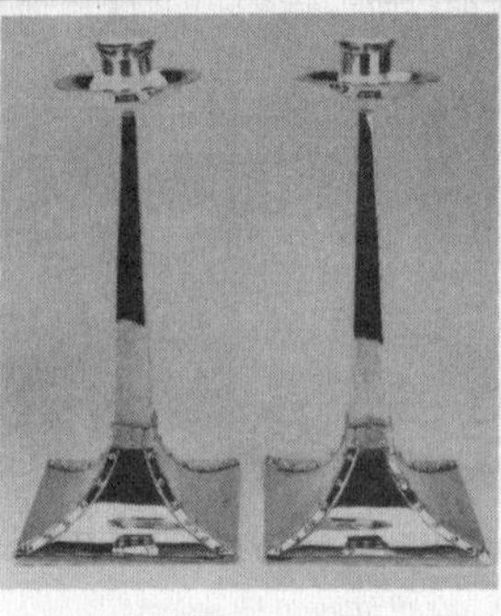

A pair of late 18th century German candlesticks, chased festoons of foliage and wreathes, by Philipp Friedrich Bruglocker, Augsburg 1785-7, 24.5cm. high. 22.5oz.
(Christie's) $1,641

A pair of Edwardian Arts & Crafts candlesticks with tapering square columns and sloping square bases, James Dixon & Sons, Sheffield 1907, 22.5cm. high.
(Christie's) $2,299

A pair of Victorian tapersticks, in the George II/III manner with knopped columns, by Walker & Hall, Sheffield 1904, 17.5cm. high.
(Christie's) $589

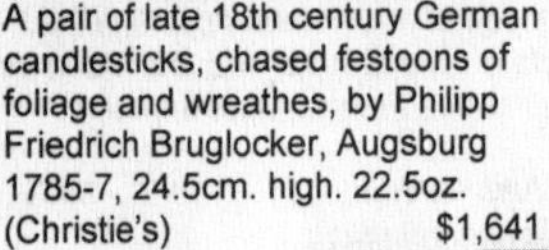

A rare pair of George II Irish cast candlesticks with circular bases, sunken centers and knopped columns, by John Hamilton, Dublin, 1736, 18cm. high, 26oz.
(Christie's) $4,225

A pair of George III dwarf candlesticks with vase shaped capitals, bevelled square bases and beaded borders, by William Abdy I, 1784, 10.75cm. high, loaded.
(Christie's) $2,689

A pair of late George II candlesticks, having gadroon edges, 9¾in. high, John Hyatt & Charles Semore, London 1759, 41oz.
(Woolley & Wallis) $4,740

A pair of mid 18th century Dutch candlesticks on shaped square bases with leaf-capped scroll feet, by Jacob van der Hoop, Amsterdam, 1743, 18.75cm. high, 19.25oz.(Christie's) $14,720

A pair of George III cast tapersticks with knopped columns, stepped square bases, fluted decoration 1767, 16.5cm. high, 19.5oz.
(Christie's) $3,649

A pair of mid 19th century Continental candlesticks, the ribbed stems with leaf and cartouche repoussé decorated bowls and candleholders, 11.9in. high.
(Woolley & Wallis) $864

A pair of George III Old Sheffield plated columnar candlesticks, with circular top, bright cut and reeded stem, 10¾in. high.
(Andrew Hartley) $269

A pair of Edward VII dressing table candlesticks, the bases and detachable nozzles with gadroon edging, 18cm. high, Thomas Bradbury, London, 1902, weighted.
(Bearne's) $922

Two very similar George II cast candlesticks, one by Thomas Gilpin, 1755, the other by Edward Wakelin, 1748, 21.5cm high each, 39oz. (Christie's) $2,689

Emick Romer, a pair of early George III tapersticks, the stop fluted columns to pierced Corinthian capitals, the detachable square nozzles with concave gadroon edges, 7in. high,London 1764.
(Woolley & Wallis) $2,370

A set of four George III candlesticks, engraved a stag crest, the baluster stems with gadroon knops, 12in. Makers James Gregory & John Stainiforth, Sheffield 1800/1802.
(Woolley & Wallis) $3,200

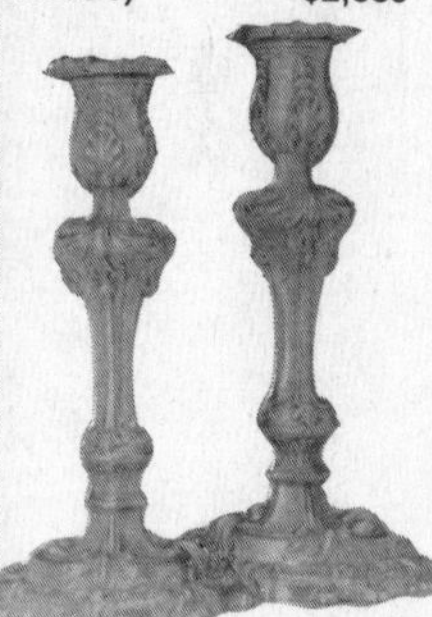

A pair of early Victorian candlesticks, the Silesian stems with leaf and scroll shoulders to scaled shell candle holders, 9.5in. high.
(Woolley & Wallis) $284

A pair of George III cluster column candlesticks on fluted, domed square bases with bead borders, maker W.E.I.K. (incuse) 1767, 34.5cm. high.
(Christie's) $3,680

Pair of Russian candlesticks, late 19th century, on shaped square base with scrolling stylized dolphins to corners, the stem with flat leaf motifs, 13¾in. high, 26 troy oz. approximately,
(Skinner) $805

A pair of late 18th century Old Sheffield plate neo-classical candlesticks, the columns with trailing oak leaves a acorns, circa 1785. (Christie's) $643

A set of three George II casters, one large and two smaller of vase form with knop finials and high domed covers, Samuel Wood, 1737, 18.5 x 15cm. high, 19.5oz.
(Christie's) $2,760

A Queen Anne sugar caster, pear-shaped with a molded girdle, pierced with two bands of pierced work, the body engraved with a coat of arms, by Charles Adam, 1708, 18.5cm. high, 7oz.
(Christie's) $2,302

An early 18th century Belgian caster and matching mustard pot, with a beaded scroll handle, each of plain vase form on circular pedestals, Brussels, 1710-172, 17.25cm. high. 16.25oz.
(Christie's) $12,751

A pair of George II embossed casters, of baluster form with pine-cone finials and asymmetrical cartouches by Samuel Wood, 1750, 18cm. high. 17.75oz.
(Christie's) $2,917

A set of three George I silver casters, Charles Adam, London, 1714, with detachable pierced domed cover and baluster finial, two 17cm. and one 20cm. high, 21oz. (Christie's) $5,485

Pair of early George III silver muffineers of circular baluster form on spreading circular bases, the pierced domed lids with wrythen finials, 5in. tall, London, 1767.
(G.A. Key) $576

An Art Deco sugar caster, the cylindrical body with a detachable pierced molded domed cover, 6in. high, Hamilton and Inches Edinburgh, 1937, 7oz.
(Woolley & Wallis) $308

Two George III vase-shaped pepper casters, on circular pedestals, by James Sutton, 1782, the other by Samuel & Edward Davenport, 1796, 14.5cm. and 15.5cm. high, 6oz.
(Christie's) $1,173

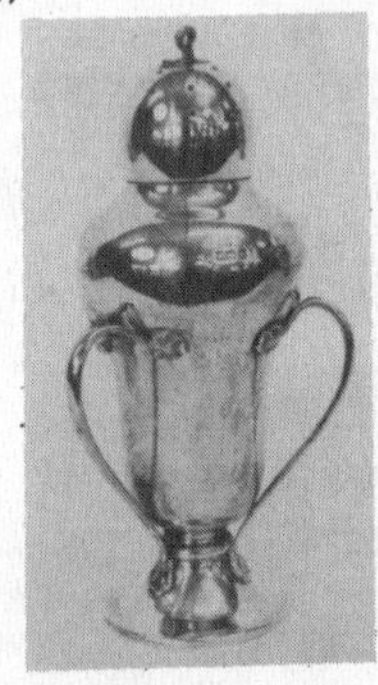

Good large Art Nouveau styled silver sugar caster of inverted baluster form to a circular foot, having three looped handles, 8in. high, Sheffield 1904 by H.E. Limited, 12oz.
(G.A. Key) $400

A German silver centerpiece, late 19th century, 800 standard, the top chased to simulate water and with a shell, drawn by a swan with seated winged putto, 12½in. high, gross 93oz. (Christie's) $10,605

German silver centerpiece, 19th century, lobed panelled navette form, raised and chased design, children finials, 12¼in. high. approximately 121 troy oz. (Skinner) $4,025

A George IV silver centerpiece, William Eaton, London, 1821, the frame on four Ceres mask, cornucopiae, reeded anthemion supports, 13in. high, 143oz. (Christie's) $14,628

A Victorian cast electroplated table centerpiece, modelled as a Bedouin and his camel taking shade under a palm tree with twin trunks and drooping fronds, by T. Bradbury & Sons, circa 1870, 42cm. high. (Christie's) $1,714

Edwardian silver plated table centerpiece on circular slightly domed base with beaded edge, emitting three scrolled arms, 12in. tall, circa 1900 (G A Key) $102

A George IV silver four-light candelabrum centerpiece, Paul Storr, London 1822, the stem formed as acanthus foliage and applied with the figures of Bacchus, a bacchante, goat, kid, and a putto, 29½in. high, 637oz. (Christie's) $155,800

A Victorian silver centerpiece, Elkington & Company, Birmingham, 1865, applied with detachable stag, doe and fawn beneath two entwined palm trees, 21½in. high. 124oz. (Christie's) $7,314

A George IV table centerpiece, with bevelled oblong base and paw feet, four detachable foliate branches, caryatid figure in each corner, probably by Edward Turnpenny, Birmingham 1825, height 42cm., 77oz. weighable silver. (Christie's) $4,782

A late Victorian electroplated centerpiece, 20in. high. (Dockrees) $544

George III silver taper stick, the tray formed base with reeded edge, complete with snuffer on chain, 2½in. diameter, Sheffield 1801, by Thomas Law.
(G.A. Key) $352

A late Victorian silver chamberstick, London 1894, Richard and Richard Hodd, stylized leaf form, wavy edge border, approximate weight 7oz., 22.5cm. long.
(Bonhams) $412

An Edwardian silver chamberstick/vesta holder, London 1902, John Thomas Heath & John Hartsborne Middleton, of pear form, tapering circular candle holder, weight 8oz.,17.5cm. long.
(Bonhams) $628

Edward Wakelin, a George III bedroom candlestick, the circular tray with a raised gadroon edge border, with a leaf scale and shell handle, London 1760, 13oz.
(Woolley & Wallis) $1,162

Two George III silver chambersticks, Ebenezer Coker, London, 1770 and 1771, shaped circular and on three shell and scroll feet, 5¼in. diameter, 16oz.
(Christie's) $1,728

Small chamberstick, London, 1804, maker's mark *AK*, ribbed borders, lacking extinguisher, 2in. high, 2 troy oz. approximately.
(Skinner) $172

Victorian small chamber candlestick in the form of a shell, the support and candle holder as a flower, by Robinson, Edkins & Aston, circa 1844, 3½in., 2½oz.
(Ewbank) $277

A pair of William IV Sheffield plate bedroom candlesticks, with panelled edge circular trays and detachable nozzles to the candleholder.
(Woolley & Wallis) $440

Georgian silver tray candlestick of shaped circular design with scrolled edge, detachable nozzle and complete with snuffer, the base 6in. diameter, Sheffield Assay, circa 1820. (G A Key) $303

A George III silver-gilt taperstick, John Scofield, London 1782, of chamberstick form, with circular base and leaf-capped scroll bracket handle, 1½in. high, 3oz.
(Christie's) $1,132

A pair of late Victorian chamber sticks, each of trefoil form, gadrooned rim, single carrying handle, 4in. wide, Chester 1893.
(George Kidner) $417

A George III chamberstick with a gadrooned circular base, leaf-capped scroll handle and conical snuffer, crested by William Stroud, 1807, 15cm. diameter, 14oz.
(Christie's) $1,728

A chocolatière, designed by Lucien Bonvallet, manufactured by Cardeilhac, circa 1895-1900, waisted cylinder decorated with repoussé 'ancolie' leaves, 8¼in. high. (Christie's) $4,800

Hallmarked silver café-au-lait set in Queen Anne style, of tapering cylindrical form with side handle, urn finials to lids, 6in. tall, London 1901, 18oz all in. (G A Key) $558

A rare George II/III chocolate pot, Robert Calderwood, Dublin, circa 1760, of baluster form with a leaf-capped double scroll handle, a cushion domed cover with a detachable finial, 25cm. high, 28.75oz.(Bonhams) $15,444

CHRISTENING MUGS

An early Victorian silver mug, London 1844, J and J Angell, engraved with Gothic and scroll decoration, and the figures of Charles I and Sire De Courcy, approximate weight 7oz., 12.3cm., high. (Bonhams) $428

Fancis Higgins, a Victorian christening set, of a porringer and spoon, engraved with initials and a coronet, the porringer with a flared rim to two bead and scroll handles, London 1866, 6.25oz. (Woolley & Wallis) $185

A Victorian christening mug, the bucket shape body engraved with initials to vine pendants, ivy swags and scrolls, Alexander Macrae, London 1866, 4.75oz. (Woolley & Wallis) $231

CIGARETTE CASES

A Continental white metal and enamelled cigarette case of rounded oblong form, depicting a horse's head, 3¾in. wide. (Andrew Hartley) $512

A German silvered metal cigarette case, the cover polychrome enamelled with female nude, seated on chaise longue dusting her feet, 8.5cm. high. (Christie's) $480

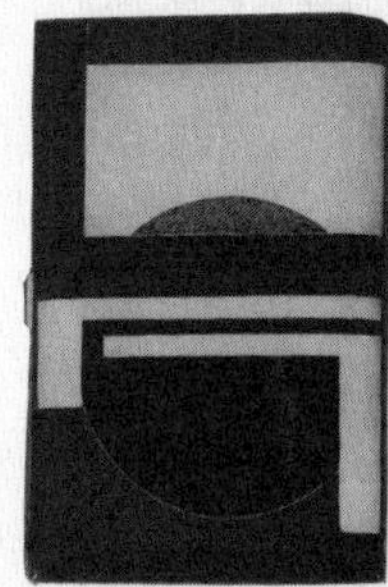

Raymond Templier, cigarette case in original fitted case, 1929, silver-coloured metal, decorated with a geometric design in eggshell and black and blue lacquer, 13 x 8.5cm. (Sotheby's) $13,972

A silver mounted claret jug maker D (S) Ltd., Birmingham, 1957, the hinged domed cover and finial above a loop handle and star cut sides, 29cm.
(Cheffins) $318

A pair of Victorian silver-mounted cut-glass claret jugs, Charles Reily and George Storer, London, 1842, the partly-frosted cut-glass bodies with stylized foliage decoration, 10¾in. high.
(Christie's) $10,971

A late Victorian mounted cut-glass claret jug with an embossed mount with a cast mask spout, by J. Heath & J.H. Middleton, 1900, 28cm. high.
(Christie's) $2,113

A Victorian silver-mounted cut-glass claret jug, John Figg, London, 1867, cylindrical body with spreading base, cut with star decoration, with beaded lower mount and bracket handle, 12¾in. high. (Christie's) $4,936

A late Victorian cased pair of silver gilt mounted cut-glass claret jugs, with bark textured handles, Charles Boyton, 1892, 28cm. high.
(Christie's) $11,040

A mid Victorian Scottish silver claret jug, Glasgow 1845, maker's mark of Robert Gray & Son, of baluster form, the body embossed with entwined foliate scroll and floral decoration, approximate weight 27oz., 27cm. high.
(Bonhams) $1,570

A claret ewer, the glass of ovoid shape engraved with a golfer taking a swing, and ladies with parasols, circa 1880, 24cm.
(Tennants) $706

A pair of Edwardian silver mounted glass claret jugs, Sheffield 1909, maker's mark of R. B., of tapering circular form, the glass bodies with cut-glass decoration, 30.5cm. high.
(Bonhams) $1,334

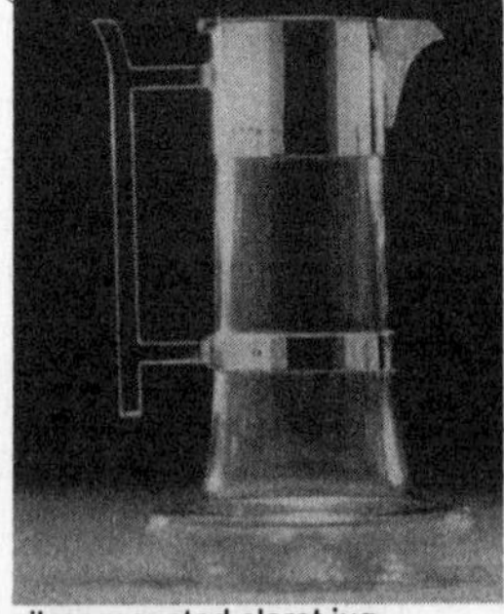

A silver mounted claret jug, designed by Christopher Dresser, manufactured by Hukin & Heath, 1879-80, the slender tapering glass body on a compressed baluster base, 8½in. high.
(Christie's) $4,844

A pair of George III wine coasters, with gadrooned rims, the sides pierced with latticework, William Allen (III) 1803, 14cm. diameter. (Christie's) $3,430

19th century silver and plated double wine coaster on spoke wheels, each coaster 6in. diameter. (G.A. Key) $350

A pair of George III wine coasters with reeded rims and turned wooden bases, by Peter & Ann Bateman, 1790, 12.25cm. diameter. (Christie's) $3,430

A pair of George III silver wine coasters, Paul Storr, London, 1819, circular with turned wood bases, the fluted sides with gadrooned border, 6¾in. diameter. (Christie's) $10,971

A set of four George III decanter stands, the pierced fret trailing foliage sides interspersed with vertical bands, probably Francis Spilsbury II, London 1768. (Woolley & Wallis) $4,582

A pair of wine coasters with waisted scroll-pierced sides and applied husk and scroll rims, Messrs John & Joseph Angell, 1846, 14cm. diameter. (Christie's) $2,888

A set of three electro-plated wine coasters, with turned wooden bases and everting lattice-work sides, by Elkington & Co, 1863, 20cm. diameter. (Christie's) $1,263

A rare pair of George III Irish wine coasters with beaded rims, the sides pierced with horizontal rows of holes and slots between two bands of wrigglework engraving, Thomas Jones or Thomas Johnston, Dublin circa 1785, 12cm. diameter.(Christie's) $4,694

A set of three George III silver wine-coasters, Edward Aldridge, London, 1771, the sides pierced with scrolls and flowers, with corded rim, 11.5cm. diameter, 20oz gross. (Christie's) $4,754

A large George III coffee pot, the baluster body with a cast leaf decorated swan neck spout having a pendant drop, 10½in. high, possibly Francis Crump, London 1769, 27.75oz. all in.
(Woolley & Wallis) $1,386

A matched pair of Edwardian café-au-lait pots, one by Goldsmiths & Silversmiths Co Ltd, 1906, the other by Holland, Aldwinkle & Slater, 1902, 17cm. high, 23oz.
(Christie's) $1,288

An Edwardian embossed coffee pot of baluster form, decorated in the 1760s style with embossed rocaille cartouches, trailing flowers and a fruiting bud finial, by Skinner & Co., 1903, 28cm. high, 29oz.
(Christie's) $744

A sterling silver coffee pot by Sigurd Persson, Stockholm, 1952, of tapering cylindrical form, with hinged lid and hard wood handle, 24.2cm. high.
(Stockholms AV) $5,492

A pair of modern octagonal café-au-lait pots with scroll handles and ring finials, by George Howson, 1911, 13.5cm. high, 15oz.
(Christie's) $515

A George III coffee pot of pear shape embossed and chased with swags and floral pendants, London 1772, by Charles Wright, 29oz. all in. (Russell Baldwin & Bright)
$2,438

A George II silver coffee-pot, Ayme Videau, London, 1754, the body and cover chased with scrolls, foliage and rococo ornament, engraved with coat-of-arms, 10½in. high, gross 38oz.
(Christie's) $3,657

A pair of Edwardian ivory mounted café au lait jugs, each cylindrical with tucked-in base and waisted neck, by R. Martin & E. Hall, Sheffield, 1904, 17.5cm. high.
(Christie's) $885

Paul Storr, a Regency coffee pot, the vase shape body engraved with a seahorse crest, a collar of a repoussé band of shells, scrolls and tulips, 10in. high, London 1815, 31oz. all in.
(Woolley & Wallis) $6,160

A late Victorian silver coffee pot, Sheffield 1889, retailed by Walker and Hall, baluster form, embossed foliate decoration, domed hinged cover, weight 26oz., 30.5cm. high. (Bonhams) $507

Robert Garrard, a Victorian coffee pot, the cylindrical tapering body engraved with a crest of a demi lion issuant regardant, to a slightly flared neck, 6.75in. high, London 1854, 20oz. all in. (Woolley & Wallis) $832

George II coffeepot, London, 1754, Richard Gurney & Co., the body engraved to both sides with monograms within foliate cartouches, 10½in. approximately 29 troy oz. (Skinner) $1,840

Charles Fox, a fine William IV coffee pot, in Rococo Revival style, the pear shape body having a vacant cartouche to chased repoussé scrolls and applied cast foliage decoration, 10in. high, London 1837, 31.75oz. all in. (Woolley & Wallis) $1,232

A William IV embossed coffee pot, of baluster form on a circular pedestal with four cast floral scroll feet, a scroll handle and a fruit finial, by Johnathan Hayne, 1833, 26cm. high, 36oz. (Christie's) $1,240

An early George III baluster coffee pot, with a cast leaf and scroll decorated swan neck spout, a scroll wood handle, 10in., probably Thomas Wallis 1st., London 1766, 21oz. all in. (Woolley & Wallis) $1,649

A small George II coffee pot of tapered cylindrical form with a side handle, domed cover and knop finial, by Humphrey Payne, 1735, 17.5cm. high., 14oz. (Christie's) $2,833

A Victorian baluster shaped coffee pot, the vacant cartouches engraved with foliage, a leaf swan neck spout, on leaf spray appliqué scroll bead feet, 9½in. (Woolley & Wallis) $146

A Sheffield plate George IV plate coffee pot, the baluster body with gadrooning to the tuck-in base, a ribbed and foliage capped repoussé swan neck spout, 11in. high. (Woolley & Wallis) $185

A Victorian sparrow beak cream jug of baluster form with scrolled handle and spreading foot, 3in. high, London 1881, 2oz 5dwt. (Andrew Hartley) $157

A rare George II/III Irish cream boat of oval boat form with a cast oval foot, probably by Andrew Goodwin Dublin, circa 1760, 18cm. long, 5.75oz. (Christie's) $999

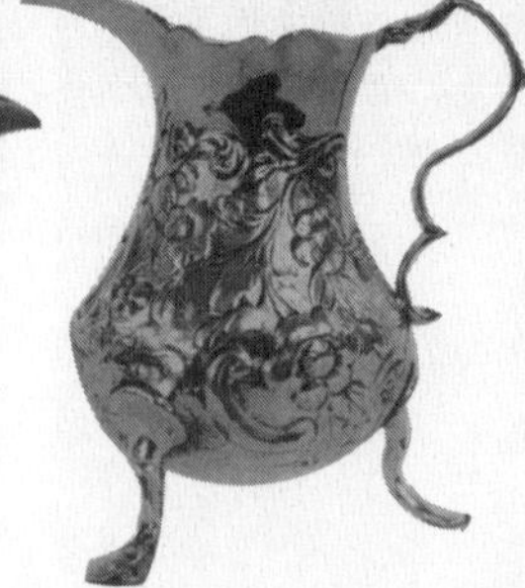

Early George III silver cream jug, card cut rim, the body embossed with trailing flowers and foliage, London 1763 by David Mowden. (G.A. Key) $288

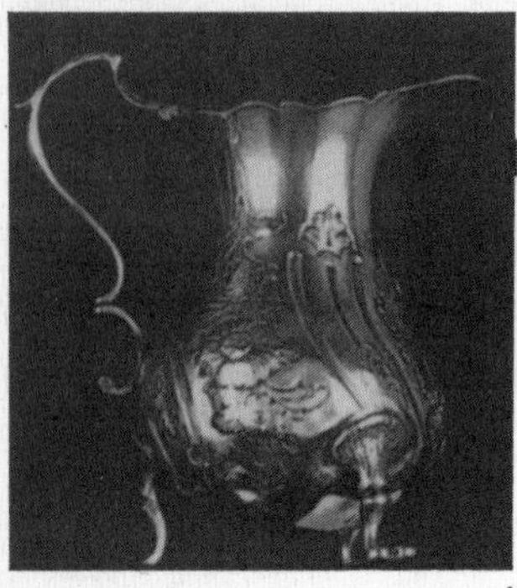

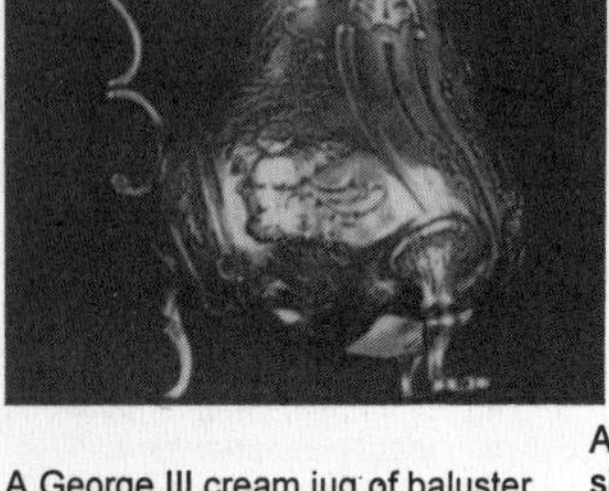

A George III cream jug of baluster form on three feet, embossed with floral sprays and chased wrythen fluting, 1760, 9.5cm. high, 2.25oz. (Christie's) $269

Arts & Crafts small hallmarked silver cream jug of circular baluster form with spot hammered decoration, snake design entwined handle, 3in. tall, Sheffield 1906, maker L W. (G.A. Key) $215

Early George III large silver cream jug of circular baluster form, fluted and gadrooned spreading circular foot, chased with simple scroll designs, scrolled handle, 5in. tall, London 1762, maker S M. (G A Key) $407

George III silver cream jug of inverted pear form to a shaped spreading circular foot, punch beaded and floral chased decoration, 3½in. tall, London 1779. (G A Key) $272

Liberty and Co. silver cream jug of tapering circular design with plain looped handle and supported on three ball feet, 3in. tall, Birmingham 1904. (G A Key) $365

Large George III silver helmet cream jug in neoclassical style, the body engraved with garlands and foliate swags, 5in. tall, London 1791, maker H C. (G.A. Key) $332

Victorian silver plated cruet stand of Warwick type, having pierced sides, applied wheatsheaf and scrolled rims, supported on pierced wheatsheaf feet, holding six faceted glass bottles. (G A Key) $384

Fine Victorian silver six cup egg cruet of shaped circular design, limited engraved swag and anthemion decoration, London 1870 by the Barnards, 20½oz. (G.A. Key) $631

Early George III oil and vinegar bottle stand of two trellis pierced conjoined cylindrical holders with rope twist rims, pierced divider, 8in. tall, London 1773 by Thomas Nash I . (G A Key) $1,088

George III cruet stand, London, 1765, possibly John Darwall, hexafoil, with five later cut glass bottles, two with glass stoppers, others metal mounted, 9½in. in., 24 troy oz. approximately. (Skinner) $747

A George II Warwick cruet with one large caster, pair of smaller casters and two silver lidded cut-glass bottles, London 1740, three casters London 1742s, Samuel Wood. (Russell Baldwin & Bright) $5,802

A Victorian electro-plated cast figural condiment set, in the form of an Indian wallah or bearer, carrying two mounted frosted glass condiments in the form of barrels on a beam over one shoulder, 16.5cm. high.(Christie's) $729

A George III cruet frame with a square base, bracket feet, gadrooned borders and a gadrooned ring handle, by I. E. Terry, 1815, 24cm. high. (Christie's) $1,875

George III cruet stand with cut glass bottles, London, 1797, the body with bands of bright cut engraving and monogramed cartouche, 10¼in. high. (Skinner) $1,035

Attractive Victorian circular silver cruet stand, the foliate pierced gallery with wavy gadrooned edge, central carrying handle with shell detail, 6in. diameter, London 1846 by the Barnards. (G.A. Key) $267

A George I tumbler cup of plain circular form with a curved base by Arthur Dicken, 1720, 5.5cm. diameter, 2.75oz.
(Christie's) $999

A George III silver-gilt cup and cover, Daniel Smith and Robert Sharp, London, 1770, the body with two vine capped double scroll handles, 17¾in. high, 128oz.
(Christie's) $57,615

A Queen Anne silver dram cup, John Gibbon, London, 1705, Britannia standard, 2in. high, 1oz 8dwt. (Sotheby's) $1,247

A Charles I stem wine cup, with tapered bowl, baluster stem and spread foot, the rim pricked *IK*, 7in. Walter Shute, London 1639, 10.75oz.
(Woolley & Wallis) $18,170

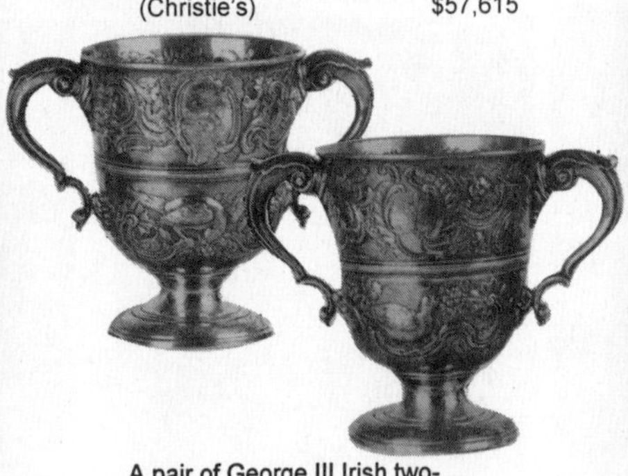

A pair of George III Irish two-handled cups with campana shaped bodies and leaf capped double scroll handles, by either James Warren or John West, Dublin circa 1760, 12.5cm. high, 27oz.
(Christie's) $2,784

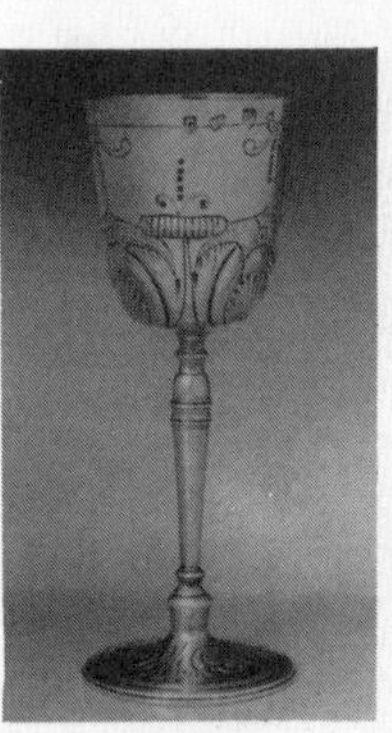

A Charles I silver gilt stem wine cup, chased formal foliate decoration with a tapered stem and spread foot, 5⅞in. high, maker W C, heart below, London 1631, 3oz.
(Woolley & Wallis) $10,424

A George III coconut cup, with a silver lining, gilded inside, the rim with bright cutting, the nut with a vacant wood cartouche, 6.75in., by T Phipps & E Robinson, London 1791. (Bristol) $684

A Regency coursing cup, the campana shape body applied with a chased oval plaque cast in relief, a scene of a hound catching a hare, 7⅝in., William Burwash, London 1814, 22.25oz.
(Woolley & Wallis) $980

A modern Art Nouveau cup, on an extended trumpet foot with globular bowl and two entwined scroll handles, Messrs Barraclough & Sons, Sheffield, 1910, 26cm. high, 38.5oz. (Christie's) $686

A George I silver cup and cover, Thomas Tearle, London, 1726, the body with molded mid-rib and two leaf-capped scroll handles, 12½in. high, 96oz.
(Christie's) $9,603

A George I campana shaped cup and cover with double handles and molded girdle and later embossed decoration, George Wickes, 1725, 19cm. high, 34.5oz.
(Christie's) $2,305

A George II/III two-handled cup of baluster form with a domed cover and foot, by William Grundy, 1760, 23.25cm. high, 28oz.
(Christie's) $1,055

A Queen Anne communion cup on a flared pedestal foot with a molded border and a tapering bowl, inscribed, by John Porter, 1705, 19cm. high, 9.5oz.
(Christie's) $1,440

A Victorian presentation three handled loving cup, chased strapwork and raised on three ball feet, 8in. high, London 1873, maker's mark for Bernard, 41oz. 6dwt. (Andrew Hartley) $940

A Victorian parcel-gilt silver cup and cover, Robert Garrard, London 1845, the body cast and chased overall with foliage, scrolls and strapwork on a reeded and matted ground, 9¾in. high, 23oz.
(Christie's) $3,772

A rare Charles II tumbler cup, (probably from a campaign/canteen set), engraved on one side with the coat of arms of a widow, probably by Thomas Jenkins, circa 1680, 9.5cm. diameter x 8.25cm. high, 6.5oz. (Christie's) $9,987

A Charles I stem wine cup, with tapered bowl and stem with molded bands and spread foot, 8¼in., Walter Shute, London 1631, 10.5oz.
(Woolley & Wallis) $16,590

A Queen Anne two handled cup with a campana shaped bowl, plain narrow girdle and s-scroll handles, by John Reed, 1710, 14.25cm. high, 13.5cm. diameter, 23.5oz.
(Christie's) $4,609

Italian silver gilt covered entrée dish, Rome, 20th century, applied flat leaf border at top and bottom, stylized loop handles with goose head terminals, approximately 14½in. long. (Skinner) $863

An Art Deco French metalware vegetable dish and cover with a circular body, lug handles and a low domed cover, maker's mark *H.L*, 28.5cm. wide overall. (Christie's) $773

An Old Sheffield plated warming dish, with ivory loop handles and lion paw feet, 13½in. wide and an Old Sheffield plated oblong entrée dish and cover. (Andrew Hartley) $346

Attractive large Victorian silver plated entrée dish and lid of shaped oval design with heavy shell and scrolled edges, supported on four claw feet, 12 x 9in., circa 1850. (G A Key) $393

A modern silver gilt fruit dish of circular outline with two handles and a cast border of fruiting vines, by Walker & Hall, Sheffield 1947, 31cm. diameter, 41oz. (Christie's) $840

A dish ring, the pierced and embossed sides with cartouches flanked by birds, scrolling foliage and vases of flowers, 8¼in. wide, London 1913, 16oz 12dwt. (Andrew Hartley) $739

A W.M.F. scallop shape meat dish in soft metal with cast squirrel handle holding a nut in its paws, 11in. long. (Woolley & Wallis) $185

Pair of Matthew Bolton silver plated entrée dishes, late 18th century shaped oval form applied shell and scroll decoration, 14½in. long. (Skinner) $6,325

A Victorian chinoiserie fruit dish, of shaped oval form on a domed oval foot with a cast border of flowerheads and scrolls, by John S. Hunt, 1849, 34cm. long, 29oz. (Christie's) $832

A silver Imperial presentation kovsh, Russia, probably Moscow, 1682-1696, the domed center repoussé, chased and engraved with the Imperial double-headed eagle, 27cm. long, 390gm. (Christie's) $21,126

Small Georg Jensen footed compôte, circa 1925-32, ten-sided base with ten applied beads, leafy stem, and hammered flared bowl, 5in. long, approximately 3 troy oz. (Skinner) $374

A George III silver vegetable dish and cover, John Edwards, London, 1800, plain circular and with two leaf-capped reeded scroll handles, 10in. long, 41oz.
(Christie's) $6,146

A late 19th century Russian niello work kovsch, chased around the upper body with panels of scrolls and a Cyrillic inscription, by Pavel Ovchinnikov, Moscow 1886, 14cm. long, 4.25oz.
(Christie's) $1,104

A muffin dish with turned ivory finial on domed lid, removable liner and gadrooned banding, 7¼in. wide, Sheffield 1938, 19oz. 16dwt.
(Andrew Hartley) $235

Tiffany sterling compôte, 1853, shallow bowl with upright handles, Renaissance Revival band around bowl column, gold washed interior, 8⅝in. diameter, approx. 35 troy oz.
(Skinner) $1,783

English silver bun warmer, late 19th/early 20th century, by Elkington, roll-away cover, engraved decoration and crest, 13in. across.
(Eldred's) $319

Early Victorian Scottish silver pedestal fruit dish on pierced scrolled four footed base and having elaborate pierced and scrolled edges, 12in. diameter, Edinburgh 1847, probably James Howden and Co., 24½oz.
(G A Key) $793

An Edwardian Irish dish ring of spool form, pierced and embossed with figures, birds and architecture, West & Sons, Dublin 1903, 20cm. high, 12oz. weighable silver. (Christie's) $2,208

A late 19th century German Art Nouveau shaped oval dish with two handles, resting on four cast dragonfly feet, circa 1900, 36cm. long, 13oz. (Christie's) $405

A caviar dish and liner, designed by Josef Hoffman, circa 1903, the deep bowl set on circular dipped base, decorated with repoussé rectangular panels, 9¼in. diameter.
(Christie's) $23,184

A Spanish parcel-gilt silver shaped oval sweetmeat dish, 17th century, the center flat-chased with foliage on a partially stippled ground, approx. 4oz., 5in. long.
(Sothebys') $4,600

Good quality large Victorian silver bon bon dish, the top pierced with floral and ribbon designs, 7½in. diameter, London 1894, 11oz.
(G.A. Key) $365

ÉPERGNES

A modern épergne or centerpiece with a cylindrical column, an octagonal dish with a central vase and two small baskets dependent, by Fenton Bros Ltd, Sheffield, 1922, 49.5cm. high, 60oz.
(Christie's) $3,457

A modern épergne or centerpiece with a central detachable trumpet vase flanked by three detachable smaller vases, H. Matthews, Birmingham 1927, 28cm. high, 11oz weighable silver.
(Christie's) $922

A modern épergne, the plain bowl with molded band, on openwork pedestal foot and four winged paw feet, with four matching smaller pendant baskets, by Roberts & Belk, Sheffield 1920, 29cm. high. 45oz. (Christie's) $1,594

EWERS

A large silver ewer, probably Portugal, circa 1810, the domed center repoussé with swirling flutes, the scrolling handle with foliate thumbpiece and terminals, 23in. high, 142.5oz.
(Christie's) $7,314

A pair of silver ewers, Richard Martin and Ebenezer Hall, Sheffield 1907, the bodies chased and applied with winged male and female demi-figures, 12¼in. high, 60oz. gross.
(Christie's) $5,281

A William IV Scottish silver ewer, Elder & Co, Edinburgh, 1833, with additional maker's mark of D. C. Rait of Glasgow, body chased and repoussé with scrolls, flowers and foliage on a matted ground, 9in. high, 36in. high.
(Christie's) $4,205

FLAGONS

A William IV silver church flagon, London 1829, maker's mark of William Bateman II, tapering circular form, scroll handle, domed hinged cover with a cross finial, approximate weight 52oz.
(Bonhams) $1,491

A Victorian Irish flagon of tapering form with a domed and spreading base, probably by John Scriber, Dublin 1873, 34cm. high. 62oz.
(Christie's) $3,457

A Victorian flagon of baluster form with a large ivory insulated scroll handle, the whole embossed with flowers and scrolls, by Martin Hall & Co, Sheffield 1858, 29.5 cm. high, 45oz. (Christie's) $2,302

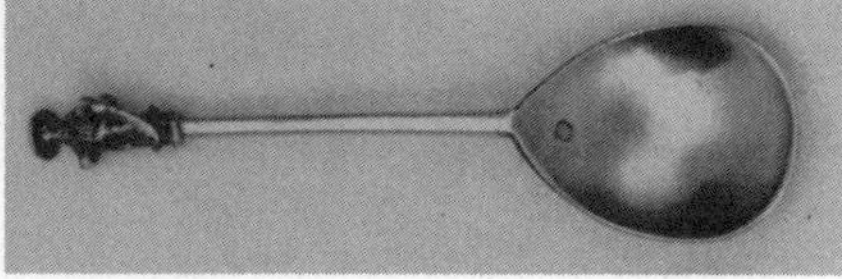

An Elizabeth I apostle spoon; St. Simon Zelotes, the gilt figure of the saint with a saw and sacred dove nimbus, maker's mark a bird's claw, 1562, 17.5cm. long, 2oz. (Christie's) $12,719

A rare pair of Elizabeth I apostle spoons, St. John and St. Simon Zelotes, with pierced, spoked nimbuses, traces of gilding, both with broad, tapering stems and fig-shaped bowls, by William Cawdell, 1589, 18.2cm. and 18cm. long respectively, 4oz. (Christie's) $19,078

A set of three mid 19th century bright engraved tablespoons, initialled *E.J.G.* on the tops of the stems with double skeletal drop bowls, by Thomas de Gruchy & John Le Gallais, Jersey, circa 1840, 21.5cm. long; together with another similar tablespoon initialled and dated *Marr Feb 16 1840* by the same maker, 22.75cm. long, 7oz. (Christie's) $690

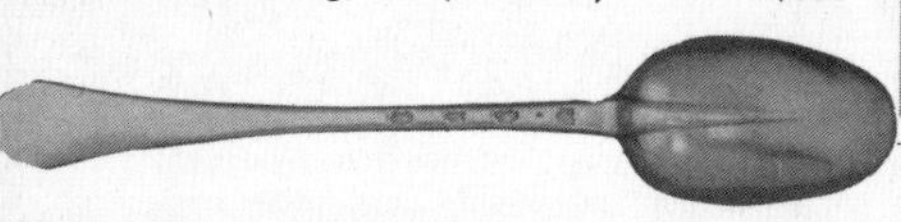

Richard Freeman of Plymouth, a large rat tail basting spoon with dog nose terminal, circa 1705. (Woolley & Wallis) $2,173

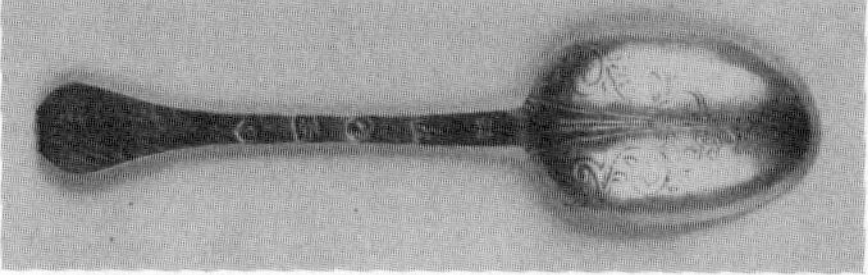

A Queen Anne ascribed West Country lace-back wavy-end or dog-nose spoon, pricked *I.K. E.S. 1708* on the back of the terminal, the oval bowl with a reeded rat-tail, by Edward (II) Sweet, (of Dunster), Exeter 1707, 20cm. long, 1.25oz. (Christie's) $1,725

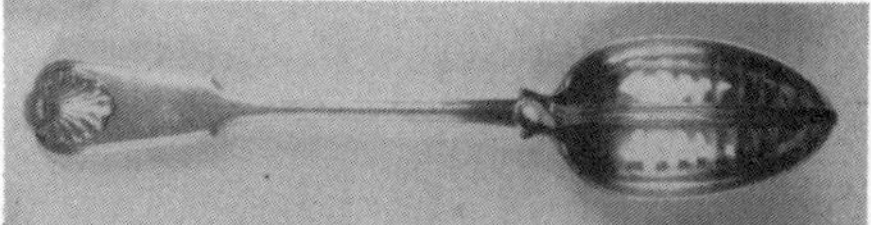

A mid 19th century Indian colonial fiddle, thread and shell pattern strainer spoon, with a detachable slot-pierced strainer secured by a thumbscrew, by Lattey Bros., Calcutta circa 1840, 29cm. long, 9oz. (Christie's) $1,362

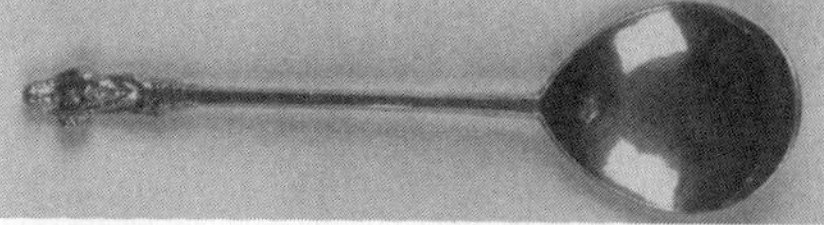

A James I/Charles I silver-gilt unascribed Wessex/West Country apostle spoon, probably St. Matthew, the figure of large proportions without a nimbus on a straight-sided hexagonal stem, pricked on the back of the bowl with the initials and date *R.V. S.M. 1627*, unascribed, probably Salisbury area circa 1625, 20cm. long, 1.75oz. (Christie's) $3,452

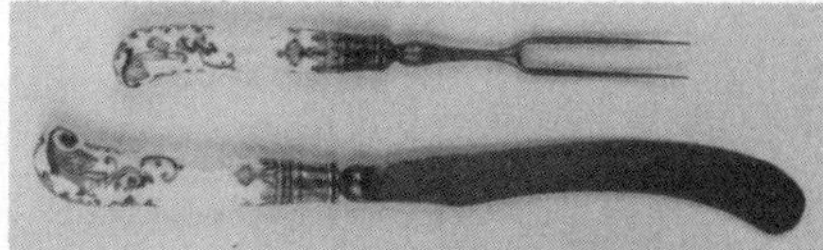

A mid 18th century French silver mounted steel knife with a scimitar blade and a matching two-pronged steel fork with blue and white soft paste porcelain (St. Cloud) pistol handles, circa 1745, the knife 28.5cm. long, the fork, 21cm. long. (Christie's) $581

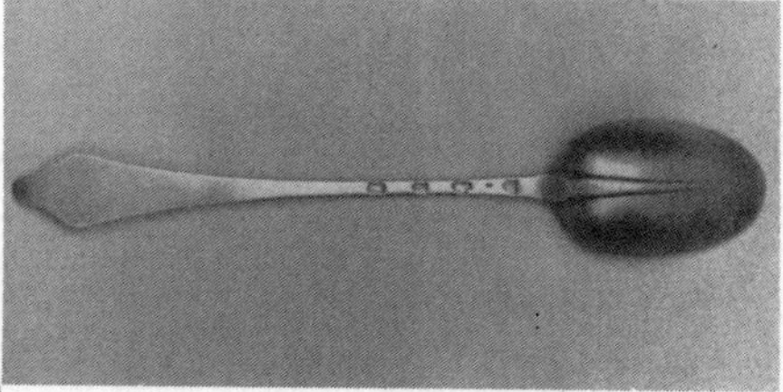

A Queen Anne/George I ascribed West Country wavy-end or dog-nose, basting spoon with a plain rat-tail bowl, maker's mark for Richard Freeman Plymouth, circa 1715, 35.5cm. long, 6oz. (Christie's) $1,454

A George III meat skewer with a cast shell and faceted ring terminal, initialled by T. Whipham and C. Wright, 1766, 31.5cm. long, 3.5oz.
(Christie's) $515

A silver-handled tortoiseshell caviar scoop, designed by Henry Van de Velde, circa 1900, the handle with sweeping linear decoration, 7½in. long.
(Christie's) $1,117

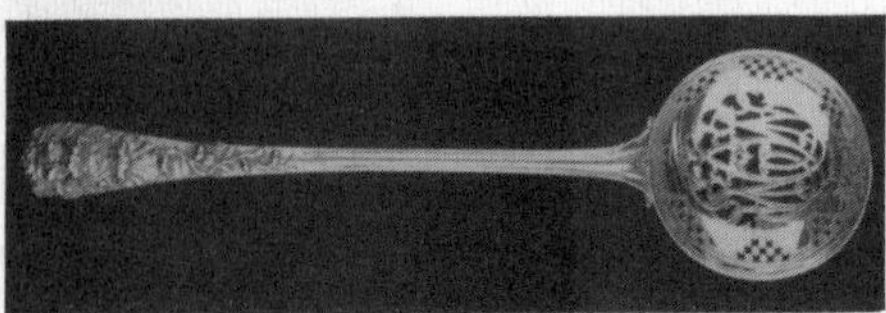

A George II silver straining spoon, unmarked, circa 1740, attributed to Paul de Lamerie, with circular bowl pierced and engraved with a cypher with basket of flowers above within panels of diaperwork, 10½in. long, 4oz. (Christie's) $5,281

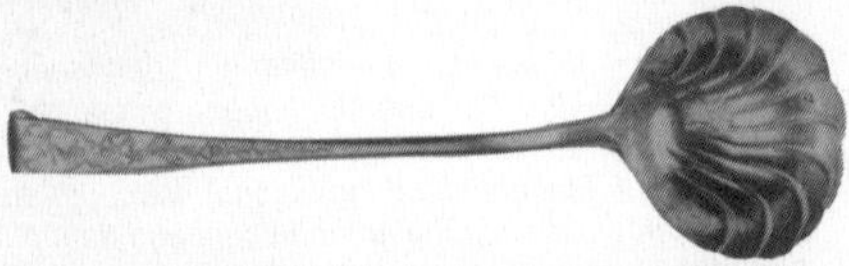

A good, George III Irish hook-end soup ladle with a fluted circular bowl, chased on the back with foliate scrolls, crested, by Christopher S. Kinner, Dublin 1763, 33cm. long, 7oz. (Christie's) $1,728

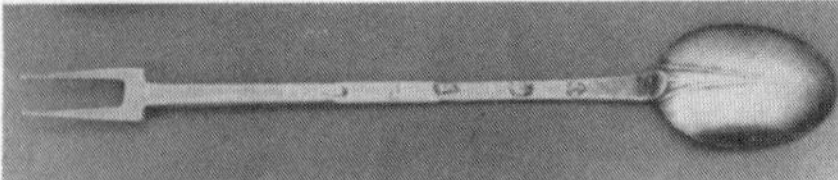

A James II sucket fork, with rat tail bowl, plain apart from engraved initials *T.S.,* maker E H with a star below in a shield, London 1688.
(Woolley & Wallis) $2,923

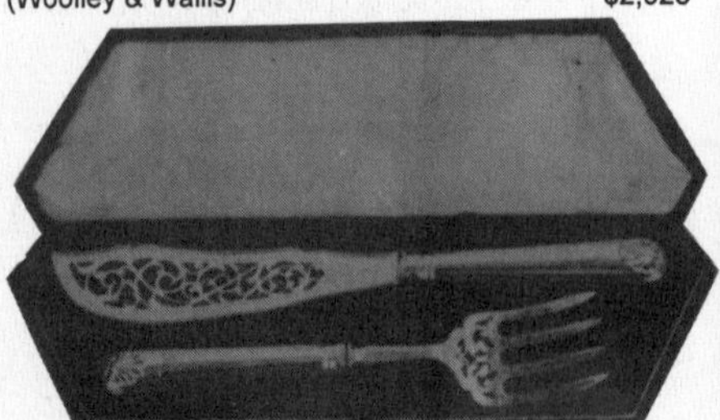

Attractive pair of Victorian silver fish servers with foliate pierced blades, shell and reeded handles, Sheffield 1854, by Martin Hall and Co.
(G A Key) $288

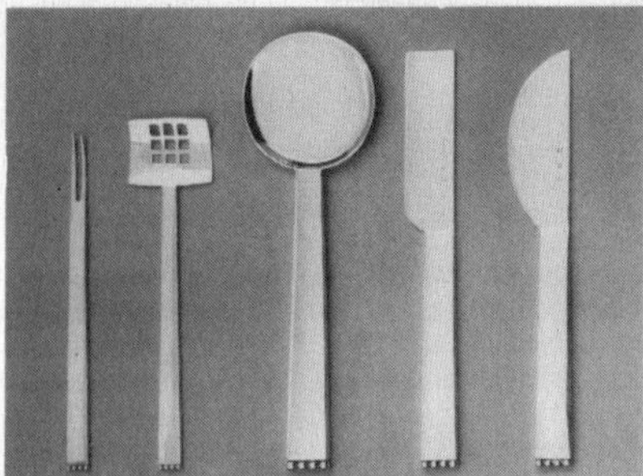

A five piece serving set, designed by Josef Hoffmann, manufactured by the Wiener Werkstätte, 1904, 6¾in. length of serving spoon. (Christie's) $40,572

A rare 17th century Belgian spoon and four-pronged fork with faceted hexagonal stems and flared slip-top terminals and initialled *IH*, the fork by an unascribed maker *IO* or *OI* with a crossbow between, both items probably last quarter 17th century, 3.25oz.
(Christie's) $1,195

A five piece serving set, designed by Josef Hoffmann, manufactured by Sturm, circa 1900, comprising: 1 ladle, 1 sauce spoon, 1 meat fork, 1 serving spoon, 1 salt spoon, 12in. approximate length of ladle.
(Christie's) $13,041

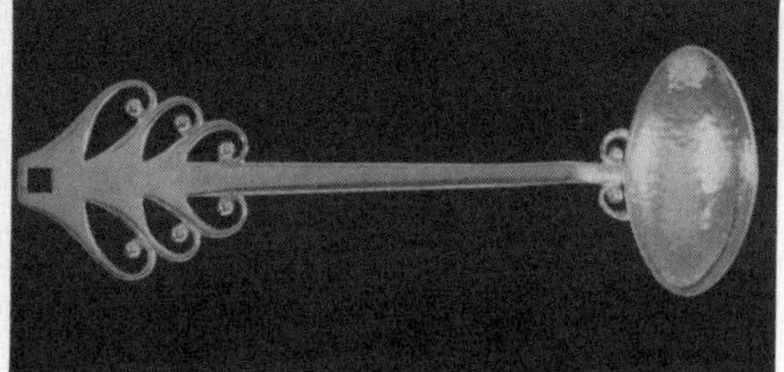

Josef Hoffman for the Wiener Werkstätte, executed by Alfred Mayer, scroll motif spoon, 1905, silver-colored metal, the bowl with martelé finish, 6¼in. long. (Sotheby's) $12,975

Japanese silver spoon, late 19th century, the twig-form handle with twining leaves and flower blossoms, the bowl chased and embossed with chrysanthemums, 7½in. long, 2 troy oz. approximately. (Skinner) $230

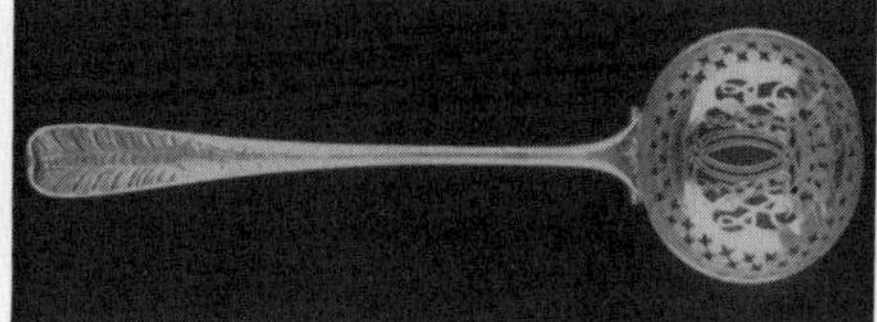

A George II straining spoon, unmarked, circa 1740, Old English pattern with circular bowl pierced and engraved on both sides with the cypher *WHC*, 9¾in. long, 3oz. (Christie's) $3,583

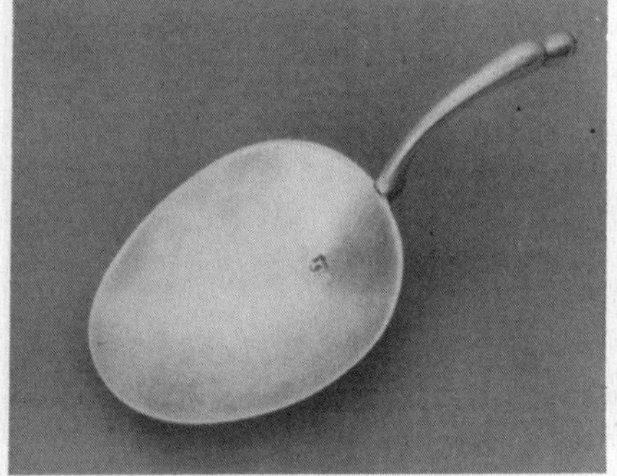

A Charles II hoof end spice spoon, maker's mark only of John King, circa 1665. (Woolley & Wallis) $1,327

A George II Hanoverian pattern basting spoon with a single drop bowl, by Richard Gesling, 1745, 33.25cm. long, 5oz. (Christie's) $589

A good gilt grape scissors, with tapering handles cast with scallops, scrolls, lion masks and fruiting vines, with wavy edged cutters, by Charles Rawlings, 1823, 4½oz. (Tennants) $596

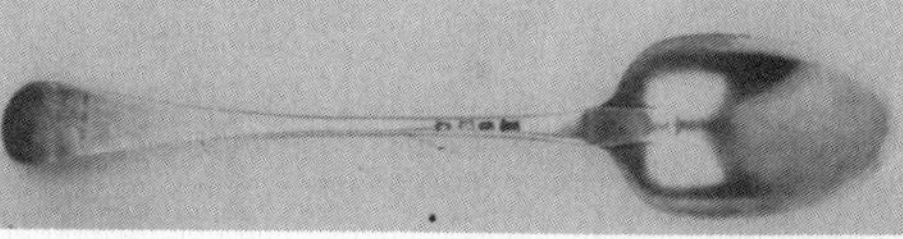

A George II Hanoverian pattern basting spoon, with a single drop bowl, engraved with two crests, (one contemporary), by Robert Perth, 1751, 37cm. long, 7oz. (Christie's) $1,440

A George III Old English thread pattern straining spoon, serving or basting size with a slot-pierced divider, crested and initialled on the back of the stem, by George Smith & William Fearn, 1793, 4oz. (Christie's) $671

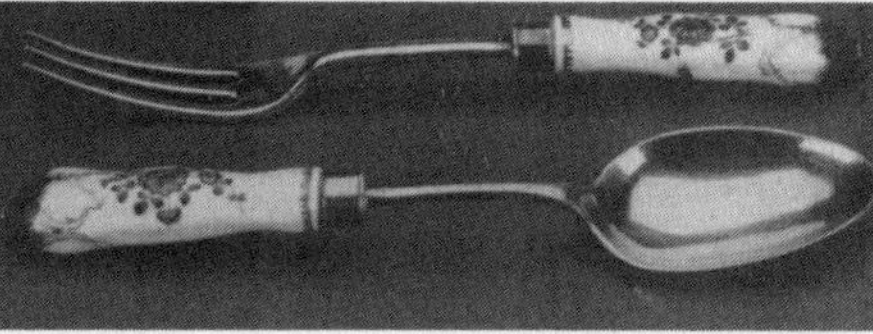

Six Meissen cutlery handles from the Mollendorf service, circa 1761, each of oval section and slightly tapering form, painted in iron-red with bouquets of indianische Blumen enriched with gilding, the handles 3½in. long. (Christie's) $2,362

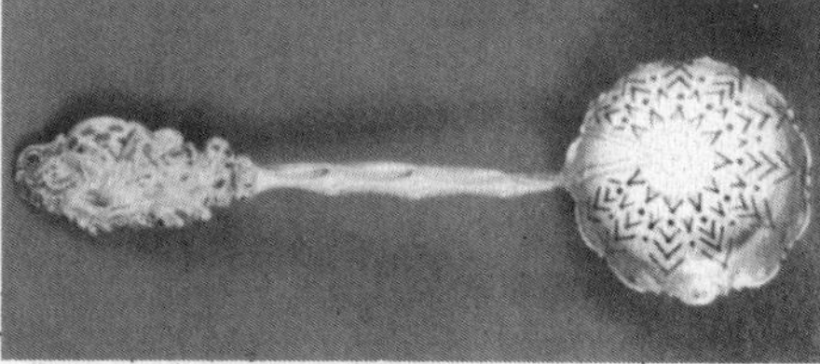

Chicago Columbian Exposition 1893, an American silver sugar sifter, Tiffany & Co., New York, circa 1893, of Indian War Dance pattern, the round bowl with shaped rim, 3oz, 7¾in. long. (Sotheby's) $3,162

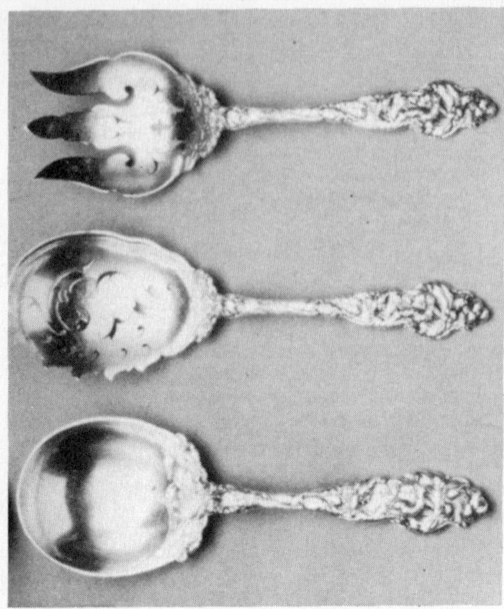

Three Reed & Barton Sterling flatware serving pieces, 1901, Les Six Fleurs pattern, salad servers, macaroni spoon, gold washed bowls, approximately 15 troy oz. (Skinner) $920

A good George III feather-edge pattern soup ladle, and a circular bowl with a shaped and fluted rim, engraved with a cypher, by T. & W. Chawner, 1764, 37cm. long. 6.5oz. (Christie's) $693

A rare silver flatware service, Gorham Mfg. Co., Providence, 1917, martelé, the handles hand-hammered and with flowers and foliage, the front of the handles with monogram *EFS*, 374 pieces, 512oz. 10dwt. weighable silver. (Christie's) $68,500

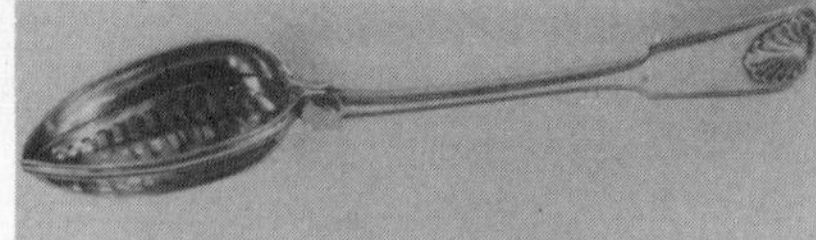

Interesting Indian Colonial silver straining spoon in fiddle, thread and shell pattern by Lattey Bros of Calcutta, circa 1850-55, 11in. long, 7oz. (G.A. Key) $304

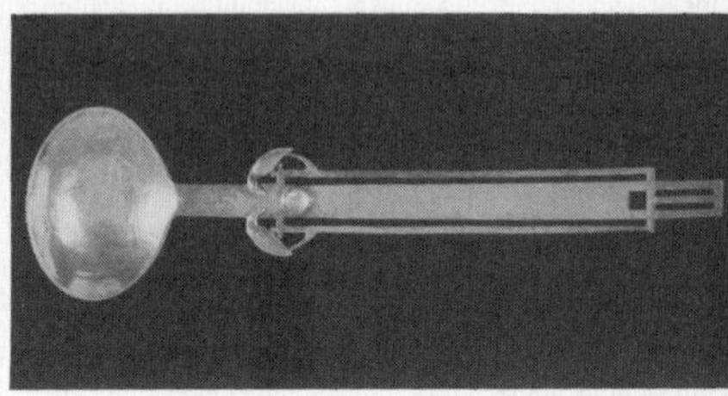

Josef Hoffmann for the Wiener Werkstätte, stylized bird and geometric motif spoon, 1905, silver colored metal, inset with moonstone, martelé finish, 15.4cm. long. (Sotheby's) $12,975

A rare George III large spoon, for marrow bone jelly with a long Old English pattern stem and an elongated oval bowl, by Thomas Northcote, 1793, 30.5cm. long, 2.75oz. (Christie's) $1,003

A table service, of Hanoverian thread, shell and drop (or Lamerie) pattern, comprising twelve settings, by Manoah Rhodes, Sheffield, 1927, in a mahogany cabinet, 108cm. (Tennants) $6,908

A Charles I Moor's head spoon, maker's mark indistinct, possibly Benjamin Yates, London 1633. (Woolley & Wallis) $3,318

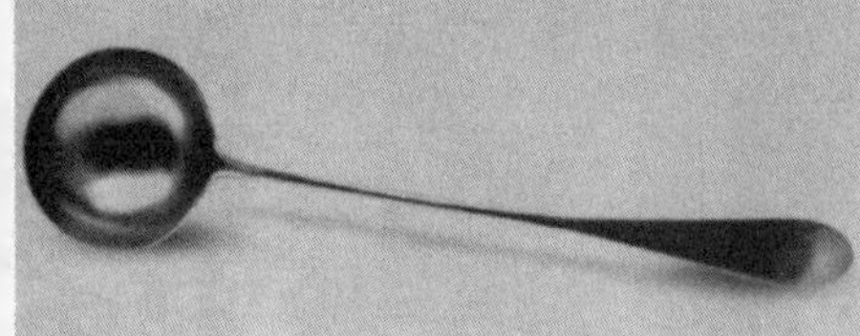

An early 19th century Scottish Provincial soup ladle, the Celtic pattern stem monogramed, Thomas Davie, Greenock, circa 1820, 228gm. (Bearne's) $661

A late 17th century sucket fork, the stem leaf engraved, the bowl engraved a rat tail, maker S H, a pellet between and below, a heart above. (Woolley & Wallis) $1,138

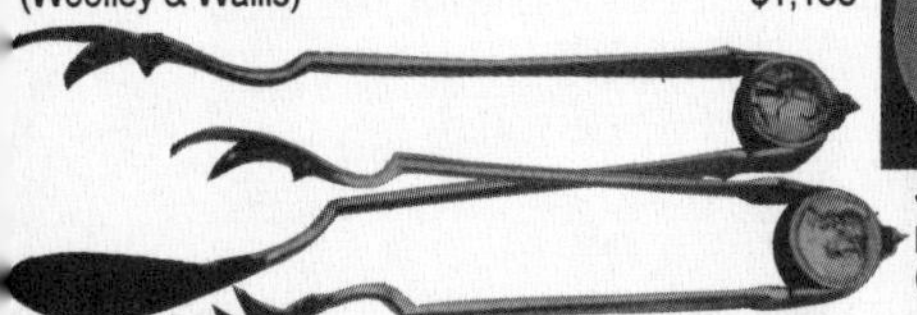

Two pairs of Gorham medallion sterling tongs, 1860s, monogramed, 10¹/8in. long, approx. 11 troy oz. (Skinner) $2,070

Georg Jensen flatware service for twelve, Cactus pattern, sixty-seven pieces total, approximately 89 troy oz. weighable silver. (Skinner) $4,600

Georg Jensen flatware service for eight, Acanthus pattern, post 1945, seventy six pieces in total in storage box, approximately 75 troy oz. weighable silver. (Skinner) $4,140

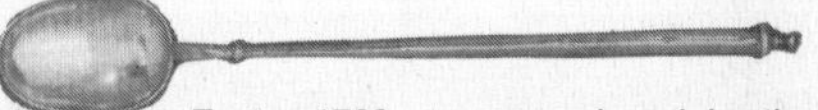

John Avery, Exeter 1703, a cannon barrel basting spoon, pricked *IB 1704*, maker's mark also on handle. (Woolley & Wallis) $5,635

John Parnell of Truro, circa 1620, a lion sejant spoon, pricked to back of bowl *CL 86.* (Woolley & Wallis) $3,864

A trefid spoon, the terminal engraved *I*, Exeter, circa 1683. (Woolley & Wallis) $1,256

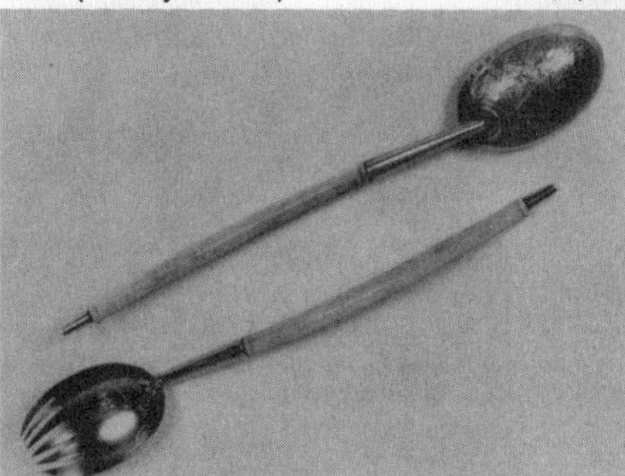

A Victorian pair of silver gilt salad servers, engraved in the manner of Dr Christopher Dresser, with curved octagonal ivory handles, B'ham 1873 by Fredk Elkington, length 32.3cm. (Bristol) $503

An early 18th century German silver-gilt engraved trefid spoon, the plain rat-tail flanked by foliate motifs, the front and back of the stem decorated with fruit and foliage within a thread border, by Johan (II) Schuch, Augsburg 1705, 18.75cm. long, 2oz.
(Christie's) $1,544

Two William & Mary/ William III engraved trefid coffee spoons/teaspoons, one with a partially discernible maker's mark *?H*, the other initialled *E.N* and unmarked, 1690-1700, approximately 10.75cm long each, 0.75oz. (Christie's) $291

A German silver soup ladle, maker's mark probably that of Christian Gottfried Müller, Dresden, 1727, with faceted baluster-shaped handle and plain circular bowl with gilt interior, 40.5cm., 10oz.
(Christie's) $4,388

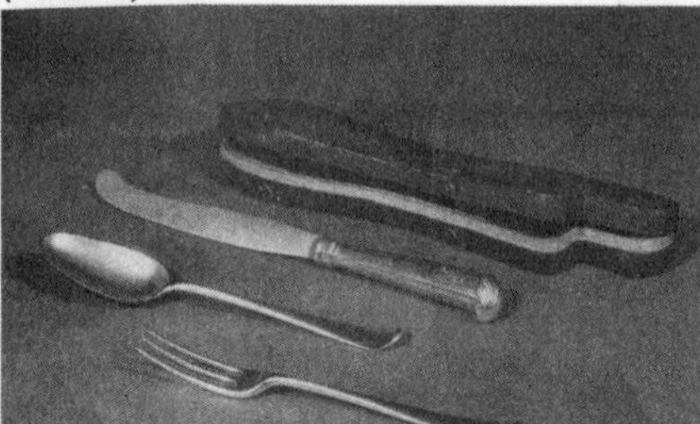

A rare George III gold dessert knife, fork and spoon, Thomas Whipham and Charles Wright, London, 1769, the spoon and fork of Hanoverian pattern, the knife with Onslow pattern handle and silver blade, each engraved with a coat-of-arms within rococo cartouche, all in green velvet lined black shagreen case the spoon and fork 4oz. (Christie's) $29,256

A rare, Edward VI apostle spoon, the figure probably St. James the Greater, gilded and with a pierced, spoked nimbus on a broad tapering stem with a fig-shaped bowl, maker's mark a crescent enclosing a mullet, 1552, 18.1cm. long, 2oz.
(Christie's) $17,262

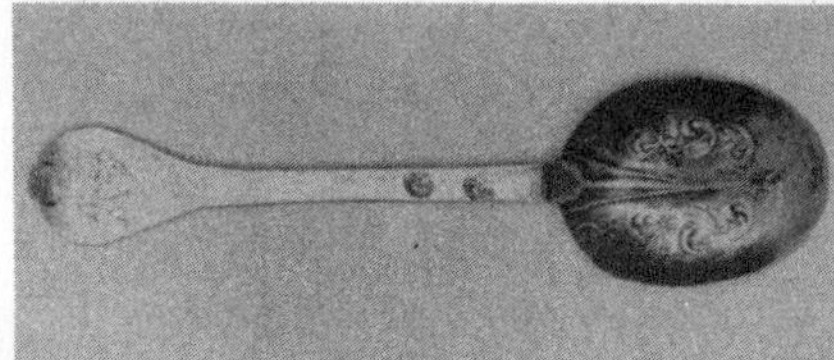

A Charles II ascribed West Country lace-back trefid spoon with a ribbed rat-tail and a rounded cleft terminal pricked *A.W M.W 1683* on the reverse, crowned X mark struck twice on the back of the bowl, no maker's mark, Exeter circa 1680, 19.75cm. long, 1.75oz. (Christie's) $909

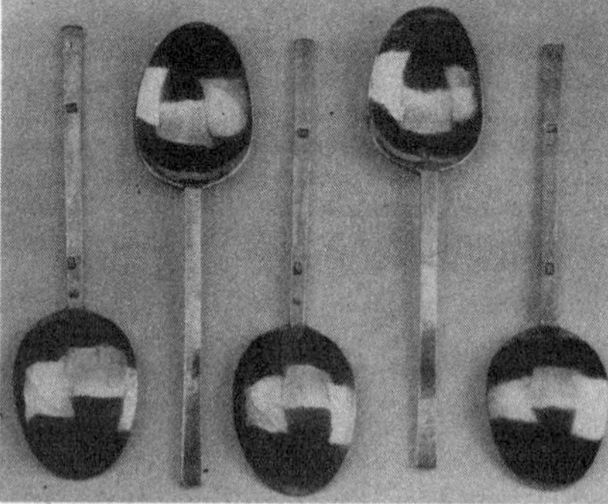

A rare set of five of five Commonwealth Puritan spoons, of good gauge with rudimentary rat-tails, scratched *P* over *W.M.* on the back of the stems, by Stephen Venables, 1651, lengths varying from 17.75cm. to 18cm. long, 8oz.
(Christie's) $10,902

A George I Provincial silver basting spoon, maker's mark of Anthony Tripe, Exeter, 1719, Hanoverian pattern and with rat-tail bowl, the reverse of the handle engraved with a crest, 12¾in. long, 5oz.
(Christie's) $5,302

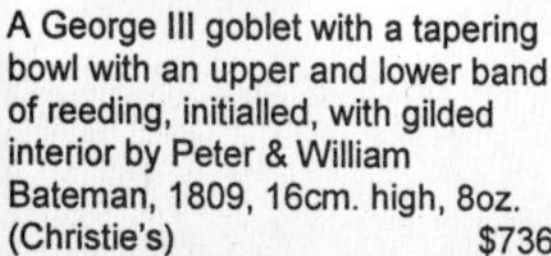

A George III goblet with a tapering bowl with an upper and lower band of reeding, initialled, with gilded interior by Peter & William Bateman, 1809, 16cm. high, 8oz.
(Christie's) $736

Interesting pair of hallmarked silver covered goblets with engraved knopped stems, the slightly domed lid with knopped stems, 5½in. tall, Sheffield 1931 by Walker and Hall.
(G A Key) $319

A rare Commonwealth wine goblet, on a spreading circular foot with a baluster pedestal and a tapering cylindrical bowl, 1651, 15.75cm. high, 8.5oz.
(Christie's) $11,511

A George III goblet and part fluted campana shaped bowl, a gilded interior, by William Elliott, 1818, 18.5cm. high, 21.25oz.
(Christie's) $1,440

A pair of George III goblets, each hemispherical on conical stem, decorated with pricked and bright-cut engraved band of foliage and flowers, by Thomas Wallis and Jonathan Hayne, 1812, 13.5cm. high. 15oz. (Christie's) $2,567

A Regency goblet, the campana shape body with a chased band of grape vines above an engraved wreath cartouche, 6.75in. high, by Joseph William Story, London 1809, 13oz.
(Bristol) $977

A matched pair of modern goblets with squat, knopped pedestals, one chased all over with a design of iris flowers, the other with poppies, by Rod Kelly for Garrard & Co., 1993, 19cm. high.
(Christie's) $2,125

A matched pair of George III silver goblets, maker's mark of Francis Howden, Edinburgh, 1797/1801, engraved with bright-cut bands of Vitruvian scrolls, lambrequins, and circular cartouche, gilt interiors, 6½in. high, 15oz.
(Christie's) $4,416

Pair of Gorham medallion silver goblets, 1860s, heads applied to an engraved floral band, panelled base, $7^{1}/_{16}$in. high, approx. 15 troy oz. (Skinner) $1,265

A Victorian electro-plated inkstand, fitted with a central taperstick, flanked by two cut-glass inkbottles and covers, flashed with pale ruby, by Martin Hall & Co, circa 1865, 32.5cm. long overall.
(Christie's) $349

A Victorian oblong inkstand with a scroll pierced gallery, Messrs E & J Barnard, 1852, 33cm. long, 37oz weighable silver.
(Christie's) $2,392

George III silver ink stand, boat shaped in Adam style with reeded edges and reeded feet, holding an oval cut glass bottle with plated mounts, 10 x 3in., London 1788, maker John Wall.
(G A Key) $451

An early George III inkstand of rounded oblong form, fitted with box section and taperstick, cover with snuffer, by R. Emes and E. Barnard 1809, inkstand by William Plummer, 1760, 26cm., 24.5oz.
(Christie's) $4,784

A commemorative silver inkstand, John Wanamaker, Philadelphia, circa 1885, in Colonial style, the stand shaped oblong with scrolls and shells at intervals, 10½in. long, 28oz. (Christie's) $2,070

A William IV inkstand, the foot and border cast in high relief with various flowerheads, husks and scrolls, by Messrs Barnard, 1835, 31cm. long, 42oz. weighable silver.
(Christie's) $3,496

A Victorian rectangular two-division inkwell with gadroon edging and central presentation inscription, 24cm. long, Charles Stuart Harris, London 1896, 18.1oz.
(Bearne's) $708

A Victorian inkstand, of shaped form with a foliate scroll border and scroll feet, by Henry Wilkinson & Co, Sheffield 1863, 27cm. long, 17.5oz weighable silver.
(Christie's) $2,005

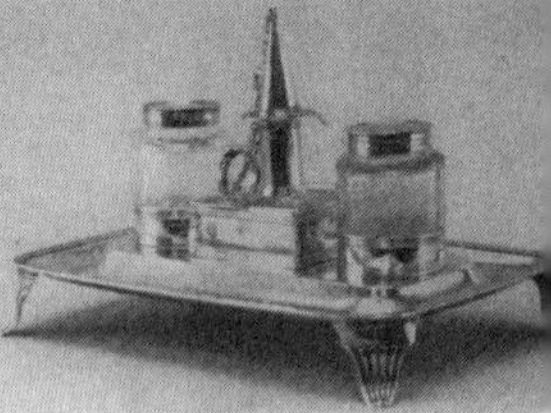

George III silver inkstand, with marks for Henry Chawner and John Eames, London, 1797, rectangular form with reeded rim and four supports, 8½in. long, 17oz.
(Eldred's) $2,750

A George III partners' rectangular inkstand, fitted with three glass bottles, with pierced covers, Andrew Fogelberg. 10in., London 1780, 25oz. (scratch weight 27.5oz.)
(Woolley & Wallis) $1,680

Early 20th century solid silver ink stand, rectangular shaped with rounded corners, gadrooned edges and supported on four curved beaded feet, 9 x 5½in., London 1910 by the Goldsmiths and Silversmiths Co., 21oz.
(G.A. Key) $795

An oblong gallery inkstand with pierced sides and a wavy gadrooned rim, resting on four cast scroll feet, by Charles Thomas & George Fox, 1846/56, 31oz weighable silver.
(Christie's) $3,611

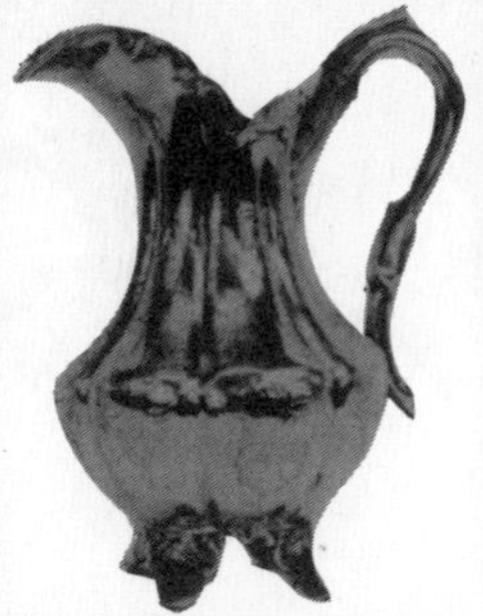

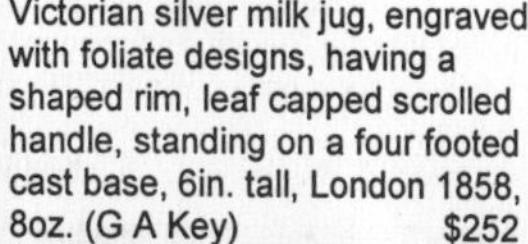

Victorian silver milk jug, engraved with foliate designs, having a shaped rim, leaf capped scrolled handle, standing on a four footed cast base, 6in. tall, London 1858, 8oz. (G A Key) $252

Unusual pair of Victorian wine jugs in the form of nautilus shells, each on three scroll feet, Sheffield, 1897, 11in. high, 32oz.
(Ewbank) $2,618

A wine jug by Georg Jensen, the hammered tapering body with folded rim and shaped spout, 9½in. high, import mark for London 1922, 19oz. 3dwt.
(Andrew Hartley) $3,110

A George III bright-cut hot water jug of vase form with a pedestal circular base, initialled by Henry Chawner, 1792, 31.25cm. high, 26oz.
(Christie's) $2,689

A pair of lidded jugs, designed by Omar Ramsden, 1937, each hinged cover surmounted with a flared finial inset with a precious stone, above an octagonal baluster body, 7¼in. high.
(Christie's) $10,805

A rare George I Provincial hot milk jug, of octagonal pear shape, the high dome cover with orb finial, 5¾in. high, Francis Batty II, Newcastle 1717, 7½oz. all in.
(Woolley & Wallis) $11,376

Victorian silver milk jug in mid 18th century style of pear shape, embossed and chased with scrolls, floral and foliate designs, all supported on three case shell feet, 4½in. tall, London 1851.
(G A Key) $272

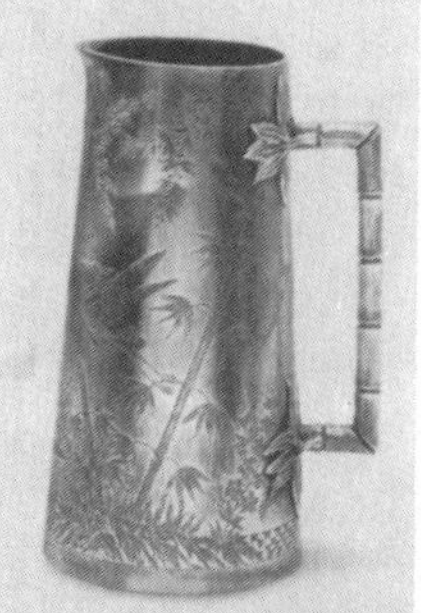

A Victorian water jug, decorated in the Aesthetic taste with engraved cranes amongst bamboo, 20cm. high, Elkington & Co, London 1883, 572gm., 18.3oz.
(Bearne's) $1,809

William IV silver baluster milk jug with limited chased and embossed floral and scrolled decoration, leaf capped scrolled handle, 5in. tall, London 1836, 8oz.
(G A Key) $126

Heavy late Victorian silver mark jug of compressed circular design, quarter straight fluted decoration, gilt interior, 3½in. tall, London 1897, 6oz. (G A Key) $159

A pair of Edwardian lidded jugs of pear shape with foliate finial, gadrooned rim, caned scroll handle, 7in. high, London 1902/3, 18oz. 17dwt. (Andrew Hartley) $454

E, E J & W Barnard, a George IV milk jug, with foliage and rococo spray decoration, London 1830, 9.5oz. (Woolley & Wallis) $345

A Queen Anne silver milk-jug, Anthony Nelme, London, 1710, pear-shaped and on spreading circular foot, with short curved spout, 6½in. high, gross 10oz. (Christie's) $6,399

Good quality late Victorian silver water jug of circular baluster form to a spreading circular foot, the body with half fluted ribbon, tie and festoon decoration, 6in. tall, London 1885, 14oz. (G A Key) $503

An ale jug, George II with later repoussé decoration as a coursing club prize, the baluster body with a coursing scene beneath an extended spout, 8.25in. high, London 1745, 27.75oz. (Woolley & Wallis) $1,309

An Elizabeth I silver-gilt mounted tigerware or Rhenish jug, of baluster form with a c-shaped handle, the hinged cover embossed with mask cartouches, 1573, 22cm. high. (Christie's) $29,221

A George III bright-engraved hot water jug, the sides engraved with a shield shaped cartouche with drapery mantling and later armorials, by Charles Hougham, 1791, 33cm. high, 27oz. (Christie's) $1,858

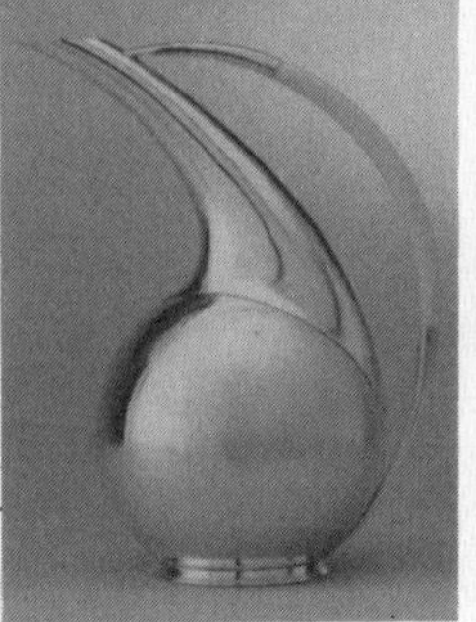

A carafe stamped *Frantz Hingelberg Århus*, designed by Svend Weihrauch, of spherical shape with long curved spout, curved ivory and silver handle, 1940s, 18.5cm. high. (Stockholms AV) $4,656

A George IV nutmeg grater, engine turned with reeded sides, the rectangular hinged cover with a chased foliage thumbpiece, 1.65in. Thomas Shaw, Birmingham 1827.
(Woolley & Wallis) $785

A George IV brandy saucepan, with an ivory knop finial, a squat domed cover, a hinged flap over the spout and a turned wooden handle, by Rebecca Emes & Edward Barnard, 1822, 11.5cm. high, 12oz.
(Christie's) $2,834

Ornate Dutch import hallmarked silver casket, rectangular shaped, heavily embossed with children in orchards and fields etc., having caryatid mounted corners, hinged lid 3¾ x 2½in., London import hallmarked for 1903, 10oz.
(G.A. Key) $540

Elkington & Co., a duck press, the wheel on a screw, the whole encased by simulated oven doors chased an initial *D*, 21in.
(Woolley & Wallis) $1,413

A modern cased child's dish and spoon, engraved with scenes from 'Peter Pan', by R.E. Stone, 1939/40, the dish with facsimile signature, 16.75cm. diameter, 8oz.
(Christie's) $773

An Edwardian mounted cut-glass cuboid inkwell, the hinged cover set with an eight day, dual faced plated timepiece, J. Gloster & Sons, Birmingham, 1909, 10cm. square.
(Christie's) $2,024

A George III cream pail with wirework sides and a twisted swing handle, centered by a rose motif, probably by Thomas Rowe, 1769, 11.5cm. high overall, 3oz.
(Christie's) $1,536

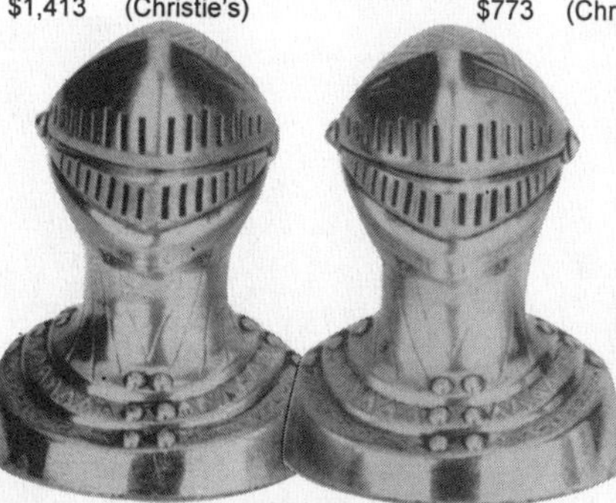

A pair of Victorian novelty pepperettes, modelled as knight's helmets with slot-pierced and hinged visors, round bases and engraved decoration by George Unite, Birmingham 1876, 6.5cm. high, 4oz. (Christie's) $1,328

Coin silver cann, William Swan, Boston, 1757–74, bulbous form with molded rim and applied molded circular foot, 5⅛in. high.
(Skinner) $1,840

A late 18th century Dutch brazier with a circular waisted bowl, pierced sides and rim, probably by Johannes Jansen, Rotterdam 1793, 15cm. diameter, 8.75oz.
(Christie's) $1,152

A jeweled silver and enamel desk seal, apparently unmarked, late 19th century, decorated with spiralling translucent blue and opaque white enamel bands, 3in. high.
(Sotheby's) $3,457

A Victorian letter rack, with five divisions, each separated by a gothic letter spelling *Mother*, on flattened bun feet, 6¼in.
(Woolley & Wallis) $269

BUYER BEWARE

Some tips to note when buying silver:

Tongue scrapers in use before the age of toothbrushes, may have been adapted from sugar tongs!

Many toastracks may have been made from teaspoon handles. If so, each division will bear a hallmark, sometimes these may even be quite different!

(Clarke Gammon)

A late 19th century Austro-Hungarian toothpick holder in the form of a sailor standing next to a barrel and an anchor, circa 1880, 13cm. high, 2.25oz.
(Christie's) $499

IVth Olympiad, London, 1908, umpire's badge, in embossed silver bronze and blue enamel, designed by B. McKennal, together with an Olympic Games 1908 Programme.
(Sotheby's) $2,153

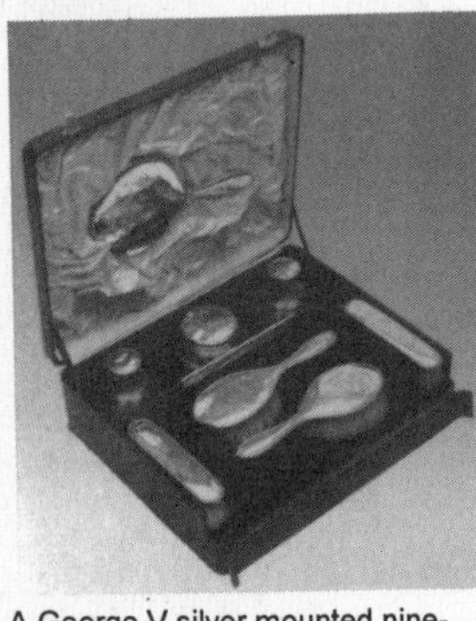

A George V silver mounted nine-piece dressing table set, monogramed and with engraved foliate decoration, Mappin & Webb, Birmingham 1917.
(Bearne's) $412

Unusual Edwardian silver case, the hinged lid opening to reveal two sprung compartments for sovereigns, one for half sovereigns and one for stamps, 2½ x 2in., Birmingham 1903.
(G.A. Key) $922

A silver hipflask, Birmingham 1919 Mappin & Webb, oval form, engine turned decoration, bayonet fitting cover, 15.3cm. long.
(Bonhams) $240

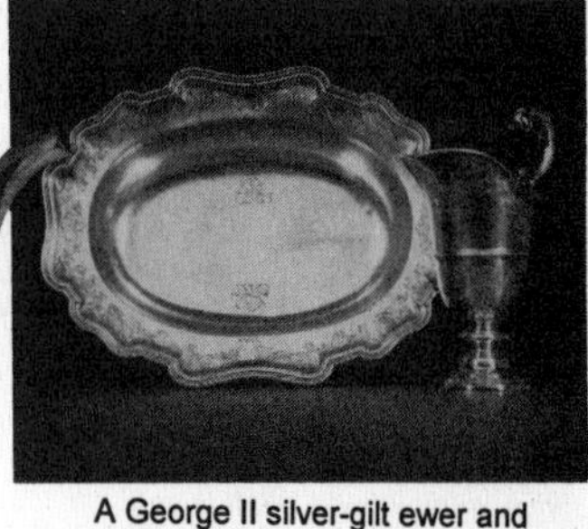

An egg cup and small spoon designed by Josef Hoffmann, manufactured by the Wiener Werkstätte, 1903-4, the egg cup on four cylindrical supports with bead brackets, 2in. height of egg cup.
(Christie's) $9,274

A Victorian silver argyle by John Tapley, London 1838, the detachable cover opening to reveal a central warmer compartment, 15cm., 15.5oz.
(Cheffins) $1,304

A George II silver-gilt ewer and basin, the basin with maker's mark of John White, London, 1734, helmet-shaped ewer with a border engraved with shells, scrolls and geometric pattern, the ewer 9½in. high, 70oz.
(Christie's) $38,398

A modern novelty watch stand on a circular base, formed by two propped-up tennis rackets and a ball, by Gilbert & Co, Birmingham 1912, 8cm. high.
(Christie's) $863

A silver gilt bezoar stone case in two sections, with bands of pierced scroll work and lined, with stone, probably Anglo-Indian or English, late 17th/18th century, 7.5cm. diameter, 8cm. long.
(Woolley & Wallis) $9,164

A gentleman's silver lodestone, French, possibly late 17th century, the mounts with engraved scallop decoration, 5cm. high.
(Bonhams) $1,648

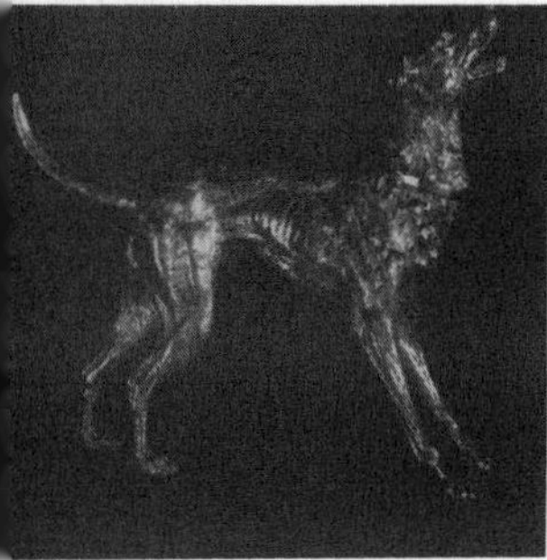

A late 19th/early 20th century cast model of a hound or hunting dog, standing with tail raised and head erect, import marks for Bertholt Muller, 1902, 33cm. long. 41oz.
(Christie's) $9,026

An early Victorian card case, scrolling foliage chased, with St Paul's Cathedral in relief, Nathaniel Mills, 4in., Birmingham 1845.
(Woolley & Wallis) $1,216

A Continental plated metal and painted figure of a racehorse with jockey up, 17¼in. high, indistinctly signed *W. Lwick*(?).
(Canterbury) $393

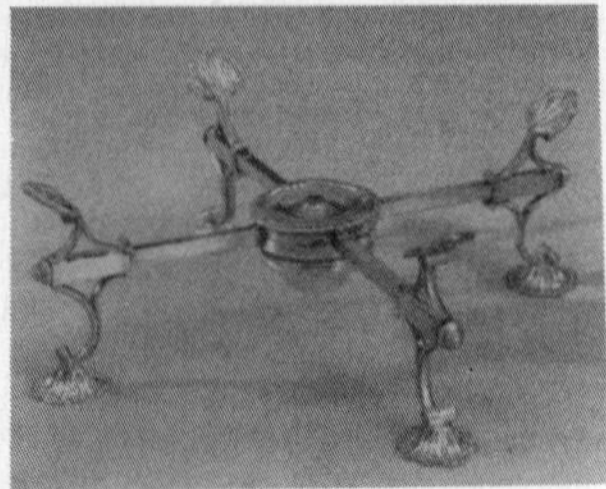

A George III Sheffield plate dish cross, with gadroon borders and shell rests to scroll adjustable legs.
(Woolley & Wallis) $676

A rare George III cream pail, the openwork sides forming a pastoral scene in high relief, by Charles Clark, 1775, 13cm. high, 2.25oz.
(Christie's) $2,113

English cigarette box and matchsafe, both London, 1865, maker's mark *WW FD*, the rectangular box with ribbed edge and central roundel, 3 x 2¹/5in., approximately 6 troy oz.
(Skinner) $173

A rattle, silver, formed as a baby holding a rattle, the body engraved with initials, import marks for London 1881, sponsor's mark Sampson Mordan, 7.3cm.
(Christie's) $772

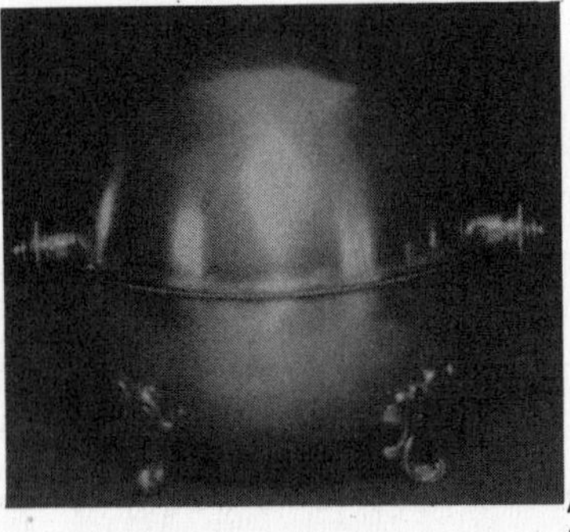

A caviar dish, marked *M. Ovchinnikov* with Imperial warrant, Moscow, 1896-1908, the base with gadrooned rim, 6¾in. wide, 730gm.
(Christie's) $1,536

A Scottish silver mounted mother of pearl and tortoiseshell banded capstan snuff mull, unmarked, circa 1750, with scallop-edge shaped border, the hinged cover with silver oval initial disc, ivory interior, 2½in. high.
(Christie's) $3,323

A pair of French silver plate warmers, last quarter 18th century, of circular form, with turned wooden handle and on wooden ball feet, 10.5cm. high, 1030gr. total weight.
(Finarte) $3,536

A swivel toilet mirror, with foliate borders, the stand with central oblong toilet box and cover with pair of circular boxes mounted between the pillars, probably French, 71.5cm. long.
(Christie's) $1,063

An early 20th century Continental parcel gilt nef on a domed oval base with a cast dolphin and putto finial, three masts fully rigged, with English import marks for 1928, 38cm. high, 29oz.
(Christie's) $2,834

Rare Chinese export silver mug, circa 1800, marked with the cipher of the East India Company, 5³/8in. (Eldred's) $935

A George II small mug of bellied form with a tucked-in circular base and an s-scroll handle, probably by Richard Brayley, 1732, 9cm. high, 8.25oz. (Christie's) $1,444

Andrew Worth of Plymouth Dock & Modbury, Exeter 1718, a small mug, the tapering body engraved with a crest. (Woolley & Wallis) $2,334

A William III mug of tapering form with a skirted base and a flat-section, reeded scroll handles, by Tomothy Ley, circa 1697, 9cm. high, 5.5oz. (Christie's) $1,986

William Parry of Plymouth, Exeter 1746, a baluster pint mug, with a double scroll handle, 12oz. (Woolley & Wallis) $1,449

A silver mug by Hayne & Cater, London, 1852/3, the sides applied with figures in a wooded landscape, the circular foot with foliate ornament, 12cm. high, 230gm. (Finarte) $578

A late 18th century mug with a tucked-in circular pedestal base, tapering bowl, Jersey, circa 1776, 8.75cm. high, 4.5oz. (Christie's) $1,632

A George III mug, by William Grundy, 1764, 10.5cm. high, 8oz. (Christie's) $999

S. Kirk & Sons repoussé silver mug, 1846–61, baluster form, chased overall floral design, 4in. high, approximately 8 troy oz. (Skinner) $517

Fine extra large George IV silver mustard and liner of compressed circular form, embossed with bands of flowers, leaves etc, the domed lid with cast floral finial, London 1823 by Craddock and Reid, 8oz. free.
(G.A. Key) $763

Scarce 18th century early George III Provincial silver drum mustard of plain form with raised edges, reeded lid in traditional Newcastle tankard style, Newcastle 1779.
(G.A. Key) $970

Large Georgian silver drum mustard of plain design with beaded lid, angular handles, plus blue glass liner and spoon, 3in. tal London 1807 by John Emes.
(G A Key) $35

A Victorian drum mustard pot with a gadrooned border, the body and cover engraved with birds, flowers and scrolls, blue glass liner, probably by William Martin, 1859, 8.5cm. high. (Christie's) $352

A Victorian silver novelty owl mustard pot by Charles Thompson and George Fox, the body with textured plumage, mustard spoon with a cast field mouse finial. London 1865, 4in. high.
(David Lay) $3,662

A Victorian mustard pot by Charles and George Fox, London 1859, modelled as a bandsman's drum, the handle formed as a strap, plain glass liner, 8.25cm., 6oz.
(Cheffins) $1,64

Large Victorian silver drum mustard with beaded foot and rim, scrolled handle, limited banded engraved decoration, pierced thumbpiece plus blue glass liner and spoon, 2½in. tall, London 1869.
(G A Key) $412

A silver mustard pot and spoon, of cylindrical form with gadrooned ring, the flat hinged cover with a stylised shell thumb rest, William Eley II and William Fearn, London 1824, 155gm., 5cm. high.
(Lempertz) $837

Attractive large Victorian silver drum mustard with foliate pierced sides, scrolled handle, shell thumbpiece, plus blue glass liner and spoon, 2¼in. tall, London 185 by Hyam Hyams.
(G A Key) $254

A late Victorian oblong photograph frame with a pierced surmount and two mask spandrels, by H. Matthews, Birmingham 1900, 26cm. high. (Christie's) $576

An Edwardian Art Nouveau mounted oak photograph frame, embossed with a border of flowerheads, surmounted by a shaped cartouche, Birmingham 1904, 32cm. high. (Christie's) $699

A late Victorian heart shaped mirror frame, embossed and pierced around the border with putti and harpies amidst foliate scrolls, by William Comyns, 1890, 43cm. high. (Christie's) $1,108

An Edwardian Art Nouveau photograph frame, embossed symmetrically with a rising sun flanked by a pair of peacocks, maker's mark *J.A.& S., Birmingham 1904,* 23cm. high. (Christie's) $699

An Edwardian Art Nouveau mounted oak photograph frame, embossed with trailing honeysuckle flowers, by F.H. Adams, Birmingham 1910, 21cm. high. (Christie's) $699

A late Victorian Art Nouveau photograph frame of shaped oblong form, embossed with stylized scroll and flowers, by W. Nicholson, Chester 1900, 19cm high. (Christie's) $1,011

An American metalware photograph frame with a floral scroll-engraved border, by Tiffany & Co., circa 1925, wooden easel back, 29.5cm. high. (Christie's) $699

An Edwardian Art Nouveau photograph frame, embossed in relief with lilies on a pond and flowering waterplants, by William Davenport, Birmingham, 1905, 21cm. high.(Christie's) $827

An Edwardian Art Nouveau photograph frame, embossed in low relief with wading birds in a swamp and lily pads and flowers, by W. Atkin, Birmingham, 1906, 32cm. high. (Christie's) $920

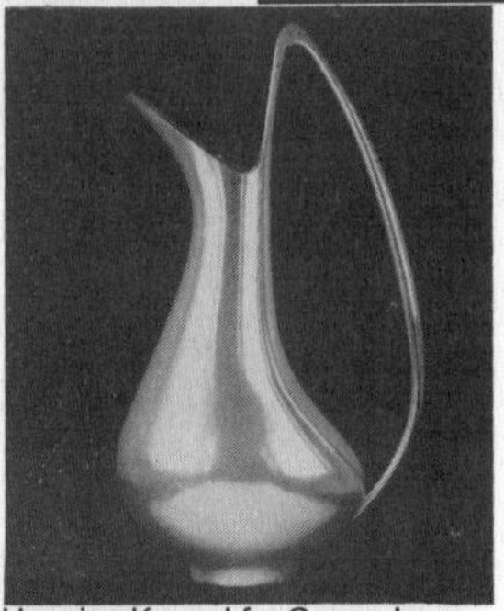

Henning Koppel for Georg Jensen, pitcher, designed 1952, silver colored metal, hand raised and sculpted with bulbous lower part tapering into circular foot, 41.5cm.
(Sotheby's) $32,437

Sterling silver water pitcher by Frank Whiting, lobed body, monogramed and dated 1904, 7½in. high, 20.8 troy oz.
(Eldred's) $330

A silver-mounted cut-glass pitcher, Whiting Mfg. Co., circa 1885, the silver-mounted foot rim applied with flowerheads at intervals, the cut-glass faceted body part-fluted, 8½in. high.
(Christie's) $4,600

George René Lecomte, retailed by G. Carré et Cie., pitcher, circa 1925, hammered silver colored metal, 9½in. high.
(Sotheby's) $1,622

A matched pair of pitchers, of recent manufacture, with helmet shaped rims, curved handles and slightly bellied lower bodies, Keith W. Redfern, retailed by Asprey & Co., 1997, 28cm. high, 55oz.
(Christie's) $1,948

A modern water jug or pitcher of recent manufacture, with a part swirl-fluted body and a flattened ring handle, by Garrard & Co., 1993, 22.5cm. high, 32.5oz.
(Christie's) $1,063

PLATES

A set of twelve George III silver dinner plates, John Wakelin and William Taylor, London, 1788, shaped circular, with gadrooned rim, 25cm. diameter, 178oz.
(Christie's) $7,314

A set of fifteen silver dinner plates, Gorham Mfg. Co., Providence, 1917, martelé, each circular, the wavy rims repoussé and chased with flowers and foliage, 11in. diameter, 321oz.
(Christie's) $36,800

A set of twelve George III silver dinner-plates, William Stroud, London, 1804, circular with gadrooned borders, each engraved with a coat-of-arms, 25cm. diameter, 223oz.
(Christie's) $16,056

A Queen Anne porringer, slightly flared, with two scroll handles, the body engraved *E S*, the base *E K*, maker William Gamble, London 1703, 4½oz.
(Woolley & Wallis) $3,002

A William and Mary silver porringer, John Jackson, London 1690, the lower part of the body chased with spiral flutes, 5¼in. high, 18oz.
(Christie's) $8,405

A Queen Anne porringer with an embossed ropework girdle and swirl-fluting around the body, by John Martin Stocker, 1703, (gilded interior), 10.25cm. diameter, 5.5oz.
(Christie's) $2,113

A Charles II silver porringer and cover, Marmaduke Best, London, second half of the 17th century, the lower part of the body chased and repoussé with flowerheads and foliage, 6½in. high, 21oz.
(Christie's) $13,713

A William III small porringer, with a part fluted lower body, ropework girdle and twisted wirework s-shaped handles, by John Cory, 1700, 7.25cm. high. 3oz.
(Christie's) $2,005

A Victorian large porringer and cover, London, 1878, embossed in Restoration style with a stagshead and a lion pursued by a hunting dog, the handles in caryatid form, 12cm. diameter, 19oz.
(Dreweatt Neate) $954

A Charles II porringer, the cylindrical body engraved chinoiserie decoration of birds and trees, 3¾in. high, maker's mark *A R* with pellets, London 1681, 8oz.
(Woolley & Wallis) $2,765

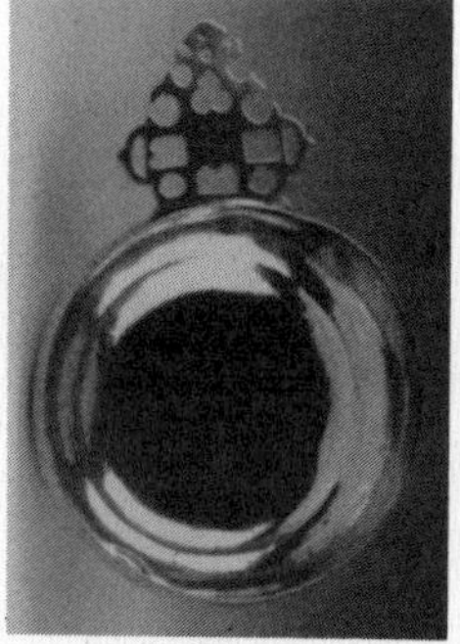

A late Victorian Britannia Standard silver porringer, London 1894, Joshua Vander, of circular form, pierced handle, initialled, approximate weight 7oz., diameter 13.5cm. (Bonhams) $396

A Charles II silver porringer and cover, porringer with maker's mark of *WM*, London, 1664, the cover with maker's mark *RD*, London, circa 1668, the body chased with flower heads and foliage, 7in. high, 26oz. (Christie's) $6,399

A pair of Victorian electroplated cast salts, modelled as eagles with spread wings, supporting gilt shell bowls on their backs, complete with two matching spoons, by Elkington & Co, the salts, 9cm. high.
(Christie's) $722

A pair of Regency salts, rectangular with panelled borders, gilded inside, with reeded leaf spray borders, John Watson & Son, Sheffield 1814, 7oz.
(Woolley & Wallis) $282

A pair of Scottish thistle shaped salts, on three leaf feet with gilded interiors and two matching spoons, by McKay & Chisholm, Edinburgh 1890/1, the salts 5.5cm. high, 3oz.
(Christie's) $816

A set of four William IV circular salts, ogee everted melon panelled bodies, Charles Gordon, London 1835, 10oz.
(Woolley & Wallis) $822

A pair of William IV cast nautilus shell salts with shaped oval bases of husks and flowers and textured sides (gilded interiors) by J. & J. Angell, 1834, 9.25cm. long, 9.5oz.
(Christie's) $3,365

A set of four George III silver salt-cellars, Paul Storr, London, 1804, each circular and on three lion's mask and paw feet, the bodies cast and chased with flowers, 4½in. diameter, 36oz.
(Christie's) $7,314

A pair of George III salts, of squat circular form on waisted circular pedestals, chased with a border of husks and scrolls against a matt ground, by Henry Green, 1786, 8.75cm. diameter, 18oz.
(Christie's) $911

A French late 19th/early 20th century cast silver-gilt salt cellar, supported by two winged beasts on a mask and scroll foot, 14cm. high.
(Christie's) $1,063

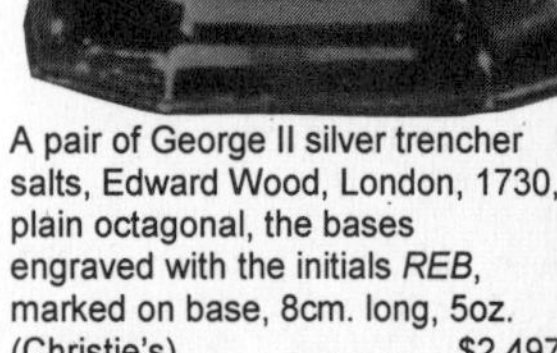

A pair of George II silver trencher salts, Edward Wood, London, 1730, plain octagonal, the bases engraved with the initials *REB*, marked on base, 8cm. long, 5oz.
(Christie's) $2,497

Humphrey Payne, a good George II pap boat, engraved with a goat crest, London 1749.
(Woolley & Wallis) $632

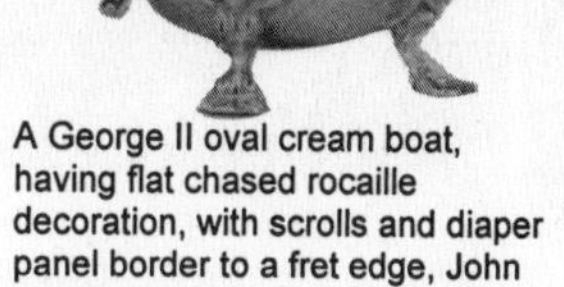

A George II oval cream boat, having flat chased rocaille decoration, with scrolls and diaper panel border to a fret edge, John Montgomery, London 1737, 7oz.
(Woolley & Wallis) $2,449

Well marked George III Scottish silver pap boat of usual plain form, 4in. long, Edinburgh 1809 by Cunningham and Simpson.
(G A Key) $309

Attractive George II silver sauce boat with card cut rim, flying scrolled handle and supported on three hoof feet, later chased and embossed with floral and foliate designs, gilt interior, London 1746.
(G A Key) $326

Good quality early George III silver sauce boat, with heavy gadrooned rim, leaf capped scrolled handle and supported on three shell and hoof feet, 7in. long overall, London 1764, 8½oz.
(G A Key) $644

A George IV oval sauceboat, with shaped rim and leaf-capped flying scroll handle, 17cm. long, John, Henry and Charles Lias, London, 1828, 8.6oz.
(Bearne's) $572

A pair of George II silver sauce boats, Christian Hillan, London 1739, cast and chased with flowers, foliage and scrolls, 6¾in. long, 33oz. (Christie's) $4,526

A fine pair of Edwardian decorative sauceboats, in the form of sleighs with curved runners, a demi-putto figurehead and lamp finial, by William Comyns, 1903, 19.5cm. long, 27oz.
(Christie's) $2,377

A pair of George III sauceboats with oval bodies, resting on three feet with 'pinch-beaded' rims, William Cattell, 1774, 14.5cm. long, 8oz.
(Christie's) $1,247

An early George III sauceboat of bellied oval form with shell feet, a gadrooned border and a leaf-capped scroll handle, 1763, 20.5cm. long, 15oz.
(Christie's) $1,986

A pair of William IV sauce boats with leafage cast reeded borders, splay feet embossed with anthemion, 9in. , London 1836, by Benjamin Smith, 23oz.
(Russell Baldwin & Bright) $1,053

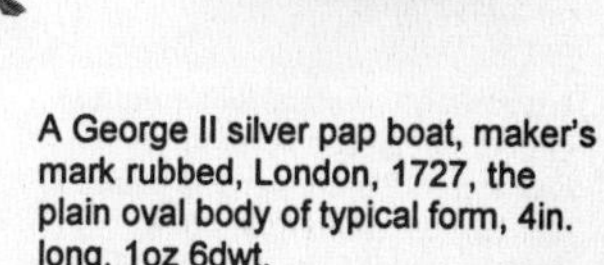

A George II silver pap boat, maker's mark rubbed, London, 1727, the plain oval body of typical form, 4in. long, 1oz 6dwt.
(Sotheby's) $192

A George IV table snuff box, in casket style with a repoussé foliage border to the engine turned hinged lid, 3½in. Maker Thomas Shaw, Birmingham 1829, 4.5oz.
(Woolley & Wallis) $496

An early Victorian 'castle top' snuff box, of flat oblong form, probably depicting a view of Kenilworth Castle, with an engine turned base, by Nathaniel Mills, Birmingham 1837, approximately 7.25cm. long, 2oz. (Christie's) $744

A George IV rectangular snuff box, the hinged cover with a panoramic view of Abbotsford, 3in. Thomas Shaw, Birmingham 1822.
(Woolley & Wallis) $368

A Victorian rectangular snuff box with engine-turned and acorn leaf decoration, 10cm. long, Edward Edwards, London, 1840, 7.5oz.
(Bearne's) $880

A Regency oblong snuff box, in the form of a purse, foliage bright cut decoration, with thumbpieces, 2.25in., probably Thomas Edwards, London 1816.
(Woolley & Wallis) $392

Attractive Victorian silver snuff box of shaped rectangular design and having an unusual opening action, the base and top naturalistically engraved with owls and other birds, 2 x 1¼in., London 1889.
(G A Key) $419

A papier mâché lacquer snuff box by the Lukutin Factory, Moscow, 1841-1863, the cover painted with an oval scene of five men in a rowing boat, 9.2cm. long.
(Christie's) $4,225

A tortoiseshell rectangular snuff box, with silver mounts and hinges, the lid applied with a silver hound, 3¼in. (Woolley & Wallis) $442

A 19th century Japanese carved tortoiseshell curved snuff box, panels with figures, trees and buildings, 3.15in.
(Russell Baldwin & Bright) $517

STIRRUP CUPS

A good and unusual silver double-ended stirrup cup relating to Richard Daft's cricket and baseball tour to North America, 1879, William Henry Dee, London, 1879.
(Sotheby's) $5,382

A boar mask stirrup cup, with textured hair and snarling mouth, by Messrs Slater, Slater & Holland, 1896, 14cm. long.
(Christie's) $6,499

A Scottish cast hare-mask stirrup cup, with textured fur and erect ears, unascribed, Edinburgh 1899, 16.5cm. ear tip to nose.
(Christie's) $7,222

An American silver tankard, Joseph Anthony, Jr., Philadelphia, circa 1785, double-scroll handle with heart-shaped endpiece, 43oz., 9in. high. (Sotheby's) $27,600

A Scandinavian silver tankard, maker's mark *LB* in a shield, circa 1700, probably Norway, the hinged domed cover inset with a coin, 18.5cm. high, 23oz. (Christie's) $2,194

Russian silver-gilt and enamel tankard, Moscow, late 19th century, tapered cylindrical body, serpentine handle lid with thumbpiece and ball finial, 5¾in. high, 15 troy oz. (Skinner) $1,955

A Continental parcel-gilt tankard, probably German, 19th century, the gilt cover cast and chased with three bands of classical figures, 1830, 9¼in. high. 82oz. (Christie's) $4,754

A German parcel-gilt tankard, Hamburg, circa 1680, maker's mark a fleur-de-lys, the body embossed with an allegory of Autumn, 1in. high, 65oz. (Christie's) $14,628

A George III silver tankard, Andrew Fogelberg and Stephen Gilbert, London, 1784, tapering and with two reeded bands, with plain handle and hinged flat cover, 7¼in. high, 28oz. (Christie's) $2,925

Attractive George II Newcastle silver tankard of tapering cylindrical design with hollow scrolled handle, spreading foot, later engraved with foliate designs and cartouche, 4in. tall, circa 1750/60 by John Langlands, 9ozs. (G A Key) $602

A Commonwealth tankard, engraved with the arms of Chapman of Thringston, 5½in. high, maker H W, mullet below, London 1651, 14oz. (Woolley & Wallis) $7,900

Omar Ramsden hallmarked silver tankard of slightly tapering cylindrical design to a spreading circular foot, having applied foliate chased body bands, 5in. tall, inscribed to base, 1936, 5in. tall, 16½oz. (G A Key) $994

An Edward VII three-piece tea service of semi-reeded circular form, the everted rims with tongue and bead, shell and acanthus edging, Walker & Hall, Sheffield 1908, 40oz. (Bearne's) $610

A George VI four-piece tea and coffee service of plair circular form, crested above motto, on spreading bases, Sheffield 1948/9, 55.3oz., and a pair of George III sugar tongs. (Bearne's) $561

A Victorian Scottish four piece tea set in the Neo-classical Revival manner, the teapot of tapering circular form, 11in. wide, and a coffee pot with mask headed spout and flared base, 11in. high, Edinburgh 1878, 96oz. 18dwt. (Andrew Hartley) $3,429

A George III four-piece tea and coffee service, o oblong form monogramed within fern sprays with gadroon edging, on ball feet, John Robertson anc John Watson, Newcastle 1811, 64.6oz (Bearne's) $4,125

An Edwardian E.P.N.S. tea service by Elkington & Co, elaborately embossed and engraved with floral scro cartouches, with heraldic beast finials, comprising tea kettle on stand, teapot, hotwater jug, cream jug and suga basin. (Russell Baldwin & Bright) $1,28

A late Georgian three piece service by Chas. Marsh, Dublin 1809. (G. E. Sworder) $1,472

Gorham three-piece coffee set, late 19th century, pot of waisted ovoid baluster form, on spreading foot with beaded border and bands of foliate repoussé, all pieces monogramed, pot 9¾in. high, approximately 28 troy oz. total. (Skinner) $1,035

Georg Jensen six-piece tea and coffee service, Denmark, post 1945, Blossom pattern, comprising kettle on stand, coffeepot, teapot, covered sugar, covered creamer and large tray, kettle 10½in. high, 228 troy oz. approximately, total weight. (Skinner) $25,300

A good three piece silver tea set, well chased with cartouches of scrolls and flowers upon matting and scales, the milk jug and sugar basin with gilt capes and interior, by John Figg or John Fraser, 1836, 49oz. (Tennants) $1,962

A three piece Irish silver teaset, engraved by Edward Power, 1824/1825. (G.E. Sworder) $1,320

A three piece teaset by the Cooper Bros. & Sons, Sheffield 1917, comprising a teapot of circular shape, the lower body panelled over a circular pedestal base, 18cm. high, with matching milk jug and sugar bowl, 36oz. (Cheffins) $565

A George III bright-cut tea caddy of panelled oval form with shaped ends, Henry Chawner, 1792, 15cm. high, 11oz.
(Christie's) $3,265

A pair of early 18th century Dutch tea caddies, embossed with a central band of fluting, above stiff leaves and below banded swirls, Pieter de Both, Haarlem, 1729, 13.5cm. high. 6.5oz.
(Christie's) $2,826

A George III tea caddy of plain oblong form with slab sides and a flat base, probably by William Purse, 1789, 12.5cm. long, 12.5oz.
(Christie's) $2,113

A George III tea caddy, of straight sided oval section with bright-cut decoration and detachable cover, Thomas Hayter, London, 1808, 4.3oz. (Bearne's) $826

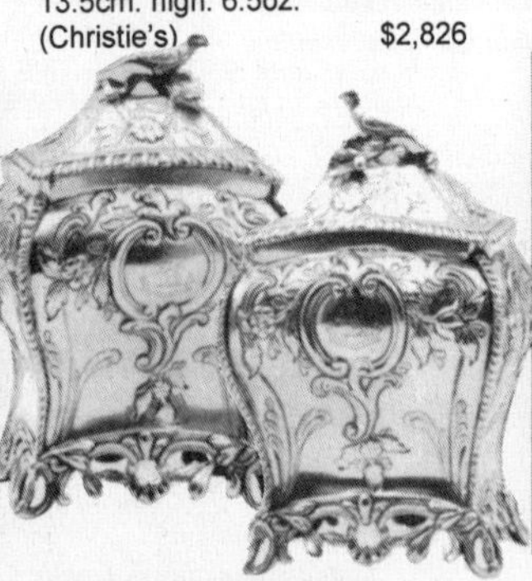

A pair of George III tea caddies and covers crested within foliate scroll cartouche with gadroon edging London 1770, 14cm. high, makers mark *S.W.*, London 1770, 19.2oz.
(Bearne's) $5,920

Attractive Edwardian silver tea caddy, oval shaped with gadrooned rim, scrolled articulated handle to lid, 3½in. tall, Chester 1907.
(G.A. Key) $302

An Edwardian tea caddy, the ogee cube body repoussé decorated with scrolls and foliage, 3.75in. wide, by Samuel Walton Smith & Co, London 1901, 8.75oz.
(Bristol) $846

Attractive early 20th century silver tea caddy of baluster shape, having a gadrooned rim to the hinged lid, side ringlet handles, all supported on four shell and curved feet, 4 x 2½in., Sheffield 1910 by S W Hutton, 5½oz.
(G A Key) $593

Attractive George III silver tea caddy, oval shaped with beaded rims, later chased and embossed with exotic birds amongst trailing foliage and scrolls, 5 x 3½in., London 1784 by Daniel Smith and Robert Sharp.
(G A Key) $1,221

Victorian silver plated spirit kettle, burner and stand, the kettle of oval compressed design, the stand of openwork with slot pierced detail, 12in. tall, circa 1890.
(G.A. Key) $272

A William IV tea kettle, by James Fray, Dublin 1835, of melon fluted form on a stand with scroll work supports, openwork cast feet and a lift-out burner, 36cm. high, 111oz.
(Bonhams) $4,360

A. Jacobi & Co. repoussé kettle on stand, Baltimore, late 19th century, on serpentine legs ending in flattened rocaille feet, 11in. high, approximately 52 troy oz.
(Skinner) $1,955

A George I octagonal tea kettle and stand, with leather covered swing handle, engraved later with armorials, the stand with three scroll legs and fixed burner, by John Sanders I London 1717, 75oz. all in.
(Woolley & Wallis) $47,400

Late Victorian silver plated spirit kettle of half fluted oval design, together with a matching four footed base and spirit burner, 12in. high, circa 1900.
(G.A. Key) $165

A late Victorian kettle, burner and stand, the former of rounded rectangular section, embossed with bands of gadrooning, flowers and foliage, London 1900, Goldsmiths and Silversmiths Co., 38oz. gross.
(Dreweatt Neate) $874

A George II silver tea kettle, stand and lamp, Edward Wakelin, London, 1757, the melon-fluted spherical kettle with leaf-capped curved spout, 14½in. high, 79oz.
(Christie's) $3,841

Hallmarked silver spirit kettle, burner and stand, the kettle of flattened circular design with bone handle, 7in. diameter, Sheffield, 1930, 37oz. all in.
(G.A. Key) $512

Victorian silver plated tea kettle and stand, the kettle of melon design with fluted decoration and well embossed with naturalistic cricket amongst foliage, in George II style, 13in. tall, circa 1875.
(G.A. Key) $270

A William IV teapot, domed hinged cover with a detachable flower finial, George Burrows II & Richard Pearce, London 1831, 22oz. all in. (Woolley & Wallis) $506

Robert Hennell I, a George III oval teapot, having bright cut decorated bands and ribbon tied oval cartouches, a straight tapering spout, London 1783, 12.5oz. all in. (Woolley & Wallis) $246

A Georgian teapot of compressed circular segmented form, embossed with flowerheads, Chinaman finial on domed lid, 11¼in. wide, London 1823, 28oz. 11dwt. (Andrew Hartley) $606

George III rectangular teapot, together with matching stand, teapot by John Robins, stand by Charles Hougham, both London 1791, the teapot 7½in., the stand 7in., gross weight 21oz. (Ewbank) $521

George III teapot, London, 1805, Peter, Ann and William Bateman, oblong body on four ball feet, serpentine spout, fruitwood handle, 7¾in. high, 21 troy oz. approximately. (Skinner) $632

George III plain oval teapot with ebonised handle and knob, with matching stand on four reeded feet, by Thomas Robinson, London 1804, gross weight 12oz. (Ewbank) $716

E, E J & W Bernard, a George IV teapot, the circular compressed body with a band of foliage with crested and vacant cartouches, 1830, 28oz. all in. (Woolley & Wallis) $691

A George III small teapot and stand of oval outline with bright-engraved borders and wreath cartouches, crested by Thomas Wallis (II), 1804, 14oz. (Christie's) $827

Attractive Victorian silver plated teapot, oval shaped naturalistically engraved with herons amongst river foliage, angular handle, circa 1885. (G A Key) $90

An Arts & Crafts teapot, with a detachable cover, made in the form of a classical lamp with a plain lower body and collet foot, by Liberty & Co, Birmingham, 1900, 17oz. (Christie's) $2,708

George III silver teapot of slightly tapering oval design, bright cut engraved, angular spout, treen handle and finial, marked for London 1797, by George Smith and Thomas Hayter, 14oz all in. (G A Key) $754

A George IV silver teapot by Emes and Barnard, London 1827, of melon shape, the upper body foliate embossed, with insulated leaf capped handle, 14.5cm. high, 23.5oz. (Cheffins) $608

A tea pot, of sixteen lobed straight-sided form with bands of bright cutting and fluted spout, by Henry Chawner, 1788, 14oz. (Tennants) $816

A George III teapot and stand of elliptical form, engraved with vacant leafage scroll cartouches, floral and trellis borders, 7in. high, London 1798, by Andrew Fogelberg, 20oz. all in. (Russell Baldwin & Bright) $977

A tea pot, engraved with bands, cartouches and swags of flowers between beaded edges, maker perhaps Samuel Wood, 1784, 14½oz. (Tennants) $1,256

A George III teapot and stand, of plain navette form with reeded borders, by Peter, Ann & William Bateman, 1800, the stand 17cm. long, 18oz. (Christie's) $1,444

A George III silver teapot and stand, London, 1784, the teapot with maker's mark of Hester Bateman, the stand with maker's mark of Elizabeth Jones, the teapot 9¾in. long, the stand 6¼in. long. gross 17oz. (Christie's) $3,457

An early 18th century Dutch teapot, the body decorated with bands of embossed fluting and stiff leaves, probably by Wieger Schrender, Sneek 1728, 11.25oz. (Christie's) $3,464

A Regency tea pot, the long sides with bowed bands of bright cut decoration and floral cartouches above the paw feet, Dublin 1815, James LeBass, 21oz. gross. (Dreweatt Neate) $556

A William IV teapot for the Dutch market embossed with buildings amongst trees, scrolls and foliage, 19cm. high, possibly Edward Farrell, London, 1835, 29.4oz. (Bearne's) $636

A tea pot, oval straight sided, with alternating bright engraved and plain fluting with fluted tapering spout, the flat cover with pineapple knop, by Robert Hennell, 1781, 18½oz. (Tennants) $1,413

A George III silver teapot, London 1812, of compressed circular form, gadroon and shell borders, part fluted decoration, 10.5cm. high. (Bonhams) $317

Good Victorian silver plated teapot of compressed circular design, having engraved garland decoration, bud finial to lid, circa 1875 by Elkington and Co. (G A Key) $155

Victorian oval engraved teapot with beaded borders and flat top, ebonized handle and knob, London 1872, 8in., gross weight 10oz. (Ewbank) $456

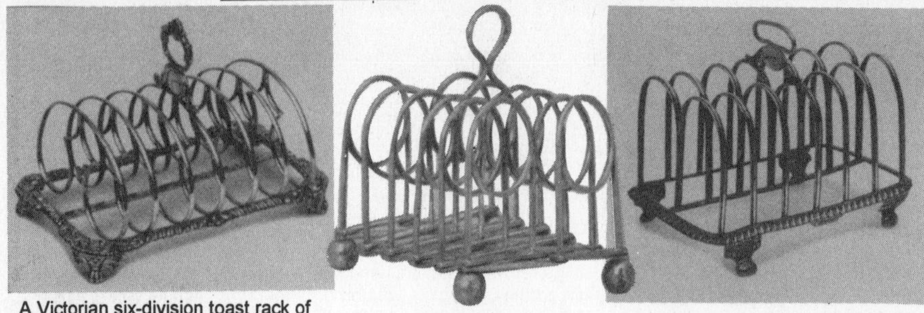

A Victorian six-division toast rack of openwork scroll design with gadroon and scrolling foliate decoration, 19cm. long, Sheffield 1811, maker's mark *I.S.* over *T.S.*, 375gm., 12oz.
(Bearne's) $612

A late Victorian expanding toast rack, the six ring dividers with a central handle, the telescopic base frame on bun feet (plating wearing).
(Woolley & Wallis) $308

A George III rounded rectangular six-division toast rack with reeded double arch dividers, 16cm. long, Rebecca Emes and Edward Barnard, London 1819, 272gm.
(Bearne's) $408

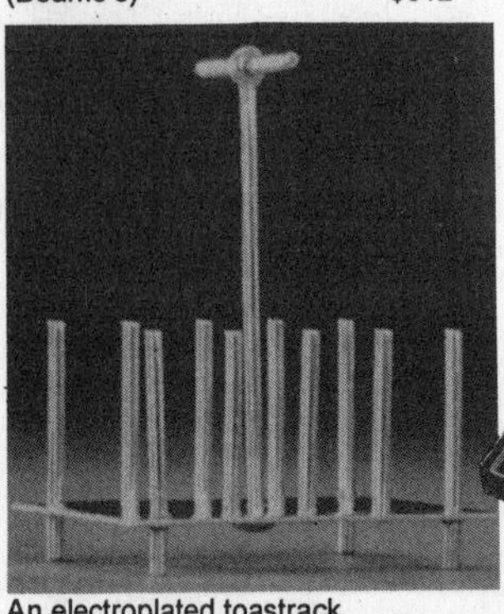

An electroplated toastrack, designed by Christopher Dresser manufactured by Hukin and Heath, 1878, the flat rectangular base with five vertical rods on each of the longer sides, 5¼in. high.
(Christie's) $2,235

Cased pair of two small hallmarked silver toast racks of five wirework bars to a rectangular base and supported on four ball feet, 2½ x 1½in., Sheffield 1911.
(G A Key) $174

An electroplated toastrack, designed by Christopher Dresser, manufactured by James Dixon & Sons, circa 1881, the rectangular frame with triangular supports, on four spike feet, 6½in. high.
(Christie's) $10,246

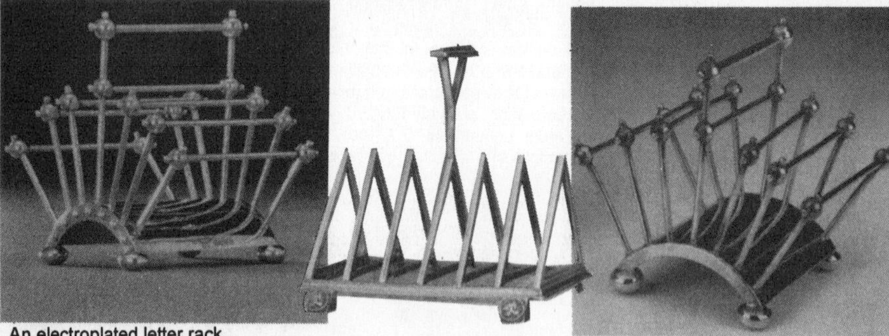

An electroplated letter rack, designed by Christopher Dresser, manufactured by Heath and Middleton, 1881, the six divisions separated by articulated rods and spheres, 5in. high.
(Christie's) $1,490

A Victorian toast rack, in Aesthetic style, the six triangular divisions with a central handle, on classical mask decorated block feet.
(Bristol) $75

A late Victorian toast rack, in the style of Christopher Dresser, with arched base on ball feet and seven radiating angular bars, by Heath & Middleton, London 1899, 14cm. long. 10.5oz. (Christie's) $619

A George II kettle stand, of shaped triangular outline with a molded border and cast shell and scroll feet, engraved in the center with a coat of arms, by Hugh Mills, 1745, 26cm. wide, 20oz.
(Christie's) $3,011

An early Charles II salver on foot, or stand for a porringer, plain well center bordered by a broad rim embossed with assorted fruit, birds and animals, attributed to Gilbert Shepherd,1663, 28.5cm. diameter, 16.5oz.
(Christie's) $10,626

A George II waiter, the center engraved with a coat of arms within a husk and scroll cartouche, by David Willaume (II), 1737, 15.25cm. diameter, 9oz.
(Christie's) $922

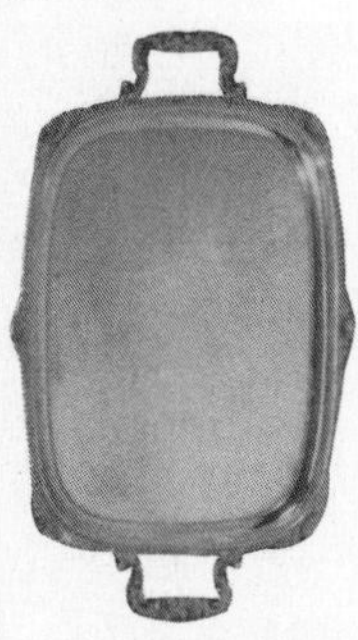

A silver tray, Chester, 1914, maker's mark *HEB* over *FEB,* oblong and on four shell and scroll feet, with shell, scroll and gadrooned border, 27¾in. long, 112oz. (Christie's) $2,743

A pair of early George II waiters, of square outline with serpentine corners, bracket feet and a plain molded border, by David Willaume (II), 1729, 15.75cm. square, 19.35oz. (Christie's) $7,970

A Victorian oval tray, engraved borders of Greek key and petal motifs, the raised sides with a ribbon and bead edge, 29½in. across handles.
(Woolley & Wallis) $314

William Kerr Reid, a William IV circular salver, the center engraved with a crest of a sword hanging from an oak tree with motto above of the Waller family, 10in. diameter, London 1837, 31oz.
(Woolley & Wallis) $1,201

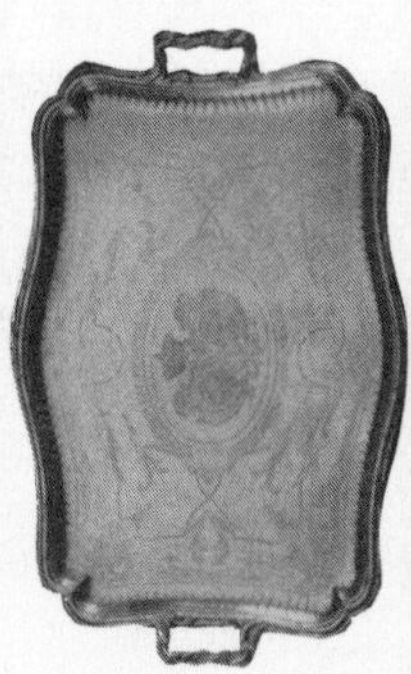

A French silver-gilt tray, stamped *Froment-Meurice, Paris*, 1838-1850, shaped oblong and with ribbon-tied border, 31in. long. 152oz. (Christie's) $7,314

A George II silver waiter, Edward Cornock, London, 1729, shaped circular and on three scroll feet, with molded rim, 17cm. diameter, 9oz. (Christie's) $2,925

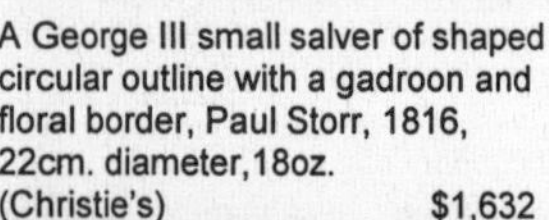

A George III small salver of shaped circular outline with a gadroon and floral border, Paul Storr, 1816, 22cm. diameter,18oz.
(Christie's) $1,632

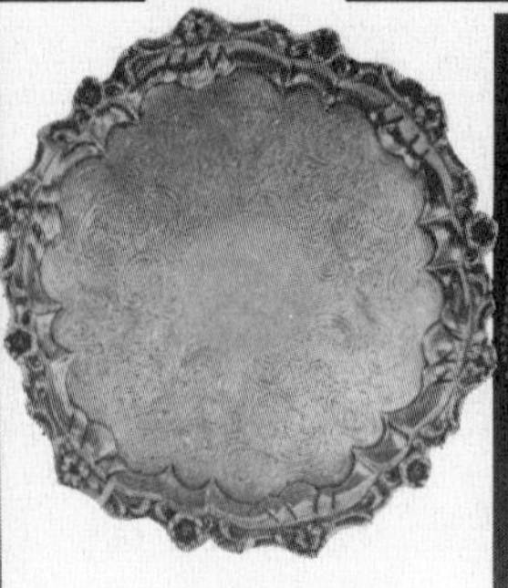

William IV silver salver, circular shaped with applied cast floral and acanthus scrolled edge, foliate engraved center, 11in. diameter, London 1833 by Charles Reily and George Storer, 23oz.
(G A Key) $856

A rare, George III salver with a domed shaped and beaded border, by Matthew Boulton & John Fothergill, Birmingham 1774, 25.5cm. diameter, 17oz.
(Christie's) $999

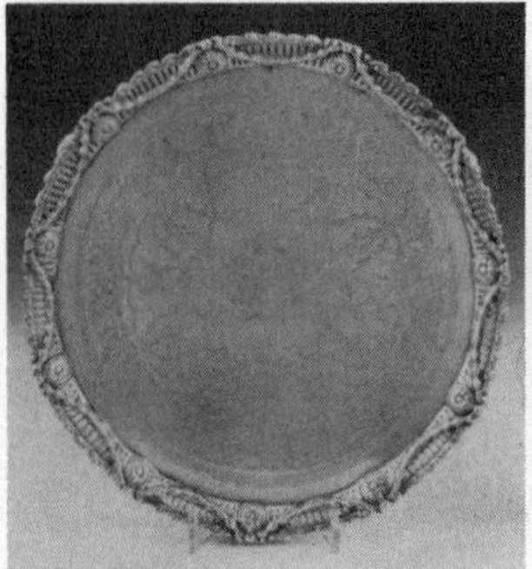

A Victorian engraved salver, of shaped circular outline with cast feet and a cast border of paterae, festoons and pierced slots, Robert Harper, 1881, 23.5cm. diameter, 15¼oz. (Christie's) $583

An early 18th century Continental salver on foot of square outline with incurved corners, a 19th century Dutch duty mark, possibly Belgian, first half of 18th century, 23cm. square, 16.5oz.
(Christie's) $2,392

A George IV salver of shaped circular outline with a border of foliate scrolls engraved in the center, probably by Messrs Blagdin, Hodgson, Kirkby, Elliott & Woolin, Sheffield, 1826, 45.5cm. diameter, 66oz. (Christie's) $1,921

A George II waiter of shaped circular outline with a shell and scroll border, by John Carter (II) 1769, 18cm. diameter, 8.75oz.
(Christie's) $589

An early George III salver of shaped circular outline with a cast border of repeating floral sprays and cast bracket feet, Ebenezer Coker, 1764, 33.5cm. diameter, 38.25oz. (Christie's) $2,208

A George II salver of circular outline with shell and scroll border and scroll feet, by William Peaston, 1755, 32½cm. diameter, 30oz.
(Christie's) $1,563

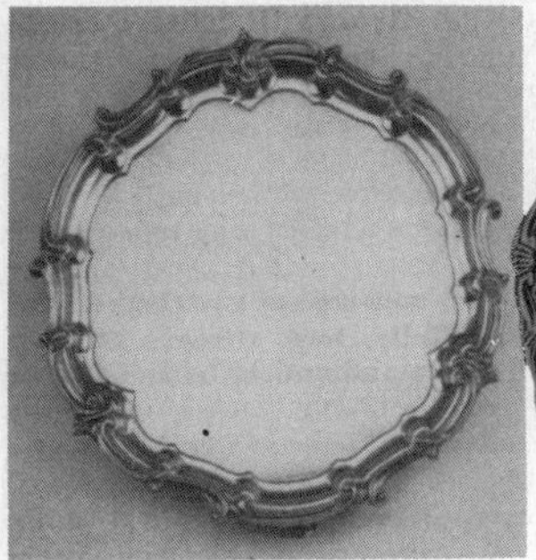

A modern salver of shaped circular outline with a border of scrolls and leafy scroll feet, by Mappin & Webb, Sheffield 1918, 42cm. diameter, 71.5oz.
(Christie's) $1,379

A George II salver with a shell and scroll border and pad feet, by William Peaston, 1748, 24.25cm. diameter, 16oz.
(Christie's) $1,152

Robert Abercromby, a George II circular salver, uninscribed with a raised molded border with repoussé scrolls and interspersed shells to the channelled cast edge, 12in. diameter, London 1740, 31.5oz. (Bristol) $1,302

A late 18th century Portuguese salver, with a husk and scroll border and flat chased floral decoration, by an unascribed maker, Lisbon, second half of 18th century, 27.5cm. diameter, 16.5oz.
(Christie's) $1,416

A George III oval salver engraved at the center with a monogram within a surround of flowers, shells and scrolling foliage, 38.5cm. long, Timothy Renou, London 1800, 1210gm. (Bearne's) $743

A fine George II salver, engraved with contemporary armorials in a wide chased band of flowers and fruit with a shaped scroll and leafage border, 15in. diameter, by Isaac Cookson, Newcastle 1748, 64oz.
(Woolley & Wallis) $5,846

A George III salver, circular with a cast border of gadrooning, interrupted by alternating husks and shell motifs, by Ebenezer Coker, 1764, 28cm. diameter 23.75oz.
(Christie's) $3,972

A presentation silver salver, Ashes Series 1924-5, by W.M. Co. Birmingham, engraved *To Herbert Sutcliffe*.....8in. diameter.
(Sotheby's) $1,703

A George V shaped circular salver with reeded edge on four pad feet, 36cm. diameter, R & W Sorley, London 1929, 1250gm.
(Bearne's) $511

Tiffany & Co. covered tureen, 1875-91, ovoid, on stepped foot, with square section handles with beaded cube to center and flat leaf terminals, 15in. long, approximately 56 troy oz. (Skinner) $5,175

English silverplate covered tureen, circa 1900, oval shape with acanthus leaf and Rococo shell motifs,10¼in. high. (Du Mouchelles) $1,700

A soup tureen, of oval bellied shape with gadrooned edge and scrolling projecting loop handles, by Walter Brind, 1773, 93oz. 42cm. including handles. (Tennants) $7,850

A pair of sauce tureens, with gadrooned edges and lion mask and ring handles, by William Fountain, 1803, 39oz, 14cm. diameter. (Tennants) $5,626

A silver plated soup tureen by Christofle, Paris, circa 1890, of oval form, the cover surmounted by a pomegranate, raised on a tray cast with scrolls and foliage, 31cm. high. (Sotheby's) $16,871

John Emes, a pair of George III oval sauce tureens, the boat shape partly ribbed bodies each with two molded angular loop handles, 9½in., London 1798, 30oz. (Woolley & Wallis) $4,424

An electroplated soup tureen, designed by Christopher Dresser, manufactured by Hukin and Heath, 1880, ivory bar handles and turned finial, separate liner, 12¼in. maximum width. (Christie's) $4,443

A Sheffield plated oval two-handled soup tureen and cover, early 19th century, length over handles 15in. (Sotheby's) $1,955

Christopher Dresser for J.W. Hukin & J.T. Heath, tureen, cover and ladle, design registered 28 July 1880, electroplated metal and ebonised wood, tureen 12¼in. width over handles. (Sotheby's) $8,832

A George III Sheffield Plate tea urn, the faceted leaf shape body with an applied draped shield shape cartouche engraved a phoenix crest, 13½in., circa 1800.
(Woolley & Wallis) $512

An early Victorian samovar and cover, melon lobed body with acanthus cast detail, quatrefoil platform base, 42cm. high.
(Wintertons) $492

A George III silver tea urn, Thomas Whipham and Charles Wright, London 1767, the plinth with openwork sides and gadrooned borders, 20in. high, 79oz. gross.
(Christie's) $4,149

Good quality plated tea urn of bulbous form with ring carrying handles and tap, fluted and gadrooned decoration to a stem square base, squat circular feet, late Victorian period.
(G A Key) $657

A Regency copper water urn, early 19th century, the barrel shaped body with reeded banding and twin ring handles, with a stained green ivory cone knopped fitment to the tap handle, supported on a square plinth on bun feet, 11½in. high.
(Christie's) $588

A middle period, Old Sheffield plated samovar or tea urn with a squat circular body, on a shaped square pedestal, circa 1820, 43cm. high. (Christie's) $1,288

A William IV silver tea-urn, Paul Storr, London, 1833, the baluster-shaped body with two bifurcated branch, flower and quilted scroll handles, 18½in. high, 152oz.
(Christie's) $13,714

Antique English Sheffield silver plated hot water urn in the Adams style, urn form, 16in. high.
(Eldred's) $440

An electro-plated urn, on a four-legged stand with detachable burner, the body modelled as a barrel with a hinged cover and two angular handles, circa 1875, 36.5cm. high.(Christie's) $722

A pair of Victorian massive parcel-gilt vases, Charles Frederick Hancock, London 1852, the campana shaped vases cast and chased as openwork fruiting vine tendrils, 29½in. high, 1,158oz.
(Christie's) $255,020

An Edwardian copy of the Warwick Vase, the campana shape body decorated with lion pelts and applied Bacchic masks beneath trailing fruiting vines, 12in. across, by Messrs Barnard Brothers, London, 1904, 62.25oz.
(Bristol) $4,232

A pair of late Victorian flower vases with flared rims and embossed with stylized foliage with two vacant cartouches, J. & F. Hall, London 1898, 28cm. high, 32oz.
(Christie's) $1,536

A French silver-gilt and cut-glass sugar-vase and cover, Marc-Augustin Lebrun, Paris, 1819-1838, the cup raised on four chased dolphins on circular plinth, 13¼in. high.
(Christie's) $5,485

A pair of Victorian vases with spiral fluted neck and wide scroll edged rim, applied figure handles, flower embossed body, 4in. high, London 1891, 6oz. 14dwt.
(Andrew Hartley) $271

A Victorian silver-gilt vase, John Hunt and Robert Roskell, London 1868, the detachable openwork campana shaped vase formed as fruiting vine tendrils, with ruby glass liner, 20½in. high, 267oz.
(Christie's) $56,580

A George III silver vase and pedestal, Paul Storr, London, 1815, the vase formed as the Warwick vase on a square plinth, the vase engraved on the reverse with the initial *B*, 20in. high, 369oz.
(Christie's) $57,615

A pair of Austro-Hungarian silver dessert stands, late 19th century, 800 standard, the baluster stems each applied with a winged putto and floral garlands,13¾in. high. 142oz. (Christie's) $13,165

An American silver and other metals vase, Tiffany & Co., New York, circa 1880–85, with hammered surface engraved and applied with trailing vines, a copper ladybug and spider, 16oz., 2dwt. gross, 6½in. high.
(Sotheby's) $26,450

A late Victorian vesta case of rectangular form, the front enamelled with a steam engine, R.C., Birmingham 1900, 5cm.
(Christie's) $2,407

An Edward VII small oval vesta case with fox mask motif, 52mm. long overall, Chester 1907.
(Bearne's) $785

A silver vesta case of rectangular form, the front decorated with an enamelled study of a 'society' lady holding a fan, A. Buckley Ltd, Birmingham 1923, 5cm.
(Christie's) $2,222

A silver vesta case of rectangular form, the front enamelled with a study of a nude reclining on her bed, within a black enamel scrollwork border, J.B.S., Chester 1911, 5.5cm.
(Christie's) $1,573

A tortoiseshell vesta case of rectangular form, the mount enamelled with white line decoration and applied with a diamond set clasp and hinges, French, late 19th century, 5cm.
(Christie's) $1,111

An Edwardian vesta case of rounded rectangular form, the front enamelled with a reclining nude female seated on a shoreline, waves and skyline beyond, import marks for London 1905, 5cm.
(Christie's) $1,481

A silver vesta case of rounded rectangular form, the front enamelled to one side with a rectangular study of a nude female standing beside a lake, probably German, late 19th century, 4.5cm.
(Christie's) $1,573

A silver-plated vesta case of rectangular form, the front enamelled with a view of a cross-country runner surrounded by engraved ferns, probably English, late 19th century, 4cm.
(Christie's) $926

A silver vesta case of rounded rectangular form, the front with applied gold bands, terminating in flower petals set with synthetic rubies, import marks for London 1904, 4.3cm.
(Christie's) $481

An Edwardian vesta case of shaped rectangular form incorporating a vesta case and map reader, maker's mark rubbed, London 1909, 8.2cm.
(Christie's) $2,037

A Victorian vesta case in the form of a lock, A.W., Birmingham 1882, 4.3cm.
(Christie's) $592

A Victorian vesta case of rectangular form, the front enamelled with a dancer, C.C., Birmingham 1894, 5cm.
(Christie's) $1,388

A silver vesta case formed as a male bust portrait study, the flattened back engraved with a name, with interior striker pad, French import marks, late 19th century, 6.6cm.
(Christie's) $889

An owl, silver vesta case realistically chased with plumage and with applied boot button eyes, probably Sampson Mordan, London 1894, 5.7cm.
(Christie's) $1,685

A brass vesta case of rectangular form with sloping cover, the front with an enamelled scene of a girl and her servant in her boudoir, French, late19th, 4.7cm.
(Christie's) $741

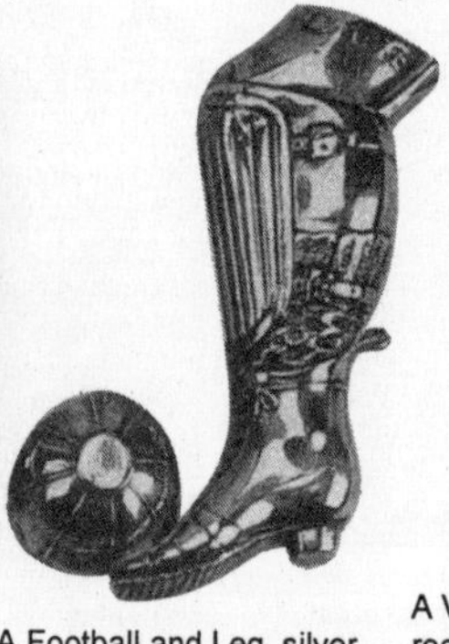

A Football and Leg, silver, formed as the lower leg of a footballer, a ball balanced on his foot, the lid stamped, *C & M. Patent*, Birmingham 1884, 5.5cm.
(Christie's) $736

A Victorian vesta case, rectangular with a pointed dome, the front enamelled with a seaside Punch and Judy tent, Sampson Mordan, London 1887, 5.5cm.
(Christie's) $12,03

A silver vesta case of shaped rectangular form, the front with an applied copper head of a Native American Indian, American, late 19th century, 7cm.
(Christie's) $370

An Edwardian vesta case of horseshoe form, one side inset with Connemara marble and part engraved with foliage, J.Cook and Son, Birmingham 1905, 4cm.
(Christie's) $889

A Victorian vesta case of rectangular form, the front enamelled with the head of a dog, W.T. & S., Birmingham 1887, 4.9cm.
(Christie's) $889

The Benevolent and Protective Order of Elks, silver, formed as an elk's tooth, the front stamped with an elk head, American late 19th century, 6.5cm.
(Christie's) $76

A George IV silver gilt vinaigrette, Birmingham 1826, by J. Betteridge, of good gauge, oblong, engine turned and with cast scroll and floral edging and with gilt interior, 3.6cm. (Bonhams) $474

A George III multi-compartment box, James Henzell, Dublin 1812, vinaigrette and patch/tablet compartment at each end; toothpick compartment along each side; central snuff compartment and a further compartment in its cover, 4.5oz. (Bonhams) $30,889

An early Victorian silver vinaigrette, Birmingham 1853, Edward Smith, lobed oval form, with bands of engine turned decoration, vacant cartouche, 4cm. (Bonhams) $284

A Regency purse style vinaigrette, the engraved hinged cover with a strap and raised foliage borders, 1in. Joseph Taylor, Birmingham 1818. (Woolley & Wallis) $480

A mid-Victorian novelty silver vinaigrette, London 1870, Henry William Dee, modelled as a lantern, the front with a hinged lid (lacking glass) that opens to reveal the pierced grille, 3cm. high. (Bonhams) $1,975

A William IV rectangular vinaigrette with engraved design, having floral pierced silver-gilt grille, Birmingham 1836, by Nathaniel Mills. (Russell Baldwin & Bright) $354

WAX JACKS

An early George III silver wax jack, London 1763, John Langford and John Febrille, with a pineapple finial above pierçed nips, on a slender column and pierced octagonal base with scrolled paw feet, 6¾in. high. (Bonhams) $2,400

A George III wax-jack with a reeded circular base, the pillar with a cone finial, by John Scofield 1789, 14.5cm. high, 5.5oz weighable silver. (Christie's) $2,497

A modern wax-jack in the early 19th century style, on an oblong base with gadrooning, a reeded framework and a conical snuffer on a chain, by George Howson, 1911, 11.5cm. high, 6oz. (Christie's) $920

A pair of Regency Sheffield plate wine coolers, the campana shape bodies partly ribbed, with two leaf tied spray appliqué reeded scroll handles, on a circular molded foot, 9¼in. high.
(Woolley & Wallis) $2,002

Attractive Victorian silver plated wine cooler, melon shaped with fluted circular foot, beaded rim, serpent formed handles, plus liner, 12in. tall, circa 1860.
(G A Key) $707

A pair of Victorian silver gilt wine coolers, Robert Gray & Sons, Glasgow, 1841, the bodies with scrolled cartouche between chased strapwork panels on a matted ground, detachable plain liners, 12¼in. high, 185oz.
(Christie's) $13,685

A pair of Russian silver wine-coolers, Carl Jacob Tegelsten, St. Petersburg, 1840, with two detachable acanthus foliage scroll handles, the everted rim applied with acanthus foliage, 10½in. high. 235oz.
(Christie's) $54,855

A pair of Sheffield plate Regency wine coolers, the compressed circular bodies with ovolo molding and a pair of shell appliqué open side handles, 8.25in. high. (Bristol) $1,465

A bronze and silvered wine cooler Paris, circa 1890, the bowl cast with a rosette and guilloche border, supported by three putti, 36cm. high. (Sotheby's) $7,498

A Georgian wine funnel, with spiral fluting to the body, on circular stand with reeded rim, 4½in. high, maker's mark *PR*, 3oz 18dwt. (Andrew Hartley) $462

Good George III two piece silver wine funnel of usual design, reeded edge, shell clip, well marked for London 1822 by Rebecca Emes and Edward Barnard, 5in. tall. (G.A. Key) $382

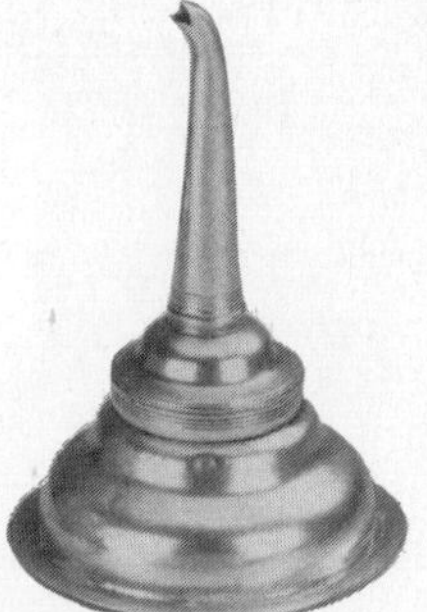

A George III wine funnel with reeded borders and a circular bowl with a pointed tang, initialled by Crispin Fuller, 1813, 13cm. high, 3.5oz. (Christie's) $999

A George III silver wine funnel, ondon date letter worn, maker's nark of Charles Aldridge and Henry Green, circular bowl, plain border, lip broken, monogramed, pproximate weight 2oz. Bonhams) $408

A George IV Scottish wine funnel, Philip Grierson, Glasgow, 1825, chased and embossed with a band of fruiting vines on a matted ground, 16cm. high, 4.5oz. (Bonhams) $2,725

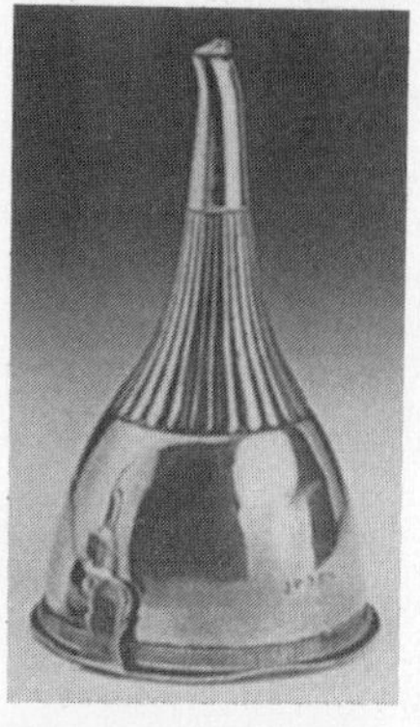

A George III silver wine funnel, London 1804, Solomon Hougham, domed circular form, part fluted decoration, approximate weight 5oz. (Bonhams) $659

WINE TASTERS

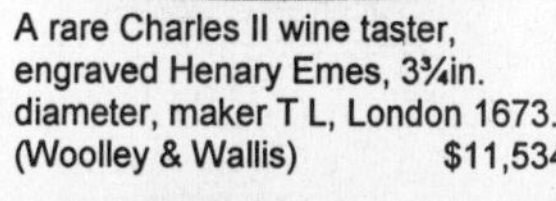

A rare Charles II wine taster, engraved Henary Emes, 3¾in. diameter, maker T L, London 1673. (Woolley & Wallis) $11,534

A Commonwealth silver wine taster, ondon, 1655, shaped circular and vith two wirework handles, the enter chased with stylized flowers, 3cm. long, 2oz. Christie's) $5,485

A late 19th century French wine taster with an oval thumbpiece, ring handle and part fluted and part lobed bowl, *inscribed Eduard Voleau a Niort*, 9cm. diameter, 4oz. (Christie's) $529

A Charles II silver wine taster, London, 1661, maker's mark of *RL* with three pellets above and below, with two wirework scroll handles, 4in. long, 1oz. (Christie's) $4,023

A Symphonion No. 25A de-luxe musical box for 30cm. discs with 2 x 42 tone double comb, in walnut case, circa 1900.
(Auction Team Köln) $3,150

A 7⅝in. Symphonion in simulated carved walnut case of Renaissance style, with single-comb movement with zither attachment and crank wind, 11½in. wide, with 23 discs.
(Christie's) $2,208

A 13⅝in. table Symphonion with sublime harmony combs, glass inner lid and inlaid lid with internal monochrome print, 21¾in. wide, with 37 discs.
(Christie's) $4,154

A rare 27½in. Symphonion, with double comb movement, oak case with carved columns, 85in. high, with 42 discs.
(Christie's) $20,240

A 19⅛in. upright Symphonion with two sublime harmony combs, coin mechanism, with typical walnut case with glazed door, pediment, 84½in. high, with 24 discs.
(Christie's) $7,586

An 8¼in. Symphonion, No. 348248, with diagonal sublime harmony combs and ratchet wind, in black case, 11in. square, with 46 discs.
(Christie's) $814

A 17¾in. table Symphonion No. 329794, with sublime harmony combs, in unfigured walnut case with quarter-veneered lid and reproduction monochrome print inside, 23½in. wide, with sixteen discs. (Christie's) $2,87

A coin operated Symphonion mechanical music box for 30cm. discs, with 84-tone double comb, 1895. (Auction Team Köln)
$2,009

A Flemish historical tapestry, second half 16th /early 17th century, woven in wools, depicting a King in Roman armour seated on a scallop-shell encrusted and scrolling throne beneath a canopy, before him four attendants, one paying tribute, 7ft6in. x 12ft.5in. (Christie's) $29,072

A 17th century Audenaerde tapestry of a landscape with trees and foliage, a village with bridge and waterfall in the background, with floral border, 280 x 428cm. (Galerie Moderne) $11,054

A Brussels mythological tapestry, second half 16th century, woven in wools and silks, depicting a youth carrying a book and surmounted by a plaque inscribed *Eyphka*, 97in. x 91in. (Christie's) $45,816

A Louis XV Aubusson pastoral tapestry, woven in wools and silks, in the foreground with a courtly man pursuing a young maiden in blue dress, to the right with a seated lady and before her with a child, 9ft.6in. x 8ft.9in. (Christie's) $33,615

A Marche Game-Park tapestry, second half 16th century, woven in wools and silks, depicting an ostrich hunt with various hunters on horseback attacking ostriches, within a flowerhead-filled foliate guilloche border, 8ft.6in. x 11ft.9in. (Christie's) $63,200

An Aubusson Biblical tapestry, early 18th century, possibly by François Grellet, woven in wools, depicting Armida before Godefroy of Bouillon from The Story of Godefroy of Bouillon in Jerusalem Delivered, 116 x 168½in. (Christie's) $10,499

A rare center seam teddy by Steiff, German, circa 1904, the cinnamon bear with thick, curly mohair, black boot button eyes, straw filled jointed body, hump to back, 19in.
(Bonhams) $4,740

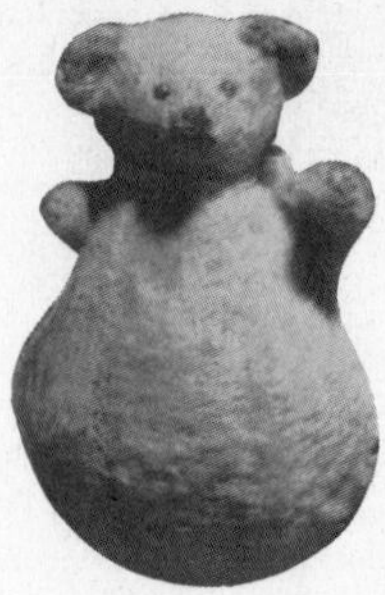

A rare Steiff 'Roly Poly' bear with blond mohair, black shoe button eyes, ball shaped body with weighted base containing rattle and button in ear, 7in. tall, circa 1909.
(Christie's) $13,628

A Steiff center seam teddy bear with golden mohair, black boot button eyes, swivel head, long jointed shaped limbs, felt pads and hump, 16in. tall, circa 1908.
(Christie's) $3,089

A white Steiff teddy bear with curly mohair, black boot button eyes, pronounced clipped snout, beige stitched nose, cream felt pads and hump, 20in. tall, circa 1908.
(Christie's) $10,902

A white Steiff teddy bear with curly mohair, black boot button eyes, pronounced clipped snout, felt foot pads lined with blue felt and hump, 20in. tall, circa 1908.
(Christie's) $3,634

A fine Steiff center seam teddy bear, with rich golden mohair, black glass eyes, brown felt pads, growler, hump and button in ear, 18in. tall, circa 1908.
(Christie's) $16,146

'Albert', a Farnell teddy bear with rich golden mohair, webbed paw claws, felt pads, large card lined feet and hump, 28in. tall, 1920s.
(Christie's) $8,728

A large and rare teddy bear by Steiff, German, circa 1910, the golden mohair bear with black boot button eyes, light brown stitched nose, mouth and claws, 30in. tall.
(Bonhams) $3,950

A Steiff teddy bear, with apricot mohair, 19in. tall, circa 1908, with a studio photograph of original owner as a young girl with this teddy bear.
(Christie's) $6,831

Harry', a Steiff center seam teddy ɔear, with blond mohair, black boot ɔutton eyes, pronounced clipped snout, growler and button in ear, 28in. tall, circa 1908.
(Christie's) $10,764

'Cecil', a Steiff teddy bear, with center seam, blond curly mohair, large shaped paws and feet, felt pads, hump and button in ear, 24in. tall, circa 1908.
(Christie's) $6,810

A Steiff teddy bear, German, circa 1920, with golden mohair and clipped snout, orange glass eyes, black stitched nose, mouth and paws, filled with straw, felt paw pads and button to left ear, 20in. tall. (Bonhams) $2,054

A Farnell teddy bear, with white mohair, brown and black glass eyes, pronounced snout, beige stitched nose, mouth and claws, rexine pads, hump and squeak, 27in. tall, circa 1930.
(Christie's) $4,305

'Cedric', a Steiff teddy bear, with honey golden mohair, black boot button eyes, long jointed shaped limbs, felt pads, hump and blank button in ear, 19in. tall, circa 1907.
(Christie's) $7,176

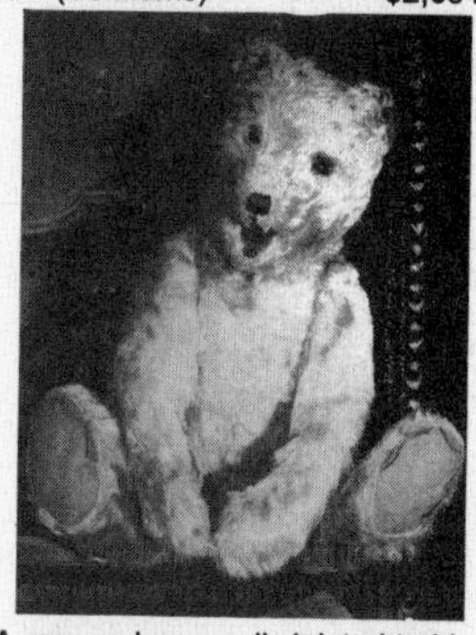

A rare and unusually jointed teddy bear, with golden mohair, clear and black glass eyes painted brown on reverse, beige felt claws, 16in. tall, circa 1920, English.
(Christie's) $986

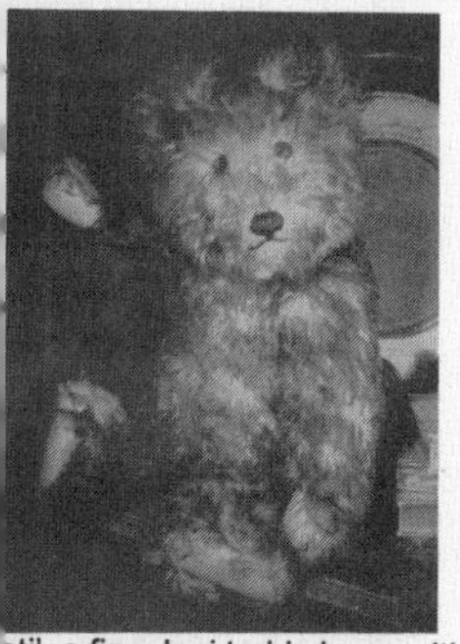

ɔti', a fine Jopi teddy bear, with ırk brown tipped silver white ɔhair, brown and black glass es, jointed shaped limbs, cream t pads and growler, 19in. tall, 20s. (Christie's) $2,332

Zandra Rhodes bear, dyed in deep pink, dressed in a cerise chiffon sari, earrings, nosering, sequinned bindhi and painted henna tattoos on paw and foot pads.
(Christie's) $4,149

An Alpha Farnell teddy bear, with long curly golden mohair, large brown and black glass eyes, black stitched nose, mouth and claws, 25in. tall, circa 1930.
(Christie's) $6,279

A Farnell teddy bear with blond mohair, black button eyes, linen pads, cardlined feet and hump, 13in. tall, circa 1912. (Christie's) $726

A Merrythought teddy bear with golden mohair, deep amber and black glass eyes, clipped snout, brown stitched nose, mouth and claws, 12in. tall, 1930s. (Christie's) $327

A Chad Valley teddy bear, with blond mohair, large gold and black glass eyes, hump, growler and button attached below neck, 23in. tall, 1920s. (Christie's) $86

A rare Laughing Roosevelt Bear by the Columbia Teddy Bear Company, with short rich golden mohair, squeeze box growler and open/close mouth movement by squeeze of tummy or turning of head, 16in. tall, circa 1907. (Christie's) $1,272

A Chiltern Ting-A-Ling Bruin with golden mohair, clipped plush cut muzzle, inner ears and upper feet, jointed limbs and rexine pads, 16in. tall, 1950s. (Christie's) $278

An early German teddy bear with pale blond mohair, black boot button eyes, pronounced clipped snout, hump and large round card lined feet, 25in. tall, circa 1910. (Christie's) $635

A Steiff teddy bear with white mohair, brown and black glass eyes, pronounced snout, brown horizontally stitched nose, mouth and claws, 10in. tall, 1920s. (Christie's) $726

A Chiltern teddy bear with golden mohair, deep amber and black glass eyes, pronounced clipped snout, swivel head, velvet pads and card lined feet, 19in. tall, 1930s. (Christie's) $364

A Schuco 'Yes/No' teddy bear wit short golden mohair, large brown and black glass eyes, pronounced clipped snout, and tail operating 'yes/no' head movement, 19in. tal 1920s. (Christie's) $72

A Steiff teddy bear with beige curly mohair, brown and black glass eyes, jointed limbs, cream felt pads and growler, 25in. tall, 1950s. (Christie's) $817

'Head Boy', a Steiff teddy bear, with golden mohair, black boot button eyes, swivel head, jointed shaped limbs and felt pads, 9in. tall, circa 1910. (Christie's) $509

A Chiltern Ting-A-Ling Bruin bear, with golden mohair, jointed shaped limbs, rexine pads and ting-a-ling in tummy, 14in. tall, circa 1953. (Christie's) $574

A Farnell teddy bear with golden mohair, black button eyes, pronounced clipped snout, swivel head, jointed shaped limbs and card lined feet, 14in. tall, circa 1912. (Christie's) $272

A Merrythought Bell Hop bear with golden cotton plush head, paws and feet, dressed in fixed blue felt and red velvet bellhop costume with fixed bellhop cap, 12in. tall, 1940s. (Christie's) $400

A Strunz teddy bear with golden mohair, brown stitched nose and mouth, swivel head, long jointed shaped limbs, felt pads and button in left ear, 19in. tall, circa 1905. (Christie's) $2,907

An American teddy bear with bright golden mohair, deep amber and black glass eyes, clipped tip of snout, pinched ears slotted into head, 21in. tall, circa 1920. (Christie's) $436

An unusual bear cub by Merrythought, English, circa 1930, the blonde mohair bear in sitting position, with large brown glass eyes, chunky straw and kapok filled body, tan felt paw pads, 17in. tall. (Bonhams) $980

A Steiff teddy bear with golden mohair, black boot button eyes, large shaped paws and feet, felt pads, hump and button in ear, 22in. tall, circa 1910. (Christie's) $4,361

A wooden extension telephone with button and box earphone. (Auction Team Köln) $86

A Danish metal desk telephone, with gold decoration and dial on front. (Auction Team Köln) $65

A Swedish L M Ericsson, Stockholm extension telephone with desk case and conductor. (Auction Team Köln) $1,123

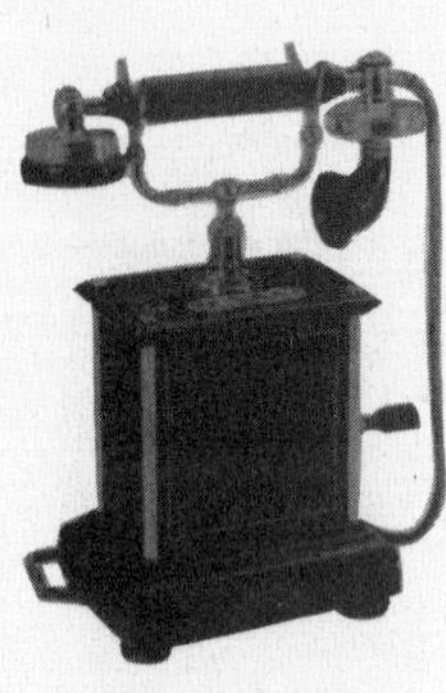

A K.T.A.S. Danish desk telephone, metal case with gold decoration, on wooden plinth, with call button, cable and horn receiver. (Auction Team Köln) $111

A Reichspost model desk telephone in metal case, receiver bracket and cable restored, lacking receiver horn. (Auction Team Köln) $334

A Swedish local battery desk telephone, with conical handset, black metal casing with wooden plinth, circa 1903. (Auction Team Köln) $200

A ZBSA 19 desk telephone by Siemens & Halske, Berlin, in metal case. (Auction Team Köln) $217

A large telephone exchange for 150 lines, possibly by Bell Telephone, Antwerp, with plugs and weights, with diagram of connections. (Auction Team Köln) $1,674

A Danish line-dial desk telephone with two buttons, handset and speech button, lacking receiver horn. (Auction Team Köln) $393

A French desk telephone by the Société Française des Téléphones, Berliner System, Paris, wooden plinth with brass lion's paw feet.
(Auction Team Köln) $1,320

An L M Ericsson line dial desk telephone, in wooden case, with button and call button.
(Auction Team Köln) $891

A Danish Ericsson 'Skeleton' model desk telephone, with press button and connection socket, receiver with speech button.
(Auction Team Köln) $1,574

An L M Ericsson wall telephone, wooden casing with metal battery box, handset with hygienic receiver, 1914.
(Auction Team Köln) $401

An Ericsson desk telephone, with dial, second earpiece and press button, metal case, circa 1922.
(Auction Team Köln) $157

A French desk telephone by the Société des Téléphones Système Picart Lebas, Paris, with second receiver and call key, 1910.
(Auction Team Köln) $201

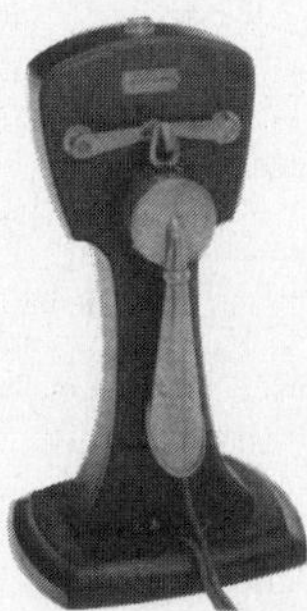

An early French S.I.T. mahogany desk telephone, with chromed receiver and open speaker, second receiver and call button, circa 1903.
(Auction Team Köln) $721

A very rare highly decorative and undocumented desk telephone by L M Ericsson's Argentinian factory.
(Auction Team Köln) $726

A mahogany telephone, Système Microphonique, M & M, Paris, the turned speaker with bell at rear, on baluster support, 9½in. high, late 19th century.
(Christie's) $1,011

A terracotta figure of a gnome wearing a red hat and holding a broom, 35in. high.
(Russell Baldwin & Bright) $2,557

A pair of terracotta busts of Moorish servants on spool turned bases, first half 19th century, 88cm. high.
(Finarte) $7,161

A mid 19th century terracotta bust of a young peasant girl, signed *Foresterie*, on turned base, 62cm. high. (Finarte) $1,494

An Art Nouveau terracotta figure, modelled as a crowned maiden, wearing loosely draped costume applied with opalescent glass cabochons, standing with arms raised, 78cm. high.
(Christie's) $699

A pair of terracotta roundels of circular form, each modelled in deep relief with the winged face of a cherub, 15½in. diameter.
(Christie's) $736

A Goldscheider terracotta bust cast from a model by Petri, of a young woman wearing cape with hood, incised signature, 36.5cm. high.
(Christie's) $331

TRICKS OF THE TRADE

There is nothing particularly difficult about cleaning terracotta, whether it's a precious bust or an old flowerpot.

It responds admirably to hot water and a few soda crystals. A stiff paintbrush will get into the detail.

To rinse, use warm water and leave to dry.
(Hobbs Parker)

A large Goldscheider terracotta figure, cast from a model by E.Tell, modelled as Loie Fuller dancing with billowing, diaphanous costume, incised signature, 72cm. high. (Christie's) $2,944

A patinated terracotta figure from a model by Horejc, incised signature, 23.5cm. high.
(Christie's) $270

Framed needlework panel depicting house, flowers, birds, animals, fish and insects, carved frame once part of a pole screen, 13 x 16in. overall.
(Eldred's) $605

A fine pair of ladies ivory kid shoes covered with bizarre brocaded silk woven in shades of pink, ivory and pale green, trimmed with metallic threads, circa 1730.
(Bonhams) $3,080

A needlework panel in polychrome, possibly American, late 19th/20th century, churchyard landscape depicting a figure in a window.
(Sotheby's) $460

A good Paisley shawl woven with an intricate design of scrolling foliate sprays and a mihrab decorated central panel, 170 x 86cm. (Bonhams) $616

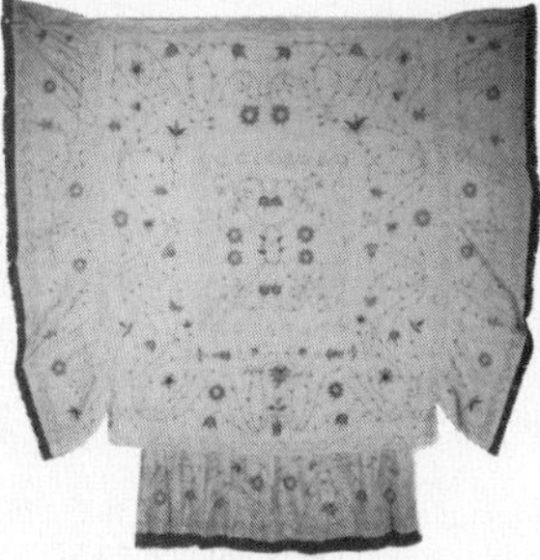

Crewel embroidered coverlet, America, initialled and dated *E.H. 1804*, scrolled flowering vine design on linen ground, 98 x 104in.
(Skinner) $6,900

TOP TIP

Early 19th century Paisley shawls were comprised of a separate patterned border sewn on to a plain square center, but by the 1840s they were woven in one piece. The smaller the plain center, the later the date, but from the 1860s all-over patterns were used. Early shawls were woven and single-sided, while printed examples date from the 1850s onward. The last shawl was woven in 1903.

(Cotswold Auction Co.)

Silk needlework picture, England, 19th century, depicting Jesus as a gardener meeting Mary Magdalene in the garden after the Resurrection, worked in a multi-layered format, 16 x 18¾in.
(Skinner) $575

Political campaign parade apron, America, mid-19th century, *Lincoln and Hamlin* within a flag with thirty-one stars on an irregular patterned field, 1860, above a later addition *Harrison and Morton* in stencilled black letters, 1888, 24¾ x 23⅛in.
(Skinner) $9,200

A Victorian woolwork picture of a young boy, showing a dead rabbit to a woman seated by a tree stump with a small girl, framed, 15½ x 13¾in.
(Dreweatt Neate) $380

An iron thimble, the sides cast with scrollwork, the tip cast with a single flowerhead, Italian, 18th century, 2.2cm.
(Christie's) $1,779

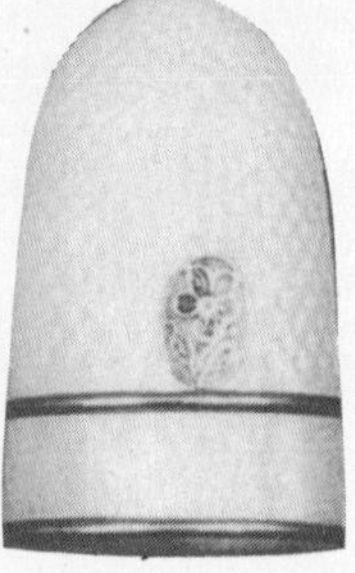

A mother of pearl thimble, with applied oval shield enamelled with a pansy and foliage, French, circa 1820, 2.6cm.
(Christie's) $749

A silver thumb thimble, with plain border, the rim engraved with a geometric design, probably English, early 19th century, 2.5cm.
(Christie's) $487

An iron thimble, cast with zoomorphic scenes within scrollwork above a beadwork rim, Italian, 18th century, 2cm.
(Christie's) $2,05

A silver thimble, the border chased with the legend, *A Stitch In Time Saves Nine*, American, Simons Brothers, early 20th century, 2cm.
(Christie's) $449

A silver-gilt thimble, the tip with applied glazed compartment, and with lift-off cover, Central European, late sixteenth century, 2.3cm.
(Christie's) $1,217

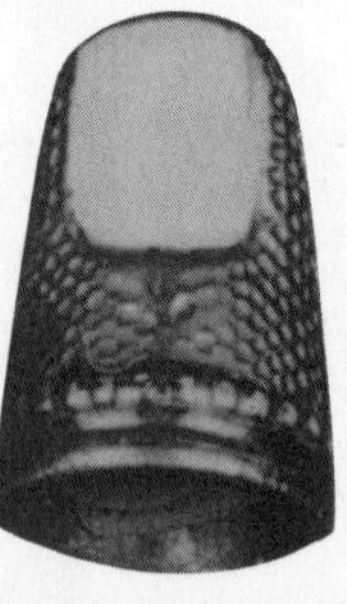

A porcelain thimble, in the form of a finger, painted gilt overall apart from a white fingernail, possibly Meissen, early 19th century, 2.3cm.
(Christie's) $656

A steel thimble, the indentations running down the sides of the thimble, the border with applied pierced and engraved gold frieze, French, early 19th century, 2.5cm.
(Christie's) $1,030

A gold thimble, the plain sides engraved with initials and conjoined hearts within reeding, French duty marks, early 19th century, 3cm.
(Christie's) $898

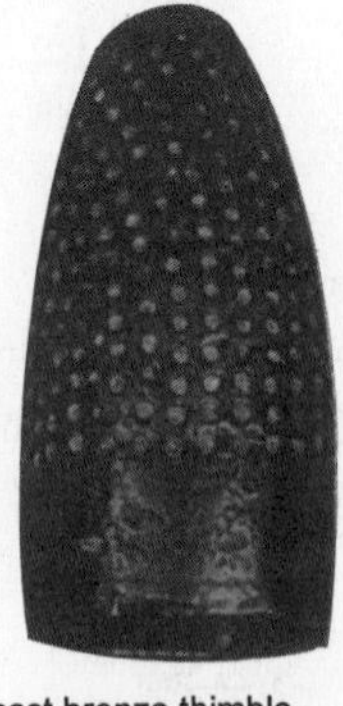

A cast bronze thimble, indentations running the length of the body to a plain border, the tip holed, Hispano-Moresque, circa 13th century, 4.4cm.
(Christie's) $656

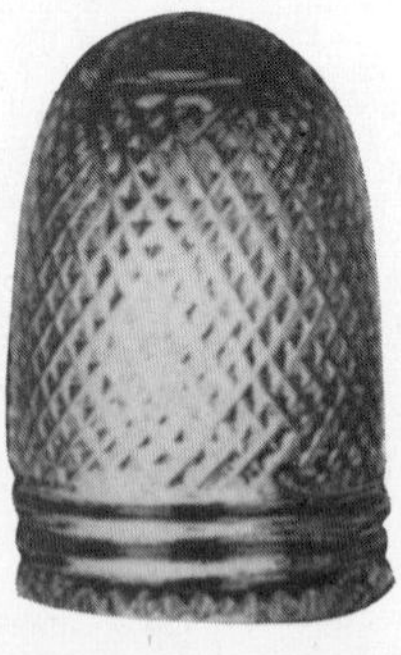

A glass thimble, simulated knurling running down the sides to a ribbed and faceted border, probably English, late 19th century, 2.6cm.
(Christie's) $599

A silver combination thimble and pin cushion, the thimble unscrewing to reveal the pin cushion, English, late 18th/early 19th century, 3.4cm.
(Christie's) $93

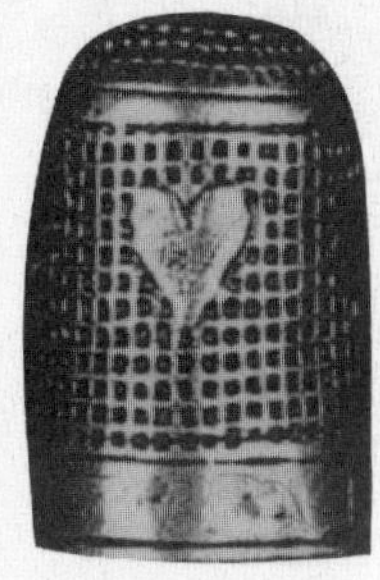

A silver thimble, the sides engraved with two flowerheads and two hearts, English, early 17th century, 2.3cm.
(Christie's) $1,748

A silver thimble, the wide border chased with a scene of a group of girls sewing, French, early 20th century, 2.4cm.
(Christie's) $2,433

A gold thimble, the wide border applied with trailing ivy on a matted ground, English, late 19th century, 2.3cm.
(Christie's) $599

A silver thimble, the sides chased with flowers, foliage and scrollwork, with scalloped rim, Indian, late 19th century 2.5cm.
(Christie's) $244

A gold thimble, the wide border with two applied scrollwork friezes enclosing engine-turning and a vacant cartouche, English, late 19th century, 2.4cm.
(Christie's) $412

An enamel thimble, the sides painted with flowers, foliage and scrollwork on a white ground, English, South Staffordshire, circa 1780, 1.8cm.
(Christie's) $599

A gold thimble, the wide border with applied contrasting color gold foliage and berries on a matted ground, English, mid 19th century, 2.6cm.
(Christie's) $487

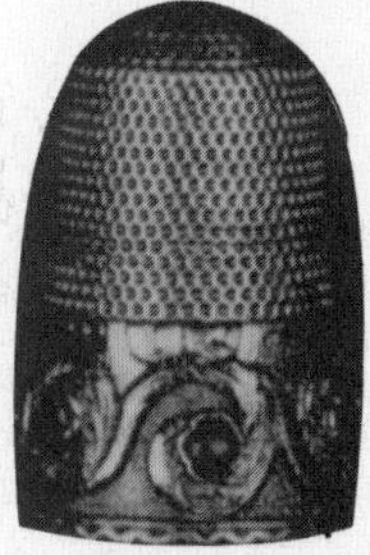

A 15ct gold thimble, the wide border with applied scrollwork on a matted ground and with applied coral beads, probably Birmingham 1885, 2.2cm.
(Christie's) $561

A silver combination thimble and seal, the thimble unscrewing to reveal a clear cut-glass scent bottle and stopper, English, early 19th century 3.5cm.
(Christie's) $1,160

A silver combination thimble and seal, the base engraved with initials and unscrewing to reveal a cut-glass scent bottle and stopper, English, early 19th century, 2.7cm.
(Christie's) $898

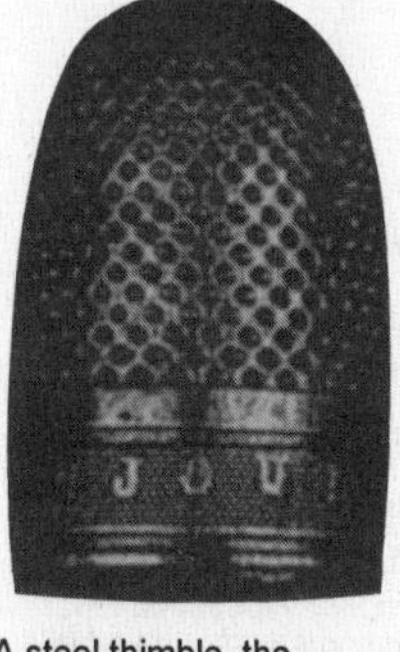

A steel thimble, the indentations extending down the sides, the border cast with the phrase, 'Toujours Fidele' on a matted ground, French, early 19th century.
(Christie's) $936

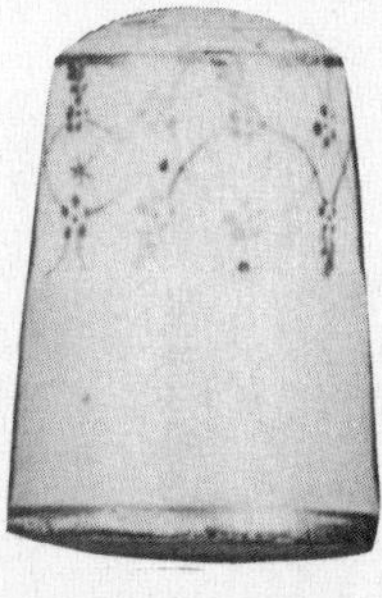

A porcelain thimble, the sides painted with flowerheads and foliage extending down to a wide plain pink border and gilt rim, English, early 19th century, 2.5cm.
(Christie's) $524

A pair of French lacquered tôle-peint trays on later japanned stands, the trays 19th century, the interiors painted with flowers, roses, honeysuckle and berries, 29¼in. wide. (Christie's) $5,451

Painted tin dome top document box, America, 19th century, red, yellow, green fruit and foliage, yellow stylized leaf borders, 9½in. wide. (Skinner) $5,462

Painted tin coffee pot, America, 19th century, gooseneck spout, dome top, yellow birds, red pomegranates, 10½in. high. (Skinner) $1,092

Pair of tôle urns, probably France, 19th century, covered two-handled urns with acorn finials, decorated with floral sprays and birds. (Skinner) $575

Paint decorated tin coffee pot, America, early 19th century, the sides decorated with fruit and leaves in a diamond formation in shades of orange, yellow, and green on a black ground, 10¼in. high. (Skinner) $862

Pair of painted chinoiserie decorated tea bins, marked *Henry Troemner Maker Philad'a Pa.*, mid 19th century, tinned sheet iron rectangular bins with projecting curved fronts, 23½in. high. (Skinner) $3,737

A chinoiserie decorated metal coal box, mid 19th century, the domed cover with twisted rocaille style handle and conforming side handles, the re-decorated red ground with gilded foliate ornament, 21¼in. high. (Christie's) $1,600

A painted and decorated toleware bread basket, signed *D. Fredley*, American, 19th century, black painted interior enclosed by a conforming brown band with red, green, and brown-painted strawberries and foliage, 11½in. wide. (Christie's) $345

Painted tin cylindrical canister, America, 19th century, red cherries, green leaves on a white border, yellow stylized leaves and swag borders, 6in. high. (Skinner) $402

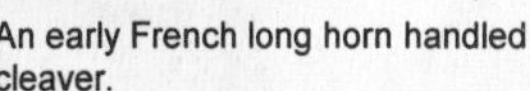

An early French long horn handled cleaver.
(Tool Shop Auctions) $22

A heavy beheading ax head, 10in. blade.
(Tool Shop Auctions) $368

A French cooper's doloire, original handle, some worm.
(Tool Shop Auctions) $224

An important medieval ax, 18in. overall, cutting edge thicker than the main blade, handle in poor condition but conceivably the original. Probably 15/16 century.
(Tool Shop Auctions) $512

A French coachbuilder's side ax.
(Tool Shop Auctions) $192

An early hand forged shipwright's masting ax, 17in. head, 6in. edge.
(Tool Shop Auctions) $288

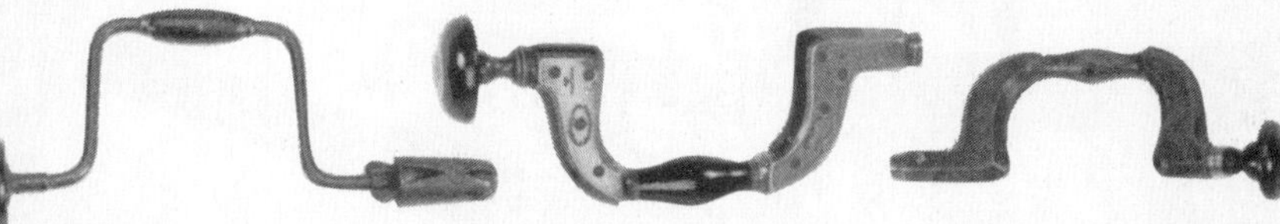

A huge side ax by Robert Sorby, 18in. head with 8in. edge. Unused.
(Tool Shop Auctions) $224

A Pic-cul, Pioche de Vigneron, predominately used in horticulture.
(Tool Shop Auctions) $128

A double bitted ax, *The Kelly Registered Axe No.2289*, hand made. (Tony Murland) $83

BRACES

An early iron brace, spring loaded bit retention device.
(Tool Shop Auctions) $80

A rare ebony Sims type framed brace.
(Tool Shop Auctions) $1,216

A gas fitter's brass brace, early 20th century.
(Charles Tomlinson) $30

A very unusual brace, the chuck closes by tightening a large wing nut behind the chuck which forces the jaws together.
(Tool Shop Auctions) $128

A brass framed ebony Ultimatum brace by William Marples, original condition, some factory lacquer remaining.
(Tool Shop Auctions) $440

A rare beech ladies' brace by J. Buck. These braces were historically used by pianoforte manufacturers.
(Tool Shop Auctions) $160

An elaborate 18th century cage head brace with forged twisted cage bars.
(Tool Shop Auctions) $344

A brass framed Ultimatum brace with rosewood infill and head.
(Tool Shop Auctions) $696

A Horton gunmetal and rosewood brace, No. 2528, registered Nov. 8th 1850.
(Tool Shop Auctions) $640

A French copper glue pot, 4in. diameter.
(Tool Shop Auctions) $147

An early copper glue pot with dovetail jointing, late 18th/early 19th century.
(Charles Tomlinson) $120

A lovely Victorian copper oil can with brass top, punch decorated with a floral array.
(Tool Shop Auctions) $284

EEL SPEARS

A 3 prong eel gleave.
(Tool Shop Auctions) $192

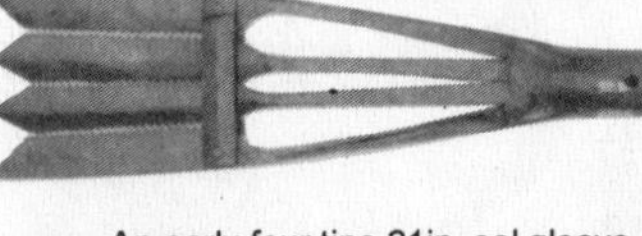

An early four tine 21in. eel gleave.
(Tool Shop Auctions) $96

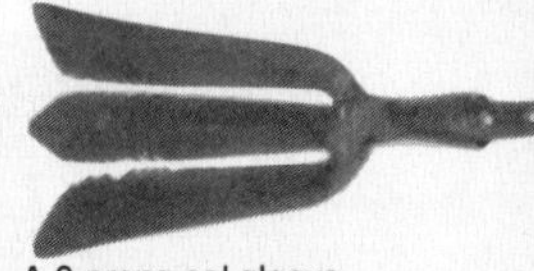

A 3 prong eel gleave.
(Tool Shop Auctions) $136

A 5 prong eel gleave.
(Tool Shop Auctions) $144

A 15in. four tine eel gleave.
(Tool Shop Auctions) $96

A 5 prong eel gleave.
(Tool Shop Auctions) $160

HAMMERS

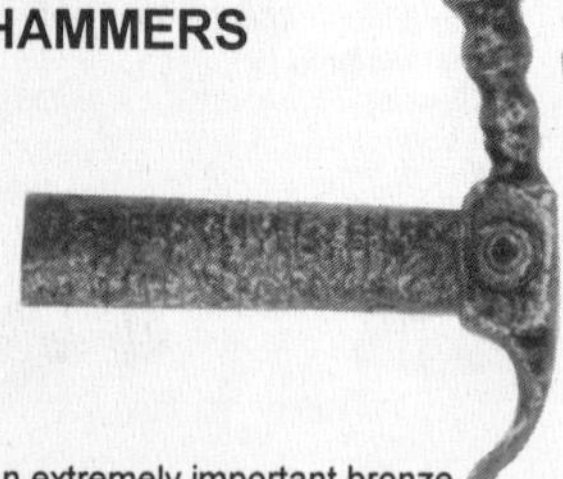

An extremely important bronze hammer head, 2 x 1¾in. displaying ornate decoration. Excavated near Thetford, Norfolk, probably Roman.
(Tool Shop Auctions) $400

A combination hammer, file, knife, awl and spike, made in Germany.
(Tool Shop Auctions) $72

A clever ash handled combined hammer and pliers, the pliers activated by pulling a knob on the bottom of the handle.
(Tool Shop Auctions) $163

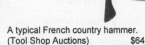

A Coopers' hammer by Sorby.
(Tool Shop Auctions) $52

A typical French country hammer.
(Tool Shop Auctions) $64

A rare hammer adze by Brades.
(Tool Shop Auctions) $96

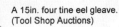

A 28½in. Norris A1 jointer plane, dovetailed body and rosewood infill. These planes were only available as a special order from the Factory. (Tool Shop Auctions) $6,112

A 16in. embossed iron panel plane, extremely attractive casting and infill with Masonic pierced lever cap. (Tool Shop Auctions) $419

A dovetailed Norris A7 shoulder plane with rosewood infill, early 20th century. (Charles Tomlinson) $900

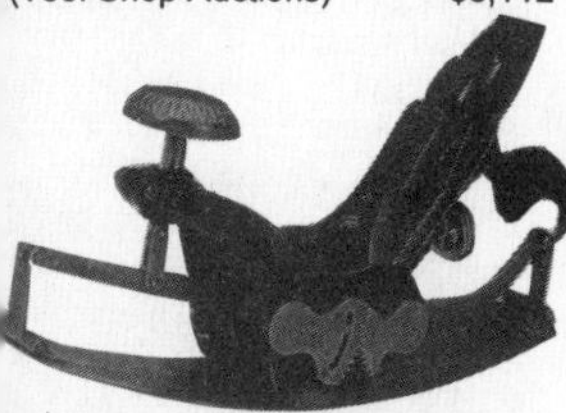

A Stanley No. 113 ship's plane of all metal construction, for planing convex or concave surfaces, circa 1890. (Auction Team Köln) $99

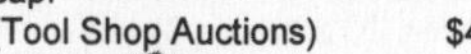

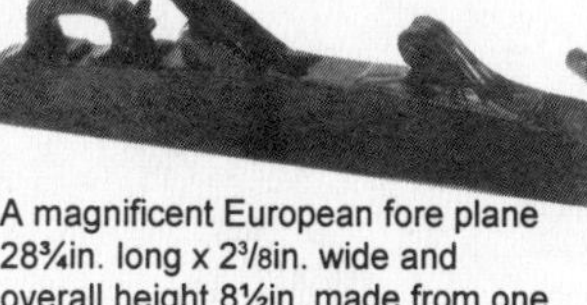

A magnificent European fore plane 28¾in. long x 2³/8in. wide and overall height 8½in. made from one piece of Quercus ilex and with a bold magnificent carving on the front of the handle of a sea serpent surrounded by waves, dated *1780.* (Tool Shop Auctions) $6,240

A beech sash fillister by Greenslade with brass screwstems and rosewood locking nut. (Tool Shop Auctions) $1,120

A massively important 4 iron complex molding plane by Macguire & Jago, Glasgow, possibly the first 4 iron molding plane with this configuration of wedges and cutters. (Tool Shop Auctions) $1,216

An 8⁵/8in. dovetailed Norris smoothing plane with rosewood infill and closed handle, dovetailed steel with *steel* stamped on the toe, apparently yet another unrecorded model from this quality tool company. (Tool Shop Auctions) $800

An extra wide beech sash fillister by King & Company, Hull, with the unique feature of an adjustable fence, with two brass screws on the side of the body, maybe a prototype. (Tool Shop Auctions) $368

SAWS

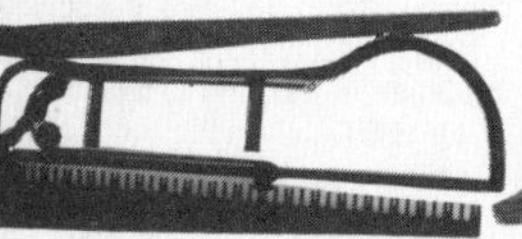

A most unusual, forester's spring loaded folding one man tree felling saw, late 19th century. (Charles Tomlinson) $225

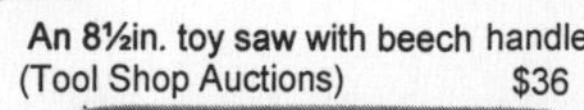

An 8½in. toy saw with beech handle. (Tool Shop Auctions) $36

A heavy brass craftsman made hacksaw of considerable early appearance. (Tool Shop Auctions) $66

A typical 17th century European surgeon's saw with original horn handle, 17in. overall, nicely decorated ironwork. (Tool Shop Auctions) $816

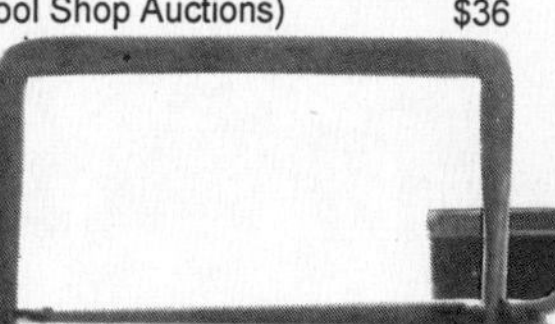

An early iron chairmaker's saw with ram's horn wing nut, late 18th century/early 19th century. (Tool Shop Auctions) $188

A rare 18th century/early 19th century brass backed saw, 18in. blade, by Ibbotson, Sheffield, saws from this early period have only two screws, the third screw in this example is a later addition. (Tool Shop Auctions) $225

A Schuco red tinplate clockwork 'Texi' toy, the driver with fabric clothing, turns round when reversing, post 1960.
(Auction Team Köln) $736

A large lithographed tinplate toy horse-drawn 'Ice' caravan,by the Morton E. Converse Co., Winchendon MA. , 45cm. long, circa 1913.
(Auction Team Köln) $236

A TippCo motorcycle and sidecar, lithographed tinplate clockwork toy labelled *Made in US Zone, Germany*, 19cm. long, post 1945,
(Auction Team Köln) $602

A rare blue Chrysler Imperial Le Baron tinplate push-and-go toy by the Asahi Toy Co., Japan, in original box, 1962, 39cm. long.
(Auction Team Köln) $10,141

A Dean's Rag plush Mickey Mouse, with fully articulated wired limbs, felt and leather hands, ears and shoes, stitched eyes, 21cm. high, 1933.
(Auction Team Köln) $459

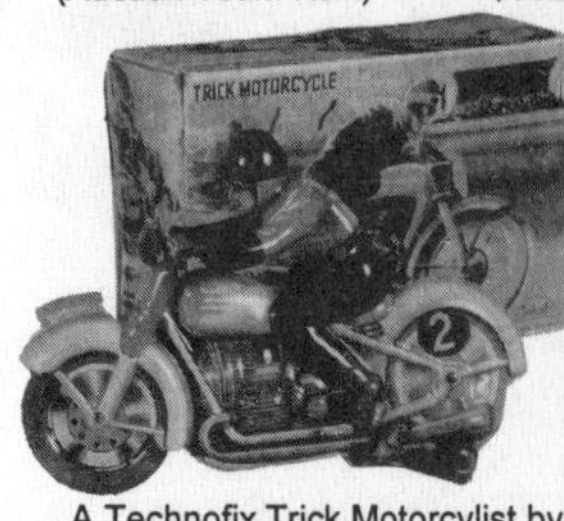

A Technofix Trick Motorcylist by Gebr. Einfalt, Nürnberg, lithographed tinplate clockwork toy, 18cm. long, 1950.
(Auction Team Köln) $569

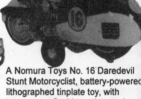

An Arnold Mac 700 lithographed tinplate motorcyclist by Karl Arnold, Nürnberg, early black version without sidecar, 20cm. long, 1948.
(Auction Team Köln) $1,071

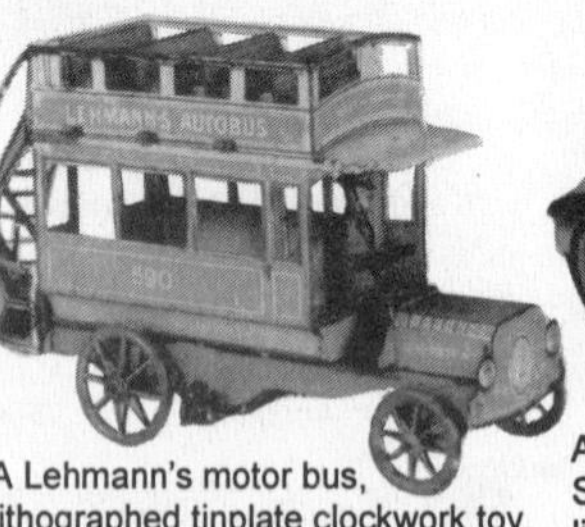

A Lehmann's motor bus, lithographed tinplate clockwork toy, red with yellow stairs and gray roof, post 1907.
(Auction Team Köln) $1,875

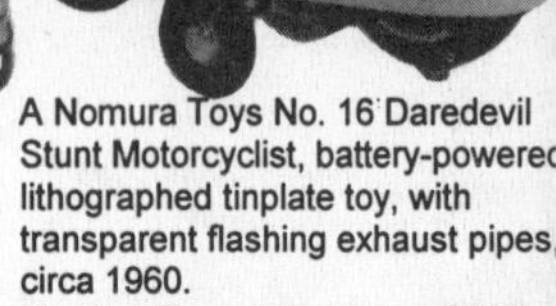

A Nomura Toys No. 16 Daredevil Stunt Motorcyclist, battery-powered lithographed tinplate toy, with transparent flashing exhaust pipes, circa 1960.
(Auction Team Köln) $557

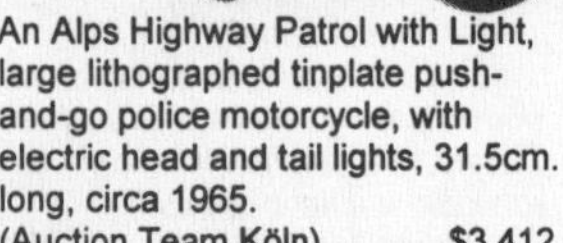

An Alps Highway Patrol with Light, large lithographed tinplate push-and-go police motorcycle, with electric head and tail lights, 31.5cm. long, circa 1965.
(Auction Team Köln) $3,412

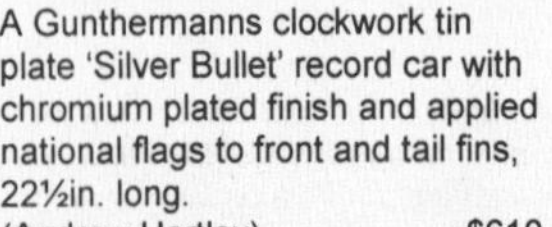

A Gunthermanns clockwork tin plate 'Silver Bullet' record car with chromium plated finish and applied national flags to front and tail fins, 22½in. long.
(Andrew Hartley) $610

A lithographed tinplate Auto Scooter by Hoch & Beckmann, with plastic steering wheel and paste driver, 12cm. long, circa 1955.
(Auction Team Köln) $113

A unique French Delaunay-Belleville model car by Jouets Français, with clockwork motor, and turning front axle, hand-made and painted, 28.5cm. circa 1910.
(Auction Team Köln) $5,493

A CKO lithographed tinplate clockwork fire engine by Georg Kellermann, the bonnet functioning as an alarm bell, 16cm. long, circa 1950.
(Auction Team Köln) $160

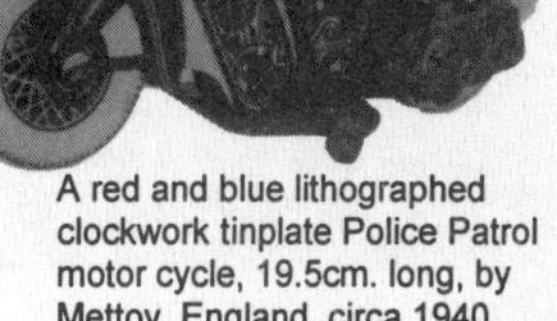

A red and blue lithographed clockwork tinplate Police Patrol motor cycle, 19.5cm. long, by Mettoy, England, circa 1940.
(Auction Team Köln) $262

A lithographed clockwork tinplate motor coach by Lehmann, Brandenburg, with hand painted driver, 13cm. long, after 1897.
(Auction Team Köln) $983

A Dinky No. 4 Racing Cars gift set, in original box, base dated *9.53.*
(Christie's) $736

A Technofix lithographed tinplate clockwork bulldozer, with forward and reverse action and moving shovel, 19cm. long, 1957.
(Auction Team Köln) $234

Boby the Tricycling Monkey, by Karl Arnold, Nürnberg, lithographed tinplate clockwork toy, 10cm. high, blue and white US Zone edition, circa 1950.
(Auction Team Köln) $160

A black- and grey-painted child's rocking horse, New England, 19th century, gazing forward with peaked ears, the padded seat below on carved legs and shaped rockers. (Sotheby's) $1,610

A Schuco Motodrill Clown, lithographed tinplate clockwork toy, rider with felt clothing and plush hair, post 1952.
(Auction Team Köln) $669

A very rare and unusual Tipp & Co. No. 696 lithographed tinplate clockwork motorcycle and sidecar, with adjustable steering, 31cm. long, circa 1935. (Auction Team Köln) $15,747

A Steiff wild boar, with ginger and cream mohair with airbrushed features, brown and black glass eyes, 22in. long, 1950s.
(Christie's) $339

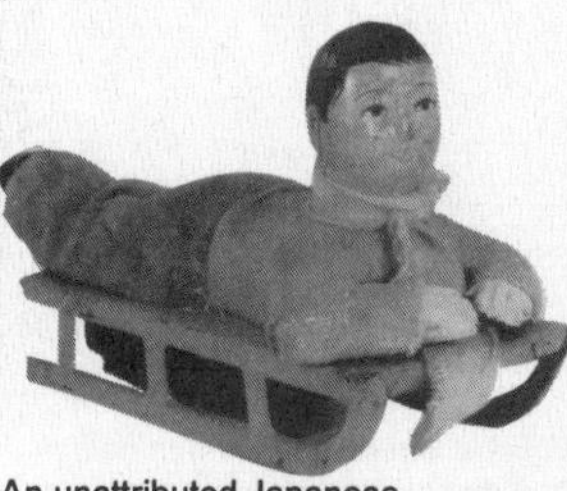

An unattributed Japanese clockwork sledger toy, lithographed face and hair, plush clothing, 16.5cm. long, circa 1940.
(Auction Team Köln) $200

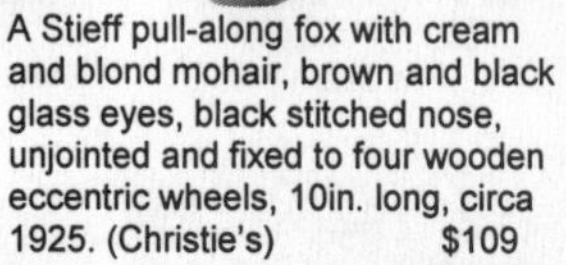

A scarce Dinky Toys Farmyard Animals No. 2, comprising 2 standing cows, 2 standing horses, a standing sheep and similar pink pig, on original card in original 2 part green covered box.
(Wallis & Wallis) $220

A Stieff pull-along fox with cream and blond mohair, brown and black glass eyes, black stitched nose, unjointed and fixed to four wooden eccentric wheels, 10in. long, circa 1925. (Christie's) $109

A large Steiff bear 'ride-on' toy with dark brown mohair, large brown and black glass eyes, steering handle to back, pull-cord growler to back, standing on metal wheeled frame, 32in. long,1930s.
(Christie's) $817

An exhibition standard 1/16 scale 3½in. gauge electric model of the Glasgow Corporation Tramways Car No.472 built by D. Orchard with glazed upper and lower saloons with full interior seating and furniture detailing, 12½ x 21½in.
(Christie's) $6,360

A 1950s Palitoy ventriloquist doll, Peter Brough's Archie Andrews, approximately 15in. tall, light blue felt jacket, plastic head with black hair and opening mouth, in original box, with instruction sheet.
(Wallis & Wallis) $110

A Meccano No1. Aero constructor set, comprising full set of silver finished parts for 6 models shown on instruction sheets, some taping and dissected; in original box.
(Wallis & Wallis) $235

Steiff lion on wheels with golden mohair, white mohair mane, pink stitched nose, pull-cord growl, standing on four spoked wheeled metal frame, 29in. tall, circa 1920.
(Christie's) $327

A rare Dean's Rag Book, Flip The Frog, red, yellow and blue velvet covered, with plastic loose pupil eyes backed with pink felt, cotton bow tie, 8in. tall, circa 1930.
(Christie's) $2,152

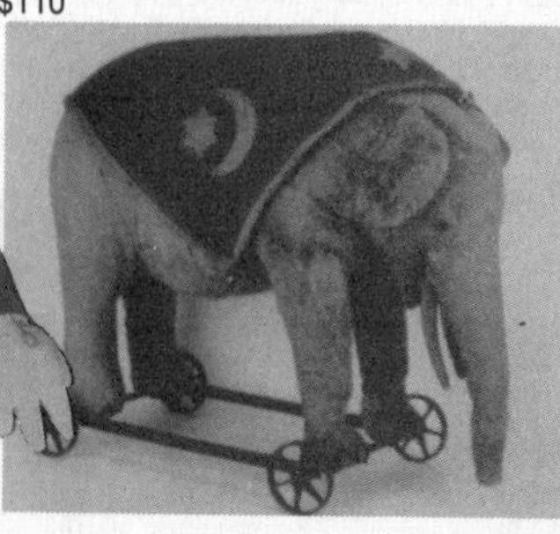

A Steiff elephant on wheels with black boot button eyes, white felt tusks standing on metal wheeled frame, 22in. long, circa 1910.
(Christie's) $581

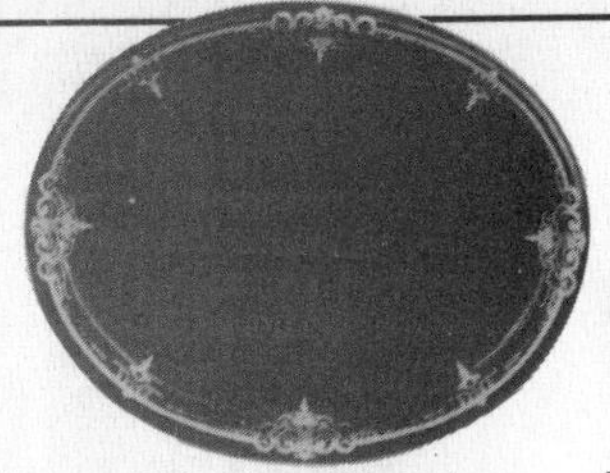

Jennens & Bettridge 19th century oval papier-mâché tray, the border gilded with stylized geometric design, on a burr walnut effect ground, 19th century, 24in.
(G A Key) $640

A Robert 'Mouseman' Thompson oak cheese platter, elliptical form with handle, carved in relief with mouse motif, 37cm. wide.
(Christie's) $862

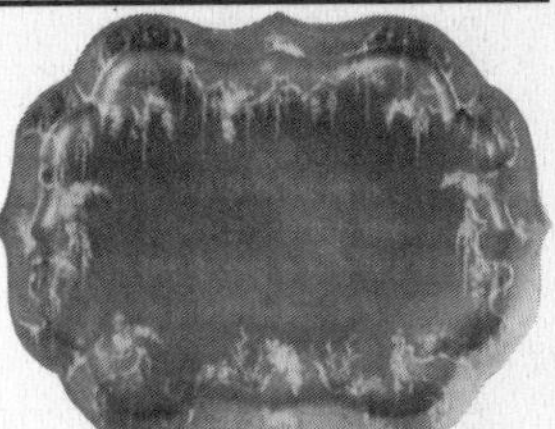

A Victorian green lacquered tray, the shaped surround to a stylized painted centre in a surround of apple blossom and gilt pendants, 32in. wide.
(Boardmans) $902

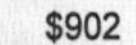

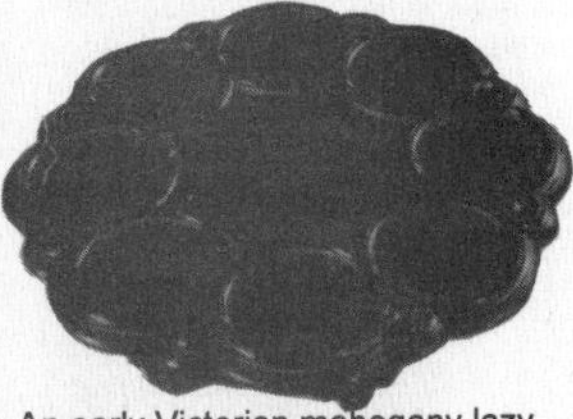

An early Victorian mahogany lazy susan, attributed to William Harrison, the lobed circular top with eight molded circular recesses separated by spandrels, 23¾in. diameter. (Christie's) $4,629

An early 19th century mahogany 'Lazy Susan', the circular edge carved in relief with fruiting vine, the top revolving on step turned circular foot, 24in.
(Dreweatt Neate) $745

A Regency tôleware oval tray with gilt leafage decoration on a red ground, around a central painting of a classical landscape, 30in. wide.
(G.A. Key) $1,431

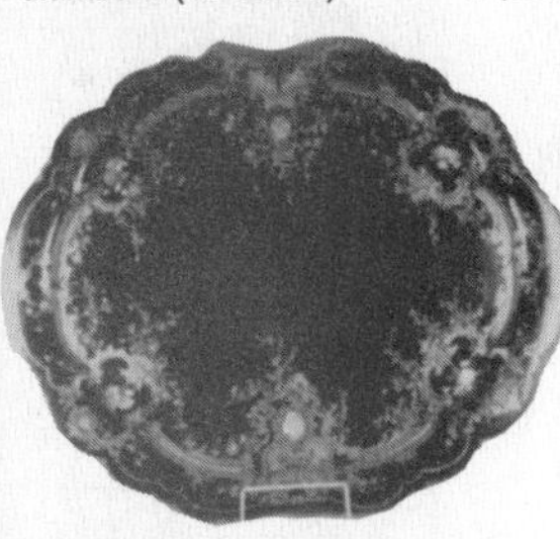

A Victorian 'Jennings & Bettridge' papier mâché tray, 79cm.
(Bonhams) $1,101

A fine Chippendale figured mahogany piecrust serving tray, American or English, circa 1780, with a shaped circular top and moulded edge, 19in. diameter.
(Sotheby's) $18,400

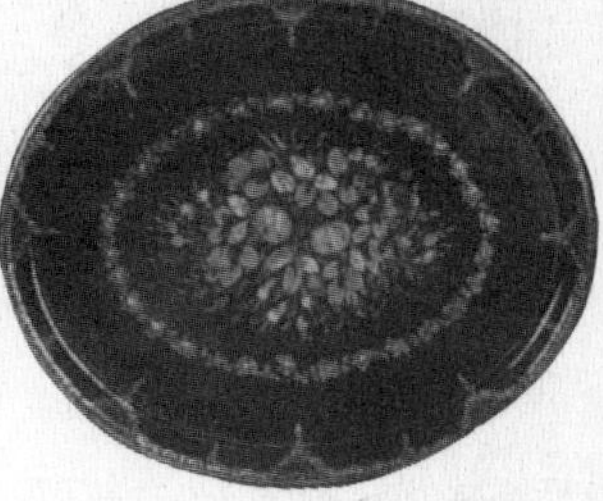

A Victorian black papier mâché oval tray, mother of pearl inlaid, gilt and painted with oval of fruit and flowers, 75cm. wide.
(Bristol) $593

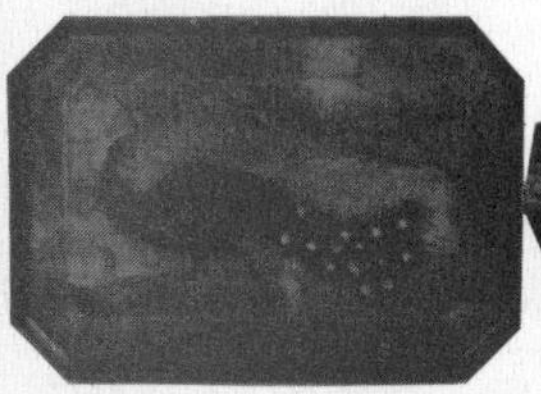

A late 19th century Aesthetic style tray, inlaid with a peacock cartouche, 60cm. wide.
(Bonhams) $284

Carved and inlaid walnut cutlery tray, America, mid-19th century, centre divider carved in a patriotic motif with eagle heads at the handle, 13in. long.
(Skinner) $2,530

19th century rectangular tray, gilded with birds amidst foliage and butterflies etc., on a black ground, 24in. (G A Key) $800

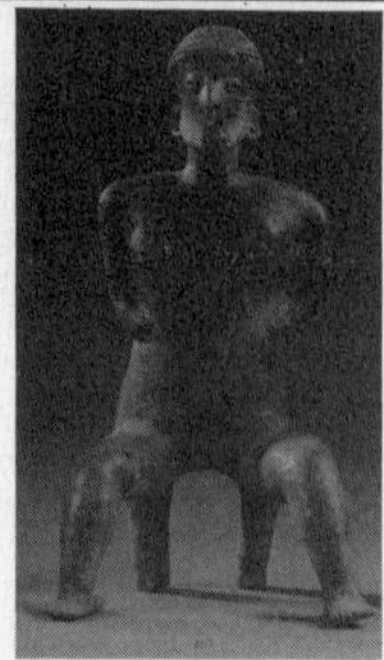

A Nayarit seated female pottery figure, San Sebastian-style, West Mexico, modelled with typical deformed 'guitar-shaped' head, 53cm. high.
(Bonhams) $3,454

Pair of seated male and female figures (Nigeria, West Africa), constructed from carved hardwood, probably used to ensure good harvest/guard crops from pests, 24in. (G.A. Key) $230

A Maori model war canoe stern, taurapa, New Zealand, elaborately carved with a seated figure wearing moko tattoos, 35cm. high.
(Bonhams) $6,594

A Kuba helmet mask, bwoom, Democratic Republic of Congo, the almond eyes pierced around the perimeter, above flat sloping cheeks painted with cream stripes, 46cm. high.
(Bonhams) $1,570

A Colima standing dog, West Mexican Highlands, of strong youthful proportions, the upraised head with openwork growl, distended abdomen, 36cm. long.
(Bonhams) $3,768

An Nguni Colonial figure, South Africa, of a man with circular ears and concentric circular eyes, standing holding a briar pipe and tobacco box (?), 26cm. high.
(Bonhams) $659

A fine Koryak Eskimo hide cap, Kamchatka, of domed form with earl panels, embroidered with bands of white, blue and black Russian trade beads, probably 19th century, 28cm. high.
(Bonhams) $1,884

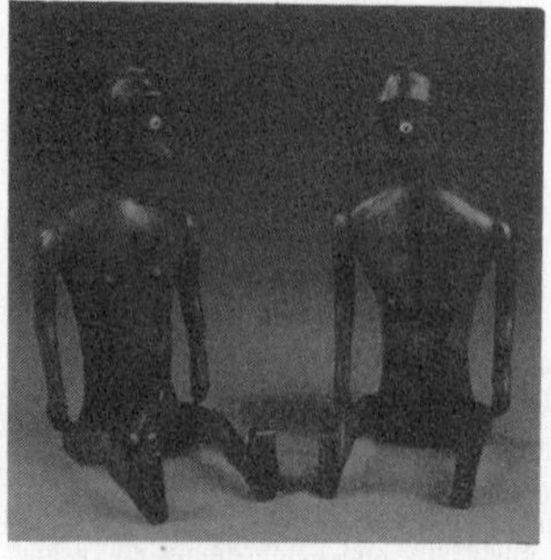

A pair of Batak funerery puppets, Sumatra, the male and female with articulated limbs and necks, bone inlaid eyes, animal hair tufts, 37cm. high. (Bonhams) $550

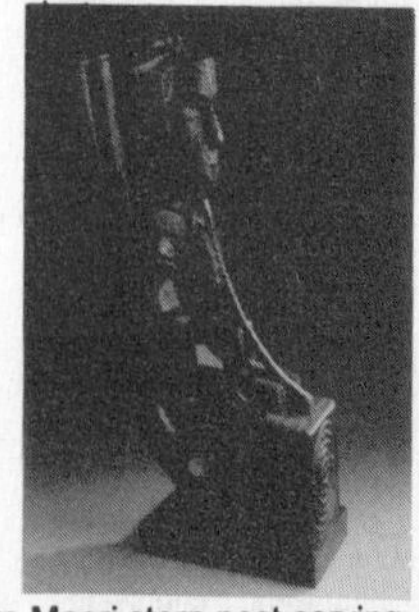

A rare Maori stern post carving taurapa, East Coast, North Island, New Zealand, pierced and carved with a large crouching figure grasping its chest with both three-fingered hands, probably early to middle 19th century, 89cm. high.
(Bonhams) $23,550

An Aboriginal bark painting, Groote Eylandt, North Australia, painted in natural yellow, red ocher and white pigments on a black manganese ground, with a scene of human figures with weapons, 56 x 43cm. (Bonhams) $706

A Tridacna and tortoiseshell kapkap, New Ireland or Solomon Islands, the circular white clam shell disc pierced through the center and tied to a smaller thin filigree tortoiseshell shell disk with fibre cord, 13cm. diameter. (Bonhams) $628

An Aboriginal bark painting, Groote Eylandt, North Australia, painted in typical pigment on a manganese ground, with a central circle containing the morning star, fish, reptiles and plants, 52 x 58cm. (Bonhams) $1,099

A Ngbaka mask, Northwest Democratic Republic of the Congo, the pigmented heart-shaped face with straight nose and pierced nostrils, pierced almond eyes, open mouth and wood teeth, 23cm. high. (Bonhams) $440

A fishing box, Tokelau, Micronesia, of slightly tapering cylindrical form, with serrated base, square lug handles to the sides, 27cm. high. (Bonhams) $1,884

A Yoruba Ifa drum, Ijebu area, possibly Ijebu-Igbo, Nigeria, of slightly tapered cylindrical form, carved in shallow relief with a stylized figure holding its two fish tails in each hand, 71cm. high. (Christie's) $942

A Quimbaya seated figural vessel, Western Colombia, the round head with narrow slit bean eyes and mouth, pierced ears, traces of orange and cream paint, 24cm. high. (Bonhams) $550

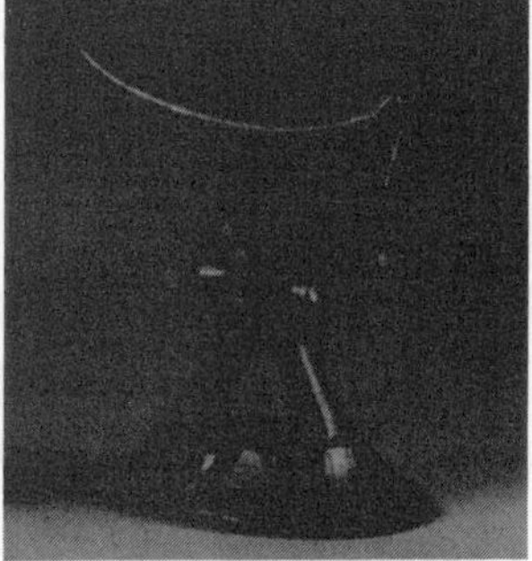

A Shona neckrest, mutsago, Southern Zimbabwe, conceived as a highly abstract female form, the oval base with sloping sides and triangular pubic bosses, beneath an X-form frame, 13.5cm. (Bonhams) $1,492

A Tairona blackware figural vessel, Northern Colombia, modelled as a seated male, with hands held to the cheeks, circular open mouth, 21.5cm. high. (Bonhams) $283

An unusual American Burnett typewriter with sloping typebasket, only seven models known, lacking front cover and ribbons, 1907.
(Auction Team Köln) $7,546

An early model of the decorative American Odell's pointer typewriter, unrestored, circa 1890.
(Auction Team Köln) $924

An American Monarch Pioneer portable typewriter with upright typebars as with the Remington Portable, 1932.
(Auction Team Köln) $98

An American Pittsburgh Visible No.10 typebar machine, solving the problem of visible type by total removal of the keyboard and all typebars by means of two levers, 1902. (Auction Team Köln)
$1,717

A German Liliput Model Duplex German index machine by Justin Bamberger, Munich, black, on cast base, with original tin cover, 1907.
(Auction Team Köln) $5,943

An American Hammond Multiplex type shuttle machine with straight Universal keyboard, in elegant leather case with green velvet lining, 1913.
(Auction Team Köln) $360

An red Mignon Model 2 from an early production run of the first German pointer typewriter by AEG, 1904.
(Auction Team Köln) $990

A Smith Premier No. 1, the decorative first model of the American understrike machine with full keyboard, spare keys on both sides and integral type cleaning brush, with tin cover, 1889.
(Auction Team Köln) $590

A Yost No. 1, the first model of the early American understrike machine with the 'Grasshopper' typebar mechanism and remarkable inkpad printing, 1887.
(Auction Team Köln) $426

The Fox, an American understrike machine with swivel carriage, with tin cover, 1902.
(Auction Team Köln) $787

A British Imperial Model B three-row typebar machine with round keyboard and dual shift keys, 1914.
(Auction Team Köln) $360

A Mignon Model 2 British export version of the German pointer typewriter, with Electric Company Ltd., London decal, 1905.
(Auction Team Köln) $301

An American Bar-Lock No. 6 type bar machine with full keyboard and stamped sheet copper basket front, 1894. (Auction Team Köln) $1,849

An Edison Mimeograph Typewriter No. 1, an upstrike machine for use with the Edison Mimeograph wax plate copier. Only very few were produced, 1894.
(Auction Team Köln) $13,398

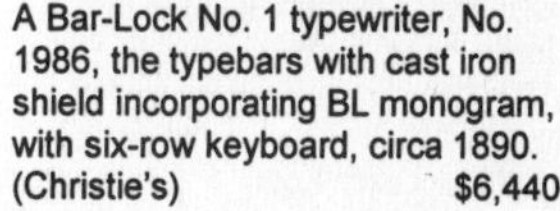

A Bar-Lock No. 1 typewriter, No. 1986, the typebars with cast iron shield incorporating BL monogram, with six-row keyboard, circa 1890.
(Christie's) $6,440

A rare edition of the Draper American type cylinder machine with unusual ribbon layout and backward hammer strike, 1898.
(Auction Team Köln) $1,574

A Swiss Hermes 2000 4-row portable typewriter by Paillard & Cie., Yverdon, with mottled gold housing and original box, Hebrew type, circa 1958.
(Auction Team Köln) $466

A black Imperial Model D British three row portable typewriter with high type basket and straight Universal keyboard, 1919.
(Auction Team Köln) $396

A Yost No. 4 American full keyboard upstrike typewriter in original condition, 1895.
(Auction Team Köln) $669

The Fox, an American front strike machine with swivel cylinder, 1906.
(Auction Team Köln) $459

A very rare edition of the Densmore No. 4 American understrike machine, incomplete, 1898.
(Auction Team Köln) $360

The Daugherty Visible, an American typebar machine, the whole typebar arrangement interchangeable by means of two levers, 1890.
(Auction Team Köln) $2,034

The first mass produced typewriter, the Malling Hansen Writing Ball, developed in Denmark by Pastor R.A. Malling Hansen in 1867, only thirty now known worldwide.
(Auction Team Köln) $59,431

A Smith Premier No. 2, the second model of the American understrike machine with full keyboard and integral type cleaning brush, with metal cover, 1895.
(Auction Team Köln) $459

A Pittsburgh Standard No. 11 American typebar machine with really visible type, 1908.
(Auction Team Köln) $622

A Remington Standard No. 6 American understrike machine with shift keys and wooden typebar posts, 1894.
(Auction Team Köln) $426

A Remington Monarch No. 3 4-row American front strike machine, 1906.
(Auction Team Köln) $217

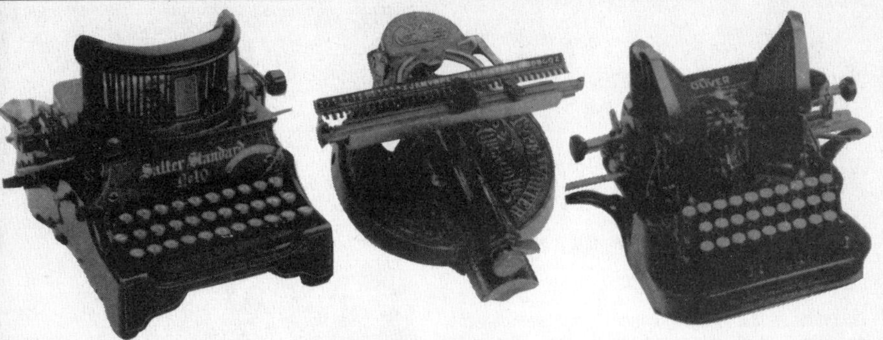

The Salter Standard No. 10 3-row overstrike typebar machine, British, 1908.
(Auction Team Köln) $788

An Odell No. 4 decorative American pointer typewriter by Farquhar & Albrecht, Chicago, 1889.
(Auction Team Köln) $1,050

An Oliver No. 5 American typebar machine, with tin cover, 1906.
(Auction Team Köln) $459

A very rare Williams No. 1 round typewriter with curved 3-row keyboard and 'Grasshopper' typebar mechanism, American, 1891.
(Auction Team Köln) $6,561

A German Frister & Rossmann understrike machine with so-called 'Berlin restboard', 1900.
(Auction Team Köln) $936

A Remington No. 5, an unusual version of this American upstrike machine with carriage return and wooden shift, 1888.
(Auction Team Köln) $602

A Nova three-row American type-bar machine with special ribbon color, lacking carriage return, 1901.
(Auction Team Köln) $320

A Postal Model 5, a rare version of the American typewheel machine, circa 1905.
(Auction Team Köln) $1,312

A Hammond No. 2 American type shuttle machine with Ideal keyboard and back hammer strike, with wooden cover, 1893.
(Auction Team Köln) $426

A molded and gilded copper fox weathervane, American, third quarter 19th century, fullbodied, molded zinc figure of a leaping fox, 23¼in. long. (Sotheby's) $9,200

Leaping stag with bush gilt-molded copper weathervane, attributed to Harris & Co. Boston, late 19th century, on a cast iron stand with cardinals, 29½in. long. (Skinner) $16,100

A molded copper horse and jockey weathervane, American, third quarter, 19th century, the full bodied stylized figure of a jockey astride a galloping horse, 32½in. wide. (Sotheby's) $5,750

Gilt molded copper cow weather vane, attributed to Harris & Co., Boston, late 19th century, with weathered gilt verdigris surface, 33in. long. (Skinner) $23,000

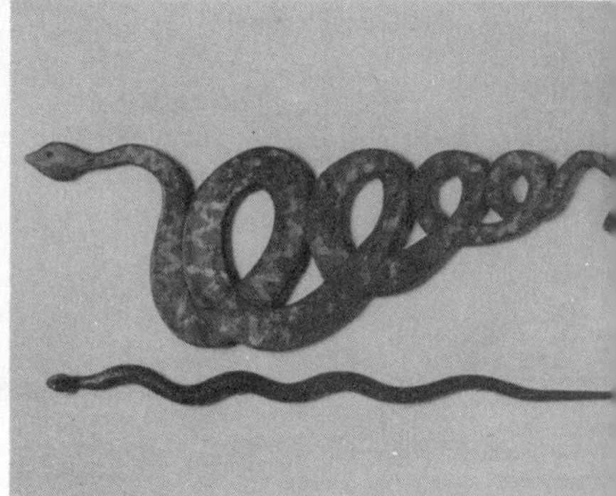

An unusual carved and painted rattlesnake weathervane, American, late 19th century, carved from a single thickness of pine in the form of a curled serpent painted red with yellow markings. (Christie's) $6,612

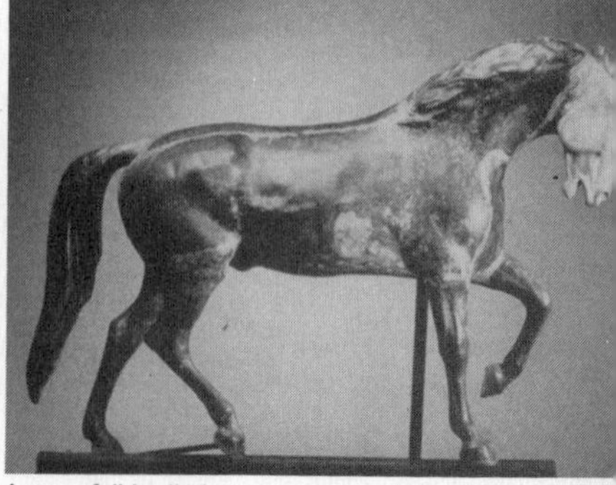

Large full-bodied copper and zinc horse weather vane, America, late 19th century, copper body and cast zinc head, identified as 'Washington' and probably by J.W. Fiske, 33in. long. (Skinner) $6,900

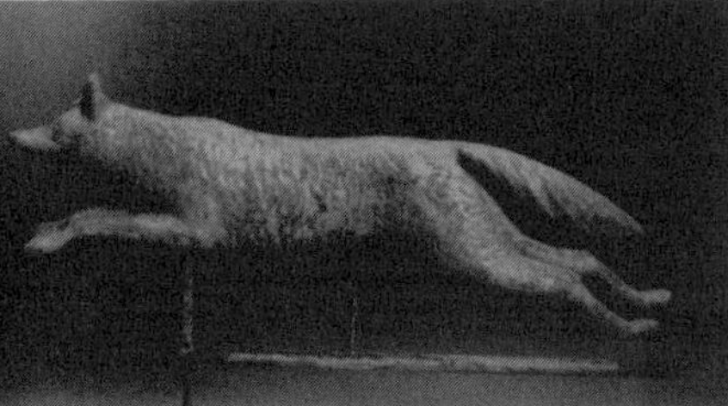

Copper running fox weathervane, L.W. Cushing & Sons, Waltham, Massachusetts, circa 1883, traces of gilding, 22in. long.
(Skinner) $5,750

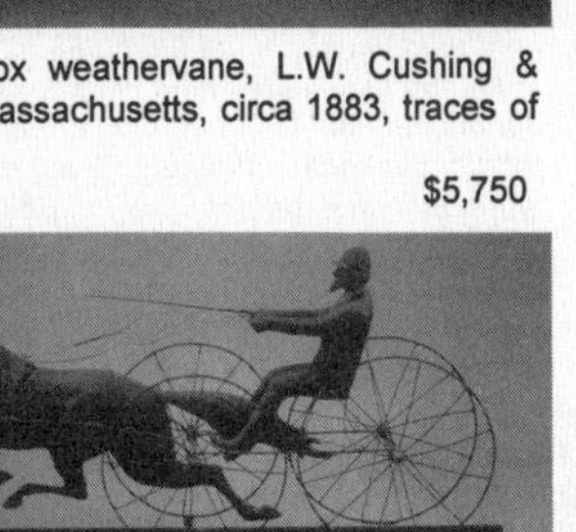

Four wheeled sulky and driver molded copper weathervane, attributed to J.W. Fiske, Boston, late 19th century, mounted on a wooden base, 50in. long.
(Skinner) $17,250

A painted sheet iron flying horse weathervane, American, late 19th/early 20th century, the silhouetted figure of a galloping horse painted black and red, 43in. long. (Christie's) $2,587

Copper Dexter with jockey weather vane, Cushing & White, Waltham, Massachusetts, circa 1868-72, copper horse and rider with cast zinc heads, 28in. long. (Skinner) $10,350

Figural hunter sheet iron weathervane, America, late 19th/early 20th century, depicting a black painted silhouette of a hunter taking aim, 25in. long.
(Skinner) $1,265

A wrought iron weather vane, 19th century, modelled as a twin masted ship, with pole bracket, 19¼in. wide.
(Christie's) $1,463

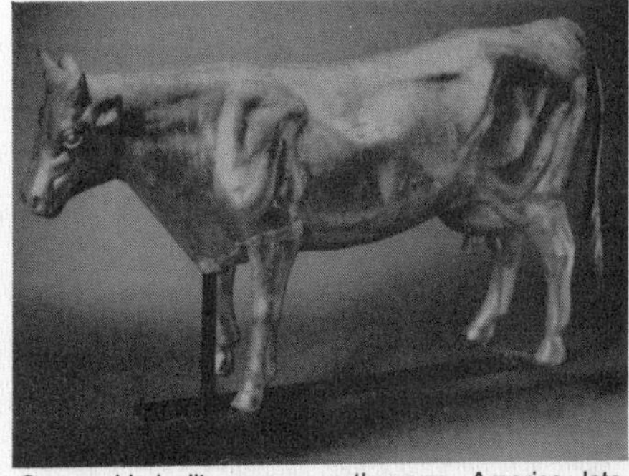

Cow molded gilt copper weathervane, America, late 19th century, traces of verdigris, 28in. long.
(Skinner) $2,185

A horse and sulky molded copper and zinc weathervane, American, third quarter 19th century, the swell-bodied figure of a running horse hitched to a sulky with driver, 35in. long.
(Sotheby's) $11,500

Black Hawk copper molded weathervane, America, late 19th century, 18½in. high, 33in. long.
(Skinner) $6,555

A molded and gilded copper sheep weathervane, American, third quarter, 19th century, the swell-bodied figure of a standing sheep with repoussé fur and sheet metal ears, 18in. long.
(Sotheby's) $3,450

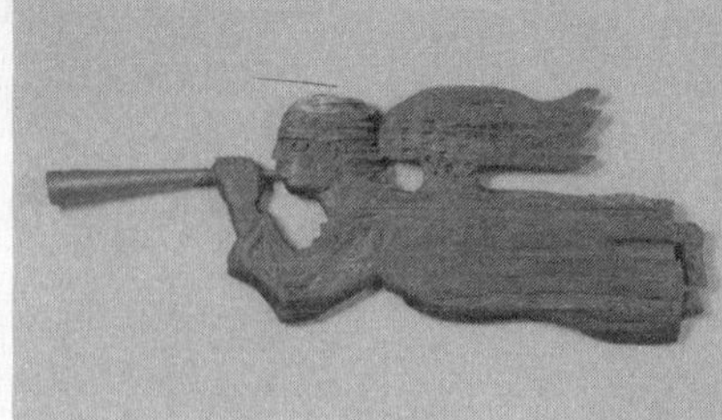

A carved and gilded pine Angel Gabriel weathervane, American, late 19th century, the figure carved from a single thickness of pine, fitted with a sheet metal trumpet covered in new gilding, 45¼in. long.
(Christie's) $4,600

A fine leaping horse weathervane, A.L. Jewell and Co., Waltham, Massachusetts, third quarter, 19th century, the swell bodied figure with forelegs tucked and rear legs extended, 39in. long.
(Sotheby's) $40,250

A molded copper and zinc running horse weathervane, American, third quarter 19th century, the full bodied figure of a running horse with a molded cast zinc head, 42in. long.
(Sotheby's) $9,775

Glen Nevis – Early 20th century, John M Scott & Co., Leith. Clear glass bottle, driven cork, slightly shrinking at base, lacking capsule.
(Christie's) $846

Laphroaig – Circa 1940, distilled and bottled by D Johnston & Co., Laphroaig Distillery, Islay. Green colored glass bottle, single malt.
(Christie's) $2,930

The Clan Campbell – Late 19th century, Blended by John M. Scott & Co., Leith & London. Clear glass bottle, short driven cork, lacking capsule.
(Christie's) $684

Royal Dukennet, Special Scotch Whisky. Special Purveyors To H.H. The Duke of Teck Jamie & Co, London. Stopper cork, lead capsule.
(Christie's) $488

Calleyvat – 7 year old – Early 20th century, bottled by W. Glendinning & Sons Ltd., 9 Granger Street, Newcastle-On-Tyne. Brown colored large glass flask, stopper cork, paper seal. (Christie's) $895

Titanic Old Scotch Whisky – Early 20th century, distilled in bottle by Duncan Manning and Black, hand blown green colored glass bottle, driven cork, lead capsule embossed.
(Christie's) $1,546

Monarch O' The Glen – Early 20th century, MacGregor, Caldbeck & Co., London & Glasgow. Green colored square angled bottle, driven cork, lead capsule.
(Christie's) $1,009

Old Vatted Glenlivet – 1862, Importation label printed *From M.E. Bellows' Son & Co., Agent and Importer of Wines and Spirits, 77 Broad Street, New York.*
(Christie's) $1,790

Dunville's Special Liqueur Whisky, circa 1930, Distilled and bottled by Dunville & Co. Ltd., Belfast. Product of Ireland. Clear glass bottle.
(Christie's) $1,302

Smith's Glenlivet – 1899, Shipped to Sydney N.S.W. August 1912 in sailing ship Port Jackson, returned from Sydney N.S.W. May 1914 in S.S. Swazzi.
(Christie's) $2,116

Old Tobermory – 1912, distilled by John Hopkins & Co., Distillers, Tobermory Distillery, Isle of Mull. Brown colored dumpy glass bottle, single malt.
(Christie's) $4,557

Glenleven – Late 19th century, John Haig & Co. Ltd., Markinch, Scotland, excellent label, driven cork, lead capsule, level: 5.5cm. from base of capsule.
(Christie's) $4,883

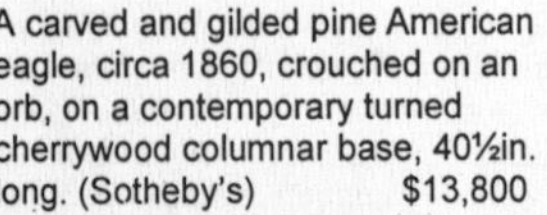

A carved and gilded pine American eagle, circa 1860, crouched on an orb, on a contemporary turned cherrywood columnar base, 40½in. long. (Sotheby's) $13,800

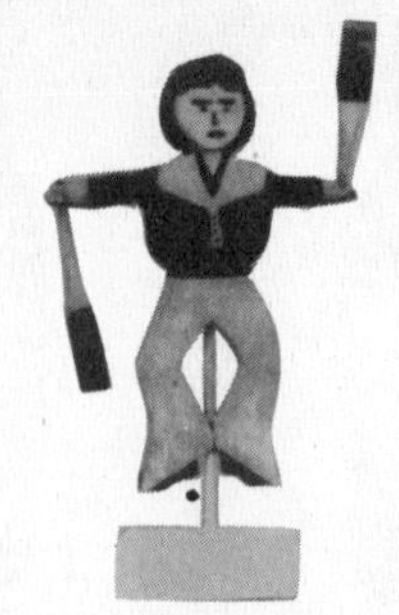

'Happy Jack' whirligig, in red, white, and blue paint, some retouching, 13in. high. (Eldred's) $605

A polychrome carved wood panel of the Duke of Grafton's arms, bearing the date *1687*, set within a later associated painted and parcel-gilt frame, the arms panel, 21½in. wide, 15¾in. high. (Christie's) $15,640

A carved oak heraldic panel fragment, 19th century, modelled as helmet with visor, 16 x 12 x 5½in. (Christie's) $1,656

A pair of carved and stained wood busts of Byron and Milton, circa 1900, 21in. and 20¼in. high respectively. (Christie's) $3,200

A Friesland chip carved oak foot warmer box, 18th century, of typical form, with brass swing handle, the underside carved with the initial *G.P.* and the date *1746*, 9¾in. wide. (Christie's) $460

A rare group of three oak figures, English, mid 15th century, the figure on the left a knight in armour, the central figure possibly a nobleman and to the right a page, 43in. high. (Sotheby's) $178,400

One of an impressive pair of carved wood lions, each fully maned beast in a seated position, on a canted rectangular plinth, 46½in. high. (Bonhams) (Two) $1,280

A carved wood and polychrome fairground bust, first quarter 20th century, depicting a Turk wearing a head-dress, his robe with lion's mask brooch, 37in. high. (Christie's) $640

A boxwood root tea caddy, probably Scottish, late 18th or early 19th century, of naturalistic form, with a hinged cover, 6¾in. wide.
(Christie's) $3,997

An articulated artist's lay figure, 19th century, 23in. high.
(Christie's) $2,751

Carved and paint decorated storage box, Massachusetts, first quarter 19th century, the rectangular hinged top with an applied carved crouching cat handle, 16¼in. wide.
(Skinner) $26,450

A Northern French polychrome wood equestrian figure of St. Bavo, early 16th century, holding the reins in his right hand whilst his right is raised holding a falcon, 73cm. high.
(Sotheby's) $45,080

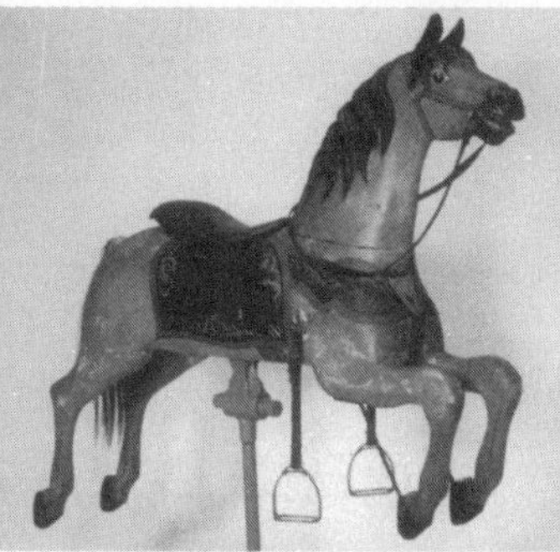

Carved polychrome prancing horse carousel figure, attributed to Armitage Herschell Company, late 19th century, the tan horse with black mane, rust colored bridle, glass eyes, brown saddle, 48in. long. (Skinner) $12,650

An early 16th century South German carved limewood figure of St Michael, polychrome decorated, his right arm raised with a clenched fist, (formerly clasping a lance) with the devil at his feet, 4ft.high.
(Woolley & Wallis) $25,280

A carved and painted cigar store Indian, American, late 19th century, standing with fully articulated musculature, holding a spear and gilt-acanthus-edge red-painted shield, 50¼in. high.
(Christie's) $19,550

Continental burl walnut and horn mounted tankard, late 17th century, with flower shaped cover and scrolled handle, with leaf carved base, 6½in. high.
(Skinner) $2,185

A Northern French polychrome wood donor group, late 15th century, with kneeling figures of a noblewoman and nobleman donor, behind, the standing figures of a bishop saint and St. Antony, 26½in.
(Sotheby's) $18,400

Two polychrome carved wood figures, 19th century, a kneeling male figure and a lady, standing carrying a basket of fruit, 14¼in. and 17in. high.
(Christie's) $1,553

A carved painted pine and gesso American eagle, Wilhelm Schimmel, Cumberland Valley, Pennsylvania, with outstretched lappet-carved wings dovetailed into the body, 9½in. wide.
(Sotheby's) $17,250

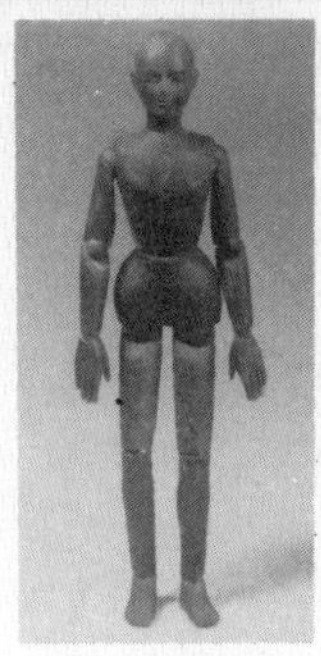

A carved pine artist's model articulated figure, 19th century, carved in the round, the head with defined features, 20in. high.
(Sotheby's) $1,265

An 18th century wood figure of a Northumbrian piper, carved in a seated pose, wearing a red coat with white collar and cuffs, 32.5cm.
(Tennants) $9,749

A pair of George III style carved pine eagle brackets, shown contra posto, mounted on stylized rockwork, 13in. high.
(Christie's) $1,207

A carved and painted pine Neptune ship's figurehead, American, 19th century, carved in the round, the bare-chested, white haired figure grasping a blue cloak, 54in. high.
(Sotheby's) $5,462

A carved walnut panel, in the German 16th century style, modelled in relief depicting two warriors in combat on horseback, 26½ x 16½in.
(Christie's) $1,555

Stephen Hunick, 20th century, a coiled serpent, carved and painted basswood, 18in. high.
(Sotheby's) $920

Painted wooden child's sled, late 19th century, painted *Kelley*, solid wood frame with iron runners, dark green, mustard and red paint, 34in. long. (Skinner) $805

\ carved and painted pine \merican eagle wall plaque, \merican, third quarter, 19th :entury, carved in the half round, he eagle with talons grasping hirteen arrows, 36½ x 31½in. Sotheby's) $21,850

A carved and painted pine American eagle, probably New England, 19th century, the stylized rotund figure of an eagle with upraised wings painted with speckled feathers, 10¼in. high. (Sotheby's) $5,175

Treenware goblet, England, late 18th/early 19th century, heavily incised decoration with panels of animals and Royal crest between religious verses, 8¼in. high. (Skinner) $9,200

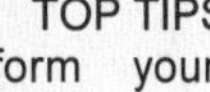

TOP TIPS

Transform your carved wood with colored shoe polish, no less! Put it on with a small brush. (This provides your discarded toothbrush with a second career.) Leave to dry for a few hours, then rub the carving with a stiff brush or wooden burnisher. Parts in relief turn lighter, while the undercuts will stay dark because the brush or burnisher can't reach them.

(Hobbs Parker)

A carved and gilded pine mermaid, 19th century, the buxom female figure wearing a diadem, with tail curled mounted on a rod, 15 x 16½in. (Sotheby's) $1,495

A carved and stained wood figure of a Red Indian, late 19th century, shown standing holding a lacquer tray, 15¼in. high. (Christie's) $1,271

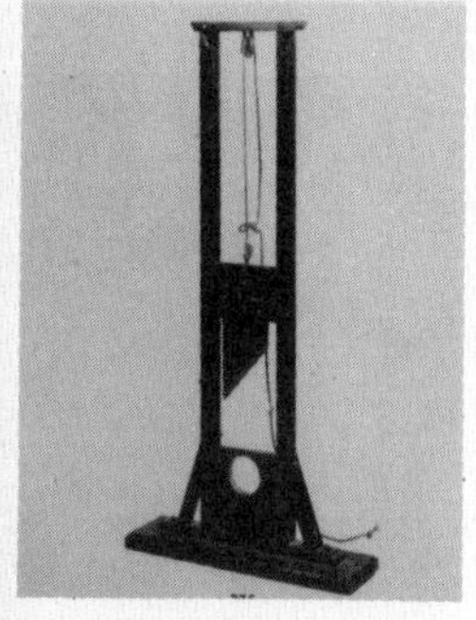

. French wood and iron model of a uillotine, 19th century, the ectangular frame with pulley and lade, 48½in. high. Christie's) $1,372

A pair of George IV polychrome carved wood models of a lion and a unicorn, 19th century, each shown passant holding a vacant shield, 15¾in. high. (Christie's) $6,400

A carved and painted pine ship's figurehead, American, circa 1850, the sweet faced figure of a dark haired young woman wearing a blue gown, 13½in. (Sotheby's) $4,600

A section of Napoleon's writing desk, the mahogany and fruitwood strung top section with raised ebony outer banding, with pastel label, *The Gift of Madame Bertram 1819 St. Helena,* 31 x 25cm.
(Bonhams) $1,236

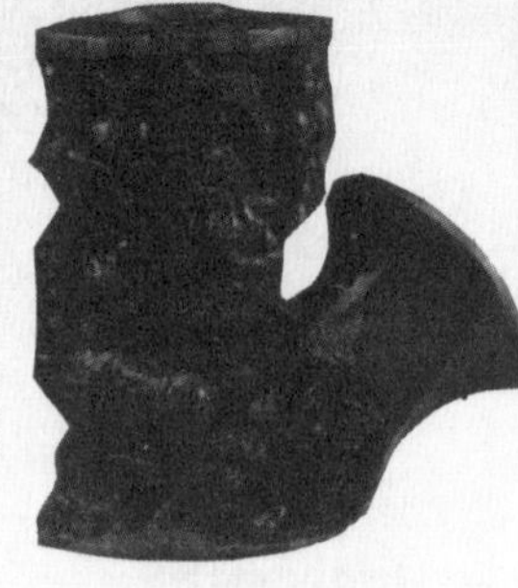

A Swedish birch pipe bowl by Sofia Isberg, carved with an allegorical scene depicting Napoleon, 11cm. high.
(Stockholms AV) $2,865

A polychrome wood model of a butcher's shop, late 19th/early 20th century, showing the shop front with carcasses and joints of meat hung to the façade, with three figures beside their carving blocks, 20 x 28in. (Christie's) $11,885

A German carved torchère, 19th century, in the form of a stooping elf, hands aloft supporting a cornucopia, on a plinth base, 44in. high. (Christie's) $3,634

An English lignum vitae 'York' tankard, mid 17th century, lacking cover and bun feet, handle re-mounted, silvered band to the rim, 4¾in. high.
(Christie's) $5,486

A carved and painted pine ship's figurehead, American, 19th century, the full bodied figure of a dark haired young woman wearing a blue gown with red and white sashes, 56in. high.
(Sotheby's) $9,775

One of a pair of carved giltwood Chinese Dogs of Fo, 62cm. high.
(Bonhams) (Two) $551

A carved oak relief bust of a lady, in the manner of Rysbrack, shown with a garland of beads entwined in her hair, with head to sinister, 14½in. high. (Christie's)
(Christie's) $1,651

A baroque money box, probably 17th century, burl birch with iron locks, 14cm. high.
(Stockholms AV) $2,8[illegible]

INDEX

C

G

N

O

P

T